COLLECTED ESSAYS

VOLUME III

THE LITTMAN LIBRARY OF
JEWISH CIVILIZATION

Life Patron
COLETTE LITTMAN

Dedicated to the memory of
LOUIS THOMAS SIDNEY LITTMAN
who founded the Littman Library for the love of God
and as an act of charity in memory of his father
JOSEPH AARON LITTMAN
and to the memory of
ROBERT JOSEPH LITTMAN
who continued what his father Louis had begun
יהא זכרם ברוך

'Get wisdom, get understanding:
Forsake her not and she shall preserve thee'
PROV. 4:5

The Littman Library of Jewish Civilization is a registered UK charity
Registered charity no. 1000784

COLLECTED ESSAYS

VOLUME III

HAYM SOLOVEITCHIK

London
The Littman Library of Jewish Civilization
in association with Liverpool University Press

The Littman Library of Jewish Civilization
Registered office: 14th floor, 33 Cavendish Square, London WIG OPW

in association with Liverpool University Press
4 Cambridge Street, Liverpool L69 7ZU, UK
www.liverpooluniversitypress.co.uk/littman

Managing Editor: Connie Webber

Distributed in North America by Longleaf Services
116 S Boundary St, Chapel Hill, NC 27514, USA

First published 2020
First published in paperback 2024

Catalogue records for this book are available from the
British Library and the Library of Congress

ISBN 978-1-802075-85-4

Publishing co-ordinator: Janet Moth
Copy-editing: Agnes Erdos
Proof-reading: Philippa Claiden
Indexes: Agnes Erdos
Designed and typeset by Pete Russell, Faringdon, Oxon.

Printed and bound by CPI Group (UK) Ltd, Croydon, CR0 4YY

To Ezra and Laurie

Preface

LIKE THE PRECEDING TWO VOLUMES, this one also draws upon material written over some five decades; while the external unity seems obvious—*Sefer Ḥasidim* and Provençal halakhah, most notably Ravad of Posquières—it is linked with the preceding volumes by the underlying question of how one reads medieval Jewish sources, be it halakhic or ethical ones. The tool that I employed in the halakhic texts, which ran like a scarlet thread through the preceding volumes, was that of 'angle of deflection'. That is to say, is there some noticeable swerve from the 'straight and narrow' road of halakhic thinking that would entitle the historian to say that external factors were impinging on the argument of the halakhist? Otherwise, he could not have written as he did. This principle was challenged by some of my colleagues, and I replied to them in the preceding volumes. New criticisms have emerged and, in the concluding essay of this volume, I attempt to demonstrate that the principle of 'angle of deflection' has nothing to do with the old jurisprudential debate about realism and formalism.

The first section, on *Sefer Ḥasidim*, is also dominated—explicitly or implicitly—by the same methodological issue of historical inference. When is one justified in drawing conclusions about the values of the authors of moral and ethical works—of another era, or even those of our own time? Until well into the twentieth century, and in the Diaspora to this day, Hebrew was and is a learned and not a spoken language, a language which draws both its vocabulary and its mandate from the classical Jewish literature, and thus will constantly use such terms as 'good and bad' (*tov ve-ra'*), 'with or without an ulterior intention' (*li-shmah ve-shelo li-shmah*), God-fearing men and reprobate ones (*yir'ei shamayim u-feritsim*), charity, grace (*tsedakah, ḥesed*), and the like. The categories are thus timeless, and their meanings multifarious. They can assume, and have assumed, innumerable forms. Most ethical writers have specific sins in mind, sins that their generation is most prone to commit and which therefore are in most need of correction. When is decrial of a sin a standard remark, a simple restatement of an ethical norm of which every generation is in need of being reminded, and when does it constitute the 'front', as it were, of the writer or the movement, its contemporary agenda, a sin in a specific form and guise, to which their generation is especially inclined, and which for this reason is most in need of reprimand and rectification?

Moral ideas, moreover, can be entertained in different ways. One must often ask four questions to sort out the different levels at which ideas can be held: Is this simply a passing thought in the work? (Of which, I would add, *Sefer Ḥasidim* has a good number.) Is it a thought seriously entertained but only abstractly, or is it a value that the author seeks to impress upon his readers to stir them to action? For example, *contemptus mundi* (scorn of the world or total disregard of what people think) is an idea which figures in any ethical (*mussar*) group bent on self-improvement, not to speak of self-transcendence. However, only the *mussarniks* of Novardok (Navahrudak) in the late nineteenth and early twentieth centuries sent their novitiates into stores with a fork to buy a glass of milk or ask to purchase screws in a bakery. To them alone was negation of the ego an animating principle. Finally, is this an idea that lies at the heart of the thinker's agenda, a message which this movement flies on its mast, as is, for example, 'custody of the eyes', avoiding looking at women, for medieval German Pietism?

The first essay in the section on *Sefer Ḥasidim* was my first venture in analyzing that protean work and sought to dislodge the dominant view of Ḥasidei Ashkenaz that obtained in the 1960s and 1970s. The third essay was an attempt to discern different ideological groups in the movement, while the fifth essay expresses my mature views on German Pietism. The problem of historical inference from ethical or hortatory literature occupied me throughout the 1960s and 1970s. I put down my conclusions in the early 1980s and have polished and rounded them out in the two essays that appear as Chapters 8 and 9 of this volume.

The second section, 'Ravad and Provençal Studies', has two of my studies of the famed twelfth-century Talmudist Ravad of Posquières (known now as Vauvert, situated some 22 miles west of Arles and 27 miles east of Montpellier). The first essay sought to change the image of Ravad (d.1198) that has dominated both halakhic and historical literature since the sixteenth century. The second essay addresses his conflict-laden relationship with R. Zeraḥyah ha-Levi of Lunel (d. before 1186), the author of the *Sefer ha-Ma'or*, the renowned critique of the rulings of R. Yitsḥak of Fez (d.1103), a halakhic authority before whom even Maimonides often bent. It seeks to uncover the reason for the personal enmity between these two scholars, which was further fueled by their sharply different intellectual temperaments. The head of a traditional yeshivah took strong exception to my first article and wrote a vigorous and lengthy dissent. His objections and my reply are found in Chapters 12 and 13. Currently the writings of the thirteenth-century Provençal Talmudist R. Menaḥem ha-Me'iri are much in use; however, for centuries they had been ignored. Chapter 15 seeks to draw his intellectual portrait and explain the reason for this strange history. The concluding chapter, as already stated, returns to the issue of the disputed 'angle of deflection' and points out new areas of Jewish history in which this principle can be fruitfully employed, such as the study of the Marranos (the crypto-Jews of the Iberian peninsula), the religious reform of the nineteenth century, and the women's movement of today.

None of the previously printed essays have been altered. Any additions or changes in opinion are noted either in an Afterword or enclosed in braces { } in the footnotes. The additions to the footnotes are generally ones of fact; those in the Afterwords are mostly my current reflections on the subject, responses to criticism, or reactions to other scholars' treatment of the material. All bibliographical additions have also been placed in braces, with one exception. The last thirty years have seen a flood of scholarly editions of medieval halakhic works; I have updated these references without marking them. For example, a citation of the *Ḥiddushei ha-Ramban* has automatically been updated from the Meltzer edition of 1928 to the relevant volume in the series of the *Shas ha-Yisra'eli ha-Shalem*.

As closely as the previously published studies hew to the original formulations, I did not perceive them as masoretic texts, demanding absolute fidelity of transmission. If I or the editors at Littman found a phrase infelicitous, we edited it out; if a clause seemed over-complicated, we simplified it. I did alter two overstatements. In one, I changed 'never' to 'rarely'; in the other, I changed '[wine was] the most important article of trade' to 'one of the most important articles of trade'. (I tell my students to avoid, as much as possible, the use of 'ever', 'never', and the superlative form of comparison, but in preparing this volume I discovered that occasionally I had failed to practice what I preached.)

Written, as these essays were, at different times and for different audiences—some for scholars of rabbinic literature, some for laymen or for scholars not necessarily Jewish who were interested, for example, in the medieval Jewish attitude to usury—there are occasional explanatory asides which may appear to the better-informed reader to be superfluous; I have left them untouched. Several of the essays began as lectures. In these oral presentations, I sometimes borrowed an apt phrase or sentence or two from a previous article and subsequently published the presentation. When several of these lectures are placed side by side, the occasional repetition can be jarring. In one instance, I have altered the formulation (and so noted in a footnote); in the two or three other instances, I have let them stand, and appeal simply to the reader's forbearance.

Acknowledgments

ANY ACKNOWLEDGMENT of an intellectual debt in a series of collected essays whose publication stretches back some forty-five years should begin with the 'creditors' who can never be repaid, not simply because they are no longer with us, but because their perspectives and ways of thinking are embedded in everything that one has written. First and foremost is my father, who bestowed upon me no less than a decade and a half of talmudic instruction—and much more; then Jacob Katz, from whom I learnt historical method. I am also under obligation to Ḥayyim Hillel Ben-Sasson and Joshua Prawer, under whom I studied at the Hebrew University in Jerusalem.

Not all learning takes place in the classroom, and I would be sorely remiss if I did not record my obligations to Michael Bernstein, Eliezer Shimshon Rosenthal, Shraga Abramson, and Saul Lieberman. For reasons best known to them (certainly not because of any merit of mine), they privileged me with hundreds of hours of conversation. What those sessions imparted to me, both in knowledge and in method, has nourished every aspect of my scholarly life.

The idea of collecting my essays of some forty years, scattered in books and journals both known and unknown (some in works possibly deserving oblivion), was first suggested to me by my cousin, Morry Gerber. When I broached the idea to Connie Webber, the managing editor of Littman, she received it enthusiastically; without her involvement, the project would not have come to fruition. I had heard from colleagues about the superb editing at Littman; what I received exceeded all expectations. I had not one, but two editors. Agi Erdos did painstaking and meticulous work, and Janet Moth then provided me with the finest English editing that I have ever received. Philippa Claiden's patient checking of the Hebrew and correcting the proofs was likewise much appreciated; Pete Russell's design has improved the readability of the text, for which I am grateful; while Ludo Craddock's handling of the bureaucratic technicalities connected with signing the original contract for a three-volume work made them less bureaucratic and technical.

I hired Hanna Caine Braunschvig of Jerusalem, an experienced Hebrew editor, to check all the titles, places of publication, and pages of the articles and books cited, and to keep a watchful eye on some of the other paraphernalia of scholarship. However, the intelligence of her comments on the articles and our conversations about the manner of their improvement has turned our relationship from that of author/assistant to one of collegiality. Ezra Merkin, Jerry Balsam, and Sheon Karol read and commented perceptively on every essay in the collection. I am indebted to all of them. (Jerry's eye for errant commas proved a further blessing.) Elisabeth Hollender graciously checked my German references (especially their case endings). Without the assistance of the staffs of the Gottesman and Pollack libraries of Yeshiva University, little of my research would have been possible. I would like to single out Zvi Ehrenyi, John Moryl, and Mary Ann Linahan for special thanks.

Given the state of the currently printed medieval rabbinic texts, no serious research is possible without sustained recourse to manuscripts. Everything that I have written over the past forty-five years is based, without exception, on the treasures of the Institute of Microfilmed Hebrew Manuscripts at the National Library of Israel in Jerusalem. Their holdings and their catalogue provide countless scholars with undreamt-of riches. The helpfulness of their staff, especially their cataloguers, is fabled. I am obliged to each and every one of them; however, I would like to note my special indebtedness to Binyamin Richler and Ezra Chwat.

Other than the obligation that I owe to my teachers, my greatest debt is to the past president of Yeshiva University, Richard Joel, and its provost, Mort Lowengrub. They appointed me the Merkin Family Research Professor, thus freeing me from all teaching obligations so that I could devote myself entirely to research and writing. The current president of Yeshiva University, Ari Berman, the current provost, Selma Botman, and the Special Assistant to the Provost, Timothy Stevens, graciously extended the life of that appointment. Without their gift of time and resources, the entire project—a multi-volume series of my collected essays—would simply have been inconceivable.

H.S.

Contents

Note on Transliteration and Conventions Used in the Text

HEBREW

The transliteration of Hebrew in this book reflects consideration of the type of book it is, in terms of its content, purpose, and readership. The system adopted therefore reflects an academic approach to transcription, such as that of the *Encyclopaedia Judaica* or other systems developed for text-based or linguistic studies. The aim has partly been to reflect the pronunciation prescribed for modern Hebrew, as well as the spelling or Hebrew word structure, and to do so using conventions that are generally familiar to the English-speaking reader.

In accordance with this approach, no attempt is made to indicate the distinctions between *tet* and *taf*, *kaf* and *kuf*, *sin* and *samekh*, since these are not relevant to pronunciation. The *dagesh* is indicated by double consonants, except when the doubling would result in a string of consonants unacceptable to the English reader's eye, as in *kitstsur*. Following the principle of using conventions familiar to the majority of readers, however, transcriptions that are well established have been retained even when they are not fully consistent with the transliteration system adopted. On similar grounds, the *tsadi* is rendered by 'tz' in such familiar words as barmitzvah. Likewise, the distinction between *ḥet* and *khaf* has been retained, using *ḥ* for the former and *kh* for the latter; the associated forms are generally familiar to readers, even if the distinction is not actually borne out in pronunciation, and for the same reason the final *heh* is indicated too. Although in Hebrew no capital letters are used, the transcription of titles and names in lower case may be strange to the English-speaking reader's eye and in this volume we therefore adopt the English system of capitalization (for example, *Shulḥan 'Arukh*).

No distinction is made between *'alef* and *'ayin* in the intervocalic position: both are represented by an apostrophe; *'ayin* is also marked at the beginnings and ends of words.

The *sheva na'* is indicated by an *e*—*perikat 'ol, reshut*—except, again, when established convention dictates otherwise.

The *yod* is represented by *i* when it occurs as a vowel (*bereshit*), by *y* when it occurs as a consonant (*yesodot*), and by *yi* when it occurs as both (*yisra'el*).

The definite article and those conjunctives and prepositions that in Hebrew are attached to the word have been separated by a hyphen in our transcription to help distinguish the individual elements.

Medieval Hebrew names follow the above system, whereas contemporary names are transcribed as they appear in Western literature.

The names of scholars who have published in European languages are given in Latinized form, even when referring to Hebrew articles of theirs. Thus Yaakov Katz is uniformly referred to as 'Jacob Katz' and registered in bibliographical entries as 'J. Katz'. Similarly, Yoel Miller is registered as 'J. Müller'.

The page numbers of the original essays have been shown thus in the text: |99| to enable readers to swiftly find references to passages in these articles registered in the scholarly literature of the past. Bibliographical and other additions are enclosed in braces { } in the footnotes. More extensive additional comments are noted in an Afterword to the relevant chapter.

YIDDISH

The transcription of Yiddish in this volume follows the conventions of the YIVO Institute.

PART I

SEFER ḤASIDIM

SPECIFIC STUDIES

MUCH of *Sefer Ḥasidim* reflects a common religious outlook and shared climate of opinion; most of it is equally written in an inimitably poor Hebrew. Clearly it is the work of a single author/compiler or a small, cohesive band of authors/compilers. Their identity, however, is anything but clear. I chose to call the author/compiler of *Sefer Ḥasidim* 'the Ḥasid'.

German Pietism is also a unique form of pietism, unlike any other in Jewish ethical tradition. To distinguish between the two in my essays, I refer to Ḥasidei Ashkenaz as 'Pietists' and to other groups of religious virtuosi as 'pietists'. The differentiating markers imply no higher evaluation of one over the other. Throughout the essays in Part I of this volume, all references to the distinctive German Pietism or Pietists are capped—such as Ḥasidut Ashkenaz, the Ḥasid, Ḥasidut; all references to generic pietism, such as that of *Sefer Ḥasidim I* (*SH I*, which I shall later define and discuss), Rabbenu Baḥya, R. Yonah mi-Gerundi, R. Yisra'el Salanter, and the like are not capped.

CHAPTER ONE

Three Themes in *Sefer Ḥasidim*

This is an early essay—two of its three sections were written a decade before its publication in 1976—and, like one or two of my studies of that period, it assumed that the reader was familiar with the state of the field and realized what I was arguing against and to what extent the terse formulations differed from the scholarly consensus of the time. Unlike my essay on pawnbroking,[a] which went unread, this essay was well received, so perhaps I was right in my assumptions at the time. Forty years later, those assumptions are no longer true, and it is best to tell the reader at the very outset what the climate of opinion was when the essay was written. The understanding of *Sefer Ḥasidim* and of medieval German pietism (Ḥasidut Ashkenaz) was dominated for over a generation by Yitzhak Baer's famous essay of 1938 (below, n. 10). In it, he compared R. Yehudah he-Ḥasid, *mutatis mutandis*, to his Christian contemporary, St Francis of Assisi. Baer portrayed the humility, gentle demeanor, and meek acceptance of mockery that R. Yehudah advocated to his followers to the similar demands made by Francis of his acolytes. Both R. Yehudah and St Francis were deeply sensitive to the feelings of their fellow man, even displaying a concern for the treatment of animals. R. Yehudah's sense of right and justice, what he termed *din shamayim* (heavenly law), had little in common with halakhic norms; it resembled instead the 'natural law' of the Stoics,[b] a sense of justice imprinted in all men's minds that guided them to

Professors Gershom Scholem, Jacob Katz, Haim Hillel Ben-Sasson, and Morton Bloomfield were kind enough to comment on the manuscript. For the errors and perversities still remaining the author alone bears responsibility.

[a] 'Pawnbroking: A Study in Ribbit and of the Halakhah in Exile', *Proceedings of the American Academy for Jewish Research*, 38–39 (1970–1), 203–68; reprinted in an expanded form in *Collected Essays*, i (Oxford, 2013), 57–166.

[b] See Y. Baer, 'Ha-Megammah ha-Datit ha-Ḥevratit shel Sefer Ḥasidim', *Zion*, 3 (1938), 1–50 {repr. in id., *Meḥkarim u-Masot be-Toledot 'Am Yisra'el* (Jerusalem, 1985), and in I. G. Marcus, ed., *Dat ve-Ḥevrah be-Mishnatam shel Ḥasidei Ashkenaz: Leket Ma'amarim* (Jerusalem, 1977); Y. Baer, 'Shenei Perakim shel Torat ha-Hashgaḥah be-Sefer Ḥasidim', in B. Yaron, ed., *Meḥkarim be-Kabbalah u-ve-Toledot ha-Datot Mukdashim le-Gershom Shalom* (Jerusalem, 1968), 47–62; id., 'Torat ha-Shivyon ha-Tiv'i ha-Kadmon etsel Ḥasidei Ashkenaz', *Zion*, 32 (1967), 47–62; repr. in id., *Meḥkarim u-Masot be-Toledot 'Am Yisra'el* (Jerusalem, 1985), ii. 225–32, 233–50, and in I. G. Marcus, ed., *Dat ve-Ḥevrah be-Mishnatam shel Ḥasidei Ashkenaz: Leket Ma'amarim* (Jerusalem, 1977), 183–98, 199–206.}

a common perception of the right and the equitable. Indeed, this central notion of *din shamayim* occasionally dissented explicitly from the talmudic norm, and co-existed at all times in deep, if latent, tension with the halakhah, a disharmony to which R. Yehudah and his followers could never admit, not even to themselves, challenge as they might—and did—the primacy both of the scholar and of Torah study in Jewish religious life.

In the concluding section of the essay, 'Retrospect and Points at Issue' (pp. 58–61 below), I summed up my differences with the reigning view of the man and the movement and the larger implications of this dissent. I think the contemporary reader would do well to begin with that section and, with it as outline and guide, turn to the body of the essay. Knowing from the outset where the essay is heading, what conclusions the author seeks to draw, he or she will also be in a better position to judge the strength or weakness of the arguments being advanced.

To further facilitate such a critical reading, I have thickened the footnotes with citations. In the original essay, I frequently supplied only references to passages which I thought supported and occasionally amplified my argument. In this volume, I have—for the reader's convenience—often reproduced in the notes the passages that I had in mind when I referred to these sources for corroboration.[c]

[c] All numerical references are to *Sefer Ḥasidim*, ed. J. Wistinetzki (Berlin, 1891), based on Parma, Biblioteca Palatina 1133; henceforth *SHP*. This edition was photo-offset in Frankfurt am Main in 1924 and provided with indices and a large and important introduction by J. Freimann. When in the course of a sentence a simple numeral would be unclear, it has been prefaced with *SH*. When reference is made to the earlier and far briefer Bologna edition of 1538, this is specifically indicated as e.g. *SHB*, #10.

The original essay did not provide the Hebrew original of the axial opening citations. The newly added footnotes 2 and 3 fill this lacuna. All references to footnotes of this article must therefore be raised by two, e.g. n. 25 in the original is n. 27 in this volume.

The cited sections of *Sefer Ḥasidim* in the footnotes are often not in numerical order. This is intentional. Those passages which constituted proof or clear instantiation of the point being made in the text are cited first. Those which take on new meaning after the point has been accepted are then cited. I have divided these two groups by a semicolon.

The 1913 Safed edition of the *Ḥokhmat ha-Nefesh* by R. El'azar of Worms was used in the original article, together with some minor corrections from manuscripts of that work such as Parma, De Rossi 1390 and Oxford, Bodley 1569. A somewhat superior text has been published by the Makhon Sodei Razaya in the second volume of *Sifrei ha-Ra mi-Germaiza, Ba'al ha-Roke'aḥ* (Jerusalem, 2006), sect. 2, pp. 1–132. It is based on an Ashkenazic manuscript copied in 1343/4 (currently owned by an anonymous Australian), whose microfilm (f 43104) is available in the Institute of Microfilmed Hebrew Manuscripts at the National Library of Israel.

Both volumes of that set contain a number of the shorter works of R. El'azar, each with its own pagination. 'Sect. 2' refers to the second work in that volume. (The editor, A. Eizenbach, entitled the 2015 reprint of the set *Sifrei Rabbenu Ba'al ha-Roke'aḥ*, further complicating the lives of bibliographers.) The differences between the two versions in the passages cited from the *Ḥokhmat ha-Nefesh* in this essay are quite minor, the majority even trivial. In the original essay I naturally cited the Safed edition. In this series I have followed the superior text of the Makhon Sodei Razaya. However, when

I

לא מצאנהו שגיא כח לא דברה כנגד רצון הבורא ולא כפי הצורך לאדם.

Sefer Ḥasidim, #1076

It is not simply the bounty of novel directives found in *Sefer Ḥasidim* that constitutes the most puzzling feature of that work, nor even their occasional strangeness, but rather the awesome authority claimed for these prescripts. Divine punishment of the direst sort awaits those who fail, even unwittingly, to comply with them. Indeed, entire communities have been doomed by just such unintended transgressions. Yet the behests that fill |312| the pages of *Sefer Ḥasidim* are frequently neither simply aids to moral edification nor genuine extrapolations of talmudic dicta—two types of dictates that could be supposed to possess God's tacit endorsement. What is mandated there amounts to a new world of ritual, a fresh religious sensibility, at times even a new morality, and all these make bold claim to Divine sanction. What is the basis, we are led to ask, of the hasidic mandamus? What sustains the Pietists' profound assurance that they are privy to God's will? Have they had some recent revelation authorizing them to speak in the name of the Lord?[1]

I thought that the Safed version or some of the manuscripts of the *Ḥokhmat ha-Nefesh* had a somewhat better reading, I incorporated it into the citation.

All the manuscripts cited were viewed at the Institute of Microfilmed Hebrew Manuscripts of the Jewish National and University Library in Jerusalem. {In recent years, I have made free use of the Princeton University *Sefer Hasidim* Database. It seemed bootless to attempt to sort out which new references originated from the notes and jottings that have accumulated in my books in the forty years since the essay appeared and what I took out from that database. I can state with certainty that all the references to the Boesky manuscript come from the Princeton project. One should note that the database is not entirely complete. It does not contain very brief extracts of *Sefer Ḥasidim* found in MSS Oxford, Bodley 453, fos. 231b–232a (##1–5, 99–101 of Bologna); Hamburg Stadtsbibliothek 213, fos. 24b–25a; Oxford, Bodley 1098, fo. 104b. (I have not listed any manuscripts copied after 1700.) A fuller description of the manuscripts of *Sefer Ḥasidim* can be found below, pp. 120–4.}

[1] Prophecy is a phenomenon known to hasidic circles, and R. Shemu'el he-Ḥasid is called in certain sources R. Shemu'el ha-Navi (G. Scholem, *Ursprung und Anfänge der Kabbala* [Berlin, 1962], 211–18; {see now id., *The Origins of the Kabbalah*, ed. R. J. Z. Werblowsky (Philadelphia, 1987), 238–42}). However, prophetic authority does not underlie *Sefer Ḥasidim*, nor is any such claim, explicit or implicit, ever set forth. Throughout the book, the Ḥasid or Ḥakham is not a figure who has been vouchsafed communication with the transcendental world, but one who is *baki be-'inyan ha-Borè* {which can be translated either as 'insightful in matter[s] of the Borè' or '[has] comprehensive knowledge of the matter[s] of the Borè'} (*SH*, #1328). Knowledge and perception of a unique sort rather than illumination empower the Ḥasid to speak. {On *baki* as 'insightful' or 'perspicacious', see H. Yalon, *Pirkei Lashon* (Jerusalem, 1971), 313–15. The reference to Scholem is an error. He does discuss there the use of the term *navi* in Ashkenaz, but makes no mention of its being an appellation

We might begin by turning to the introductory words with which both compilers of the *Book of the Pious*, *Sefer Ḥasidim*, thought it proper to open their respective collections:

[This book] is written for those who fear God and are mindful of His name [*le-yir'ei ha-Shem u-le-ḥoshevei shemo*; cf. Mal. 3: 16].

There is a Ḥasid whose heart desires, out of love for his Creator, to do His will, but he is unaware of all these things [i.e. demands]—which thing to avoid and how to execute profoundly [*le-ha'amik la-'asot*] the wish of the Creator . . . For this reason the *Sefer Ḥasidim* was written so that all who fear God and those returning to their Creator with an undivided heart may read it and know and understand what is incumbent upon them to do and what they must avoid. (*SHB*)[2]

For those who fear God and are mindful of His name do I write this book of remembrance [Mal. 3: 16] so that they may learn [how] to fear God . . . There is a Ḥasid whose heart goes out to [i.e. aspires to do] the will of his Creator but he does not perform as many good deeds as the wise Ḥasid . . . for [these demands] were not passed on to him by his teacher and he was not wise enough to infer them by himself, but had he known he would have accepted and fulfilled them. For they [our Sages] have said [*Berakhot* 17a], 'A man must be cunning in the fear [of the Lord] [*'arum be-yir'ah*]'.

And we find in the Torah that anyone who was capable of understanding [a demand] even though he was not [explicitly] commanded is punished for not realizing [the requirement] on his own. As it is written, 'And |313| Moses was angry with the officers of the army . . . who had come from the service of the war. And he said to them, "Have you let all the women live?"' [Num. 31: 14–15]. Why did they not reply, 'You did not command us, for you did not tell us to kill the women'? But Moses knew that they were wise and perspicacious enough to infer [this command] on their own . . . Similarly, why did not Balaam reply to the angel's question, 'Why have you struck your ass?' by saying, 'What sin was there in striking my ass, seeing she crushed my foot against the wall [for no good reason]? . . . How have I sinned?' But he should have thought that perhaps God was opposed, for He only gave him permission to foretell the future . . . [Similarly Balaam] said, 'I have sinned for I knew not that you stood in the way against me' [Num. 22: 34]. Quite the contrary, the reverse conclusion should be drawn: because he was unaware that the angel stood against him, he did not sin. But

of R. Shemu'el he-Ḥasid. The correct reference is A. Epstein, *Kitvei Avraham Epstein*, ed. A. M. Habermann (Jerusalem, 1950), i. 253. See now E. Kanarfogel, *Peering through the Lattices: Mystical, Magical and Pietistic Dimensions in the Tosafist Period* (Detroit, 2000), 206 n. 37.}

2 ונכתב ליראי ה' ולחושבי שמו—כי חסיד אשר לבו חפץ באהבת בוראו לעשות כל רצונו ואינו יודע לשום על לב הדברים כולם ומאיזה דבר צריך להזהר ואיך להעמיק לעשות רצון בוראו . . . לכך נכתב ספר חסידים למען יראו בו יראי ה' וכל השבים לבוראם בלב שלם וידעו ויבינו מה שעלי לעשות ומאיזה דבר צריכין ליזהר.

{See the Afterword, sect. A, #4 below.}

> [what he meant in saying 'I have sinned' was] that 'I have sinned in that I did not give heed to think, I did not probe and investigate what [other] sin might have caused this.' From here we may infer that man must be cunning in the fear [of God] since they punish him for his ignorance; for one must know and probe, for in the presence of the Ruler you cannot acquit yourself by saying, 'It was a sin committed out of ignorance.'
>
> For this reason I set myself to writing a book for the God-fearing [*yir'ei ha-Shem*], lest they be punished and think [it is] for no reason. Far be it from God to do such a thing! [Gen. 18: 25] . . . Therefore I have set forth this Book of Fear so that those who fear the word of God can take heed. 'More than these, my son, must you take heed' [Eccl. 12: 12]. (*SHP*)[3]

Embodied in these passages and others, underlying much of *Sefer Ḥasidim* is the idea that God's will, or, as they often call it, the Will of the Creator, the *retson ha-Borè*, has not been cabined or confined within the overt dictates of the Torah, written or oral. A few of the Law's imperatives mirror the Divine wish only imperfectly, for that supreme volition was occasionally tempered by the Creator in consideration of the frailties of man[4] and the practical demands of life.[5] The very act of legislation effected a further diminution, for dealing necessarily with the generality, little provision could be made for the broad spectrum of individual cases, and thus no expression could be given to the infinite gradation and nuances inherent in the fullness of God's will.[6]

But far more significant than the occasional instances of contraction are the domains of silence. There are tracts, vast tracts, of human feeling and behavior of which the Divine Will is profoundly aware, indeed, acutely |314| demanding, but for which no directive as to their governance is to be found in the pages of the Law. Unincorporated, this Will did not fade away, nor was it

3 ליראי יי ולחושבי שמו—אכתוב זה ספר זכרון לפניהם למען ילמדו ליראה את יי ואת בניהם ילמדון . . . ויש חסיד שלבו דולק אחרי רצון בוראו ואינו מרבה מעשים טובים כחסיד וחכם מפני . . . שלא קבל מרבו ולא היה חכם להבין מלבו ואילו היה יודע היה מקבל ומקיים לפי שאמרו לעולם יהא אדם ערום ביראה . . . ומצינו בתורה שכל מי שיכול להבין אע"פ שלא נצטוה נענש עליה שלא שם על לב שנאמ[ר] ויקצוף משה על פקודי החיל שרי האלפים ושרי המאות הבאים מצבא המלחמה ויאמר אליהם החייתם כל נקבה. ולמה לא ענו לו למה לא צוית לנו והלא לא אמרת לנו להמית הנשים אלא שידע משה שהיו חכמים ובקיאין לדון קל וחומר . . . וכן למה לא אמר בלעם כשאמ[ר] לו המלאך על מה הכית את אתונך, מה עון שהכיתי את אתוני . . . שלחצה רגלו אל הקיר . . . מה עון עשיתי, אלא שהיה לו לחשוב שמא שלא ברצון הקב"ה שהוא לא נתן לו רשות אלא להגיד להם העתידות . . . וזהו שאמר חטאתי כי לא ידעתי שאתה נצב לקראתי, אדרבה איפכא מסתברא, לפי שלא ידע שהוא נצב לקראתו לא חטא. אלא כך אמ[ר] חטאתי שלא שמתי על לב לדעתי שלא פשפשתי וחקרתי באיזה עון הוא. מכיון שיהא אדם ערום ביראה הואיל ומענישין אותו על שאין יודע, שיש לדעת ולחקור שהרי לפני השליט לא תוכל לאמר כי שגגה היא . . . על כן אמרתי אכתוב ספר ליראי יי פן יענשו והם סבורים שעל חנם הוא, וחלילה ליי מרשע כי לא חפץ רשע . . . על כן ערכתי ספר היראה למען יזהר הירא את דבר יי, ויותר מהמה בני הזהר.

4 ##1004, 1100, 1110, 1111, 1143.

5 #1076.

6 ##914, 1289.

buried in the innermost recesses of the Divinity, inscrutable and irrelevant to man. The vast disparity between biblical and rabbinic norms, and the testimony of God's actions (both His wrath and His favor) both in the Bible and in daily experience, stand witness to the operation in history of standards of judgment other than those articulated in the Torah.[7] This potent norm is the Divine Will in its plenitude, and the fabric of human destiny is woven by compliance with and disobedience to its commands.[8] This is the key to many surprising biblical narratives and contemporary events. Man's destiny, however, could not be shaped by this norm had he not been first summoned to compliance and given the instrument of its discernment.[9]

[7] ##1006, 228, 15 (p. 21), and by implication much of *Sefer Ḥasidim*.

[8] Unwittingly much of *Sefer Ḥasidim* is a reproof of their doctrine of predestination (*gezerah*, as the Pietists called it), an indication of how little organic relationship there is between the received theoretical principles of the movement and its living thought.

[9] For the conscious formulation of R. Yehudah he-Ḥasid that new religious directives lie buried in every biblical passage, see *Moshav Zekenim 'al ha-Torah*, ed. D. Sassoon (London, 1959), 84, taken from the *Perush ha-Torah li-Shelomoh b. R. Yehudah he-Ḥasid*, MS Cambridge, Add. 669.2, fo. 23v {printed as Y. S. Lange, ed., *Perushei ha-Torah le-R. Yehudah he-Ḥasid* (Jerusalem, 1975), 55–6}:

> My father used to ask why we make a blessing on three verses of the Torah [when called up in the synagogue to read it], seeing as there are many verses that have no *torah* [i.e. no religious imperative]. He was wont to say that from the beginning of Genesis to 'in the sight of all Israel' [i.e. the last verse of the Pentateuch] there are no three consecutive verses which do not contain a ruling in civil law or in ritual matters. And I raised many objections to this statement and he [my father] answered all. I asked what we can learn from the passage of 'the generations of Esau' [Gen. 36: 1] and he answered . . . And I objected, what can be learnt from the *parashah* [i.e. pentateuchal section] of 'Mi-Kets'—Pharaoh's dream [Gen. 41: 1–32]—and he answered that one may learn a matter of ritual law from this . . . And so he said that one must study with great care the Torah of Mosheh, for it is impossible that there should be three verses without some [teaching about] ritual laws or without some ruling in civil law.

> **אבי היה מקשה למה אנו מברכין על ג' פסוקים ברכת התורה, והלא כמה פסוקים יש שאין בהם תורה, והוא היה אומר שמבראשית ועד לעיני כל ישר[אל] אין ג' פסוקים זה אצל זה (אם) [ש]אין דין יוצא מהן או איסור והתיר. והקשתי לו הרבה ותירץ הכל. והקשתי לו מפרשת אלופי עשו ותירץ . . . והקשיתי מן ויהי מקץ, וחלום של פרעה ותי' איסור והתיר יוצא מזה . . . וכך אמר שיש כך לדקדק בכל תורת משה שאי אפשר לג' פסוקים בלא איסור והתיר או בלא הוראת דין.**

This is taken up and elaborated by his pupils in *SH*, ##1826, 1829, 1831. See also #1514:

> There are hints and secrets of the Torah [whose meaning] will not be known until many generations later . . . and God said, *tsaddik* X is destined to reveal them in his generation after such and such a number of years, and he will reveal those secrets which were not known previously. And that X will write a book on that [newly discovered] matter . . . and he will make it a religious imperative [*mitsvah*], as did Josiah [of the paschal lamb; 2 Chr. 35: 18]. Three hundred and thirty-two years elapsed . . . before they [i.e. the Jews] brought the paschal lamb . . . And so it is written: 'His secret is with the righteous' [Prov. 3: 32], and it is written: 'He revealeth his secrets unto the righteous' [Amos 3: 7] . . . And a similar destiny awaits all [the other] hidden matters that are hinted at in the Torah. And He [God] did not write them [explicitly in the Torah] so as

|315| To recover, to lay bare this Will in its fullness, to mold their lives in its accord, and to guide others through its sinuous paths was the self-appointed task of the German Pietists, Ḥasidei Ashkenaz.

> to increase the reward for those who fear him [*li-yere'av*] and who should search [this hidden] meaning out, as it is written: 'If thou seekest her as silver and searchest for her as for hidden treasures, then shalt thou understand the fear of the Lord and find knowledge of God' [Prov. 3: 4–5]. . . . And a further reason [for the encoding of the covert commandments is] that He did not wish the unworthy to know of them.
>
> **כי יש רמזים וסודי התורה ולא יכלו לדעת עד כמה דורות . . . והקב"ה אמר עתיד אותו צדיק פלוני שידע באותו דור לאחר כך וכך שנים יעמד ויגלה אותם סודות שלא נודעו קודם. אותו פלוני יעשה ספר מאותו דבר ופלוני מאותם דברים ויעשה אותם מצוה כמו שכתוב ביאשיהו כמנין יאשיה"ו שנים עד שנעשה הפסח . . . וכתיב סוד ה' ליראיו וכתיב את ישרים סודו . . . כן כל הנסתרות שרמוזים בתורה ולא כתבם בפירוש כדי להרבות שכר ליראיו שיחפשו אחריהם שנא' תבקשנה ככסף וכמטמונים תחפשנה אז תבין יראת ה' ודעת אלהים תמצא, ועוד לא רצה שידעו אותם שאינם ראוים להם.**

See also *Roke'aḥ*, *Hilkhot Ḥasidut*, *Shoresh Rosh ha-Ḥasidut bi-Teḥillato*, ed. B. S. Shne'orson (repr. Jerusalem, 1960), 11; *Ha-Roke'aḥ ha-Gadol* edn. (Jerusalem, 2014), 19:

> And one should search the Talmud and the Yerushalmi and the Midrash for [new] virtues [or good deeds] and he should perform them and [further] act for the common good [by informing others of their existence], and he should think, perhaps this is the will of his Creator.
>
> **וכל מעלות יש לו לחפש בתלמוד ובירושלמי ובמדרש ויעשה ויזכה את העולם ויחשוב בלבו שמא זה רצון בוראו.**

{As to the element of doubt in Roke'aḥ's remarks, see below, pp. 24–5. He is hedging his bets when addressing a wider audience. I forgo citing the first edition of *Roke'aḥ* (Fano, 1505) as it is seriously defective. At the moment, the best edition is *Ha-Roke'aḥ ha-Gadol*; the most readily available one is that of Shne'orson.} The scanning of *midrashim* for new imperatives is echoed in #1667. (Cf. the remarks of R. El'azar of Worms published by J. Dan in 'Sefer ha-Ḥokhmah le-R. El'azar mi-Vorms u-Mashma'uto le-Toledot Toratah ve-Sifrutah shel Ḥasidut Ashkenaz', *Zion*, 29 [1964], 171 {repr. in id., *'Iyyunim be-Sifrut Ḥasidut Ashkenaz* (Ramat Gan, 1975), 46}, cited in part below, n. 126.) {I am aware that as a result of D. M. Sigal's study 'Sefer ha-Ḥokhmah ha-Meyuḥas la-Roke'aḥ', contained in his *Sodei Razei Semukhin*, 2nd edn. (Jerusalem, 2001), 31–69, the authenticity of much of that work has been compromised. However, the passages that bear upon my argument are not affected. See the authentic text of the introduction to the *Sefer ha-Ḥokhmah* (ibid. 51), and the authentic text of the *Sefer Sodei Razei Semukhin* (ibid. 53). The passages cited below in n. 126 follow the text of Sigal. I would like to thank Daniel Abrams for discussing Sigal's work with me. See also Abrams's article, 'Ketivat ha-Sod be-Ashkenaz ve-ha-Ma'avar li-Sefarad', *Maḥanayim: Riv'on le-Meḥkar, le-Hagut u-le-Tarbut Yehudit* (1994), 94–103.} (The bulk of the first section and the entire second section of this essay were written in the spring of 1967. J. Dan informed me at the time of the existence of the Cambridge manuscript [Add. 669.2], which had previously been in the possession of S. D. Luzzatto, and which was described by him in *Kerem Ḥemed*, 7 (1843), 68–71; see *Sefer Ḥasidim*, ed. J. Wistinetzki, with introduction and indices by J. Freimann (Frankfurt am Main, 1924), introduction, p. 7. Prior to Y. S. Lange's publication of the text in the late 1970s, H. H. Ben-Sasson had drawn attention to this manuscript in 'Ḥasidei Ashkenaz 'al Ḥalukkat Kinyanim Ḥomriyyim ve-Ruḥaniyyim bein Benei Adam', *Zion*, 35 (1970), 61–79; {repr. in id., *Retsef u-Temurah*: *'Iyyunim be-Toledot Yisra'el bi-Yemei ha-Beinayim u-va-'Et ha-Ḥadashah*, ed. J. Hacker (Jerusalem, 1984), 177–97. In the original article, I transcribed the passage from this manuscript. In this edition I have reproduced the text of Lange (which is often eclectic, that is to say, a synthesis of several sources) in

When the Pietists refer to this Larger Will, especially in their declarative moods, they often speak of it as the *retson ha-Borè*, the Will of the Creator.[10] In hasidic thought, the Borè denotes the hidden Divinity as opposed to the revealed Kavod. The Borè is hidden not in the sense that He is unknowable or unfathomable, but that, unlike the Kavod, He is not subject to direct sense perception. His existence, however, may be inferred from hints and signs strewn by Him throughout nature (*zekher 'asah le-nifle'otav*) if they are but viewed in the proper light.[11] A corresponding duality in the nature of Revelation underlies hasidic thought and their terminology is not wholly fortuitous. There is the manifest revelation of the Written and Oral Law (*Torah she-bi-khetav u-ve-'al peh*), a myriad of directives given to Moses at Sinai and to be found explicit in the traditional corpus. Then there is the far more vast hidden revelation of the Creator's Will encoded into Scripture and history and awaiting its decipherment.[12]

accordance with the policy throughout this series that where there is no meaningful difference between print and manuscript, the readily available printed version is cited.

I have intentionally written that Lange published the work 'in the late 1970s', despite the fact that the date on the title page is 1975, for it would appear that the work was intentionally pre-dated and that the actual printing took place some two years later. See below, Ch. 6, n. 1.}

[10] See the opening sections of both editions of *Sefer Ḥasidim* cited briefly above, pp. 8–9. See also *SH*, ##27, 28, which form part of the same programmatic introduction, and see the use of *retson ha-Borè* in the passages cited in n. 50 in light of my remarks there. Note also להעמיק לעשות רצון הבורא, עומק הלכות הבורא, רצון הבורא in the above passages, in #984 and *SHB*, #10, in light of the use of the term *'omek* in hasidic writings for hidden Divine lore (Dan, 'Sefer ha-Ḥokhmah' [above, n. 9], 170 n. 9 {repr. in id., *'Iyyunim be-Sifrut Ḥasidei Ashkenaz* (above, n. 9), 46 n. 9}). See also Y. Baer, 'Ha-Megammah ha-Datit ha-Ḥevratit shel Sefer Ḥasidim' (above, preliminary n. b), 8; {repr. in id., *Meḥkarim u-Masot* (above, n. b), ii. 182, and in Marcus, ed., *Dat ve-Ḥevrah be-Mishnatam shel Ḥasidei Ashkenaz* (above, n. b), 88. An English translation/adaption of the article, without the footnotes, appeared in J. Dan, ed., *Binah: Studies in Jewish History, Thought, and Culture*, ii: *Studies in Jewish Thought* (New York, 1989), 57–95. Our passage is found at p. 62}. Ḥasidei Ashkenaz had a congenital difficulty in adhering to any fixed terminology, even in their esoteric teachings (G. Scholem, *Major Trends in Jewish Mysticism* [New York, 1946], 110; see also my remarks below, pp. 174, 202), and not surprisingly *retson ha-Borè* is often used colloquially with no special connotation (e.g. ##114, 244, 305), just as it is sometimes referred to as the Will of the Holy One, Blessed be He (*retson ha-Kadosh Barukh Hu*, below, n. 52). {As to the Bologna introduction cited in the text, see the Afterword below, sect. A, #4, and sect. B.}

[11] J. Dan, *Torat ha-Sod shel Ḥasidut Ashkenaz* (Jerusalem, 1968), 84–94.

[12] It should be emphasized that the idea of implicit revelation or Will of the Borè is not being inferred from hasidic terminology (a hazardous task at best), but from the content of the entire *Sefer Ḥasidim*. The correspondence of this notion with other aspects of thought is simply being pointed out and a correlation suggested. If the reader feels that these similarities are fortuitous and prefers to speak of this second revelation simply as a 'Larger Divine Will' rather than as 'the Will of the Creator', I have, basically, no quarrel with him. (The subsequent remarks in the text [pp. 15–16] should preclude any misunderstanding that each aspect of the Deity is responsible for a separate and distinct revelation. Nothing could be further from the thoughts of the Pietists.)

This implicit doctrine of dual revelation bears a familial resemblance to the common idea of the 'book of creatures', which, in one form or another, shaped the entire medieval perception of the outside world and, as |316| it also underlay most of its art, found expression in every relief and sculpture attached to fronts and doors of cathedrals of the time and their stained-glass windows. The doctrine taught that God has declared Himself in two manifestations: in the Holy Scripture and in the Book of Nature.[13] The world of the senses is what it appears to be—a structure of physical objects—but it is at the same time a mirror and mystical typology of the attributes of the Creator Himself.

> The world is a book written by the hand of God, in which every creature is a word charged with meaning. The ignorant see the forms—the mysterious letters—understanding nothing of their meaning, but the wise pass from the visible to the invisible, and, in reading nature, read the thoughts of God.[14]

The differences between the Larger Will of the German Pietists and the Christian idea of the Book of Nature that went back ultimately to the Epistle to the Romans[15] are, of course, considerable. The hasidic doctrine dealt with Divine imperatives, the Christian one with Divine attributes; the former asserted deductions of new truths, the latter symbolic reflections of known ones. They share, however, one common assumption: outside the binding, canonized corpus,[16] a 'larger Scripture', as it were, exists which can yield up religious truths upon proper inspection. Did some Ḥasid perhaps hear an outdoor preacher who followed the advice that Guibert of Nogent (d.1124) gave in his sermon manual and brought proof of the faith from natural phenomena?[17] The doctrine of 'hints and signs' (*zekher 'asah le-nifle'otav*) seems clearly patterned on the widespread notion of *vestigia dei*,[18] and it

[13] See e.g. R. Javelet, *Image et ressemblance au douzième siècle: De Saint Anselme à Alain de Lille*, 2 vols. (Paris, 1967), especially i. 227 ff.; E. R. Curtius, *European Literature and the Latin Middle Ages* (New York, 1953), 319 ff. (though I am in no way arguing for any 'book' topos in hasidic thought).

[14] E. Mâle, *The Gothic Image: Religious Art in France of the Thirteenth Century* (New York, 1958), 29 ff.

[15] 1: 20: 'Invisibilia enim ipsius a creatura mundi per ea quae facta sunt intellecta conspiciuntur.'

[16] Binding corpus amongst Jews meant the halakhic portions of the Pentateuch as interpreted by the Oral Law. All narrative portions of the Bible would be part of the 'larger Scripture'.

[17] Curtius, *European Literature and the Latin Middle Ages* (n. 13 above), 318.

[18] Certain ideas suggest themselves naturally to the imagination, and their occurrence in two adjacent societies does not necessarily indicate influence. Others are so strange and novel that they can emerge only in a specific climate of opinion. Though the hasidic system of penance was probably of alien derivation (see below, pp. 24–5), one can easily imagine such practices springing up indigenously. That sin must be expiated is instinctive enough a feeling, and similar doctrines of penance

is possible that |317| the Will of the Borè is ultimately no less derivative of medieval commonplaces. Not that this idea of a second, implicit revelation was consciously adopted by the Pietists—note that while everywhere assumed, it is never explicitly formulated; the notion (a neutral one in essence) was, rather, absorbed from the environment unawares and evolved in time into the major unarticulated premise of *Sefer Ḥasidim*.

But so radical and alien an idea could hardly have achieved unquestioning acceptance unless it answered a profound anterior need. Underlying the movement of Ḥasidei Ashkenaz was the recent discovery of man's hitherto unsuspected capabilities and ingenuity. In the first fresh look at human nature since the Midrash, the Pietists uncovered a creature who (among other qualities) possessed infinite resourcefulness and restless energy, and was capable of heroic exertion in achieving its own ends, and they insisted that religion actively and vigorously demand of man the equivalent mobilization of his abilities for the Divine service.[19] The traditional requirements touched only a

could well emerge in two parallel cultures independent of one another. The notion of inferring God's omniscience from the skills of a bloodhound in tracing its quarry (J. Dan, *Torat ha-Sod shel Ḥasidut Ashkenaz* [Jerusalem, 1968], 90) does not on its own present itself to the mind. Dogs are not naturally associated with the Divinity, nor do the faithful as a rule draw sustenance for their belief from the canine population around them. Only in a culture that systematically viewed the world and its creatures as symbols of religious truths, and which, as a consequence, engaged in religious exegesis of bestiaries, could some thinker find confirmation of Divine attributes in the proficiency of a bloodhound. {On religious exegesis of bestiaries, see Mâle, *The Gothic Image* (n. 14 above), 29ff.; D. Hassig, ed., *The Mark of the Beast: The Medieval Bestiary in Art, Life, and Literature* (New York, 2008); W. B. Clark, *A Medieval Book of Beasts: The Second-Family Bestiaries* (Woodbridge, 2006). On my use of *zekher 'asah le-nifle'otav*, see Afterword, sect. B below.}

[19] #985:

> A man should always . . . think of the craftiness that the world exercises for the purpose of advancement and honor. How so? He should see [i.e. take note of] how a man risks his life and goes to dangerous places for his honor, as do the knights who plunge into the thick of battle so that they not be shamed. And how many acts of cunning have women of high standing performed who have become pregnant through adultery? How many crafty things did they think up so that they should not lose their honor? The same do thieves [that they be not caught]. If for transient honor men toiled [i.e. toil] thus, how much more [must one toil] for the honor of Heaven, and how much cunning must one exercise for the honor of the Creator!
>
> לעולם יהא אדם . . . לחשוב ערמות העולם כנגד תקנתם וכנגד כבודם. כיצד? יראה היאך אדם משים נפשו בכפו והולך במקום סכנה בשביל כבודו כגון הפרשים ההולכים בעומק המלחמה ומוסרים עצמם בשביל כבודם שלא יתביישו. ועוד כמה ערמות הנשים הנכבדות שנתעברו מנאפופיהם, כמה ערמות חשבו שלא יבא לידי הבשת. וכן הגנבים. ומה אילו לכבוד שעה עבדו, בשביל כבוד שמים על אחת כמה וכמה, וכמה צריך להערים בשביל כבוד בוראו.

The Princeton University *Sefer Hasidim* Database registers all three manuscripts containing this passage as reading in the final sentence: מה אילו לכבוד שעה אבדו, and indeed, MS Parma 1133, from which Wistinetzki published, reads אבדו (fo. 91v, col. 1). I find the unwitting emendation of

fraction of his capacities, and he who contented himself with this was no true worshipper of God. This discovery of man and his potentialities was not an opening to Humanism, as in several strands of Christian thought of the time,[20] but a summons to an infinitely more comprehensive submission to the heavenly yoke. It was self-evident to the Pietists that far more had been exacted of man than what the received literature recounted—'"We have not found it [the Torah] of ample strength" [Job 27: 23]: the Torah did not express the [full] Will of the Creator, nor did it address itself to the [full] needs of man'[21]—a second, more demanding revelation simply *had* to exist, and any |318| passing remark about another, 'larger Scripture', as it were, containing religious truths would have fallen on fertile soil. The basic impetus was indigenous; the Will of the Borè was simply the mold into which hasidic aspirations were cast.

What the Pietists envisioned, and this must be emphasized, was not two bodies of rules founded on distinct principles running parallel to one another, but rather a single Divine point radiating outward, forming ultimately two concentric circles. The expansion of both these perimeters was the object of their endeavors, indeed had a common impulse. To scan the horizon for new dictates of God could take on full meaning only if the many already revealed had been fulfilled to their utmost. In their quest to reach the uttermost limits of the Law and to ensure its compliance, the Ḥasidim fashioned a policy of systematic stringency (*haḥmarah*) and of erecting fences about the Law (*seyyagim la-Torah*),[22] which, though beginning as the program of an elite, in the end altered the contours of their community's conduct and outlook. In the early fourteenth century, the halakhic cultures of Ashkenaz and Sefarad were moving ever closer together as R. Asher assimilated in his work the accomplishments of Spanish and Provençal scholars and the school of Gerona

Wistinetzki preferable. Similarly in ##2 (p. 4), 15 (p. 17), 359, 476 (775, 755, 960). *Roke'aḥ, Hilkhot Ḥasidut, Shoresh Zekhiyot 'Arum be-Yir'ah*, ed. Shne'orson (above, n. 9), 17; *Ha-Roke'aḥ ha-Gadol* edn. (above, n. 9), 29. The concept of *'arum be-yir'ah* (cunning or, better yet, unremitting resourcefulness in the fear [i.e. true worship] of God) is a leitmotif of Pietist thought. {I have added in brackets 'true worship' as *yir'ei ha-Shem* is one of the monikers used by Ḥasidei Ashkenaz for members of their movement. See below, n. 52 (end) and p. 121.}

20 R. W. Southern, *Medieval Humanism and Other Studies* (New York, 1970), 29–60 (and more questionably C. Morris, *The Discovery of the Individual, 1050–1200* [London, 1972]). {J. Chydenius, *The Friendship of God and the Two Ends of Man: A Study of Christian Humanism, 1100–1321*, Societas Scientiarum Fennica: Commentationes Humanarum Litterarum 68 (Helsinki, 1981); Rachel Fulton, *From Judgement to Passion: Devotion to Christ and the Virgin Mary, 800–1200* (New York, 2002), 1–192. See also below, Afterword, sect. B end.}

21 *SH*, #1076: לא מצאנוהו שגיא כח—לא דברה תורה כנגד רצון הבורא ולא כפי הצורך לאדם.

22 ##1661, 1664, 1006, 1939, (1838 end); cf. 1503.

adopted and refined the tosafist approach. Yet when the next historical confrontation took place at the end of the sixteenth century, it was clear that Ashkenazic and Sephardic thought were operating in effect in separate worlds. The Code represented the normal increment of halakhic development; the glosses of R. Mosheh Isserles represented the equivalent increment permeated by a sense of inadequacy and proudly molded by both a popular and judicial tendency for stringency.[23]

The Pietists had no quarrel with the dialectical revolution of the French and German Tosafists. That movement had transformed the skeletal demands of the *Ma'aseh ha-Ge'onim* and the *Ha-Oreh* into the comprehensive regulations of the *Sefer ha-Terumah*, *Or Zarua'*, and *Ravyah*. It had elicited principles upon principles long buried in the Talmud and had pushed the religious norm to undreamt-of frontiers. The tosafist achievement was in consonance, then, with the deepest drives of the Pietists. Though Hasidism was born in part as a reaction and corrective to the burgeoning legalism of the twelfth century, the movement was at the same time committed to the latter's dynamic. The very aspirations of Ḥasidei Ashkenaz bound them |319| fast to the dialectic of their French and German brethren with its ceaseless aggrandizement of the Divine dictate. In the mind of the yoke-seeking, norm-intoxicated Pietist, there was little doubt that a double duty had devolved upon the true believer: to develop to the utmost the Law that had been revealed, and to seek out those Divine prescripts embedded elsewhere—in history and Scripture, in historical events both biblical and contemporary, and in passages of the Scripture which had been hitherto viewed as simple narratives.

The outer of the two concentric circles, the Larger Will of God, which the Ḥasidim reverently decoded and made explicit, shows upon inspection to be, not surprisingly, the cumulative cluster of hasidic traditions, principles, and beliefs elevated to normative status,[24] and, as such, precludes unitary definition. The image of an unseen force shaping man's fate formed easy alliance with the popular demonology of their age once it was stripped of its Satanism,[25] and in the thicket of hasidic dicta it is often difficult to disentangle

[23] Y. Sirkes, *Teshuvot ha-Baḥ ha-Yeshanot* (Frankfurt, 1697), #79. It is fashionable nowadays to decry the historiography of the men of the nineteenth-century Jewish Enlightenment (*maskilim*), notably *Dor Dor ve-Dorshav*, and not without justice. However, it should be remembered that they recognized stringency (*ḥumra*) when they saw it. Their error was not so much of fact as in the belief that stringency and leniency are meaningful, indeed *the* meaningful, rubrics of halakhic history.

[24] On my use of the term 'normative', see below, pp. 24–5.

[25] Despite one or two references to *ha-shed* (*diabolus*—see Baer, 'Ha-Megammah ha-Datit ha-Ḥevratit' [above, preliminary n. b], 16 {repr. in id., *Meḥkarim u-Masot* (above, n. b), 190; Eng. translation/adaption in *Binah* (above, n. 10), 70}), the very rich hasidic world of demons has been

ritual from magic. Scrolls, phylacteries, *mezuzot*, and books of the Law, any repository of *kedushah*, are hedged with a multitude of new restrictions, a number of which can be understood only as designed to protect against the mighty taboo of the 'holy', as are all their directives concerning matters involving the Divine name, such as oaths and interdicts. Frustrated in their efforts at communal reforms,[26] they strove to build, at least, pure family units. These efforts, coupled with the traditional concept of good lineage (*yiḥus*) and their own conviction of ancestral merit (*zekhut avot*) as one of the major instruments of Providence, turned their attention |320| to marriage. Popular notions of romantic predestination fused with their own doctrine of celestial archetypes and provided a theoretical framework for the elaborate principles of matchmaking that the hasidic movement produced. Prayer, not surprisingly, received its set of detailed instructions, as did Sabbath, charity, Torah study, dietary laws, and the very prominent relationships with the world of ghosts. Influenced by their Christian environment, they developed from sundry biblical and midrashic tales an elaborate doctrine of penance,[27] and emphasis was placed upon the importance of humility in the life of the Ḥasid. Honesty of the highest order was made imperative and directives abound for

stripped of its satanic properties. In *Sefer Ḥasidim* (as in most Jewish literatures, Professor Scholem informs me) *shedim* are troublesome, at times even physically dangerous, but they are not evil. They are never agents of Lucifer seeking to ensnare man in sin. This is all the more remarkable in view of the fact that contemporary Christian demons are invariably the emissaries of the Kingdom of Darkness (cf. e.g. Caesarius of Heisterbach, *Dialogue on Miracles* [London, 1929], vol. i, Bk. IV, pp. 309–90). The Ḥasid was impervious to such influences, for the purity of Sa'adyah's Deity and the awesome omnipotence of the Throne-God of hasidic Merkavah traditions prevented him from seriously entertaining the idea of a force standing in opposition to His will. Contemporary demons were accepted as a natural but not theological force. For an extreme formulation of this position, see *Or Zarua'*, ii (Zhitomir, 1862), #147:

> 'Perhaps these reports were given by Joseph the Demon' [*'Eruvin* 43a]. Rashi explained that he [the demon] does not observe the Sabbath. [However], my teacher R. Yehudah [he-Ḥasid] used to say that the demons believe in the Torah and [even] observe all that the Sages [of the Talmud] have said. And they asked him, if so, how does he [the demon] have sexual relations with a married woman, and he [R. Yehudah] replied . . .
>
> דילמא יוסף שידא אמרינהו [עירובין מג ע"א], פירש רש"י דלא מנטר שבתא. מורי ה"ר יהודה זצ"ל היה אומר שהשדים מאמינים בתורה ועושים כל מה שאמרו חכמים. ושאלו ממנו א"כ למה בא על אשת איש והשיב וכו'.

See also the passage in the Bodley manuscript cited in Dan, *'Iyyunim be-Sifrut Ḥasidei Ashkenaz* (above, n. 9), 142. (The second word in the passage should read *niv'elet*.) See also J. Trachtenberg, *Jewish Magic and Superstition: A Study in Folk Religion* (New York, 1939), 35.

[26] Cf. below, pp. 24–30.

[27] Baer, 'Ha-Megammah ha-Datit ha-Ḥevratit' (above, preliminary n. b), 18–20 {repr. in id., *Meḥkarim u-Masot* (above, n. b), 192–4; Eng. translation/adaption in *Binah* (above, n. 10), 70–2}.

the conduct of private and communal affairs in the spirit of humaneness and equity.[28]

[28] The phrase *humaner Billigkeit* is Scholem's, *Major Trends in Jewish Mysticism* (above, n. 10), 94, and deserves, I think, wider currency.

A number of these directives are assumed under the name of *din shamayim*, a category which has achieved such prominence in recent historiography that a few words may be in place. After reading the relevant sections in Aquinas on *jus divinum* or *lex divina* (*Summa Theologica*, I, II, Q. 91, A. 4, 5), it becomes difficult to see what it has to do with *din shamayim*, understood as 'the natural law implanted in man's conscience'. *Lex divina* is the exact reverse of that. It is a revealed code given to man precisely because the fallibility of his reason and instinct left him in need of explicit directives. The passage sometimes cited in proof of the similarity of these two concepts (*Sum. Theol.*, I, II, Q. 96, A. 2) deals with Divine Providence and not at all with Divine Law. Another writer has cautiously termed *din shamayim* a 'kind of natural law'. But then the identity of terms is lost, and it is this identity that provides the simplest evidence of overt influence. It is wisest to eschew the term 'natural law' altogether, for it assumes conceptions of an ordered cosmos, a universal reason, a community of mankind, and the like, ideas as alien to Ḥasidei Ashkenaz as a motor car. The dozen or so instances of *din shamayim* scattered about the 2,000 sections of *Sefer Ḥasidim* in no sense represent the perception of a fixed and eternal body of general truths that serve as a basis for the construction of a natural ethic. They are, rather, a spotty group of glosses. All are 'ad hoc' dicta, the predominant number of which treat restitution in cases of theft or damage (##22 [twice]; 43; 90, 89, 1888, 1964; 632; 1323 [164]), as do the dozen cases of *din shamayim* in the Talmud clustered thickly in the sixth chapter of *Bava Kamma* (55b–56a, 118a) and in *Bava Metsi'a* 37a, and after which those of Ḥasidei Ashkenaz are clearly patterned. They form a limited and, occasionally, sensitized expansion of the talmudic principle of *din shamayim*, namely, that the moral obligations in tort exceed the legal ones. This is expanded in one or two rulings to include waivers where the full exercise of one's rights would lead to, or would in itself be, an injustice (##1207, 1214, 1313), and then to certain specific judicial corrections when the execution of the general (and of necessity uniform) ordinance would be palpably unfair (#1381 [see #1005] and #1289 [see #1840], and see above, p. 12). The term is employed once with regard to filial piety (##1725–6), again in admonishing against supping heartily at a miser's table (#848), and yet once more in emphasizing the importance of intent in evaluating human actions (#1673; see below, p. 22). If correlatives must be had for its predominant use, a rough approximation would be found in equity, which, as Maitland has eloquently reminded us, is never a body of law but a collection of appendices. {F. M. Maitland, *Equity: A Course of Lectures*, ed. A. H. Chaytor and W. J. Whittaker, 2nd, rev., edn. (Cambridge, 1949), 18.}

Din shamayim is but a small and rather prosaic fragment of the larger, revolutionary *retson ha-Borè*. As S. Assaf has already noted, there is little in the hasidic *din shamayim* that has neither geonic precedent nor Spanish parallel. (Baer, 'Ha-Megammah ha-Datit ha-Ḥevratit' (above, preliminary n. b), 13 n. 25 {repr. in id., *Meḥkarim u-Masot* (above, n. b), 187 n. 25. As I remarked in n. 10, the English article in *Binah* is a translation only of the text, not of the notes.}) For sooner or later any legal system must provide for effectual redress where, by reason of the special circumstances of the case, the redress at law is inadequate. This universally felt need could be taken by Ḥasidei Ashkenaz as part of God's Larger Will and a ready-made term, *din shamayim*, easily given it, for it was only an elaboration of that talmudic principle enunciated in passages known to every schoolboy. The quotidian significance of *din shamayim* was minuscule. How often was one involved in torts and thefts? Its invocation by a judge of hasidic persuasion would awaken few murmurs among his non-hasidic colleagues for they shared similar goals. (Anyone who imagines that many judges let an instance of

|321| Personal ethics and sensitized social relations form a considerable, and certainly attractive, part of the Divine Will. However, it is, as we have seen, far from the whole of the Pietists' conception of that imperative. The traditions upon which they drew had ever refused to admit a distinction between ritual and morality, nor could the hasidic mentality have ever maintained one. Significantly, the trenchant terms 'commandments between man and God' (*bein adam la-makom*) and 'between man and his fellowman' (*bein adam la-ḥavero*) make no appearance in their writings. Before one rashly locates the movement's center of gravity, it would be wise to recollect that in the classical formulation of *hilkhot ḥasidut* by R. El'azar of Worms, the social teachings, as distinct from those of personal virtue, are anemic if not altogether absent,[29] and that the famous will |322| attributed to the move-

talyuha ve-zaben, a coerced sale [*Bava Batra* 47b], pass unimpeded through their hands is rather naive.) There is no precedent or parallel to the hundreds of prescriptions of the Borè that flowed ceaselessly from the hasidic pen. They altered the contours of the Pietists' daily life and could only arouse astonishment, consternation, and opposition among those in whom the ideals of the movement struck no responsive chord. It is in the sweeping *retson ha-Borè* that we can grasp the hasidic daring, and it was here that the clash with the establishment was brewing. (As to the claims of 'latent antagonism' between *din shamayim* and *din torah*, see below, p. 59.) {On *din shamayim*, see now A. Kirschenbaum, *Equity in Jewish Law: Beyond Equity* (Hoboken, NJ, 1991), 137–77. See also J. L. Rubenstein, 'The Laws of Heaven in *Sefer Hasidim*', in R. M. Geffen and M. B. Edelman, eds., *Freedom and Responsibility: Exploring the Challenges of Jewish Continuity* (Hoboken, NJ, 1998), 79–99. See Afterword, sect. D below.}

[29] Ben-Sasson, in 'Ḥasidei Ashkenaz 'al Ḥalukkat Kinyanim' (above, n. 9), 61–79 {repr. in id., *Retsef u-Temurah* (above, n. 9), 177–97} has drawn attention to the absence of social protest in R. El'azar's writings. The latter's indifference to our way of thinking goes much further than that. Not only is he without any desire to alter the social order, but even on a personal plane, the quality of man's relationships with his fellow man scarcely interests him. In the exposition of Pietism that he prefaced to the *Roke'aḥ*, the qualities of justice and benevolence receive little emphasis, and in his portrait of the Ḥasid sensitized social relationships are barely adumbrated. The *Hilkhot Ḥasidut* of R. El'azar is a propaedeutic to spiritual ascent and self-perfection, in which man's dealings with his brethren hardly figure. When they do appear, it is primarily to the extent that such intercourse affects not the other person's life but the Ḥasid's own moral development. Yet the formulations of the Ba'al ha-Roke'aḥ, inward-turning and 'self-centered' as they are, were accepted by friend and foe alike as the classic summary of the movement's aspirations, something incomprehensible had social ethics occupied anything near the importance commonly attached to them. Moreover, could the two figures of R. El'azar of Worms and R. Yehudah he-Ḥasid have been so identified and interchanged with one another for 700 years had they parted company over issues which, we are told, constituted the very core of the movement? In *Sefer Ḥasidim*, thoughts of social reform are few and far between, but (following here R. Yehudah rather than R. El'azar) many passages indicate a deep and abiding concern with refinement and considerateness in human relations. Real as these sentiments are, they form (as noted in the text) only part of hasidic concerns. German Pietism was a religious rather than social movement, and for this reason a person could achieve a commanding, indeed an authoritative, position among its adherents even though he was almost bereft of any social consciousness.

ment's founder, R. Yehudah he-Ḥasid, is without any ethical prescriptions whatsoever.[30]

The significance of *retson ha-Borè* lay not in the tension between two concurrent norms—this is largely illusory—but in the proclamation of the inadequacy of the Law to encompass experience, to bring within its orbit both the larger and more interior spheres of human activity. It went yet deeper. The Larger Will of Ḥasidei Ashkenaz was an assertion that man, in his relationship to himself and to God, to the Divine worship and to his fellow man, to the demons and the dead, to places and to things, was in need of unremitting guidance that the traditional corpus of halakhah and aggadah could not provide. This notion marked for Ashkenazic Jewry the advent of the Middle Ages. Even in the most norm-oriented society, law is only a skeletal structure. The patterns of thought and of imagination, the values and ideals of conduct, the ethos and *areté* are the flesh and blood of any civilization. By their twin achievements in halakhah and Midrash, the *tanna'im* and *amora'im* had produced such an integrated whole and provided Jewry with its cultural matrix. For many generations, while outer life was regulated by the Law, the spiritual sensibilities of a nation were nurtured on the aggadah. From the writings of R. Mosheh ha-Darshan, one can see that in the early eleventh century the midrashic outlook had not only sustained itself, but was still creatively alive. By Rashi's time creativity had ceased; yet it is clear from his commentary on the Torah that the world of the aggadah remained the basic frame of reference, and that the mind and soul of pre-Crusade Jewry still found rest in it. Rashi extracted from midrashic sources what he was most attuned to, but he experienced those parts traditionally. There is selectivity in his outlook but not reinterpretation. In the course of the twelfth century, however, renascent |323| Europe pressed in on Ashkenazic culture and succeeded in medievalizing it. The categories that had long given to experience its reliable and coherent character had disintegrated. Midrash, understood on its own terms, could no longer provide a *Weltanschauung* for succeeding generations. Romantic predestination, celestial archetypes, *din shamayim*, genius loci, demons, the enormous panoply of *gematriyot* of the Pietists are all attempts to develop some conceptual apparatus to order anew the facts of experience and to invest them with significance. But new modes of perception and a fresh religious sensibility would be inconceivable unless they were discovered to have been long implicit in the sacred literature. A new world of aggadah would have to arise—expounding, exploiting, and reinterpreting the traditional corpus. In

[30] The actual authorship of R. Yehudah is questionable, but the testament is certainly a product of the movement.

many senses *Sefer Ḥasidim* and R. Yehudah's radical commentary on the Torah[31] are simply a medieval German *midrash*. They reflect the attempt of a new religious culture to find its values in the canonized literature and to see them not as their own thoughts but as the expression of the Divine Will.[32]

If the halakhic hierarchy of sanctions and traditional classification of *mitsvot—ḥayyavei mitot bet-din, ḥayyavei keritot, lo ta'aseh, issur 'aseh*—had reflected a corresponding scale of values, no opportunity would have been afforded for the newly discovered norms to take on any significance, even for

[31] MS Cambridge Add. 669.2 {subsequently published as *Perushei ha-Torah le-R. Yehudah he-Ḥasid*, ed. Y. S. Lange (Jerusalem, 1975)}.

[32] R. Yehudah's drive to renarrate the Bible according to his outlook, and his profound conviction that he was only eliciting the meaning of the text, can perhaps be illustrated by his interpretation of the *maḥatsit ha-shekel* reported by his son (MS Cambridge Add. 669.2, fos. 43r–44v {*Perushei ha-Torah le-R. Yehudah he-Ḥasid*, 110–11}) and reproduced partially by Ben-Sasson in 'Ḥasidei Ashkenaz 'al Ḥalukkat Kinyanim' (above, n. 9), 64–6 {repr. in his *Retsef u-Temurah* (above, n. 9), 180–1}. The passage concludes thus:

> וכל אלו הדברים אמ' לי גם מ"א [מורי אבי] על פסוק אחר כי היה מקש' שני פסוקים אהדדי, פסוק אחד אומ' כל העובר על הפקודים מחצית השקל ופסוק (חד) [אחר] אומר כל העובר על הפקודי' וגו' הא כיצד אלא כל העובר נותן הפקודי' זהו המקבל. והקש[יתי] לו א"כ מה שעשה הפייט . . . ועוד מהו ויכפר על נפשותיכ', ועוד מהו לא יהיה בכם נגף ונתנו איש כופר נפשו. ופי' לי שמשה צוה לו לגזבר ליתן לו במתנה גמורה (ולא) ולא במתנה על מנת להחזיר, הרי אם היו רוצים היו תופשי' לעצמן בטוב. ואע"פ היו נותנין. ועוד שאר היה תי' לי, ולא נראה לי. ואמרתי מעולם לא עלתה על דעת משה רבי'. וגער בי מ"א ואמר לי הלואי שהייתה כל התורה כולה סדורה כדבר זה.

> Similar things he [my father] used to say on another verse. He used to point out the contradiction between the verse 'This they shall give all who passed the census, half a shekel' [Exod. 30: 13] and the verse 'half a shekel . . . *to* all who passed the census' [Exod. 38: 26; emphasis mine]. [He replied,] 'to all who passed'—this refers to the receivers. And I asked him. 'The *payyetan* [liturgical poet] [on this weekly portion of the Torah reading, Parashat Shekalim,] writes . . . How can [the half-shekel] "make an atonement for your souls" [Exod. 30: 1]? Furthermore, "and there will be no plague among them". And "Then shall they give a ransom for his soul"' . . .
>
> And he [my father] answered me that Moses ordered the treasurer to give him [them, i.e. the poor, the half-shekel] as an outright gift, and they could well have kept it for themselves; nevertheless, they gave [the half-shekel] to Moses. And he gave me other answers that did not persuade me, and I said, '[All] this never occurred to Moses our Master.' And my father angrily reprimanded me saying, 'Would that the entire Torah was as ordered [i.e. clear] to me as is this matter [i.e. my interpretation of these verses].'

{The text in some places is elliptical, but here, as opposed to Ch. 6 below, it is of no matter, as even an elliptical text proves the point that R. Yehudah he-Ḥasid radically reinterpreted Scripture.}

The practical significance of this interpretation, or more accurately its inspiration, is to be found in *SH*, #914 as H. H. Ben-Sasson pointed out. {See my remarks on this passage below, pp. 157–60.} (The last two lines of our citation are missing in MS Moscow, RSL Günzburg 82, fo. 179r. A brief summary of R. Yehudah's interpretation is found in MS London, British Library 243, fo. 21v, and is reproduced in A. Marmorstein, 'Sur un auteur français inconnu du treizième siècle', *Revue des Études Juives*, 76 [1923], 117—though at p. 118 he mistakenly attributes the passage to the Tosafist R. Yehudah Sirleon of Paris.)

Ḥasidim. For lacking such sanctions, they would be regarded as trivia, present but peripheral. Hence the Pietists insisted that the official penalties were a necessary convention only and threw no light on the |324| intrinsic worth of any deed. They foretold not what retribution would be meted out to man either in this world or in the next, and certainly the Bible provided ample documentation of how seeming minutiae evoked Divine wrath.[33] A psychological rather than a practical disruption was intended. Parts of the traditional hierarchy of emphasis in the Jewish way of life were to be altered, and the process demanded the breaking of the commonly accepted yardsticks of importance.

Pietism entailed a further axiological displacement. As the intuitive religious perception of the Ḥasidim was interior, they tended to look less upon the deed itself, as law by its nature must, than upon the thoughts and feelings that lay behind it. It was in the immolation of desire, the contravention of instinct, that they located the significance of the religious act.[34] God's will, in its fullness, measures all deeds, great or small, according to the extent to which they were performed despite one's deepest inclinations. Continence rather than temperance makes the moral man. From this perspective halakhic hierarchies were leveled. Different acts could be ultimately of identical value, just as identical acts might be of differing value to different people, or to the same person at different moments. Besides introducing a permanent freshness into the round of religious performances and a persistent incentive for self-conquest, the doctrine of 'action in the line of greatest resistance' was able to hold out promises of ever-increasing reward as the Divine Will was discovered to demand the curtailment of man's more elementary drives and its fulfillment encountered mounting difficulties.

Accompanying this shift from the formal and overt to the interior was the notion that moral responsibility for one's deeds did not begin at the fixed age of legal adulthood but came rather with the advent of intellectual discernment, and accordingly Divine retribution was meted out to minors.[35] It was circumstances, the Ḥasidim further noted, that allowed or disallowed a per-

[33] ##15 (p. 21), 157, 986, 1046, 1146, 1287, 1289, 1519, 1840.

[34] ##15 (p. 21), 43, 47, 986, 1289, 1518, 1836, 1964, 1967; *Ḥokhmat ha-Nefesh* (Safed, 1913), fo. 22c; {Sodei Razaya edn. (Jerusalem, 2006), 92b–93a.}

[35] *Moshav Zekenim 'al ha-Torah*, ed. D. Sassoon (London, 1959), 74–5; MS Cambridge, Add. 669.2, fo. 21v {subsequently published as *Perushei ha-Torah le-R. Yehudah he-Ḥasid* (above, n. 31), 52–3}; *SH*, ##16, 217, and reflected in #1966 (in conjunction with #1725). {*Minḥat Yehudah: Perush la-Torah me-et Rabbi Yehudah b. El'azar mi-Ba'alei ha-Tosafot*, i: *Bereshit*, ed. Ḥ. Touitou (Jerusalem, 2012), 38: 10 (p. 152); *Tosafot ha-Shalem: Otsar Perushei Ba'alei ha-Tosafot*, ed. Y. Gliss (Jerusalem, 1985), iv. 64.}

formance. Only the inner decision to act was wholly in man's hands, and so in God's eyes, in instances where execution proved to be beyond man's power, the inner (might we say autonomous) resolution for action was equivalent to the deed itself.[36] This interior perspective was a departure |325| from formal legal thinking and arose as a corrective to the growing legal consciousness of the period. Needless to say, the aim of the Ḥasidim was only axiological. No Ḥasid dreamt of hanging a 10-year-old or of thinking of a *lulav* instead of taking it. He sought, rather, to endow transactions of the soul with significance equal to those of the body.

II

כל הדברים אשר דבר ה׳ נעשה—נַעֲשֶׂה

R. Shemu'el he-Ḥasid

The talmudic dictum that a public benefactor was credited with all the good done by his beneficiaries as a result of his act[37] provided a backdrop for another major theme of the Pietist movement: that of acting for the common good (*le-zakkot et ha-rabbim*). No one could doubt that such conduct was highly commendable, for the Talmud speaks admiringly of it. In a sense it may even have been understood to be obligatory. However, its fluid and amorphous nature eluded capture in the net of normative thought, and no directive for its performance is to be found in the literature of the Franco-German communities from their dawn until the rise of the Pietist movement some two centuries later. It was inevitable, then, that most people had a less than vibrant awareness of their duties in this sphere.

A broadened and sensitized awareness of the social consequences of one's actions was demanded by the Ḥasidim,[38] as they sought to break the traditional narrow categories of causation and to imbue man with a wider sense of responsibility for the outcome of his deeds.[39] Praise for the benefactor (*mezakkeh*) of the public[40] and opprobrium for one who causes the public to sin

[36] ##4, 5, 6, 47, 110, 199, 424, 1325, 1376, 1530, 1673 {and see #1052 end (p. 266)}.

[37] *Avot* 5: 18: משה זכה וזיכה את הרבים זכות הרבים תלוי בו.

[38] ##56–160, 478, 600, 738, 1555, 1819, *et ad libitum*.

[39] ##18, 157, 158, MS Oxford, Bodley 1566, fo. 178r: חסיד אחד היה מלמד בנותיו לכתוב. אמר שאם לא ידעו לכתוב הרי צריכות לבקש שיכתבו להם כתבים למשכונות כשמלוין מעותיהן וייתיחדו עם הכותבים ויחטאו. וזה יהיה כפשיעתי שכל מי שבידו לעשות גדר לעבירה ואינו עושה, כאילו הוא גרם (and previous note).

[40] ##{34,} 125, 158, 641, 745, 1035, 1036, 1038. *Talmud Torah* is to be structured so as to enable maximum public benefit (##762–5, 1495), and innumerable similar instructions are found with regard to the writing of books, e.g. ##1739, 1740 *et ad libitum*.

(*maḥti*) are so frequent as to constitute one of the leitmotifs of *Sefer Ḥasidim*.[41] Acting for the common weal becomes now a standard characteristic of the hasidic image of the righteous man |326| (*tsaddik*),[42] and, conversely, failure to take a public stand against wrongdoing is seen as one of the potent sins shaping history which unleash retribution upon the seemingly innocent.[43] Incorrigible sinners are to be systematically sacrificed to the common good.[44] Conversely, despite their profound horror of sin, *yir'at ha-ḥet* (which is one of their deepest legacies to the Ashkenazic community), they counsel, contrary perhaps to the Talmud, performing minor sins to prevent major trespassing by the public.[45]

Communal responsibility and action of set purpose for the general good were partly an outgrowth of the aristocratic traditions of the movement's leaders, the Kalonymides, who for centuries had stood at the helm of the German communities. But in part they were an outcome of the Pietists' ideology.[46] Actually, the Ḥasidim were ambivalent as to the nature of their doctrines. They knew that nothing that they would ever elicit from the pages of the Bible or from history could take on the obligatory character of, say, the eating of matzot, and, in view of the rigid legal connotations of the term *ḥovah* (obligation) they would have shied away from ascribing a binding nature to their teachings. Yet, on the other hand, they had discovered God's will in its

[41] ##122, 187, 191, 192, 198, 208, 358, 747, 790, 1968. R. El'azar of Worms singles this sinner out in *Roke'aḥ, Hilkhot Yom Ha-Kippurim*, #216 {ed. Shne'orson (above, n. 9), 105; *Ha-Roke'aḥ ha-Gadol* edn. (above, n. 9), 226. The phrase **בזה [ו]לעולם הבא** is an idiomatic expression for this world and the world to come. See e.g. the subsequent remarks of Roke'aḥ in #217: **והחוטא העושה תשובה יתכפר לו לעולם הבא, אך בזה יהיה לו יסורין** (ed. Shne'orson, 110; *Ha-Roke'aḥ ha-Gadol* edn., 237).}

[42] *SH*, #815, where the description of the ideal love of God runs thus: **וכל חיבת שעשוע לב האוהב את ה' בכל לבבו ובכל הרהוריו איך לעשות רצון הבורא ולזכות את הרבים ולעשות קידוש השם ולמסור את עצמו באהבת את הבורא זהו יראת ה' שלא תעבור וכו'** {taken from *Roke'aḥ, Hilkhot Ḥasidut, Shoresh Ahavah*; *Sodei Razaya* in *Sifrei ha-Ra mi-Germaiza, Ba'al ha-Roke'aḥ*, ed. A. Eizenbach (Jerusalem, 2006), i, sect. 1, 9a; *Ḥokhmat ha-Nefesh* (Safed edn., fos. 13c, 14a, 25d; Sodei Razaya edn., 55a [**כי מורים כהלכה ומזכים את הרבים**], 57b–58a [**ומזכה אחרים**], 105a–b). On the editions of the *Ḥokhmat ha-Nefesh*, see above, p. 6, preliminary note.} (See also *SH*, #1557.) On what that ideal may have meant in practice to the ordinary Ḥasid, see below, n. 76. {N. A. van Uchelen has underscored the role of *kol yisra'el 'arevim zeh la-zeh* in the notions of acting for and against the public good; see his 'Aspects of Pietist Solidarity in *Sefer Hasidim*: Analysis of a Motif', *Frankfurter Judaistische Beiträge*, 21 (1994), 69–79.}

[43] ##1, 115–16, 225, 305 (p. 98), 361 (end), 1273, 989, 1295, 1345, based on *Shabbat* 54b, *'Avodah Zarah* 5a. Obligations extend even to Gentiles (#1968).

[44] ##181–5.

[45] #125. Cf. *Shabbat* 4a: **וכי אומרים לאדם חטא כדי שיזכה חבירך.**

[46] Professor Morton Bloomfield has drawn my attention to the theme of *bonum commune* in Aquinas (*Sum. Theol.*, I, II, Q. 90, A. 2; II, II, Q. 58, A. 5, 6) and the rich literature it has engendered in recent times. I am, however, unaware of the twelfth- and thirteenth-century antecedents of this idea and the measure of its popular diffusion, if any, and therefore cannot say whether it played a role in shaping the Pietists' outlook.

plenitude and, surely, obedience to this was not optional. In this spirit they spoke of converts to Ḥasidism as penitents,[47] viewing as sins the past deeds performed in obliviousness to *retson ha-Borè*, and, again, they warned of the obligation incumbent upon all to consult the Ḥasid or Ḥakham, who was wise and learned in the laws of the Borè, so as to ascertain the will of God on any doubtful point.[48] More significant than the fullness of the Divine Will was its potency. Those who |327| transgressed it, even unwittingly, were subjected to the most dire punishment in this world and in the next. Did not chastisement presume obligation? How could the Ḥasid desist from guiding the ignorant through the tangled wilderness of God's covert wishes by the light of his newly discovered truth? To have so refrained would have been to sit idly back as his brethren went to their destruction. The ideology of the movement and its deepest sentiments called for action. Now that we know how the supposedly quietistic Ḥasidim carried their convictions about liturgy to the point of book-burning,[49] we should not at all be surprised by their declaration 'Be in matters of "God-fearingness" [i.e. religious matters] among the victorious and not among the vanquished. For example, if it lies within your power to make fences [about the Law] and to protest [successfully] against transgressors.'[50] This only echoed the words of the movement's founder, R. Shemu'el he-Ḥasid, who wrote: '"All the words which the Lord has spoken we will do [*na'aseh*]" [Exod. 24: 3]. [Instead of] *na'aseh* [we will do] read *ne'asseh* [we will compel], i.e. [concerning all the words which the Lord has spoken], we will compel those Jews who refuse to obey.'[51] Given the nature of *Sefer Ḥasidim*, we could not expect to read there an account of their efforts of reform and correction. Nevertheless, scattered passages and keywords betray a pungent and

[47] *SHB*, ##1, 7, 29. Cf. Y. Baer, 'Ha-Megammah ha-Datit ha-Ḥevratit' (above, preliminary n. b), 9 {repr. in id., *Meḥkarim u-Masot* (above, n. b), 181; Eng. translation/adaption in *Binah* (above, n. 10), 64. As to the Bologna citations, see the Afterword, sect. A, #1 below.}

[48] ##1324, 1506, 110, 1328 (1941–2).

[49] *'Arugat ha-Bosem*, ed. E. E. Urbach (Jerusalem, 1963), iv. 80–3. {See now S. Emanuel, 'Ha-Pulmos shel Ḥasidei Ashkenaz 'al Nusakh ha-Tefillah', in Y. Sussman and D. Rosenthal, eds., *Meḥkerei Talmud: Kovets Ma'amarim be-Talmud u-vi-Teḥumim Govlim Mukdash le-Zikhro shel Professor Ephraim A. Urbach* (Jerusalem, 2005), iii. 2, 591–625.}

[50] *SHB*, #648. The passage in the Berlin edition (#117) is truncated and should be corrected accordingly. (The successful nature of the protest envisioned is clear from the context.) {See the description in the *Ḥokhmat ha-Nefesh* of the ideal *tsaddik*, who, in the afterlife, earns the greatest proximity to the supernal Kavod: **יש שנכנס כבר בבירית הכבוד, כי יש צדיק גמור ומוחה ברבים וסובל בעולם הזה . . . אז יזכו כי מורים כהלכה ומזכים את הרבים על כן יהיו תחת כסא הכבוד כמו חיות [הקודש]** (Safed edn., fo. 13c; Sodei Razaya edn., 55a–b).}

[51] **כל הדברים אשר דבר ה' נעשה—נְעָשֶׂה (ונברך) [ונכריח] את ישראל הממאנים לשמוע**. Thus in MS Munich, Bayerische Staatsbibliothek 15, fo. 152v, cited in *Kitvei Avraham Epstein* (above, n. 1), 256. The emendation is Epstein's.

acrimonious reality,[52] and we find the thought of the Pietists marked, perhaps even scarred, by their struggles for acceptance and influence, apostolic contentions more lost than won.

[52] See the lengthy exposition on 'thorns and thistles' (*kots ve-dardar*) in *Ḥokhmat ha-Nefesh* (Safed, 1913), fo. 23a {Sodei Razaya edn., 94a–b} (cited in full below, pp. 31–3), which clearly reflects contemporary conflicts (and see below, n. 68 for their demands for slow recitation of the *pesukei de-zimra* and n. 72 for its interminable length). Reference is made in *Sefer Ḥasidim* to certain rules as being operational only if 'the good men [*tovim*, *boni*] have the upper hand [*yad ha-tovim tekefah*]' #1591 (##1770, 1372, 1382), and elsewhere (#1343) the Ḥasidim are described as being foiled: 'Most of the communal heads are good men [*tovim*], who wish to institute the Will of God, but are unable because of the arrogant ones [*ge'im*]' (**ורוב ראשי הקהל טובים וברצונם לתקן רצון הקב"ה ואין יכולים מפני הגאים**). Similarly #989: 'And this one [i.e. communal leader] was arrogant [*ge'eh*] and did as [whatever] his [base] inclinations desired and aided the sinners, and [others] were unable to protest because of this arrogant man, who made the good men greatly fear him' (**וזה מתגאה ועושה מה שייצרו מתאוה ומסייע עוברי עבירה ואין יכולין למחות בידם מפני זה גאה שחיתתו על הטובים**). See #1326: 'One should not put fear in the good men' (**אל יפיל אדם אימה על הטובים**), and equally #1325: 'if those who feared heaven [*yir'ei shamayim*] wished to enact [new] ordinances and were unsuccessful because others would not listen to them' (**ואם עסקו יראי שמים לתקן תקנות והנה לא (מסייע) [איסתייע] מילתא (היא) שלא היו נשמעים להם**).

R. El'azar of Worms repeats the theme of thorns and thistles in *Ḥokhmat ha-Nefesh* (Safed edn.), fo. 19a {Sodei Razaya edn., 78b}, and sums up thus:

> If the men of the city are worthy, then the wicked are defeated by the righteous [*tsaddik*] and the good men [*tovim*] are able to confer benefits upon the wicked [i.e. institute ordinances which prevent them from sinning], and the righteous are able to enact the Will of the Creator—there is joy before Him [a circumlocution to avoid the anthropomorphism 'He rejoices'] . . . However, if the men of the city are not worthy, He hands the city over to the arrogant and the cruel and the iniquitous . . . And the righteous are unable to do the Will of the Creator and [institute] their [i.e. His] enactments because of the wicked.
>
> **אם זכו אנשי העיר נופלין הרשעים מפני הצדיקים ומזכין הטובים את הרעים ויכולין הצדיקין כל רצון הבורא לעשות, ושמחה לפניו . . . ואם לא זכו בני העיר מוסר העיר ביד גאים ואכזרים וביד עוולנים . . . וגם הצדיקים לא יכלו רצון בוראם ותקנתם לעשות מפני הרעים.**

Similar significance should be attached to such actual descriptions of communal leaders as that in #1344 (see below, n. 72), which concludes: 'because he used to put fear and dread in the hearts of God-fearers [*yir'ei ha-Shem*], and he would, out of spite, hurry [the recitation of] the "praises" [*ha-shevaḥot*, i.e. *pesukei de-zimra*] in the synagogue, and he prevented the righteous ones [*tsaddikim*] from performing their religious duties [*mitsvot*] and would expel from the synagogue whomever he wished, and he gave aid to the transgressors [of God's will], and he scorned the God-fearers [*yir'ei ha-Shem*]' (**כי היה מטיל יראתו ואימתו על יראי השם ולהכעיס היה ממהר השבחות [=פסוקי דזמרא] בבית הכנסת ומונע צדיקים מן המצות ומגרש מבית הכנסת מי שירצה, ומסייע לעוברי עבירה ויראי ה' מנאץ**). This is echoed in #1968: 'He who causes others to sin or he that frightens people [into submission] and they are afraid to do the will of their Creator' (**המחטיא את הרבים או מי שחיתתו נופלת על העם ויראים לעשות רצון בוראם**). These communal opponents and their doubly sad fate won special mention in the *Hilkhot Yom ha-Kippurim* of Roke'aḥ: 'He who causes the public to sin or prevents the public from acting properly and mocks and hates the good men will be punished both in this world and in the world to come' (**אבל המחטיא את הרבים או מונע את הרבים מלזכות ומתלוצץ ושונא את הטובים לוקה בזה [ו]לעולם הבא**). {For the source and the idiomatic expression **בזה [ו]לעולם הבא**, see above, n. 41. I suspect that the correct reading in the *Roke'aḥ* is **ומונע מלזכות את הרבים** ('and prevents others from acting for the public good', a major and often-stressed point in the hasidic agenda, as is its opposite—causing the

|328| Their so-called doctrine of ataraxy sprang, it would seem, less from any spiritual or historical kinship with Cynicism than from the pressing needs of the movement.[53] The Franco-German community was permeated by a profound |329| conviction of its religiosity and its dedication to the Law, and

public to sin; see above, p. 23 and nn. 40, 41). However, I have translated the passage as it stands. Little help can be had from manuscripts as there is only one full manuscript of the *Roke'aḥ*, Bibliothèque Nationale, 363, and to all intents and purposes, it is identical with the printed version.} The isolation felt by the Ḥasid and his need for authoritative support in his struggles is reflected in his wistful interpretation of the Psalmist's words, in #1037:

> 'I am a friend [*ḥaver*] to all that fear you' [Ps. 119: 63]. Is it possible to be a friend to the entire world? There were those who didn't know David and whom David didn't know, however, [this is the interpretation] . . . when the fearers of God [*yir'ei ha-Shem*] would give a ruling in civil law or render a decision in ritual law and the sharp-minded, wicked men would testify and rule wickedly—forbidding that which was permitted and contaminating that which was pure—they [the *yir'ei ha-Shem*] would send to David, and he would join them [***u-mitḥaber lahem***] and agree with the ***yir'ei ha-Shem*** in his **writings**. (emphases mine)

> **חבר אני לכל אשר יראוך [תהילים קי״ט, ס״ג] וכי אפשר להיות חבר לכל העולם, יש שלא היו מכירים את דוד ודוד לא היה מכירם אלא . . . כשהיו יראי ה׳ עושים דין או הוראה וחריפי רשעים מעידים ומורים לרעה מאסור מותר ומטמא טהור, והיו שולחים לדוד ומתחבר להם דוד להסכים עם יראי ה׳ בכתביו.**

{The last word reveals its contemporary moment. The *yir'ei ha-Shem* would appeal the wicked ruling, and King David would uphold their position in his responsa! See below, n. 87 for another form of necessary support in their struggles with their intellectual adversaries: an added measure of wisdom (*ḥokhmah yeterah*), which would be bestowed upon the Ḥasidim by God so that they could best their wicked opponents in argument. In the absence of King David or Divine intercession, as was currently the case, public humiliation was often the lot of the Ḥasid; see below, n. 59.}

Terminology and realia: (*a*) *yir'ei ha-Shem* and, to a lesser extent, *yir'ei shamayim* and *tovim* are often used by the Pietists to describe those who sought to accept the yoke of the Larger Will; ##1, 27–8, 38 (end), 86, and *passim*; see also below, p. 201. (*b*) The will of the Holy One, Blessed be He (*retson ha-Kadosh Barukh Hu*), in the aforementioned #1343 refers to the Will of the Creator (*retson ha-Borè*). Compare similarly: 'to probe deeply and execute the will of the Holy One, Blessed be He' (**להעמיק לעשות רצון הקב״ה**) in #774 with the opening programmatic statement in #27: 'For there is a Ḥasid whose heart aspires . . . to probe deeply and execute the Will of the Creator' (**כי יש חסיד שלבו חפץ . . . להעמיק לעשות רצון הבורא**). (*c*) On *salms*(!) (**שלמש**), *shevaḥot*, or *tishbaḥot* as *pesukei de-zimra*, see below, n. 68. (*d*) In the above-cited #1344, the wicked communal leader is vividly described as having taken the *tallit* of the *tsaddik*, given it to a mocker, and humiliated the *tsaddik* (**וגם לקח טלית של צדיק אחד ונתן לליצן להתעטף והלבין פני הצדיק**). The hooded *tallit* of Ḥasidei Ashkenaz was highly distinctive (see below, n. 57) and worn at all times (below, n. 56). A common, visible symbol of the movement, it was a natural target of derision. This is no abstract portrayal of wickedness, but a description of a contemporary reality, as is clearly the clash over the *pesukei de-zimra*, the introductory psalms recited in the morning prayer.

[53] Cf. Scholem, *Major Trends in Jewish Mysticism* (above, n. 10), 92–3, 96–7. The difficulty entertained in describing the hasidic demand for indifference to praise or blame as ataraxy, absence of passion, and thus linking their outlook with certain elements in Cynicism that influenced both eastern and western monasticism, lies in the emphatic position that they adopted in the age-old controversy of continence versus temperance (above, p. 22). Had the Ḥasid aspired to a state of 'absence of passions', it is hard to see how he could have announced repeatedly that the moral man is he who curbs

possessed unquestioned pride in the wisdom and customs of its ancestors.[54] The appearance of new ideals of personality and patterns of conduct that its

rather than eviscerates his appetites. The passions animating the people in *Sefer Ḥasidim* are intense, and no interest is displayed in combating this state of affairs. Much advice is given on how to restrain and channel those drives, but little, if any, direction is provided as to how to deaden them. That this is not simply a *pis aller* is evidenced by ##52–3 of *Sefer Ḥasidim*. The Ḥasid there received an inquiry, in great detail and vividness, whether it was permissible, perhaps even commendable, for someone to cultivate his baser passions intentionally so as to curb them all the more dramatically at the crucial moment. Was it allowable to stimulate regularly one's appetite for revenge, theft, or sex by either lying in ambush, fingering buried treasures, or engaging in incestuous sexual foreplay for the purpose of stopping short just as the impulse was coming to climax? The hasidic mentor (*he-ḥakham*) to whom the question was put found himself at a loss for an answer(!) and, in his perplexity, referred the inquirers to a *rosh yeshivah*, who replied decisively in the negative. This story is admittedly extreme and quite possibly a literary invention, but it does bespeak an atmosphere where 'action in the line of greatest resistance' is held up as an ideal and one wholly alien to any aspirations to 'absence of passion'. (One can hardly imagine Diogenes or Benedict being asked such questions.) There is no attempt in *Sefer Ḥasidim* to deaden any feelings other than those of humiliation and hurt. Answer could be made that the Ḥasidim were anything but consistent, and while they gave free range to feelings in some spheres, they sought to dull them in others. But then the question arises, why this particular configuration of inconstancy? Why were the Pietists immune to contemporary notions of ataraxy in all areas other than that of social opprobrium? Was it need that determined this pattern of acceptance and rejection? The contention that the Pietists could not aspire to deaden the sexual drive because of the traditional importance of marital life in Judaism collides with the fact that there is no attempt at ataraxy in other spheres either. Furthermore, the hasidic acceptance of marital sex was not an attitude forced upon them by tradition. Had the Pietists wished to denigrate, or even to downplay, carnal enjoyment, numerous talmudic dicta (such as מגלה טפח ומכסה טפח ודומה כאילו כפאו שד and the like) lay readily to hand to be invoked and elaborated upon. Numerous ascetically oriented writers, from Ravad of Posquières to R. Yosef Karo, expatiated on these passages; the Pietists scarcely mentioned them. Contrast e.g. *Sefer Ḥasidim* with *Shulḥan 'Arukh*, 'Oraḥ Ḥayyim', 240: 8; 'Even ha-'Ezer', 25: 2. *Sefer Ḥasidim* advocates, or at least exudes, an almost lusty enjoyment of marital life. {See now Ḥ. Ben-Artsi, 'Ha-Perishut be-Sefer Ḥasidim', *De'ot*, 11 (1983), 39–43; Y. Kiel, 'Toratam ha-Musarit-Datit shel Ḥasidei Ashkenaz: bein Sagfanut ve-Ḥushaniyut', *Da'at*, 73 (2012), 85–101.

Regarding sections 52–3 of *Sefer Ḥasidim*, see Eli Yassif, 'Ha-Sippur ha-Ekzemplari be-*Sefer Ḥasidim*', *Tarbiz*, 57 (1988), 236 n. 49, who cites Joseph Dan's (apparently oral) disagreement with my interpretation of the stand of the *rosh yeshivah* as being wholly negative, because the *rosh yeshivah* says 'ki ha-sakhar taluy be-ha-Kadosh, Barukh Hu', which Dr Dan takes as stating that in the next world they will be rewarded for their actions. To my thinking that runs contrary to everything that follows that statement, where the *rosh yeshivah* cites a talmudic proof text and damns their action in the strongest terms. What that scholar said was, 'You seek to increase your Divine reward in the world to come by getting yourselves into compromising situations, stimulating your baser instincts and then pulling back. This is both dangerous and illegal. Leave all matters of your Divine reward up to God. He knows enough about you to apportion your lot correctly. Your task in the here-and-now is to act responsibly and in accordance with the halakhah, which strictly forbids such conduct.' See also T. Alexander-Frizier, *The Pious Sinner: Ethics and Aesthetics in the Medieval Hasidic Narrative* (Tübingen, 1981).}

[54] See my forthcoming *Circumstance, Custom and Halakhah in the Thought of the Tosafists*. {This

traditions had never known evoked feelings of antagonism and contempt in those in whom the new movement did not strike a sympathetic chord. The new Ḥasid, who lowered his eyes at the passing of women, who spoke little of the doings of the world and not at all of his neighbor, who eschewed all recreation and elementary social intercourse,[55] who passed the day in *tallit* and *tefillin*[56] (a distinctive *tallit*—with a hood—at that[57]) and expounded the strange minutiae of God's newly discovered Will,[58] was the inevitable butt of

appeared in a much-expanded form as *Ha-Yayin bi-Yemei ha-Beinayim: Yein Nesekh—Perek be-Toledot ha-Halakhah be-Ashkenaz bi-Yemei ha-Beinayim* (Jerusalem, 2008), see pp. 223, 269–70, 303–4, 318, 358–71. A free translation of 358–71 is found in *Collected Essays*, i (Oxford, 2013), 258–76. See also the preceding article in that volume, 'Religious Law and Change: The Medieval Ashkenazic Example' (239–57), which first appeared in the *AJS Review*, 13 (1987), 205–21.}

[55] *Roke'aḥ, Hilkhot Ḥasidut, Shoresh Ahavah*; *SH*, ##815, 978, 986. See *She'elot she-Nish'alu le-Rabbi Yehudah he-Ḥasid zts'l 'al 'Iskei Teshuvah*, MS Munich, Bayerische Staatsbibliothek 232, fos. 110v–111r:

> Response about forbidden sexual acts: First and foremost, he should not look at women. Know that the major part of the reward is for closing his eyes when he sees women . . . and there is no limit to his reward because he is constantly being tested, [moreover,] others shame him and laugh and mock him [for this], therefore his reward is 'doubled and then doubled again' [i.e. very great].
>
> **תשובה על העריות: תחילה תחילה שלא יראןה] בנשים. ודע כי עיקר שכר שהוא עוצם עיניו בראות בנשים . . . ואין קץ לשכרו כי תדיר בא לידי נסיון [ועוד] שבושת עושין לו שמתלוצצין בו ומלעיגין עליו, לכך שכרו כפול ומכופל.**

{Emese Kozma has edited the private penitentials of the German Pietists. The above-cited passage, with minor variants from MS Vatican 183, is found in her doctorate, 'The Practice of *Teshuvah* (Penance) in the Medieval Ashkenazi Jewish Communities (A *tesuva* [vezeklés] gyakorlata a középkori askenázi zsidó közösségekben)' (Ph.D. diss., Eötvös Loránd University, Budapest, 2012), vol. ii, Texts, 46.}

[56] ##1036, 986, 976, 1589; *SHB*, #57 (and see *SH*, #439). The *tallit* as a symbol of *ḥasidut* is reflected in #1344 (see above, n. 52). {In light of my subsequent essay (below, Ch. 3), *SHB* #57 should be stricken from the list. The conventional pietists equally insisted that a *tallit* should be worn for prayer every day and not just on the Sabbath, though their *tallit* was not distinctive, unlike that of the German Pietists (see next note). On the general laxity in both the Ashkenazic and Provençal communities in the observance of *tallit*, *tefillin*, and *mezuzah*, see A. Ravitzky, '"Hatsivi Lakh Tsiyyunim" le-Tsiyyon: Gilgulo shel Ra'ayon', *'Al Da'at ha-Makom: Meḥkarim ba-Hagut ha-Yehudit u-ve-Toledoteiha* (Jerusalem, 1991), 37–41. The same article appeared in *Erets Yisra'el ba-Hagut ha-Yehudit bi-Yemei ha-Beinayim* (Jerusalem, 1991), 1–39; our passage is at pp. 4–8; E. Kanarfogel, 'Rabbinic Attitudes toward Non-Observance in the Medieval Period', in J. J. Schacter, ed., *Jewish Tradition and the Non-Traditional Jew* (Northvale, NJ, 1992), 7–14; S. Emanuel, ed., *Teshuvot ha-Ge'onim ha-Ḥadashot ve-'Imam Teshuvot, Pesakim u-Ferushim me-et Ḥakhmei Provence ha-Rishonim* (Jerusalem, 1995), #161, 234–7, and nn. 16–18, 38.}

[57] *Teshuvot R. Me'ir mi-Rotenburg* (Prague, 1608), #287. {The largest collection of the medieval Ashkenazic responsa commonly attributed to R. Me'ir of Rothenburg was first printed in Prague, 1608. The defective text was critically edited by M. A. Bloch and published in Budapest in 1895.}

[58] Even the Pietists realized that their new prescription would appear strange in the eyes of the world; see *Sefer Ḥasidim*, #28: 'Should a wicked man see in the words [that follow] statements that

protracted caricature and abuse. The adherents of Hasidism soon learnt to associate their way of life with the blanch of humiliation,[59] and, from the outset, proclaimed the cornerstone of Ḥasidut to be the capacity to persist in God's will despite scorn and mockery. Perseverance no less than |330| indifference was the immediate goal of the Ḥasidim, and it was sought as much as a mechanism of defense as a moral trait.[60]

The doctrines of the Ḥasidim concerning prayer and synagogue, focal points both in their thought[61] and in the daily life of the community, were such that, when acted upon, they would have antagonized large segments of their society and led the Pietists to be regarded as saintly pests, or worse yet, as reprehensible snobs. Only the truly righteous, the Ḥasidim claimed, should be called to the Torah, given honors in the services,[62] or be a *sandak* at a circumcision.[63] The most vigorous action must be taken to prevent an unrighteous man from being the cantor (*sheliaḥ tsibbur*), for his functioning in this capacity literally endangers the community, since his prayers will necessarily be rejected. Any religious act performed by an unworthy person—such as blowing the shofar (ram's horn) on Rosh Hashanah—should be discounted and repeated by the Ḥasid himself.[64] Strictly speaking, the unworthy should not be allowed into the synagogue, for their sight stirs evil thoughts in the hearts of the worshippers.[65] Hymns written by sinners should not be recited,[66] and prayer books copied by them should not be used.[67] Finally, the morning psalms (*pesukei de-zimra*) should be recited at great, indeed, interminable, length.[68]

appear to him as nonsense and if you speak them to him, he will mock (him) [you]' (אם יראה רשע באלה הדברים [דברים ה]נראין בעיניו כדברי שטות ואם תדברם באזניו ילעג למו). {The parallel passage in *SHB*, #1 is more grammatical.}

59 R. Shemu'el he-Ḥasid in *SH*, #2 (p. 5), *Roke'aḥ, Hilkhot Ḥasidut, Shoresh Rosh Ḥasidut*; *'Arugat ha-Bosem* (above, n. 49), 103 {*Perushei Siddur ha-Tefilah la-Roke'aḥ*, eds. M. Hershler and Y. A. Hershler (Jerusalem, 1992), ii. 513}; *SH*, ##118, 119, 975–8, 982, *et ad libitum*.

60 It should be emphasized that once the doctrine of indifference was developed, it may well have served the further purpose of spiritual ascent. For this reason the adjective 'immediate' was employed in the text. Though one might note that nowhere does *Sefer Ḥasidim* counsel the would-be Pietist to commit acts that would invite ridicule, rather, it emphasizes that to become a Ḥasid one must be ready to endure it. The line between immanent development and practical necessity is a thin one. Too thin, perhaps, to be discerned from a distance of 700 years, and it is wisest when the two forces may be at work to eschew assigning pride of place to one over the other.

61 The largest bloc of regulations in *Sefer Ḥasidim* touches on these topics: ##393–543; ##1568–1632, not to speak of innumerable other mentions of and references to prayer throughout that work.

62 ##470–1.

63 #585.

64 #1591 (see ##443, 444).

65 #403 (for further isolation see #60).

66 ##470, 1619–20; *Ḥokhmat ha-Nefesh*, Safed edn., fo. 23a; {Sodei Razaya edn., 94b}.

67 ##404–5, 1621.

68 ##418, 450, 839, 1620, 1344, and see n. 70 below.

Much depends, of course, on just who was considered 'unrighteous' or 'wicked', for only too often the Pietists' epithets have been taken at their face value. No doubt they refer at times to violent and immoral individuals,[69] but the widespread presence of *resha'im* according to the |331| hasidic account leads us to one of two conclusions: either the political and spiritual leadership in thirteenth-century Germany was frequently in the hands of evil men or the Pietists used this term after their own fashion. We may obtain a glimpse of what the Ḥasidim had in mind if we compare three parallel passages which have come down to us (emphases are mine):

Initially the *paytanim* did not incorporate their names in the poems' acrostics . . . for they did not compose [these poems] to perpetuate their names . . . Once the wicked [*resha'im*] began to compose *piyyutim* [liturgical poems], one should [have] recite[d] no *piyyut* whatsoever, for is it conceivable that the *piyyut* of the wicked will be heard? 'Surely God does not hear an empty cry!' [Job 35: 13] And people did not know which were the poems of the righteous. To prevent people from [mistakenly] saying 'the wicked composed these poems [and so we should refrain from reciting them]', the righteous [began to] incorporate their names in their *piyyutim*.

If a righteous man composes a *piyyut* and its language is not as good as that of a wicked person [*rasha'*], better that people recite the [poem] of the righteous, for the merit of its author is remembered [by God, and He looks favorably] on the one who recites it, while the evil-doing of the wicked is held against those who recite their poems. Once the righteous began to incorporate their names in their poems, the wicked could no longer say, 'We composed them, and they were jealous'. When the wicked achieved the upper hand, they used to recite the *piyyutim* of their relatives, and for this reason there was much Divine retribution. When the righteous got the upper hand, they decreed that no one could pray [i.e. serve as cantor] unless the righteous had given him permission to pray . . . and they instituted *reshuyot* [the formal permission-taking by the cantor] because some used to recite the *piyyutim* of the wicked or the dishonest would at times pray and raise their voice in chant, and it is written, 'She has lifted up her voice against me, therefore I hate her' [Jer. 12: 8].

'Thorns and thistles it shall bring forth to you' [Gen. 3: 17]. It is decreed upon every generation that it should have its thorn, and the wicked man is the thorn. And He planted them in each generation: Abraham had Amraphel for his thorn, Isaac—the shepherds of Gerar; Jacob—Esau. . . . And so in every generation the righteous man always has his thorn—'And these are [the men] that the Lord left to test Israel' [cf. Judg. 3: 1]. When a righteous man in the city [is involved] in benefiting the community

[69] #444. (There are two passages where the Ḥasid is advised to use caution in translating his precepts into communal reform. However, the material gathered in this section of the essay indicates, I hope, that the Pietists did not always allow themselves to be guided by such pragmatic counsel.)

[*tsibbur*], he has his thorn—the wicked man [*rasha'*], who seeks to lead it astray, just as the prophets of the Lord had their thorn [in the form of] the prophets of Ba'al and Ashtoret. And when the community is worthy, they do what the prophets of the Lord say, and the prophets of Ba'al are as naught. |**332**| But if the community is unworthy, the prophets of the Lord are ignored and their words go unheeded. Similarly the righteous man in the city will seek to benefit [i.e. improve] it in all ways he deems fit [*mezakkeh le-khol ḥeftso*]—benefiting both himself and others. And he will have a thorn in the city who shall overturn his words and aggravate him in every way that the wicked can aggravate the good. If that were not bad enough, the good man will speak justly and rule truthfully and justly, while the evil man will pervert justice and his words will be wrong and the words of the good man will go unheeded while those of the evil man [will be accepted]. And he will lead the public astray. And all this was predetermined then [after Adam's fall, by the curse] 'Thorns and thistles it shall bring forth to you'. And this takes place because the people of the city are deemed [by God] unworthy of heeding the good man and so He inclines their hearts after the wicked so that they should stumble. And He makes the words of the wicked man successful [i.e. attractive], so that they should be drawn to him and stumble. *If that were not bad enough, the wicked man will yet write books which will last for generations, and write piyyutim which will be recited by* [*succeeding*] *generations*, but not so the good man [i.e. he will neither write books nor compose liturgies, or, if written, they will remain unread and unrecited]. And all this happens because future generations are also unworthy and so God allows all this to come to pass in order that they too shall stumble.... And because He knows posterity to be unworthy he allows the dishonest *to write books and piyyutim*, for had the [future] generations been worthy He would have allowed the good men to write the good books and the *piyyutim*. 'Thorns and thistles', in *gematriyah*, is the numerical equivalent of 'posterity'. And *thus a wicked man is enabled* [*by God*] *to earn* [*richly*] *in this world in an iniquitous way and to establish a synagogue or a cemetery or some other important thing*, for posterity is unworthy [to benefit from] the deeds of the good, and God does not want the deeds of the good to[benefit] the dishonest.[70]

From these two selections we see that, by the Pietists' own admission, the

[70] #470; *Ḥokhmat ha-Nefesh*, Safed edn., fo. 23a; {Sodei Razaya edn., 94a–b}:

בראשונה לא היו פייטנין עושין חורוזות ולא שמם מיוסד עליתם בשירות . . . כי בשביל להזכיר שמם לא יסדום . . . ומאחר שהרשעים עושים פיוטים לא נאמר כלום, כי איך יתכן שפיוטי הרשעים ישמע? (איוב לה יג) אך שוא לא ישמע אל! ולא היו יודעים איזה פיוט של צדיקים וכדי שלא יאמרו רשעים אמרום תיקנום הצדיקים שמם בפיוטיהם.

אם צדיק עשה הפיוט ושאין הלשון טוב כפיוטי הרשע מוטב שיאמרו של צדיקים, שזכות מי שעשה הפיוט נזכר לטובה לאומרו, ורשעת הרשעים נזכרת לרעה לאומרי פיוטיהם. וכיון שהתחילו הצדיקים לעשות פיוטים ושמם רמוז בהם ולא יוכלו הרשעים לומר 'אנו עשינו אותם והיו מקנאים'. ומשגברה יד הרשעים היו מתפללים פיוטי קרוביהם, ולכך פורענות רבות. וכשגברה יד הצדיקים תקנו שלא יהיו מתפללין אלא מי שיתנו הצדיקים רשות להתפלל . . . ותקנו רשויות לפי שהיו אומרים פיוטים של רשעים או היו מתפללים שאינם הגונים ומנגנים בקול וכתיב (ירמיה יב ח) נתנה עלי בקולה על כן שנאתיה.

rasha' is a scholar who makes contributions of some permanence to halakhic thought, and, not surprisingly, sits on the courts, or, at the very least, gives influential rulings on religious problems. He is graced with the soul of a poet, and his words celebrating the majesty of God or mourning the sufferings of his people strike a responsive chord in the hearts of the people. Knowledge of |333| Midrash is clearly his, as is a sense of public weal and a willingness to give of himself to it. Wherein lies, we wonder, his wickedness? The third parallel passage provides us with the answer.

There are *piyyutim* to which the following biblical verses may be appropriately applied if they are recited: 'She has lifted up her voice against me, therefore I hate her' [Jer. 12: 8] and 'Your mediators have transgressed against me' [Isa. 43: 27]—even *piyyutim* written by the righteous if they are recited by a bad man. . . . Should there be a scholar, an expert in the Law, and he composes *piyyutim* and he hurries the blessing and the psalms of the morning prayer in the synagogue, it is improper to recite his *piyyutim*. For what David composed by Divine inspiration he scorns and hastens to cast out

וכשאמר 'קוץ ודרדר תצמיח לך' (ברא', ג: יח) נגזר על כל דור ודור שיהא קוץ עמו ובליעל כקוץ. ושתלן בכל דור ודור, היה אברהם, היה אמרפל קוץ שלו; היה יצחק , היו רועי גרר; יעקב היה עשו . . . וכן בכל דור ודור יש לצדיק קוץ, 'ואלה אשר הניח ה' לנסות בהם ישראל' (שופטים ג: א). לעולם כשיש צדיק בעיר המזכם, יש לו קוץ אחד–רשע המחטיא את הרבים, כמו נביא ה' קוץ שלהם נביאי הבעל ונביאי האשרה. וכשזוכים הציבור עושים מה שנביא ה' אומר ונביאי הבעל [כ]אין נחשבו. ואם לא יזכו, [שומעים לנביאי השקר ונביאי ה'] לא יחשבו ולא יהיו נשמעים דבריהם. וכן לצדיק שבעיר, ויהיה מזכה לכל חפצו לזכות ולזכות אחרים, ויהיה לו קוץ בעיר שמהפך דבריו ומעציבו בכל מה שיוכל הרע לצער את הטוב. ולא עוד אלא שהרע מצליח, וכשמפייס לרע ואין דברי הטוב נשמעים ואינם נחשבים לכלום כגנגד הרע. ולא עוד אלא שהטוב מדבר דברי יושר ודן באמת וי[ו]שר, [והרע מטה הדין] ואין דבריו נכונים, א[ף] ע[ל] פ[י] כ[ן] אין דברי הטוב נשמעים אלא דברי הרע המחטיא הרבים, ונשמעים לו ונכשל הטוב בפני הרע. כל זה [נגזר אז 'קוץ ודרדר] תצמיח לך'. והכל שאין בני העיר ראויים לכך שיהיו נשמעים לטוב ומטה את לבם אחרי הרע כדי שיכשלו, ומצליח את דברי [הרע] כדי [שיהו נמשכים אחריו] ויכשלו. ולא עוד אלא שהרע יעשה ספרים ויהיו [ל]דורות ויעשה פיוטים ויאמרו לדורות. והטוב לא יהיה לו כן. [כל זה] (כדי) שגם הדורות שעתידין להיות אינם ראויים וכדי שיכשלו אף הם, מניחים מן השמים כל זה . . . לפי שגלוי לפניו שהדורות אין ראויים ומניח לזה שאינו הגון (קודם לכן) [ל]עשות ספרים ופיוטים. שאם זכו הדורות היה מניח אלה הספרים ופיוטים טובים לעשותם. 'וקר"ץ ודרד"ר' בגימ[טריא] דורר"ת. וכן מספיקין לאדם רע שירוויח בעוולה ויתקן בית כנסת או בית הקברות או דבר גדול שאין זוכים הדורות במעשה הטוב, והטוב אין הקב"ה חפץ שיהיו מעשיו לשאינם מהוגנים.

{In the Safed edition, several words and phrases were missing and were so noted by the printer/editor. These lacunae were filled in from the Sodei Razaya edn. and from MSS Bodley 1569 and Parma, De Rossi 1390. They appear in brackets in the citation.}

This section in its entirety was written in the spring of 1967. Since then, Professor H. H. Ben-Sasson has called attention to these passages to illustrate, among other things, the deep tension that existed between the Pietists and the establishment, a point with which, needless to say, I concur. The purpose of my lengthy citations is to align them with coming sections of *Sefer Ḥasidim* so as to demonstrate just how idiosyncratic the hasidic terminology is and how meaningless it is to take hasidic descriptions and evaluations at face value. Ben-Sasson, 'Ḥasidei Ashkenaz 'al Ḥalukkat Kinyanim' (above, n. 9), 72–7 {repr. in id., *Retsef u-Temurah* [above, n. 9], 189–94}.

from his mouth, while that which he composes he recites slowly. Similarly if a scholar does not give charity or do personal favors, or if he is a scholar and is quarrelsome or proud, it is improper to recite his *piyyutim*.[71]

'Wicked' to the hasidic mind meant, then, not only men violent and immoral, but even scholars, poets, and men of quality who took less time in reciting the psalms than the Ḥasidim deemed appropriate, or in any way fell short of their novel and exacting standards. And lest we again take the Ḥasidim at their word and imagine that what was at stake in their demand for slow recitation was a few more minutes of devotion (*kavvanah*), their own remarks elsewhere in *Sefer Ḥasidim* should be cited:

There were once two synagogues in a city and the Ḥakham went . . . sometimes to one and sometimes to the other. Then he prayed only in the smaller one. They asked him, 'Why have you left the larger synagogue, where both the many and the prominent pray?' He replied, 'In the large synagogue they hasten [the recitation of] the morning blessings and the psalms . . . but not so in the smaller synagogue. There they recite the morning blessings and psalms slowly and I gain in this that, while I recite [the psalm] slowly, I count on my fingers how many *alef*s there are [in each psalm], how many *bet*s, and similarly for each letter, 'and upon my return home I attempt to find a reason for each sum.'[72]

[71] #1620:

There are liturgical poems [*piyyutim*] that if they are recited, it was said of them, 'She has lifted up her voice against me, therefore I hate her' [Jer. 12: 8] . . . Liturgical poems, even if they were composed by good men [*tovim*] but a bad one recited them, or those poems which were composed by a good man [*tsaddik*], however, they contain the name of his father and his father was not a good man . . . Similarly, if there is a scholar who commands the entire Torah and he composes *piyyutim*, and he hurries the praises of God which are called 'Salms' [the psalms said before 'Barkhu'] in the synagogue, it is improper to recite [his] poems, for what David wrote by Divine inspiration, he despises and rushes to spit them out of his mouth, but what he has composed, he recites at stately length. Similarly a scholar who does not do deeds of loving kindness with his money [if he has money], nor does he do deeds of loving kindness with his body, or he is a scholar but is quarrelsome or haughty, it is improper to recite his *piyyutim*, even if he has all the [other] virtues.

יש פיוטים אם יתפללו אותם נאמר עליהם (ירמיה יב ח) נתנה עלי בקולה על כן שנאתיה . . . פיוטין אפילו עשאום טובים ומתפלל אדם רע אותם או אותן פיוטין שעשאו צדיק ובפיוט יש שם אביו ואביו לא היה צדיק . . . וכן אם יש תלמיד חכם שבקי בתורה והוא עשה פיוטין והוא ממהר את הברכות ואת השבחות שקורין שלמש בבית הכנסת, אינו ראוי שיאמרו פיוטים שהרי מה שדוד ברוח הקדש אמר הוא מואס וממהר לזרוק מפיו ואשר הוא עשה מושך. וכן תלמיד חכם ואינו גומל חסדים בממונו אם יש לו ממון או בגופו אינו גומל הסדים או הוא תלמיד חכם ובעל מחלוקת הוא או גאה הוא ואינו ראוי לומר פיוטיו ואפילו יש בו כל מידות טובות.

See above, n. 70 for further examples of individuals who would be deemed flawed but quite honorable, even distinguished, members of the community, but who are labeled as wicked by the Pietist.

[72] #1575 (see also *Tur*, 'Oraḥ Ḥayyim', 113). See *Tashbets* (Jerusalem, 1951), #219:

[334] Epithets of *rasha'*, *ra'*, and *ra' ma'alalim* were applied not just to the quarrelsome, the arrogant, and the stingy,[73] but also to those who simply denied the new revelation and the apostolic claims of the Pietists.[74] Thus defined, few would pass muster and, not surprisingly, many a communal

[A report] is found in a book composed by R. Barukh of Mainz that he sent an inquiry to R. Yehudah Ḥasid as to how he could do what occurs regularly on Pesah and Shavu'ot and on [the Sabbath following] a wedding, [namely] that the [psalms, *pesukei de-zimra*, that precede] the recitation of the Shema are not completed until after the third hour [of daylight, by which time the Shema halakhically needs to have been recited], thus the time for recitation of the Shema has passed.

יש בספר שתקן רבינו ברוך ממגנצא ששלח לרבינו יהודה חסיד ושאל היאך היה עושה בפסח ובשבועות ובנישואין שקריאת שמע נמשך לפעמים עד לאחר שלש שעות ובכן עבר זמן קריאת שמע וכו׳.

Perhaps the great scholar mentioned by R. Yehudah he-Ḥasid has not received the sympathy he may well have deserved: 'And I heard from R. Yehudah he-Ḥasid that there was a great rabbi whose authority was widely accepted, and he used to decry in the synagogue those that prolonged the [morning] blessings because he wished to hasten to study. And he was punished for this in the other [i.e. next] world' (**ואני שמעתי מפי ר״י החסיד זצ״ל שהיה רב גדול ומובהק לרבים אחד והיה גוער בבית הכנסת שהיו מאריכין בברכות והיה בדעתו למהר ללימוד ונענש על כך באותו עולם**). *Or Zarua'*, ii (Zhitomir, 1862), #42, cited in a gloss in *SHP*, #126. See also #1344 cited in full above, n. 52: 'because he used to put fear and dread in the hearts of the God-fearers [*yir'ei ha-Shem*], and he would, out of spite, hurry [the recitation of] the "praises" [i.e. *pesukei de-zimra*] in the synagogue . . . and scorned the God-fearers [*yir'ei ha-Shem*]'. (See above, n. 51 for the connotation of *yir'ei ha-Shem*, and above, nn. 56–7 for the significance of *tallit* in the preceding description.)

[73] #1620.

[74] The harsh accusations of the Pietists that the religious establishment had failed in its duties of leadership in not admonishing their community and repairing the breaches of observance (**שהיה בידם למחות ולא מיחו** and the like) should be taken at a similar discount. No doubt there were instances of scholars and communal leaders who were lax in enforcing religious norms, but the Pietists' indictment was more a product of their outlook than a reflection of reality.

Among the manifold talents of man discovered by the Pietists was his capacity for foresight, and much of *Sefer Ḥasidim* is a summons to anticipate the consequences of one's conduct and to act accordingly. This sense of foresight, together with the Pietists' 'fear of sinning' (*yir'at ha-ḥet*), induced the doctrine of making fences around the law (*seyyag*) to prevent errors from occurring. Preventable errors to the Ḥasid came perilously close to being considered deliberate acts of will (e.g. ##875, 1439). Religious life must be so structured as to put a large and untraversable distance between man and sin, and a good part of their instructions are an attempt at just such an organization. The standard canons of religiosity, with their allowances for unintended failings and occasional inability to perform a commandment, were then wholly inadequate, and indeed verged on condoning the criminal.

Furthermore, the demands of the Pietists for the full mobilization of man's abilities in the service of God, and their concomitant refusal to allow for any routinization of the religious imperative, made their clash with the establishment inevitable. The tendency of any established order to turn a blind eye to certain entrenched infractions, or infractions difficult to prove and even more difficult to correct, its awareness that a measure of laxity among some members of the community was inevitable and that attempts to improve matters might strain the social fabric or bring a measure of unreasonableness in religious demands, were all anathema to the Pietists. They knew man as few of their contemporaries did, but they probed his frailties to overcome them, not to rest content with them. Whether a whole society would tolerate such sustained correction, whether it would agree to live at a

|335| leader, and even eminent rabbi, grew antagonistic to the hasidic practices[75] and battled them on numerous fronts. Humble as to themselves, sweeping as to their claims, the Pietists were scarcely lacking in the meek presumptuousness of the saintly.[76] It may be wise to remind ourselves from

level of unremitting religious tension, were questions they felt that a concerned believer had no right to ask before he acted. Others thought differently.

[75] Cf. above, nn. 72, 74. Every movement, one might add, has its lunatic fringe that gives it a bad odor, and Ḥasidei Ashkenaz were no exception. What were the feelings, one wonders, of a weary Tosafist returning home on Friday from a six-day stint in the *bet ha-midrash*, to shed his boots for the first time in a week (E. E. Urbach, *Ba'alei ha-Tosafot: Toledoteihem, Ḥibbureihem, Shitatam*, rev. edn. [Jerusalem, 1980], 18), passing by the house of an otherwise undistinguished Ḥasid and witnessing this distinctive *imitatio dei* (#628):

> And all that we find God doing in honor of the Sabbath, [we should also do. It is written:] 'and on the Seventh Day he ascended and sat on the Throne of Glory'. There was a Ḥasid who said that all that he found [about God on the Sabbath], he would equally do. And he had a special, beautiful chair and he would sit on it on the Seventh Day for the glory of the Day of Rest.

> וכל מה שמצינו שהקב"ה מכבד שבת שאמרו 'וביום השביעי נתעלה וישב על כסא כבודו', הרי היה חסיד אחד ואמר כל מה שמצא כאן עשה כן, היה לו כסא יפה ומיוחד שהיה יושב עליו בשביעי להתפאר ליום המנוחה.

If the Ḥasid yet took to preaching to him on his religious inadequacies, little needs to be left to the imagination.

[76] See e.g. #1272:

> Once a Ḥasid requested of the king that he should fine any Jew who swears taking God's name 12 *peshitim* [pfennig]. And he intended thereby to stop people from swearing falsely, for in that country they used to take the name of the Lord in vain and swear falsely, even when there was no civil suit. He requested of the king and the king authorized him to take a dinar [solidus] from any Jew who swore, whether truly or falsely, when not involved in a civil suit, so as to prevent them from swearing in vain. And the inhabitants of that country bribed [the authorities] to expel him, and the men of the country excommunicated him so that he had to go to another country, taking with him family and friends. And all those that excommunicated him, they and their seed, were punished, some killed [by sword], some by fire, because he [the Ḥasid] had good intentions.

> מעשה בחסיד אחד שביקש למלך שכל יהודי שישבע בשם שיקח מאותו יהודי י"ב פשי[טים] ונתכוון שלא ישבעו לשקר. כי באותה מדינה היו מוצאין שם שמים לבטלה ונשבעין לשקר בלא תביעת ממון. וביקש מן המלך ונותן לו ממשלה: כל יהודי שישבע בין באמת בין לשקר בלא תביעת ממון שיקח ממנו דינר כדי למנוע מפיהם שלא ישבעו לבטלה. והשחידו בני המדינה לגרשו, וגם בני המדינה נידוהו עד שהלך ולקח קרוביו ואוהביו והלך לארץ אחרת. וכל אותם שנידוהו וגם זרעם לקו ומהם נהרגו ומהם נשרפו כי הוא נתכוון לטובה.

Whether this dangerous alliance with the secular authorities to ensure religious observance is fact or fiction we do not know, but clearly the author of *Sefer Ḥasidim* sees nothing improper in this unprecedented conduct and cannot understand why the instigator was run out of town. He also considers fire and sword an appropriate punishment for those who thwarted this well-meaning Ḥasid. {E. Shoham Steiner, in his recent article 'Exile, Immigration and Piety: The Jewish Pietists of Medieval Germany, from the Rhineland to the Danube', *Jewish Studies Quarterly*, 244 (2017), 121–42, has suggested that the Ḥasid mentioned here is the famed R. Shemu'el he-Ḥasid, R. Yehudah's father. If correct, the story adds splendor neither to R. Shemu'el's reputation nor to his judgment.}

time to time that while many in their day (and apparently in ours) found in their new ways a moral tonic, and in their thought an answer to some of the larger problems of life, a good number of the religious and the scholarly, the poetic and the sober, the retiring and the communally active, felt their novel demands to be absurd and their humble pretentiousness insufferable.

|336| The number of actual Ḥasidim in most towns was small,[77] and anyone who lived up to their standards of honesty would of necessity be poor. Disliking extensive contact with Gentiles—the *sine qua non* of leadership—and steadfastly refusing to lie or flatter or even to make small talk, which is the stuff of human relations,[78] the Pietists stood little chance against the hard-nosed men of the world in the area of communal struggle. Not surprisingly, their attempts to institute the Divine Will in its fullness met with little success.

Frustrated in their efforts to effect communal reform, the Ḥasidim retreated into themselves. Circumstances reinforced the ancient values of good lineage (*yiḥus*) and, in order to insure pure family units—the most they could hope to achieve—endogamy was recommended, if not actually practiced.[79] Numerous dicta against dwelling in the environs of *resha'im* are found

See further *SHB*, #534: 'One God-Fearer fell mortally ill, and he cried during his sickness and said, "I am not crying for my personal loss, but rather [for the public loss] for as long as I lived I used to admonish the public [to mend its ways]"' (אחד היה ירא שמים והיה בוכה בחליו. אמר לא מפני הנאת עצמי אני בוכה אלא כל זמן שהייתי חי הייתי מוכיח הרבים).

Whether a man who lived for the sole purpose of correcting others was an easy or a pleasant person to deal with is something to contemplate. See also *SH*, #1946: 'The wiser and more saintly one is than others, the more he doubts his place in Paradise. And so it was with R. Yoḥanan ben Zakkai [*Berakhot* 28b], who wept [on his deathbed] and said, "I know not where they will take me [to Heaven or to Hell]"' (מי שהוא חכם וצדיק מחבירו יותר מסתפק מן העולם הבא. וכן רבן יוחנן בן זכאי בכה ואמר איני יודע אנה יוליכוני). Our weeping Pietist, however, seems not to have any worries as to his final destination in the hereafter. In the parallel passage in the Berlin edition (#1557), the mortally ill God-fearer says that 'as long as I am alive, I act for the common good' (שכל זמן [שאני חי] אני מזכה את הרבים), which leads one to suspect that a great deal of the much-vaunted 'acting for the public good' (זכיית הרבים) practiced by the usually isolated and powerless Ḥasid (see below) consisted in his admonishing others, not exactly a *Beruf* that endeared German Pietists to their communities. Is it accidental that in the Bologna edition of *Sefer Ḥasidim*, which opens with something akin to a presentation of the principles of the movement (##1–20), the imperative of *tokhaḥah* is discussed at the very outset (#5)? {(*a*) See the Afterword, sect. A, #1 below. (*b*) שאני חי in the citation of #1557 has been bracketed as these two words have been inserted in the Berlin text by its editor—and correctly so—on the basis of the parallel passage in the Bologna edition. They are not found in the manuscript from which the Berlin edition was published, Parma, De Rossi, 1133, fo. 144v, col. 1.}

[77] #1952, and see G. Scholem, 'Three Types of Jewish Piety', *Eranos-Jahrbuch*, 38 (1969), 344 {repr. in *Ariel: A Review of the Arts and Sciences in Israel*, 22 (1973), 5–24}.

[78] ##815, 980, 984, 986.

[79] ##1300–1 and numerous passages on the importance of marrying *benei tovim* (the sons of good people, i.e. men from good families) and the like.

in *Sefer Ḥasidim*,[80] as is a correlative pessimism regarding the ability of the righteous to reform the wayward.[81] Thought was given to forming pure hasidic settlements where the will of God could be realized unhindered.[82] The sober awareness that wealth and prestige are necessary to achieve influence appears,[83] and the imperative of admonition (*tokhaḥah*) is generally given a strict construction.[84] Constant collision with their opponents led them to evolve a nemesis theory of history. Every representative of the forces of good must, sooner or later, contend with a predestined |337| opponent from the ranks of the powers of evil. The outcome of this struggle, the Pietists argued defensively, would hinge not on the merits of the righteous (*tsaddik*) but on whether his generation was worthy of his victory.[85]

The Ḥasid was opposed not only by the communal leadership but also by the intellectual establishment, and minds trained in distinction and riposte could, and did, make short shrift of many a hasidic argument. The Ḥasid attributed his defeats to a Divine spirit that entered and confounded him so as

[80] ##116, 181, 233, 305 (end), *Ḥokhmat ha-Nefesh*, Safed edn., fo. 19a {Sodei Razaya edn., 78b}: ונפקא מינ[ה] לבקש רחמים שירחיקם מן העיו.

[81] #1373 (end, indicative also); cf. #116.

[82] ##1300–1, see the remarks of Y. Baer, 'Ha-Megammah ha-Datit ha-Ḥevratit' (above, preliminary n. b), 47 {repr. in id., *Meḥkarim be-Toledot 'Am Yisra'el* (above, n. b), 221; Eng. translation/adaption in *Binah* (above, n. 10), 91–2}. (This is also implied by #786.)

[83] ##1337, 1340, 1341, 1795, 1845, 1286; a concrete example of this frustration is provided by the vivid description in #1344, cited in part above, nn. 52, 72.

[84] One would expect a broad and insistent doctrine of admonition similar to that of R. Eli'ezer of Metz in *Sefer Yere'im ha-Shalem* (Vilna, 1892–1902), #223, or analogous to that of Maimonides in *Mishneh Torah*, 'Hilkhot De'ot', 6: 7. One finds instead (##1338, 1971) the limited one of R. Mosheh of Coucy and R. Yitsḥak of Corbeil (*Semag: Sefer Mitsvot Gadol*, ed. E. Schlesinger [Jerusalem, 1995], *'aseh* #11; *Semak: Sefer Mitsvot Katan* [Jerusalem, 2005], #112). R. Mosheh and R. Yitsḥak, as good dialecticians, arrived at their doctrine out of a desire to harmonize the central passage in *'Arakhin* 16b, with its sweeping mandate of admonition, with the passing remark in *Yevamot* 65b against administering rebuke that will be rejected out of hand. The Pietists are aware of *'Arakhin*, but appear unaware of *Yevamot*, as is clear from #1338. Experience, not dialectic, speaks here. (*SHB*, #39 proves much less, for the people there act out of ignorance. מוטב שיהו שוגגין ואל יהו מזידין [better that they sin unwittingly than wittingly] is an old halakhic principle, and was generally accepted as restricting *tokhaḥah*. See *Tosafot Shabbat* 55a, s.v. *af*.) However, *SHB*, #5 does reflect an unrestricted doctrine of *tokhaḥah*. For this reason, I have used the term 'generally'. {The word 'generally' should now be struck from the formulation and the statement stands without qualification. See the Afterword below, sect. A, #1.}

[85] *Ḥokhmat ha-Nefesh*, Safed edn., fos. 23a, 25d {Sodei Razaya edn., 94a (cited above, pp. 32–3), 104d–105a; *Sefer ha-Shem* in *Sifrei ha-Ra mi-Germaiza* (above, n. 42), vol. i, sect. 3, 78b}; *SH*, #1049. Some caution should be employed with #225, as it is simply one of forty examples of *middah keneged middah*; see ##222–4. Cf. Scholem, *Major Trends in Jewish Mysticism* (above, n. 10), 90–1; Ben-Sasson, 'Ḥasidei Ashkenaz 'al Ḥalukkat Kinyanim' (above, n. 9), 74–7 {repr. in his *Retsef u-Temurah* (above, n. 9), 188–92, and see above, n. 70.}

to increase his share in the world to come.[86] But Divine reward was not all that a Ḥasid yearned for. He dreamt long dreams of the world to come, where not only would his just cause be vindicated, but the sweet taste of victorious argument would be his at last. An added wisdom (*ḥokhmah yeterah*) would be given to him, and his opponents would soon lie vanquished in disputation.[87]

The struggle of Ḥasidei Ashkenaz with those who did not see their light, and their humiliation and frustration at the hands of their opponents, only intensified the streak of harshness which can be detected in hasidic thought,[88]

[86] *Ḥokhmat ha-Nefesh*, Safed edn., fo. 25a {Sodei Razaya edn., 105a}:

> In this world [unlike in the world to come], it will occur that a righteous man will argue with an unrighteous man and at times a spirit will enter the heart [i.e. mind] of the righteous man or a spirit from heaven and mislead the righteous man so that he is defeated by the unrighteous man, so that the unrighteous man should enjoy this world to the full.
>
> **ובזה העולם יהיה שיתווכח צדיק עם שאינו צדיק ופעמים נכנסה רוח נשמה(!) בלב הצדיק או רוח מן השמים ומתעה את הצדיק עד שנוצח [על ידי] שאינו צדיק, כדי שיהיה לו (זאת אומרת, ה"אינו צדיק") עולם הזה מלא.**

(See above, p. 32 and notes ad loc.; *SH*, ##1037 [cited above, n. 52], 811, [1536], and the Ḥasid's dreams of ideal *talmud Torah* at the end of #1838. One might possibly begin to take with a grain of salt such famous passages as ##1816 and 1375, though no doubt there could have been cases of genuine *resha'im*. See below, p. 180.)

[87] *Ḥokhmat ha-Nefesh*, Safed edn., fo. 20b {Sodei Razaya edn., 83a}:

> But in the world of the souls the righteous man is given an added wisdom in proportion to the depth of his fear of God, so in that world of the souls they give to the righteous man an added wisdom to triumph, also to raise objections and to answer them, and the issue is decided according to his views—which is not the case in this world.
>
> **אבל בעולם של נשמות, נותנים לצדיק חכמה יתירה כמו [זאת אומרת, באותה מידה] שהוא מעמיק ביראת שמים, כך באותו עולם של נשמות נותנים לצדיק חכמה יתירה לנצח גם להקשות ולתרץ ועל פיו נגמר הדין מה [שאינו] בזה העולם.**

Despite what his defense mechanism may have told him of the disruptions worked by an outside spirit, the Ḥasid's sense of realism (a sense that accounts for much of the impact of his movement and forms a good part of its disarming charm) did not here abandon him. Even when daydreaming, the Ḥasid realized that even were he left undisturbed and unconfounded in the world to come (as he had every reason to believe he would be), unless his present intellectual equipment were strongly reinforced, he would prove no match for his protagonists.

[88] e.g. above, pp. 23–4; *Sefer Ḥasidim*, MS Zurich Zentralbibliothek, Heid. 51, fo. 9v {Princeton University *Sefer Hasidim* Database, par. 9, beginning}:

> He who has a mentally disturbed son, if he [the father] requests [of Heaven] mercy on him [the son] that he may live or [mercy] for a wicked man who has caused others to sin and does evil things, they should not answer 'amen' after his words, for he [the son or the wicked man] is better dead than alive.
>
> **מי שיש לו בן שוטה ואין בו דעת אם מבקש רחמים עליו שיחיה או על רשע שהחטיא ועושה רעות, אל יענו אמן אחריו כי טוב יותר במיתתו מבחייהו**

(*SH*, #1272, cited and commented upon above, n. 76).

(Need I mention the sensitive, yet at the same time elitist, doctrine of charity set forth in *SH*, ##857–929, 1675–1738, which, if implemented, would have slashed severely the alms available to the

and their posture toward the *resha'im* assumed chilling proportions. If one who had thwarted them fell sick, it was forbidden to pray for |338| his recovery, and if he died, rejoicing was in place.[89] An obscure *midrash* about 'not having pity on the cruel' was seized upon, embroidered, and repeated again and again.[90] Few lines harsher than those of R. Yehudah he-Ḥasid have been penned in Jewish ethical writings. Unable to comprehend how Abraham could have sought mercy for the sinners of Sodom, he wrote:

'Wilt Thou destroy [the *place* and not spare it for the fifty righteous]?' [Gen. 18: 24]. Explanation: He [Abraham] is not concerned about the wicked [*resha'im*] if You kill them, but do not overturn the city, leave it for the righteous and their seed. And this is what [he says], 'Shalt Thou destroy the entire city? Leave the land alone and kill the inhabitants.'[91]

Equally unmatched are the words of his disciples, who, faithful to his spirit, gave to the communities which sought their spiritual guidance this counsel in times of persecution, when refugees would flock to their gates seeking shelter and residence:

If *resha'im* and sinners should *flee* to you seeking *refuge under your wing*, do not *protect* them [i.e. take them in], for if you will receive them [i.e. allow them residence] in the end they will become an implacable adversary of yours or of your seed.[92]

Words more in the spirit of Dominic than of Francis. |339|

non-hasidic poor?) {See now Y. Y. Stal's addendum to *Teshuvot Rabbenu El'azar mi-Vormaiza ha-Roke'aḥ* (Jerusalem, 2014), 104.} *SH*, #112 uses *benei tovim* in the traditional sense, well-born or formerly wealthy individuals whose current need of charity is a source of great embarrassment to them.

[89] ##187, 191, 358 (cf. 1968), 392, (388), and previous note. The nature of the *rasha'* comes out clearly in #191, where his sin is not in declining guidance in halakhah but in *tsaddikut* and *yir'at shamayim*. {Note the description of the *rasha'* as causing the public to sin (*maḥti et ha-rabbim*) in ##181, 191, and 358, and see above, n. 41. Even more revelatory is the description of the *rasha'* in #1968 as 'one who caused the public to sin and whom the people so feared that they were afraid to perform the Will of the Creator [*retson ha-Borè*]'. However, #388, which in the original article I cited parenthetically and have reproduced here, cannot serve as evidence as there is no indication that it refers to opponents of the Pietists rather than to wicked individuals of the ordinary variety.}

[90] #2 (p. 5; this passage was apparently authored by R. Shemu'el he-Ḥasid), ##181, 852, 853.

[91] *Moshav Zekenim 'al ha-Torah* (above, n. 9), 24; MS Cambridge, Add. 669.2, fo. 9v {= *Perushei ha-Torah le-Rabbi Yehudah he-Ḥasid* (above, n. 9), 22}: **האף תספה רשע עם צדיק. פי[רוש] על הרשעים איני חושש אם תמיתם, רק את העיר אל תהפוך ותניח לצדיקים ולזרעם. וזהו 'התשחית בה[ן'] [=בחמישה] כל העיר'? הקרקע תניח ובני העיר תמית**. I have cited the passage as found in *Moshav Zekenim*, as the Cambridge manuscript reproduced by Lange is slightly abridged; the text of *Moshav Zekenim* is corroborated by MS Moscow, RSL Günzburg 82, fo. 65r. In the Cambridge manuscript the heading is **האף תספה צדיק עם רשע**. However, it is clear that R. Yehudah referred to the next verse. This form of abbreviated reference is a common occurrence in manuscripts.

[92] #181:

III

תורת ה' תמימה—כשיוצאה מפי תמים

Sefer Ḥasidim, #747

If ever halakhah had a confident hour it was around the year 1200. The past sixty years had witnessed an advance unparalleled since the days of Abbaye and Rava, as the dialectical method dormant since the fourth century sprang to life again. The multiple armor thrusts of Rabbenu Tam's intellect had smashed the front of the old, simplistic interpretation, and under the quiet but relentless generalship of R. Yitsḥak of Dampierre the land of the Talmud was occupied, reorganized, and administered by tosafist thought. In Germany developments were less concentrated and dramatic but no less massive and far-reaching. Beginning in Speyer with the teachings of R. Yitsḥak ben Asher (Riva, d. before 1133), dialectics spread in the next generation to Mainz and Regensburg in the figures of R. Eli'ezer ben Natan (b. *c.*1090), R. Yitsḥak ben Mordekhai (Rivam), and the stormy R. Efrayim, and then on to Bonn and Cologne in the activities of R. Yo'el ha-Levi and R. Shemu'el ben Natronai. Collation, contradiction, and distinction had now transfigured the works of the *amora'im* in no less a measure than the tannaitic inheritance had been transformed by the Babylonians. Creativity in France peaked at the turn of the century,[93] but continued on in Germany for another two decades, as

> *יברחו* רשעים וחטאים אצלך *לחסות בצל כנפיך* אל תהיה עליהם *מגן*, שאם תקבלם יהפך הדבר שיהו לך לסטן או לזרעיך. כי כאשר יבא רשע בעיר, אם תוכל למחות בידו אל תתנהו לבא בעיר, וכל שכן בביתך, שאם תקבלהו הוא או זרעו יהיה לך או לזרעיך לשיכים בעיניכם ולצנינים בצדיכם [במדבר, ל"ג: נ"ה] . . . ואם צדיק בא לעיר לדור . . .

The opening sentence of that section is indeed a paraphrase of the Talmud's advice (*Niddah* 61a) against harboring suspected murderers. The connotation of *rasha'* in the second sentence—the one I have quoted—would appear, then, to be at best ambiguous and my use of it open to question. However, the term 'or to your seed' (*le-zar'akha*) in that passage indicates that we are not dealing with any clear and present danger. Indeed, the term 'implacable adversary' (*le-satan*), or the biblical phrase that is employed with regard to these wicked Jews in the elaboration that follows—'barbs in your eyes and thorns in your sides'—indicates that what is feared is not physical danger (as is very much the case in the talmudic narrative), but some ultimate religious-cultural clash of the type described by the Ḥasid in #1301 or those cited above, pp. 31–4. Note also that in the concluding sentence of that section, the figure used as contrast to the aforementioned *rasha'* is neither *adam eḥad* nor *adam hagun* but a *tsaddik* who wishes to settle in a community. All of which leads me to conclude that the term *rasha'* is being used here in a distinctly hasidic fashion, and that the distance traversed by the Ḥasid by his association of this case with that of the Talmud is correspondingly immense. {See Ch. 8 below.}

93 The burning of the Talmud in 1240 precipitated an institutional crisis in talmudic studies, not an intellectual one. The creative period of the French Tosafists may be said to have come to a close

R. Eli'ezer ben Yo'el (Ravyah) toiled on the completion of his massive oeuvre, which summed up the labors of some four generations. Their successors would spend a century digesting these accomplishments, and much of halakhic history is a reinvestment and exploitation of the capital then accumulated. But even this was in the future. At the turn of the thirteenth century there was every reason to imagine that the next hundred years would be like the last and that halakhic progress would continue indefinitely. Unlike Polish hasidism, which arose during the nadir of legal thought in eastern Europe, German Hasidism grew up alongside a halakhah triumphant. And it is against the backdrop of the tosafist movement that Ḥasidei Ashkenaz must be viewed.

The immortal accomplishments of the French and German Tosafists in creating a European Talmud and in restoring to halakhah the mandate of thought should not, however, blind us to the genuine abuses that, in all |**340**| probability, followed in their wake. And the remarks of *Sefer Ḥasidim* should be read in this light. They are less a criticism of *talmidei ḥakhamim* in general than a censure of certain contemporary phenomena. The cutting edge of dialectic is distinction, and it is an edge which can cut both ways. The ability to perceive differences between things ostensibly comparable is the beginning of precise thought and, at the same time, an invitation to specious argument. The danger is inherent, and had been so recognized from the beginning. At the dawn of Western thought, when dialectic first evolved, Plato and Isocrates had immediately warned that the newly forged tool could be misused as a weapon of controversy,[94] and the same abuses attended the rediscovery of dialectic by a renascent Europe. Alexander Neckam, a contemporary of R. Shemu'el he-Ḥasid, soon wrote: 'Dialectics teaches how to distinguish between true and false. However, no one is worthy of being called a dialectician who knowingly proposes something false to win public approval.' Nor was he alone in his criticism.[95] Unless Jews were immune to human temptation, many students returned home from the schools of Troyes, Dampierre, Speyer, or Mainz to confound for their own advancement scholars of the old school, and used the training that they had there acquired to crush their

with R. Shimshon of Sens' departure for the Holy Land in 1211. If one insists on viewing the year 1240 as a watershed I have no quarrel, for it would only strengthen the argument. {For a fuller presentation of the claim made here, see my *Collected Essays*, i (Oxford, 2013), 3–40.}

[94] W. Jaeger, *Paideia: The Ideals of Greek Culture* (Oxford, 1939–45), ii. 316–17; iii. 56.

[95] *De Naturis Rerum et de Laudibus Divinae Sapientiae*, ed. T. Wright (London, 1863), 284, and see the entire chapter. (Speaking of the *trivium* generally, Alexander writes [p. 283]: 'Potestas est, quae in utramque partem disserit ac si gladium teneat ancipitem.') See below, n. 116, for other critics of the new dialectic and for parallels between contemporary Jewish and Christian strictures.

opponents rather than to arrive at the truth.[96] Dialectic is separated from cleverness only by the thin line of integrity; and character, unfortunately, is much rarer than talent.[97] Only too easily could this new tool be employed by the unscrupulous to pervert justice. Even when the method was honestly practiced, much, if not most, of what was said was of poor quality. Every great book gives rise to a hundred bad ones. When we speak of the Tosafists in France, we actually speak of the work of one school, that of Ramerupt-Dampierre, and our image of the movement in Germany is essentially that of several small circles in Bonn, Mainz, Speyer, and Regensburg. We could make no greater error than imagining that all else that was said in the numerous *battei midrash* scattered about Ashkenaz at the time was of |**341**| equal worth.[98] There is every reason to assume that much nonsense was marching at the time under the banner of Rabbenu Tam and Ravyah, and that a great deal of energy was being expended on 'creativity' that could have been far better employed in simple study.[99] This was the opinion of the Tosafist R. Eli'ezer of Metz no less than of R. Yehudah he-Ḥasid. Indeed, if full credence be given to the reports of the reliable R. Shelomoh Luria, the prickly genius of Ramerupt expressed himself as bitingly as the German Pietists ever did concerning what was being perpetrated in his name.[100]

The uneven diffusion of the works of the Tosafists rendered dishonesty a permanent temptation. Ravyah, for example, knew next to nothing of the labors of Dampierre, and many years later *Sefer Ḥasidim* could speak of cities

[96] ##1049 (end), 814, 752 (end, a *derashah* very indicative of just what the Pietists favored and to what they were opposed). Cf. ##784, and possibly #1312.

[97] ##1816, 1838, 1375, 1037. For the extent to which the *rish'ut* of these scholars was real and not simply a product of the hasidic perspective, see above, p. 31.

[98] ##746, 1440 end: 'Some men were causing a scholar a great deal of aggravation, and he would say that he would gladly live to see his revenge on them. The wise man said, "Better had you wished to live so that you could write *tosafot* in this [world], and you would receive reward for this in the world to come"' (בני אדם ציערו לאחד תלמיד חכם צער גדול, והיה אומר ברצון היה חי עד שיראה נקמה מהם אמר לו החכם מוטב שהייתה מתאוה להיות חי כדי שהייתה כותב תוספות בזה הייתה מקבל שכר טוב לעוה"ב וכו'). Do we have any guarantee that his *tosafot* would have been of any worth? (See below, pp. 45–6.)

[99] #648. The need for practical halakhic knowledge in the period prior to the publication of the *Semak*, *Sha'arei Dura*, and the like was acute. See e.g. #765.

[100] Urbach, *Ba'alei ha-Tosafot* (above, n. 75), 26: כשראה תוספות כתובות דקדוקים וגלגולים על פירושים, וירע בעיניו ונצטער על התורה שנתמעט. The continuation of R. Mosheh Taku's report is fully in keeping with what we know of Rabbenu Tam's and Ri's personalities. Rabbenu Tam's reaction was apparently unrepeatable—'and he said what he said' (ואמר מה שאמר); his nephew's, milder and wistful. Widespread use of the dialectic, he felt, was more appropriate for messianic times, when God will pour his spirit on all flesh ראוי להמתין עד ביאת הגואל עד שיתקיים המקרא ואשפוך רוחי על כל בשר (Joel 3: 1). Until then resolution by distinction and radical reinterpretation was best left to the competent few.

which lacked *Tosafot* to certain tractates.[101] Nothing was easier for the ambitious than to pass off the questions and resolutions of the Tosafists as their own[102] and to claim title to a position of authority for which they were wholly unqualified. Dialectic also opened the gates to a new phenomenon—reputation via éclat. While there have been exhibitionists and frauds in all societies, in the previous culture, the path to eminence lay in massive scholarship[103]—comprehensive knowledge which could be acquired only by many years of study. If the emblem of excellence, however, was *ḥiddush* (literally 'something new', i.e. an original insight or doctrine), making several subtle distinctions could bring a man |342| rapidly into prominence,[104] at least in the outlying cities. And prominence ill-deserved will often be prominence ill-used. Some people, morally undistinguished, perhaps even deficient, could now claim a place in the religious hierarchy that would have been previously inconceivable. The traditional yardsticks of religious merit may well have been shattered by a triumphant dialectic, without the latter offering any standards of its own other than that of intellectual excellence. Moreover, dialectic was in every sense a revolution, and revolutionaries tend to be arrogant. Many of the adherents of the new school may have looked down on the intellectual patrimony of their fathers and on the scholars who embodied it. In sum, it would be surprising if the tosafist movement, with all its immortal achievements, had not at the same time set loose some little foxes who were spoiling the vineyards of the Ashkenazic community.

Or so at least it might appear to a conservative contemporary.

But the problem confronting the Pietists went far deeper than these distortions. In the course of the twelfth century the Talmud was transformed from a static to an expanding universe. Nevermore could it be mastered—as Maimonides, living in splendid isolation in a pre-tosafist world, still dreamt it might. It could only be probed and elaborated; and the process has continued to this day. It is difficult for us, heirs to 700 years of ongoing development, to imagine how new the phenomenon of *ḥiddush* was and what a heady brew it could prove for many who first tasted of it. For over half a millennium the efforts of an entire people had been dedicated to preserving its Babylonian heritage. The Talmud was to be conserved, explained, and applied. Commen-

[101] ##664 (cf. 1478), 1748. {In view of my subsequent early dating of *Sefer Ḥasidim* (below, p. 112), the phrase 'many years later' should be struck from this sentence.}

[102] #1707. For a contemporary example of this from Italy, see the remarks of R. Yesha'ayah of Trani, cited by Urbach, *Ba'alei ha-Tosafot* (above, n. 75), 26–7. The full text is to be found in *Sha'arei Toharah*, ed. S. Goronchik (Jerusalem, 1940), fo. 88; *Teshuvot ha-Rid* (Jerusalem, 1967), col. 100. See also *SH*, #1732.

[103] See below, pp. 47–8.

[104] ##1707, 648.

tary required great talent, and the application of law to a world as different from Sassanian Babylonia as was medieval Germany demanded a good measure of originality. But all this took place within the traditional halakhic perimeter—as did codification, which usually meant simply writing handbooks, unless, of course, one had a sweeping new conception, as did Maimonides. And sorry to tell, even these fields were reserved for the great. For centuries there was little for the average, or even above-average, scholar to do. Responsa-writing is not self-initiatory, and the fame of the author will determine heavily the measure of acceptance to be won by a small code of restricted scope. Commentary had meaning only if performed on the scale of a tractate or more, and *explication de texte* of that magnitude was so grueling a test that not even the greatest could enter the lists alone. The circumscribed ambience of pre-tosafist thought is reflected in its literary |343| remains. It consists of one collective, and perforce anonymous, effort at talmudic commentary,[105] responsa and brief reports of the rulings of the famous, and sundry little handbooks scattered in the *Sifrut de-Vei Rashi*—useful enough, but uninspiring. No work of any scope is to be found there. There are slender *livres de circonstance*, but there is little literary creativity, certainly no *personal* literary creativity, in pre-Crusade Germany.

In the next century halakhah burst out of its traditional confines. Every line of the Talmud became potentially problematic, and the men of the time accepted the challenge of detecting every latent contradiction in that vast corpus and suggesting its resolution. Within two generations the Talmud had been rewritten. In few periods of Jewish history has so much talent been liberated so rapidly. The achievement was breathtaking, perhaps intoxicating. Communal pride, the collective sense of being part of a heroic age of Torah, animated the Ashkenazic community, and it would be strange if it had left individuals untouched.[106] Scholars or would-be scholars were busily writing

[105] The commentary of the Mainz academy published under the title *Perush Rabbenu Gershom*; see A. Epstein, 'Der Gerschom Meor ha-Golah zugeschriebene Talmud-Commentar', in *Festschrift zum achtzigsten Geburtstage Moritz Steinschneiders* (Leipzig, 1896), 115–43. {When writing this section of the essay in the early 1970s, I was unaware of the revolutionary nature of the Mainz commentary and the magnitude of the accomplishment of the yeshivah of Mainz. See now 'The Third Yeshivah of Bavel and the Cultural Origins of Ashkenaz—A Proposal' in *Collected Essays*, ii (Oxford, 2014), 159–61, 210; see also 32–5. I would scarcely describe now the Mainz Commentary as 'useful but uninspiring'. This in no way affects the central point of the argument that—other than for the Promethean figure of Rashi—there was no 'personal literary creativity' in eleventh-century Ashkenaz.}

[106] It is the academic scene and its pride in creativity that springs first to the Ḥasid's mind when he speaks of the need for modesty; see #815:

The principle of modesty: where there is great gain and honor, he should distance himself and

ḥiddushim or *Tosafot*, *their ḥiddushim* and *their Tosafot*, to the Talmud.[107] Authorship had come into being, and is it surprising that pride followed close behind?[108] Ambition too, as creativity now opened the doors to career and fame, and the Pietists inveighed regularly against |344| the growing phenomenon of *torah she-lo li-shmah* (study of the Law not for its own sake).[109] Intellectual excellence was fast becoming the *areté* of the age, and he who possessed it was often only too easily tempted to dispense with the humbler and more inconvenient virtues. Repeatedly the Pietists warned their generation that intellectual accomplishment was neither a substitute for spiritual growth nor even a guarantee of religious integrity.[110]

not include himself in it. How so? If one is studying before his teacher and he remembers a good question or a good solution [that he had once propounded], he should not say, 'Thus I asked' or 'Thus I answered', instead he should say 'Thus you asked' and 'Thus you answered'... [the Lord says,] 'Whom shall I send and who will go *for us*?' [Isa. 6: 8]—the Bible taught here modesty to scholars ... and when he sits in the yeshivah and knows a question or [has] a solution [to one], he should not leap up and say it until he sees that no one will notice and then he should speak.

שורש ענוה: במקום שיש ריוח גדול וכבוד ירחיק את עצמו ולא יכליל את עצמו. כיצד? הרי לומד לפני רבו וזכר קושיא ותירוץ טוב, לא יאמר לרבו או לחבירו כך הקשיתי וכך תירצתי אלא כך הקשית וכך תירצת... וכתיב 'את מי אשלח ומי ילך לנו' [ישעיה ו: ח], מכאן למדה תורה ענוה לרבנים... וכשיושב בישיבה ויודע קושיא או תירוץ טוב לא יקפוץ לאומרו עד שיראה שלא ישימו על לב, אז יפתח פיו.

{Similarly, *Sodei Razaya*, in *Sifrei ha-Ra mi-Germaiza* (above, n. 42), vol. i, sect. 1, 9a.} See material cited in n. 108. The Pietists' reaction was doubly sharp for they were unaware that the creativity that they took for granted in sections 1950 (p. 473), 1052, and 774 was actually a new phenomenon. The Berlin edition {corroborated by MS JTS Boesky 45} reads *anavah le-rabbanan*, but the Bologna reading (#9) *anavah le-rabbanim* seems preferable. The term *rabbanim* has often a contemporary connotation; see, for example, #648. {See also the identical phrase *mi-kan limmed derekh anavah le-rabbanim* in *Sefer ha-Shem* in *Sifrei ha-Ra mi-Germaiza* (above, n. 42), vol. i, sect. 3, 30b.}

107 ##746, 1440, 15 (p. 21); note the hasidic aspirations in ##1950 (p. 473) and 1052.

108 ##1052, 355. The disappearance of anonymous authorship, which the Pietists mourn (##1558, 1955), and the phenomenon of plagiarism (#1748, and see above, n. 102) are parts of the same development. (One cannot help feeling that the giant shadow cast by Rabbenu Tam should somehow figure in this account. The towering intellect of R. Ya'akov and his leonine personality inspired awe and admiration among his contemporaries, and such sentiments, especially among students, lead to imitation. It is, however, far easier to copy the style of a man than his genius. The famous in all societies are mimetic figures, and one may wonder whether in this regard the bold and overbearing personality of Rabbenu Tam was a wholly salutary image for a number of people. At the very least, R. Ya'akov legitimized, for those whom nature so inclined, a greater measure of pride and self-assertion than had hitherto been acceptable in the conventional Ashkenazic image of the *talmid ḥakham*.)

109 To the material cited in the above note add ##15 (p. 21), 648; *SHB*, #958. See also ##860, 862, 919, and 753.

110 #15 (p. 21), 746, and the endless warnings against *talmud Torah* without *yir'at shamayim*, e.g. ##752, 1029, 1053, 1093, 811, 820, 814.

With their congenital inability to adhere strictly to any terminology, the Pietists used the term *she-lo li-shmah* at times as synonymous with *lilmod she-lo 'al menat le-kayyem* (study without the intention of fulfilling the Law),[111] which in their hands meant not simply study by the religiously lax, but the reduction of *talmud Torah* to a purely intellectual experience. Any expansion of the Divine norm was certainly in consonance with the goals of *ḥasidut*, and the Pietists had no quarrel with the new *pilpul* as such. But the purpose of dialectic to them was not simply the solution of logical difficulties, but the detection by man of new demands made upon him by God. One thought in order to discover to what to submit. Unlike early Polish hasidim, the German Pietists did not seek to empty *talmud Torah* of its intellectual content, for that would have been self-defeating. They rather demanded *in* study the ongoing experience of law as an imperative.[112] Only then was study integrated with and productive of religious growth, and anything less than that bordered on the criminal. A scholar who attained a deeper understanding of the halakhah—that is to say, a fuller comprehension of the Divine demands—but whose religious observance did not intensify concomitantly, could only be viewed, in the final analysis, as being in a state of rebellion.[113] *Talmud Torah* could |345| not coexist with a static religious commitment. As dialectic marched from triumph to triumph, growing daily more sophisticated, more time-consuming, and more self-justificatory, the danger that loomed was precisely the detachment of learning from spiritual growth, the disassociation of comprehension from commitment.

The possibility of psychic imbalance now threatened the Ashkenazic community. The tosafist movement had turned a corpus into a problem. In place of apprehension and application came now question and resolution. The act of knowing became creative and infinitely more time-consuming. The breathtaking accomplishments in talmudic studies could not go unnoticed, and the desire to participate in them was only natural. Preoccupation with the brave new world of dialectic tended to crowd out other activities and the menace of hypertrophy of the intellect made itself felt, as the old educational models—

111 ##754, 756 (note contrast); *SHB*, #17. Compare #862 with #1707: אלא . . . יתן [הצדקה] ליראי ה' העוסקין בתורה לשמה / אלא יתן ליראי ה' הלומדים לקיים המצוות. (MS Oxford, Bodley 875, fo. 134v reads in *SHB*, #17: אלא לומד על מנת לקיים לשמור ולעשות זו היא תורה לשמה.)

112 We are here focusing on what was distinctive in the hasidic conception of *talmud Torah*. As all uniqueness in a traditional society is only partial, these orientations prevented neither the Polish nor the German Ḥasid from often engaging in the traditional modes and experiences of study.

113 *SHB*, #17; ##1474 (end), 1475. {For a fuller analysis of *lilmod 'al menat le-kayyem* in hasidic thought, see Ch. 8 below, pp. 203–4.}

geared more to *Gestalt* than to accomplishment—were shaken. Prayer had played a central role in the old Ashkenazic culture and religious poetry had been reverently cultivated. People found in *piyyut* an expression of their deepest feelings and incorporated it, apparently on their own initiative, into the Divine service. The composition of liturgical poetry was widespread enough in the old Ashkenazic culture to be viewed as one of the desirable accomplishments of the *talmid ḥakham*, and its detailed study and explication formed an important scholarly pursuit.[114] There could be no writing of *piyyut*, no understanding of *piyyut*, without a deep orientation in Bible and Midrash. As learning in this world was assimilative rather than creative, the scholarly style was milder, the profile lower. Many of the traits that we associate with Rashi—reticence, modesty, temperateness of expression—are common to the literature of the eleventh century.[115] In cultivating simultaneously |**346**| talmudic scholarship, poetry, prayer, biblical exegesis, and midrashic interest, the old Ashkenazic ideal had nurtured a wide range of human faculties, had drawn upon and developed a broader spectrum of man's capabilities. The equilibrium of the intellectual, imaginative, and moral faculties was being upset by this pre-emption of aspiration on the part of *talmud Torah*. On a deeper level, much of *Sefer Ḥasidim* is an attempt to redress this imbalance.[116] On this I shall have more to say later.

[114] *'Arugat ha-Bosem* (above, n. 49), 1 ff. {On the explication of *piyyut* in France, see A. Grossman, *Ḥakhmei Tsarfat ha-Rishonim: Koroteihem, Darkam be-Hanhagat ha-Tsibbur, Yetsiratam ha-Ruḥanit*, 3rd edn. (Jerusalem, 2001), 249–50, 325–7, 381–95, 507–38.}

The late Daniel Goldschmidt once remarked to me that the reason Rashi penned his *piyyutim* (which added no luster to his name) was that at that time the well-rounded *talmid ḥakham* was expected to be able to compose some religious poetry upon the proper occasion. 'Oh, roughly analogous', he added, 'to a *derashah* in our days. He [a scholar] needn't be a *darshan*, but he should be able to say some appropriate words as occasion demands.'

[115] This is the type of statement for which it is difficult to cite book and verse. Yet close to a decade's work in the literature of the eleventh century has given me the sustained impression that Rashi is unique in the near-total cohesion of his thought and in the lucidity of his presentation, but hardly atypical in character and general bearing. Rashi is simply a sterling (and prominent) example of a pre-Crusade Rhineland scholar. Avraham Grossman of the Hebrew University, who has made the most exhaustive study of the figures of the period (soon to be published), has concurred with this impression. {Grossman's expanded version of his thesis was published in Jerusalem in 1981 as *Ḥakhmei Ashkenaz ha-Rishonim: Koroteihem, Darkam be-Hanhagat ha-Tsibbur, Yetsiratam ha-Ruḥanit mi-Reshit Yishuvam ve-'ad li-Gezerot Tatnu* (Jerusalem, 1981).}

[116] On a simple, technical level, see e.g. *'Arugat ha-Bosem* (above, n. 49), 110–11. Parallels can be found, *mutatis mutandis*, in contemporary Christian literature for much of the Pietists' strictures, such as the pre-emption of interest by dialectic, the crowding out of other disciplines and the cultural imbalance that follows, curriculum distortions and the precipitous introduction of the student to the new technique, the opening of positions to the unqualified, and the increasing study for the sake of fame and self-advancement. See e.g. J. W. Baldwin, *Masters, Princes and Merchants: The Social Views*

It is in no small measure as a corrective to the growing intellectualism of the time that the movement of the Ḥasidei Ashkenaz arose. That morals outweigh scholarship and that knowledge is no safeguard of virtue are statements that would win assent from all segments of normative Judaism, and they imply no challenge to the axiological primacy of *talmud Torah*. Study of the Law is the most desirable and sublime pursuit of man, and it occupies the center of hasidic aspirations in this world and, more significantly, in some of their dreams of the world to come.[117] *Sefer Ḥasidim* overflows with panegyrics to *talmud Torah*, and it should be emphasized that it is *talmud Torah* understood in the traditional sense of the phrase.[118] Much advice is given on how to achieve maximum results from study, |347| and the standards of talmudic knowledge aspired to by the Pietists would satisfy the most demanding.[119] They pointed freely to the blemishes of many scholars, but their writings

of Peter Chanter and His Circle (Princeton, 1970), i. 81–6, 100, 130–1, and notes ad loc.; U. T. Holmes, 'Transitions in European Education', in M. Clagett, G. Post, and R. Reynolds, eds., *Twelfth-Century Europe and the Foundations of Modern Society* (Madison, 1961), 22–5. The Pietists' critiques are few and their language mild indeed in comparison with what Alexander Neckam, Gerald of Cambridge, Jacques de Vitry, and John of Salisbury, among others, had to say about the misuse of the new logic and its adverse effects. What must be kept in mind, however, is that Jews had no tradition of rhetoric whose avowed aim was suasion rather than truth—a tradition which would instantly adopt dialectic to its purpose—no institution of *disputatio*, and no curriculum of *sophismata logicalia*, both of which would at once hasten and heighten the ill uses to which dialectic could be put. Nor could halakhic eminence open the gate to any equivalent career of high service to prince or churchman as could Roman or canon law. Tosafism was prestigious but hardly a 'lucrative science'.

117 Ben-Sasson ('Ḥasidei Ashkenaz 'al Ḥalukkat Kinyanim [above, n. 9], 74–7; repr. in his *Retsef u-Temurah* [above, n. 9], 193–5) has drawn attention to this fact. See also *Ḥokhmat ha-Nefesh*, Safed edn., fo. 14a {Sodei Razaya edn., 58a}. (*SH*, #1546 says the same thing as *Ḥokhmat ha-Nefesh*, but I do not believe that it can be cited as proof of an aspiration.) Section 1838, to which Ben-Sasson draws attention, is probably the best description of the hasidic ideal of *talmud Torah*. {See now the requirement of sixteen hours a day of Torah study found in *Sefer ha-Gematriyot le-R. Yehudah he-Ḥasid*, ed. Y. Y. Stal (Jerusalem, 2005), i. 11—12, and the sources cited in n. 72, to which Rabbi Mordechai M. Honig has added *Sefer ha-Shem* in *Sifrei ha-Ra mi-Germaiza* (above, n. 42), vol. i, sect. 3, 191–2. Both volumes of that set contain a number of the shorter works of R. El'azar, each with its own pagination. 'Sect. 3' refers to the third work in that volume.}

118 *Talmud Torah* is never a means for achieving another and higher religious end, although if undertaken in the proper spirit, it should lead to a deepening of *yir'at shamayim* (see above). Furthermore, there is no passage, to the best of my knowledge, where *talmud Torah* even connotes the exclusive study of hasidic lore, though quite naturally such an inquiry is often included in the term. (See e.g. Dan, 'Sefer ha-Ḥokhmah' [above, n. 9], 171 n. 18; repr. in id., *'Iyyunim be-Sifrut Ḥasidei Ashkenaz* [above, n. 9], 47 n. 18; {see my remarks in n. 9 above for the strictures of D. M. Sigal}.)

119 e.g. ##1474, 768, 769, 771 (this last section—which addresses the problem of a man who cannot cease from cogitating on Torah matters when in the privy—seemed excessive to some subsequent generations, and the parallel passage in *SHB*, #954 was omitted in several printings of that work, such as Sulzbach [1685], Frankfurt [1743], Żółkiew [1785]), ##774, 775.

contain no indictment of a class. It never occurred to the Pietists that in being relieved of paying taxes, the *talmid ḥakham* was possessed of an undeserved prerogative. Indeed, the privileged economic position of the scholar is upheld by the Ḥasidim in stronger terms than those of the Talmud.[120] The remarks of

[120] Contrast *Bava Batra* 8a: 'Rabbi Yohanan said: all [must contribute the impost of paying for the city watchman. This money must be collected] even from the estates of orphans, but not scholars, as they are in no need of watchmen [as the Torah stands watch over them]' (אמר רב יוחנן הכל לפסי העיר ואפי' מיתמי, אבל רבנן לא, דרבנן לא צריכא נטירותא) with *SH*, #807: 'Scholars who study day and night need not pay any taxes, because this burden has fallen on the community because of the sins of the ignorant, whereas [scholars], the Torah of the Lord stands watch over them' (ותלמידי חכמים שעוסקין יומם ולילה לא יתנו עמם דבר כי לא בעבורם הוטל אלא בעון עמי הארץ, ותורת אלהים משמרתן). To the hasidic mind the point of the biblical narrative of Joseph's treatment of the landed holdings of the Egyptian priests is to teach us that scholars are exempt from taxation. This is the very raison d'être of the passage (see above, n. 9.) The hasidic tradition reported by R. Yosef Ibn 'Ezra, to which Ben-Sasson has drawn attention ('Ḥasidei Ashkenaz 'al Ḥalukkat Kinyanim [above, n. 9], 66 {repr. in his *Retsef u-Temurah* (above, n. 9), 183}) is entirely in keeping with what we know of their outlook:

> Once there was a tax assessment and there were two rich talmudic scholars and they sought to exempt themselves from the tax because they were halakhically exempt from taxation, and most of the community were agreeable to this claim. Two wealthy members [however] protested and they [the scholars] were taxed. They [the wealthy people who protested] all died within a month . . . On the night of Hoshana Rabbah, the Pietist dozed off, and he saw two of the rich men [who had protested], and a donkey was [repeatedly] biting the shoulder of one of the men . . . The Pietist asked [them] . . . what was your sin that you should suffer such cruel blows? They answered, 'Because we blocked those who sought to help the talmudic scholars.'
>
> שפעם אחת בא עריכה בקהל, והיו שם ב' ת"ח עשירים, רצו לפטור עצמן מהמס מטעם שהם פטורים, כפי הדין. וכל הקהל היו מרוצים, וקמו עשירי הקהל ומיחו בידם והעריכום. ולא מלאו חודש ימים שמתו . . . ובליל הושענה רב' נתנמנם החסיד. וראה את ב' עשירים אלו שהיה חמור אחד נושך לאחד על כתיפו . . . שאל החסיד . . . מה פשעתם לה' שתוכו מכה אכזרי' כזאת? השיבו לו: על שעכבו ביד המסייעין לת"ח בענין הערכין וכו'.

The attitude in the above story is slightly tempered by their remarks in #1392, where they counsel a scholar to share in the communal burden if he is only able. Note, however, that this is a voluntary participation on his part and not an obligatory one, and they never counsel the community to make it such. While the attitude of Ḥasidei Ashkenaz to *'ammei ha-arets* is beyond the scope of this essay, one simple example may indicate how much more complex and ambivalent was their relationship to the unlettered than is commonly imagined. One would hardly expect to find on the pages of *Sefer Ḥasidim* the chilling dictum of the Yerushalmi (*Horayot* 3: 4) that, when aiding and ransoming captives, it is preferable to expend money to provide the captive wife of a scholar with clothes than to spend that money to save the life of an ignoramus (כסות אשת חבר קודמת לחיי עם הארץ). Yet it does make its appearance in section 1676, without any apparent qualms on the part of the writer, such as those which troubled such halakhists as the author of the *Penei Mosheh* (ad loc.) and R. Shabbetai Kohen (*Shakh*, 'Yoreh De'ah', 251: 16). That this is no mechanical citation nor literary ballast carried without any real awareness of its import can be seen from the end of the section. The Ḥasid proceeds to qualify the definition of clothing to mean decent rather than fancy clothes and restrict the priority of a 'wife of a scholar' to a woman who is deeply religious and attends to the needs of her scholarly husband—so as to align the Yerushalmi's dictum with the writer's own sense of right and wrong. However, he leaves the 'life of the ignoramus' unqualified, taking that phrase quite literally and with-

Sefer Ḥasidim constitute no revolutionary evaluation of *talmud torah* or fundamental critique of *talmidei ḥakhamim*; they were simply a reassertion of certain truths that may have been overlooked in the intellectual enthusiasm of the late twelfth century. Significantly, their words were read for 700 years without anyone taking offence.

Yet—after all this has been entered on the ledger, one confronts a remainder of bitterness in the Pietists' remarks still unaccounted for. This acrimony is partly due, as I have already noted, to their defeats and humiliations at the hands of the intellectual establishment. Anger, however, is discernible in the *Ḥokhmat ha-Nefesh*, which issued from the pen of R. El'azar of Worms, as prominent a member of that establishment as one could desire—author of the *Roke'aḥ*, signatory of the Takkanot Shum, and |348| scion of one of the most distinguished families of Ashkenaz.[121] Bitterness, of course, need not be the result of one's own experiences; it could reflect indignation at the fate suffered by well-meaning followers. But it may be that there is indeed a personal dimension to the resentment that has been detected in the writings of R. El'azar.

From a reading of the *Roke'aḥ* one would never suspect that an intellectual revolution was sweeping through the schools of Ashkenaz. It is a work in the tradition of the *Sifrut de-Vei Rashi*[122] and has little connection with the world of the Tosafists. This is not a consequence of brevity or practical purpose, as is sometimes suggested. The *Semak* is no less a brief popular handbook, but the problems there treated are those created by the new dialectic, and the doctrines cited are drawn from the writings of the Tosafists. R. El'azar's work, however, in no way reflects those of Ravan, R. Efrayim, or Ravyah, nor does it seek in any way to sum up their achievements. It lives in a world that is still

out any apparent compunction. {On the attitude of *Sefer Ḥasidim* to the talmudic exemption of scholars from taxes, see now Y. Altschuler, 'Hitpatḥutam u-Mashma'utam shel Misei ha-Kahal be-Ashkenaz mi-Reshit ha-Hityashvut ve-'ad la-Magefah ha-Sheḥorah' (Ph.D. diss., Bar-Ilan University, 2009), 224–30. (Despite his gracious correction at p. 225 n. 277, there is no misprint in this note; I intentionally cited #1392 and not #1493. The latter concludes, *she-ein yadam tekefah 'al ha-tsibbur*, that is to say, when the Ḥasidim do control the community, those who devote themselves to study but earn an income on the side would be relieved of paying taxes. In MS Parma, De Rossi 1133, the text is *ein yadam* without the *she-* and this reading is corroborated by JTS Boesky 45. It thus appears that both the printed *SHP* and *SHB* editions are scribal emendations. Both *she-ein* of *SHP* and *ve-ein* of *SHB*, however, seem to be making the same qualification, taking *ein yadam tekefah* as a temporal clause meaning 'when', i.e. '*ka-asher ein yadam tekefah*, then the above applies; however, *ke-she-yadam tekefah*, the aforesaid does not apply'.) On *yadam tekefah*, see above, n. 52.}

121 This was noted by Ben-Sasson, 'Ḥasidei Ashkenaz 'al Ḥalukkat Kinyanim (above, n. 9).

122 Cf. *'Arugat ha-Bosem* (above, n. 49), 328 ff.

unbedeviled by the contradictory results of talmudic collation and the multiple possibilities of resolution. To the author of the *Roke'aḥ* the Talmud still means one thing, and it is this straightforward meaning, together with the traditions of the Rhineland and the rulings of its great, that constitutes his halakhic world. The *Roke'aḥ* is in direct line of descent from the *Ma'aseh Ge'onim* and the *Pardes*, and this fact may be of significance. Unless R. El'azar was a unique throwback, this would indicate that alongside the great creative centers of Mainz, Bonn, and Regensburg there existed a conservative circle, which, while in no way opposed to dialectic—indeed, it could even break a dialectical lance if |349| need be[123]—never really assimilated the achievements of the new *pilpul* or made them part of its halakhic *Anschauung*. Being conservative, this circle wrote little, but was nonetheless very much alive. Ḥasidei Ashkenaz, I suggest, arose from a group that still lived in a world of simple rather than multiple reference. If this be going beyond the evidence, this much is certain: the one certified Talmudist among the movement's founders was closer halakhically to the spirit of the eleventh century than to that of the thirteenth.[124]

But the thirteenth century was the one in which they lived, and this was a French century—even in Germany. German scholars studied regularly in France, while the Frenchman who studied in Germany was rare indeed. Rarer yet is any reference to German works in the writings of R. Yehudah of Paris, R. Mosheh of Coucy, or R. Yitsḥak of Corbeil. Though Ravyah and R. El'azar of Worms both studied with a pupil of Rabbenu Tam, each in his own way still represented a distinctive German tradition. Their pupil, R. Yitsḥak Or Zarua', belongs as much to Tsarfat as to Ashkenaz. There is a great deal of Germanic material in the *Or Zarua'*, but it is not a work of Germanic tradition. From the days of Rabbenu Tam and R. Yitsḥak of Dampierre, a French wave beats upon the shores of the Rhineland, and in the second quarter of the thirteenth century inundates it. R. Me'ir of Rothenburg is in his thought and rulings no more German than French, and the same holds true for R. Mordekhai ben Hillel. As for R. Asher (Rosh), who would know of the achievements of Ravan and Ravyah if he took his instruction from the *Piskei ha-Rosh*? There is far more of Spain and Provence in that work than there is of his German homeland.[125] And when he turned to commentary, it was the

123 See *'Arugat ha-Bosem* (above, n. 49), 334 ff. The precise level of R. El'azar's attainments in dialectic deserves a separate study.

124 I add 'certified' because R. Shemu'el he-Ḥasid has also a halakhic work to his credit. However, since next to nothing of it has survived, we can evaluate neither the man nor his posture.

125 H. Soloveitchik, 'Mashkon ve-'Arev: Shenei Meḥkarim be-Ribbit u-ve-Toledot ha-Halakhah

Tosafot of Dampierre that he edited and preserved and not those of Riva or Rivam. Germany as a distinct halakhic culture ceases to exist somewhere around the year 1230, and the lament of R. El'azar of Worms in his *Sefer ha-Ḥokhmah* that he has no one to whom to transmit his esoteric traditions |**350**| is only part of a wider phenomenon.[126] R. Yehudah he-Ḥasid and R. El'azar of Worms lived out their days watching the decline and fall of Ashkenaz.

It was from the aristocratic center of the Jewish community and not from its periphery that German Hasidism arose.[127] And total and unswerving indeed was the devotion to *talmud Torah* on the part of these families, who, for centuries, had embodied the ideals of the Ashkenazic community. This fact cannot be stressed enough.[128] But it should equally be understood and

ba-Galut' (Ph.D. diss., Hebrew University of Jerusalem, 1972), 52 ff. {This appeared as *Halakhah, Kalkalah ve-Dimmuy 'Atsmi: ha-Mashkona'ut bi-Yemei ha-Beinayim* (Jerusalem, 1984), 97–8; id., 'Can Halakhic Texts Talk History?', in *Collected Essays*, i (Oxford, 2013), 169–223. The relevant passage is found in the former source at 194–5 and in the latter at 221–2.} I have, in this paragraph, borrowed several formulations from that article.

126 Sigal, 'Sefer ha-Ḥokhmah ha-Meyuḥas la-Roke'aḥ' (above, n. 9), 51–2; Dan, 'Sefer ha-Ḥokhmah' (above, n. 9), 171 {repr. in id., *'Iyyunim be-Sifrut Ḥasidei Ashkenaz* (above, n. 9), 47}:

לא זכיתי לבני יחידי אשר קבלם והלך בחצי ימיו, נאמן הדיין יתברך שמו ויתעלה זכרו, ולא זכיתי ללמוד[!] השערים לאחרים כי פסקו אנשי מעשה ונתמעטו הלבבות [מבלי להבין איך] יוצא התלמוד מה' חומשי תורה.

[For] I was unworthy [to the extent that] my only son who received [this lore] died young. I accept [the judgment of] the Judge, may His name be blessed and His memory held most highly, and I have not been able to teach these gates [i.e. modes of interpretation] to others because worthy people no longer exist and the hearts [i.e. minds] have become too small [to comprehend how] the Talmud is derived from the Five Books of Moses.

{As noted above, n. 9, D. M. Sigal's study has shown that much of the text of *Sefer ha-Ḥokhmah* is spurious; however, our passage is authentic, and has been cited as given by Sigal. The three words that the later editor/author of *Sefer ha-Ḥokhmah* added, and which I have placed in brackets, appear to be a reasonable emendation to fill a clear ellipsis in the original text. The authentic text (in Sigal, 'Sefer ha-Ḥokhmah') also speaks of the prior death of R. El'azar's only son, leaving him with no worthy recipient of what has been hitherto an oral tradition. All of which explains why the writer has taken the crucial step of writing down the secret lore of the Kalonymides and disseminating it. Whether or not R. Yehudah preceded R. El'azar in the inscription of their vital arcanum is irrelevant. The two were the first to record and promulgate the esoteric teachings of the Kalonymides, so the time frame for the disappearance of successors to carry on the Kalonymide traditions remains unchanged.} I inquired of the late Professor Efrayim Gottlieb whether he felt these words were a stock-in-trade preface penned simply to justify committing esoteric knowledge to writing. His reply was in the negative.

127 It is doubtful whether anyone less than a certified aristocrat could have risked propounding in Ashkenaz the strange and novel demands of the *retson ha-Bore* and not be run out of town, let alone win a hearing. {See p. 246 below.}

128 German Hasidism is often described as a popular movement. Much depends on the sense in which the term is used. If by 'popular' one wishes to say that it reflects beliefs and attitudes current

emphasized that this elite was now helplessly witnessing the erosion of its own position. Anyone reared upon the *Tosafot* of Dampierre would find the world of the *Roke'aḥ* woefully inadequate. But challenge Dampierre and Ravyah the Pietists could not, for not only traditional values but their own ideology bound them fast to the revolution that was sweeping through the yeshivot and *battei midrash* of Germany. Far from being antinomian, the very ark of the hasidic covenant was the aggrandizement of the Divine norm, and this quest for self-fetterment made the Pietists one with the spirit of the new dialectic with its unremitting expansion of the halakhic dictate.[129] The success of this dialectic, however, was destroying the very world that the hasidic leadership represented. It was supplanting the primacy of their traditions, undermining their communal pre-eminence, and sorely limiting their capacity for effective action. R. Yehudah Ḥasid and R. El'azar Roke'aḥ were committed thus to the instruments of |351| their own destruction, of their own dislodgement, at the very least,[130] and from this sprang their profound ambivalence towards *talmud Torah* and *pilpul*. Hasidic literature is the work of a spiritual elite; much of it is, at the same time, the work of a displaced aristocracy or one in the process of being stripped of its intellectual and political patrimony.

Where are the Kalonymides or the other old and famous families of Ashkenaz after the 1220s? It is Bohemia and not the Rhineland that provides Germany with its leaders in the next generation, and these men did not distinguish between the Seine and the Rhine, the Aube and the Tauber; neither did their successors—R. Me'ir of Rothenburg, R. Asher, R. Me'ir ha-Kohen,

in Germany at the time in contradistinction to the outlook of the received 'canonized' literature, there is a good deal of truth to this description. If it denotes sympathy with the victims of injustice and a desire to right things, the term is again being used accurately. If the statement means that German Hasidism arose from the 'populus', from the simple or underprivileged sectors of the community, it is demonstrably false. If 'popular' implies that hasidic ideas found a receptive audience in those downtrodden segments and drew from them adherents, the assertion is unproven. We know absolutely nothing of the social origins of any Ḥasid other than the three founders and theoreticians of the movement, R. Shemu'el, R. Yehudah, and R. El'azar, bluebloods all.

[129] I should hasten to add that the vehicles of expansion were utterly different. The Ḥasid did not derive the Larger Will through any use of the new dialectic, but rather (to put it roughly) made normative the moral suggested to him by a biblical or talmudic narrative. His approach was intuitive rather than technical, associative rather than discursive.

[130] Is it accidental that R. Yehudah he-Ḥasid, when struggling angrily to uphold the liturgical text of his movement, labeled other variants as 'the French practice', even though these variants were no French innovation, but had been recited equally in Ashkenaz and go back to geonic times (*'Arugat ha-Bosem* [above, n. 49], 92 ff.)? Or was this simply an admission that the legitimation for these variants, so contrary to *his* ideas and traditions, stemmed from its receiving French endorsement? Was he not saying in effect that his text was under French pressure?

and R. Mordekhai ben Hillel—of whom only the latter was a scion of a once-famous family. The importance of lineage in the thought of the Ḥasidim, the repeated protests on their part against the marriage of the well-born (*benei tovim*) with the unworthy rich, and their laments about the seizure of communal leadership by the base and the wicked reflect, I suggest, this loss by the old Rhineland aristocracy of the commanding heights of prestige and power. And one wonders whether one of the sources nourishing their sympathy for the deprived was not their own sense of disinheritance. For German Ḥasidut was shaped by men who had been adversely affected by the events of their time: not by any loss of material possessions, but by a diminution of the deference and authority that had been hitherto accorded them.

What the early decades of the thirteenth century witnessed was not simply the displacement of an elite but the passing of an entire culture, though this properly is the subject of another essay and I can give it only the barest of intimations here. It would be surprising indeed if, in a society centered to an extraordinary degree around *talmud Torah*, talmudic studies could be transformed and intellectual traditions ruptured without this having far-reaching effects. The inability of R. Yehudah he-Ḥasid and R. El'azar Roke'aḥ to find pupils worthy of being taught the esoteric lore of |352| Ashkenaz, of continuing its oral tradition, was one such consequence. The drop in the volume and quality of, and interest in, *piyyutim* was another. Liturgical creativity flags after 1230,[131] and except for one pupil of R. Yehudah, R. 'Azri'el of Bohemia, the study of *piyyut* ceases to interest the German community, or interests it to a much lesser extent. This too I would relate to the French 'invasion'. *Piyyut* never struck deep roots in France. Rashi's generation and the generation of his early pupils and younger contemporaries—R. Me'ir of Ramerupt, Rashbam, and R. Yosef Kara—were raised in an Ashkenazic world and, faithful to their upbringing, they either composed or interpreted religious poetry.[132] Their successors—R. Yitsḥak of Dampierre, R. Shimshon of Sens, the French Tosafists—had little contact with the Rhineland, knew next to nothing of its

[131] Professor Aharon Mirsky has confirmed this impression of mine and further informed me that the material in manuscripts presents the same picture. {This statement must be qualified by Ephraim Kanarfogel's observations in *The Intellectual History and Rabbinic Culture of Medieval Ashkenaz* (Detroit, 2013), 404–44. However, Kanarfogel's portrait does not go beyond the early years of the fourteenth century, and so the modification entailed by his researches is that the transformations outlined in prayer, *sod*, halakhah, and *piyyut* did not proceed at the same pace. The first three developments were completed by the end of the first third of the thirteenth century, whereas that of liturgical poetry took some three-quarters of a century longer. Elisabeth Hollender's future essay on the hitherto unkown R. Aharon b. Yosef will further nuance the state of *piyyut* in the thirteenth century.}

[132] *'Arugat ha-Bosem* (above, n. 49), 6–23.

traditions, and evinced no interest in *piyyut*.[133] From the days of R. Yitsḥak to those of the exile in 1306, poetry is noticeably absent from the center of the French stage. With the French conquest of Germany, *piyyut* becomes peripheral even in the Rhineland. Finally, there is the decline of prayer, communal prayer at least, in Germany from an encounter between man and his Lord to the status of a *mitsvah*, albeit one which required *kavvanah*, together with the concomitant transformation of the cantor (*sheliaḥ tsibbur*) from his eleventh-century role as the communal ambassador to the Divine court to that of a religious functionary.[134]

[133] Rabbenu Tam is a transitional figure in this regard. The correlation in France between knowledge of the pre-Crusade literature and the involvement in *piyyut* is perhaps worth noting. R. Me'ir of Ramerupt and Rashbam possessed a firm familiarity with this lore, Rabbenu Tam far less. R. Yitsḥak of Dampierre was either ignorant of this world or oblivious to it. (See H. Soloveitchik, 'Pawnbroking: A Study in Ribbit and of the Halakhah in Exile', *Proceedings of the American Academy for Jewish Research*, 38–39 [1970–1], 255 n. 98. {Reprinted in an expanded form in *Collected Essays*, i (Oxford, 2013), 137 n. 190.})

[134] A few salient points of a theme that will be developed in detail elsewhere: no cantor of the thirteenth century possessed anything approaching the standing of R. Me'ir Sheliaḥ Tsibbur of the eleventh century or that of R. El'azar Ḥazan of Speyer in the early twelfth. Elections of cantors first appear in the latter half of the twelfth century, as do salaries. I do not mean to imply by the phrase 'religious functionary' a low communal standing for the cantor—R. El'azar Ḥazan is, after all, one of the signatories of the Takkanot Shum—but that he is no longer a central religious figure, no longer a keeper of the secrets of prayer or arbiter and guardian of its potent text. This cannot be attributed to the decision of the Pietists to disseminate their lore, for the decline is noticeable before the decision of R. Yehudah and R. El'azar to 'go public' as it were. (See Dan, 'Sefer ha-Ḥokhmah' [above, n. 9], 171 {repr. in id., *'Iyyunim be-Sifrut Ḥasidei Ashkenaz* (above, n. 9), 47; as to M. D. Sigal's critique in 'Sefer ha-Ḥokhmah ha-Meyuḥas la-Roke'aḥ', see above, n. 9}.) Needless to say, this decline was accelerated and intensified in the outlying settlements and slower in the old centers; see *Or Zarua'*, i, #113. (One could object that the question of elections first appears in the literature of the early thirteenth century not because elections were relatively new, but because the traditional principle of election—unanimity—was coming under increasing pressure from the new concept of majority rule. I can only counter that to my mind the received picture of communal organization is in error. Ashkenazic communities were at all times run on the majority principle. This position will be argued in detail in the forthcoming *Shut ke-Makor Histori*.) {It was published by Merkaz Shazar (Jerusalem, 1990).}

It may be instructive to draw attention to the codicological discoveries of M. Beit-Arié and his staff at the Institute of Hebrew Paleography. 'Bookmaking' in Germany undergoes a transformation during the thirteenth century. From 1233 on a novel process of preparation of hides is discernible, which is fully developed by 1264. By the same date a new system of rulings and prickings comes to the fore. We do not know how French manuscripts were prepared as almost no manuscripts with French colophons have survived. Thus we have no right to attribute this transformation to the growing French influence. One might, however, note that two of the three codicological changes that took place in German Hebrew manuscripts during the thirteenth century occurred in England amongst Latin manuscripts in the wake of the Norman conquest. (See M. Beit-Arié, 'Tekhunot Kodikologiyyot ki-Veḥanim Pale'ografiyyim be-Khitvei Yad 'Ivriyyim bi-Yemei ha-Beinayim', *Kiryat Sefer*, 45

The intellectual perception of the Ashkenazic community had been transformed by the early decades of the thirteenth century, its religious experience altered, and its traditions, both in law and in mysticism, threatened with extinction. The movement of Ḥasidei Ashkenaz was in one sense a reactionary one. It was an attempt by the leaders of the old Ashkenazic culture to defend the received values and customary modes of understanding. The irony was that while some of the *postures* and *values* defended |353| by the Ḥasidim —low personal profile, temperateness in dealings with others, the centrality of prayer, and the importance of balanced knowledge as distinct from exclusive preoccupation with novellae—were indeed old Ashkenazic ones,[135] the *doctrines* of the movement—the myriad prescriptions |354| of God's Larger Will (*retson ha-Borè*), not to speak of its folklore and demonology—were more thoroughly medieval than anything produced in the schools of Ramerupt and Dampierre. The creative spirit of the twelfth century had, all unawares, touched R. Shemu'el he-Ḥasid, his son R. Yehudah, and R. El'azar of Worms

[1970], 435–46, especially 444 n. 30. The dates given in the article are 1254 and 1272. Subsequent research, however, has advanced them respectively, Dr Beit-Arié tells me, to 1233 and 1264. It is these dates that I have employed.) {These dates still hold, though there is some foreshadowing of these developments in the early decades of the thirteenth century. See the online 2015 pre-print version of *Kodikologiyah 'Ivrit: Tipologiyah shel Melekhet ha-Sefer ha-'Ivri bi-Yemei ha-Beinayim*, 168–71, 282–4, 304–9; <http://web.nli.org.il/sites/NLI/Hebrew/collections/manuscripts/hebrewcodicology/Documents/Hebrew-Codicology-continuously-updated-online-version.pdf>.}

135 Some of these traits had achieved, as early as the eleventh century, an intensified embodiment in certain isolated individuals, as for example the excessively humble style of the Makirites, the self-effacement of R. Ya'akov b. Yakar (not to speak of his unique Divine service of floor-sweeping [#991]), and the literalism, *perishut*, and possible stringency of R. Sasson. From a study of the literature of pre-Crusade Jewry one obtains the impression that certain general values of the period, which attained occasionally extreme individual realization, were adopted and intensified by the Pietists, placed in a fresh conceptual framework, and made normative. For the traits of the above-mentioned scholars, see A. Grossman, *Toledot ha-Sifrut ha-Rabbanit be-Ashkenaz u-ve-Tsarfat ha-Tsefonit ba-Me'ah ha-Aḥat-'Esreh* (Ph.D. diss., Hebrew University of Jerusalem, 1973), 320–1; cf. 172 ff., 243 ff. {a much-expanded version was published eight years later as *Ḥakhmei Ashkenaz ha-Rishonim* (above, n. 115), see pp. 246–7, 334–5, 369–70}. See his remarks about R. Yitsḥak b. Mosheh, better known as R. Me'ir Shats, *Toledot ha-Sifrut ha-Rabbanit*, 297–8 {*Ḥakhmei Ashkenaz ha-Rishonim*, 293–4}. Though I would take exception to some of the instances that Grossman adduces for his portrait of R. Sasson, I nevertheless find myself in agreement with his overall evaluation of that scholar. {I now would take exception to much of the characterization of R. Sasson; see *Collected Essays*, ii (Oxford, 2014), 106–21.

I must qualify the second sentence in this footnote in light of my article 'Piety, Pietism, and German Pietism' (Ch. 3 below). What is found in the eleventh century served as a prelude to, perhaps even was part of, conventional pietism. It had nothing in common with the unique and idiosyncratic one of Ḥasidei Ashkenaz; or, put differently, it was a prelude to the conventional aspects of the ideology of Ḥasidei Ashkenaz, not to those that originated in the *retson ha-Borè*. See also the Afterword below, sect. A—introductory paragraph and part 1.}

no less than it had R. Ya'akov Tam, and despite the most conservative intentions, they could not help but transform what they touched. In retrospect, the movement of Ḥasidei Ashkenaz appears as a natural complement and corrective to that of the Tosafists. The explosion of European halakhic thought demanded a similar expansion of the ethical and imaginative world. The altered modes of perception made it, moreover, impossible for the Midrash —now speaking a distant language—to communicate directly with the men of the late twelfth and thirteenth centuries and to provide them with a comprehensive *Weltanschauung*. Spiritual atrophy threatened unless the new European Talmud was provided with its own aggadah. While seeking to defend the old, the German Pietists were actually engaged in creating the new, in composing a new Midrash. And with partial success. The ethic of medieval Jewry did in time become that of the German Ḥasid, but its imaginative and theosophical world was to be that of the Spanish kabbalah, the true Midrash of Europe.

IV

RETROSPECT AND POINTS AT ISSUE

The meaning often given to *din shamayim*, the centrality attributed to it in the Pietists' thought, and the image of the Ḥasid as torn (consciously or not) between two competing sources of authority tell us, I suggest, more about the outlook of modern Jewish historiography—its attraction to the simple and the intuitive or its fascination with the antinomian and paradoxical—than about the thinking of those medieval German Jews who so aspired to the epithet 'Ḥasidim'. The interpretation which would make the perception of a natural ethic a focal point in hasidic thought, possibly even its motor force, must fall back on the categories of unconscious tension or paradox when confronted with the Pietists' relentless policy of stringency (*haḥmarah*) and their passionate concern for halakhic minutiae—not to speak of the hundreds of ritual prescriptions of their own making.[136] Far from being antinomian, the

[136] Cf. Y. Baer, 'Ha-Megammah ha-Datit ha-Ḥevratit' (above, preliminary n. b), 12–13. {Repr. in id., *Meḥkarim u-Masot* (above, n. b), 186–7; English translation/adaption in *Binah* (above, n. 10), 66–8.

Ithamar Gruenwald has drawn attention to the fact that pietism in the Christian context is inward and devotional and is invariably contrasted to legalism and to the established, long-entrenched, if you wish, routinized forms of religious practice. (I. Gruenwald, 'Social and Mystical Aspects of Sefer Ḥasidim', in K. E. Grözinger and J. Dan, eds., *Mysticism, Magic and Kabbalah in Ashkenazi Judaism: International Symposium held in Frankfurt a. M. 1991* [Berlin, 1995]}, 106–16.) However, as Shemuel Safrai has pointed out, the first hasidim that we know of, the *ḥasidim rishonim*

Pietists were norm-hungry, and their threefold activity of safeguarding the given, developing the revealed, and discovering the hidden flowed from one psychological and conceptual |355| center. To reduce the multitudinous and varied prescriptions of God's Larger Will to a few ethical and social demands, or to make them peripheral, is to shut one's eyes to much of the Pietists' writings and almost entirely to their religious aspirations. Not *din shamayim* but the Will of the Borè is the proper foil to *din ha-Torah* in hasidic thought. And these two revelations—the explicit and the implicit—should hardly be conceived of as competing poles of allegiance but as concentric circles emanating from a unitary (and ever-expanding) Divine Will, the outer perimeter of which takes on meaning only because of the wide ambience of the inner.

But does not *din shamayim* imply a notion of natural law that at least latently challenges the positive norm?[137] The answer is yes, but that yes takes on meaning only after two more basic questions are answered—implied to whom, and in what sense are ideas latent? For over a millennium natural law has played a prominent and catalytic role in Western history as it provided men with an ultimate measure of right and wrong, a touchstone of existing institutions, and a justification of rebellion. Two, possibly three, of the four major revolutions of modern times—the American, the French, and the English—have taken place (ostensibly at least) under the banner of this ideal. The contemporary historian is understandably attuned to the slightest whisper of such a notion in his readings. Whether such a sensitivity has a place in the study of *Sefer Ḥasidim* is open, however, to question. It is a fact that neither Ḥasidei Ashkenaz nor anyone else in the Ashkenazic community over the course of 700 years was aware of the explosive nature of *din shamayim*. A Confucian philosopher reading Aquinas would no doubt perceive many startling implications. If, however, neither Thomas himself drew those conclusions nor have they been perceived by subsequent scholastic thought or by Western culture to this day, the implications would not 'exist' in any historical sense of the word. They would be present only in a philosophical fashion—in the mind of the Perfect Knower. What we could learn from the Chinese thinker's observation would be precisely the reverse—that these ideas were

of tannaitic times, were hypernomian and sought a more rigorous observance of the religious practices than was commonly the case. See S. Safrai, 'The Teaching of the Pietists in Mishnaic Literature', *Journal of Jewish Studies*, 16 (1965), 15–33, and in an expanded Hebrew version in id., *Erets Yisra'el ve-Ḥakhameiha bi-Tekufat ha-Mishnah ve-ha-Talmud* (Jerusalem, 1983), 144–60, and id., *Bi-Yemei Bayit Sheni u-ve-Yemei ha-Mishnah* (Jerusalem, 1994), ii. 518–39. When discussing *ḥasidut*/pietism in Jewish history, we need to free ourselves from the 'anomian' or antinomian connotations of the term. This is an important point and deserves to be more widely known.}

137 Cf. Scholem, *Major Trends in Jewish Mysticism* (above, n. 10), 94.

without resonance in Western culture. The fact that *din shamayim* remained for 700 years within the exact confines in which the German Pietists left it—though it could easily have developed into something akin to natural law—indicates that while Ashkenazic culture was not unreceptive to antinomianism, it was singularly unresponsive to natural law and all that this idea entailed, and that if a source of competing authority were to arise |**356**| indigenously to challenge the primacy of the halakhah, it would not be able to base itself upon a self-confident, humanistic, and universalist intuition.

'Every man is a moon', wrote Mark Twain, 'and has a dark side.' The German Pietist was no exception, and the second theme of this essay takes issue with the romanticized portrait often drawn of Ḥasidei Ashkenaz. Though meek and quiescent in their private dealings, they were in communal matters assertive, presumptuous, and elitist to the bone. No doubt the Ḥasid looked upon himself as filled with the milk of human kindness—and perhaps justly so. But the phenomenon of overflowing love turning to fury and hatred when the bearer of new religious tidings finds his claims denied is common enough. We meet it frequently in the Gospels, and it will be found in *Sefer Ḥasidim*, if we will but read that book with open eyes. Historiography has tended to accept both the Pietist's self-image and his idiom at face value and has not questioned whether terms such as *resha'im*, *peritsim*, *yir'ei ha-Shem*, *lilmod she-lo 'al menat le-kayyem*, *le-zakkot et ha-rabbim* have a distinctive (and revelatory) connotation in his writings. So deeply has scholarship sympathized with the Ḥasidim that it has not wondered how the Ḥasid appeared to others or why the opposition to his ways from what was possibly the most God-fearing and martyrdom-tested community in Jewish history. Were his new religious demands reasonable? Were his pre-emptive claims and conduct not downright insulting? It was, ironically, the conjunction of an admirable humility and concern for others with the nature and ideology of Pietism that produced the antagonistic amalgam. The humble Pietist did not view his submission to God's will (as he conceived it) as something out of the ordinary; he saw himself simply as one who strove to fulfill his duties as a Jew. From this it followed that those who did less than he were lax or non-observant Jews (*resha'im*). Though the conclusions to be drawn from this were bitter, the Ḥasid did not shrink from them. The result was a religious elitism that many found repugnant. Hasidism as an ideal religious type, German Hasidism certainly, is characterized by exaggerated and supererogatory behavior. 'He [the Ḥasid] is the enthusiast, whose radicalism and utter emotional commitment are not to be deterred by bourgeois considerations.'[138] So long as these

[138] Scholem, 'Three Types of Jewish Piety' (above, n. 77), 341 {repr. in *Ariel* (above, n. 77), 18}.

tendencies are confined to the private domain all is well. But when a spirituality of extremism is coupled with an ideology of public service |357| (*le-zakkot et ha-rabbim*), the clash with the communal order becomes inevitable. Defeat follows, and bitterness, with all its psychological distortions, soon sets in.

Finally this essay questions whether the celebrated remarks of *Sefer Ḥasidim* about *talmud Torah* and *talmidei ḥakhamim* constituted a theoretical evaluation of these institutions and thus expressed a basic axiological critique, or whether these words arose from a distinct historical context and possessed a specific address. It is the tosafist movement—surely not one of the more bashful events of Jewish history—that forms the backdrop to Ḥasidei Ashkenaz. Much of *Sefer Ḥasidim*, both good and bad, is a product of and a response to the disruptive effects of the new dialectic. The hasidic movement was a reaction to, and at the same time part of, the intellectual revolution sweeping Ashkenaz in the twelfth century. That so much of importance could be written about German Pietism without a reference to the Tosafists is a tribute to the brilliance of modern historiography. It also may say something about its orientation. It bespeaks an outlook that sees halakhah as an intellectual discipline rather than as a cultural and 'political' force, and hence of no wider significance. Halakhah may well have become in modern times—even for the Orthodox—simply a *regula*; in the medieval period, it formed a good part of the cultural matrix of society and was at the same time a pathway to power. Constituting the major source of legitimacy, it inevitably invested its interpreters with authority and influence. A revolution in Jewish law, a swift and complete *bouleversement* in the major system of Jewish thought—in Ashkenaz the only structured system of thought—could well entail a transformation of perception and a change in elites. Forty years ago, we knew little about the ebb and flow of legal thought. Things have changed considerably since. And the historian, even if he should choose to speak of matters purely spiritual or social, can now neglect halakhic developments only at his own peril.

AFTERWORD

A

This essay, as I said at the outset, was published in 1976. In 2003 I published an essay entitled 'Piety, Pietism, and German Pietism' (reprinted below as Chapter 3), in which I argued that the first 152 sections of *Sefer Ḥasidim* found in the 1538 Bologna edition were unlinked to what followed. It was a separate work (which I termed *Sefer Ḥasidim I*) and reflected the outlook of a pietistic group in Germany or France who sharply dissented from the radical and idiosyncratic pietism of Ḥasidei Ashkenaz, had no use for the novel claims of *retson ha-Borè* or for its harsh penance, let alone that group's massive acceptance *in its teachings and writings* of the contemporary Germanic notions of the returning dead, witches, werewolves, and the like.[139] This naturally puts in question those statements in this earlier study where I drew upon those first 152 sections for support, namely nn. 47, 76 end, 84 end, and 111.

1. In three out of the five cases (nn. 76, 84, 111) there is sufficient evidence from the Berlin edition to prove the points made in the essay. Nor should the fact that *Sefer Ḥasidim I* holds similar views surprise us. The two groups had many ideas in common. Let us not forget that the German Pietists were pietists and then some. They shared with conventional pietists the belief that a vital link existed between knowledge and piety—intellectual growth had to be linked with spiritual development. The greater and more detailed the knowledge of the Divine norm, the greater the duty to obey that norm in all its newly found complexity (n. 111). The conventional pietists agreed with their German brethren that it was incumbent upon a pietist to reprove others for their religious failings. As their demands were for greater observance of *mitsvot* whose existence had universal assent and made no claim to radical social reform or to novel Divine dictates, they seem to have had somewhat more success than did their German confrères. At least, they never had to pull back (as did Ḥasidei Ashkenaz) and restrict the imperative of admonition (*tokhaḥah*) to cases where there was a realistic chance that it would be effective. As their prescriptions were neither strange nor unprecedented, Ḥasidim were duty-bound to rebuke those who failed to observe them, even if their admonition invited scorn and their shaming of the wayward incited physical retaliation (nn. 76, 84). No one ever claimed that a conventional pietist with a sense of mission was an easy person to live with.

2. All the documentation for the claim that the German Pietists viewed all those who sought to become Pietists as penitents stems from *Sefer Ḥasidim I*, and one may well claim that this assertion is undocumented (n. 47). I have no quarrel if one insists on striking that sentence from the text; however, it seems to me to be true of Ḥasidei Ashkenaz *a fortiori*. If conventional pietists, who emphasized simply the obligations of humility, modesty, love and fear of God,

[139] See below, pp. 80–3. I emphasize 'in their teachings and writings' because the conventional pietists, such as the author of *Sefer Ḥasidim I* and R. Yonah mi-Gerundi, in all probability shared together with Ḥasidei Ashkenaz the notions of the natural world of the surrounding society. However, they never invoked any of these forces when expounding their outlook.

and the like, viewed all those who joined their ranks as penitents—and justly so, for the newcomers had not observed fully, if at all, these commandments—a group that claimed that there were myriad new commandments of the Borè that people transgressed daily would certainly view its novitiates as penitents. This does not mean that there were any initiatory rites to be observed in becoming a Pietist, nor did penitential expiation ever serve as such a rite.

3. The conventional pietists shared the view of Ḥasidei Ashkenaz regarding the need to avoid the sight of women, and even mention once 'custody of the eyes'. However, these ideas have none of the centrality and intensity that they possess in the thought of Ḥasidei Ashkenaz. There is no single section devoted to them; they are always mentioned as one of a set of desirable ideas. Compare the passages cited above in n. 55 with *SHB*, ##16, 140. They did believe, as pietists usually do, that knowledge obligates: the deeper the understanding of God's demands, the greater the duty of their realization. However, there is no evidence that they thought that having a stray sexual thought constituted a betrayal of one's knowledge of its illicit nature and a 'learned' Pietist was thus doubly damned for such passing notions.[140] They seem to have accepted, de facto at least, that such momentary experiences were simply human nature.

4. Finally, we come to the first citation of the essay (n. 2)—the opening remarks of the Bologna *Sefer Ḥasidim*. As I remarked in my later essay,[141] the author/editor of *Sefer Ḥasidim I* stole some of the clothes of the German Pietists. First, he entitled his work '*Sefer Ḥasidim*'; he further employed in his introductory remarks some of the key words of Ḥasidei Ashkenaz—*yir'ei ha-Shem*, *le-ha'amik la'asot*, *retson ha-Borè*—and then proceeded to expound a detailed program of conventional pietism, wholly at odds with that of Ḥasidei Ashkenaz. Strictly speaking, the citation should be removed; I left it in primarily because of the policy of not changing the original text, but also because these skillfully chosen words can well serve as an introduction to German Pietism and were intended to give that impression. That what followed in the subsequent 152 sections was anything but German Pietism is another matter.

B

The role played by *zekher 'asah le-nifle'otav* in hasidic thought has been given an entirely new cast and significance by David I. Shyovitz in his Ph.D. dissertation "'He Has Created a Remembrance of His Wonders": Nature

[140] See p. 47 above, pp. 202–4 below.   [141] See p. 81 below.

and Embodiment in the Thought of the Hasidei Ashkenaz' (University of Pennsylvania, 2011), written under the direction of Talya Fishman and now published in a revised and expanded form as *A Remembrance of His Wonders—Nature and the Supernatural in Medieval Ashkenaz* (Philadelphia, 2017). It compels me to retract an argument advanced in 'The Midrash, *Sefer Ḥasidim*, and the Changing Face of God' (below, p. 151); however, it has little bearing on this essay. Shyovitz addresses my formulations here about *vestigia dei* and the *retson ha-Borè* in his thesis (pp. 36–8), and in his book (p. 226 n. 10) he refers the reader to this discussion. After citing several sentences, he writes: 'the notion that the hidden, rigorous *retson ha-Borè* may be linked with the remembrances that God implanted in the physical world is indeed a suggestive one. But in linking the two, Soloveitchik seems to squeeze the concept of *zekher 'asah le-nifle'otav* too forcefully into the mode of the *retson ha-Borè*.'[142] He is absolutely correct. I am also flattered that he writes that I am the only scholar other than Joseph Dan who has 'devoted detailed attention to the doctrine of *zekher 'asah le-nifle'otav*'. The compliment, however, is undeserved, as I gave that concept little consideration if any. The purpose of the first section of this essay was to locate the *retson ha-Borè* as the center of the hasidic enterprise rather than *din shamayim* as advocated by Y. Baer. I introduced *vestigia dei*, a 'medieval commonplace' (as I recalled from my undergraduate days), simply as a parallel phenomenon and gave it no further thought. Nor could further thought then have helped much, as the publication of R. Yehudah he-Ḥasid's *Zekher 'Asah le-Nifle'otav* lay some thirty years in the future.

At note 38, Shyovitz writes: 'Interestingly, Soloveitchik admits that in seeking to locate God's will in the natural world, the Pietists mirrored the contemporaneous Christian notion of *vestigia dei*. Nonetheless, he denies that this parallel points to any noteworthy interaction: their approach "was absorbed from the environment unawares and evolved in time into the major unarticulated premise of *Sefer Ḥasidim*."' I stated specifically that the notion of '*zekher 'asah le-nifle'otav* was clearly patterned on the widespread notion of *vestigia dei*'. I did not know then, nor do I know now, of any Christian notion parallel to the *retson ha-Borè* that the Ḥasidim could draw on. I left open the possibility that the well-known idea of the Book of Nature with its implicit dual revelation may have played some unwitting role in the evolution of the idea of *retson ha-Borè*. What led me to say that this was 'unwitting' was the fact that *zekher 'asah le-nifle'otav* is an oft-repeated, clearly articulated idea with a classic proof text from the Bible. It is a crisp concept in its Christian form and so too in its Hebrew adaptation. The same is not true of *retson ha-Borè*.

142 pp. 36–8.

The phrase appears on numerous occasions, at times in the conventional, at times in the radically new sense of the Pietists.[143] There are also other code words that point to it;[144] however, it is never stated as a central doctrine. It is, as I wrote, 'the major unarticulated premise of *Sefer Ḥasidim*'. (Had it been clearly articulated, there would have been no need for my essay.) One consciously borrows what one can use, that which answers a need. Why acquire an alien idea if it serves no purpose? When, however, foreign notion X evolves in the thinking of an out-group into notion Y, that alien idea is usually a product of osmosis rather than of appropriation. It is part of the climate of opinion of the time; one imbibes it in childhood or early youth, as one does other commonplaces of one's surroundings. Or so, at least, it seemed and still seems to me. Should someone discover a Christian or Germanic notion of *retson ha-Borè*, I will be the first to admit the foreign origin of this fundamental hasidic premise.

The only point in Shyovitz's account to which I would take exception is his claim that I linked the new discovery of man's potential of the Ḥasidim to the 'discovery of individualism' of the twelfth century (pp. 37–8). I wrote: 'This discovery of man and his potentialities was not an opening to Humanism, as in several strands of Christian thought of the time' (above, p. 15), and the footnote to this statement read: 'R. W. Southern, *Medieval Humanism and Other Studies* (New York, 1970), 29–60 (and more questionably C. Morris, *The Discovery of the Individual, 1050–1200* [London, 1972]).' Intuitively, I had doubts about Morris's theory and took care not to use the term 'individualism' in my essay. My essay appeared in 1976, and C. Bynum's essay 'Did the Twelfth Century Discover the Individual?' had yet to appear (*Journal of Ecclesiastical History*, 31 [1980], 1–17; it was reprinted in an expanded form in id., *Jesus as Mother: Studies in the Spirituality of the High Middle Ages* [Berkeley, 1982], 82–109). See now W. Pohl, 'Introduction to Ego Trouble', in R. Coridini, M. Gillis, R. McKitterick, and I. van Renswoude, eds., *Ego Trouble. Authors and their Identities in the Early Middle Ages*, Forschungen zur Geschichte des Mittelalters 15 (Vienna, 2010), 9–21.

C

As regards the *retson ha-Borè*, I would differ from C. N. van Uchelen, 'Aspects of Pietist Solidarity in *Sefer Ḥasidim*: Analysis of a Motif', *Frankfurter Judaistische Beiträge*, 21 (1994), 69, who describes the *retson ha-Borè* as a 'motif' rather than a 'theme'—a 'theme being a comprehensive abstraction' whereas a

[143] See above, n. 10. [144] See pp. 26–34 above and pp. 200–4 below.

motif 'is explicitly present in the text and is to be derived from the textual wording'. To a historian at least, the term 'present in the text' needs qualification. The phrase *retson ha-Borè* does, indeed, appear with some frequency in *Sefer Ḥasidim*; however, unlike *kol yisra'el 'arevim zeh la-zeh*, which Uchelen discusses, the 'charged' meaning of *retson ha-Borè* has to be deciphered as it can be equally understood as simply 'God's will', no different from *retson ha-Kadosh Barukh Hu.*[145] Indeed, the author of *Sefer Ḥasidim I* took just such key phrases as *yir'ei ha-Shem* and *retson ha-Borè* and employed them traditionally, stealing, as it were, the clothes of the movement, as noted above (Afterword, sect. A, #4).[146] Drawing attention to the unique notion of a 'covert Divine Will' denoted by the term *retson ha-Borè* and its underlying centrality was the very purpose of the first part of the essay.

D

In an informative essay, 'The Laws of Heaven in *Sefer Ḥasidim*', J. L. Rubenstein writes: 'I am in full agreement with Soloveitchik's claim that *dinei shamayim* is not a dominant concept in the thought of the pietists; it is an ad hoc approach to specific situations that they found troubling. Yet I think that there is much more to the use of the talmudic concept than Soloveitchik concedes.'[147] I am perplexed how my formulations here gave so discerning a reader as Rubenstein the impression that I was minimizing the relationship between *din shamayim* of the Pietists and that of the Talmud. If they nevertheless did, I can only state that it never was, nor is it now, my intention. The point of the footnote was, as Rubenstein correctly asserts, to minimize the significance of *din shamayim* in the *Weltanschauung* of the Pietists, especially in comparison with the *retson ha-Borè*.

E

My disagreements with Ivan G. Marcus's interpretation of German Pietism in general and his manner of reading *Sefer Ḥasidim* in particular are set forth in '*Sefer Ḥasidim* and the Social Sciences' (below, Ch. 9) and 'On Reading *Sefer Ḥasidim*' (below, Ch. 8). I will here address only his criticism leveled at a specific point in my essay (other than the meaning of the words *tsaddik* and *rasha'*, which are the subjects of the second of the above-mentioned essays).

1. In the introduction to an excellent collection of essays on *Sefer Ḥasidim*

[145] See n. 10 above. [146] See Ch. 3 below, especially pp. 91–2.

[147] 'The Laws of Heaven in *Sefer Ḥasidim*' (above, n. 28), 97 n. 18.

that Marcus edited,[148] he notes that Y. N. Simhoni had already pointed out in his 1917 essay[149] that Ḥasidei Ashkenaz were not appreciated by Ashkenazic Jewry as representing their highest ideals, as the romantic picture of them would have it. On the contrary, they were mocked and humiliated by the larger community, and, according to Marcus, I and others failed to note that we had been anticipated in this matter by Simhoni.

If the second section of my essay had any purpose, it was not to note that the German Pietists were frequently humiliated—that seemed to me obvious, seeing that they repeatedly speak of their abasement by others, indeed, interpret the word 'Ḥasid' as stemming from the Aramaic word for 'white', that is to say, with the blanch of humiliation.[150] To be a Ḥasid was to be humiliated. I sought to explain why they were so mocked and derided and why the bitter opposition that they encountered was understandable. As I wrote in the summary, 'though meek and quiescent in their private dealings, they [Ḥasidei Ashkenaz] were in communal matters assertive, presumptuous, and elitist to the bone.... So deeply has scholarship sympathized with the Ḥasidim that it has not wondered how the Ḥasid appeared to others or why the opposition to his ways from what was possibly the most God-fearing and martyrdom-tested community in Jewish history. Were his new religious demands reasonable? Were his pre-emptive claims and conduct not downright insulting?'[151] Simhoni noted the opposition; however, in so far as I can see, he shared the 'romantic' perception of the Ḥasid as an innocent, suffering servant.

2. Marcus writes: 'Although the French tosafist innovation may underlie certain emphases in *Sefer Ḥasidim*, Soloveitchik's claim that the Qalonimides as a whole felt displaced as leaders of Ashkenazic Jewry and that the critique in *Sefer Ḥasidim* is directed against French talmudists is not demonstrated. Within the context of the book itself, Judah's critique seems aimed at local Jews not French ones.'[152] I never contended (pp. 52–4) that French Talmudists displaced the Kalonymide aristocracy. I contended that the French tosafist movement undermined the supremacy of the old Rhineland aristocracy and that after 1220, the leadership of the German community was in the hands of new leaders and scholars from other regions of the German Empire. I wrote: 'Hasidic literature is the work of a spiritual elite; much of it is at the same time the work of a displaced aristocracy or one in the process of being stripped of its intellectual and political patrimony. Where are the Kalonymides or the

[148] *Dat ve-Ḥevrah be-Mishnatam shel Ḥasidei Ashkenaz* (Jerusalem, 1987), 16 and n. 27 ad loc.

[149] 'Ha-Ḥasidut ha-Ashkenazit bi-Yemei ha-Beinayim', in Marcus, ed., *Dat ve-Ḥevrah* (above, n. 148), 47–80. The passage cited is at p. 65.

[150] Above, p. 30.

[151] Above, p. 60.

[152] *Piety and Society: The Jewish Pietists of Medieval Germany* (Leiden, 1981), 168 n. 28.

other old and famous families of Ashkenaz after the 1220s? It is Bohemia and not the Rhineland that provides Germany with its leaders in the next generation, and these men did not distinguish between the Seine and the Rhine, the Aube and the Tauber; neither did their successors—R. Me'ir of Rothenburg, R. Asher, R. Me'ir ha-Kohen, and R. Mordekhai ben Hillel—of whom only the latter was a scion of a once-famous family.'[153] See the essay of Simcha Emanuel cited in the next note.

F

Simcha Emanuel, in a very rare memory lapse, forgot the concluding section of the essay (above, pp. 53–5) when he penned his critique in 'Ḥakhmei Germanyah ba-Me'ah ha-Shelosh-'Esreh: Retsef o Mashber?', *Tarbiz*, 82 (2014), 556–8, and in the English presentation 'German Sages in the Thirteenth Century: Continuity or Crisis?' *Frankfurter Judaistische Beiträge*, 39 (2014), 7–9. His essay (in the Hebrew version, pp. 549–67, in the English one, pp. 1–19) documents in greater detail—with all the erudition and precision characteristic of its author—one aspect of the cultural break sketched here in four areas—prayer, *sod*, halakhah, and *piyyut*.

G

Robert Chazan has suggested that the martyrdom practiced by the Rhineland community in 1096—suicide and murder of children—which has no foundation in halakhah, was a proto-Ḥasidei Ashkenaz version of the *retson ha-Borè*.[154] It's an interesting idea; however, he himself admits that 'Unfortunately there seems to be no literature outside of the Hebrew First Crusade chronicles which presents the early development of what I have called proto-Ḥasidei Ashkenaz.'[155] Another objection that could be raised against this filiation is that Ḥasidei Ashkenaz have no special doctrine about martyrdom, nor can any aspiration to martyrdom be detected in their writings. Indeed, not only do they not advocate suicide, let alone murder of children, they argue against getting oneself into a situation in which martyrdom may be required. As pietists of all denominations know, dying for God is easy; living under His ever-watchful eye is hard.[156]

153 Above, pp. 54–5.

154 'The Early Development of Hasidei Ashkenaz', *Jewish Quarterly Review*, 75 (1985), 199–211.

155 Ibid. 211.

156 See my essay 'Halakhah, Hermeneutics and Martyrdom', *Jewish Quarterly Review*, 94 (2004), 289–91; reprinted with revisions in *Collected Essays*, ii (Oxford, 2014), 274–6.

H

Peter Schäfer has linked the piety of Ḥasidei Ashkenaz to the *yordei merkavah* of the Heikhalot literature.[157] Given my ignorance of the Heikhalot literature, I am incapable of judging this evaluation.[158] I would simply like to point out that the distinctive piety of Ḥasidei Ashkenaz is one thing, the hundreds of new dictates of the *retson ha-Borè* another. To the best of my knowledge, no one has found any precedent, let alone a source, for this axial doctrine.

[157] 'The Ideal of Piety of the Ashkenazi Hasidim and Its Roots in Jewish Tradition', *Jewish History*, 4 (1990), 9–23.

[158] See further parallels between the Heikhalot literature and Ḥasidei Ashkenaz in D. Abrams, 'Sod Kol ha-Sodot: Tefisat ha-Kavod bi-Tefillah ve-Khavvanat ha-Tefillah be-Khitvei R. El'azar mi-Vormaiza', *Da'at*, 34 (1995), 69 n. 40.

CHAPTER TWO

On Dating *Sefer Ḥasidim*

I WOULD LIKE TO SUGGEST a point of departure for a problem that has occupied scholars since Leopold Zunz: When was *Sefer Ḥasidim* written?[1] The question is not 'Did R. Yehudah he-Ḥasid write a *Sefer Ḥasidim*?' No one has ever doubted that he did. The question is when that agglomeration of booklets (*maḥbarot*, *kuntresim*) of the Pietists that we currently possess was first composed—be it the shorter, strung-together compilation published in Bologna in 1538 (henceforth *SHB*) or the far larger such assemblage published in 1891 from a fourteenth-century manuscript in the Parma-Palatina Library (henceforth *SHP*).

The question is not antiquarian, but one rich with implications. First, what society is being described in *Sefer Ḥasidim*—is it Ashkenaz in the early years or the late ones of the thirteenth century, perhaps even of the fourteenth? Second, to what extent does *Sefer Ḥasidim* accurately reflect the outlook of R. Yehudah he-Ḥasid (d.1217) and R. El'azar of Worms (d. *c.*1238), or of one of the two? If the composition of the sundry booklets of the Pietists is relatively late or if their 'composition' stretched out over many years, then we have the collective work of a movement, a spirituality, and an outlook that was years in the making and which probably reflects the basic ideas and perspectives of its founders, but scarcely can be taken as an accurate statement of them. However, if the composition of *Sefer Ḥasidim* took place during the lifetimes of R. Yehudah and R. El'azar, it is difficult to imagine that someone would dare disseminate his own ideas in their name and in the name of their movement, or, had he rashly done so, that protests would not be swiftly heard and denials issued.

[1] See J. Freimann's introduction to the reprint of Wistinetzki's 1891 publication of the Parma manuscript of *Sefer Ḥasidim* (Berlin, 1924), 12–14. Professor Yeshayahu Tishbi treated this problem at length in his course on *Sefer Ḥasidim*, which unfortunately never appeared in print. More recently, I. G. Marcus has addressed this issue in his *Piety and Society: The Jewish Pietists of Medieval Germany* (Leiden, 1981), 136–43. I am in agreement with his early dating of the work, but for reasons different from those advanced by him. {See below, Ch. 9. For the statement that R. Yehudah he-Ḥasid added to *Sefer Ḥasidim* shortly before his death, see Freimann's introduction, p. 11.}

Third, it is clear from *Sefer Ḥasidim* that, while there were not many Ḥasidim in any one town, there were a few Ḥasidim in a number of towns. German Pietism was not a mass but an elite movement, a group of spiritual virtuosi, small in numbers but still enough to constitute a movement. If *Sefer Ḥasidim* is the labor of writers that stretches on to the mid-fourteenth century, we are talking of a movement that lasted four or five generations, or, at the very least, that reflects ideas that gestated for decades and then developed into a movement of *âmes d'élite*. If, however, *Sefer Ḥasidim* is the product of the early thirteenth century, it would then appear to be a movement coeval with the lives of the two famous figures associated with it, for there is no mention of its existence at any later date. If so, the movement of Ḥasidei Ashkenaz (in contradistinction to some of the ideas it bequeathed to Ashkenazic Jewry) was a short-lived affair, lasting no more than a generation or two. The question naturally presents itself: Why was this movement of so brief a duration? Was it some inherent weakness that condemned it to an early death or did outside forces lead to its demise, and if so, what were they? Matters of no small moment hinge on the question of the date of *Sefer Ḥasidim*.

One can identify some fifty to seventy sections in *Sefer Ḥasidim* as authored by R. Yehudah or R. El'azar, but what about the other 1,900 sections of *SHP*? Manuscripts provide no solution. MS Oxford, Bodley 875 contains the first 152 sections of *SHB* and it was written in 1299, but is this a copy of a recent work or one from the early years of that century? And what about the hundreds of other sections in *SHB*? As for *SHP*, almost twice the size of *SHB*, it issues from the fourteenth century, but is it from the early or late years of that century, or even possibly a copy of an earlier manuscript?

I would like to tackle the issue of dating from a new standpoint—by observing the financial institutions mentioned in that work. More precisely, I would like to study the modes of intra-Jewish credit as they appear in *Sefer Ḥasidim*.

Throughout the Middle Ages Jews lent to Gentiles at interest. At the outset, this was but one facet, possibly simply a by-product, of their involvement in trade. In the course of the twelfth century in France and in the next century in Germany, Jews were pushed out of trade, and usury became the staff of life of the Ashkenazic Jewish community.

Lending to a Gentile at interest is permissible; however, every lender—including banks today—must replenish their funds from other sources. For example, an opportunity presented itself to a Jew to make a major loan to a Gentile. Lacking at the moment the necessary liquidity, he naturally turns to a co-religionist and asks him to loan him that sum of money. In other words, the widespread profession of lending to Gentiles at interest presumes a parallel infrastructure of Jews lending to one another at interest. Such lending, however, is strictly forbidden by the Torah; indeed, he who does so violates no fewer than four biblical injunctions.

The only available manner of intra-Jewish loan permitted by the Talmud is that of *maḥatsit sakhar* (very similar to the widespread *commenda* employed in the Middle Ages), that is to say, an arrangement which is half loan, half partnership, and in which the silent partner pays the active one a salary for his work. For example, Reuven needed a loan of 1,000 dollars. He requested that sum from Shimon, 500 dollars of which was a loan and 500 a deposit for investment. If the investment of 500 dollars made money, the profits were divided; if it lost money, the loss was divided between the two. With the 500-dollar loan unit, there was no division. If the borrower lost money, he remained under obligation, as would any debtor, to repay in full the borrowed sum; if he made money, the profits were all his. His only obligation was to repay the initial loan. Shimon was thus a semi-partner. However, if Shimon took his full half of the profits, it would mean that he was getting the initial investment back plus half the profits without paying Reuven for his work as investor. He would be getting Reuven's work gratis because he had allowed Reuven the use of his money. This would constitute usury.

To avoid this, the Talmud requires that Shimon either pay Reuven for his services or take a smaller cut of the profits. For example, someone who invested 66 percent of the principal would receive only 50 percent of the profits. The 16 percent forgone was salary for services rendered. This arrangement was called *maḥatsit sakhar* (half-profit), that is to say, the silent partner took two-thirds of the investment and the risk, but only half of the profits.

If recourse to credit was an occasional occurrence, this cumbersome arrangement could yet suffice; in a commercial economy, whose lifeblood is credit, however, it was impractical. Jews in medieval Europe were initially traders and later moneylenders. When Jews turned to their co-religionists for credit, they were not seeking business partners but creditors to finance a business project. Put differently, they were seeking a straightforward lender–creditor relationship, something the *maḥatsit sakhar* arrangement could not provide.

In the latter half of the eleventh century and over the course of the twelfth, French scholars circumvented the usury injunction by means of a bold legal fiction—the Gentile 'straw man'. Reuven could say to a Gentile in his employ, 'Go and get a loan at interest from Shimon.' Shimon would give the Gentile the money, who would proceed to hand it over it to his employer. Even though the Gentile was clearly an agent of the Jew, he was viewed as being a principal. Legally, two loans were seen to have taken place. Shimon had lent at interest to the Gentile employee, who in turn lent that money at interest to his employer. Since both transactions involved a Gentile, first as borrower and then as lender, the usury injunction did not apply.

The originator of the device of the Gentile straw man was Rashi (d.1104), and his grandson, the great Rabbenu Tam (d.1170), boldly extended the scope of the allowance. The latter's nephew and pupil, R. Yitsḥak of Dampierre, the famed Ri (d.1189), entertained some doubts as to his teacher's radical expansion, but he fully endorsed Rashi's allowance. Not surprisingly the straw man arrangement was swiftly adopted by French Jewry and became the central instrument of intra-Jewish credit in northern France (Tsarfat) and in Norman England, whose halakhic culture was predominantly French.

In Germany, things were entirely different. The first German Tosafist, R. Yitsḥak b. Avraham (Riva) of Speyer (d. before 1132), wrote a small but influential halakhic guide to pawnbroking, part of which was a vigorous (if unnamed) critique of Rashi's straw man and a strong defense of the traditional and far stricter German restraints on intra-Jewish credit. The leading German Talmudist of the next generation, R. Eli'ezer b. Natan of Mainz, discounted entirely the French allowance, and his grandson, R. Eli'ezer b. Yo'el ha-Levi, the famed Ravyah (d. *c.*1225–30), concurred fully with his grandfather's disallowance.

Such was the state of affairs around 1225.

In the second quarter of the thirteenth century, the intellectual climate changed radically. The two halakhic cultures met, and the impact was one-sided. French Jewry retained in full its intellectual independence and proceeded to ignore the dialectical accomplishments of its German brethren. Germany, on the other hand, was inundated by the French wave and ceased, for all practical purposes, to exist as a distinct halakhic culture. In the first quarter of the thirteenth century the works of both R. El'azar Roke'aḥ, the leader of the conservative school of German thought, and R. Eli'ezer b. Yo'el, Ravyah, the leader of the German school of dialectics, reflect fully the halakhic thought of Germany, in which the French component (invariably the writings of the great Rabbenu Tam) played a relatively minor role. Their pupils (such as R. Yitsḥak Or Zarua'), however, and their pupils' pupils (such as R. Me'ir of Rothenburg) belong to a Franco-German school in which the cultures are intermingled. As for the famed Rabbenu Asher (Rosh), whose flight from Germany ended the era of German Tosafism, he is—intellectually—a Frenchman to his fingertips. One knows more about the writings of the Spanish and Catalan halakhists from his works than about those of the scholars of his homeland.

These developments are reflected in the issue of intra-Jewish credit. Ravyah's pupil, R. Yitsḥak Or Zarua', cited in full both the French and German positions about the Gentile straw man without taking any stand on the issue. His pupil, R. Me'ir of Rothenburg, endorsed in full Rabbenu Tam's expansion of the concept and saw no place for any emotional hesitancy, as Rashi had, in employing this legal fiction. His pupil, Rabbenu Asher, adopted in full the position of Ri of Dampierre, both in his code (*Sefer Pesakim*) and in his *Tosafot*. No mention is made in either work of the more stringent position of the great German scholars of the preceding two centuries.

If R. Yitsḥak Or Zarua' thought that as good a case could be made for the use of a Gentile straw man as against it, it is difficult to imagine that the average German merchant had any religious scruples in employing it. Unsurprisingly, R. Me'ir of Rothenburg writes a generation later that the use of the Gentile straw man was the common popular practice. True, there were some who still refrained from employing the French innovation, but one can reasonably say that from the mid-thirteenth century, perhaps even a decade or two earlier, the French straw man was in widespread use.[2]

The picture that emerges from the halakhic material is reflected in another genre of German writings, that of communal ordinances. In the years 1220–1, the three venerated communities of Germany, Speyer, Worms, and Mainz, enacted the famed Ordinances of Shum (the Hebrew acronym of these three communities), one of which reads: 'And no one should lend money to his fellow man [at interest] in any form other than *maḥatsit sakhar*.'[3] The exclusionary purpose is clear—precluding the use of the Gentile straw man. In the third decade of the thirteenth century, German communal leaders sensed that in matters of usury, as in several other areas, the German traditions were under French pressure. They also sensed the growing impetus to exchange the cumbersome *maḥatsit sakhar* for the simpler and swifter arrangement of the Gentile straw man and sought to prevent its spread in Germany. To no avail—as attested by the remarks of R. Me'ir of Rothenburg, who wrote, after citing the

[2] This process is described in detail in my *Halakhah, Kalkalah ve-Dimmuy 'Atsmi* (Jerusalem, 1985), 46–9, 52–7, and see there p. 65 n. 25. {A more expansive and updated English presentation of these developments can be found in *Collected Essays*, i (Oxford, 2013), 103–39.}

[3] L. Finkelstein, *Jewish Self-Government in the Middle Ages* (repr. New York, 1975), 125; R. J. Barzen, *Taqqanot Qehillot Šum. Die Rechtssatzungen der jüdischen Gemeinden von Mainz, Worms und Speyer im hohen und späten Mittelalter*. Monumenta Germaniae Historica. Hebräische Texte aus dem mittelalterlichen Deutschland 2 (Wiesbaden, 2019), 289–91.

allowance of Rabbenu Tam, 'And so people conduct themselves' (*ve-khen 'ama de-bar*).

Whether the Gentile straw man had already penetrated Germany by 1220–1 or whether the German communal leaders foresaw its imminent arrival is an open question. One thing, however, is clear: between 1210 and 1230, that is to say, sometime between a decade prior to and a decade after the Ordinances of Shum, the use of the Gentile straw man had begun to penetrate Germany, and it swiftly became the backbone of intra-Jewish credit.

What financial arrangements are described in *Sefer Ḥasidim*—those of the pre-Shum or of the post-Shum era?

There is no mention whatsoever in either of the two versions of *Sefer Ḥasidim* that we possess, *SHB* or *SHP*, of a Gentile straw man. Whenever intra-Jewish credit is mentioned, and it appears seven times in *SHP* and four times in *SHB*, in many differing contexts, the arrangement is always that of *maḥatsit sakhar*. And the range of the distribution in *SHP*, at least, is very wide, extending over 900 sections, from #774 to #1682.[4] Moreover, it is clear from #1423 in *SHP* that the augmented straw man arrangement that Rabbenu Tam had publicly declared to be 'absolutely permissible' (*ḥeter gamur u-mitsvah min ha-muvḥar*) was wholly unknown even to a businessman who possessed more initiative than religious scruples. The passage reads:

> Reuven was rich and he could not lend all of his capital to Gentiles. He went to Shimon, and Shimon was a good Jew [i.e. scrupulously religious], and [Reuven] said, 'A Gentile gave me this money to lend at interest; if you wish I can arrange that the Gentile will lend it to you.' Shimon agreed. Reuven told Levi that he would gladly have arranged that Shimon would receive the money from him, because the Gentile is not allowed to give the money to anyone other than the one I [i.e. Reuven] wish. Levi realized that the money was [actually] Reuven's and told Shimon. Shimon replied, 'But Reuven told me it belonged to the Gentile.' Levi said, 'I have inquired closely into the matter and the money is Reuven's, not the Gentile's.' Shimon declined to accept the money.

A Jew had a surplus of capital and wished to lend to both Gentiles and Jews. To achieve that end, he lied to Shimon, telling him that the money belonged to a Gentile (what is called 'false fronting'), and proceeded to lie again to Levi. Had the Gentile straw man been in use, what need had he of deception? He could have made his money openly available to his co-religionists by employing a Gentile intermediary, an arrangement that the great Rabbenu Tam had

[4] *SHP*, ##774, 864, 889, 1205, 1233, 1678, 1682. Four of these sections appear also in *SHB*, #953 (= #774 in *SHP*); #1028 (= #1678 in *SHP*); #1063 (= #1205 in *SHP*); 1075 (= #1233 in *SHP*).

declared 'absolutely permissible'. The story, the exemplum if you wish, loses its contemporaneity, its practical religious message, in an era in which the straw man is in use. It could never have been written in France after the early years of the twelfth century. In addition, unlike the Shum assemblage, *Sefer Ḥasidim* contains neither remonstrance against Jews employing a Gentile straw man nor any admonition against adopting this French invention. The Gentile intermediary is simply not on the horizon of that work.[5] From the perspective of business financing, *Sefer Ḥasidim* seems to have been composed prior to the second quarter of the thirteenth century.

If this be correct, it would imply that *Sefer Ḥasidim* is more or less an accurate representation of the thoughts of R. Yehudah he-Ḥasid and R. El'azar of Worms (or one of the two of them). The existence of any movement stretching over several generations would therefore seem questionable.

If we are confronted with a short-lived movement the question becomes: Is this due to some central flaw in its ideology or did this high-minded but self-righteously truculent movement run up against the combined opposition of the communal and religious establishment, and when their two famed, blueblood leaders passed from the scene, the movement lost its protective cover and soon disappeared?[6]

I have not intended in this essay to decide these weighty questions or even to discuss their pros and cons. One could still insist and argue that some 'booklets' in *Sefer Ḥasidim* are old and some more recent, and it is merely happenstance that matters of credit figure in the old booklets. I have simply tried to provide a temporal point of departure for the discussion, a starting point that avoids the hitherto vicious circle of literary attributions and anchors itself in the concrete and datable realities of the thirteenth century.

AFTERWORD

1. On the central questions whether German Pietism was a movement, and if a movement, of what duration, see now J. Dan, 'Ashkenazi Hasidim 1941–1991:

[5] There are some scattered references to Jews lending to one another at interest—e.g. *SHP*, ##111, 1232, 1295, 1422—something one would only expect, as every society has a measure of deviant behavior {doubly understandable in view of the desperate need for intra-Jewish credit, as German Jewish society was moving in those decades from trade to an economy based predominantly on moneylending to Gentiles}. However, there is no mention whatsoever of any use of the Gentile straw man.

[6] On the infuriating conduct of the humble Pietists and some of their less endearing if high-minded communal aspirations, see Ch. 1 above and the heightened portrait of I. G. Marcus, *Piety and Society: The Jewish Pietists of Medieval Germany* (Leiden, 1981), 92–106. {The reasons why I opted for a less radical portrait than Marcus are spelled out in Chs. 8 and 9 below.}

Was there Really a Hasidic Movement in Medieval Germany', in P. Schäfer and J. Dan, eds., *Gershom Scholem's* Major Trends in Jewish Mysticism *50 Years Later* (Tübingen, 1993), 87–102; I. G. Marcus, 'The Historical Meaning of *Hasidei Ashkenaz*: Fact, Fiction or Cultural Self-Image?', ibid. 103–115. I. Gruenwald, 'Social and Mystical Aspects of Sefer Ḥasidim', in K. E. Grözinger and J. Dan, eds., *Mysticism, Magic and Kabbalah in Ashkenazi Judaism: International Symposium held in Frankfurt a. M. 1991* (Berlin, 1995), 106–16. See also J. Dan's recent survey in his *Toledot Torat ha-Sod ha-'Ivrit* (Jerusalem, 2011), v. 64–74. Dan's article was republished in his *Jewish Mysticism* (Northvale, NJ, 1998), ii. 313–31. Marcus's study was reprinted in his collection of essays, *Jewish Culture and Society in Medieval France and Germany* (Farnham, Surrey, 2014), no. XIV.

From the study of tombstone inscriptions, Avraham (Rami) Reiner has recently arrived at the conclusion that the movement of German Pietism was of brief duration, and by the last decade of the thirteenth century was on the verge of extinction, as the death of one, and only one, such Ḥasid is found among the many hundreds of names recorded in the *Memorbuch* of the Rintfleisch massacres of 1298. See his article 'Even she-Katuv 'Aleiha: To'arei ha-Niftarim 'al Matsevot Bet ha-'Almin be-Virtsburg, 1147–1346', *Tarbiz*, 78 (2009), 142–4. If he is correct in his surmise that the title *ḥasid* in the thirteenth-century inscriptions refers to Ḥasidei Ashkenaz, then my statement (above, p. 73) that there is no mention of the existence of such Pietists after the death of the movement's two leading figures, that is to say, after *c.*1230, is in need of correction. It lasted a generation, perhaps even two, after the demise of its founders. See G. Scholem, 'Three Types of Jewish Piety', *Eranos-Jahrbuch*, 38 (1969), 344 (repr. in *Ariel: A Review of the Arts and Sciences in Israel*, 32 [1973], 21).

2. The question of the duration of German Pietism is independent of the question of its influence on German, French, and Spanish communities. There may have been only two such Pietists, R. Yehudah and R. El'azar, however, they influenced many—both near and far. I have addressed the issue of influence in the essay 'Piety, Pietism, and German Pietism: *Sefer Ḥasidim I* and the Influence of Ḥasidei Ashkenaz', reprinted as Chapter 3 below.

3. The reader might well ask how I could have written, in an essay on the authorship of *Sefer Ḥasidim*, that there are three to five passages attributable to R. Yehudah he-Ḥasid or R. El'azar of Worms,[7] and then turn around and state in this essay that the number of passages attributable to the same

[7] See p. 226 below.

individuals amounts to fifty to seventy. The answer is quite simple. The heading of the closing booklet (*kuntres or maḥberet*) in *SHP*, ##1129–72, reads: 'This was copied from another *Sefer Ḥasidim*.' Most of it is a copy of sections of *Ḥokhmat ha-Nefesh*, a work by R. El'azar of Worms on the esoteric doctrine (*torat ha-sod*) on the soul.[8] The printer or copyist of this text recognized that it stemmed from the German Pietists and entitled it *Sefer Ḥasidim*. In the essay on authorship where I disagreed with Ivan Marcus, both he and I took it for granted that that addendum could in no way be viewed as another *kuntres* of *Sefer Ḥasidim* and should be left out of any tabulation of passages that could be attributed to one or the other of the movement's two leaders. The present essay did not address the issue of attribution of the authorship of *Sefer Ḥasidim*, but the dating of that work. Whether or not this final section is actually part of *Sefer Ḥasidim* makes no difference, and without giving the matter a second thought, I included it in my count. In retrospect, I should not have done so; fortunately, there are no adverse side effects to my inadvertency.

4. This essay was written long before the notion of *Sefer Ḥasidim I* had occurred to me. Otherwise, I would have discounted manuscripts containing only the first 152 sections of *SHB*, such as MS Oxford, Bodley 875, as having any connection with the authorship of *SHB* and *SHP*. Fortunately, I drew no conclusion from this manuscript or other ones like it,[9] so here too there were no adverse effects of my ignorance of the time. Rabbenu Tam's statement *heter gamur u-mitsvah min ha-muvḥar* is found in the *Or Zarua'*, iii (Jerusalem, 1890), #202. His proclamation is discussed in detail in my essay on pawnbroking in *Collected Essays*, i (Oxford, 2013), 133–6.

5. I first advanced the notion of the French wave in my early essay 'Three Themes in *Sefer Ḥasidim*' (1976; reprinted as Ch. 1 above), illustrated it in 'Can Halakhic Texts Talk History?' (1978), which can be found in the first volume of this series (pp. 214–15, 221–2), and elaborated on it in *Halakhah ve-Khalkalah bi-Yemei ha-Beinayim* (Jerusalem, 1985), 97–8. The last two sources also register the resistance to the growing French influence reflected in the Ordinances of Shum. See also R. J. Barzen, *Taqqanot Qehillot Šum* (above, n. 3), 293–5. (For a cautionary note, see my *Ha-Yayin bi-Yemei ha-Beinayim—Yein Nesekh: Perek be-Toledot ha-Halakhah be-Ashkenaz* [Jerusalem, 2008], 230–1.)

On the matter of 'false fronting', a stratagem that plagued the German Jewish community but seems to have been infrequent among French Jews, see my 'Pawnbroking', in *Collected Essays*, i (Oxford, 2013), 126–8.

[8] See above, pp. 6, 80 n.3. [9] See below, pp. 120–4.

CHAPTER THREE

Piety, Pietism, and German Pietism: *Sefer Ḥasidim I* and the Influence of Ḥasidei Ashkenaz

MORE THAN 135 YEARS AGO, Jacob Reifmann noted that the first 152 sections of *Sefer Ḥasidim* (what we now call |455| the Bologna edition, but what was then called simply *Sefer Ḥasidim*, as the existence of another version was yet unknown) constituted an independent work.[1] Section 153 was no continuation of what had preceded, but an introduction to a second *Sefer Ḥasidim*. (And, indeed, several decades later, a larger and considerably different version of *Sefer Ḥasidim* was published by Judah Wistinetzki,[2] and its opening section was none other than section 153 of the Bologna edition.) Reifmann further noted that sections 1–152 (henceforth *SH I*) had numerous Maimonidean citations from 'Hilkhot Teshuvah', 'De'ot', and 'Tefillah', and that the author evinced in one passage, in striking contrast to other sections of *Sefer Ḥasidim*, a negative attitude towards soothsaying (*niḥush*), as did Maimonides. In addition, he remarked there were fewer infelicities of language in

A shorter form of the first section of this essay was presented at the annual convention of the Association for Jewish Studies in Boston on December 16, 1998, and again at the quadrennial conference of the World Union of Jewish Studies held in Jerusalem in August 2001. The second and third sections were delivered in an abridged form at a conference held by the University of the Negev at Be'er Sheva in May 1999. My thanks to Avishai Braverman, Daniel Lasker, and Ed Fram for their gracious hospitality at the conference. I would also like to thank Talya Fishman for reading and commenting on this essay.

Appendix III contains a short collection of ethical dicta found in a manuscript. In this edition, I have made two corrections to my transcription and registered each change in a note. Thus, after n. 109, the note numbers are upped by one, and after n. 120 upped by two.

[1] *Ma'amar Arba'ah Ḥarashim: Yedabber 'al Tekhunat Arba'ah Sefarim* (Prague, 1860), 6–20. This edition of *Sefer Ḥasidim* will be referred to henceforth as *SHB*.

[2] *Sefer Ḥasidim*, ed. J. Wistinetzki (Berlin, 1891). Henceforth designated as *SHP* when giving a citation, or simply *Sefer Ḥasidim* when speaking generally of the work authored by Ḥasidei Ashkenaz.

SH I than in the subsequent sections. Moritz Güdemann, while disagreeing somewhat with Reifmann's division, pointed out that in fact there existed a manuscript comprising only sections 1–152, which would militate in favor of its separate existence.[3] More recently, Ivan Marcus further observed that the |456| Rhenish penance of mortification of the flesh is noticeably missing from *SH I*, and in its place are found extensive passages from Maimonides. Following Reifmann, he tentatively suggested that this block (*SH I*) was written by 'French or Rhenish Jews who rejected the Rhenish Jewish penitential system in favor of the less ascetic views of Maimonides'.[4]

I would like, first, to amplify the remarks of Reifmann and Marcus and then attempt to show that the differences between *SH I* and *Sefer Ḥasidim* are not incidental but systematic, radical, and far-ranging rather than narrow and circumscribed. I will proceed to propose that *SH I* emerges from a group of religious virtuosi other than Ḥasidei Ashkenaz and expresses a spirituality thoroughly unlike that of *Sefer Ḥasidim*. Finally, I will suggest some of the broader conclusions that may be drawn from the separate existence of *SH I*.

I

SEFER ḤASIDIM AND *SEFER ḤASIDIM I*

What I take to be the most distinctive element of *Sefer Ḥasidim*, *retson ha-Borè* (the Will of the Creator), is missing from *SH I*.[5] The hundreds of novel demands, making bold claim to Divine mandate as God's covert will, that fill the pages of *Sefer Ḥasidim* and set it apart from all other ethical works are

[3] M. Güdemann, *Geschichte des Erziehungswesens und der Cultur der abendländischen Juden, während des Mittelalters und der neueren Zeit* (Vienna, 1880), i. 286. The manuscript is that of the Bodleian Library, Oxford, Opp. 340 (Neubauer 875), fos. 131r–151r. (Sections 103–16 of the printed Bologna text are missing, apparently as a result of a scribal error.) Further note that while almost all of the shorter text of the Bologna edition is contained within the larger and far more comprehensive Wistinetzki text, this is true only of the 982 sections that follow section 152. Of the first 152 sections of that edition, what I have termed *SH I*, only forty-three are reproduced in Wistinetzki's text. Thus, more than two-thirds of *SH I* is not found in the comprehensive statement of German Pietism recorded in the Parma manuscript. Even after one subtracts from this count the numerous sections of Maimonides, still close to 50 percent of *SH I* is without parallel in the comprehensive Parma text. There is no similar gap in any other part of the Bologna edition. I say '982 subsequent sections', because sections 1135–1179 of the Bologna edition are not taken from any manuscript of *Sefer Ḥasidim*, but rather from the *Ḥokhmat ha-Nefesh* of R. El'azar of Worms, as Güdemann and others have long noted. The printer of the Bologna text was not a scholar versed in the bibliographic intricacies of German Pietism. To him, one work of these Pietists was the same as another, and he noted the change in manuscript by simply writing '[taken] from another *Sefer Ḥasidim*'.

[4] I. G. Marcus, 'The Recensions and Structure of *Sefer Ḥasidim*', *Proceedings of the American Academy for Jewish Research*, 45 (1978), 152–3.

[5] Above, pp. 7–23.

missing from these sections. Nothing is demanded in *SH I* that might not be found in any other ethical work. The virtues of love of God, fear of God, humility, Torah study, and the like are found without the distinctive cast that *Sefer Ḥasidim* usually gives them. True, *retson ha-Borè* is mentioned several times, and there is a reference or two to acting for the common good (*le-zakkot et ha-rabbim*), a passing mention of 'cunning in God-fearingness' (*'arum be-yir'ah*), and an allusion to 'study [of Torah] for the sake of performing' (*lilmod 'al menat le-kayyem*),[6] all of which were key words that the cognoscenti would recognize as referring to distinctive hasidic doctrines.[7] However, these, and other scattered terms with strong hasidic overtones, are never expounded on in the text of *SH I*. They lie there encoded and unexplicated and will pass unnoticed by the uninitiated. There is no overt reference to, let alone advocacy of, the hundreds of novel dictates of the |457| covert Will of God that figure so prominently in the other sections of *Sefer Ḥasidim*. The hasidic doctrine that the sins of the fathers are visited upon the children, that misfortune befalls individuals for the sins of their ancestors, runs like Ariadne's thread through the tangled text of *Sefer Ḥasidim*, yet it too is totally absent from *SH I*. Neither ancestral guilt nor unwitting violations of God's covert will constitute the theodicy of *SH I*. The individual, and the individual alone, is wholly responsible for his own fate.

Numerology (*gematriyah*) was not simply a major instrument of hasidic exegesis, but a basic mode of hasidic thinking. Ubiquitous in *Sefer Ḥasidim* and other writings of the movement, it is almost entirely absent from *SH I*. Two simple numerologies (*gematriyot*), both on the word *ḥerem*, emphasizing the dread power of the communal ban—the key instrument of social discipline in the Middle Ages—are all that we find in the 152 sections that comprise *SH I*.[8]

[6] *Retson ha-Borè—SHB*, ##1, 2, 29, 53; *le-zakkot et ha-rabbim—SHB*, #13 and see #65; *'arum be-yir'ah—SHB*, #13; *lilmod 'al menat le-kayyem—SHB*, #17, and see below, p. 201.

[7] On the charged meaning of these words, see above, Ch. 1, especially pp. 9, 12 with emphasis on nn. 8, 17, 40, 42, 73 end, 109.

[8] *SHB*, ##106, 143. The dual *gematriyah* given in #106 was apparently a common one. R. Avraham Ibn Yarḥi of Provence cites it in his work *Sefer ha-Manhig*, ed. Y. Raphael (Jerusalem, 1978), i. 33, in the name of R. Yitsḥak ha-Lavan. The first equivalence of *ḥerem* and the first and last letters of the final word of each book of the Pentateuch is found also in the medieval biblical commentary *Da'at Zekenim* (on Gen. 23: 5), repr. in *Tosafot ha-Shalem*, ed. Y. Gellis (Jerusalem, 1983), ii. 235; R. Tsidkiyah ha-Rofè, *Shibbolei ha-Leket II*, ed. S. Ḥasida (Jerusalem, 1987), i. 231; *Kol Bo*, ed. D. Avraham (Jerusalem, 1993), iv, #66 (col. 214). The second equivalence of *ḥerem* and the number of limbs of the body is found also in the late thirteenth-century French work of Yitsḥak b. Yehudah ha-Levi, *Pa'ane'aḥ Raza* (Warsaw, 1860), fo. 41a ('Ekev', beginning). {On *Sefer Pa'ane'aḥ Raza*, in addition to the editor's introduction, see Joy Rochwarger's Master's thesis written under the direction of

The fierce penance of the Pietists, the very ark of the hasidic covenant and the subject of so many and so widely diffused handbooks,[9] makes no appearance in *SH I*. Not penance but repentance—inner and experiential—is advocated in *SH I*. Maimonides' 'Hilkhot Teshuvah' ('Laws of Repentance') replaces the esoteric teachings of penance (*sod ha-teshuvah*) that Ḥasidei Ashkenaz so widely proffered, both to the God-fearing (*yir'ei ha-Shem*), who rendered unto God the full measure of His due, and to the broader community at large, which sought to escape the hellfire of the world to come.[10] Prayer alone could rival penance for pride of place in hasidic thought. Proper prayer formed the focal point of the |458| Ḥasid's quotidian aspiration, and its public practice generated fierce antagonism. It occupied hours of the Pietists' days as they pondered its esoteric meanings and intents and sought to put them into practice.[11] Finally, in an effort to secure its future, they stripped the centuries-old veil of secrecy and disseminated publicly their esoteric lore of the Divine service.[12] Yet the hasidic doctrines of prayer are wholly absent from *SH I*. The lengthy sections on prayer are made up of selections from Maimonides' 'Hilkhot Tefillah'.[13] Most of what Maimonides wrote on prayer, and all that is found in the edited form that it assumes in *SH I*, would be accepted by all. The significance of these passages in *SH I* lies, not in the adoption of any Maimonideanisms, for no significant ones are to be found there, but in the total absence of the Pietists' own doctrine of prayer, so central to their movement, to their world-view, and, most important, to their own religious experience. What emerges from the comprehensive presentation in *SH I* is a

Ephraim Kanarfogel, 'Sefer Pa'ane'aḥ Raza and Biblical Exegesis in Medieval Ashkenaz' (Touro College, Graduate School of Jewish Studies, 2000), and A. Zion's 'Pa'ane'aḥ Raza le-R. Yitsḥak ben Yehudah ha-Levi: Mavo Kelali u-Farshiyot Lekh Lekha–Va-Yera 'al pi Ketav Yad 'im Ḥillufei Nusḥa'ot ve-He'arot' (Ph.D. diss., Yeshiva University, 1974).}

[9] I. G. Marcus, 'Ḥasidei Ashkenaz Private Penitentials: An Introduction and Descriptive Catalogue of their Manuscripts and Early Editions', in J. Dan and F. Talmage, eds., *Studies in Jewish Mysticism* (Cambridge, Mass., 1982), 57–83.

[10] *SHB*, ##19, 20, 21, 23, 27, 43. (A passage from Sa'adyah Gaon's equally experiential doctrine of repentance is cited in #42.) See Y. Elbaum's remarks in his *Teshuvat ha-Lev ve-Kabbalat Yissurim: 'Iyyunim be-Shitot ha-Teshuvah shel Ḥakhmei Ashkenaz ve-Polin, 1348–1648* (Jerusalem, 1992), 13 n. 7, 17 n. 19.

[11] Above, pp. 30–4.

[12] J. Dan, 'Sefer ha-Ḥokhmah le-R. El'azar mi-Worms u-Mashma'uto le-Toledot Toratah ve-Sifrutah shel Ḥasidut Ashkenaz', *Zion*, 29 (1964), 168–91. {D. M. Sigal's study 'Sefer ha-Ḥokhmah ha-Meyuḥas la-Roke'aḥ' (*Sodei Razei Semukhin*, 2nd edn. [Jerusalem, 2001], 31–69) has demonstrated that much of that work is a forgery. Fortunately, the passages that treat Roke'aḥ's decision to commit esoteric lore to writing are unaffected by his findings. See the authentic text both of the introduction to the *Sefer ha-Ḥokhmah* (ibid. 51) and of the *Sefer Sodei Razei Semukhin*, ibid. 53.}

[13] *SHB*, #18.

meticulously envisioned but still traditional image of prayer—one to which all might aspire and with which none could take issue.

If the Maimonidean passages from 'Hilkhot Tefillah' are not transformative, the passages from 'Hilkhot De'ot' are very much so. *SH I* rejects not only the harsh asceticism of *Sefer Ḥasidim*, but even the milder and far more widespread forms of such spiritual discipline as articulated by Rabbenu Baḥya, for example. The Golden Mean replaces asceticism in *SH I* as the model of spirituality. Physical impulses are not to be eradicated by persistent mortification of the flesh; rather, an equilibrium is to be sought between the legitimate needs of the body and those of the soul. Supererogation, the very essence of German Pietism, is rejected. Extremes of all sorts are cast out, and Maimonides' formulations of the Golden Path of balanced living are cited at length and presented as the religious ideal to which all people should aspire.[14] The only minor concession—if concession it be—that the author of *SH I* makes to the severe ascetic regimen of the German Pietists is to implicitly advocate |459| fasting one day a month so as 'not to enjoy too much the pleasures of this world.'[15]

No less striking than the absence of *retson ha-Borè*, asceticism, and other defining themes of the Pietist movement is the parallel absence in *SH I* of exempla, which abound in the other sections of *Sefer Ḥasidim*. *Sefer Ḥasidim* is a casuistic work, in the classic sense of the word. It deals with the concrete and problematic issues of life on a case-by-case basis. Indeed, these vivid, individuated discussions account for a good part of the work's staying power. They shifted the focus away from the clear-cut realm of theory, where most ethical works reside, to the messy and ambiguous real world, and offered to readers the concrete guidance they sought. Yet exempla are scarcely to be found in *SH I*, if at all.[16] Concomitantly, *SH I* lacks topical specificity. What characterizes

[14] *SHB*, ## 51–2.

[15] *SHB*, #97. There may be no advocacy even here. The case given is simply to illustrate the unwitting sinfulness of the so-called 'righteous'. However, *SH I* does qualify Maimonides' strictures against fasting by adding that fasting is permitted to stop a growing sexual drive that threatens to overpower the believer (#52 end). Contrast #97 with #225: **שלא יעברו עליו שמונה ימים בלא תענית**. The latter is adopted by *Sefer ha-Yir'ah*, #102. This weekly regimen, though mild in itself, was apparently appropriated by some aspiring pietists, and the author of *Yesod ha-Teshuvah*, possibly R. Yonah mi-Gerundi, cites Ravad of Posquières' critique: **אל יחשוב אדם לגמרי שלא יאכל בשר ולא ישתה יין, כי די לנו במה שאסרה תורה. אך בעוד שהמאכל לפניו ועודנו תאב לאכול ממנו ימשך ממנו לכבוד בוראו ולא יאכל כדי תאותו. וזה יזכירנו אהבת הבורא יותר מתענית אחת בשבוע כי זה כל יום מידי אכלו**. The passage is found in *Orḥot Ḥayyim* (repr. Jerusalem, 1956), 228a, 'Hilkhot Rosh ha-Shanah', end. Significantly, *SH I* also draws upon this passage from Ravad's *Ba'alei ha-Nefesh* in #12.

[16] #18 end, 46, 58, 97, 122, 135. Strictly speaking, none of these are exempla but simply reports of punishment. They are not independent narratives that illustrate a moral lesson, nor do they portray

Sefer Ḥasidim is the particularity of its directives. It does not simply set forth general |460| principles, as do other ethical works, but provides a handbook of guidance to some of the thornier of life's problems. It addresses explicitly and in much concrete detail such topics as marriage and matchmaking, marital relations, parental relations, care and handling of books, child-rearing, educational curriculum, and instruction. Indeed, large sections of *Sefer Ḥasidim* are headed 'On Books', 'On Charity', 'On Study', 'On Honoring Father and Mother', 'On Women', 'On Trusting Other People', 'On the Dead', 'On Oaths and Malevolent Forces [*Mazzikim*]', 'On Demons [*Shedim*]', and the like. There are, at most, a few passing references to these topics in *SH I*, and in those rare instances where instruction is given, the singular doctrines of German Pietism are noticeably absent. There are three indistinctive passages regarding holy books that stress their sanctity rather than their dangerous potency, which was so emphasized by German Pietism.[17] The elaborate and highly distinctive marital directions of *Sefer Ḥasidim* are reduced to one phrase: 'that God should destine for him a good woman'.[18] The complex pietistic doctrine of charity is reduced to one paragraph, and its elitist tendencies, which would have denied access to charity to all those who were not of the hasidic persuasion,[19] are thoroughly tempered. In *SH I*, only wastrels and whoremongers are excluded from personal and communal benevolence.[20] *SH I* exhibits the customary doctrines, abstract dicta, and admonitory formulae found in other ethical works. This is not to say that it is indistinguishable from the writings of Rabbenu Baḥya or R. Yonah mi-Gerundi. Emphasis, style, and mix of topics differentiate each work from the others. However, there are few passages in *SH I* whose messages we could not envisage reading in these

borderline cases so common to the situational ethics of *Sefer Ḥasidim*. They are simply accounts of seemingly righteous individuals who, appearing in a dream, state that retribution is being exacted from them in the Other World for transgressing a principle spelled out in detail by the author of *SH I*. They are proofs of penalty, not ethical narratives or illustrations of a moral principle or dilemma. The same holds true for #4, which is simply an application of the talmudic dictum כל השומע הזכרה מפי חבירו צריך לנדותו (*Nedarim* 7b), cited at the end of the preceding section. (For #122 see #149, which is probably out of place, as it makes a far better preface to #122 than does #121, which strictly speaking is unrelated to what follows.) The only apparent exception to the dream pattern is #18, which simply reads: הראו מן השמים לאותו חכם. The oldest manuscript of *SH I*, copied in 1299 (Oxford, Bodley 875), however, reads (fo. 137v): הראו מן השמים בחלום לאותו חכם. {The reading of *SHB* is corroborated by MS Moscow, RSL Günzburg 103; MS Oxford, Bodley 875; MS Nîmes, Bibliothèque Municipale 26, and partly by *SHP*, #424: ובא לחכם בחלום.}

[17] *SHB*, ##97, 101, 141. (Perhaps one should add #136. However, these are instructions to scribes how to transcribe holy texts and not instructions how these potent texts are to be handled.)

[18] *SHB*, #135.

[19] Above, p. 39 n. 86; and see Ch. 8, pp. 197–212.

[20] *SHB*, #61.

other works. There are hundreds upon hundreds of passages in the rest of *Sefer Ḥasidim* that would be inconceivable in any other work of the Middle Ages. Soothsaying (*niḥush*) is, indeed, frowned upon in *SH I*, as Reifmann noted long ago,[21] but this is only part of a larger difference. There is not a trace in these sections (1–152) of the rich supernatural world, and a heavily Germanic one at that, |461| with which the rest of *Sefer Ḥasidim* is deeply infused. Missing entirely from the pages of *SH I* are *shedim* and *genii loci*, revenants, and the all-too-alive dead. One hears nothing whatsoever of the frequent and easy intercourse between the dwellers of this world and those of the other (*alterius mundus*) so prevalent in *Sefer Ḥasidim*.[22] Of soothsaying and necromancy, of dreams and miracles, of foreboding and foretelling, of the dangerous power of the sacred, of the taboo—not a word is to be found in all of *SH I*. *SH I* is culturally disembodied—uprooted from the rich soil of Germanic folkways and stripped clean of the thick underbrush of local beliefs in which the rest of *Sefer Ḥasidim* is so enmeshed.

SH I is also set apart in language. Not only is the Hebrew smoother, as Reifmann noted, but its language is of a wholly different order. Phrases of classical rabbinic Hebrew abound here that, while scarcely unusual, are not found in the other sections of *Sefer Ḥasidim*: **דרשו חכמים, צא ולמד, בוא וראה, הזהר ושמור נפשיך, במעלת היראה**.[23]

The language of *Sefer Ḥasidim* is translated Middle High German, and is invariably clumsy and asyntactic, as its writers sought to render the language and speech patterns of spoken German into a Hebrew they had not entirely mastered. Awkward and prone to circumlocution, the Hebrew is, at the same time, choppy, and the thought often digressive. The shorter paragraphs abound in anacolutha, that is, shifts of grammatical constructions in mid-sentence from one subject or predicate to another. The longer paragraphs are full of ideas interrupted by other associations. Easy access is thus denied to the reader of *Sefer Ḥasidim*, and only too often the text does not yield its meaning on first encounter but demands a second or even third reading by those unaccustomed to its diction. These difficulties are only aggravated by citations of verses, frequently entire strings of verses, whose bearing on the subject at hand seems tenuous, if not outright idiosyncratic, to the contemporary |462| reader.

21 *SHB*, #59 and above, n. 1.

22 Any knowledge in *SH I* of punishment in the world to come (above, n. 16) is by means of dreams, not through direct communication with the dead, as is common in *Sefer Ḥasidim*. This difference is preserved even when the authors narrate the same story. *SHP*, #555 reads **מעשה באחד שראה את מי שמת בפני כמה שנים**, while the parallel passage in *SHB*, #46 reads **ומעשה באדם אחד שמת לפני זמנו נתגלה (להם) בחלום לאחד ממקורביו . . . .**

23 *SHB*, ##121, 135, 45, 53, 32, 56, 30, 151.

Certainly, *Sefer Ḥasidim* can make no claim to literary merit or to brief and apt exegesis.

In *SH I*, on the other hand, the verses cited are few and invariably apt, the Hebrew clear and idiomatic. For example:

> קרוב אתה בפיהם ורחוק מכליותיהם [ירמיהו י״ב, ב] אלו בני אדם המוציאים חטא ונבול פה או דבר רע על חבריהם בכונה ואומרים ׳המקום ימחול לנו׳ ואינם במעלת היראה כי אינם יראי חטא, ולא שבט אלהים ואימתו עליהם.[24]

It is difficult to convey in English the at times aphoristic style of the author, and, more generally, his rich, associative prose that blends seamlessly many fragments of verses of the Bible with other biblical passages that echo and enrich the preceding quotations. My best efforts yield only a rough translation.

> 'You are always on their lips, but far from their hearts' [Jer. 12: 2]. These are men who utter sinful words and indecent speech and speak evil of their neighbors intentionally, and say 'May God forgive us'; they have not even attained the level of fearing God [in the crudest sense] for neither [fear of] the rod of God nor dread of Him is upon them [cf. Job 21: 9, Exod. 15: 16].

So smooth is the language that multiple sentences and even entire sections of Maimonides are interwoven with the words of *SH I*, and the mix that results seems so natural, the transitions so seamless, that one is hard pressed to detect where one ends and the other begins. For example in section 145, the first nine lines (in Margolies' edition) on anger are those of Maimonides, while the following five are those of *SH I*. The text blends with the *Mivḥar Peninim* no less smoothly in section 36:

> ברוב השתיקה יהיה המורא. הירא מהאלהים השומעו ורואהו ויודעו וחוקרו והוא שותק מיראתו, הוא מוסיף על המורא. ואם מתנשא ומגביה קול מפסיד את המורא, כי שכח שהוא עומד לפני האלהים. הרי הוא כסומא העומד לפני המלך, שמרבה דברים ואינו ירא ממנו,לפי שאינו רואה את מי שיש לו ליראה ממנו. והמרבה לשתוק מחמת המורא, לא במהרה הוא חוטא.

> In much silence will come the fear [of God]. One who fears God and hears Him and sees Him [standing before him] and knows Him and examines Him and is silent [in his awe of Him], he adds to the fear. But one who is arrogant and raises his voice, he loses his fear [of Him] because he forgets that he stands before God; he is like a blind man who stands before the king, who talks a lot for he is not in fear [of the king], because he doesn't see him of whom he should be in fear. One who is very silent out of fear [of God] will not sin swiftly [i.e. easily].

Only the first four words are those of *Mivḥar Peninim*.

24 *SHB*, #151.

The diction of *SH I*, like that of the other sections of *Sefer Ḥasidim*, is often oral. However, the orality embodied is that of the preacher's sermon, not that of a layman's daily discourse. Indeed, its oral, hortatory cadences have few, if any, parallels in medieval literature. Not only does the text literately and effectively meld biblical verses and midrashic phrases with its own articulations, but it even rises occasionally to the level of eloquence, as, for example, in sections 30–1:

> הזהר ושמור נפשך, פן תלכד ברשתו של יצר הרע, המדיחך מארץ החיים והמשיאך לדבר עבירה קטנה להמשיך לבך לגדולה, השפילהו והכניעהו להמסר בידך, ואתה לא תהיה נמסר בידו, פן יביאך לבאר שחת באש לא נופח. ולא יהיה יצרך הרע נמסר בידך אם לא על ידי תשובה לבוראך. ולהרחיקך מבשר תאוה זכור נא לימים אשר יבואו ולרב טוב הצפון. כי אם תיטיב שאת, ואם לאו לפתח חטאת רובץ. ואתה בן אדם, שוב ליוצרך בכל לבבך, והכן לבבך שלם לבוחן כליות ושא עיניך אל השמים, ויאר אליך בשמחה. ואל יכשילך יצר הרע בחייך. ובכל יום ולילה שוב אל לבבך: כי אחר המות יש חבוט הקבר, ואחריו דינה של גיהנם המר, כי במר יבכיון (ישעיהו לג, ז) שיתנו כח לאדם |463| שיסבול כח היסורין. ועוד, אחר שינצל מדינה של גיהנם, יש דינים אחרים קשים ומרים. גם הרמה אשר תצא מבשרך, תאכל את נבלתך. ואמרו חכמים: קשה רימה למת כמחט בבשר חי.
>
> גם בכל עת ועונה יש לך לאהוב את בוראך בכל לבבך ובכל נפשך השב אל לבך וקח משל מאנוש רמה . . . בוא וראה, כמה יש לך לאהוב את בוראך, המפליא חסדו עמך: הוא בוראך מטפה סרוחה ונתן בך נשמה, מוציאך מבטן, אחרי זאת נתן לך פה לדבר ולב להבין, אזנים לשמוע דברי פיו הטהורות והמזוקקות ככסף ומצורפות כזהב, הוא המוליכך על פני הארץ, הוא הנותן מחיה לכל, הוא ממית ומחיה כל, אשר בידו נפש כל חי ורוח, הוא המטריף לחם חוקיך, מה אומר? כי אין הפה יכולה לדבר, והאוזן יכולה לשמוע, כי לו דומיה תהילה (תהילים סה, ב). אין קץ לאורך ימיו, לא יתמו שנותיו, הוא מלך מלכי המלכים, הקדוש ברוך הוא, יתברך שמו ויתברך זכרו, הוא שברא שמים וארץ הים וכל אשר בם, הוא הזן את הכל, כי עיניו פקוחות על כל דרכי בני אדם, לתת לאיש כדרכיו וכפרי מעלליו, הן טוב הן רע.
>
> והנה הוא נותן לפניו שני דרכים: דרך החיים ודרך המות, ואומר לך: ובחרת בחיים (דברים ל, יט). ובכל זאת אנו, המלאים רמה ותולעה, לא חשבנו ולא שמנו על לבבנו כיאם למלאות תאותינו לרצון. וכי צבא לאנוש ימיו?[25] היום כאן, ולמחר בקבר! הלא בפתע פתאום ימות,[26] כי אין אדם שליט ברוחו לכלוא את הרוח.[27] לכן אין טוב לו לאדם כי אם להרחיק עצמו מכל תאוה, ולתת לבו לאהוב וליראה את הצור בכל לבבו ובכל מאדו, ולמאוס בחיי הבל.

Take care and watch thy soul carefully lest you be ensnared by the Evil Instinct, who seduces you from the land of [eternal] life [Paradise], who tempts you to commit a small sin to further induce you to a greater one. Cast him and subdue him so that he is in your power and you are not in his, lest he bring you to the Pit of Destruction, which burns with an unfanned fire. And the Evil Instinct in you can be subdued only by your return to your Creator. And to keep your distance from fleshly desires—remember the

[25] Cf. Job 7: 1. [26] Cf. Num. 6: 9. [27] Cf. Eccles. 8: 8.

days that will come [i.e. after death] and the great good that is stored up [for the righteous]. 'If you do what is right, will you not be accepted? But if you do not do what is right, sin is crouching at your door' [Gen. 4: 7].

And you, son of man, return to your Creator with all your heart, and prepare fully your heart to be examined by Him who examines men's minds [*boḥen kelayot*, Jer. 10: 17]. Lift your eyes [sincerely] to heaven and He will turn His light upon you. Let not your Evil Instinct cause you to stumble [into sin] during your life. Every day [and every] night remember that after life there is the tumbling of the grave and after that the judgment of bitter Gehenna, [as is written,] 'they will cry in anguish' [Isa. 33: 7]; and [hope] that you will have the strength to withstand the force of suffering. Furthermore, after the punishment of Gehenna there are other punishments, hard and bitter. And the maggot that works its way through your flesh will devour your carcass, and our Sages said: 'The maggots in a dead body are as painful [to the corpse] as is a needle to a living body' [*Berakhot* 18b].

You must love your Creator with all your heart and might at all times and in all seasons... Contemplate [*bo u-re'eh*] how much you must love your Creator, who overflows with loving kindness to you. He created you from a soiled drop of sperm and instilled in you a soul. He took you out of the womb and gave your mouth the power of speech and your heart [mind] the ability to understand and your ears [the ability] to hear His pure words, purged of all dross, pure, refined gold. He leads you across lands and provides sustenance to all; He deadens and quickens all life, [as is written,] 'In whose hand is the soul of every living thing and the breath of all mankind' [Job 12: 10]. He gives you your daily bread [*leḥem ḥukekha*]. What can I say—no mouth is adequate [to tell all his loving kindness], nor is any ear capable of hearing [it], [as is written,] 'Silence is your praise [for all human speech is inadequate; Ps. 65: 2 as understood by Rashi and the author of *SH I*], for there is no limit to the length of His days and His years have no end [cf. Ps. 102: 28; Eccles. 4: 8]. He is the king of kings, the Holy One, Blessed be He, may His name be blessed and His memorial/appellation too [see Exod. 3: 15]. He created the heavens and the earth and the sea and all that is in them; He nourishes all, for His eyes are always set on seeing men's ways and giving each his deserves and what is due to him, for better and for worse.

And He places in front of you two ways: the Way of Life and the Way of Death and says to you 'Choose life' [Deut. 30: 19]. Despite this, we, [mere] maggots and worms [Job 25: 20], did not think, did not take to heart other than to fill our lusts at will. Is there an appointed time to man on earth?! [Job 7: 1] Today he is here; tomorrow he is in the grave. Cannot a man die suddenly? For no man controls his living breath, to keep it imprisoned [contained] in his body [Eccles. 8: 8]. Therefore, nothing could be better for man than to keep himself from all [fleshly] desire and to devote his heart to love and fear the Rock with all his heart and all his might, and to reject with disgust the life of vanity.

If parallels to these oratorical cadences exist in other medieval works, they are unknown to me. From the vantage point of language, diction, and voice, few ethical works of the Middle Ages are further apart than *Sefer Ḥasidim* and *SH I*.

Lacking *retson ha-Borè* and *gematriyot*, penance and asceticism, bereft of ghosts, demons, dreams, and soothsaying, and without miracles and exempla —what then is left in *SH I*? What is left is pietism, though not German Pietism. What is left in *SH I* is introspection and religious inwardness, an aspiration for virtue and not just for good deeds (important as the latter may be), an accountability for thoughts and feelings no less than for actions, a call for moral education and for the cultivation of virtue (for virtue, if inborn, is a tender shoot that needs vigilant nurture), a Divine discontent with the pygmy-like standards of the common herd, together with refusal to compromise with the way of the world or to accept man as he is, and a haunting fear of sin coupled with an acute and heavy sense of |464| God's abiding presence and especially of His ever-watchful eye. In short, pietism as is found the world over.

What does this mean? It means that not all pietists in Germany were German Pietists. Indeed, the most influential pietists in Germany were not German Pietists, for *SH I* had a diffusion far greater than that of *Sefer Ḥasidim* itself. Four of the seven extant manuscripts of *Sefer Ḥasidim*, including the oldest dated one, contain only *SH I*.[28] In other words, more than half the manuscripts of *Sefer Ḥasidim* are *not* manuscripts of *Sefer Ḥasidim* and their existence does not attest to the influence of German Pietism, but, on the contrary, to the influence of an ideology opposed to many of the basic tenets of German Pietism. Two of the three remaining manuscripts contain all of *SH I* followed by sections of *Sefer Ḥasidim*.[29] That is to say, they are composites, as is the standard *Sefer Ḥasidim* itself. The standard *Sefer Ḥasidim*, first printed in 1538 and reprinted over twenty times before the twentieth century,[30] is, in reality, a compound. It contains two separate and distinct *Sifrei Ḥasidim*, each with its own religious vision. It embodies the teachings of two sharply divergent groups of religious virtuosi, who proffered to their readers radically different itineraries to God. Only one manuscript, that which Wistinetzki

[28] MSS Moscow, RSL Günzburg 103; Milan, Biblioteca Ambrosiana X 111 Sup.; Nîmes, Bibliothèque Municipale 26 (contains *SHB*, ##1–62), and Oxford, Bodley 875, which is the oldest extant manuscript, copied in 1299. I should add that MS Oxford, Bodley 453 does not contain any copy of *Sefer Ḥasidim*.

[29] MSS Bodley 641, Cambridge Add. 379,2.

[30] C. B. Friedberg, *Bet 'Eked Sefarim: Bibliographical Lexicon* (Tel Aviv, 1952), ii. 385, #1076.

published in 1891,[31] lacks *SH I*, that is to say, only one manuscript is cut wholly from the cloth of Ḥasidei Ashkenaz. One fourteenth-century manuscript and only one accurately reflects the teachings of German Pietism. Apparently the radical and idiosyncratic doctrine of that movement awakened little interest, found very few followers, and, to all appearances, had little to no cultural resonance. Whatever pietism there may be in French writings of the thirteenth century, such as the *Semag* and *Semak* (I believe, as we shall see, that there was none; however, let us grant for argument's sake the opinion of many |**465**| that it existed), it is entirely conventional pietism, not of the radical sort. As for the borrowings from *Sefer Ḥasidim* by Rabbenu Yonah mi-Gerundi (of Gerona) in his *Sefer ha-Yir'ah*, of which so much has been recently made, all such borrowings are, I must sadly report, from *SH I* and *SH I* alone.[32] All in all, reports of the influence of German Pietism would appear to be rather exaggerated.

II

PIETY, PIETISM, AND GERMAN PIETISM

I have said that the most influential pietists in Germany were not German Pietists. But are we even sure that *SH I* is a product of Germany? All the glosses in the printed *SH I* are French. The oldest dated manuscript[33] has three times as many glosses as the printed text, but they too are all French. To be sure, French was spoken in the Rhineland until the mid-thirteenth century, and we have works of unquestioned German provenance, such as those of R. Eli'ezer ben Natan of Mainz (Ravan) or of R. El'azar of Worms himself, which are extant with French glosses.[34] Nevertheless, we must be open to the

[31] Above, n. 2. The manuscript is registered as Parma, De Rossi 1133. {See my reformulation of this sentence below, p. 120.}

[32] N. Brüll, 'Zur Geschichte der jüdisch-ethischen Literatur des Mittelalters', *Jahrbuch für jüdische Geschichte*, 5–6 (1883), 83–7. More than half of Brüll's list of 'borrowings' are simply similar statements or parallel quotations of talmudic or midrashic texts. However, there are enough statements lifted almost verbatim from the first 152 sections of *SHB* to fully validate his claim. See below, pp. 97–100. {This conclusion is confirmed by M. Beit-Arié's study of the indifference of German scribes to the admonitions of the German Pietists against certain scribal practices and their dire warnings of the fate of those who ignored these prescriptions. See his 'Ideals versus Reality: Scribal Prescriptions in *Sefer Ḥasidim* and Contemporary Scribal Practices in Franco-German Manuscripts', in G. Sed-Rajna, ed., *Rashi, 1040–1990: Hommage à Ephraïm E. Urbach* (Paris, 1993), 559–66.}

[33] MS Oxford, Bodley 875, dated 1299.

[34] M. Güdemann, *Geschichte des Erziehungswesens und der Cultur der abendländischen Juden* (above, n. 3), 273–80. He contends that in the Rhineland, Jews spoke French among themselves. This would not have been particularly anomalous, since while French was scarcely the first language of commu-

possibility that the widely disseminated *SH I* is of French rather then Rhenish origin, that it was a Frenchman who stripped the teachings of Ḥasidei Ashkenaz of all its Germanic folklore, expunged its eccentric notion of *retson ha-Borè*, eliminated its pervasive *gematriyot*, and substituted the Golden Mean for severe asceticism and mortification of the flesh. Conceivably, a Frenchman rewrote the bad Hebrew of sections of *Sefer Ḥasidim* and eliminated the rest of it, substituting |466| the sober words of Maimonides together with the eloquent ones of an unknown preacher, and thus supplanted the singular, indeed, peculiar agenda of R. Yehudah he-Ḥasid with a conventional pietistic one. Whoever the editor was and wherever he stemmed from, he capped off his labors by entitling his work *Sefer Ḥasidim* or *Sefer Ḥasidut*,[35] thus appropriating the name of the movement's handbook.[36]

The next step appropriated its historical image. Over the course of time, different editors appended *SH I* to various collections of material of *Sefer Ḥasidim*, always taking care that *SH I* opened the collection, ensuring that the reader would first encounter not the startling tenets of Ḥasidei Ashkenaz but rather page after page of conventional pietistic discourse on love of God, fear of God, humility, and so on. One of these composites made it into print quite early, in 1538, and achieved wide popularity. It is remarkable to what extent *SH I* and those passages in *Sefer Ḥasidim* that were in the spirit of *SH I* shaped the historical image of Ḥasidei Ashkenaz. Study of the influence of *Sefer Ḥasidim* on the subsequent literature of Ashkenaz, whether halakhic or ethical, shows that not only were the new ritual world of *retson ha-Borè* or the book's radical social teachings (not to speak of its numerous idiosyncratic counsels) wholly without influence, but also that they went literally unnoted. One will search in vain the literature of the subsequent centuries for any reference to them. What was absorbed from this composite work were the messages of conventional pietism, not the extremist ones.[37] Indeed, the radical passages went

nication of the German aristocracy, it was widely known. Indeed, knowledge of French may well have been part of a well-rounded education for German 'gentry' in the thirteenth century. The cachet attached to French in the governing classes may well have encouraged its maintenance as the primary internal language among the Jews of the old Rhineland communities. See V. H. Suolahti, *Der französische Einfluss auf die deutsche Sprache im dreizehnten Jahrhundert*, Mémoires de la société Néo-philologique à Helsingfors 8 (Helsinki, 1929), 5–41.

35 *SHB*, ##1, 38. (The referent in #2 is not clear.)

36 See Appendix II below.

37 As for ghosts and the like: as long as Jews in central and eastern Europe lived in a culture that saw itself populated with the 'living dead', and as long as their notions of the active creatures of the 'other world' coincided with that of *Sefer Ḥasidim* (the demonology did change in part with the spread of Lurianic kabbalah), the counsels of *Sefer Ḥasidim* were probably heeded by most. To act otherwise would have been viewed as defying the forces of nature and inviting disaster. However, the literary and, in a sense, ideological innovation of *Sefer Ḥasidim*, that is, the incorporation of such

wholly unnoted even by |467| scholars. It is the visage of the meek, humble, and God-intoxicated pietists that confronts us (until very recently) in the *Wissenschaft* literature, not the harsh and elitist reformers who had uncovered God's previously hidden will with its multitude of novel demands, and sought to reshape both man and society in light of the revelation to which they alone were privy.

In one area alone did the viewpoint of *Sefer Ḥasidim* triumph over that of *SH I.* Its notion of penance struck a deep, responsive chord in Ashkenaz, not through the agency of *Sefer Ḥasidim*, but rather through penitential handbooks. Expiation for sin is a common enough impulse, and it ran strong in thirteenth- and fourteenth-century Germany. R. El'azar of Worms, one of the founders of the hasidic movement (d. *c.*1227), and certainly its leading literary exponent, wrote a handbook of penitential demands, detailing the penance that must be done for a lengthy list of sins. The work apparently answered an acute need and urgent impulse of the community, for it was widely copied, freely edited, and broadly disseminated. There are some fifty extant manuscripts of it, and it is clear from the Germanic literature of subsequent centuries—both ethical and halakhic—that penitential expiation was seen as obligatory. The rigors of the hasidic penance became the cultural norm of Ashkenazic communities of the late Middle Ages.[38] A few of these Ashkenazic works, such as the *Orḥot Tsaddikim*, were adopted by the Safed kabbalists, with the result that hasidic penance ultimately achieved very wide diffusion in the early modern period.

Before I turn to the impact of *Sefer Ḥasidim* in other cultures, it may be wise to say a few words about another source of misunderstanding concerning the extent of the influence of Ḥasidei Ashkenaz. The German Pietists were the carriers of two separate and distinct messages. They bore the message of God's Covert Will in all its distinctiveness, and they were also the proud

notions and counsel into ethical works, went wholly unemulated in the Europe of the Middle Ages. Kabbalah did, indeed, incorporate *shedim* into its *Weltanschauung*; but *shedim* were intrinsically part of the kabbalistic system. They were generated by kabbalistic theory. *Sefer Ḥasidim* stands out because it incorporates—wholesale—the *shedim* of the surrounding world into its normative system. Admittedly, *shedim* from the surrounding culture are also present in the kabbalistic world. This is inevitable as the invisible forces governing the visible world tend to cross cultural lines. However, *shedim* are naturalized citizens in a domain richly populated by indigenous residents.

38 {See E. Kozma, 'The Practice of *Teshuvah* (Penance) in the Medieval Ashkenazi Jewish Communities (A *tesuva* [vezeklés] gyakorlata a középkori askenázi zsidó közösségekben)' (Ph.D. diss., Eötvös Loránd University, Budapest, 2012). The Hebrew section at the end of the thesis contains an annotated edition of all penitentials in print and manuscript.} See Y. A. Dinari, *Ḥakhmei Ashkenaz be-Shilhei Yemei ha-Beinayim* (Jerusalem, 1984), 85–93; Elbaum, *Teshuvat ha-Lev* (above, n. 10), 18–36.

inheritors of an esoteric tradition, *torat ha-sod*, about the mysteries of the Godhead, the structure of the soul, and the esoteric meanings encoded in prayer. The new religious message was the work of R. Yehudah he-Ḥasid. Those of *sod* were the traditions that his family and that of R. El'azar of |**468**| Worms, the Kalonymides, had brought with them from Lucca, Italy sometime in the prehistory of Ashkenaz. Admittedly, R. Yehudah he-Ḥasid and R. El'azar may well have amplified this esoteric lore, even added boldly to it, but these teachings, whether new or old, were viewed as ancient and authoritative by the Ashkenazic community. They were viewed as the traditions of the Kalonymides, the founding family of Ashkenaz—guardians of its secret lore and authors of much of its sacred poetry. While most Jews were skeptical of the new revelations of the Pietists, no one, other than the singular R. Mosheh of Taku (Tachau), doubted the veracity of their traditions of *sod*. Whoever aspired to know the nature of God, the mysteries of the Kavod, or the true intent of the prayers and how they acted upon the Divine potencies would turn to Ḥasidei Ashkenaz for instruction. There were no other competing systems of explanation. However, to follow R. El'azar of Worms and R. Yehudah in the esoteric understanding of prayer is not to follow them in Ḥasidut, because there is no organic link between the two, nor was any perceived to exist at the time. The writings of R. 'Azri'el of Bohemia, a pupil both of Rabbenu Tam and of R. Yehudah he-Ḥasid, vividly illustrate this. In his encyclopedic commentary on the prayers, *'Arugat ha-Bosem*, R. 'Azri'el draws extensively on the esoteric teachings of Ḥasidei Ashkenaz; however, there is not a word of German Pietism—not even penance!—in his work.[39] The acceptance of *torat ha-sod* of the Kalonymides and the influence that these guardians of the covert, potent meaning of prayer may have had over the exact text of prayer and its understanding[40] is no indication of the spread of German Pietism as a social and religious ideology or movement.

The same holds true for the use of numerology. The mighty reputation of R. El'azar of Worms probably popularized the use of numerology in Ashkenazic culture. Numerology, however, is not an ideology. It is a method of showing how information found in one place is encoded in another. The

[39] Cf. *'Arugat ha-Bosem*, ed. E. E. Urbach (Jerusalem, 1963), iv. 179–80; Elbaum, *Teshuvat ha-Lev* (above, n. 10), 43.

[40] See e. g. the kabbalistic commentary of R. Naftali Hirts Treves (Drifzan) on the prayerbook, *Dikdukei Tefillah*, published in Thiengen in 1560. (I am indebted to the anonymous reviewer of the *Jewish Quarterly Review* for drawing my attention to this work.) The other use of prayer, as a mystical technique as opposed to a hermeneutical device, spread so far as Spain. See D. Abrams, 'From Germany to Spain: Numerology as a Mystical Technique', *Journal of Jewish Studies*, 47 (1996), 85–101. Needless to say, a mystical technique is not an ideology.

information discovered depends on the interpreter. He can unearth numerical equivalents of any and all varieties of truth. Use of numerology does not a German Pietist |469| make—unless the contents discovered by *gematriyah* are the distinctive teachings of Ḥasidei Ashkenaz.

Finally, we would do well to remind ourselves of what Joseph Dan pointed out over a decade ago: other than a single passing reference to their distinctive *tallit* (occasioned by a halakhic question about *tallit*), not a trace of Ḥasidei Ashkenaz as a social or religious movement is to be found in the entire medieval literature of Ashkenaz.[41] R. El'azar of Worms makes no reference to any such group in his voluminous esoteric writings, nor does R. Avraham ben 'Azri'el in his multi-volume and wide-ranging commentary. The religious and social programs of the Pietists should have triggered numerous communal controversies, however, not a whisper of this is to be found in all the responsa of the period, indeed in the entire halakhic corpus of Ashkenaz. The German Pietists were too few, their doctrines too radical and idiosyncratic to merit any mention by their contemporaries. True, many passages in *Sefer Ḥasidim* evince the air of a virtuous and embattled elite,[42] however, those who sharply divide the world into states of grace and damnation generally see life as a clash between themselves and the sons of darkness. The people standing in Times Square with placards inscribed 'Repent Now—The Day of Judgment is Near' envision themselves as engaged in a titanic struggle with the forces of evil. Others see them differently, if they see them at all.

If the impact of *Sefer Ḥasidim* on its native soil was minimal except in the realm of penance, what was its impact on other cultures, such as France and Spain? The answer is: it had even less impact than in Germany. With the partial exception of penance, *none* of the distinctive doctrines of *Sefer Ḥasidim*, which I will elaborate, are to be found in the literature of France or Spain.

As for penance, in France it was pointedly ignored by R. Mosheh of Coucy in his great code, *Sefer Mitsvot Gadol* (*Semag*), composed in the fourth decade of the thirteenth century. It first attained muted mention a generation later, though we do hear dissenting voices. R. Yitsḥak of Corbeil (d.1280) refers elliptically in his code to the fourfold penance that the German Pietists advocated but gives no explanation what these four terms mean, which is atypical of this |470| remarkably clear codifier.[43] His glossator, R. Perets of Corbeil (d.1298), fills the noticeable lacuna, spelling out fully what the fourfold ways

[41] J. Dan, 'Ashkenazi Hasidim, 1941–1991: Was there Really a Hasidic Movement in Medieval Germany?', in P. Schäfer and J. Dan, eds., *Gershom Scholem's Major Trends in Jewish Mysticism 50 Years After* (Tübingen, 1993), 94–101.

[42] Above, pp. 23–37.

[43] *Sefer Mitsvot Katan* (henceforth *Semak*) (repr. Jerusalem, 1965), #53.

were.[44] Was R. Yitsḥak a reluctant advocate of the Pietist penance or was this explanatory lapse simply an oversight? We shall never know.[45] We do know that a pupil of his and of R. Mosheh of Evreux, or at least one who recorded their practices, did register dissent from the Pietists' penance, writing, 'And if one sinned, he should study more Torah than before, for the Torah atones, as is written [Prov. 16: 6], "By charity and truth shall sin be atoned" and there is no charity and truth other than the Torah.'[46] Similarly, R. Avraham ben Efrayim, the author of a second, and less successful, abridgment of the *Semag*, makes no mention whatsoever of penance.[47] The northern French community was effectively dispersed a few years later by the exile of 1306, and one can only conjecture whether penance would have taken as deep a hold as it did in Germany.

The penitential handbook of R. El'azar also made its way into the last halakhic work composed in England, the *'Ets Ḥayyim* of R. Ya'akov Ḥazan of London, penned in 1286, four years before the expulsion.[48] In the second half of the thirteenth century, an unknown author, apparently a Frenchman living in a port town of Italy, penned a manual with strong ascetic overtones and under the clear influence of German Pietism. The author remains anonymous to this day. This work was wholly unknown in the Middle Ages and was first published in the twentieth century.[49] Historically it is of little importance. More significant and far more typical of Italy is the work of R. Tsidkiyah ha-Rofê, scion of the leading Jewish family of Rome. He studied in Germany and his *Shibbolei ha-Leket*, a frequently cited and much-copied work, is a rich repository of German writings. He cites a responsum from an unknown German master imposing penance for unwitting Sabbath violation. This is the only instance of |471| penance mentioned in that two-volume work. He never refers to, much less cites, the widespread penitential handbooks with which he was undoubtedly familiar.[50] Is Sabbath violation somehow different because there was some geonic precedent for penance in this instance? Too little has

44 *Haggahot Rabbenu Perets* ad loc.

45 I do not include R. Yitsḥak's remarks in #123 as evidence for a critical stance toward penance **ומה תקנתן של מספרי לשון הרע? יעסוק בתורה שנאמר [משלי טו: ג] מרפא לשון עץ חיים** because he is here referring to the cure for gossip, not its penance.

46 MS Cambridge Add. 3127, fos. 165b–166a. See below, Appendix III, #27.

47 A. Havatselet, 'Kitsur Semag shel R. Avraham ben Efrayim', in Y. D. Frankel and Y. Booksboim, eds., *Sefer ha-Zikkaron li-khevodo u-le-zikhro shel Rabbi Yitsḥak Yedidyah Frankel* (Jerusalem, 1992), 282.

48 *'Ets Ḥayyim: Halakhot, Pesakim u-Minhagim*, ed. I. Brodie (Jerusalem, 1962), i. 203–5.

49 M. Z. Weisz, 'Sefer Minhag Tov', *Ha-Tsofeh le-Ḥokhmat Yisra'el*, 13 (1929), 217–45.

50 *Shibbolei ha-Leket*, ed. S. K. Mirsky (New York, 1966), 276.

survived from Italy of the thirteenth and fourteenth centuries for one to speak with any degree of confidence. In Provence, one early fourteenth-century florilegium, the *Orḥot Ḥayyim* (and its abridgment, the *Kol Bo*), cites sections of the German penitentials, alongside contrary instructions for a repentance that is wholly internal and experiential.[51] What the compiler himself advocated, if anything, is difficult to say. However, no other writer of southern France ever advocated penance, and no one else, to the best of my knowledge, even mentions it.[52]

The story of penance in Spain is identical with that of Provence. R. Yisra'el Al-Nakawa, the author of one large ethical compendium, reproduces a German penitential tract, though it is not clear how this penance squares with other passages in that work, as the editor of that compendium already noted.[53] Be that as it may, this is the sole appearance of penance in Spanish sources known to me. No writer ever actually advocated it and no one ever troubled himself to oppose it. This silence, it should be emphasized, occurs at a time when a growing number of German emigrés made their way to |472| Spain, as fourteenth-century German Jews sought to escape their increasingly precarious position. The rich religious literature of Spain makes no more mention of penance than of any of the other distinctive doctrines of Ḥasidei Ashkenaz.

Rabbenu Yonah mi-Gerundi is sometimes presented as a German Pietist, or at least as having been decisively influenced by that movement. To my mind, this is a result of failing to differentiate pietism, a well-known mode of spirituality, from the radical and idiosyncratic mode of Ḥasidei Ashkenaz, a distinction which I have already adumbrated. For all the varieties of religiosity that the venerable term *ḥasid* has encompassed over the past millennium, and for all the differences that exist between Rabbenu Baḥya, Rabbenu Yonah,

[51] *Orḥot Ḥayyim* (Jerusalem, 1955), #22 (224–6); *Kol Bo* (above, n. 8), iv, #66 (cols. 201–18). (It is irrelevant here whether the *Kol Bo* is an abridgment of the *Orḥot Ḥayyim* or whether it is a first draft of it. The important point from the perspective of intellectual history is that these two works effectively constitute only one reference. They register but a single occurrence of an idea.)

[52] R. Ya'akov Anatoli opposes penance as well as all other forms of asceticism. See his *Malmad ha-Talmidim* (Lyck, 1866), fo. 174b; he views penance and asceticism as distinctly Christian practices, not Jewish ones. See M. Saperstein, *'Your Voice Like a Ram's Horn': Themes and Texts in Traditional Preaching* (Cincinnati, 1996), 61–71, especially nn. 33–4. There is no evidence of any penetration in Provence of the penance of Ḥasidei Ashkenaz.

[53] Yisra'el Ibn 'Al-Nakawa, *Menorat ha-Ma'or*, ed. H. G. Enelow (New York, 1931), iii. 113–19. How this passage is to be reconciled with that of pp. 43–7, especially p. 44, ll. 11–14, is problematic. The inquirer in *Teshuvot ha-Rosh*, 19: 16 is, as we now know from Y. S. Yudlov's new edition of that work (Jerusalem, 1994), a nephew of R. Asher, and thus his query does not evidence any penetration of penance among Spanish Jews. For the tradition of the specific penance cited there by R. Asher, see *Teshuvot Maharil ha-Ḥadashot*, ed. Y. Satz (Jerusalem, 1973), #89 and notes ad loc.

and R. Yisra'el Salanter, there remains, nevertheless, a core meaning to that word and some quintessential commonality to those figures. *Ḥasidut* has long and aptly been translated as 'pietism', for it has much in common with a religious type found in Christianity (whence the term is borrowed) and Islam. Roughly speaking, pietism is characterized by introspection and religious inwardness, ethical accountability, and an emphasis on the experiential over the intellectual. Possessing a keen understanding of individual sinfulness and of the frailties of the will when pitted against instinct, pietism calls for sustained moral training and provides a program for the vigilant disciple of the soul. *Sefer Ḥasidim* has much, though not all, of this spirituality. What characterizes it, however, and sets it apart from all other Jewish movements is, as I have previously noted: first, its harsh asceticism and even harsher penance; next, its religious elitism together with its claims to a new revelation (*retson ha-Borè*) and its myriad of new dictates; and further, its complete identification with the popular beliefs of medieval Germany—not simply the belief in demons, vampires, and werewolves, not to speak of romantic predestination, but rather the large role that these notions play in religious counsel.

R. Yonah was, indeed, a pietist, as was Rabbenu Baḥya before him, but he was not a German Pietist. Not a trace of any of their distinctive and radical notions is found in his writings, major or minor, early or late. To be a pietist doesn't require being a German Pietist, and to become a pietist one doesn't have to have been a German Pietist or to have been influenced by them. The passage from believer to pietist is far simpler and the footway well trodden. The same mounting path has been taken in every century by *âmes d'élite* the world over, and though variously inscribed, its mileposts are identical. |473| Influence of the very distinctive German brand of pietism on the classical pietism of R. Yonah can be claimed only if such an influence can be documented, yet there is not a trace of the teachings of Ḥasidei Ashkenaz in any of the works that were unquestionably authored by R. Yonah and on which his fame is based—the *Sha'arei Teshuvah*, or his commentaries on *Avot* or on Proverbs. All claims of filiation hinge on the borrowings from *Sefer Ḥasidim* found in a small pamphlet entitled *Sefer ha-Yir'ah*, attributed in some sources to R. Yonah. Passing the problematic issue of attribution,[54] suffice it to remark that all the passages borrowed are from *SH I* and from *SH I* alone.[55] Whatever influence *Sefer Ḥasidim* in any of its guises had south of the Pyrenees, and

[54] See below, n. 89.

[55] Above, n. 32. Further parallels are noted in the text of *Sefer ha-Yir'ah* contained in the 1990 edition of *Sha'arei Teshuvah* published in Jerusalem by the Siftei Chachamim Institute for the Dissemination of Torah and Mussar. It lists four more parallels. Section 69 of *Sefer ha-Yir'ah* is listed

I believe it to have been trivial, it was *SH I* that exercised that influence, not the *Sefer Ḥasidim* of Ḥasidei Ashkenaz.

Let us linger a moment or two on R. Yonah before turning north to France. How much of *SH I* actually is there in *Sefer ha-Yir'ah*? Very little; and of substance nothing at all. Of the thirty-two parallels |474| cited by Brüll (all taken from *SH I*), only fifteen are genuine parallels; the others are simply common citations of indistinctive talmudic or midrashic passages. However, there is no doubt that the author of *Sefer ha-Yir'ah* had in front of him *SH I*. Passages in *SH I*, such as 'Do not comb your hair over a book and do not kill a flea on the table, for the table has been called an altar'; 'One should not think Torah thoughts in an impure place [i.e. outhouse]; but rather one should do arithmetical calculations [of one's budget], and this is what is called "being cunning [far-sighted] in God-fearingness"' appear in *Sefer ha-Yir'ah*, as do instructions such as 'Do not join others suddenly if they are whispering to one another [i.e. they are probably gossiping]' or 'If you hear people speaking evil about someone, pretend to believe [them], but do not believe them.'[56] These ideas, however, are of no significance to the *Sefer ha-Yir'ah*.

The central thrust of that small pamphlet entitled *Sefer ha-Yir'ah* is to create a morning and evening regimen, so that so long as the Jew is found in his private space, from the moment he rises in the morning to the moment he steps into the alien, public, Gentile space to earn his daily bread, his thoughts are directed uninterruptedly toward God. A full 50 percent of this short work is dedicated to that goal. The other 50 percent is devoted to virtues to be prac-

as parallel to *SHB*, #459. However, this is simply a translation of the talmudic dictum in *Pesaḥim* 110b. Anyone seeking to discourage soothsaying, as do both *Sefer ha-Yir'ah*, #69 and *SHB*, #59, and seeking to allay his reader's fears, will cite the passage in *Pesaḥim*. The parallelism lies in the strong and uncustomary position of opposing the ubiquitous soothsaying. Citing the talmudic passage in support follows naturally. Sections 18 and 27 are listed as parallels to *SHB*, #822. This is correct. They are, however, also parallel to *SHB*, #57. Section 75 is parallel to *SHB*, #313, but this is simply a statement of universal practice. Section 93 has indeed partial parallels with *SHB*, ##546 and 949, as does section 95 with *SHB*, #917. Note, however, that all the parallels and borrowings deal with one and the same subject, soiled places (*mekomot metunnafim*) and their relationship to sacred objects and the recitation of sacred words. Clearly the author of the *Sefer ha-Yir'ah* had a few more sections in his *SHB* on soiled places which fleshed out the position stated more generally in *SHB*, #57. (There is, after all, nothing canonical in the number 152, and copies of *SH I* may well have circulated with 160 or 170 sections.) Also, note that *SHB*, #917 deals with the fear of passing wind in the presence of sacred books, while *Sefer ha-Yir'ah* deals with nakedness in their presence. The religious sensitivity is the same but there is, strictly speaking, no literary borrowing. Be that as it may, other than on the topic of *mekomot metunnafim*, all parallelisms between *Sefer ha-Yir'ah* and *Sefer Ḥasidim* are actually between *Sefer ha-Yir'ah* and *SH I*.

56 *SHB*, ##101, 102, *Sefer ha-Yir'ah*, #75; *SHB*, #949, *Sefer ha-Yir'ah*, #93; *SHB*, #64, *Sefer ha-Yir'ah*, #51.

ticed in the public sphere of human intercourse: humility, courtesy, sensitivity to other human beings, and honesty both in deed and speech. A few phrasings of these directives come from *SH I*, but not many. Only three directives are found in *Sefer ha-Yir'ah* that are probably distinctive to *SH I*. The first is that a Jew should contribute weekly a penny or halfpenny to charity so as to show that he is a tenant (*rentier*) of God. A lovely idea found in *SH I*, but one that is in no way developed in either of these two works.[57] The second is the injunction against scribes encoding their names in the works that they copy.[58] The third is the injunction to fast once a month. (*Sefer Ḥasidim* itself suggests once a week, *SH I* characteristically reduces the demand to once a month.[59]) Yet these very cases of influence reflect, at the same time, a contrary tendency of *Sefer ha-Yir'ah*, that is, to mute or soften the very dictates that it occasionally does borrow from *SH I*. *Sefer ha-Yir'ah* qualifies the monthly fast, writing: 'One should fast [i.e. abstain totally from food and drink] one day in the month or [at the least] eat only bread and water [one day a month].[60] *SHB* opens the section |475| against the scribal practice of encoding one's name in books thus: '"The name of the wicked shall rot" [Prov. 10: 7]—these are the scribes who add or subtract letters', and concludes: 'Is it conceivable that for the sake of their disgusting name, they should add or subtract letters [from the text]?!' *Sefer ha-Yir'ah* simply writes: 'If you are a scribe do not add a letter or subtract a letter [from the text] to sign your name at the head of a column' without any derogatory remarks. Both forbid raising one's hand in anger against one's fellow man, but *SHB* adds: 'the only correction is cutting off his hand'.[61] Again, when advocating walking in a bent posture (*be-komah shehuḥah*), *Sefer ha-Yir'ah* writes, 'he should not bend over excessively . . . lest he become an object of mockery'.[62] And yet again, while advocating *kavvanah* in prayer, *Sefer ha-Yir'ah* writes: 'He should not stretch out his prayer for too long lest he be thought a "heavy" [*le-kaved*] or a clown.'[63] In other words, the very few facets of extremism that *SH I* does share with *Sefer Ḥasidim*,[64] namely, the occasionally sharp language and the willingness, indeed the insistence, on suffering mockery for the public practice of its forms of piety, are repudiated by *Sefer ha-Yir'ah*. That work insists that such a path is counterproductive.[65]

57 *Sefer ha-Yir'ah*, #62 (= *SHB*, #61).

58 *Sefer ha-Yir'ah*, #90 (= *SHB*, #136).

59 *Sefer ha-Yir'ah*, #102, *SHB*, #97, though see n. 15 above.

60 See *SHB*, #617.

61 *Sefer ha-Yir'ah*, #67, *SHB*, #49 (ואין לו תקנה אלא קציצת ידו).

62 *Sefer ha-Yir'ah*, #42, *SHB*, #57.

63 *Sefer ha-Yir'ah*, #29.

64 Above, pp. 33–4.

65 Interestingly, the author or compiler of the ethical passages in MS Cambridge Add. 3127 (see Appendix III below) was also aware of the dangers of counterproductive behavior—apparently both had seen enough supererogatory conduct in their times and the reaction it provoked—and when

All in all, the influence of *SH I* on *Sefer ha-Yir'ah* is real but trivial, that of *Sefer Ḥasidim* and Ḥasidei Ashkenaz non-existent.

North of the Pyrenees, a finger has been pointed at two figures as having been influenced by Ḥasidei Ashkenaz: R. Mosheh of Coucy, the author of the great French code *Sefer Mitsvot Gadol* (*Semag*), and R. Yitsḥak of Corbeil, the author of the abridgment of that work, commonly known as the *Semak*. R. Eli'ezer of Metz—a city situated in the Empire, but, Jewishly speaking, culturally part of France—the late twelfth-century author of the *Sefer Yere'im*, has also been suggested a number of times as a forerunner of the German Pietists and has been portrayed as a prototypical Ḥasid Ashkenazi.

Confusion has arisen on this issue from the start, repeating the mistake made with Rabbenu Yonah, namely, failure to distinguish between pietism and German Pietism. This error is compounded |476| by a further failure to distinguish between pietism and piety. The latter error is largely a product of the English language and is less likely to occur in German, in which piety is termed *Frömmigkeit* (whence the Yiddish *frumkayt*) while pietism is termed *Pietismus*. Piety, unlike pietism, is not a distinctive mode of spirituality. It is simply, as Webster's Dictionary puts it, 'devout fulfillment of one's religious obligations', whatever those obligations may be, as external as oblation or as internal as meditation.

That these three halakhists are not German Pietists is clear. There isn't a word of that group's distinctive teachings in all of their writings. Are they pietists at all? Do we find in them—as we do in R. Yonah—a concern for the religious formation of the whole person? Are their writings suffused with a pervasive sense of God's power and presence and with the fear that this presence should instill in man? Do they possess a pungent sense of individual sinfulness and are they animated by concerns for constant vigilance against the evil instinct? Since guiding the heart and the will is at least as difficult as guiding the hand, as every pietist from R. Baḥya to R. Yisra'el Salanter knew only too well, do they attempt to show a path to the attainment of these inner goals? Do they provide us with some regimen for the maintenance of the health of the soul? The answer to all these questions is one and the same: not at all. On occasion these writers urge their readers to greater piety, to greater *Frömmigkeit*, that is, to a fuller and more scrupulous fulfillment of their religious duties, including those 'of the heart'—but they are in no way pietists, nor do they advocate pietism to their readers.

What has possibly led some astray is the fact that these writers, unlike most

advocating abstemious eating habits on all days other than Sabbath and holidays (#19), he used the same words of counsel: ובפני רבים מותר פן יחשב ללעג.

of their fellow Tosafists, do address such imperatives as 'love of God', 'fear of God', and 'cleaving to Him', and speak of the injunctions against pride and covetousness, or against testing God. Unnoted has been the less than bashful fact that these authors are not simply codifiers but *monei mitsvot*, 'counters of commandments'. That is to say, they are codifiers who have chosen to organize their work by enumerating and then discussing the nature and specifics of each imperative (*mitsvah*). This is significant. A chronological framework for presentation such as that adopted by the school of Rashi (*Sifrut de-Vei Rashi*) or later the *Tur* would begin with the morning prayers, blessings on food, and the grace after meals, then move on to the evening prayers, and then to Sabbath and so on. This approach might never get around to discussing the more |477| interior duties of loving God, fearing God, and cleaving to Him, or injunctions against anger or pride, which have no set time or framework for their fulfillment. However, if one adopts a framework of *minyan ha-mitsvot*, one must address the commandment 'And thou shalt love thy God with all thy heart', and that of 'And Him shalt thou fear and to Him shalt thou cleave'. Thus, the discussion of these topics does not reflect any choice on the part of the individual authors. Rather, we should ask how these commandments are discussed. How large do they bulk in the respective works? Do the various authors seek to give the 'duties of the heart' some centrality in the halakhic system, as Maimonides does in the *Sefer Madda*'? Do the writers content themselves with a few talmudic quotations, or do they seize these occasions for extended discussion on the nature of these 'duties of the heart'? The answer is that these commandments occupy a minute part of each respective code, and there is either no discussion at all (as in the *Sefer Yere'im*),[66] or no extended or even serious discussion (in the other two works) of these 'duties of the heart'. And needless to say, none of the above authors provides any spiritual regimen, or anything even vaguely resembling it.

These authors are codifiers who composed works that spell out in detail the full range of religious obligations. On occasion, they exhort their readers to observe the laws in which there had been laxity, *tefillin* and *mezuzah*, and summon them to greater intentionality (*kavvanah*) in prayers.[67] They call heatedly for more decorum in the synagogue and plead for greater honesty in

[66] See the perfunctory treatment of the commandments to love and fear God, and to cleave to Him and walk in His ways in ##404–8, ##153–4. The discussion consists entirely of citations of rabbinic passages. The imperative of 'cleaving to Him', which lies at the heart of pietism, is taken simply in the rabbinic sense of cleaving to scholars. As for interpersonal conduct, see the brief and purely technical discussions throughout the fifth section (*'amud ha-ḥamishi*) of the work.

[67] *Sefer Mitsvot Gadol* (henceforth *Semag*), ed. E. Schlesinger (Jerusalem, 1989–95), ii, *'aseh* #3; *Semak*, #11.

their dealings with their fellow men, especially Gentiles.[68] They inveigh against the dangers of pride, covetousness, and anger and remind people to ever walk humbly before God.[69] But all this scarcely constitutes pietism. Indeed, the author of the *Semak*, R. Yitsḥak of |478| Corbeil, sometimes called *he-ḥasid* or *ha-kadosh* ('the saintly' or 'the holy'),[70] who fasted one day a month as suggested by the *Sefer ha-Yir'ah*,[71] and who, in good supererogatory fashion, waited twenty-four hours between consuming meat and milk as did the father of Mar Ukba in the Talmud,[72] nevertheless was heard remarking that 'he regretted that he had gotten so accustomed to going to the synagogue [to pray] as he enjoyed study so much'.[73]

Should such admissions surprise us? Not at all. The Ashkenazic community in the high Middle Ages was, indeed, lax in observance of *tallit* and *tefillin*,[74] as were most other European Jewish communities. And has there ever been a community that was free of pride or lust or quarrel, or one that did not merit admonition about the earnestness of its prayer or its decorum in synagogue? Nor is the presence of such exhortations in these codes surprising. French writers never adopted Maimonides' Olympian notion of a *summa*, a comprehensive and impersonal statement of the totality of the Oral Law. Their codes are far more mundane than Maimonides' Olympian work. They have clear practical purposes in mind that they state openly in their respective

[68] *Semak*, #11; *Semag*, i, *'aseh* #74; ii, *lo ta'aseh* #2, and see also *lo ta'aseh* ##152, 170. For a possible context to R. Mosheh's exhortation, see J. Woolf, 'Some Polemical Emphases in the *Sefer Misvot Gadol* of R. Moses of Coucy', *Jewish Quarterly Review*, 89 (1998), 81–100; *Semak*, #85.

[69] *Semag*, ii, *'aseh* #16, *lo ta'aseh* #64; *Semak*, ##14, 19, 22 (#9).

[70] E. Kanarfogel, *Peering through the Lattices: Mystical, Magical, and Pietistic Dimensions in the Tosafist Period* (Detroit, 2000), 90.

[71] MS Cambridge Add. 3127, fo. 166a. See below, Appendix III, #32. R. Yitsḥak's compatriot and glossator, R. Perets of Corbeil, spoke approvingly of fasting for one's sins; *Haggahot Rabbenu Perets* on the *Semak*, #175.

[72] *Piskei Ri mi-Corbeil*, MS Cambridge Add. 3127, fo. 167b, and see *Ḥullin* 106a. This set of rulings immediately follows the ethical prescriptions described below and reproduced in Appendix III. On the various versions and manuscripts of these rulings, see S. Emanuel, 'Ha-Sefarim ha-Avudim shel Ba'alei ha-Tosafot' (Ph.D. diss., Hebrew University of Jerusalem, 1993), 237–43 {published as *Shivrei Luḥot: Sefarim Avudim shel Ba'alei ha-Tosafot* (Jerusalem, 2007), 198–207; see also G. Vajda, 'Likkutim mi-Sefer Mussar Bilti Yadu'a le-Eḥad mi-Rabbanei Tsarfat', in S. Abramson et al., eds., *Sefer Ḥayyim Shirman: Kovets Meḥkarim* (Jerusalem, 1970), 108: **וטוב להיזהר לאכילת חלב עד מעת לעת [מ]אכלו בשר בהמה**}.

[73] **פעם אחת אמר מצטער אני שהורגלתי כל כך לילך לבית הכנסת, שטוב לי ללמוד** (*Piskei Ri mi-Corbeil*, fo. 169a). {See Emanuel, *Shivrei Luḥot* (above, n. 72), 207 n. 89.}

[74] A. Ravitzky, *'Al Da'at ha-Makom: Meḥkarim ba-Hagut ha-Yehudit u-ve-Toledoteiha* (Jerusalem, 1991), 37–40; E. Kanarfogel, 'Rabbinic Attitudes Toward Nonobservance in the Medieval Period', in J. J. Schachter, ed., *Jewish Tradition and the Non-traditional Jew* (Northvale, NJ, 1992), 7–14.

introductions. They intend to enlighten their fellow Jews as to the fullness of their duties, to inform people of laws of which they may be insufficiently aware, to raise their religious sensitivities, and to encourage them to seal the breaches in their observances. Hortatory remarks are integral to the spirit of these works and their avowed goals. However, religious exhortation isn't piety, piety isn't pietism, and pietism itself is scarcely German Pietism. |479|

III

PIETY AND RELIGIOSITY

While these authors are not pietists, do they breathe religiosity, does one discern passion in their exhortations? In the *Sefer Yere'im* and the *Semak*, one senses conviction more than passion. The *Semag*, however, evinces a passion whose force is not diminished for being a quiet one. It was not simply hortatory skills that made its author, R. Mosheh of Coucy, the 'preacher' among the Tosafists but also his animating impulse to improve and uplift his fellow Jews. R. Mosheh the Preacher, while in no way a pietist, nevertheless exudes a religiosity that is palpable.

He sees man as a day laborer of God who must daily fulfill his *opus dei*, which is the end and purpose of his existence. God must be worshipped and obeyed for His own sake and not out of fear of punishment, nor from seeking to win favor in His eyes. Anger is sinful, but the greatest of all sins is the sin of pride, for it means forgetting one's nothingness before God and becoming oblivious to God's infinite grace in giving one existence.[75] As sinning is human, penance always befits us. R. Mosheh penned a special prayer for penitents, which he mentions but does not reproduce in his code, a prayer which R. Yonah mi-Gerundi found so admirable that he apparently copied and embellished it and, as often happened with short devotional works in the Middle Ages, it soon went under R. Yonah's name in his homeland.[76] R. Mosheh further suggested that his readers spend an hour a day on their knees supplicating God's forgiveness for their inevitable sins.[77] But

[75] Y. D. Galinsky, 'Rabbi Mosheh mi-Coucy ke-Ḥasid, ke-Darshan u-Fulmusan' (MA thesis, Bernard Revel Graduate School, Yeshivah University, 1993), 27–59. To date, Galinsky's work, written under the direction of David Berger, is the most sober treatment of R. Mosheh of Coucy generally, and of R. Mosheh's putative relationship to German Pietism in particular. See also his articles: '"Ve-lihyot le-Fanekha 'Eved Ne'eman Kol ha-Yamim": Perek be-Haguto ha-Datit shel R. Mosheh mi-Coucy', *Da'at*, 42 (1999), 13–31; '"Kum 'Aseh Sefer Torah mi-Shenei Ḥalakim": le-Verur Kavanot Rabbi Mosheh mi-Coucy bi-Khetivat ha-Semag', *Ha-Ma'ayan*, 35/1 (1995), 23–31, especially 25 n. 10.

[76] Y. Gilat, 'Shetei Bakashot le-Rabbi Mosheh mi-Coucy', *Tarbiz*, 28 (1959), 54–8.

[77] *Semag*, i, *'aseh* #16.

recommending this protracted kneeling posture is the closest that R. Mosheh of Coucy comes to a pietistic stance.

His contemporary, R. Mosheh of Evreux, the author/compiler of the *Tosafot* of Evreux, similarly emphasized in a small ethical |**480**| broadside the danger of anger, the importance of humility—always walking, in good medieval fashion, with bent head and downcast eyes—of seeking repentance for one's inevitable sins, and of weeping honest tears in prayer, 'for he who weeps [in prayer] in the night, the stars and constellations weep with him and his prayer is heard'.[78] For a brief moment the author/compiler of the *Tosafot* of Evreux,[79] who partook very lightly of meat so as to deny himself one of the pleasures of the world,[80] drops the impersonality of 'Objection' and 'Reply may be made' in which his other writings are couched, and we glimpse a deeply religious man, not crushed by his sin but aware of its existence and disturbed by it. No less aware is he of the harsh, adamantine ego, and mindful that only by contraction rather than by expansion, by withdrawing rather than by asserting oneself, can the resistant, inviolate self be conquered.

There were those who did not pen spiritual advice but drew up lists of vices to be avoided and practices to be encouraged. Spurning penance, not to mention the ascetic rigors of the German Pietists, one writer, apparently a pupil or votary of R. Yitsḥak of Corbeil, the author of the *Semak*, suggests minor denials of bodily wants designed to remind man of his higher nature and calls upon him to partake very lightly of meat on weekdays and only as much as is necessary 'to sustain and strengthen the body'; not to partake in festive meals unnecessarily (except Sabbath, of course, which was to be fully celebrated at the table); to fast twice or three times |**481**| a year, or once a month or once a week (he is not sure what to endorse); and on those fast days to confess to a

[78] *Orḥot Ḥayyim* (repr. Jerusalem, 1956), 228, end of 'Hilkhot Rosh ha-Shanah'; *Kol Bo* (above, n. 8), iv, #66, col. 220. The phrase is talmudic (*Sanhedrin* 104b), but R. Mosheh of Evreux is the only writer, to the best of my knowledge, who draws on this passage. The entire passage on prayer found favor in the eyes of R. Yitsḥak of Corbeil and he quoted it in his glosses on the *Semak* (#11). I say 'in good medieval fashion', for while walking with a bent head has talmudic precedent (*Berakhot* 43b), walking with eyes downcast, to the best of my knowledge, does not. (See Rashi, *Niddah* 24a, s.v. *simi at*; *Menaḥot* 110a, s.v. *simi at*. Rashi has *heard* this explanation; however, he has no explicit source for it. See the *'asarah milei de-ḥasiduta* cited in *Sefer ha-Oreh* [Lvov, 1905], 3–4.) Yet this is a trait advocated by *SHI* (*SHB*, #53), *Sefer ha-Yir'ah* (#42), and R. Mosheh of Evreux. Downcast eyes are taken to be emblematic of piety by all three, not surprisingly, as 'custody of the eyes' to avoid temptation. An indication of humility, this practice was viewed as a hallmark of the religious and was widespread in the surrounding society.

[79] E. E. Urbach, *Ba'alei ha-Tosafot*, rev. edn. (Jerusalem, 1980), 479–85.

[80] MS Cambridge Add. 3127, fo. 165b. See below, Appendix III, #21. His action was probably a compromise between not forbidding what the Torah had permitted and not partaking in the pleasures of the world.

rabbi and repent bitterly of one's sins. He also enumerates the need to walk humbly, to deal justly with one's neighbor, neither to flatter nor to lie, to respect all men, not to offend anyone with word or deed, nor seek power over others.[81] Self-improvement rather than self-abnegation was the goal. Abstemious habits, moral conduct, and some sense of human worthlessness and sin had to accompany the quotidian Jewish life of ritual.

There were still others who neither wrote manuals nor even drew up lists, but, finding a line or two in one of these lists that resonated with them, inserted those lines right into the long catalogue of ritual prescriptions and judicial rulings that they were copying—with no sense of incongruity.[82] And then, of course, there were the hundreds of owners of manuscripts who instructed their scribes to include the widest variety of ethical writings and prescriptions into their copies of halakhic works.[83]

Should all this surprise us? Not at all. The voluminous writings of the Tosafists tell us of their thoughts, not of their feelings and muted aspirations. We have every reason to suppose that in this large group of thinkers, as well as in their eager audience, every variety of individual existed. There were 'once-born souls' and 'twice-born' ones, the religiously indifferent, the spiritually casual, the somewhat interested, the wholly dedicated, and those who had indeed passed through the light and darkness of religious travail. 'The spirit blows where it listeth', and we would do well not to tie its coming and going to any specific movement, nor should we think that, were it not for some eccentric Rhenish pietists, there would have been no spiritual hunger in France and Germany in the high Middle Ages. |**482**|

IV

FRANCE OR GERMANY?

Truth to tell, if we were to judge on the basis of the written remains, there was more spiritual hunger in France than in Germany. Perhaps the time has come to remind ourselves that the traveler and inveterate recorder R. Avraham Ibn

[81] MS Cambridge Add. 3127, fos. 165b–166a. It is reproduced in full in Appendix III below.

[82] The scribe or editor of *Piskei Rabbenu Perets* (found in MS Paris, Bibliothèque Nationale 407, fos. 236b–237a) inserted several ethical prescriptions from MS Cambridge Add. 3127 into his transcriptions of the *Pesakim*. See Ḥ. S. Sha'anan, 'Piskei Rabbenu Perets ve-Aḥerim be-'Inyanei Oraḥ Ḥayyim', *Moriah*, 17/9–10 (1991), 12 (##15–16). See below, Appendix III, ##19, 21, 29.

[83] In fact, many of the owners themselves transcribed the ethical works. At least 50 percent of Hebrew manuscripts are owner-copied. See M. Beit-Arié, *Hebrew Manuscripts of East and West: Towards a Comparative Codicology* (London, 1993), 79–83.

Yarḥi mentions *ḥasidei Tsarfat* at least as often as *ḥasidei Alamania*.[84] I have already noted that all the glosses in *SH I* are in French, which in itself proves little. However, *SH I* speaks approvingly of swaying in prayer and cites as support Psalm 35: 10: 'All my limbs should say, God, who is like Thee?'[85] Ibn Yarḥi mentions this swaying in prayer (together with the very same verse as proof text) as a hallmark of the 'rabbis and *ḥasidim* of Tsarfat'.[86] It should be further noted that the version of *Sefer Ḥasidim* published by Wistinetzki, which faithfully reflects the teachings of German Pietism, makes no mention of swaying in prayer.[87] The *Sefer ha-Yir'ah* equally recommends swaying, citing the same proof text.[88] All three seem to reflect the tradition and practice of a religious and spiritual elite in France. While debate continues over the authorship of *Sefer ha-Yir'ah*, even those who argue for the authorship of R. Yonah mi-Gerundi concede that it was composed during his stay at the yeshivah of Evreux or very soon afterwards, when he was still under its influence.[89] The *Sefer ha-Yir'ah* |483| is thus a product of northern French culture. The similarities between that work and *SH I*, together with the clear literary borrowings, would strengthen somewhat the claims of *SH I* to be a French work. A community of emphases has also been noted between *SH I* and the writings of R. Mosheh of Coucy.[90] If to this evidence we add the brief but

84 *Sefer ha-Manhig*, i. 85, 363; ii. 607, 626 (a repetition of the same report).

85 *SHB*, #56.

86 *Sefer ha-Manhig*, i. 85.

87 Noted by Y. (Eric) Zimmer, 'Tikkunei ha-Guf bi-She'at ha-Tefillah', in his *'Olam ke-Minhago Noheg* (Jerusalem, 1996), 100 n. 166.

88 #33. One must distinguish between swaying in Torah study, swaying during the Torah reading, and swaying in prayer. Each has its separate source and advocates. See Zimmer, *'Olam ke-Minhago Noheg* (above, n. 87), 98–101.

89 I. M. Ta-Shma, 'Ḥasidut Ashkenaz bi-Sefarad: R. Yonah mi-Gerundi, ha-Ish u-Fo'olo', in A. Mirsky, A. Grossman, and Y. Kaplan, eds., *Galut Aḥar Golah: Meḥkarim be-Toledot 'Am Yisra'el Mugashim le-Professor Ḥayyim Beinart li-Melot lo Shiv'im Shanah* (Jerusalem, 1988), 168–70. I have serious doubts whether Benjamin Richler's argument for north European authorship has been effectively refuted. See B. Richler, ''Al Kitvei ha-Yad shel *Sefer ha-Yir'ah* ha-Meyuḥas le-Rabbenu Yonah Girondi', *'Alei Sefer*, 8 (1980), 51–9. The manuscript evidence is very strong and the citation of Ritva seems to me an instance of misplaced authority. We know that this slender work went under R. Yonah's name in Spain and we have every reason to believe that even if R. Yonah was not its actual author, he endorsed both its halakhic and moral contents and gave them currency and no little authority in the Iberian Peninsula. In doing so, he tacitly endorsed whatever halakhic positions were contained in the *Sefer ha-Yir'ah*. A halakhist would be wholly justified in citing these passages as proof of R. Yonah's stand. The question here, however, is not legal endorsement but ascription of actual authorship. The issue is not halakhic but bibliographic, and I know no reason why the attribution of a cousin's pupil's pupil—which is what the great Ritva's connection to R. Yonah was—is somehow authoritative in these matters, especially against the overwhelming evidence of the manuscripts.

90 Galinsky, 'Rabbi Mosheh mi-Coucy' (above, n. 74), 36–66, with notes ad loc., especially nn. 55, 108.

moving remarks of R. Mosheh of Evreux against anger and pride and on the importance of humility and tearful prayer,[91] there is every indication that intense legal thinking had not stifled the aspiration for virtue among the French Tosafists, nor had dialectic desiccated their spirit. Some aspired to pietism, some to piety, and some simply wished to be humbler, better men and to insure somehow that the world would not be too much with them.

APPENDIX I

MINHAG OSTREYKH AND THE EAST

I have discussed the putative influence of German Pietism in Germany itself, to the south in Italy, to the west in France, and south-west in Provence and Spain. A word may be in order about its supposed influence in the east, namely in Austria and Poland. This discussion can be divided into two parts: the underlying assumptions of influence and the actual documentation of specific influences.

In my laudatory review of Eric Zimmer's *'Olam ke-Minhago Noheg* I indicated how the book's premises on this subject are problematic.[92] In that fine work Zimmer sees hasidic influence on *minhag* Ostreykh, the rite of Austria and Poland. I quote from my review:

Zimmer draws upon Ta-Shma's important article on the presence of numerous pupils of R. Yehudah he-Ḥasid in Slavic countries. Ta-Shma conjectured that R. Yehudah he-Ḥasid moved from Speyer to Regensburg |**484**| because of the opposition that he encountered in the old Rhineland city to his radical program and sought out the 'frontier' zone as being more receptive to his innovative ideas. Similarly, pupils of his settled in the East precisely because in the new settlements there was a greater chance of instituting Hasidic doctrines. Adopting this line of thought, Zimmer sees in German Pietism a major force in shaping the rite of Ostreich and Poland. It is an interesting thesis and certainly worth pursuing. It should be noted however, that Regensburg in the twelfth century was a burgeoning commercial center. Situated on the Danube, this imperial city was a gateway to trade with southeastern Europe and the lands of Islam and quite possibly was also already playing a major role in financing the *Ostsiedlung*. And Jewish settlement in medieval times often followed commercial opportunity. To ask why R. Yehudah he-Ḥasid settled there is equally to ask why other prominent Tosafists, such as R. Isaac ben Mordecai (Ribam), R. Isaac ben Jacob (Ri Lavan),

[91] Above, p. 104.

[92] 'Yishaq (Eric) Zimmer, "*'Olam ke-Minhago Noheg*: A Review Essay", *AJS Review*, 23 (1998), 222–34.

> R. Ephraim, R. Baruch, and R. Shemaryah all made their new homes in Regensburg. Moreover, Regensburg, while considerably east of the Rhineland, was no *tabula rasa* waiting for the imprint of some distinguished émigré. It housed a distinguished line of Tosafists, who antedated R. Yehudah in residence by a half century.[93]

I would now add that many of these scholars had studied under Rabbenu Tam and maintained ongoing contact with him because, until the second half of the thirteenth century, Regensburg had some of the closest connections with France of any German city. If R. Yehudah he-Ḥasid's distinguished lineage did not obviate problems in his hometown of Speyer, he could scarcely have imagined that his singular doctrines would be welcomed in the French beachhead on the Danube, and certainly not by the stormiest petrel of the tosafist movement, R. Efrayim of Regensburg. A man who once sent Rabbenu Tam a letter containing all the hairs he had torn out of his beard in exasperation at one of his teacher's rulings could scarcely be expected to put up with R. Yehudah's private revelations, his newly discovered covert will of God. If R. Yehudah he-Ḥasid was seeking in his move to Regensburg to outflank his opposition, he couldn't have been more mistaken.

Regensburg was also the seat of one of the most venerable Jewish communities in Germany, whose recorded history stretched as far back as that of the Rhineland cities. It is customary to picture the expansion of the German |485| Jewish community as radiating eastward from the settlements on the Rhine. The written record, however, documents the simultaneous emergence in the tenth century of Jewish communities both in the Rhineland and in the trading centers near and along the eastern borders of the Empire (the Empire' in medieval times was the term for the German Empire, as all other countries had monarchies)—Regensburg, Magdeburg, Merseburg, and Prague. True, the oldest academies were in Mainz and Worms, but the other ancient communities were scarcely deferential about their local customs and practices. R. Yitsḥak Or Zarua'—who numbered R. Yehudah he-Ḥasid among his teachers—juxtaposed with no sense of inferiority the traditions of his native Bohemia with those of the Rhineland.

As to the alleged influence of German Pietism on the Eastern rite, we would do well to remember two things. First, important as Ta-Shma's article is and rich in new information about little-known medieval Polish sages, the connection between these scholars and Ḥasidei Ashkenaz remains, nevertheless, conjectural. For example, that the scholar R. Ya'akov ha-Kohen belonged to the circle of German Pietists is based on the assumption that the Ya'akov

[93] 'Yishaq (Eric) Zimmer, "*'Olam ke-Minhago Noheg*: A Review Essay", *AJS Review*, 23, 229–30.

ha-Kohen (neither a very rare nor a distinctive name) mentioned in the halakhic sources is one and the same person mentioned in a now-lost kabbalistic manuscript. All that we know for certain is that R. Yehudah he-Ḥasid had Slavic pupils in his Bible classes. There is no evidence that these pupils were scholars of any standing or that they exercised any authority in their homeland.[94]

So much—to my thinking—for the premises; let us now investigate the evidence for specific influences. Zimmer cautiously suggests influence in five areas: swaying in prayer, postnatal sexual relationships, added days of menstrual abstinence, restriction of priestly blessings to holidays, and spread of a certain formula in prayer. I see no evidence for any of these influences. In my review, I expressed my reservations about Zimmer's arguments for priestly blessings and postnatal relations,[95] and I have indicated above that swaying in prayer was a French practice rather than a German one.[96] I would like to register here my demurrals on the other two topics.[97]

First, no doubt the German Pietists opposed the French addition to the 'El Erekh Appayim' prayer, however, there is no evidence that the French version was ever recited in Germany. Thus, Ḥasidei Ashkenaz |**486**| were but defending the German practice. The French rite had little to no influence on the Eastern rite, which is almost entirely German. Why attribute the victory of the German version of 'El Erekh Appayim' to Ḥasidei Ashkenaz? The German rite triumphed here as in hundreds of other instances. Furthermore, I know of no evidence whatsoever that the German Pietists ever advocated an added seven-day menstrual abstinence. Indeed, as I pointed out in my remarks on postnatal relations, all the evidence that we possess of the hypersensitivity of Ḥasidei Ashkenaz to any form of pollution, whether physical or ritual, is with regard to *sancta* with their powerful taboo, not with regard to mundane sexual relations. Moreover, in light of the vibrant awareness of Ḥasidei Ashkenaz of sexual temptations and their almost lusty endorsement of marital sex, such a position is not only undocumented but also unlikely.

The proud claims of later cultures to be the heirs of Ḥasidei Ashkenaz, like that of R. Yo'el Sirkes (*Teshuvot ha-Baḥ ha-Yeshanot* [Frankfurt am Main, 1697], #79), should be carefully weighed, as I wrote in my review:

For time had passed and the more radical bent of the medieval Pietists had been long forgotten. Little now remained of the Pietists' legacy in the collective memory of pre-Chmielnicki Poland other than sensitivity in human relations, personal humility, rites

[94] Ibid. [95] Ibid. 226–7. [96] Above, pp. 105–6.

[97] Zimmer, *'Olam ke-Minhago Noheg* (above, n. 87), 114–23, 240–50.

of penance and an inclination to stringency (*ḥumra*). A new culture finding its voice (as Poland did in the late sixteenth and early seventeenth centuries) is often in search of distinguished antecedents, and in this case, a claim was easily made for descent from the venerated Ḥasidei Ashkenaz. Such assertions, however, may be more in the nature of acquired heraldry than actual lineage, or, if that be too strong a metaphor, more a pious self-image than a fact.[98]

Zimmer's most recent book confirms these suspicions. R. Yo'el Sirkes spoke proudly of Poland's being the heir of hasidic traditions. A generation earlier, R. Ḥayyim ben R. Betsal'el of Friedburg inveighed against the growing Polish influence—best embodied in the growing sway of R. Mosheh Isserles—in Germany and claimed that these upstarts from the East were displacing the traditions of Ḥasidei Ashkenaz, of which the German community was the proud bearer![99]

I yield to few in my esteem of Zimmer's sober scholarship. However, the hasidic influence that he occasionally invokes is not a |487| conclusion but a postulate and one I believe that we are best off without, for it obscures rather than solves the problems that he has so finely posed.

APPENDIX II

THE TEXT OF RADICAL PIETISM ANTECEDES THAT OF *SEFER ḤASIDIM I*

While not essential to my argument (though it may be of wider significance), I do believe that the author of *SH I* knew of the basic doctrines of Ḥasidei Ashkenaz and had in front of him some ur-text of *Sefer Ḥasidim*,[100] rather than the other way around—that a German Pietist wove sections of a wholly independent *SH I* into the text of *Sefer Ḥasidim*. Parts of *SH I* were ultimately included in both texts of *Sefer Ḥasidim* that have come down to us, however, sections of *SH I* were originally written, in my view, with at least some of the work and doctrines of the German Pietists in mind.

The author of *SH I* opens his work, as does the author of the *Sefer Ḥasidim*, with an announcement of the desire of many to follow the covert Will of the Creator (*retson ha-Borè*) and who only refrain from doing so out of ignorance

[98] Zimmer, *'Olam ke-Minhago Noheg* (above, n. 87), 233.

[99] Y. (Eric) Zimmer, *Gaḥaltan shel Ḥakhamim* (Be'er Sheva, 1999), 233–4.

[100] Let us remember that *SHP* (#1589) writes וכבר כתוב בספר חסידים and that shortly before his death, R. Yehudah he-Ḥasid wrote שנים [!] כרכין מן ספר חסידים, as cited by J. Freimann in his introduction to *SHP* (Frankfurt am Main, 1924), 11.

of its demands. He therefore undertakes to lay bare the demands and prescriptions of this Divine Will. He pre-empts arguments against its strangeness or even nonsense (*shetut*), which some readers may register upon perusal of the work. However, what follows in *SH I* is not the tale of Balaam's ass or that of the Midianite war advanced in the opening section of *Sefer Ḥasidim* as proof of an entirely new world of ritual and religious demands encoded in Scripture and in history,[101] which the following pages go on to partially explicate. This, indeed, would and did awaken astonishment and laughter in the minds of most Jews. The apologetic introduction of *SH I* is followed by a presentation of the 'duties of the heart', an exposition of the religious demands made of the interior man with which few would take issue. The introduction of *SH I* makes little sense on its own. It appears as if the writer is borrowing the defensive introductory style used, understandably, by German Pietists when they introduce the novel demands of the *retson ha-Borè*. |**488**|

Further, I find it difficult to conceive that only by chance does the author of *SH I* use key terms in the thought of German Pietism, such as *retson ha-Borè*, *le-zakkot et ha-rabbim*, *'arum beyir'ah*, and *lilmod 'al menat le-kayyem*, and highlights them in the early, programmatic segment of his work (sections 1–17).[102] He neutralizes these pivotal phrases by generally employing them in a general, traditional sense. *SH I* has the introduction and the idiom of *Sefer Ḥasidim* but not its distinctive doctrines. This of course may be accidental; it may also be accidental that the author entitled his work *Sefer Ḥasidim* or *Sefer Ḥasidut*,[103] a name that bears some similarity to the name of a contemporary work of R. Yehudah he-Ḥasid, *Sefer Ḥasidim*. Indeed, the titles are so similar that most scribes did not notice the difference, labeling both *Sefer Ḥasidim*.

There are some forty-three parallel passages in the two works. To my untutored eye, a number of these passages in *SH I* appear as a reworking of material found in an ur-*Sefer Ḥasidim* rather than the reverse. For example, I have difficulty seeing why someone would take the smooth formulation of *SHB*, #137 and turn it into the rough one of *SHP*, #125. The same holds true for *SHB*, #84 and *SHP*, #1000.

Again, it seems to me that the author of *SHB*, #138 noted that a moral is more effectively made with a single biblical citation in clear Hebrew, and that the further talmudic examples in Aramaic of the same point found in *SHP*, #126 only weaken its force. He further noted that the final, alternative explanation in *SHP*, #126 (*ve-'od keivan she-ḥarah apo*) makes a very effective ending for the biblical example originally given. A similar smoothing of the

[101] See pp. 8–11 above.

[102] Above, nn. 6–7.

[103] *SHB*, ##1, 38.

formulation, coupled with compression of multiple verses and elimination of alternative explanations, is found in *SHB*, #11, in contrast to *SHP*, #1979.

The issue of who copied from whom may have a bearing on the early diffusion of German Pietism. *SH I* was employed by the author of the *Sefer ha-Yir'ah*, a work either written by R. Yonah mi-Gerundi or adopted by him in his stay in northern France.[104] R. Yonah appears to have left the French academies in the mid-1220s at the latest; *SH I* had to be written well before then. Thus we can conclude that some of the major doctrines of Ḥasidei Ashkenaz |**489**| and parts of *Sefer Ḥasidim* were circulating in France even earlier, perhaps as early as the turn of the thirteenth century.

APPENDIX III

MS CAMBRIDGE ADD. 3127 (FOS. 165B–166A)

Nestled between the *Piskei R. Yitsḥak mi-Corbeil* and the *Sefer ha-Tashbets* is a brief collection of moral dicta. It lacks the pietistic intensity of *SH I* and shares nothing with the emerging system of *Sefer ha-Yir'ah*. In fact, it even contains internal contradictions in the brief span of a page or two. Who the editor was we do not know. We do know that alongside his desire to transmit all the finer minutiae of ritual performance, as reflected in the practices of the great R. Me'ir of Rothenburg and the 'saintly' (*ha-kadosh*) R. Yitsḥak of Corbeil, he also aspired to better his ways with his fellow men, to distance himself a bit more from the vanities of the world, and to regularly confront his own sinful nature. I publish here this collection in the belief that there were others in his time and place who shared these aspirations.

[סליק תשב"ץ]

[לקוטי מוסר][105]

אתחיל ליקוטים אחרים

[1] שלא להביט בנשים ובמלבושיהם[106] ולא בפני רשע[107] ולא בפני צלם.[108]

[2] שלא לעשות לחבירו דבר השנוי לו.

[104] Above, n. 89.

[105] The title is my own, as is the numbering of the sections.

[106] *'Avodah Zarah* 21a–b. Significantly, the editor of the earlier *Sefer ha-Oreh* (Lvov, 1905) opened his work with the same talmudic passage (p. 3).

[107] *Megillah* 28a.

[108] Likely the writer's own aversion, possibly one acquired from the spirit of the teachings of Ḥasidei Ashkenaz (see J. Katz, *Exclusiveness and Tolerance: Studies in Jewish–Gentile Relations in Medieval and Modern Times* [Oxford, 1961], ch. 8, though no specific ban on looking at a cross is found, to the best of my knowledge, in hasidic literature). {See S. Sassoon, ed., *Moshav Zekenim 'al ha-Torah* (London, 1959), 344:

[3] שלא לרדוף אחרי הכבוד ולא לשמוע [חסר].
[4] שלא לעשות דברים של קלות [רא]ש ולא גנאי של תורה ולומדיה.
[5] שלא לה[ו]נות לחבירו ושלא להקניטו בדברים.[109]
[6] שלא להקניטו בדברים [שלא לגנ]וב דעת בריות וכל שכן ממונם.
[7] שלא לחשוד בכשרים.|490|
[8] שלא ליטול שררה על איש אלא לשם שמים.
[9] שלא לחניף [!].
[10] שלא לשנוא התוכחות.
[11] שלא לזלזל בכבוד אב ואם וחכמים.
[12] שלא להזכיר ולישבע שם[!] שמים לבטלה.
[13] שלא ליהנות מסעודת הרשות ר"ל [רצה לומר] כמו הזמנת שכיניו אם לא לדבר מצוה. נר[אה] שהוא הזמנת רבו או ר"ח [ראש חודש] וח"ה [וחול המועד] זהו סעודת מצוה.
[14] שלא למלא פיו שחוק מן הלב.
[15] שלא להתלוצץ.
[16] שלא לקפח שכר חבירו.
[17] שלא לתת תפארת בעצמו לשום דבר.
[18] שלא לטייל בחינם.[110]
[19] שלא ליהנות מן העולם דרך תענוג בחול כ"א [כי אם] לקיים חיזוק גופו. ובפני רבים מותר פן יחשב ללעג.[111]
[20] שלא לפרוש מן התורה.
[21] והר"ר משה היה מחתך הבשר דק דק שלא לטעום טעם בשר חשוב.[112]
[22] שלא להלבין פני חבירו.
[23] שלא לקרותו בכינוייו.[113]
[24] אדם חייב להיות כשכיר יום[114] להיות זהיר ביום שאם תבטל ת"ת [תלמוד תורה] ביום שישלם בלילה.

אל תפנו אל האלילים (ויקרא יט, ד) פרש"י לעובדם. וקשה דבמס[כת] שבת בפ[רק] השואל [קמט ע"א] מוכח דאפי[לו] לראותם אסור, דתניא התם ודיוקנא עצמה אפי' בחול אסור, שנא' אל תפנו אל האלילים מדעתכם לראותם. ותי[רץ] הר' שמואל דמוקמ[ינן] לה ביחידאה ולית הלכתא כותיה. ונהגו בני עירו לעיין בצורות שעל התועבה. והרי"ח [כינוי רווח לר' יהודה החסיד] אומר הואיל וסתמא דתלמודא דידין מסיק בפ[רק] השואל אסור, ודאי כך ההלכה. וכן כתב רב ניסים גאון הלכה דאסור לראותם. וראוי להחמיר הואיל וכתיב (משלי ה: ה) הרחק מעלי[ה] דרכיך ואל תקרב אל פתח ביתה.

On the use of *vadai*, see Daniel Goldschmidt's remarks cited in my *Yeinam: Saḥar be-Yeinam shel Goyim—'al Gilgulah shel Halakhah be-'Olam ha-Ma'aseh*, rev. edn. (Jerusalem, 2017), 54 n. 54.}

109 Correction on the basis of S. Emanuel, *Shivrei Luḥot* (above, n. 72), 202 n. 66.

110 Strolling in the town was one of the few entertainments available in this period. See, for example, the medieval ruling, endorsed by the *Shulḥan 'Arukh* ('Oraḥ Ḥayyim', 554: 21), against strolling in the market on Tish'ah be-Av 'lest one come to שחוק וקלות [ראש] והתול'. More probable, however, is that טיול here denotes 'relaxing', as in *Sukkah* 28b: אוכל ושותה ומטייל בסוכה. This secondary meaning also obtained in medieval rabbinic Hebrew, e.g. in *Tosafot*, *Betsah* 12a, s.v. *dilma* (end): דהא אשכחן נמי דמשחקין בכדור ביו"ט ברה"ר אע"ג דליכא אלא טיול. Several of the exhortations in *SHP* against טיולין (##278, 770, 815) refer to relaxation rather than to strolling.

111 This passage, together with #21 and #29, was copied into the *Piskei Rabbenu Perets* in MS Paris, Bibliothèque Nationale 407, fo. 326d (above, n. 82).

112 Thus also in the above manuscript.

113 *Megillah* 28a.

114 The metaphor is that of the *Semag* (above, p. 99); however, it is used here differently.

[25] ואמת כי התורה נמשלת למים שיורדים בנחת לזכוכית.[115]

[26] וחייב לעשות מדברי תורה קבע ומכל דבר עראי, לבד מן המצות שהם חובה עליו בגופו כגון תפילין כתיק[ו]נו, ובשאר מצוות שאי אפשר לעשותן ע״י |491| אחר, ודאי הוא חייב להקדימן לתלמוד תורה.

[27] ואין לענות נפשו יותר מדאי. ואם חטא ילך וילמוד יותר מ(ל)פני שהתורה מכפרת דכת[יב] חסד ואמת יכופר עון ואין חסד ואמת אלא תורה.[116]

[28] ואין לו לאדם לטרוח יותר מדאי בממון כי משלו יתן לו.[117]

[29] אילו[118] עבירות שחייב אדם להזהיר בנו כשהוא בן ח׳ או ט׳ שנים כדי שיהא (יוכל) [רגיל][119] להיות נזהר כשיהיה גדול:

שלא ל[הוציא] שם שמים לבטלה. שלא לספר לשון הרע ושלא לדבר בחבי[רו].[120]

שלא לדבר בחמ[ה].[121]

שלא לדבר דב[רים ב]טלים ומגאווה ומניבול פה ולצון.

[30] ואין לו לאד[ם] ליצטער בעינוי[ם], לא בתעניות ולא בעינוי נפש, רק כפי היכולת כדי שלא יבא לידי ביטול עסקיו וכל שכן מצותיו. אבל טוב להתענות בכל כ״ד שבועות ב׳ או ג׳ להיות מאנשי המעמד.[122]

[31] ופעם אחד בכל חדש (המעמד) היה נוהג הק[דוש] הר״ר יצחק [להתענות].[123]

[32] ובאותן הימים יתודה וישוב בתשובה שלימה ויתחרט במעשיו הרעים, ויספרם לרב ויאמר כזאת וזאת עשיתי[124] ויבק[ש] מאת הש[ם] מחילה (ו)מהם |492| ושיזכינו מעת[ה] הוא וכל ישראל לטובה ויפרש(!)[125] מה שירצה.

115 I know neither the source nor the purpose of this statement.

116 See *Sukkah* 49b and *Pesikta de-Rav Kahana*, ed. B. Mandelbaum (New York, 1963), *piska* 15, s.v. *Rav Abba* (p. 255).

117 The last phrase should probably be translated 'for He [God] will provide for him'.

118 This section, barring **שלא לדבר בחמ׳**, was copied into the *Piskei Rabbenu Perets* (above, n. 82). On this basis, I have indented these lines in my transcription; in the Cambridge manuscript, there is no indication that these four dicta form a single unit.

119 Thus in MS Bibliothèque Nationale (ibid.).

120 Corrected according to Emanuel (above, n. 72), 110. MS Bibliothèque Nationale reads **ולא דברי כזבים** instead of **ושלא לדבר בחבי[רו]**.

121 Missing in MS Bibliothèque Nationale.

122 Fasting once every twenty-four weeks will yield two fasts a year or sometimes three, if one locates oneself at the beginning of the cycle of *ma'amadot*. (My thanks to Yaakov Sussman for clarifying this point.)

123 See above, pp. 104–5 and n. 15. At first blush, it would appear that R. Yitsḥak was relying upon the passage in the Talmud Yerushalmi in *Ta'anit* 2: 12 according to the version found in *SHB*, #617. However, in view of the fact that the reading found in our texts of the Yerushalmi is corrobor-ated by *testimoniae* of both R. El'azar Roke'aḥ (*Roke'aḥ, Hilkhot Ḥasidut* end) and R. Yitsḥak Or Zarua' (*Or Zarua'*, i [Zhitomir, 1862], #321), the passage in *SHB* would seem to be a scribal error rather than evidence of a version which was circulating in Ashkenaz in the thirteenth century. The parallel text in *SHP*, #67 equally suggests a scribal error in *SHB*. (I would like to thank Yaakov Sussman for pointing this out to me.) {Y. Y. Stal punctuates this passage somewhat differently and accepts the reading of **מעמד**; see his edition of *Teshuvot Rabbenu El'azar mi-Vormaiza, ha-Roke'aḥ* (Jerusalem, 2014), 74.}

124 This is the only influence of German Pietism in the text, though note that the confession is to a rabbi, not to a *ḥakham* or Ḥasid.

125 It is not clear whether one should emend **מה** to **ממה**, in which case the phrase would mean 'he should abstain [from which pleasures] he chooses', or whether one should emend **יפרוש** to **יפריש**,

[33] וכל אותן הימים יתן בנדבה עבור שמיע[ת] תפילה.

[34] וטוב שלא לאכול יום אחד בשבו[ע].[126] ואם לא יכול להתענו[ת], טוב שיתנדב(ד) ויפריש מידי יום [ב]יום(?) בקביעות.[127]

[סליק ליקוטי מוסר]

[מכאן ואילך פסקי ר' יצחק מקורביל]

which would yield 'he should set aside [for charity] what he wishes'. See above, n. 80.

[126] See above, p. 83 n. 15 and p. 104.

[127] The meaning is obscure. The text probably should read **ויפר[ו]ש**, i.e. if he cannot withstand weekly fasts, he should refrain regularly from eating certain foods as a mark of abstemiousness. See above, n. 15.

CHAPTER FOUR

Pietists and Kibbitzers

THIS ESSAY was written as a reply to criticism of 'Piety, Pietism, and German Pietism: *Sefer Ḥasidim I* and the Influence of Ḥasidei Ashkenaz'. It appeared in the *Jewish Quarterly Review*, 96/1 (2006), which contained a forum on *Sefer Ḥasidim*. One of the articles was that of Edward Fram, 'German Pietism and Sixteenth- and Early Seventeenth-Century Polish Rabbinic Culture', to which I referred in the opening sentence of this article. A second section has been added for this collection of essays as the current online Princeton University *Sefer Hasidim* Database has given rise to queries as to my grouping of surviving manuscripts of *Sefer Ḥasidim*. The third section ('Appendix') placed in the public domain hitherto unpublished short manuscripts that bear directly upon the argument of the original essay. For technical reasons it could not, at the time, be appended to the printed essay. It appeared only in the *Jewish Quarterly Review* web version of the article.

I

THE LACK OF INFLUENCE OF RADICAL PIETISM

Edward Fram's article shows that German Pietism as a radical religious and social movement was no more influential in Poland in the sixteenth and seventeenth centuries than it had been in medieval western Europe. In retrospect, it appears that it could hardly have been otherwise. The standard *Sefer Ḥasidim*, first published, as noted by Fram, in Bologna (1538) and quickly republished in Basel (1580) and Kraków (1581), is a compound work, opening with the conventional pietism of the first 152 sections and continuing with the radical one of the German Pietists. For every passage of radical pietism there is a counter-passage of the conventional sort, the result being that no one could infer from the work any coherent religious position. One would find there the position that one sought, and the selections would reflect more the reader's religious sensibilities than the influence of either of the two conflicting movements embodied in the work. And, as Fram points out, Polish ethicists and thinkers were singularly uninclined to the distinctive doctrines of German Pietism and never reproduced those passages that expressed the idiosyncratic agenda of Ḥasidei Ashkenaz.

His conclusions simply extend mine about the Middle Ages to eastern Europe in the early modern period. I argued in my essay that German Pietism as a radical religious and social movement was wholly without influence in France and Spain, and even in Germany itself. Although the conventional pietistic impulses expressed by the *Sefer ha-Yir'ah* and in the first 152 sections of *Sefer Ḥasidim*, which I have entitled *SH I*,[1] found an answering echo of assent in some medieval hearts, the extreme, idiosyncratic doctrines of German Pietism fell on deaf ears. I added an appendix, in which I challenged Eric Zimmer's recent contention that certain medieval religious practices continued on in Poland as a result of the influence of German Pietism.[2] I was addressing the specific arguments of Zimmer, not expressing an opinion about Poland generally, a subject in which I have no expertise. Unfortunately, I did not clearly delineate the appendix as dealing with halakhic matters only and with Zimmer's claims specifically, even though that was its exclusive content.[3] As the rest of the article dealt with the impact of German Pietism on the spirituality of medieval Jewry, it was only natural for readers to assume that the appendix addressed this issue in Poland, and my sweeping introductory two sentences in the appendix only added to the confusion.[4]

Fram points out that the notion that children's deeds affect the status of the parents in the other world is a recurrent theme in Polish Jewish literature and that it is contrary to the ideas expressed in *SH I*. Indeed it is. However, this notion has little or nothing to do with pietism. This, in turn, leads to an allied consideration and to a major criticism that has been leveled at my article by some readers, namely, that I did not reckon with the *Sefer Ḥasidim* published by M. Hershler[5] and the sundry sections of *Sefer Ḥasidim* that were copied and incorporated in various manuscripts, and that these omissions significantly alter the manuscript count that I provided in the conclusion of Part I of that essay.[6]

I wrote the essay because I felt that there was a need to distinguish between pietists and the simply pious, and an equal need to differentiate

[1] Ch. 3 above.

[2] Above, pp. 107–10.

[3] The appendix was initially written as a part of my review essay of Zimmer's book in the *AJS Review*, 23 (1999), 223–34, repr. in my *Collected Essays*, i (Oxford, 2013), 294–307.

[4] Above, p. 107: 'I have discussed the putative influence of German Pietism in Germany itself, to the south in Italy, to the west in France, and south-west in Provence and Spain. A word may be in order about its supposed influence in the east, namely in Austria and Poland.'

[5] *Genuzot*, 1 (1984), 128–62.

[6] Above, pp. 89–90.

between pietists and German Pietists. I had not realized that it was also necessary to distinguish between pietists and guidance counselors. I warned that use of numerology did not a German Pietist make, even if Ḥasidei Ashkenaz contributed greatly to the legitimacy of *gematriyah*.[7] I similarly cautioned that accepting the esoteric lore (*torat ha-sod*) of the Kalonymides and the German Pietists did not entail any assent to the radical doctrines of Ḥasidei Ashkenaz.[8] I should have added that following some of the counsel found in *Sefer Ḥasidim* did not in any way mean acceptance or even knowledge of its radical social and religious agenda.

German Pietism is characterized not simply by its extremist ideology, but also by its inveterate desire to proffer advice on all aspects of human relations. In its own way, *Sefer Ḥasidim* is a Guide to the Perplexed, not the philosophically perplexed but those perplexed by the world and its problems. Are there difficulties with parents? *Sefer Ḥasidim* has the answers. Does one have problems with children or with one's spouse or with women generally or with one's fellow man? There are words of guidance on these subjects, too. Do the forces of the unseen world bother you? *Sefer Ḥasidim* can help you in dealing with dreams, demons, ghosts, and whatnot. I mean no disrespect, but these God-intoxicated gentlemen were also inveterate kibbitzers. In this regard, they are truly unique. I know of no work like *Sefer Ḥasidim* in Christian or Jewish literature.

R. Yehudah he-Ḥasid was a mighty name in Jewish tradition, as was R. El'azar of Worms, author of the *Sefer ha-Roke'aḥ* and the greatest mystic of Ashkenaz. Their alleged authorship lent an aura of authority to the advice of *Sefer Ḥasidim*, and it was only natural for people to turn to this unique work for some guidance in the tangled world of their daily existence. Where else could the perplexed turn to? However, taking some of their advice in practical matters does not make one a pietist, conventional or radical. Pietism addresses man's approach to God: fear of God, love of God, and cleaving to Him (*yir'ah, ahavah, devekut*). It deals with self-transcendence—humility and self-abnegation—and it entails a spiritual discipline whose goal is the emancipation of the soul from the dictates of the body. Far from addressing how to deal with the vanities of this world, pietism seeks to distance man from them so that he stands at all times in God's presence only. The manuscript printed by Hershler reflects none of these concerns. All 158 sections deal with practical advice; not a single one treats a pietistic issue. The same holds true for the selections from *Sefer Ḥasidim* found in various manuscripts.

I fear that a single sentence in a somewhat dramatic, concluding paragraph

[7] Above, pp. 92–3. [8] Above, pp. 93–4.

of Part I of my essay threw some readers off course. It read: 'Indeed, the most influential pietists in Germany were not German Pietists, for *SH I* had a diffusion far greater than that of *Sefer Ḥasidim* itself.'[9] Some readers took that sentence as alleging that *SH I* was more influential than the vast potpourri of a book entitled *Sefer Ḥasidim*. Such a claim, if made, would be patently false. '*Sefer Ḥasidim*' is used in this paragraph, as throughout much of the essay, as a metonym for the distinctive pietistic doctrines of Ḥasidei Ashkenaz, as the immediately preceding sentences and the subsequent ones of that paragraph clearly indicate. My essay addressed the influence of a religious movement, not the popularity of a book.

To let readers discover for themselves what in the multifaceted *Sefer Ḥasidim* did in fact interest medieval owners and scribes, I have transcribed all the fragments of *Sefer Ḥasidim* scattered in various manuscripts. Considerations of cost make their publication unfeasible in the printed form of the *JQR*; however, they may be found in the web edition of this article on Project Muse at <https://muse.jhu.edu/article/190747>. However one may characterize these selections, they evince no pietistic interest whatsoever. Doubly revealing is MS Bodley Mich. 569 (Neubauer 1098), a copy of the prayer book in the western Ashkenazic rite, written, to all appearances, prior to 1289, possibly even before 1283, the date of death of R. Me'ir of Rothenburg.[10] As is common with medieval manuscripts, other small works were also included in the codex, some in the body of the text, some along the margins. In the miscellaneous section at the end, the copyist transcribed *Pirkei Shirah*, a calendar for the years 1289–1328, *Sefer ha-Yir'ah*, a page of *Sefer Ḥasidim*, and then *Derekh Erets Zuta*. The copying of both *Sefer ha-Yir'ah* and *Derekh Erets Zuta* reflects some quasi-pietistic leanings and an interest in proper and moral conduct on the part of the owner. What did he choose to be copied from *Sefer Ḥasidim*—its emphasis on humility and self-effacement? Its moral tone and dicta? Its radical social and religious teachings? Nothing of the sort. At most, he was seriously interested in devout prayer but nothing beyond that.

One correction, however, I must make to my count.[11] I did not include the Boesky manuscript of the Jewish Theological Seminary.[12] A scholar was working on it in the early 1980s, and the manuscript was declared out of bounds to all other researchers. As I had never seen the manuscript, nor was any statement made about it verifiable, I omitted it. I, and most other scholars, were unaware that when that scholar left the Seminary some fifteen years later,

[9] Above, pp. 89–90.

[10] See M. Beit-Arié, ed., *Addenda and Corrigenda to Vol. I* (Oxford, 1994), 171 at nos. 1098, 1097.

[11] Above, p. 90.

[12] MS 45.

the manuscript was again placed in circulation, since no announcement of its availability was made at that time. I have since consulted it and found that it is, indeed, a sixteenth-century copy of much of Wistinetzki's text. My count therefore is: four out of eight manuscripts contain *SH I*, two of the four remaining ones contain the compound text of *SH I* and *Sefer Ḥasidim*, and two out of four have only the text of *Sefer Ḥasidim*. The above-cited paragraph[13] should therefore read:

> Four of the eight extant manuscripts of *Sefer Ḥasidim*, including the oldest dated one, contain only *SH I*. In other words, half the manuscripts of *Sefer Ḥasidim* are not manuscripts of *Sefer Ḥasidim* and their existence does not attest to the influence of German Pietism, but, on the contrary, to the influence of an ideology opposed to the basic tenets of German Pietism. Two of the four remaining ones contain all of *SH I* followed by sections of *Sefer Ḥasidim*, that is to say, they are composites, as is also, after a moment's reflection, the standard *Sefer Ḥasidim* itself. The standard *Sefer Ḥasidim*, first printed in 1538, and reprinted over twenty times before the twentieth century, is, in reality, a compound. It contains two separate and distinct *Sifrei Ḥasidim*, each with its own religious vision. It embodies the teachings of two sharply divergent groups of religious virtuosi, who proffered to their readers radically different itineraries to God. Only two manuscripts, the one published by Wistinetzki in 1891 and another in the library of the Jewish Theological Seminary, lack *SH I*, that is to say, only two manuscripts are cut wholly from the cloth of Ḥasidei Ashkenaz. Only two of eight manuscripts accurately reflect the teachings of German Pietism. Apparently, the radical and idiosyncratic doctrine of that movement awakened little interest, found few followers, and, to all appearances, had little cultural resonance.

Indeed, while the revised number of manuscripts might point to some measure of diffusion of the radical pietism of Ḥasidei Ashkenaz, an investigation of the subsequent sources has evidenced none whatsoever—even in Poland.

II

THE CURRENTLY AVAILABLE PRINCETON UNIVERSITY *SEFER HASIDIM* DATABASE

The same misimpression may well arise from the classification of manuscripts found in the Princeton University *Sefer Hasidim* Database, which had not been set up when 'Piety, Pietism, and German Pietism' was published. Two factors determined my count—size and content. Before I begin my tabulation, I would like to state that in this series of collected essays, I have always listed

[13] See above, pp. 89–90.

manuscripts by catalogue number. In this count, I will use their shelf number, as the manuscripts are thus listed in the database of Princeton. The reader interested in finding the appropriate catalogue number should use the Bibliography of Manuscripts at the end of the book. The database, as I have already noted, while listing a number of fragmentary collections (MSS Universitätsbibliothek Freiburg 483; Bodley, Opp. 487; Zurich, Zentralbibliothek D 74; Zurich, Zentralbibliothek Heidenheim 51; Frankfurt hebr. oct. 94), leaves out a few other fragmentary collections (MSS Bodley Or. 608, 231b–232a; Hamburg Staats- und Universitätsbibliothek 213, fos. 24b–25a; Bodley, Mich. 569, fo. 104b). In my essay (above, p. 89, nn. 28, 29) I did not list any such brief fragments. My minimum requirement was twenty sections or more. For this reason the Freiburg and Zurich entries and MS Bodley Opp. 487 do not appear in my Parma count, nor does MS Bodley, Mich. 155 appear in my Bologna list. Similarly, I do not refer to MS Frankfurt hebr. oct. 94 and MS Zurich, Zentralbibliothek Heidenheim 51, listed by Princeton in the 'mixed groups'.

I did not list the two other Bodley manuscripts in the 'Parma group' and discounted MS Jewish Theological Seminary 2499 and MS Vatican 285 in the 'mixed group' for the simple reason stated in my reply—their content is not pietistic.

For clarity's sake, and for an evaluation of the pietistic tendencies or absence thereof in the fragments, it is wisest to address each group of the Princeton project separately. The Princeton website classified the various manuscripts and the first group reads thus:

The Parma Group
MS Parma 3280
MS Boesky 45
MS UB Freiburg 483
MS Bodl. Lib. Opp. 614
MS Bodl. Lib. Or. 146
MS Bodl. Lib. Opp. 487
MS Zurich Zentralbibliothek D 74

It is important to read the description given by the project:

MS Boesky 45 is the third largest manuscript in our collection, containing not only the major part of the Parma edition but also presenting the text in the same order. It is divided into 826 sections, some of which coincide with the beginning of the paragraphs in MS Parma. Sometimes, however, big clusters of paragraphs present in *Parma* are absent in Boesky (sections 364–383; 1235–1260, 1630–1665, 1875–1901), while some passages of MS Boesky are not included in the Parma edition, such as the major part of sections 117, 141, 411, and the whole last section, 826. Unfortunately, the ink of sections 826 and 592 faded away, rendering them impossible to transcribe.

It seems that MS UB Freiburg 483 also presents the same version as the MSS Parma and Boesky. In this short fragment, the text not only runs in the same order as in MS Parma, but is also almost (literary) [literally] identical with it. For this reason, although the Freiburg fragment is not paragraphed by the scribe, we took the liberty of dividing it into paragraphs and numbering them in accordance with MS Parma.

MS Bodl. Lib. Opp. 614 and MS Bodl. Lib. Or. 146 contain two identical compendia of *Sefer Hasidim*. Their paragraphs appear in various parts of the Parma edition (from paragraph 211 to paragraph 1152) yet in a totally different order of sequence. The phrasing also differs considerably, which would have placed these manuscripts in the 'mixed' group (see below), if it were not for a few paragraphs that can only be found in MS Parma.

MS Bodl. Lib. Opp. 487 contains three numbered paragraphs from *Sefer Hasidim* (204, 205, 206) fully corresponding to MS Parma, paragraphs 210, 211, 212.

For some reason, MS Zurich Zentralbibliothek D 74 is not described there in the section on grouping. However, a description is found prior to the grouping in the general list of manuscripts on the website. The relevant portion reads:

Zentralbibliothek Zurich D 74

Two folios of *Sefer Hasidim* are reused in cardboard binding for a collection of [Christian] sermons . . . The manuscript is a fragment of the Parma recension, fully corresponding to its paragraphs 331–338 (f. 1) and 394–397 (f. 2).

I employed the term *Sefer Ḥasidim* in the essay as a metonym for the radical pietism embedded in the *Sefer Ḥasidim* that Wistinetzki published in 1891 from MS Parma, De Rossi 1133. Keeping in mind that that manuscript is a vast collection of 1,983 paragraphs, composed of many scrolls strung together in no clear pattern and touching on the widest range of subjects, the central question is whether those radical sections are found in these other manuscripts in critical mass, if at all. The fact that some manuscripts have some fifty paragraphs that follow one another in the same sequence as that of Parma does not in any way indicate that it originally had the same radical sections as MS Parma, found some 100 paragraphs earlier (or later). It only means that one or two of the scrolls that went into the Parma manuscript formed also another self-contained manuscript.

Clearly, MS Bodl. Lib. Opp. 614, as well as MS Bodl. Lib. Or. 146 (both transcribed and annotated in the web version of this article[14]) and MS Bodl.

[14] See below, pp. 127–9.

Lib. Opp. 487 contain no doctrine of radical pietism. Indeed, they are altogether unlinked to any pietist concern. MS Zurich Zentralbibliothek D 74 has one passage (parallel to *SHP*, #335) which may reflect the sharp distinction between *resha'im* and *tsaddikim* found in the ideology of radical pietism. However, there is not enough material, to put it mildly, to make any determination as to the meaning of these terms here. We have no way of knowing what other scrolls of *Sefer Ḥasidim* this manuscript had. MS Freiburg UB 483 shares to a limited extent the conventional pietistic aspirations of *SH I* (##981–5). Even if the missing original contained the entire following section, 986, it would still be in the conventional mode, because the authors of *SH I* naturally shared with their radical counterparts—and, one may assume, also with Talmudists of all stripes—the aspiration for a daily fulfillment of the commandments of *tallit and tefillin*.[15] Thus, in terms of radical pietism, the 'Parma group' contains only two manuscripts, as stated above in the text: the original Parma manuscript published by Wistinetzki and JTS Boesky 45.

The Princeton *Sefer Ḥasidim* project also classified the Bologna group. It reads:

Bologna group:
Bologna printed edition of 1538
MS Ambrosiana X 111
MS Bodley, Opp. 340
MS Bodley, Mich. 155
MS Moscow 103
MS Nîmes Bibl. mun. Séguier 26

The project description states:

A specific feature of this group consists in the fact that all three[!] manuscripts contain a part of the first 152 paragraphs of the Bologna printed edition.

MS Ambrosiana X 111 presents nearly the same version of *Sefer Hasidim* as paragraphs 1–152 of the Bologna print; the manuscript, however, is not paragraphed. Therefore, in order to facilitate the comparison, we divided the text of the manuscript

[15] On the general laxity in both the Ashkenazic and Provençal communities in the observance of *tallit*, *tefillin*, and *mezuzah*, see A. Ravitzky, '"Hatsivi Lakh Tsiyyunim" le-Tsiyyon: Gilgulo shel Ra'ayon', in id., *'Al Da'at ha-Makom: Meḥkarim ba-Hagut ha-Yehudit u-ve-Toledoteiha* (Jerusalem, 1991), 37–41. It also appeared simultaneously in the collection edited by Ravitzky, *Erets Yisra'el ba-Hagut ha-Yehudit bi-Yemei ha-Beinayim* (Jerusalem, 1991), 4–8. E. Kanarfogel, 'Rabbinic Attitudes toward Non-Observance in the Medieval Period', in J. J. Schacter, ed., *Jewish Tradition and the Non-Traditional Jew* (Northvale, NJ, 1992), 7–14; S. Emanuel, ed., *Teshuvot ha-Ge'onim ha-Ḥadashot ve-'Imam Teshuvot, Pesakim u-Ferushim me-et Ḥakhmei Provence ha-Rishonim* (Jerusalem, 1995), #161, 233–7, and notes ad loc. There is no evidence that the conventional pietists' *tallit* differed from that of the rest of the community. R. Shimshon of Sens states that the hooded *tallit*, the 'capuchin', was, if he recalls correctly, the *tallit* worn by Ḥasidei Ashkenaz; see above, p. 29, n. 57.

into paragraphs and assigned numbers to them in accordance with the first 152 paragraphs of the Bologna edition.

MS Bodl. Lib. Opp. 340 was divided by the scribe into 63 paragraphs, which we numbered according to their order of sequence. This manuscript also contains the text of the first 152 Bologna paragraphs except for paragraphs 103–116, which literally dropped out: in the middle of the MS Bodl. Lib. Opp. 340, paragraph 47, a sentence corresponding to the one from paragraph 102 of the Bologna edition breaks off and jumps to the beginning of Bologna, paragraph 117.

MS Bodl. Lib. Mich. 155 is also sectioned by the scribe and numbered by us. It contains paragraphs 1–16 of the Bologna print.

The project does not here describe the Moscow or Nîmes manuscripts, however, a description is found in the general list of manuscripts on their website. It reads:

Moscow 103

Moscow 103 (ff. 100r–124v) is dated to the 15th century and contains the first 152 paragraphs of the Bologna edition, with the exception of paragraph 113.

Nîmes Bibl. mun. Séguier 26

Probably the earliest preserved copy of *Sefer Hasidim*, dated on paleographical grounds to the 13th century; written in Ashkenazi semi-cursive script in three columns. Pricking in hard point; lines ruled in plummet, foliated 156–175 in Roman numerals by a modern hand. *Sefer Hasidim* is subdivided by many minor and two major rubrics: *zeh niqra (sefer ha-hasidim)* (f. 155v) and *hilkhot (teshuvah)* (f. 164r). The text breaks off in the middle of paragraph 62. Then follows one folio with the table of contents of another book, which ends the codex.

The fragmentary nature of MS Bodley, Mich. 155 is clearly stated and it was discounted for this reason. For the same reason MS Bodley, Or. 608, which has Bologna ##1–5, 99–101, was omitted.

The 'mixed group' in the Princeton project reads:

MS JTS 2499
MS Vatican 285
MS Cambridge Add. 379
MS Bodl. Lib. Opp. Add. 34
MS Frankfurt Ms. hebr. oct. 94
MS Zurich, Zentralbibliothek Heid. 51

An inspection of the contents of the Frankfurt and Zurich fragments shows no pietistic intent,[16] and neither do the JTS manuscript printed below and the Vatican manuscript published by M. Hershler in *Genuzot*, 1 (1984), 128–62.

[16] Section 24 of the Frankfurt fragment has an abbreviated version of Parma #1707 which

The following appendix appeared only in the *Jewish Quarterly Review* web version of the article.

III

APPENDIX

As my concern is the subject matter of these selections rather than the meaning of any specific passage, I have simply transcribed the text as found, emended some of the more obvious errors, and provided the basic references. I have made no attempt at a critical edition. As the notes are for orientation only, I have used the standard, readily available *Yalkut Shim'oni*, even though its text may not reflect at times that of the medieval original. Given a reference in the *Yalkut Shim'oni*, the interested reader can readily trace which of the numerous parallel midrashic versions the author had in mind. In some places the transcriptions and meanings are obscure, especially in the Zurich manuscript, but never the topic addressed. I have excluded fragments from Byzantine[17] or Yemenite manuscripts, or those later than the seventeenth century, as they lie outside the period and provenance of my discussion.[18]

1. MS Bodley Mich. 569 (Neubauer 1098) (Germany, prior to 1289), fo. 104b[19]

בספר חסידים[20]

[1] **נמצא כתוב**[21] שזאת הברכה מ[ו]עילה וטובה לאומרה: יהי רצון מלפניך א להינו וא להי

concludes, 'he should rather give it to *yir'ei ha-Shem*, who study so as to perform the commandments'. However, if one doesn't know the specific meaning of *yir'ei ha-Shem* and *le-kayyem et ha-mitsvot*, as one can scarcely know from this fragment, the passage is almost a truism.

[17] MS Vatican 285, from which Hershler published (above, n. 5), is of Byzantine provenance. Nevertheless, one must reckon with this version in assessing the impact of *Sefer Ḥasidim* in the Latin West, as a 14th/15th-century Italian manuscript is found in the Jewish Theological Seminary (MS 2499) containing the same text as that of Hershler's, beginning with sect. 14 (fos. 1–29).

[18] A question mark attached to a word or letter signifies that the reading is questionable; {?} separated by a space indicates that an entire word is illegible. The marker (*) denotes that the scribe himself indicated that the word or letter should be deleted. The abbreviation *SHB* denotes the Bologna 1538 edition of *Sefer Ḥasidim*, *SHP* that of J. Wistinetzki (Berlin, 1891), *SHG* that of Hirshler in *Genuzot* (above, n. 5). I have bracketed the references of *SHP* simply to avoid confusion with *SHB*, not to privilege in any way *SHB* as a source. Whenever possible, I have preserved the spacing and paragraphing of the originals. (Several sections of the Bologna text were omitted in some subsequent editions; see, for example, above, p. 49 n. 119. None of these omitted passages are cited in our manuscripts. It thus seemed wiser to use here the numbering found in the widely available edition of Reuven Margoliot published by Mosad ha-Rav Kook rather than that of the rare first edition.)

[19] See p. 121 above.

[20] I have printed in bold those words that the scribe wrote large. Rabbi Y. Y. Stal has pointed out to me that the first six sections of this manuscript have since been published in *Sefer Pitḥei Teshuvah: Sheloshah Sefarim Niftaḥim: Seder Teshuvah, Marpe Nefesh, Teshuvah mi-Ḥayyim*, ed. E. Mantsur (Jerusalem, 2011), 41–2.

[21] *SHB*, #485 (*SHP*, #1568).

אבותי׳ שתמצא נחת רוח וקורת רוח בנו בכל מעשיך ושנמצא נחת רוח מלפניך ויגולו מידת רחמיך על מידותיך ותתנהג עם בניך במדת הרחמים ותיכנס להם מלפנים משורת הדין. ואם יראה אד[ם] שמים פתוח(!) יאמ[ר] זה התפילה כי ר׳ ישמעא׳ כהן גדול אמרה בשעה שאמ׳ לו הקב״ה בני ברכני.[22]

[2] העושה ברכה לבטלה כגון ציצית ותפילין שאינם מתוקנים כדין וסבור שמתוקנים כהלכה. אם יש אדם צדיק וחכם בעיר שיודע לתקן לתקנו ואינו שואל לו, בידוע שהוא מזיד. לכן כל אדם ישאל לחכם ממנו. וצריך לבדוק תמיד בטליתו שלא יהא מנותק חוט אחד ויברך ברכה לבטלה. ואם יש לו טלית כהלכה ולא בדק ימים רבים ואחר ימים בדק ומצא מנותק חוט אחד, יש לו להתענות באותו יום שנמצא מנותק ונתעטף בו. ואם שאר פסול נמצא בו, ידע שמתחילה לא היה מתוקן כראוי וכהלכה ובירך ברכה לבטלה, על הברכה חייב לתת עשרה זהובים.[23] ואם יש לו ליתן יתן למי שהוא ירא שמים ונצרך לכך. ולא ידבר עוד סיחת(!) חולין בבית הכנסת ולא ידבר שום דבר כשהוא משבח לקב״ה.

[3] וטוב לכל איש שהוא ירא שמים ובמצותיו חפץ לילך כל היום עם טלית קטן כדי שלא יהלך ד׳ אמות בלא ציצית, כי זאת תשובה חשובה למברך ברכה לבטלה על הטלית. ואם עני הוא [ו]מברך ברכה לבטל׳ ואין ידו משגת ליתן י׳ זהובים, אדם עשיר יאמ׳ לו או תתן זהובים או תתענה כמה ימים. כך אתה צריך להתענות על כל פעם שבירך ברכה לבטלה.

[4] או אם קיבל תפילין ממי שבקי בהן ואמר אין צריך לבודקו או ממאן דאמ׳ משנה לשנה ולא בדק לאחר מכאן, ומצא אותיות מחוקו׳, אין צריך להתענות כמו שאמרנו למעלה לגבי ציצית אע״פ שהן קדושין, מאחר שהתפילין (מכו׳) מכוסין לא הצריכו חכמ׳ לבודקן.[24] לכך כשמצאן מחוקין אין עונש דינו חמור מפני שבירך ברכה [לבט]לה כמו על ציצית. כי הציצית הוא נראה לעינים ויכול לתקן. אבל סופר עונשו חמור מאד מפני שלא היה לו לכתוב תפילן ומזוזות עד שיהא לו דיו טוב וקלף טוב. ועתה אין לו דיו וקלף טוב ואעפ״י [כן] הוא כותב וגורם לימחק ולברך ברכה לבטלה ועונש דינו חמור מאד.

[5] לכך יהו מוזהרין אותן שכותבין תפילין ומזוזות שלא לכתוב כי אם בדיו טוב וקלף טוב. ואין לכתבן בשעה שהוא מתנמנם שלא יוכל לכוין לכתו׳ לשמה.

[6] ואין נכון לעצרן[25] ולעצל לכתוב תפילין ומזוזות כי העצרן אם יכתוב שלא כדין לא יכתוב פעם אחרת.[26] לכך יהא כל אדם לעשות(!) המצוה כתיקנן ויהיה דשן ורענן.

[7] המדבר בבית הכנסת וחביריו משבחין ומשוררין, קורא אני עליו הוי על כל שכני הרעים (ירמיהו יב: יד) כי ישרים דרכי יי׳ וצדיקים ילכו בם ופושעים יכשלו בם (הושע יד: י). ולא נמנה עם חביריו ומואס לשבח קונו והוא משיג גבול הבורא ואהי להם למקדש מעט אילו בתי כניסיות[27] אין נוהגין בהם קלות ראש כדא׳ בפ׳ בתר׳ דמגילה[28] א׳הים ניצב בעדת א׳ (תהלים פב: א). והמדבר כאילו הופך עורפו ואומ׳ מדוע באתי ואין עונה (ישעהו נ: ב) נטיתי ידי ואין מקשיב לי (משלי א: כד) למה יקצף הא להים על קוליך (קהלת ה: ה). אך השתחוה לפניו ושב במורא בכפיפת ראש לפניו ובענוה ובשכיות הלב[29] התחנן לפניו ותשורר לפניו ובא לפניו ברננה (תהילים ק: ב) אז קרוב אליך ונמצא לך ובייחוד שם שמים ובכיון הלב. והמתפלל בכיוון ובשתאמר ברוך אתה, אם (תשב) [תשיח] בדברים בטלים כאילו התלוצץ בו ולא נתת יראתו על פניך ואהבתו בו, אך חשוב כי הוא ניצב לקראתך שנ׳ שויתי יי׳ לנגדי

[22] *Berakhot* 7a. [23] *Ḥullin* 87a. [24] *Menaḥot* 41b, see Rashi and *Tosafot* s.v. *tefillin*.
[25] i.e. a cheapskate. [26] See *SHB*, #990 (*SHP*, #710) end. [27] *Megillah* 29a.
[28] *Megillah* 28a. [29] See Ps. 73: 7.

תמיד (תהילים טז: ח) ותתן יראתו על פניך ואהבתו בך ותתכוין בכל לבך ותהיה צנוע לפניו והתודה על חטאך ותקדשהו והוא ימצא לך ויברכך.

[8] ואותם שנושאים נערים בשעה שהן מתפללים ונושקין אותן חוטאים ועליהם הכת' אומ' ואותי השלכת אחר גיויך (מלכים א' יד: ט). והוא מראה לכל שאוהב את בנו יותר מבוראו והא דאמ' בפ' לולב הגזול[30] כך היה מנהג אנשי ירושלים מתפלל ולולבו בידו כו', התם משום חביבי מצוה לא טרידי. וטוב לכל אדם שלא ינשק בניו ובנותיו בבית הכנסת להודיע לכל שאין אהבה כאהבת הבורא.[31]

2. MS Bodley Opp. 614 (Neubauer 2275) (Germany, 1329/30), fos. 31a–b

The section is preceded by one treating the recitation of *birkot ha-nehenin*.

ליקוטין מספר חסידים

[1] ויש שכותבין ספרים או שאר עניינים ופעמים מכוונים וכותבים [בראש השיטות את שמם ואינם עושים כדין כי[32]] לפעמים אינם מכוון כך ודוחקין התיבה(!) זו ברו(!) או מחסרין או מייתרין תיבות או מהפכין אותן. על כן אין טוב ועל מי שעושה כך עליו הכתו' אומ' ושם רשעים ירקב (משלי י"ז) שמם מחית לעולם ועד (תהלים ט: ו).[33]

[2] ולא יזמר אדם לילד פסוקים כדי שיישן או שלא יבכה.[34]

[3] אדם שכתב טעות ועוד הדיו לח והוא מקנח הדיו באצבעו מן הקלף, אל יקנח אצבעו במנעלו כי הוא בזיון.[35]

[4] טוב אשר לא תדור משתדור ולא תשלם (קהלת ה: ד) ואם נודר אדם בעת צרה כגון אם יש לו חולי מיעים(!), אל ידור שלא יאכל בני מיעים לעולם. וכן אם יש לו כאב הראש, לא ידור שלא יאכל ראש לעולם וכן כל מילי חולי.[36] (כי *הזמה)

[5] איש המשיא את בתו יצוה לה שלא תעבור על טבילתה ושלא תאמר לבעלה לא אטבול עד שתתן לי כך וכך מעות או אותו חפץ, לפי כששניהן מכוונים לשם שמים אז יהיו הבנים צדיקים.[37]

[6] לא יצא אדם מבית הכנסת עד שייסיימו כל התפילה אלא א"כ צריך לנקביו או להקיא.[38] וביום המילה לא יאמר עלינו לשבח עד לאחר שמסיים שליח צבור או המוהל הברכה.[39]

[7] מי שמת אביו בפורים, לעונה הבאה לא יניח מלשלוח מנות. ובאותו פורים ישלח המנות לעניים וכל שכן סמוך לפורים רק שלא ישלח תפנוקים כי הם עשויין לשמחה. וכל דבר העשוי לשמחה לא ישלח ולא ישלחו לו.[40]

[8] מי שמת מנודה בחרם הקהילות מרחיקים קברו משאר קברים יותר מח' אמות כדי שלא יגע תפוסת הקבר שהוא ד' אמות לתפוסת קברו.[41]

30 *Sukkah* 41b.

31 See *SHB*, #255 (*SHP*, #432), *SHG*, #87.

32 Addition made on the basis of the parallel passage in MS Bodley, Or. 146 (Neubauer 782); see below.

33 *SHB*, #136 (*SHP*, #706).

34 See *SHB*, #238 (*SHP*, #347), *SHG*, #83.

35 *SHB*, #890 (*SHP*, #714), *SHG*, #86.

36 *SHB*, #403 (*SHP*, #1282), *SHG*, #9.

37 *SHB*, #506 (*SHP*, #1154).

38 See *SHB*, #780 (*SHP*, ##464–5).

39 *SHP*, #582.

40 *SHB*, #713 (*SHP*, #292).

41 *SHB*, #707 (*SHP*, #268).

[9] אדם שישב באבילות ביום השביעי לאבילותו לא ישמש מטתו, אע"פ שהוא עושה דברים אחרים לאחר שהתפללו עמו[42] אל ישמש מיטתו עד ליל שמיני. וכן מי שיש לו מת בי"ט לאחר י"ט יש לו לישב באבילות, בי"ט אל ישמש מיטתו.[43]

[10] בירושלמ' כל הטועם קדירותיו בערב שבת מאריכין לו ימיו.[44] גם זה מספר חסידים.

[11] יש זיווגים שלא יצליחו או שניהם או אחד מהם: לשני אחים שתי אחיות. וכן אב ובן לשתי אחיות או אם ובת לב' אחים. וכן האיש שהוא אלמן ולוקח אשה אלמנה ויש לו בן ויש לה בת, מזווגי' אילו ביחד כמוכן (למפרע) [לפורעניות]. ושני נישואין בשבת אחד. והכי אית' במס' שמחות בפ' י"א ר' אלעז' אוסר משו' איבה. וכן אדם שיש לו אשה ששמה כך וכך ובנו לוקח אשה ששמן שוים. ואם בן בנו לוקח אשה ששמם ששמה כן שוים כמו כן כשמן(!), לא יצליחו לפי שהן משולשות. וכמו כן אם (אם) בת ובתה לקחו ג' אנשים ששמם שוים מן כן לא יצליחו. ושלשה או ארבעה שדרים בבית אחד ששמם שוים לא יצליחו או זרעם. והרבה כיוצא כאלה. ואע"פ שלא אסרה תורה, יש לחוש (ולא) על זה נאמ' תמים תהיה (דברים יח: יד).[45]

[12] וגם יש בני אדם שכותבין שום דבר ואירע להם בסוף הדף או בסוף העמוד תיבה של פורעניות וכותבין בסוף הדף פסוקי' של נחמה, אינם עושים כדין שהרי הוא לבטלה.[46]

[13] כשהרבה דיו על (*אמ) אות (*על) אחת, לא יקח ממנו ויכתוב השם ולא מן השם יכתוב אות אחר.[47]

[14] כל מי שעוסק בהשבעת מלאכים או בהשבעת שדים או בלחישת כשפים לא סופו טוב ויראה רעות בגופו ובבניו. לכך יתרחק האדם וגם בשאלת חלום.[48]

[15] הצמא לשתות לא יברך ואחר כך שופך אלא אם הוא חפץ לשתות מים ישפוך ואחר כך יברך.[49]

[16] ואם ראית אדם שבניו אין מתקיימים, דע לך כי השם גורם. אם אחים קורין אותם שמות לבניהן ומתקיימים ולזה אין מתקיימין, דע לך שהמקום גורם ויש לו לצאת בעיר אחרת.[50]

42 *Mo'ed Katan* 19b.

43 *SHB*, #240 (*SHP*, #350).

44 I don't know the source. {Rabbi Mordechai M. Honig of Monsey e-mailed me this characteristically erudite message soon after this section appeared on the web:

Regarding the passage of the Ashkenazic Yerushalmi in the MS Oxford, Bodley Opp. 614 that you published recently in *JQR*. See *Maḥzor Vitry*, ed. A. Goldschmidt (Jerusalem, 2004), i. 289: **תנא כל הטועם תבשילו בערב שבת מאריכין לו ימיו ושנותיו. ובירושלמי מפרש טעמא שלא לכעוס על בני ביתו מפני הקדחת תבשילו. וכתיב . . . וכל שכן שצריך להזהר פן יקדיח תבשילו**. See also Y. Goldhaber, *Minhagei ha-Kehilot* (Jerusalem, 2005), i. 162. It is possible that this custom appears or is hinted at in a few textual witnesses of the Bavli, *Shabbat* 119b. See *Dikdukei Soferim*, ed. R. N. N. Rabinowicz (repr. Jerusalem, 2002), *Shabbat*, p. 269 n. 5, [which informs us] that in MS Oxford 366 [of the Bavli, *Shabbat*], the version is **חמין בערב שבת מלוגמא פת חמה בערב שבת מלוגמא**, and similarly in *Haggadot ha-Talmud: Liket Ḥakham Sefaradi Lo Noda' Shemo: Tatslum ha-Defus ha-Yeḥidi* (Constantinople, 1511), *Shabbat*, fo. 17d, available at hebrewbooks.org. (The page number in their online photostat is 59.) See also: *Piskei ha-Rid: Berakhot, Shabbat*, ed. A. Y. Wertheimer and A. Liss (Jerusalem, 1963), 424: **פת חמה בערב שבת מלוגמא**; *Sefer Rushino: Exodus*, ed. M. Weiss (Jerusalem, 1989), 75: **חמין בערב שבת מלוגמא**.}

45 See *SHB*, #477 (*SHP*, ##1116, 1117), *SHG*, ##157, 55.

46 *SHP*, #705.

47 *SHB*, #887 (*SHP*, #716).

48 *SHB*, #205 (*SHP*, #211); see also *SHB*, #469 end, #1172 (*SHP*, #379 end), *SHG*, #48.

49 *SHB*, ##111, 852 (*SHP*, #564).

50 *SHB*, #246 (*SHP*, #366).

[17] אם ראית חלום או שום דבר של מזיקין, אל תגיד לשום אדם כי כל הרואה מזיקין ונוגע באש קודם שיוצא דיבור מפיו ואינו מגיד מה שראה לא ינזק ולא ימות.[51]

[18] אסור לכתוב בספר פלוני חייב לי כך וכך.

[19] אדם שיש לו תפילין או ספרים בתיק לא ינערם לחוץ אלא יוציאם ביד.[52]

[20] כשאדם אוכל בידיו מלוכלכות בתבשיל ליקנחם ואחר כך יברך דכת' שאו ידכם קודש וברכו את השם [תהילים קלד: ב].[53]

The selection ends here and is followed by a section on dreams:

האי מאן דחזי חילמא ולא ידע מאי חזי, ניקום מקמי כהנא לדוכתא ולימא הכי לוישמרך רבון העולמים אני שלך וחלומותי שלך וחלום שחלמתי וכו'.

3. MS Bodley Or. 146 (Neubauer 782) (Germany, 1342), fos. 69a–70a
The texts of the selections from *Sefer Ḥasidim* are identical with Bodley Opp. 614, down to most of the scribal errors. (The selection from *Sefer Ḥasidim* is preceded by a section on the recitation of *berakhot* similar to the one that preceded the selection from *Sefer Ḥasidim* in Bodley Opp. 614.)

4. MS Zurich, Zentralbibliothek Heidenheim 51 (Germany, 14th–15th centuries), fos. 9a–10b

[1] ויוסף אברהם ויקח אשה (בראשית כה: א) ואמרו על פי הדיבור[54] ואמרו היו עובדי ע"ז. א"כ למה אמ' לו הקב"ה לקחת(ו) אשה כוון[!] שאין לו הנאה מהם וכו'.[55] (*זה אומ' לקניין) הכי אמ' רב משו' ר' ראובן בן אצטרבולי דכולי מן התורה מן הנביאים ומן הכתובים. מן התורה מיי' יצא הדבר (בראשית כד: כ), מהנביאים ואביו ואמו לא ידעו כי מיי' היתה (שופטים יד: ד), מן הכתובים מיי' [אשה] משכלת (משלי יט: יד).[56]

[2] למי שמכושף אין תקנ' טובה כמו שיצא מן העיר וידור בעיר אחרת ויקח בעיר אחרת אשה.[57]

[3] אמר חכם לבנו: אל תראה את לאשתך בשעה שהיא חוטאה. ויש אדם שאשתו עושה רעה לאחרות או לאנשים ועוזר לאשתו ולבסוף נופל בידה. לכך אם רואה אדם שאשתו מריבה ואינו יכול למחות בידה וגם ירא ממנה שלא תעשה לו רעה, ישתוק ולא יכריע את אשתו לפני העולם לכף זכות אלא שלא בבפני אשתו יאמר אני מצ[ט]ער שאשתי עושה כך.[58]

[4] יהודי אחד שכח דבר גדול שנהנה ובא גוי והזכירו ואמ' ברוך זוכר הנשכחות ששם בלבו שהזכירו. אמר לו חבירו ואפי' אם היה יהודי מזכירך לא היה לך לברך אלא כשאתה בעצמך זוכר שאינך יודע אם שכח ואחר כך זכר או לא שכח. אמר זה מ"מ בא לי (ל)הנאה.[59]

[5] כל צדיק שמפרש דברי צדיק אחר כגון אמורא שמפרש דברי תנא או של אמורא (של כגון), כשמת יוצא התנא כנגדו לקבלו בסבר פנים יפות וללכת עמו ולבקש מן המל[אכים להקל עליו.[60]

51 *SHB*, #235 (*SHP*, #325).
52 *SHB*, #273 (*SHP*, #639).
53 *SHB*, #58 (*SHP*, #565).
54 *Bereshit Rabbah*, eds. J. Theodor and Ḥ. Albeck, rev. edn. (Jerusalem, 1965), ii. 661, *parashah* 61: 1, s.v. *va-yikaḥ*.
55 *SHP*, #1169; the ending there is similarly missing.
56 *Mo'ed Katan* 18b, and see *SHB*, #383 (*SHP*, #1128).
57 *SHB*, #498 (*SHP*, #1136).
58 *SHB*, #506 (*SHP*, #1154).
59 See *SHP*, #574.
60 *SHB*, #559.

[6] אם אדם כותב ה' בכתביו להיות רמז דהקב"ה, יכול למחוק, שהרי אמרו[61] כיי כ' נמחק, ליי ל' נמחק, אבל נו אינו נמחק שכבר קידשו השם.[62]

[7] אחד שאל לחכם: אמר לו עכברים אכלו מלחמי, אוכל לאכול מן הלחם? אמר לו ולמה לא תאכל. אמ' לו פן אשכח תלמודי[63] ואני נזהר מלאכול מה שמשכח (הגדול) ונזהר מכל דברי' שמשכח, ועתה אני רעב. אמ' לו החכם הרי אמרו אינו מתחייב עד שיסירם מלבו[64] ואני רואה אותך שאינך עוסק בתורה ואתה פנוי ותוכל לעסוק ,כל היום אתה בטל מדברי תורה והולך עם עמי הארץ לשמוע דברי' בטלי', מוטב לך שלא תזהר מדברי' המשכחי' כדי שתשכח דברי' הבטלי '(!) שאתה עוסק.[65]

[8] וכן אמ' החכם כל מי שרוצה לעשות סייג ומחמיר בסייג וחוטא בעיקר, הוא חוטא על חוטא, אם יש אל (אל) יזקק לו מורה כגון שאינו אוכל לחם גוי' ושוכב עם גויה.

וכן אם נפל איסור בדבר היתר ויותר מששים ואינו נותן טעם ומחמיר, אמ' לו החכם כשהקדיר' של גוים אצל האש (א) וקדירה שלך מצד אחר או באותו בית, ואינכם חוששים אם (המחלוקת {?} ואם) לוקחת הכף (שלך) [שלה] ומערבת את המאכל שלכם בעוד שאתם בית הכנסת, מי יודע אם היא עושה. על עיקר לאסור אינך חושש, (וכ) ועל דבר שמותר לכתחילה אתה מקפיד כמו שאמר [וי]אמר כן העם הזה וכן הגוי הזה לפני נאם ה' וכן כל מעשה ידיהם ואשר יקריבו שם טמא הוא (חגי ב: יד) .והיו סומכין על המקרא ויאסף כל איש ישראל אל העיר כאיש אחד חברים (שופטים כ: א), ובשביל שנאמני[ם] בחג לעמי הארץ,[66] היו מאמיני' להם כל השנה.[67]

[9] ולא אבה דוד לשתותם ויסך אותם ליי' ויאמר חלילה [לי] ליי' מעשות[י] זאת הדם האנשים {?} (שמואל ב' כג: טז). אחד שלח שלוחו לקנות לו בהמה בכפר [ו]קנה השליח הבהמה [ו]שמטה הבהמה מן הקשר וברחה ביער והיה בפחד ביער שלא יפגעוה. והיה מתבייש איך יבא לבית בלא הבהמ' פן יחשדוהו, שלא יאמרו לו לא קנה הבהמ' ותפש המעות ומשקר. טרח הרבה והלך בלילה שימצא הבהמ' בין העדר שברחה שם והביא את הבהמ'. ושחטה ונתגלגל לאחר שנמלח הבשר שאכלו הכלב והשאר בישל בקדירה ובא הכלב ולקח הבשר מן הקדירה (כך) חם (ושובר) [ושיבר] הקדירה ואכל הבשר. ואמר החכם לא על חנם נעשה, ואמרו לו מה שנעשה אומ' ברוך המקום שמנענו מלאכול המאכל שבסכנה בא לביתי.[68]

[10] מי שיש לו בן שוטה ואין בו דעת, אם מבקש רחמים עליו שיחיה או על רשע שהמחטיא ועושה רעות אל יענה אמן אחריו כי טוב יותר במיתתו מבחייהו. ויש שוטה שבקמיעה(!) לא יואיל לו שאינו מן השן[?].[69]

[11] הנה אמרו לצורך יום טוב (ללוי) [לוו] עלי ואני פורע[70] כגון שאמר העני לעשיר תלוה לי ותמתין לי עד שהבורא יזמין לי (שאשלום) [שאשלם], (יאכל) [יוכל] (לחקת) [לקחת] מידו. [אבל] בסתם, לומר לו תלוה לי לצורך יום טוב ומיד (אשלום) [אשלם], אפרע לך. והנה המלוה סבור שמיד ישלם לו והיה ממתין ואינו משלם. על זה לא אמרו לו[ו] עלי. או אם יש בידו מעות של בני אדם לחצי ריוח ואין לו כלום והוא אומ' אקח ממעות פלו' ואסמוך על

[61] *Shevu'ot* 35b. [62] *SHB*, #935 (*SHP*, #735). [63] *Horayot* 13b.
[64] *Avot* 4: 6. [65] *SHB*, #1008 (*SHP*, #1503). [66] *Ḥagigah* 26a.
[67] *SHP*, #1503. (The intent of the ending is that people relied erroneously on the verse in Judges as interpreted in *Ḥagigah*, for in reality the passage in *Ḥagigah* states that *'ammei ha-arets* are believed for the duration of the holiday only.)
[68] *SHP*, ##150–1. [69] The meaning is unclear. [70] *Betsah* 15b.

לוו עלי ואני פורע. זה לא יתכן אלא על זה אמרו עשה שבתך חול.[71] ועל זה נאמ׳ לווה רשע ולא ישלם (תהילים לז: כא), אע״פ שדעתו לשלם כיון שבלא רשות בעלים לוקח.

[12] אחד כומר שאל מהו (הוא) ושונא מתנות יחיה (משלי טו: כז)? אמ׳ לו אם בשוחד כבר אמר, אלא שמקבל מתנות ממי שנותן לעניים, הרי גוזל את העניים, שאם לא יקבל היה זה נותנם לעניים. ושלח הכומר לו מתנות. אמ׳ לא אקבל. אמ׳ לו למה? כי כבר אמרת לך ועבדך אמר לי אם לא הייתי (א) מקבל היה חפצך לשלוח אותה ליהודי אחר ואיני רוצה לקבל כי הייתי לגוזלו. וסיפר לחבריו. והיהודי עשה בעבור קידוש השם.

[13] אחד היה חולה, בא אהובו של חולה (אחד) ששמו כשמו החולה ואמר (לן) [לו] בעבור הבורא תלך לחולה שחפץ לראותך. אמ׳ הוא מבקש לי, זה לא אוכל לעשות בעבורו בספק נפשות מחללין את השבת וכת[ו]ב ושמור נפשך מאד (דברים ד: ט).[72] ואע״פ שאמרו לא נצרכ׳ אלא לבן גילו[73] בכאן (שמע) [שמא] רשם בשם מיחלף כמו מרים מגדלא[!!] בשייא[!], ודווקא בחולי שקורי׳ בלעז בלשון אשכנז זוהט שרגילין להזיע ביום (ה׳ או) [ד׳ ו]ביום ז׳.[74]

[14] מי שמושיט הסכין לחבירו (והיה) [יהיה] הקתא כלפי המקבל. אבל האב שמושיט לבנו הגדול (והיה) [יהיה] הקתא כלפי האב והברזל כלפי הבן. המושיט לקטני׳ הקתא כלפי הילד.

[15] אחד היה אומ׳ במרח[ץ] פסוקי ע״ז שהיו לגנאי, כגון פה להם ולא ידברו (תהילים קטו ה) או[מר] לעץ הקיצה וגומ׳ (חבקוק ב: יט) וכיוצ׳ בו. אמרו לו אסור לעשות שמהם יוצאים דרשות אחרות. ועוד מה יחשוב פסוקי׳ שבסמוך וכת[י]ב כל אמרת אוה[!] צרופה (תהילים יח: לא).

[16] ואל אשה בנידת טומאת׳ לא תקרב (ויקרא יח: יט). איש ואשה נעשה להם כשפים ולא יכלו להיזקק יחדיו, לא היה יכול לשמש מיטתו. שאלה האשה לחכם למה אטבול, והלא אינו יכול להיזקק אלי ואישן עמו (כשאתבי(?) ערה) כי אינו יכול לשמש. אמ׳ לה אסורה את לשכב אצלו עד שתטבלי, כי אמ׳ החכם שמא יתירה מכשף בעוד ששוכבים יחדיו ועוד שמא יבוא (עליה) [אליה] שלא כדרכה.

[17] אין משיבין על ה(כ)קלקלה,[75] שכל הצער והנזקים שבאים ע״י הצער מעלין על הגורם כאילו הוא עושה בידיים.[76] שהרי איש מבנימין (ש״א ד: יב) ואמרו שהוא שאו[ל][77] והגיד(ו)לעלי ותשב[ר] מפרקתו (ש״א ד: יז יח). ולכך ראש שאול ולא נקבר כמו הגוף אע״פ ששמן המשחה על ראשו (כא) ונשקו שמואל (ש״א י: א), אעפ״כ (ש)שמו בבית דגון (דה״א י: י) לפי שהרג כהן גדול שנמשח בשמן המשח[78] וגירש דוד וכו׳, לאמר לך עבור עליהם[79] (אחריהם) (ו)כלתו הרה ללדת ומתה וכן מיכל בת שאול מתה כשילדה.[80] לכך אין משיבין על הקל[ק]לה ואפי׳ (במלאכים) [במלכים] נוהג זה.

71 *Pesaḥim* 112a. 72 See *SHP*, #1551. 73 *Bava Metsi'a* 30a.

74 Meaning unclear. *Suht* in Middle High German means 'illness' generally, and, if my emendation is correct, it refers here to quartan fever, a cyclical fever that recurs every four days with the day of its occurrence counted as the first. (My thanks to Graeme Dumphy and Rose William of the Medtextl internet circle for their help.)

75 It apparently means that 'there is no way of repairing damage once done'. This is a strange use of the phrase, taken from *Megillah* 15a, which means 'not to return with a negative answer', and it is in this sense that it is used in *SHB*, #802 (*SHP*, #1624). 76 See *SHB*, #666 (*SHP*, #138), beginning.

77 *Yalkut Shim'oni*, *Samuel*, ed. D. Hyman (Jerusalem, 1999), #102.

78 See 1 Sam. 22: 18 and *Yalkut Shim'oni* ad loc. (#120).

79 An *'ayin* is written over the initial *alef* to indicate a correction.

80 *Sanhedrin* 21a. I am unaware of any such *midrash* about a daughter-in-law of Saul. There is the

[18] איש אחד היה נותן (חיטי) [חוטי] קנבוס למתקן מנעלים, כי לא היה רוצה ללכת אל[א] בנמעלי' רחבים רחבים[81] כדי שיהא מכניסם בהשכמה ברגליו מהרה כשהולך לבית הכנסת והיה רגיל במנעלים רחבים שקורי' בוטש והיה נותן לגוי קנבוס או משי לתפור הלבר והמנעלים [בקנבוס] כי אמר אם יהיו המנעלי' תפורי' בפשתן והלבר (*בקין) (בקנבוס או במשי) [בצמר] ואח"כ יתפור הלבר למנעל כיון שהעור של מנעל תפור בפשתן הרי הוא שעטנז. ולכך היה הגוי (*תפור) [תופר] אף המנעלים בקנבוס (לא ירדנו בפיך לעיניך) [לעיניו לפניו].[82]

[19] שני' ששונאי' זה את זה והיו בשנא' יחדיו ובמריבה כל ימי חייהם עד שמת אחד מהם ואחר"כ האחר, אל יקברוהו אצלו שאין קוברין שני שונאי' יחדיו.[83] וכן איש וגרושתו אל יקברו יחדיו.

[20] בכל מקום שאדם רואה (שמצביידים) [שמצערים] את האדם ומטריחו ויכול למחות, הרי חוטא אם לא ימחה. אם פועלין ומלמדי בניו ועבדיו עושין מלאכתו כמו שרגילין אחרי' בעיר (אחר) לעשות, לא יצערם ולא יאמ' להם פועלים אחרי' ומלמדי' אחרי' עושים יותר. כל המצער את חבירו חינם (*ס) עתיד לתת את הדין.

[21] איש אחד מתה אשתו ולקח אשה אחרת (ומתו) [ומתה] אשתו השנייה ורצו לקוברה אצל אשתו הראשונה ולא הניח אלא הרחקה מעט. וכשחלה צוה לקוברו בין שתי נשיו כי אמר שתיהן היו טובות לי.

[22] ר' יהוד' בר סימון עד שמש[ה] (ה)כותב התורה נשתייר בקולמוס קימעא [והעבירו] על ראשו ממנו נעשה לו קרני הוד.[84] ולא יתכן לסופר (שכתוב) [שכתב] (ו)אם נשתייר בקולמוס (ואם נשתייר בקולמוס) ,[אינו] מן הדין שיקנח בשער ראשו מפני שילך בבית הכסא לעשות צרכיו או שילך לאשתו.[85] ודיו שכתב השם [ו]נשתייר בקולמוס בראשו,[86] (ו)לא יתכן שיקנח בשער ראשו. ושמן שנמשחו בו כהן גדול ומלך, והלא הולך לעשות צרכיו היקרב אצל אשתו, הרי {?} [אמרו] אין לך דבר שנעשית מצותו שמועלין בו שהרי דם איברין [נמכר לגננין לזבל,[87] ומותר] אע"פ (שהמשן) [שהשמן] בזקן אהרן. וקרני ההוד מן הדיו שנשתייר ששם בראשו(ים), לפי שלא היה צריך לנקביו שהרי המן נבלע באברים ולא היה משמש מיטתו.[88] ואשר עיכב ז' ימים בענן[89] כדי למרק מה [שאכל] (ולא שמעול?) שייצא ממנו מה (שאוכל) [שאכל] ויהיה מהרה נבלע באיברים. והקולמוס שכתב השם בו אם נשבר ואינו צריך, אל יחטט בו[90] או החלב(!) ולא ישליך אלא יגנוז.[91]

[23] איש אמו ואביו תיראו ואת שבתותי תשמורו (ויקרא יט ג). אם יש לאדם אב ואם בחיים ויש לו בשר שמן ויין טוב ולחם חמודות ואומר בלבו אקדים עונג שבת שאוכל

instance of Eli's daughter-in-law (1 Sam. 4: 19–22). As the two are singled out in the *midrash* (*Yalkut Shim'oni*, *Samuel*, ##103, 120) as having died in childbirth, most probably the author cited both in the sequence of the *midrash* (and hence the dangling pronoun in *ve-khalato*), when his intended reference is only to Saul's daughter. This mode of citation is found occasionally in *Sefer Ḥasidim*.

81 *SHP*, #1665 reads *reḥavim me'od*.

82 *SHP*, #1665, whence the emendations, with the exception of *tsemer*, which is dictated by the context.

83 'Testament of R. Judah Hasid', in *Sefer Ḥasidim*, ed. R. Margoliot (Jerusalem, 1964), ##1, 10. In *Sefer ha-Roke'aḥ*, #316 the injunction is cited as originating in the *Sefer ha-Kavod* written by R. Yehudah he-Ḥasid.

84 *Yalkut Shim'oni*, ed. D. Hyman (Jerusalem, 1980), *Shemot*, #406.

85 See *SHP*, ##730, 1758.

86 i.e. the tip of the quill.

87 *Yoma* 59b, 58b.

88 *Tanḥuma*, *Tsav*, #13, s.v. *zot torat*.

89 I don't know the source.

90 See *SHB*, #890 (*SHP*, #1755).

91 See *SHB*, #894.

ואשתה, מוטב ויתן אותם תענוגים לאביו ואמו, ולעצמו יעשה שבתו חול. ואפי' אם אביו ואמו חפיצים לאכול ולשתות בחול (אותם) את מה שהכין לצורך שבת.

[24] אל תחל את בתך להזנותה (ויקרא יט: כט) את שבתותי תשמורו (ויקרא יט: יג): אם תיקן בגדי חמודות לבתו לצורך שבת וי"ט והנה מתקרבין אליה בחורים מפני יופי הבגדי' {?} במאוד מאוד, מוטב שלא יהיו לה בגדים חמודות.

[25] גם שאול חטא ששאל באוב (ש"א כח: ח) אע"פ שבעבור פיקוח נפש עשה, שהרי לא ענהו באורים ובחלומות ובנביאי', אפי' בעבור פיקוח נפש לא יעסוק אדם בכשפים.

[26] דוד קרע בגדיו ויספדו ויבכו ויצום עד ערב על שאול (ש"ב א: יא יב) אע"פ שהיה מבקש להמיתו כל הימים, הרי אם רואה אדם ששונא(י) [שלו] יהודי {?} נהרג וחיי רבים תלויים [בו] כשאול ואינו עושה רעה לאחרי', יש לו להראות צער עליו.[92] אבל נבל כשבירך דוד שנחם לפי שנבל רע לכל ושאול? כעוס לכל.[93]

[27] מי שיש לו בן או בת עומדי' על פרקן והנה יכול להשיא ביתו לאיש הגון וכשר ולבנו אשה בטוב ואביו ואמו מצא {?} {?} על כך ואומרין לו אנחנו חפיצים שתשיא את בתך לפלו' קרובינו ולבנך פלונית קרובותינו, ואם לא תעשה כן, לא נמחול לך וכל הימים אנחנו בצער. וזה אין חפצו מפני שאינה הגונה או רעה או ספק פסול יש בה, ולכך אינה [ראויה] להשיאה לבנו. {?} [וזה] שאביו ואמו חפיצי' בו אינו הגון או רעה או ספק פסול, ולכך אין חפצו להשיא בתו לו. וכל ימיו [י]היה נזהר שלא לצער את אביו.

[28] לאחר שנמחק השם פותחן פיה בעל כרחה ונותנין בפיה.[94] אם יש לפני אדם תפוח ובירך עליו בורא פרי העץ ולא היה לפניו פרי אחר ואחר שבירך [בא] פרי אחר יפה, לא יאכל אלא על מה שבירך. אם יב[י]א לו פרי לאחר שבירך על זה, כוון שלא היה הדעתו, יברך גם על זה.[95] אם בירך על המים או על שכר וסבור שהוא יין, ואמ' ברוך אי"א מ"ה בורא פרי הגפן והכיר שהיה שכר או מי דבש או מים [יאמר ברוך שם כבוד מלכותו]. וכל ברכה שישנה שם שייצא מפי האדם לבטלה ומיד ידע, (ו)[י]אמר ברוך שם כבוד מלכותו לעולם ועד.[96]

[29] כשבירך יעקב (*בניו את) [את בניו] או משה לישראל ברכם בענין העולם הזה ולא ברכם בתורה וביראת שמים ובאריכת ימים, כי לא יכלו לברכם אלא בברכה אחת (ו)לכל אחת ולכל שבט או בשתים שהן ברכה אחת [כגון] (ו)[ש]בירך ליהודה בגבורה וביין וכתי' כגבור מתרונן מיין (תהילים סח: כה) ושתו (ו)המו כמו יין (זכריה ט: טו). ואילו היה מברכם בתורה או ביראת שמים או באריכ' ימים לא היה יכול להתקיים, כי ג' דברים מעבירין על דעת קונו ועל דעתו[97] אע"פ שלבו [חפץ]. ואי אפשר לברך יותר מברכה אחת. אבל מה שהקב"ה מברך לאבות ולישר' הרבה. כי תור(*ת)ה ויראת יי בלבם ולפני מותם. ועוד הברכה לא תתקיים אלא לטובים. ועוד יראת השם באדם תלוי אע"פ שאדם אומ' וייחד לבבנו לירא את שמך. ואם תאמ' תורה, יש תלמידי חכמים שיותר רעים מן עמי הארץ, לכך לא נכתב בפירוש. ואריכת ימים [הרי] אמר ואם תלך בדרכי לשמור חקי ומצותי כאשר הלך דוד אביך והארכתי (ימים) [את ימיך] (מ"א ג: יד).[98]

ליקוטין מן ספר חסידים סיימתי ולא אחת מני אלף קיימתי כי כל ימי לא ראיתי עד שכתבתי ואותה אשמור כי קודם לכן טעיתי.

[92] *SHP*, #358.

[93] Text corrupted. *SHP*, #358 reads: ודוד שברך על נבל שחרפו, בירך לקב"ה לפי שידע שהקב"ה נגפו.

[94] *Sotah* 20a.

[95] *SHB*, ##846–7 (*SHP*, ##570–1, and see Wistinetzki's note on the non sequitur that follows the opening sentence.) [96] *SHP*, #572. [97] *'Eruvin* 41b. [98] See *SHP*, #1053.

5. MS Hamburg Staats- und Universitätsbibliothek 303 (Steinschneider 213) An Italian scribe in the seventeenth century decided to copy sections from the 1538 Bologna edition, and the passages he chose were sections 1024–68, scarcely ones treating pietistic concerns.

CHAPTER FIVE

The Midrash, *Sefer Ḥasidim*, and the Changing Face of God

THIS STUDY, an immediate follow-up of the preceding essay, is an expansion of a Hebrew lecture delivered at the Seventh Congress of the World Union of Jewish Studies, Jerusalem, August 1977, which I got around to publishing only when I turned again to studying *Sefer Ḥasidim*, some twenty-five years later. A somewhat briefer version of this essay was presented at the 34th Conference of the Association for Jewish Studies (AJS), December 15–17, 2002, and at a conference at Princeton on *Sefer Ḥasidim*, February 29, 2004.

I

Anyone who has read some twenty pages in *Sefer Ḥasidim* will recognize immediately that he is in a world wholly different from that of the Midrash. The outlook that had nurtured the religious sensibilities of Jewry for close to a millennium no longer obtains. The questions that naturally present themselves are: In what ways have the Pietists detached themselves from the religious mood and imaginative world of the Midrash and what is the significance of this change?

Rather than attempting to characterize the world of the Midrash, I would like to focus on four of its leitmotifs.

First, Avinu she-ba-Shamayim, a personal and fatherly God whose chief concern is the welfare of his children. To Him Jews may weep over their personal problems just as freely as they weep and supplicate Him for the restoration of their homeland. God himself is not above weeping at the plight of his children. Second, *palmalia shel ma'alah*: God is surrounded not simply by a host of worshipping angels, but by a Heavenly *familia*, a courtly circle over which He presides and whose members often intercede on behalf of Israel—the classic advocates being the archangel Michael, the Patriarchs, or the Matriarchs. Third, *ma'aseh avot siman le-vanim*: the present is prefigured in the classical past—contemporary occurrences are adumbrated in the archetypal events of biblical history. Finally, the notion, if you wish the hypostasis, of Keneset Yisra'el, 'corporate Israel'.[1]

All four of these leitmotifs are absent from *Sefer Ḥasidim.*

As I intend to draw inferences from this absence, a methodological remark is in place. I am not arguing from silence but from selective silence. Ḥasidei Ashkenaz quote thousands of *midrashim* in full, and fragments of many thousands more. Yet these four themes, writ large on almost every page of the |165| Midrash, are noticeably absent from these copious citations. The Midrash has been filtered by the hasidic mentality, and it is this mindset that I address.

When I state that Keneset Yisra'el is absent in the writing of Ḥasidei Ashkenaz, I do not refer simply to the noteworthy fact that this term or image is scarcely ever found in their voluminous writings,[2] but to the more important point that Ḥasidei Ashkenaz do not think in terms of a 'Jewish people', let alone work with any corporate or organic sense of nation. This is not to say that such a notion was alien to them—it runs like a scarlet thread through the liturgical poetry of Ashkenaz—but rather that it played no role in hasidic thought. When they spoke simply as Jews, they, no less than their non-Pietist brethren, drew on their common midrashic heritage. But when they came to express their own distinctive thoughts, the thoughts of their movement, the concept of Keneset Yisra'el, indeed the very term, was absent. An absence all the more remarkable in view of the centrality that they attached to the principle of 'all Jews are sureties for one another', *kol yisra'el 'arevim zeh la-zeh.* Yet their vibrant sense of collective responsibility could instill no life, invest no significance, in the traditional concept of the corporate entity of Keneset Yisra'el.

The problem of evil bulked large in hasidic thought, and in one sense *Sefer Ḥasidim* is a work of theodicy, for its avowed purpose—stated in the introduction and realized throughout the book—is to explain why one person is punished but not the other. Indeed, the attempt to discover the Will of the Creator, the *retson ha-Borè*, that is to say, to uncover a hidden code of laws for whose unwitting transgressions man is punished,[3] is part of this same

[1] G. F. Moore, *Judaism in the First Centuries of the Christian Era* (Cambridge, Mass., 1927), i. 357–444; S. Schechter, *Aspects of Rabbinic Theology: Major Concepts of the Talmud* (repr. New York, 1961), 21–115.

[2] The only instance known to me is *Sefer Ḥasidim*, ed. J. Wistinetzki (Berlin, 1891), #500. {It is equally not to be found in the Bologna, 1538 edition of *Sefer Ḥasidim* or in any other manuscript in the Princeton University *Sefer Hasidim* Database other than JTS Boesky 45, which is a sixteenth-century copy of much of Wistinetzki's text. On the manuscripts of *Sefer Ḥasidim* and their groupings, see 'Pietists and Kibbitzers', pp. 120–32 above. See also Afterword, sect. A below.}

[3] See pp. 9–12 above.

theodicy, part of their endeavor to justify God's way to man. Yet as much as the Ḥasidim wrestled with the fate of the righteous, it is remarkable that they never pondered the fate of Israel—Why does Israel suffer while the nations prosper?—despite their living in a period of relentless devolution of Jewish status, in the century that witnessed the rise of what Gavin Langmuir has called 'pathological antisemitism'.[4] The riddle of individual fates occupies their minds. Their range of vision encompasses the individual, the community, at most a cluster of communities; it does not comprehend the Jewish people in its entirety. And we will search their writings in vain for a reference to the Jewish people as an actor in history or as a nation with a historical destiny. Israel's election and her fate hold little interest for the Ḥasidim.

Accompanying this disintegration of an organic sense of nation is the detachment of the German Pietists from the past. This expresses itself in three ways.

First, as the past no longer prefigures the present, biblical occurrences are not enfolded in contemporary events. Thus, unlike the figures of the Midrash, the Ḥasid does not live simultaneously |**166**| in two planes of time—the past and the present.

Second, Ḥasidei Ashkenaz are not judged on the basis of past events—neither for better nor for worse. The Ten Martyrs, in midrashic thought, were martyred to atone for the sale of Joseph by his brothers,[5] but the Ḥasidim never attributed their suffering to the sins of their forefathers. They and they alone were responsible for their fate. The Pietists spoke frequently of *zekhut avot*, parental merit, and warned incessantly that *banim metim be'avon avot*, children die for the sins of the fathers. However, the term 'fathers' meant literally 'fathers' or 'grandfathers', not 'fathers of the nation', the Patriarchs. Their sense of closeness, of being one with the past, the foretime with which they sense a common bond and share a common fate, comprises five or six generations at most. It does not encompass millennia as in the Midrash.

Third, the dramatis personae of the Bible and Midrash are wholly absent from the world of the Ḥasidim. While Abraham, Moses, and Elijah are almost household figures in the Midrash, constantly interacting with and even interceding on behalf of its inhabitants, the Pietist has no traffic with them. They play no role in his thinking and none at all in his imagination. They simply do not exist for him. R. Yehudah he-Ḥasid is, in this regard, more removed from the world of Midrash than is Sholem Aleichem's Tevye

[4] G. I. Langmuir, *Towards a Definition of Antisemitism* (Berkeley, Calif., 1990), 195–288.

[5] *Die Geschichte von den Zehn Martyren: Synoptische Edition mit Übersetzung und Einleitung*, ed. G. Reeg (Tübingen, 1985).

the Milkman. Nineteenth-century eastern Europe was on more intimate terms with the Patriarchs and the *tanna'im* than were the German Pietists in the high Middle Ages.

The disappearance of such central notions as Keneset Yisra'el, the celestial *familia*, and the prefigurative view of history from the hasidic mindset could scarcely occur without consequences, and a few words on them are in place.

Scholars have long noted the absence of messianism in hasidic thought.[6] Nor is this surprising in light of my remarks. Restoration and redemption are events |167| in national history, events involving the Jewish people in its entirety. If the sense of nation is weak, the chance that messianism will arise is small.

Second, the hasidic world is without a dimension in time. The Pietist is cut off from the past and, bereft of a national perspective, he lacks also a future. The figures that appear on the pages of *Sefer Ḥasidim* do not move in a historical continuum. They do not issue forth from Sinai, nor do they move towards the messianic age. The hasidic world is suspended in time—static, isolated, and motionless. The only movement in time in *Sefer Ḥasidim* is the personal progression towards death, towards the afterlife, where the individual—the worthy individual—will find his bliss.

Third, as a result of their loss of a sense of historical continuity, there arises a profound feeling of loneliness that leads in turn to an intensification of the

[6] G. Scholem, *Major Trends in Jewish Mysticism*, 3rd edn. (New York, 1954), 88–90. It has been claimed that MS Bodley 268, issuing from German Pietistic circles, reflects messianic aspirations. The manuscript has been published under the mistaken name *Perush ha-Roke'aḥ 'al ha-Torah* (3 vols.). I have not found in it a trace of messianism. (On the mistaken attribution, see J. Dan, 'Perush ha-Torah le-R. El'azar mi-Germaiza (*mahadurat* Kanyevsky)', *Kiryat Sefer*, 59 [1988], 644.) One should add that the transcription is not always accurate, as the editor skipped a word or two here and a line or two there. Compare e.g. vol. i, p. 154, verse 6 with fol. 26b: **מהר׳י של׳ש סאי׳ם קמ׳ח למפר[ע] ח׳מ׳ש׳י׳ (בראשית יח: 6). לכך יצאו בניו (בחמשי) [חמושים] (ב)[מ]מצרי׳ (שמות יג: 18). יש׳מ׳ח׳ ובני ישראל יוצאים ביד רמה (שמות יד: 8), מרוממין. בו יש׳מ׳ח׳ ישראל בעושיו (תהילים קמט: 2). משיח יבא בפ׳ס׳ח׳ ק׳מ׳ח׳ וימלוך בכיפה.** However, the missing passages reflect no more messianic expectation than do the printed ones in which messiah or the messianic age is mentioned, e.g. vol. i, p. 83, verse 14; p. 157, verse 17; p. 315, verse 10. Vol. ii, p. 27, verse 13; p. 82, verse 18; p. 151, verse 7; p. 273, verse 26; p. 309, verse 26. Vol. iii, p. 104, verse 17; p. 225, verse 20; p. 272, verse 12; p. 276, verse 38; p. 281, verse 33. (The passage at p. 150 states **מהר׳י של׳ש סאי׳ם קמ׳ח למפר[ע] ח׳מ׳ש׳י׳ (בראשית יח: 6). לכך יצאו בניו (בחמשי) [חמושים] (ב)[מ]מצרי׳ (שמות יג: 18). יש׳מ׳ח׳ ובני ישראל יוצאים ביד רמה (שמות יד: 8), מרוממין. בו יש׳מ׳ח׳ ישראל בעושיו (תהילים קמט: 2). משיח יבא בפ׳ס׳ח׳ ק׳מ׳ח׳ וימלוך בכיפה**. This does not mean that the messiah will come on Passover 1348. The Midrash asserts that the visit of the three angels in Gen. 18 was on Passover [see Rashi's commentary and *Bereshit Rabbah* ad loc.], and the Talmud in *Rosh Hashanah* 11a says that the messiah will come on Passover [**משיח יבוא בפ׳ס׳ח ק׳מ׳ח׳**]. The passage states that **משיח**, whose letters are constituted in the last letters of the words in the phrase **מהר׳י של׳ש סאי׳ם קמ׳ח** [Gen. 18: 6], will come on Passover, and that the *midrash* of Passover is already adumbrated in that same verse, as the numerological equivalent of the word **קמ׳ח** is **פס׳ח**.)

sense of sin and culpability. The individual, or individual community, stands now alone before the Judgment Seat, without the support of a collective past and without intercessors to plead his individual cause. His fate will be decided solely on the basis of his own actions and God shall render judgment on him just to the last iota—and 'Who can stand alone before the Judgment Seat?' Admittedly, no one is punished for crimes of the past, and the German Pietists, unlike the rabbis of the Midrash, did not view themselves as being asked to atone for the sins of the Golden Calf or for the sale of Joseph by his brethren. However, in an era of the Crusades, ritual murder accusations, and growing demonization, such an outlook was a dubious blessing. A community experiencing sustained suffering and degradation is twice cursed if it views itself as wholly responsible for its own fate. The Midrash spread the guilt for the cataclysms of the destruction of the Second Temple and the Hadrianic persecutions across the millennia—reaching back to the sins of Israel in the desert and even to the failings of the Patriarchs. The Pietists denied the very possibility of such a shared burden of guilt. Their moral loadstar was the biblical admonition 'each is to die for his own sin [only]' (Deut. 24: 16). If the present is in no part a product of an archetypical past as in Midrash, nor a reflection of the cosmic process as in Lurianic kabbalah, then the isolated present—this little island of a century or so of time with its handful of inhabitants—simply receives its just deserts. A progressively smaller number of people then bear sole responsibility for an ever-increasing oppression. The contraction of the historical purview of the Ḥasidim thus entailed an intensification of their sense of guilt. And guilt is omnipresent in *Sefer Ḥasidim*. Indeed, I would venture to suggest that the sense of guilt is one of the major forces shaping hasidic thought. |**168**|

In one sense, much of *Sefer Ḥasidim* is a *cri de coeur*, a cry of *mea culpa*, and the concept of the Will of the Creator is in effect a quest for this *culpa*. If there exists a hidden law by which all are bound, all have then transgressed and a community of the God-fearing is in reality a band of ignorant sinners. And hundreds of passages in *Sefer Ḥasidim* conclude explicitly or implicitly with the phrase 'and for this reason were they punished'. The attempt to discover the Divine Will in its plenitude arose, as I have indicated elsewhere, from a desire for the thickening of the heavenly yoke and equally from an aspiration to more fully harness the newly discovered potential of man to the Divine service.[7] However, it should equally be understood and emphasized that this quest for the Creator's hidden law arose also from a profound, indeed frightening, sense of sin, one that echoed the psalmist's cry 'Cleanse Thou me from hidden faults!' (Ps. 19: 12).

[7] See pp. 9–15 above.

This crushing sense of guilt also explains in part the absence of the apocalyptic in hasidic thought which scholars have also noted. Palpably absent from the Pietists' mindset was the sensed injustice of their suffering—a *sine qua non* for the rise of apocalyptic thinking.

Why this sense of guilt? Was the Will of the Creator the response of some members of the German community when confronted with a world that was becoming daily more hostile and savagely oppressive? Let us remember that they, their parents, and their grandparents had experienced the demonization of the Jew, the momentous transformation, to use Langmuir's terms, of 'rational anti-Judaism' into 'pathological antisemitism'.[8] In 1096 the Jews were massacred for what they were. They were slain because they were infidels, and they were. They were slaughtered because they mocked Jesus and the Holy Mother, and they did so mercilessly. They were put to death for deicide, and though they did not actually kill Jesus, nevertheless they believed that he was justly executed as a false prophet and messiah. A century later, Jews were massacred on chimerical charges. They were slaughtered because they were part of an international conspiracy against Christianity. They were burned because they ritually slaughtered Christian children, and soon it was to be alleged and believed that they were members of a cannibalistic religion that needs the blood of infants for its rituals. How was the Pietist to justify God's way to man—and to himself? As there was no causal link between a paradigmatic antiquity and the present, the biblical and talmudic past could not explain their new and growing sufferings; the visible present did not explain them, and so one was left only with the invisible present—whence the Will of the Creator. Nothing less than a newly revealed, covert Law and, consequently, a new universe of transgression could account for the growing punishment that a newly formed 'persecuting society' was then meting out to them, their parents, and their children. Stranded in an island of time, bereft of |169| a larger historical narrative in which they could locate their condition, the bewildered Pietists were faced with a choice between existence in a meaningless universe and acceptance of fresh guilt. And they chose guilt. The result is *Sefer Ḥasidim*, which, in one sense, is a tale of 'guilt in search of sin'.[9]

This is not the whole story—I doubt whether we ever will know the whole story behind that strange work—but, I believe, it is an important part of it. The Will of the Creator was, on the one hand, as I have written in 'Three Themes in *Sefer Ḥasidim*', a proclamation of a new 'acceptance of the heavenly

[8] Above, n. 4.

[9] This phrase is the apt characterization of *Sefer Ḥasidim* made by Judith Baskin in her response to my paper at the AJS conference.

yoke', a bold statement by medieval man of both the need for and the reality of a new revelation which mandated 'a new ritual and a fresh religious sensibility'. It was, at the same time, an expression of a loss of confidence in self and in the order of things, the beneficent and comforting order of things, a confidence that the authors of the Midrash maintained even in their darkest hours.

II

We have discussed thus far three of the four differences between the hasidic world and that of the Midrash—the disappearance of Keneset Yisra'el, the Heavenly Court, and the prefigurative view of history. I would like to turn to the transformation that the notion of God underwent in hasidic thought.

The personal, fatherly God of the Midrash, the God who comforts mourners, buries the dead, suffers in Israel's exile and rejoices in their study of the Law disappeared completely. In His place came, in the esoteric writings of the Pietists, the Deus Absconditus (Borè) and the Reflected Glory (Kavod)—inner and outer. In their popular literature, that is to say, *Sefer Ḥasidim*, came a God devoid of all human traits or attributes. It is scarcely accidental that the common midrashic phrase 'To what may [God] be compared? To an earthly king who . . .'[10] is rarely, if ever, found in the writings of the Pietists. This transformation is well known and scholars have long drawn attention to the decisive influence of Sa'adyah Gaon. His vigorous opposition to anthropomorphism came to hasidic attention via the Kaliric paraphrase of his *Book of Beliefs and Opinions*. And his doctrine was received with enthusiasm by the Pietists.

Why the enthusiasm? Scarcely, one feels, out of intellectual conviction. The Ḥasidim were without philosophical training and most were ignorant even of Aristotle's ten categories, substance, accident, position, duration, and the like,[11] and so one may reasonably doubt whether they could have divined |170| Sa'adyah's argument from the emotive lines of that paraphrase, much less appreciated its logical force. The non-corporeality of God apparently answered some deep anterior need. Perhaps it served to put a further distance between their religion and that of their hated and oppressive neighbors, the Christians, who were experiencing at that time—in the course of the twelfth and thirteenth centuries—an ever greater humanization of their Deity and a

[10] משל למה הדבר דומה? למלך בשר ודם. See e.g. I. Ziegler, *Die Königsgleichnisse des Midrasch beleuchtet durch die römische Kaiserzeit* (Breslau, 1903).

[11] The most probable exception to this general unawareness is the author of the *Shir ha-Yiḥud*; see *Shirei ha-Yiḥud ve-ha-Kavod*, ed. A. M. Haberman (Jerusalem, 1948); A. Berliner, *Ketavim Nivḥarim, Meturgamim mi-Germanit* (Jerusalem, 1945), i. 168–70.

growing emphasis on, indeed preoccupation with, His human suffering.[12] Not only was there no incarnation in Judaism, but God himself, the Pietists now discovered, was bereft even of human form, indeed of any form whatsoever—biblical verses to the contrary notwithstanding. At any rate, Sa'adyah's doctrine was accepted as sacred writ and Ḥasidei Ashkenaz waged a holy war against those who dared assign to God any human attributes. They even consigned the prayer books of the anthropomorphists to the flames.[13]

However, their anti-anthropomorphism was unlinked to any underlying philosophical conception of man and the world. Though bits and pieces of Neoplatonism had filtered through to their thought,[14] the Greek or Hellenistic way of thought, feeling, and believing that underlay the Kalam and Sa'adyah's philosophy were wholly alien to them. Sa'adyah's purification of the notion of God had not arisen in a vacuum, but from an eclectic but essentially Hellenistic *Weltanschauung*, which had encompassed a theory of human nature that led to a clearly defined notion of human purpose and self-actualization. It also embraced a cosmology and a metaphysic that provided a blueprint for the soul's approaching and finally cleaving to the Divine—a regimen of spiritual exercises by which the soul slowly freed itself from the dross of the body, acquired the appropriate religious virtues, and attained the bliss of absorption in or conjunction with the Divine reality.[15] Bereft of such a world view, without such a spiritual road map, the Ḥasidim could not take the Aristotelian or Neoplatonic itinerary to God.[16] |171| In brief, the German Pietists embraced a dogma rather than reached a conclusion, and certainly did not assimilate a culture.

And it was a radical dogma that they embraced at that.

[12] See below, n. 29. [13] *'Arugat ha-Bosem*, ed. E. E. Urbach (Jerusalem, 1963), iv. 78–83.

[14] G. Scholem, 'Reste neoplatonischer Spekulation in der Mystik der deutschen Chassidismus und ihre Vermittlung durch Abraham bar Hiyya', *Monatsschrift für Geschichte und Wissenschaft des Judenthums*, 75 (1931), 172–91.

[15] G. Vajda, *L'Amour de Dieu dans la théologie juive du Moyen âge* (Paris, 1957), 73–8, 118–40, and more recently, A. Hyman, *Eschatological Themes in Medieval Jewish Philosophy* (Milwaukee, 2002), 32–89; H. Tirosh-Samuelson, *Happiness in Premodern Judaism: Virtue, Knowledge and Wellbeing* (Cincinnati, Ohio, 2003), 192–290.

[16] A glance at the passages from *Sefer Ḥasidim* cited by Vajda (above, n. 15), 149–62, or the passages from the esoteric writings of the Pietists cited by Elliot Wolfson in *Through a Speculum that Shines: Vision and Imagination in Medieval Jewish Mysticism* (Princeton, 1994), 188–269, will reveal how removed the German Pietists were from the beatitude of the philosophical tradition. (True, when describing their visions and aware of the anti-anthropomorphism of their movement, some took care to emphasize that what they experienced reflected only the human perception of the Divine rather than any ontological entity; their visions were docetic as opposed to veridic, in Wolfson's apt terminology. This is a caveat in the account of their experience, not in the experience itself.)

All the warm and intimate conceptions of God of the Midrash upon which they had been nurtured had to be discarded—ruthlessly discarded—for fear of idolatry. Thus the Merciful Father (Av ha-Raḥaman), was dethroned, but the *'inyan elohi* (Divine matter) did not and could not succeed Him. The Shekhinah disappeared from the thoughts of Ḥasidei Ashkenaz, but the Active Intellect did not appear in her place.

Who did take the place of the Merciful Father? In their esoteric or theological writings, their *torat ha-sod*, the place of the Merciful Father was taken, as I said, by the Deus Absconditus (Borè) and the Reflected Glory (Kavod). However, I would like to focus less on the hasidic theology than on their *mentalité*. How did the Ḥasid conceive of the Deity in his everyday thought? What nature did he ascribe to this all-powerful force that shaped his day-to-day existence? For this we must turn to their popular literature, *Sefer Ḥasidim*. And I would suggest that the conception of God implicit in much of that work shares, *mutatis mutandis*, a number of characteristics in common with the conception of God that obtained in Europe before the renaissance of the twelfth century, before the emergence of what has been called 'medieval humanism'.[17]

If the Will of the Creator is indeed central to hasidic thought, we would do well to explore what underlies this notion. Its implicit assumption is that the world is governed by an all-powerful ruler who visits drastic punishment on men when they transgress His will, despite the fact that this will was never made known to them. Retribution is exacted by this sovereign for acts committed in total ignorance of their culpability. Someone who accounts for events on the basis of such a premise sees the world as given over to a dangerous, eruptive, and frighteningly powerful force. Arbitrariness rather than order reigns. If Divine Providence exists, and the God-fearing Ḥasid doubted that not, the guiding hand is of an enigmatic and volatile Deity. The task of the Ḥasid is to bring that Deity to law and reason, to justify His ways to man. If he succeeds, that all-powerful force is that of a just God; if he fails, God remains an ever-threatening and fearsomely unintelligible Being. |172|

A just and retributive God is the goal of hasidic thought. It is remarkable to what extent the Merciful Father is absent from hasidic writings. There are few if any passages in *Sefer Ḥasidim* where it is told, as it is so often told in the Midrash, how God's mercy overcame His wrath and He had compassion for

[17] Needless to say, when one uses terms such as 'renaissance of the twelfth century' or 'medieval humanism', one is not signing thereby a contract with a specific theory, committing oneself to conform to all of its stipulations. These terms have entered the historical discourse and are being used here simply as monikers for the intellectual and spiritual developments of the 'long twelfth century'.

His creatures. Most stories that have been taken in this spirit[18] actually reflect, on closer examination, the principle of *suum cuique*, to each his due meed.[19] God takes note of even the minutest acts of merit and He rewards accordingly. In His infinite wisdom, God chooses the time and manner of repayment, and so it happens that, at times, an incorrigible sinner emerges from judgment surprisingly unscathed because of some minor good deed done long ago.

This motif is, of course, present in the Midrash, but it is balanced, indeed outweighed, by stories of God's overriding compassion. No equivalent counterpoise is found in *Sefer Ḥasidim*, or, for that matter, in the esoteric writings of the Pietists. Nor could there be. The Midrash is preoccupied with the dynamics of Divine judgment—an anthropomorphic God, himself divided between sternness and compassion, envisioned as surrounded by a heavenly court split between factions lobbying for mercy and retribution. In the hasidic world, however, there are no dynamics, there can be no dynamics, for there are, Heaven forbid, no divided sentiments in God, no Divine entourage, and nothing can sway His judgments. There is only reward and punishment meted out for the most microscopic acts, at a time and in a place that God in His infinite wisdom chooses. The God of *Sefer Ḥasidim* is very much an exacting God meting out measure for measure. Is it accidental that of all practices of the surrounding society, the one that struck the most sympathetic chord among the Ḥasidim and took deepest root among them was that of penance, a doctrine rooted in the demands of an implacable Deity for restitution and amends?

Nor did the universe present a beckoning image. As Joseph Dan has noted, the universe, in hasidic thinking, is empty of harmony and beauty, and above all of meaning. No image of God is to be found there, nor does it reflect His wisdom. Significance is only to be found in the strange and enigmatic phenomena.[20] Only in the marvelous and the anomalous does one find the Divinity reflected.[21]

I will not dwell on this point as Professor Dan has argued it at length, except to answer an obvious objection. What of the hasidic doctrine of Divine immanence that so awakened the wrath of R. Mosheh of Taku (Tachau)?[22] There is a difference between where God is and where man finds him. The first is a theological question, the second a religious one. From the point of

[18] *Merubbah middat ha-raḥamim 'al middat ha-din.*

[19] *Ein ha-Kadosh Barukh Hu mekappe'aḥ seḥar kol beriyah u-veriyah.* [20] *Zekher 'asah le-nifle'otav.*

[21] J. Dan, *Torat ha-Sod shel Ḥasidei Ashkenaz* (Jerusalem, 1968), 88–92, 184–200; I. M. Ta-Shma, 'Zekher 'Asah le-Nifle'otav', *Kovets 'al Yad*, 12 (1993), 123–46. {See the Afterword below.}

[22] Mosheh of Tachau, *Ketav Tamim*, *Otsar Neḥmad*, 3 (1860), 54–99.

view of heresy there may be |173| no difference, and R. Mosheh of Taku was perhaps justifiably put out, but from the point of view of spirituality there is all the difference in the world. God may well reside in nature, but if man does not actively experience His presence there, this indwelling is simply an ontological statement. Since God has no form, He resides nowhere in particular, hence, argued the Ḥasidim with impressive simplicity, He resides everywhere. However, one will search in vain the pages of *Sefer Ḥasidim* or those of their esoteric writings for any hint of communion with nature, an experience so noticeable in certain strands of Polish hasidism. There may be in hasidic writings a feeling of the Divine immanence in the human soul, but nowhere is there any sensation of an indwelling of a common Divine spirit uniting man with the rest of creation. Divine immanence was a logical corollary in their mind of Divine non-corporeality, not a part of their religious experience.

But to return. A fascination with the strange and anomalous, a perception of the universe as empty of harmony and meaning, neither reflecting God's nature nor evidencing His wisdom, a world under the sway of an overpowering, enigmatic, and eruptive force, a stern, retributive God of Judgment—all these are, without pressing the comparison too far, traits common to the perception of God and the world that obtained in the early Middle Ages and which found expression, among other places, in Romanesque iconography with its monsters and gargoyles and ubiquitous depictions of the Day of Judgment.[23]

The notion of the Deity implicit in the *Sefer Ḥasidim* was nurtured and colored by one that had previously obtained in the surrounding culture, but these regnant notions had elicited and given salience to a religious strain indigenous to the Jewish tradition, which envisioned not simply a God devoid of all human characteristics, but an inexpressible and unfathomable Deity characterized by fearfulness, absolute power, and mystery. Alongside the Midrash one finds the Heikhalot literature, and if, as some would have it, its God is not ultimately a transcendent God,[24] and some believe that He very much is,[25] much of that literature and all of its hymns celebrate the numin-

[23] E. Delaruelle, 'La Piété populaire au XIe siècle', in *Relazioni del X° Congresso internazionale di scienza storiche* (Florence, 1955), iii. 309–32 (repr. in id., *La Piété populaire au Moyen âge* [Turin, 1975], 3–32); H. Ditmar, *Das Christusbild in den deutschen Dichtung der Cluniazenserzeit* (Erlangen, 1934), 3, 25, 44 ff., 59 ff., 76, 91; G. Duby, *The Age of the Cathedrals, Art and Society 980–1420* (Chicago, 1981), 41 ff.; E. Mâle, *The Gothic Image: Religious Art in France in the Thirteenth Century* (New York, 1958), i. 101–5; R. Fulton, *From Judgment to Passion: Devotion to Christ and the Virgin Mary, 800–1200* (New York, 2002), 53–9 and notes ad loc.

[24] P. Schäfer, *The Hidden and Manifest God: Some Major Themes in Early Jewish Mysticism* (Albany, 1992), 148–66.

ous. Admittedly these hymns |174| emphasize more the fascination with the ineffable beauty and indescribable splendor than the terror it invokes, but there is no lack of either experience in the depictions of 'the blinding lights, the blazing fires, the infinite dimensions and the cacophony of sounds'.[26]

German Pietists were steeped in the Heikhalot literature; indeed, their transcriptions, together with their creative editing of it, constitute the major European channel through which these texts have reached us. Furthermore, the experience of the numinous was vigorously, indeed, creatively alive in the early Ashkenazic community, for, as Rudolph Otto himself pointed out, some of the finest hymns of the numinous are to be found in the Ashkenazic liturgy of the Yamim Nora'im,[27] the Days of Awesome Dread (which we, in our impoverished modern idiom, call the High Holidays), especially that of Yom Kippur—many written by the Kalonymides themselves, the revered ancestors of R. Yehudah he-Ḥasid and R. El'azar of Worms.

These hymns, clustered heavily in the *trisagion* (*kedushtot*), are counterbalanced by numerous prayers of supplication (*seliḥot*). Thus the medieval liturgy maintained much the same equilibrium as had the combined ancient literature of the Midrash and the Heikhalot to which it was heir—the equipoise of absolute will and plenary mercy, of a numinous Deity defying all description and comprehension and a God who seems, at times, only an imaginative enlargement of Man, what Solomon Schechter has called an 'imitatio hominis'. Against this dual Ashkenazic background, the depth of the rupture in *Sefer Ḥasidim* becomes ever more apparent. Not only has the compassionate, anthropomorphic God of the Midrash and the *seliḥot* disappeared, but also the numinous Deity of the Heikhalot and the liturgical hymns. The God of *Sefer Ḥasidim* has no inexpressible majesty, no consuming purity, no ineffable beauty. He does not fascinate and entrance. He is an unchained force, an incalculable essence, fearful and all-powerful, and who, unless some new and hitherto unknown revelation is discovered, is wholly arbitrary and unpredictable. All that was left of the numinous God of tradition was His absolute power and inscrutability.

However, this inscrutability to the thirteenth-century hasidic mind had now taken on a threatening visage. It no longer appeared as a corollary of His transcendent majesty experienced in moments of spiritual elation; it was omnipresent and ominous, and the persistent, unremitting incomprehen-

[25] Scholem, *Major Trends in Jewish Mysticism* (above, n. 6), 57 ff.; R. Elior, 'The Concept of God in the Hekhalot Literature', *Binah: Studies in Jewish Thought*, 2 (New York, 1992), 97–120.

[26] Elior, 'The Concept of God' (above, n. 25), 107.

[27] R. Otto, *The Idea of the Holy*, 2nd edn. (Oxford, 1958), 190.

sibility had by then become religiously corrosive. God's unfathomability, celebrated—in part—for over a millennium, had, in the age of *Sefer Ḥasidim*, reached crushing proportions. So much so that this volatility needed to be mitigated, even at the cost of unveiling a new universe of sin, a new burden of guilt, and a God of relentless requital. |175|

While these transformations were slowly gestating, developments in the Christian world were moving in reverse direction. In the course of the twelfth century, Christian thinkers developed an increasing sensitivity to natural phenomena, to the harmony of the cosmos, and to man's place in it. 'The world', as Marie-Dominique Chenu put it, 'was no longer an incoherent series of phenomena and events which the pious soul ascribed out of hand to the mysterious and implacable will of the Demiurge. It was an organic, homogeneous ensemble, the observation of which was not only possible but worthwhile and satisfying.'[28] And the sensed humanity of the Deity also emerges in this period. In R. W. Southern's words:

> They conquered the universe for humanity, and made God so much man's friend that his actions became almost indistinguishable from our own. The greatest triumph of medieval humanism was to make God seem human. The Ruler of the Universe, who had seemed terrifying and remote, took on the appearance of a familiar friend. The next triumph was to make the universe friendly, familiar and intelligible.[29]

Apparently, things looked somewhat different to Gentiles than to Jews in the twelfth and thirteenth centuries. While Christian thinkers were discovering a human Deity and an intelligible order of things, the spiritual elite of Ashkenaz no longer found compelling or even expressive the warm and all-too-human God of the Midrash, enthroned above a pliant universe and realizing slowly but inexorably His plan in history. In the place of the God of the Midrash and the numinous God of the Heikhalot came the Deus Absconditus (Borè), the Reflected Glory (Kavod), and a God of covert legislation and inexorable retribution.

The German Pietists sought, above all, to find reason and deservedness in the bewildering events that were then overtaking their communities—progressively more assaulted by the emerging 'persecuting society', and

[28] M. D. Chenu, *Nature, Man, and Society in the Twelfth Century: Essays on New Theological Perspectives in the Latin West* (Chicago, 1968), 232.

[29] R. W. Southern, 'Medieval Humanism', in id., *Medieval Humanism and Other Studies* (Oxford, 1970), 30–60 (the citation is at p. 36). On the transformation of the spirituality of western Europe in the course of the eleventh and twelfth centuries, see Fulton, *From Judgment to Passion* (above, n. 23), 60–3 and notes ad loc.; Chenu, *Nature, Man, and Society* (above, n. 28), 4–48; Duby, *The Age of the Cathedrals* (above, n. 23), 75 ff.; Mâle, *The Gothic Image* (above, n. 23), ii. 71–8.

increasingly demonized at the hands of their neighbors as 'rational anti-Judaism' was being transformed into 'pathological antisemitism'. They strove to justify God's way to man, even at the price of implacability in God himself. To the generations of Roman repression, the men of the Midrash had offered comfort; to the generations of the Crusades and the ritual murder accusations, the Pietists offered a vision of a perfect and unblemished Divine justice. To them perhaps this was comfort enough, but, as the swift demise of the movement was to show, it was scarcely enough for others. |176|

III

To be sure, there is a wholly different facet to *Sefer Ḥasidim*, one described by Yitzhak Baer sixty-five years ago in his famous essay on German Pietism[30]—one of 'gentility and personal sensitivity', of introspection and religious inwardness. Baer also pointed to its source. It sprung from the religious atmosphere of the twelfth century, that is to say, from the spirituality implicit in the changed face of God, in the new sense of His humanity and of His intimacy with man. Thus, much of the ethics and spirituality of the German Pietists arose and drew sustenance from the conceptions of God that obtained in their own times, while their theosophy and notions of His workings in history were rooted in the outlook of an earlier era and rested on a wholly different view of God. In this contradiction, with all its ramifications, lies one of the basic problems of their movement and, in no small measure, the source of their lasting interest. But this is the subject of another essay. |177|

AFTERWORD

A

p. 143. In a copious, far-ranging essay,[31] Moshe Idel dwells at length on the theurgic elements in the complex and often contradictory view of God in the voluminous writings of R. El'azar of Worms, and points out that I was unaware of this.[32] He is correct. I was operating in this essay with the conclu-

[30] Y. Baer, 'Ha-Megammah ha-Datit ve-ha-Ḥevratit shel *Sefer Ḥasidim*', *Zion*, 3 (1938), 1–50.

[31] ''Al Zehut Meḥabreihem shel Shenei Perushim Ashkenaziyim le-Piyyut ha-Aderet ve-ha-Emunah ve-'al Tefisot ha-Te'urgiyot ve-ha-Kavod etsel R. El'azar mi-Vorms', *Kabbalah: Ketav 'Et le-Ḥeker ha-Mistikah ha-Yehudit*, 29 (2013), 67–208, esp. 94 ff.

[32] Ibid. 156 n. 352; 203 n. 449. For his discussion of anthropomorphism, see 116 ff., 124 ff., 183 ff., 203 ff. and *passim*.

sions of Joseph Dan, the leading scholar of the esoteric teachings of Ḥasidei Ashkenaz, who has repeatedly asserted that there is no theurgic element in the esoteric teachings of the German Pietists.[33] However, I have no quarrel with Idel's richer, multifaceted perspective. There is unquestionably a very strong strand of anti-anthropomorphism in the movement of Ḥasidei Ashkenaz, as the agitated remarks of R. Mosheh of Taku indicate. R. El'azar of Worms often shared this view, and he devoted a work to its formulation—*Sha'arei ha-Sod ve-ha-Yiḥud ve-ha-Emunah*.[34] Indeed, at times, as Idel has revealingly shown, R. El'azar even strove in his commentaries to neutralize the theurgic in passages in the Midrash and liturgical poetry which reflected a theurgic outlook.[35] On other occasions, perhaps in earlier stages of his religious thinking, some of the theurgic elements in other ancient esoteric traditions which he possessed stirred his religious imagination, as Idel has demonstrated with his usual erudition.[36]

However, the startling contrast between the Heavenly Father of the Midrash and the anti-anthropomorphic Borè of the Ḥasidim—which is a central theme of this essay—is maintained if the contrast is now transformed from an all-too-human Heavenly Father to a characterless, unhuman-like Kavod, who, at the most, simply 'expands' or 'rises' as a consequence of the prayers of Israel. This enlargement of the Divine may have given a great mystic or two supreme pleasure, but it was cold comfort to most Jews, Pietists and non-Pietists alike. (Not every Pietist was a mystic; quite possibly most German Pietists were not mystics. The aspiration to religious virtuosity is one thing; the mystical urge is another.) Can one plead with the Kavod/God, appeal to Its memories, to Its past deeds of love, as one could and did to Avinu she-ba-Shamayim in the world of the Aggadah? Can the intercession of the Patriarchs sway Its decisions? Is there any appeal of Its decrees? Is this enhanced Kavod/God's governance of the world a whit warmer, more merciful, or more comprehensible than that of the Borè?

The same holds true for Idel's remarks about Keneset Yisra'el, 'corporate Israel'. He states that, contrary to my claim, such a collectivity does exist in the thought of R. El'azar,[37] though he admits that it is not to be found

[33] Dan, *Torat ha-Sod shel Ḥasidei Ashkenaz* (above, n. 21), 104–68; *Toledot Torat ha-Sod ha-'Ivrit* (Jerusalem, 2011), v. 238–92. Dan was here following Scholem, *Major Trends in Jewish Mysticism* (above, n. 6), 111–14.

[34] The work was edited by A. Jellinek and published in *Kokhavei Yitsḥak*, 26 (1862), 7–15. See J. Dan, *'Iyyunim be-Sifrut Ḥasidei Ashkenaz* (Ramat Gan, 1975), 72–88; id., *Toledot Torat ha-Sod* (above, n. 33), vi. 638–54.

[35] pp. 183–91 and *passim*.

[36] p. 191.

[37] Adumbrated at pp. 112, 147, 152–3, 180, 182, then 194 ff. Idel's references to my article are found above, in n. 32.

in *Sefer Ḥasidim*. Let me first say that, with the partial exception of anti-anthropomorphism, the subject of this essay is *Sefer Ḥasidim*, as its title clearly states. By way of the writings of Elliot Wolfson, I was aware of the passages that spoke of the Kavod's hugging and kissing the face of Jacob that is engraved on the seat or throne of the Kavod,[38] but didn't know what to make of it. Needless to say, I was unaware of the passages in the writings of R. El'azar on the theurgic power of Jewish prayer to stir the Kavod/God to renew daily Its covenant with Israel, which Idel, with his matchless erudition, has now brought to full scholarly attention—though, I must admit, this idea had been adumbrated in some of his previous articles which had escaped my notice. (Keeping abreast of Idel's output is not one of the easier tasks of scholarship.) Do I believe that this changes much the picture that I have drawn? The answer is no. Perhaps some mystics found deep satisfaction in the erotic (though not sexual, according to Idel) kissing by the Kavod of the image of Jacob's face engraved on Its throne. That, however, was precious little comfort, as I have said, for most Pietists. Keneset Yisra'el in the midrashic world is a warm, even feminine, intercessionary figure who pleads with God for her sons. She is a guarantor of Israel's salvation in the long run, and, at crucial moments of history, also in the short run.[39] Her presence in the celestial hierarchy is, as I wrote in the essay, 'an assurance of the beneficent nature of things'.

The Kavod/God of the German Pietists is not a person, as it were, but an entity without feelings or emotions. The only collective element in R. El'azar's thinking is that the daily prayers of the Jews lead theurgically to the Kavod/God's daily renewal of the covenant with Israel. This is a far cry from the centrality of the *familia* of the On High, the *palmalia shel ma'alah*. Interestingly, the Midrash saw no need for any daily renewal; the covenant of Sinai was sufficient to ensure that the Jews were the chosen people. The authors of the Midrash, however, were members of one of several minorities spread across the expanses of the Christian Roman East. Ḥasidei Ashkenaz and their co-religionists constituted the only tolerated minority in the Latin West, minute communities tightly wedged in a now aggressively supersessionary religion which had just launched a concerted and relentless campaign to convert the Jews, an offensive that insistently challenged Jewish election. R. El'azar's notion of a daily renewal of Israel's covenant appears natural enough when seen in the perspective of late twelfth- and thirteenth-century Ashkenazic

[38] E. Wolfson, 'The Image of God Engraved Upon the Throne: Further Reflections on the Esoteric Doctrine of the Pietists', in id., *Along the Path: Studies in Kabbalistic Myth, Symbolism and Hermeneutics* (Albany, 1995), 1–62.

[39] See above, n. 1.

history. Whether many of his followers or co-religionists found in it succor or sustenance is, I suggest, open to question.

B

p. 144. 'The universe, in hasidic thinking, is empty of harmony and beauty, and above all of meaning. No image of God is to be found there, nor does it reflect His wisdom. Significance is only to be found in the strange and enigmatic phenomena.' This statement and the one that follows would seem to be incorrect, or in need of serious qualification, in light of David I. Shyovitz's thesis, written under the direction of Talya Fishman, '"He Has Created a Remembrance of His Wonders": Nature and Embodiment in the Thought of the Ḥasidei Ashkenaz' (Ph.D. diss., University of Pennsylvania, 2011), and now published in a revised and expanded form as *A Remembrance of His Wonders—Nature and the Supernatural in Medieval Ashkenaz* (Philadelphia, 2017). The similarity between the image of God in hasidic thought and that of Europe prior to the late eleventh and twelfth centuries, so radically different from that of the Midrash, remains unchanged.[40]

[40] Above, nn. 28, 29.

CHAPTER SIX

Two Notes on the *Commentary on the Torah* of R. Yehudah he-Ḥasid

I

All those who deal with medieval Jewish exegesis are familiar with the storm that broke in 1976 upon the publication of R. Yehudah he-Ḥasid's *Commentary on the Torah*.[1] R. Yehudah claimed that several verses were written after the time of Moses. R. Moshe Feinstein, the leading halakhic decisor (*posek*) of the time, had apparently been shown an advance copy of choice sections of the book and declared the statement of non-Mosaic authorship to be heretical, invoking Maimonides' statements both in his *Perush ha-Mishnayot* and in *Mishneh Torah*.[2] As it was inconceivable that R. Yehudah he-Ḥasid was a heretic, the work was clearly a forgery, or certain passages had been cunningly inserted into his blameless composition to better infiltrate the bastions of the faithful. The work, Rabbi Feinstein ruled, should not be published and, if already published, should be withdrawn from circulation.[3]

That the composition is that of R. Yehudah he-Ḥasid there can be little question; there are too many citations from this commentary, specifically

[1] *Perush R. Yehudah he-Ḥasid 'al ha-Torah*, ed. Y. S. Lange (Jerusalem, 1975). I am not quite certain of the date of actual publication. The title page of the commentary gives 5735 (1975) as the year of publication. Yet the first responsum of R. Feinstein, dated 28 Adar I, 5736 (February 29, 1976), speaks of 'X, who is stubbornly insisting on publishing the book attributed to R. Y[ehudah] he-Ḥasid.' In his second responsum, dated 18 Tammuz 5736 (July 16, 1976), R. Feinstein writes that the first letter was based on select galleys that had been sent to him of the yet unpublished book. The storm clearly broke only after R. Feinstein issued his rulings in 1976. I have given the year of publication of the commentary as it is registered in the title page, even if the book may have appeared a year or even two years later, as 18 Tammuz 5736 is less than ten weeks away from Rosh Hashanah 5737 (September 25, 1976). {For some further details of the scandal, See Y. M. Ta-Shma, *Keneset Meḥkarim: 'Iyyunim ba-Sifrut ha-Rabbanit bi-Yemei ha-Beinayim*, i: *Ashkenaz* (Jerusalem, 2005), 272.}

[2] *Perush ha-Mishnayot: Makor ve-Targum*, ed. Y. Kafiḥ, iii: *Nezikin* (Jerusalem, 1965), 212–14; 'Hilkhot Teshuvah', 3: 8.

[3] *Iggerot Mosheh*, 7 vols. (photo offset, Benei Berak, 1981), vii, 'Yoreh De'ah', 3, ##114–15.

attributed to him, in medieval writings to leave room for doubt. Yet it is equally true that the work does attribute several verses of the Pentateuch to later writers.[4] How does one reconcile these two facts? How does one explain the further fact that R. Yehudah he-Ḥasid's *Commentary* is cited by medieval Ashkenazic writers? Why did the scholars of medieval Ashkenaz not share our shock at these notions?

Let us turn to Maimonides' thirteen principles, the central proof text for any charge of heresy. The seventh of his famous thirteen fundamental tenets (*yesodot* or, more commonly, *'ikarim*) of Judaism is that Moses was the *avihen* [*sic*] *shel kol ha-nevi'im*, literally 'the father of all the prophets', more aptly, 'the supreme prophet'.[5] What if someone were to say, with full conviction: 'Frankly, I think, Obadiah was a greater prophet. After all, he made it into the Bible on the basis of a single chapter, whereas Moses had to write five books to get in'? Most would think the speaker mistaken—indeed, view him as an eccentric—but few, if any, would declare him a heretic. Why don't people in America today take this *'ikar* of Maimonides seriously? Put differently: What does *avihen shel kol ha-nevi'im* mean? What sense does this term, this fundamental tenet, make?

In the Christian world in which we live, the phrase, indeed, makes little sense; in the Islamic world, it is the core of Jewish identity. The essential claim of Islam is the supremacy of the Muhammadan revelation. Muhammad was not a god but a human being, a prophet to whom God gave His fullest revelation, which superseded all previous ones, including that of Moses. In the religious orbit of Islam, the essence of Judaism lies in the supremacy of the Mosaic revelation; thus, this belief becomes a fundamental tenet of the faith, an *'ikar*.

In the Christian world, there is of course a claim to religious supersession. However, the set of beliefs that crystallized and was made dogma at the Council of Nicaea saw this supersession as occurring as a result of Incarnation, of God's appearance in the world, and of the new revelation that He then

[4] Gen. 48: 20 (pp. 64–5), Deut. 2: 8 (p. 198), and, by implication, Gen. 36: 31. See G. Brin, 'Kavim le-Ferush ha-Torah shel Rabbi Yehudah he-Ḥasid 'al ha-Torah', *Te'udah*, 3 (1983), 221–5. {B. Z. Katz, 'Judah HaHasid: Three Controversial Commentaries', *Jewish Bible Quarterly*, 25 (1997), 23–30. For a list of Brin's other publications on this topic and those of other scholars, see E. Veizel, 'R. Judah he-Hasid or R. Moshe Zaltman: Who Proposed that Torah Verses were Written after the Time of Moses?' *Journal of Jewish Studies*, 66 (2015), 98 n. 6. Veizel has suggested that R. Moshe Zaltman (or better yet, Saltman) penned those controversial pages. It's an interesting proposal, however, it changes little of my argument. These passages were incorporated into the *Perush R. Yehudah he-Ḥasid* and no opprobrium attended its absorption, as the work was widely disseminated and cited in subsequent Ashkenazic literature.}

[5] See, above, n. 2.

gave to the world. Prophecy plays very little part in Christian belief, certainly not in its self-definition, in its creed and dogma. The result is that this notion has no resonance, is of no religious significance in the contemporary world. So we view its contravention as an eccentricity but scarcely as heresy.[6]

Put differently, an *'ikar* does not arise from the fact that its negation is false, but from the fact that its negation undermines the Jewish system of belief. That Moses' prophecy was of a different order than that of other prophets is an explicit verse in the Torah (Num. 12: 7); it was a specific historical context, its denial by Islam, which turned this verse into an *'ikar*. A belief is an *'ikar* when its content is what differentiates Judaism from the surrounding creedal system.[7]

Alongside the question of the centrality or peripheral nature of prophecy was the question of the text of the Bible. The Muslims claimed that there were explicit references to Muhammad in the Bible, but the Jews in their perverseness had censored them.[8] Christians, on the other hand, differed from the Jews in the interpretation of the Bible, but not as to its text. They differed with Jews on such issues as, for example: Is the Tanakh the 'Old Testament' or not and need it be read as the prefiguration of the new one? Are such precepts of the Pentateuch as the injunctions against eating unclean animals to be read literally or only symbolically? However, as far as the text of the 'Old Testament' went, the Christians were only too aware that the Latin text that they possessed, the Vulgate, was a translation and that the Jews had the true, original text. This was called *hebraica veritas*, the 'Hebrew truth', and some

[6] Not accidentally does the seventh *'ikar* receive the briefest of discussions in the literature of the principles of Jewish faith. I should emphasize that I am not arguing that Maimonides derived the notion of *'ikarim* from his Muslim surroundings; that issue is still an open question. I am contending that he would never have raised the notion of the 'primacy of Mosaic revelation' to the level of an *'ikar* were its opposite not a defining tenet of Islam.

[7] One could qualify the statement by contending that while some *'ikarim* are, indeed, defined by their denial by others, there remain certain beliefs, such as that of monotheism, that would still be considered *'ikarim*, even were the entire world to be in agreement on the matter. I have no quarrel with such a qualification, though, as a philosophic illiterate, I would be perplexed as to how to evaluate such a confession of faith. Take, for example, a universally held notion that ever since Hume is known to be only a belief, a habit of thought without logical foundation, namely, the conviction that the sun will rise tomorrow, as it did today. What could be the creedal significance of the statement 'I believe *be-emunah shelemah* that the sun will rise tomorrow', seeing that the rest of mankind believes likewise? This, however, is an issue for philosophers and theologians to resolve, not for historians. My remarks in this essay are confined to *'ikarim* that have emerged by force of contrast.

[8] See e.g. H. Lazarus-Yafeh, *Intertwined Worlds: Medieval Islam and Bible Criticism* (Princeton, 1992), especially pp. 19–35; C. Adang, *Muslim Writers on the Bible: From Ibn Rabban to Ibn Hazm* (Leiden, 1996), 223–48.

Christian scholars even turned to the Jews for guidance in determining the literal meaning of the biblical texts.[9]

In the Islamic world, the authenticity of the Pentateuchal text was under as much question in the society that enveloped the Jews as is that same text today in our own society after some 150 years of Bible criticism.[10] Jews of Islam were as sensitive to any challenge to the totality of Mosaic authorship as are Jews of the contemporary world. Indeed, more sensitive, for Muhammad was a far weightier figure in Islamic culture than are Wellhausen and his disciples in the modern Western one. It is from this background that the Maimonidean *'ikar* of the totality of the Mosaic authorship derives, and equally its central importance to religious Jews of today.

In medieval Christian culture this idea was without resonance or implication. One *tanna* had stated, simply and with no ado, that the last eight verses were of Divine origin but not of Mosaic authorship,[11] and R. Yehudah he-Ḥasid added that there were several more verses that were not penned by Moses. Was such a position seen as being thoroughly mistaken? Most probably. Was it viewed as odd and nonconformist? Undoubtedly; though hardly more eccentric than R. Yehudah's view that King David, to flesh out his book of Psalms, lifted from the text of the 'original' Pentateuch many anonymous 'psalms' that Moses had penned![12] Were these strange and misguided views, however, perceived as being in any way heretical or even dangerous? In that time and place, certainly not. They contained no concession to the surrounding culture, opened no Pandora's box of questions. Indeed, one can take the religious temperature of R. Yehudah he-Ḥasid's explanation by the matter-of-fact way European medieval commentators (*rishonim*) treated the passages in

[9] See e.g. A. Grabois, '*Hebraica Veritas* and Jewish–Christian Intellectual Relations in the Twelfth Century', *Speculum*, 50 (1975), 613–34.

[10] The centrality of Moses in R. Maimon's *Iggeret ha-Neḥamah* and the immortal, angelic nature that Maimonides' father attributed to Moses should also be understood as part of his attempt to dissuade Jews from converting to Islam, that is to say, from accepting the supremacy of the Muhammadan revelation. See R. Maimon ha-Dayyan, *Iggeret ha-Neḥamah*, ed. B. Klar (Jerusalem, 1945), 56–9 and *passim*. It is the same contested supremacy of the Mosaic revelation that engendered Maimonides' philosophically more sophisticated but no less radical statements about the angelic nature of Moses in the afore-cited (n. 2) passage in his *Perush ha-Mishnayot* (though significantly not in *Mishneh Torah*), to which some scholars have drawn attention. Cf. A. L. Ivry, 'Ismā'ili Theology and Maimonides' Philosophy', in D. Frank, ed., *The Jews of Medieval Islam: Community, Society and Identity* (Leiden, 1995), 288–92; Y. Y. Yuval, 'Mosheh redivivus: ha-Rambam—ke-'Ozer le-Mashiaḥ', *Zion*, 72 (2007), 164–9. I doubt whether similar statements could be found in writings of Jews living in Christian countries (unless, of course, as commentaries on passages of Maimonides). As to the correctness or not of the attribution of the *Iggeret ha-Neḥamah* to Maimonides' father, see Yuval, p. 166 n. 25.

[11] *Bava Batra* 15a, *Menaḥot* 30a.

[12] *Perush R. Yehudah he-Ḥasid* (above, n. 1), Num. 21: 17 (pp. 184–6).

Menaḥot and *Bava Batra* where the tannaitic dictum of Joshua's authorship is cited.[13] In their world, these words did not abut any slippery slope of a 'documentary hypothesis' or of 'Jewish forgery'. No need, therefore, to reinterpret this passage or to forfend any untoward implications. What concerned R. Yehudah he-Ḥasid's contemporaries, the Tosafists, in this statement were its practical halakhic implications for the Sabbath Torah readings, not its theological or dogmatic ones, for to them, as to R. Yehudah, there were none.[14]

This differing attitude to the possibility of a sentence or two being of Divine but not Mosaic authorship is analogous to the opposing positions on the issue of literalism in interpreting legal passages in the Torah. R. Shemu'el ben Me'ir (Rashbam) of Ramerupt and Rouen and R. Yosef Bekhor Shor of Orléans could take such verses as 'an eye for an eye' or the one forbidding cooking a kid in the milk of its mother with a literalism that Ibn 'Ezra could never allow himself, coming as he did from a world where Karaism was flourishing. The scholars of northern France could permit themselves the hermeneutic luxury of splitting off, at times, the literal meaning of the Mosaic text from the dictates of the Oral Law, something an embattled Rabbinic Judaism could never allow itself to do.

Let us clearly delineate the parameters of our discussion. The essay addresses a historical question: How could R. Yehudah he-Ḥasid have written that several verses in the Pentateuch were not of Mosaic authorship? Whether such a work should be published in the latter half of the twentieth century poses an entirely different question: Is it permissible or religiously advisable to publish a work that expresses ideas that contravene a dogma established by Maimonides and writ into the Jewish creed for centuries—ideas, furthermore, that can be seen as inimical today to Jewish faith as they were in the time of Maimonides? Its permissibility poses a halakhic problem, its advisability—one of religious leadership; neither falls within the purview of this essay.

II

Eccentric the *Commentary* certainly is, and no one who has read ten of its 'innocent' pages, which have nothing to do with questions of Pentateuchal authorship, would question its peculiarity. However, its puzzling nature is not

[13] Above, n. 11.

[14] *Tosafot*, *Bava Batra* 15a, s.v. *shemoneh*; *Tosafot*, *Menaḥot* 30a, s.v. *shemoneh*. (Rabbi Feinstein [above, n. 3] pointed out that all *tanna'im* in the passages in *Bava Batra* and *Menaḥot* concurred that the Torah was a product of Divine dictation, not simply Divine inspiration. R. Yehudah he-Ḥasid saw little difference between the two.)

entirely the consequence of R. Yehudah's singular mode of thought. At times it is the result of a failure in communication rather than of the strangeness of the message being communicated. I would like to suggest one of the difficulties that hinder our understanding of the *Commentary*. Much of it was not written by R. Yehudah he-Ḥasid himself, but instead consists of reports of his son, Saltman, of his father's weekly Torah classes, or interpretations of his father that he heard from others. Saltman reports:

> דבר אל בני ישר׳ ויקחו לי תרומה [מאת כל איש אשר ידבנו לבו תקחו את תרומתי] (שמות כה: 2) הקשה אבי, מה ר״ל ויקחו תקחו שתי פעמים? ופי׳ כך היה המעשה: שמשה ציוה כל מי שידבנו לבו יתן, זה מאה או כ׳ זקוקים או י׳ זקוקים כל אחד לפי עשרו, וכן עשו. והלך משה ולקח כל הכסף שהתנדבו ישר׳ ותיקן מטבעות מהן, כל מטבע היה שוקל מחצית השקל. ומינה שני גזברים ונתן לאחד שק מלא מטבעות ואמר תן לכל אחד מיש׳ מחצית השקל, פי׳ מטבע אחד, וכן עשה הגזבר. והיה הגזבר השיני הולך אחריו ובידו שק ריקן והנה כל אחד מישר׳ נותן לו מחצית השקל, אותן שקיבלו מן הגזבר הראשון. וזהו ויקחו תקחו, ב׳ לקיחות היו, הראשונה כפי נדבת כל איש והשנייה מחצית השקל. ועוד היה מקשה אבי, לפי הפשט איך יתכן כשהק[ב״ה] אומר ״והדל לא ימעיט ממחצית השקל״ (שמות ל: 15), למה לא צעקו הדלים ״אדני משה, אנו אין לנו אפי׳ פרוטה לקנות צרכינו פה ואנו היינו ברצון מאחרים מקבלים, ואתה אומר ליתן מן הגורן או מן היקב״? אלא כדפי׳.
>
> וככל אלה הדברים היה אומר לי אבי על פסוק אחר. כי היה מקשה שני פסוקים זה על גב זה. פסוק אחד אומר ״כל העובר על הפקודים מח׳ השקל״ (שמות ל: 13), וכתוב אחר אומר ״לכל העובר״ (שמות לח: 26). אלא כל העובר נותן, לכל העובר זה המקבל.[15]
>
> והקשיתי לו מהו שעשה הפייט ״קיצין לבל יעוז מול מקהלים קרוא לומר הוני פדאני מעיקולים״.[16] ואם עני מה יכול להשתרר איני רוצה ליתן, מה מזיק לו לאדם שנותנין לו ביד אחת ומחזיר בידו השנייה? ועוד, מהו ״לכפר על נפשותיכם״ (שמות ל: 16)? ועוד מהו ״ולא יהיה בכם נגף״ (שמות ל: 12) ״ונתנו איש כופר נפשו״ (שם)? ותירץ לי, משה אמר לגיזבר ליתן להם מתנה גמורה על מנת שלא להחזיר, הרי אם היו רוצים היו תופשין לעצמן בטוב ואעפ[״כ] היו נותנין ועוד שאר היה תי׳ לי ולא נראה לי. ואמרתי מעולם לא עלה זה על דעת משה רבינו. וגער בי מ״א ואמר לי הלואי שהייתה כל התורה סדורה[17] כדבר זה.

S[peak] . . .' [Exod. 25: 2] My father and teacher asked what is the doubling of the verb 'to take'—'they shall take for me', 'you shall take'. He explained that the story in the

[15] See *Sefer Perush u-Fesakim 'al ha-Torah le-Rabbenu Avigdor ha-Tsarfati* (Jerusalem, 1956), 82 (on Exod. 30: 15) for a slightly different report of R. Yehudah's interpretation, namely, it was not the *gizbar* but the rich who gave the poor the half-shekel that the latter had to contribute. This passage was already noted by A. Marmorstein, 'Sur un auteur français inconnu du treizième siècle', *Revue des Études Juives*, 76 (1923), 117, though (at p. 118) he mistakenly attributes the passage to the French Tosafist R. Yehudah Sirleon, pupil of Ri.

[16] Recited on *Parashat Shekalim*; see *Seder 'Avodat Yisra'el*, ed. S. Baer (repr. New York, 2001), 650 (note of Y. S. Lange, editor of the commentary).

[17] Thus in the printed text and corroborated by the manuscript (Cambridge Add. 669.2, fo. 43r). In the parallel passage, referred to below, n. 19, the reading is *berurah*. Nevertheless, I hesitate to emend our passage in its light.

Bible occurred in this manner. Mosheh commanded everyone whose heart volunteered to give, this one 100 or 20 deniers or 10 deniers—each according to his wealth. And so they [the Israelites] did. And Mosheh went and took all the monies that the Israelites had contributed and minted coins from them; each coin weighed a half-shekel. And he ordered two treasurers, and he gave to one a sack full of coins and said 'Give every Israelite a half-shekel'. And the second treasurer followed in his wake with an empty sack, and every Israelite gave him the half-shekel he had just received from the first treasurer. And this is the meaning 'they shall take for me', 'You shall take my *terumah*': the first was the freely given contribution of individuals, the second the half-shekel [that the first treasurer was distributing]. And he further used to ask, 'How was it possible when God commanded "and the poor shall not give less than a half-shekel"? Why didn't the poor cry out, "Mosheh, our master, we don't have even a penny to purchase the necessities of life here, and we gladly receive from the [charity of] others [meaning of last clause not certain, HS], and yet you ask to give [what for us is] 'from the threshing floor to the winery' [i.e. a great sum of money; 2 Kgs 6: 27]." The answer [to this question, he said,] is as I have just explained.'

And in the same manner he used to explain to me another [problematic] verse. Because he used to point out a contradiction between two verses. One verse says . . . but [the solution is that] . . . gives, and . . . receives.

And I asked him, '[If so,] how can the liturgical poet write . . . what does a man care if what he gives with one hand is returned to his other hand? Furthermore, what meaning has the verse "to atone for your souls" [Exod. 30: 16] [if the half-shekel that he contributed is returned to him]? Similarly, what is the meaning of the verse "and there will be no plague" [Exod. 30: 12; if you count the Israelites by means of the number of half-shekels; if the money is returned, there are no half-shekels to be counted]? And what does the verse "and each shall give the ransom of his soul" [ibid.; what ransom is there, if all is returned]?' And my father and teacher replied, 'Mosheh ordered the treasurer to give [the half-shekel as] an unrestricted gift with no obligation to return it, and had they wished they could have readily retained it, but they didn't.' And he gave answers to the other questions, and they did not appear plausible to me, and I said 'Mosheh, our master, never thought of such things.' And my father got angry with me and said, 'Would that the entire Torah was as ordered [i.e. clear] to me as this is.'

The notion of Moses going about handing out half-shekels in the desert to all the Jewish males over 20 seems strange, to put it mildly. R. Yehudah he-Ḥasid's angry certainty of the truth, indeed self-evidence, of his interpretation seems odder still. That is, until we read the following passage in *Sefer Ḥasidim*:

התורה נתנה כנגד דעות בני אדם. אמרה לעשיר ולעני לתת מעשרות ותרומות ומתנות כהונה. אם יש עני בישראל וכהן עשיר, איך יתכן שהעני יתן לעשיר? אלא התורה צותה לכל עני ועשיר כדי שלא יאמר העשיר "עני אני ואיך אתן לכהן עשיר?" . . . לכך לא חילק

עני ועשיר כדי שלא יאמר העשיר "עני אני ואיך אתן לכהן עשיר?" . . . לכך לא חילק הכתוב. וכן כשצריכים הקהל לתת צדקה, אף על פי שיש עניים בעיר שמתפרנסים בצמצום, נותנין חרם לתת מן הליטר[א] כך וכך. [ו]אף על פי שזה אינו נכון להיות נותן (ל)[מ]עני לצורך העני, ופעמים שעני הנותן יותר עני מן המקבל. אלא מפני הרעים שאם לא יכנס זה באותו חרם, גם רבים לא יכנסו . . . וכל ענין הקהל מבוטלים. לכך מוטב שיתנו גם הם ויכנסו עמהם בחרם . . . *והטובים יחזירו להם לעניים כל מה שיתנו*, בסתר שלא ידעו בו הרעים.[18]

The Torah had to adjust its dictates according to the differing temperaments of people. It commanded both the poor and the rich to give [an equal] amount of tithes and priestly gifts. If there is a poor Israelite and a rich *kohen* is it just that the poor give to the rich? However, the Torah ordered both the poor and the rich equally to forestall the rich man from saying, 'I am poor, how can I give to a rich *kohen*?' . . . Therefore, the Torah did not make a distinction. Similarly when the community imposes a contribution to the communal chest, even though there are poor people who barely make ends meet, they impose—under the threat of religious excommunication—a fixed percentage of so many pennies per pound. Even though it is not right to force a poor man to give to another poor man, and at times the poor man who gives is yet poorer than the one who receives, however, this must be so because of the wicked. If one person will be exempted from the imposition, many others will equally refuse to participate, and all communal order will cease. Therefore, it is better that all give and they [the poor] be included in the ban together with the others . . . And the *tovim* [the good ones, possibly the Pietists] should return to the poor all [the money that] they contributed.

The *maḥatsit ha-shekel* (half-shekel) was a poll tax; what animated R. Yehudah's interpretation was the unjustness of such an impost. Equity dictated that Moses could not have imposed the same burden of payment on the poor as on the rich, hence his certainty as to the interpretation of the biblical passage. R. Yehudah he-Ḥasid had a vision of social justice but could not express it in discursive terms. He could speak only in biblical interpretations, parables, and numerologies. The author(s) of *Sefer Ḥasidim* grasped the vision and translated its practical implications into that work. Saltman, the son, understood nothing; he had not a glimmer of what underlay any of his father's interpretations. The exegesis that he heard was simply an explanation of biblical verses and not a hermeneutic expression of larger purposes and aspirations.

[18] *Sefer Ḥasidim* (Berlin, 1891), #914; Bologna edn. (Margoliot), #1046 (italics mine). H. H. Ben-Sasson drew attention to the connection between these two passages in 'Ḥasidei Ashkenaz 'al Ḥalukkat Kinyanim Ḥomriyyim u-Nekhasim Ruḥaniyyim bein Benei Adam', *Zion*, 35 (1970), 64–5, repr. in id., *Retsef u-Temurah*, ed. J. Hacker (Tel Aviv, 1984), 180–1. I wish here simply to draw an inference from this connection as to the character of the transcriber and shed some light on the nature of the commentary.

We are fortunate to have in *Sefer Ḥasidim* a parallel passage to R. Yehudah he-Ḥasid's exegesis here that clues us to the true intent of his remarks. One can be sure, at the very least, that the other passage, where he angrily informs his questioning son that he wished that all other passages were as clear to him as the one he had just propounded,[19] was similarly grounded in some compelling vision. Indeed, probably a number of other 'strange' interpretations found in his son's commentary issued from the same source. Unfortunately, I have found no parallels to these passages in *Sefer Ḥasidim* which would enable further decoding. Others, however, may perceive meaningful connections, new passages may be discovered in manuscripts, and the strangeness of the *Commentary* somewhat lessened.

The instance of Saltman's commentary and its contrast to the social and religious vision of *Sefer Ḥasidim* is a replay on an infinitely lower plane of the 'Socratic problem'.[20] If one reads the description of Socrates in Xenophon one has the impression of a wise and moral man and an appealing personality, but one, in intellect at least, not very different from any of the sophists that he so opposed. From the writings of Plato, whether one takes all attributions by Plato to him quite literally or views the Socrates of the later dialogues as being simply a spokesman for Plato's mature thought, Socrates still emerges as a compelling figure of genius, indeed, the father of Western philosophy. The Socratic problem is a recurrent one in the transmission of ideas, especially in traditional societies, where so much instruction is through oral teaching. And when one reads the reports of students of their master's teachings, ancient, medieval, or modern, one would do well to bear in mind Bertrand Russell's observation: 'There has been a tendency to think that everything that Xenophon says must be true, because he had not the wits to think of anything untrue. This is a very invalid line of argument. A stupid man's report of what a clever man says is never accurate, for he unconsciously translates what he hears into something that he can understand.'[21]

[19] See *Perush R. Yehudah he-Ḥasid* (above, n. 1), Exod. 19: 19 (pp. 94–5), and Ben-Sasson, 'Ḥasidei Ashkenaz 'al Ḥalukkat Kinyanim' (above, n. 18), 437 n. 4 end.

[20] See e.g. W. K. C. Guthrie, *A History of Greek Philosophy* (Cambridge, 1969), iii. 325–77; A. R. Lacey, 'Our Knowledge of Socrates', in G. Vlastos, ed., *The Philosophy of Socrates* (New York, 1971), 22–49, and the introductory essay in that volume.

[21] B. Russell, *History of Western Philosophy* (New York, 1945), 102–3.

CHAPTER SEVEN

Topics in the *Ḥokhmat ha-Nefesh*

THIS WAS A PAPER written in 1965 for a seminar on the esoteric teachings of Ḥasidei Ashkenaz given by Dr Joseph Dan, who advised publication. I am so far removed from the issues discussed here that I had no way of assessing its value. Several knowledgeable people told me that the technical analysis made here of the fluid and ever-shifting terminology of the *Ḥokhmat ha-Nefesh* still holds true, though whether this is due to my youthful insight or to the fact that nothing else on that work has been published in the past half-century is an open question.

Ḥokhmat ha-Nefesh (or *Sefer ha-Nefesh*, as it is called in some manuscripts) was first published in Lemberg in 1876 from MS Munich 81. The Safed edition, which is otherwise a replica of that of Lemberg including the identical font, corrected several errors of pagination which had occurred in it. Sections of the *Ḥokhmat ha-Nefesh* are also to be found in the Bologna text of *Sefer Ḥasidim* (Jerusalem, 1960), #1129 ff., and in the *'Arugat ha-Bosem*, ed. E. E. Urbach (Jerusalem, 1938), i. 214–15. The printed text is poor, and unfortunately the numerous manuscripts, while helpful—perhaps indispensable—for many minor points, give little aid and less comfort on central issues. The manuscripts used in the preparation of this study are: Oxford, Bodley, Neubauer 1569, 1570, 1571, 2393; Parma, De Rossi 1390; British Library, 737; London, Library of the Beth Din, 70; Florence, Biblioteca Medicea Laurenziana, Plut. I. 44; Paris, Bibliothèque Nationale 850 (fragments), all of which are available on microfilm at the Hebrew University, Jerusalem. I would like to acknowledge the kindness of the libraries in allowing photostats to be made of the respective films.

{A somewhat superior text of that work has been published by the Makhon Sodei Razaya in the second volume of *Sifrei ha-Ra mi-Germaiza, Ba'al ha-Roke'aḥ* (Jerusalem, 2006), sect. 2, 1–132. This is based upon a manuscript copied in 1343/4 and today privately owned by an individual in Australia, whose microfilm, however, is on file in the Institute of Microfilmed Hebrew Manuscripts at the National Library of Israel (f 43104). I will refer to this edition as *SR*. The Safed edition employs folio numbering; there are four columns to each folio. The *SR* edition numbers pages, each with two columns.}

A sixteenth-century Italian translation of the *Ḥokhmat ha-Nefesh* is to be found in G. Margoliouth's *Catalogue of the Hebrew and Samaritan Manuscripts in the British Museum*, no. 1057, 81a–129b.

{I would be remiss if I did not mention that the past several years have witnessed a growing interest in the esoteric lore of the German Pietists both in the *ḥaredi* and in the academic worlds, and many passages from the *Ḥokhmat ha-Nefesh* have been cited and reinterpreted. In the *ḥaredi* world, Y. Y. Stal has produced exceptionally erudite editions of texts of Ḥasidei Ashkenaz, such as the *Sefer*

I

STRUCTURE OF THE SOUL AND *DA'AT*

Introspection, often a characteristic of pietistic movements, stimulated interest in the nature of the soul. And when it was discovered in a theory of microcosm[1] that a knowledge of the structure of the soul meant insight into that of the Deity, the quest received new impetus.

The *midrashim* yield little that is concrete, though one of them does describe the respective shapes of the *neshamah* and *ruaḥ*.[2] More material was found in the translation of Sa'adyah's works,[3] but the major source was the writings of Ibn 'Ezra.

The doctrines discovered there were somewhat heterogeneous. In Ibn 'Ezra's commentary on Ecclesiastes,[4] he begins with the Aristotelian classification of vegetative, sentient, and intellectual souls, but he switches in the middle to the Platonic tripartite division and speaks at length of the appeti-

Gematriyot of R. Yehudah he-Ḥasid, 2 vols. (Jerusalem, 2005), *Amarot Toharot Ḥitsoniyot u-Fenimiyot* (Jerusalem, 2006), *Sodei Ḥomesh u-She'ar* (Jerusalem, 2009), and *Teshuvot Rabbenu El'azar mi-Vormaiza ha-Roke'aḥ* (Jerusalem, 2014). D. M. Sigal's study 'Sefer ha-Ḥokhmah ha-Meyuḥas la-Roke'aḥ', contained in his *Sodei Razei Semukhim*, 2nd edn. (Jerusalem, 2001), has challenged the authenticity of much of one of the most frequently cited works of R. El'azar of Worms. In academia, D. Shyovitz's *A Remembrance of His Wonders: Nature and the Supernatural in Medieval Ashkenaz* (Philadelphia, 2017) has shed new light on the attitude of the German Pietists to nature and the human body; while the study of Inbal Gur Ben-Yitshak, 'Bein Shamayim va-Arets: 'Iyyun be-Yaḥas ha-Koḥot bein Elyonim ve-Taḥtonim, Masa' ha-Nefesh ve-Ḥerut ha-Adam 'al pi *Ḥokhmat ha-Nefesh* le-R. El'azar mi-Vorms' (MA diss., Bar Ilan University, 2010), is the first in-depth study of the work as a coherent whole rather than as one limb of a far larger corpus of hasidic thought, which has hitherto been the scholarly practice.}

1 *Ḥokhmat ha-Nefesh* (Safed, 1913), fo. 1d; *SR*, 4a (cf. Safed, fo. 8b; *SR*, 30a). Ibn 'Ezra, *Yesod Mora ve-Sod ha-Torah: Mahadurah Madda'it Mevo'eret*, ed. J. Cohn and U. Simon (Ramat Gan, 2002), 77. Cf. *Ḥokhmat ha-Nefesh*, Safed, fos. 29c–30d; *SR*, 125b.

2 Safed, fo. 4b; *SR*, 14a–15a. The manuscript variations improve the text but little. For the sources, see *Midrash Tehillim ha-Mekhuneh Midrash Shoḥer Tov*, ed. S. Buber (Vilna, 1891), 102, on verse 11: 6 {Zikhron Aharon edn. (Jerusalem, 2012), i. 126}; *Bet ha-Midrash: Midrashim Ketanim vi-Yeshanim u-Ma'amarim Shonim*, ed. A. Jellinek (Vienna, 1878), v. 45.

3 See the term *goshem* in Safed, fo. 5c; *SR*, 20a; Safed, fo. 11d; *SR*, 48a. The word is from the famous paraphrase of Sa'adyah Gaon's *Book of Beliefs and Opinions*, MS Munich 42, fo. 361a (footnote in J. Dan's unpublished edn. of MS Oxford 1567). See below, pp. 169–70, and 176. {See now R. N. Kiener, 'The Hebrew Paraphrase of Saadiah Gaon's *Kitāb al Amānāt wa'l-I'tiqādāt*' (Ph.D. diss., University of Pennsylvania, 1984); id., 'The Hebrew Paraphrase of Saadiah Gaon's *Kitāb al Amānāt wa'l-I'tiqādāt*', *AJS Review*, 11 (1984), 1–25.}

4 Eccles. 7: 3. *Mikra'ot Gedolot ha-Keter*, ed. M. Cohn, *Ḥamesh ha-Megillot* (Jerusalem, 2012), 168–9, cited paraphrastically at Safed, fo. 5c–d; *SR*, 20a–21b.

tive, spirited, and rational souls, and, following Sa'adyah, calls them in turn *nefesh*, *ruaḥ*, and *neshamah*. These two views were not only presented in isolation, but were also unwittingly mixed. He attributes sentience to the spirited soul, a trait which must be given to the appetitive one, seeing that appetite is a desire for pleasure and pleasure is a function of sensation.[5] Similarly, in the seventh chapter of the *Yesod Mora*[6] he bestows upon the spirited element the attribute of locomotion, again transferring the Aristotelian mobility of the middle soul to the Platonic structure.[7] In that work, he also distributes the three forces between the liver, the heart, and the brain.[8]

Whereas the Aristotelian doctrine is only partially echoed in one, somewhat obscure, passage of our work,[9] the Platonic triad was lifted bodily by Roke'aḥ straight out of the *Yesod Mora* and Ibn 'Ezra's commentaries on Exodus and Ecclesiastes, and inserted into the *Ḥokhmat ha-Nefesh*.[10] Citation, however, is one thing and influence another. The title of his work is, after all, *Ḥokhmat ha-Nefesh* not *Ḥokhmat ha-Neshamah*. The new terminology of *nefesh*, *ruaḥ*, and *neshamah* was, admittedly, artificial,[11] and since it ran counter to all uses of the terms in both Bible and Midrash, the Ḥasidei Ashkenaz could not be expected to adhere to it—especially if one remembers that they did not think primarily in terms of concepts supported by biblical verses, but rather in blocks of verses.

The practical location of various qualities in sundry parts of the body was more fortunate. The liver as the seat of desire gained widespread acceptance,[12] and the intellectual element now acquired a permanent residence in the brain,[13] although it did not give up its old domicile in the heart,[14] nor could

[5] This is found at Safed, fo. 29d; *SR*, 122a.

[6] *Yesod Mora ve-Sod ha-Torah* (above, n. 1), 135–6. This may have given rise to the reduction of the heart to an instrument of perception in service of the liver found at Safed, fo. 23b; *SR*, 95a.

[7] Note cancelled. {Thus in the printed version.}

[8] *Yesod Mora ve-Sod ha-Torah* (above, n. 1), 135–6. Safed, fo. 29d; *SR*, 122a–122b.

[9] Safed, fo. 25d; *SR*, 106a. The last two lines, especially *u-ve-zeh ha-davar*, are obscure. The whole section reads like a quotation.

[10] Safed, fo. 5c–d; *SR*, 20a–21a. Safed, fo. 29d; *SR*, 122a–122b.

[11] See the language of Ibn 'Ezra on Eccles. 7: 9: **לכן אשים שמות להן** and in the *Yesod Mora*, 135: **תחפץ קרא אותם שלשה שמות 'נשמה' ו'רוח' ו'נפש'**.

[12] Safed, fo. 3a; *SR*, 9b. Safed, fo. 10b; *SR*, 42a. Safed, fo. 23b; *SR*, 95a. Safed, fo. 29a; *SR*, 119a. Safed, fo. 31d; *SR*, 129b, though sometimes the blood was viewed thus. The two may be identical—see Safed, fo. 4a; *SR*, 13b. Safed, fo. 29a; *SR*, 119a.

[13] Safed, fo. 1a; *SR*, 1a. Safed, fo. 3a; *SR*, 9a. Safed, fo. 4b; *SR*, 14a. Safed, fo. 10a; *SR*, 42a. Safed, fo. 19c; *SR*, 80b. Safed, fo. 24b; *SR*, 99b. Safed, fos. 25d–26a; *SR*, 106a. Safed, fo. 29a; *SR*, 119a. Safed, fos. 31a, 31b; *SR*, 126b, 128a. The only basis for this in the Talmud is *Yevamot* 9a; see W. Hirsch, *Rabbinic Psychology: Beliefs about the Soul in the Rabbinic Literature of the Talmudic Period* (London, 1947), 150.

[14] Safed, fo. 1b; *SR*, 2a. Safed, fo. 2c; *SR*, 7a. Safed, fo. 26b; *SR*, 36b. Safed, fo. 19d; *SR*, 81b—the lat-

it totally dissociate itself from the kidneys.[15] The pulsating heart (*lev ha-melavlev* (as the seat of locomotion) caught the hasidic fancy,[16] though its claims to being the source of anger were contested by the liver,[17] this time in virtue of the theory of humors.

But the diffusion of differing faculties is a far cry from the doctrine of separate souls,[18] and this tripartite doctrine did not penetrate deep. If one ignores the twenty-odd lines of matter in the *Ḥokhmat ha-Nefesh* taken from Ibn ’Ezra, one's understanding of the work is hardly impaired.[19] Any theory may amount to influence if it becomes part and parcel of a central, shaping tradition, but the sundry scraps gathered by the tiny band of German Pietists formed no such thing. Under such circumstances the impact of that work depended on how deeply it struck a responsive chord in its readers.[20]

The concern of the Ḥasidei Ashkenaz was not primarily with psychology per se, but with the nature of and relationship between the soul and the Kavod. As soon as the rational soul was identified with the Divine element in man, the other, mortal, forces became of marginal interest only. Even when thus contemplated, the system carried little conviction. For while the Aristotelian division is a zoological classification of living beings, the Platonic one is an analysis of human nature. Its attractiveness lay in the fact that it accurately reflected the personality of a type produced by a culture in which the cul-

ter source describes the mind as seated in the heart and the liver as the seat of desire within the very same paragraph.

[15] Safed, fo. 26c; *SR*, 108a–b. Safed, fo. 29a; *SR*, 119a.

[16] Safed, fo. 11d; *SR*, 48a. Safed, fo. 23b; *SR*, 95a. Safed, fo. 26b; *SR*, 36b. Safed, fo. 31d; *SR*, 129b, etc.

[17] Safed, fo. 31d; *SR*, 129b. Safed, fo. 14c; *SR*, 59b–60a.

[18] Ibn ’Ezra oscillates slightly between three separate souls in his commentaries on Exod. 23: 25 and Eccles. 7: 9 and a vague three faculties or forces (*Yesod Mora*). Though he claims in his commentary on Ecclesiastes to be following Sa'adyah, Sa'adyah himself insisted on diverse faculties of one soul; see Sa'adyah Gaon, *The Book of Beliefs and Opinions*, trans. S. Rosenblatt (New Haven, 1948), 1, 241–5. {I now fail to see the difference between the tripartite description in Ibn ’Ezra's commentaries and that found in the *Yesod Mora*.}

[19] Apart from the two citations of Ibn ’Ezra, there is a line and a half referring to the tripartite division in Safed, fo. 3a; *SR*, 9b, which is but one of a string of numerical threes. Another (Safed, fo. 4a; *SR*, 13a) has no connection with what follows (see below, n. 25) and there are another two lines in Safed, fo. 12a (ll. 7–9); *SR*, 29a–b. The latter is clearly a quotation, as the style indicates, as does also the fact that it locates desire not in the liver but in the lower part of the body under the diaphragm—exactly as in the *Timaeus*, 69a–70e.

[20] This is not to imply that its readership was consciously selective. Rather, circumstances accentuated the tendency toward arbitrariness and dogmatism, which often characterizes rabbinic Judaism when it encounters non-rabbinic texts. It remembers as much of the tract as seems appropriate at the time, and then invests the retained material with authority by virtue of its coming from a work of unquestioned truth.

tivation of the body, competition for excellence, and intellectual pursuit were commendable (if indeed unequal) ends of human existence. But to those who accepted as valid a disciplined satisfaction of the bodily needs but saw further physical cultivation as smacking of concupiscence, and for whom pride was, at best, a sin amongst many others and the intellect of Divine origin, the Platonic scheme was disproportionate and out of focus. Above all, the claims of the middle soul—spirit—to be a basic constituent of human nature would appear to be highly arbitrary.[21] The tripartite division found no echo in hasidic introspection and, being wholly alien to the Bible and Talmud, it could shed no light on those texts in which the Pietists were so deeply immersed. Indeed, the chance encounter between these ideas and the semi-canonized literature which did not know them merely caused perplexity.[22]

If any division of man exists in the rabbinic *Weltanschauung*, it is between the earthly and the heavenly,[23] instinct and imperative, and, in its most acute form, the good and the bad. Such a literature could have been bent to serve the purposes of dualism, but not tripartism; and indeed, a few faint traces of such a dichotomy do sometimes appear in the *Ḥokhmat ha-Nefesh*.[24] But outside citations, the spirited soul of Plato makes no appearance,[25] and the heart, its base, is assigned a number of differing functions.[26] One might, indeed, have thought that the ascetic tendencies of the movement would have been fertile soil for the development of an acrid doctrine of dualism. Yet there is nowhere noticeable in the *Ḥokhmat ha-Nefesh* any antagonism towards the body.[27] This is in part due to their being deeply imbued with rabbinic literature, but also in part to the influence of Donnolo. His detailed admiration for the structure of the body as an example of the Divine purposiveness and, above all, his elaborate theory of the microcosm which the Ḥasidei Ashkenaz adopted so prominently,[28] and to which they added the further parallelism of the body to the

[21] This idea could have become the theoretical basis for the doctrine of humility (see Safed, fo. 5d, l. 7; *SR*, 21a, ll. 6–7), so central to *Sefer Ḥasidim*. Its failure to do so underscores the fact that this tripartite doctrine was not absorbed by Ḥasidei Ashkenaz.

[22] See the inquiry of R. Shemu'el, Safed, fo. 11b, middle; *SR*, 46a–b. This is a Platonic tradition, but the question posed is identical.

[23] Cf. Hirsch, *Rabbinic Psychology* (above, n. 13), 152–4.

[24] Safed, fo. 6c; *SR*, 24b. Safed, fo. 7b; *SR*, 27a. Safed, fo. 26b; *SR*, 37a. Safed, fo. 27d; *SR*, 114a.

[25] Note that passages 3a, 4a make no mention of spirit, only of the beating of the heart (*dofeket*, *melavlev*). Even when they refer to the tripartite system, but are not actually quoting, they omit the core of the theory and quote only the physical phenomenon. Cf. above, n. 16.

[26] See above, nn. 16, 17; Safed, fo. 19d; *SR*, 81a. Safed, fo. 23b; *SR*, 95a; plus *binah*, Safed, fo. 3b; *SR*, 10b. Safed, fo. 12a; *SR*, 48b–49b. Safed, fo. 19d; *SR*, 81a; *tik ha-yir'ah*, Safed, fo. 2c; *SR*, 7a.

[27] Safed, fo. 26b; *SR*, 36a–37b and Safed, fo. 27d; *SR*, 114a are simply rephrasings of *Avot* 3: 1.

[28] Safed, fo. 23b–d; *SR*, 95b–97b. Safed, fo. 26c; *SR*, 108a–b. Safed, fo. 31a; *SR*, 126a–127a. Safed, fo. 31c–d; *SR*, 129a–130b. {On Donnolo, see now A. Sharf, *The Universe of Shabbetai Donnolo* (New York,

Tabernacle,[29] prevented the development of a 'prison' theory of the soul. This is even more remarkable in view of the fact that their etymology also yielded an interpretation of *guf* (body) similar to that which provoked the Platonic one.[30]

I have mentioned before that Sa'adyah's terminology, though formally acknowledged, was never adopted. The interchange, it should be noted, is always upward. *Nefesh* may refer also to the Divine part of man in contradistinction to *guf*, and *ruaḥ* may refer to the same in contrast with the appetitive *nefesh*. *Neshamah*, being formally assigned to the highest element, is, as a rule, fixed, and does not refer to forces other and lower than the Divine. However, the stylistic habit of Roke'aḥ of weaving semi-quotations into his own sentences leads to confusing juxtapositions, and at times makes this rule subject to exception.

Since upon this revolves a major problem both of the structure of the soul and of terminology,[31] it will be as well to go into the matter at some length.

In what may be his response[32] to a query by R. Shemu'el ben Kalonymos, Roke'aḥ writes:

> הנשמה היא נר ונתלבתה מאש הכבוד . . . והיא נתונה ברום הגוף על מקום המוח . . .
> וכן כח הנשמה בכל איברים חיותה וממשלתה ע"כ נקראת חיה. והיא יחידה בגוף הגושם.
> והדעת שבנפש היא למעלה ממנה . . . כי הדעת בחיה ואין גיד ואבר ועצם שאין שולטת בהם
> עצת הדעת . . . כי מכח דעת הנשמה נודע לנו הדבר כמו ונשמת ש די תבינם (איוב לב :ח).

The *neshamah* is a candle that was lit from the fire of the Kavod . . . and she is placed in the body at its apex, seated in the brain . . . Similarly the dominion and quickening power of the brain extend to [i.e. govern] all limbs and therefore she is called 'a living soul' [Gen. 2: 7] . . . And she rules [alone] in the physical body. And the *da'at* of the soul is at the top of the *neshamah* [i.e. governs the *neshamah*] for the *da'at* is what quickens and there is no limb or ligament that the wish of the *da'at* doesn't control . . . for what

1976) and P. Mancuso, *Shabbetai Donnolo's* Sefer Hakhmoni*: Introduction, Critical Text and Annotated Translation* (Leiden, 2010), and see D. Shyovitz's discussion in *A Remembrance of His Wonders* (above, preliminary note), 252 n. 18.}

[29] Safed, fo. 5a; *SR*, 18a. Safed, fo. 26c; *SR*, 108a–b (the origin is *Midrash Tanḥuma 'al Ḥamishah Ḥumshei Torah* [Stetin, 1865], 'Pekudei', sect. 3, p. 344; the latter half of the passage is found in Safed, fo. 5c; *SR*, 18a). Cf. Safed, fo. 26c; *SR*, 108a–b for the triple parallelism between man, Tabernacle, and the heavenly throne.

[30] Cf. Safed, fo. 14c, d; *SR*, 59b–60a (not to be confused with Safed, fo. 2c; *SR*, 7a). *Gorgias* 493d.

[31] Cf. J. Dan, 'Ha-basis ha-'Iyyuni shel Torat ha-Musar shel Ḥasidei Ashkenaz' (Ph.D. diss., Hebrew University of Jerusalem, 1964), 280–2. {See now id., *Toledot Torat ha-Sod ha-'Ivrit* (Jerusalem, 2011), vi. 595–613.}

[32] Before this section (Safed, fo. 11d; *SR*, 48a–b). MS British Library 737, fo. 536a reads: התשובה על השאלה. איני יודע אם היא כתובה פה אחר השאלה או הוא דבר בפני עצמו, כי כן מצאתיו בהעתק לפני.

we know of things is because of the powers of the *da'at* of the *neshamah*, as Scripture says: 'and [via] the *neshamah* the Almighty gives understanding' [Job 32: 8].

The impression here given is that *da'at* is distinct from the *nefesh* and *neshamah* and superior to them. In reality what has occurred is that in the course of discussing the Divine soul, Roke'aḥ proceeded to quote the famous talmudic passage (*Berakhot* 10a) which enumerates amongst the unique traits of the soul its being the source of vitality. This engendered associations of Sa'adyah's *Perush 'al Sefer Yetsirah*, wherein God is characterized as being both the life and intelligence of the universe, analogous to the soul's role in relationship to the body.[33] This passage Roke'aḥ proceeded to cite almost verbatim. But Sa'adyah, writing in Arabic, had not used the term *neshamah* for the vital element in man,[34] and thus could without difficulty write that *da'at*, intelligence, was its superior. Roke'aḥ, writing in Hebrew and having the citation of *Berakhot* clearly in mind, automatically employed the term *neshamah*, and then proceeded to quote Sa'adyah about the superiority of intelligence —with the resultant confusion of terms.

What facilitated this juxtaposition was the general use of *da'at* in the *Ḥokhmat ha-Nefesh*. In talmudic discussions of the uniqueness of the soul rationality plays little part. Indeed, in the *locus classicus* of such characterizations, that in *Berakhot* (10a), no mention is made of it at all. When the talmudic soul was identified with the Platonic *logistikon* its distinguishing trait became its rationality, at least in terms of formal definition.[35]

In the language of the paraphrase this attribute is called *binah*,[36] in that of Ibn 'Ezra *ḥokhmah*. Under the latter's influence the term *ḥokhmah* appears several times in our work,[37] but when Roke'aḥ sets out to formally define the *neshamah*, he writes: היא בעלת החכמה . . . ומחכמת ומשכלת דעת ('she [the *neshamah*] is the possessor of *ḥokhmah* . . . and she makes the *da'at* wise and understanding').[38] An examination of the use of *da'at* in the *Ḥokhmat ha-Nefesh* shows it to be only *neshamah* or *ruaḥ* expressed in Hellenic terminology and used interchangeably with it. Compare:

[33] Cited in *Perush Sefer Yetsirah le-ha-Rav ha-Nasi R. Yehudah b. Barzilai ha-Bartseloni*, ed. S. Z. H. Halberstam (Berlin, 1885), 177–8. Original text in *Commentaire sur le Sefer Yesirah, ou Livre de la création*, trans. M. Lambert (Paris, 1891), 70 (French translation, pp. 91–2 with minor variations).

[34] Contrast the Arabic text on p. 70 with p. 34.

[35] Sa'adyah Gaon, *The Book of Beliefs and Opinions* (above, n. 18), 244; *Commentaire sur le Sefer Yesirah* (above, n. 33), 55. See Ibn 'Ezra cited above. Note that Sa'adyah's definition completely displaced the midrashic quintet of purity, invisibility, etc.

[36] MS Munich 42, fo. 443b.

[37] Safed, fo. 1b; *SR*, 2b. Safed, fo. 3a; *SR*, 9a. Safed, fo. 10b; *SR*, 42a.

[38] Safed, fo. 5c; *SR*, 20a.

(*a*)

1. ודע כי כל דעת האדם נשאר לו לאחר מותו דכתיב והעוף אוכל...הראוהו שידע כי הדעת רואה העוף

Know that man's entire *da'at* continues [to live on] even after his death, as Scripture says: 'And the birds are eating' [Gen. 40: 17] . . . because the *da'at* sees the birds. (Safed, fo. 6d; *SR*, 24b)

2. והעוף אוכל אותה . . . הרי מצינו מן התורה שהנשמה רואה מה שעושין לאחר מיתה

And the birds are eating' [Gen. 40: 17]: . . . Here we find in the Torah that the *neshamah* sees what is done after death. (*SHB*, #1163 [##1129 ff. are taken from *Ḥokhmat ha-Nefesh*]; Safed, fo. 25c; *SR*, 104a)

3. הנה ידוע כי הרוח לאחר מות הגוף רואה שנא' והעוף אוכל אותו

It is well known that the *ruaḥ* sees after death, as Scripture says, 'And the birds are eating'. (Safed, fo. 14c; *SR*, 59b–60a)

(*b*)

1. רוח היא הדעת, והוא הנידון לפי מעשיו אם בטוב אם ברע, והרוח תשוב אל הא לקים

Ruaḥ is *da'at*, and he is judged according to his deeds, for better or for worse, [as Scripture says], 'and the *ruaḥ* shall return to God' [Eccles. 12: 7]. (Safed, fo. 6a; *SR*, 22b)

2. כי הנשמה מן השמים . . . ורוח תשוב אל האילקים כי הנשמה עולה לכסה"כ

For the *neshamah* is from Heaven . . . and the *ruaḥ* shall return to God [Eccles. 12: 7]. For the *neshamah* ascends to the throne of Glory. (Safed, fo. 6c; *SR*, 24a–b)

(*c*)

1. הדעת מוקף ריח הגוף

The *da'at* is ensconced in the spiritual body. (Safed, fo. 6d; *SR*, 25a)

2. כי הרוח דקה ביותר . . . ומלובשת בריח הגוף

For the *ruaḥ* is clothed in a spiritual body. (Safed, fo. 5d end; *SR*, 26b)

(*d*)

1. אבל הדעת בעודו בתוך הגוף סגור הדעת בתוכו לכך נקרא גוף ע"ש ויגיפו את הדלתות, אבל כשמת הדעת חוץ לגוף וראייתו אנה ואנה לארבע רוחות

But the *da'at*, when it is still in the body, is enclosed therein; the body [*guf*] is called thus [because the root means 'enclosed', as in the verse] 'and they closed the doors' [Neh. 7: 3]. However, when the *da'at* is outside the body, it sees simultaneously above and beneath and in all four directions. (Safed, fo. 14c; *SR*, 60a)[39]

[39] The citation concludes: ברגע אחד, שנא' והחיות רצוא ושוב וכן הנשמה לכך אחת הנה ואחת הנה (מ"א: ד ל"ה) מארבע רוחות בואי הרוח (יחזקאל לז ט). One could insist that the phrase *ve-khen ha-neshamah* implies that *neshamah* and *da'at* are separate. I believe, however, in view of the above, that this is

2. **ואחר מות האדם הנשמה רואה למעלה ולמטה לכל צדדים בפ״א כי הגוף נקרא ע״ש ויגיפו הדלתות סגורה בגוף, ואחר צאתה אין לה הקף ומסגר וכו׳**

After the death of a man, the *neshamah* sees above and below and on all four sides simultaneously, and it is called *guf* because it is enclosed in the body, as in the verse 'and they closed the doors' [Neh. 7: 3]. However, after she [the *neshamah*] leaves the body, she is unbounded and unenclosed. (Safed, fo. 14d; *SR*, 61a)

(*e*)

ואין דעת האדם לאחר שמת ברשותו אפילו צדיק גמור לענין החיים. שאם היה ברשותו עצמו היה בא בחלום לאוהביו ומזהירו. לכך הוא ברשות הממונה[40] לפי מה שגוזרים. ויש אומרים שהנשמה או בגיהנום או בג״ע או נידונית או מתענגת לכך אינה בא להזהיר את אהוביו

And man's *da'at*, after his death, is not under his control with regard to its relationship with the living, even were he a true saint. Were he to have control [of his actions], he would come to those he loves and warn them [of dangers]. For this reason, [the *da'at*] is in the hands of the appointed [the Divine supervisor], who executes what [God] decrees. And some say that the *neshamah* is either in Gehenna or in Paradise, and for this reason it does not come to warn [those whom it loves]. (Safed, fo. 14c–d; *SR*, 60a)

Further evidence of the identity of the two terms is to be found in the following passage (Safed, fo. 11d; *SR*, 48b): **מכח דעת הנשמה נודע לנו הדבר כמו ׳ונשמת שדי תבינם׳** [41] ('Because of the *da'at* of the *neshamah* do we know things, as is written, "and [via] the *neshamah* the Almighty imparts knowledge" [Job 32: 8].') Sa'adyah first quoted this verse from Job in his definition of soul both in *Beliefs and Opinions* and in the *Commentary* as proof that the soul is intellect. Roke'aḥ cites it on two other occasions in our work, both in connection with the rational faculties of the *neshamah*:

simply a repetition, with interchange of interchangeable words common to the syntax of our book. Especially so in view of the identity of the terms in the following lines which I cite in the text, item *e*.

[40] Note the assignation of a *memuneh* to exercise authority over *da'at*.

[41] (*a*) Of the other occurrences of *da'at*, the passages in Safed, fo. 3a; *SR*, 9a; Safed, fo. 4a; *SR*, 14a; Safed, fo. 19c–d; *SR*, 80b–91a are uninformative. The passage in Safed, fo. 15c–d; *SR*, 63b–64b is obscure in both printed texts and manuscripts, with phrases such as **ואין נפש רוח הדעת שנשאר לאחר מות הגוף על הרוח**. In one section (Safed, fo. 19d; *SR*, 80b–81a), sentience is attributed to the *da'at* and this is viewed as immortal; in another, the habit of terming the soul *ruaḥ* in its nocturnal visitations of the living results in the term *ruaḥ ha-da'at* (see the identical statement made about *da'at* cited in the text, item *e*). The phrase *'osek ha-da'at ruaḥ ha-adam* (Safed, fo. 15c; *SR*, 63b–64b) I take as being appositionary: *'osek ha-da'at*, i.e. *ruaḥ ha-adam*, a redundancy common to Roke'aḥ when employing a new term for old entities, e.g. *malakh mazzalo*. I may easily be mistaken in my reading of this passage, but even allowing for subsidiary meanings of *da'at*, I see no reason not to construe our passage in accordance with its predominant sense, especially in view of its Sa'adyanic origin. (*b*) As *da'at* is used only once with respect to angels (Safed, fo. 14d; *SR*, 60b), I have omitted treating it.

1. והנשמה איננה גוף ונופחה באדם על כן חכמתה מרובה ונשמת ש די תבינם

The *neshamah* isn't the body, and it was breathed into him [by God; Gen. 2: 7], as is written, 'and [via] the *neshamah* the Almighty imparts knowledge' [Job 32: 8]. (Safed, fo. 1b; *SR*, 2a)

2. ועתה כן המדה כשהנפש יוצאה מן הגוף...רואה בכל צד...מליאה בינה כמו נשמת ש די תבינם

And now this is how things are: . . . when the *nefesh* exits the body . . . she sees in all directions . . . full of understanding, as is written, 'and [via]the *neshamah* the Almighty imparts knowledge' [Job 32: 8]. (Safed, fo. 13c; *SR*, 55a)

Finally, the terminology employed to characterize the origins and destiny of *da'at* is identical with that used to describe the soul:

(*a*)

1. כי הדעת... ולא יזיק לה כל טינוף הגוף, וחיה לעולם אף במות הגוף

Because the *da'at* . . . cannot be affected adversely by any bodily filth, and she lives eternally even after the death of the body. (Safed, fo. 11d; *SR*, 48a)

2. הנשמה חי לעולם בין חי האדם בין מת האדם... והיא לא תטנף בגיעול הגוף

The *neshamah* lives forever whether a man lives or dies . . . and she cannot be affected adversely by any bodily object of disgust. (Safed, fo. 5c; *SR*, 19b–20a)

(*b*)

1. עומדת (הדעת) בכחה כפי מעשיה בכסא צרורה...ומתענגת מהוד כבוד אשר בראה משיור אשו

And the [*da'at*] stands attached, according to her deeds, to the throne [of the Kavod] . . . and delights in the glory of the Kavod, from whose fiery remnants she was created. (Safed, fo. 11d; *SR*, 48a)

2. הנשמה היא נר ונתלבתה מאש הכבוד

The *neshamah* is a candle that was lit from the fire of the Kavod. (Safed, fo. 11d; *SR*, 48a)

3. הנפש... צרורה תחת כסה"כ ומתענגת בראיית הכבוד

And the *nefesh* is attached to the underside of the throne of the Kavod and delights in the sight of the Kavod. (Safed, fo. 13a; *SR*, 55a)

II

THE ORIGIN OF THE SOUL, ITS SOJOURN IN THE BODY, AFTERLIFE

Conflicting reports are to be found in the *Ḥokhmat ha-Nefesh* as to the origin of the soul. At times it is described as originating from the holy spirit (*ruaḥ mi-ruaḥ*)[42] via a process of inbreathing (*nefiḥah*).[43] On other occasions it is said to have been lit from the flames of the Kavod or of the heavenly throne.[44] Other passages speak vaguely of its having been created (*nivra*) from the place of the heavenly spirit,[45] from a pure place, or even from *benei 'elyonim*.[46] Whether any of these processes, or all of them, are genuine acts of creation or only emanations cannot be determined from the text.

Following the Midrash[47] instead of Sa'adyah,[48] the souls are described as having been created along with the world[49] and woven into the tapestry that faces the Kavod,[50] and as passing their time in praise of the Lord. Their pre-existence thus essentially anticipates their post-existence.

Originating from the Divine,[51] the *neshamah* bears a resemblance to it,[52] and inspection of one yields knowledge of the other. And it was for the purpose of providing man with an inkling of, and avenue towards, the Kavod that he was vested with a soul.[53]

Once in the body, the soul has not yet cut its links either with God or with the world from which it came. It reports nightly to God upon the thoughts and deeds of the body.[54] It retains an instinctive knowledge of the wonders of God's works and continues, during its sojourn in the body, its adulation of the Creator.[55] It retains sufficient knowledge of its author to sense when its prayers have been accepted, and is flooded with joy when it experiences the turning of the light of the Kavod upon it. Finally, the soul possesses an

42 Safed, fo. 1a; *SR*, 1a. Safed, fo. 5c; *SR*, 19b. Safed, fo. 9d; *SR*, 40b. Safed, fo. 29b; *SR*, 120b. Also Safed, fo. 27d; *SR*, 114a.

43 The term is used very frequently.

44 Safed, fo. 11b; *SR*, 46a. Safed, fo. 13c; *SR*, 55a. Safed, fo. 23c; *SR*, 96a. One passage (Safed, fo. 5d; *SR*, 21b) speaks of *ha-nofekhet mi-kisè ha-kavod*. If the passage from Donnolo (cited in Safed, fo. 5b–c; *SR*, 19a–b; Safed, fo. 9c; *SR*, 39b) on the origin of the heavenly throne was a conscious part of hasidic thinking, then this is perhaps equivalent to the fire origin theory.

45 Safed, fo. 5a; *SR*, 17b–18a (see Safed, fo. 7b; *SR*, 26a).

46 Safed, fo. 9d; *SR*, 40b (see Safed, fo. 5a; *SR*, 17b–18a). MS London, Beth Din, 70 is unique in preserving the variant reading ממקום קדושה וטהרה.

47 *Midrash Tanḥuma* (Stettin, 1864), 'Pekudei', sect. 3, p. 344; *Niddah* 31b.

48 *The Book of Beliefs and Opinions* (above, n. 18), 235.

49 Safed, fo. 19b; *SR*, 78b (*Tanḥuma*, ibid.). The passage הנפש היתה קודם העולם in Safed, fo. 19a; *SR*, 78a means קודם שיצאה לאויר העולם as is clear from the continuation.

50 Safed, fo. 7c; *SR*, 28a. Following Rashi on *Yevamot* 62b and *'Arukh*, s.v. *guf* (cf. Kohut's notes there).

51 Safed, fo. 2d; *SR*, 8b. Safed, fo. 5d; *SR*, 21b, and *passim*.

52 Safed, fo. 5b; *SR*, 19a, *mar'ot kevodo*; Safed, fo. 1a; *SR*, 1a, בענין מראית שכינתו ובענין הווייתו. The terms are not self-explanatory within the *Ḥokhmat ha-Nefesh*. On *havvayot*, see G. Scholem, *Ursprung und Anfange der Kabbalah* (Berlin, 1962), 245–7. {See now id., *Origins of the Kabbalah* (Philadelphia, 1987), 279–93; J. Dan, *Torat ha-Sod shel Ḥasidut Ashkenaz* (Jerusalem, 1978), 94–103; id., *Toledot Torat ha-Sod ha-'Ivrit* (above, n. 31), v. 259–68.}

53 Safed, fo. 1a; *SR*, 1b–2a.

54 Safed, fo. 2d; *SR*, 8a–b, and *passim*.

55 Safed, fo. 3a; *SR*, 9a–b.

intuitive knowledge of its state in the afterlife, both its judgment and its bliss.[56]

Upon death, after a ritual immersion in fire[57]—the standard purification for celestial beings—the soul ascends heavenward. These two separate traditions award it different fates. According to the predominant midrashic theme, the souls are gathered into the treasury underneath the heavenly throne,[58] but other passages speak of the souls as gathered about the Shekhinah and exulting in its rays.[59] It is this latter view which the Ḥasidei Ashkenaz primarily adopted,[60] moved, perhaps, by their familiarity with the Heikhalot literature with its heavenly court and their own preoccupation with the Kavod and its intrinsic relation to the soul.

The seating of the souls before the Kavod in a carefully gradated hierarchy according to their merits may reflect a minute concern either for the glory of God or for the principle of justice. It may be an extension of the heavenly court, in which gradations are introduced for fear of a breach in the awesome homage that must be rendered to the Deity, or it may be concerned primarily with man, namely, that he should finally and permanently receive his exact deserts. Whilst the former image appears in one passage of the *Ḥokhmat ha-Nefesh*,[61] it is the latter which clearly predominates.[62] For the Ḥasidim, with their emphasis on humility and simplicity, were far more at ease in the deeply personal, almost familial world of the Midrash than in the rigid, ruthless, and flaming hierarchies of the Merkavah. But for all this, their congenital literary eclecticism saw to it that they were not prevented from copying passages of the latter kind here and there into their works.

The nature of these gradations is not uniform throughout the book. At times they are spoken of in terms of the distance from,[63] or of position in relation to, the Kavod, or of the soul being level with various organs of the 'figure on the throne'.[64] On other occasions, mixing his own interpretation of

[56] Safed, fo. 3a; *SR*, 9a–b. Safed, fo. 1c; *SR*, 3a–b. Safed, fo. 7b; *SR*, 27a. It may be that these last two points, without necessary root in verse or Midrash (as found for the others), hint at some religious experience of the Ḥasidim themselves, especially the phrase *nofelet pit'om simḥah*.

[57] Safed, fo. 28b; *SR*, 115a.

[58] *Shabbat* 152b and parallel passages cited in *Yefeh 'Einayim* ad loc. The term *genuzot taḥat kisè ha-kavod* is a standard one, and is the simplest interpretation of *tseror*.

[59] *Berakhot* 17a.

[60] The first opinion is found in Safed, fo. 26c; *SR*, 108b (see Safed, fo. 20b; *SR*, 93a–b), the second in Safed, fo. 7a; *SR*, 25b–26a. Safed, fo. 13c–d; *SR*, 55a–56b and Safed, fo. 28b; *SR*, 115a–116a combine both, but it is clear that the phrase *genuzot taḥat kisè ha-kavod* is literary ballast only.

[61] Safed, fo. 28b; *SR*, 115a.

[62] Safed, fo. 7a; *SR*, 55a–56b, *in extenso*; Safed, fo. 13c; *SR*, 55b. Safed, fo. 13d; *SR*, 56a. Safed, fo. 14a; *SR*, 57b.

[63] Safed, 14a; *SR*, 57b.

[64] Safed, 7a; *SR*, 25b. The image of chairs is itself composite. The chairs are drawn from *Midrash*

a famous talmudic passage with that of others,[65] R. El'azar distinguished between the vision of the Greater Light emanating from the upper half of Ezekiel's figure and the Lesser Light of the lower half.[66] Finally, there is a passage which speaks of the Outer and Inner Light.[67]

Souls enraptured by the Divine light and singing hymns to God's glory fill the dominant hasidic vision of the afterlife. But on one occasion the simpler, more common sentiments of the Ḥasidim prevail, and the world to come is portrayed as the realization of the dream of a well-rounded *talmid ḥakham*.[68]

The theory of the physical punishment of the souls of the wicked inevitably raises the question of some corporeal object capable of receiving the chastisement.[69] When this was enhanced by the desire of the Ḥasidim for a precisely corresponding retribution,[70] the doctrine of 'spiritual bodies' (*re'aḥ ha-guf*) was produced or invoked.[71]

III

DEMUT

A prominent place in the *Ḥokhmat ha-Nefesh* is occupied by *demuyot*,[72] mirror-images of man fashioned at the beginning of Creation[73] and which

Rabbah, Bamidbar, ed. M. Mirkin (Tel Aviv, 1964), 11: 1 (p. 280) (see A. Jellinek, ed., *Bet Hamidrash* [Vienna, 1872], v. 46, and *Bava Metsi'a* 85b). The individual gradations are drawn from *Shabbat* 152b (cf. *Midrash Vayikra Rabbah*, ed. M. Margolies [Jerusalem, 1953–60], 396, and notes ad loc.). That the portrayal attempts to place distance between the soul and the Kavod has been pointed out to me by Joseph Dan.

[65] *Sukkah* 45b: דעיילי בבר; cf. commentaries ad loc., and *'Arukh ha-Shalem*, ed. A. Kohut (Vienna, 1878–92), s.v. ספקלר, and B. N. Lewin, ed., *Otsar ha-Ge'onim: Teshuvot Ge'onei Bavel u-Ferusheihem 'al Pi Seder ha-Talmud*, vii: *Yevamot* (1928–43), 123–5; *Perush Sefer Yetsirah* (above, n. 33), 21; see Dan, 'Ha-Basis ha-'Iyyuni' (above, n. 31), 17–18. {See now Dan, *Torat ha-Sod shel Ḥasidut Ashkenaz* (above, n. 52), 111–12; id., *Toledot Torat ha-Sod ha-'Ivrit* (above, n. 31), v. 251–7.}

[66] Safed, fo. 13d; *SR*, 56b (cf. Safed, fo. 13c; *SR*, 55b; Safed, fo. 14a; *SR*, 57a).

[67] Safed, fo. 13b; *SR*, 54b.

[68] Safed, fo. 14a; *SR*, 57a–58b.

[69] See e.g. Nahmanides' *Sha'ar ha-Gemul* in *Kitvei ha-Ramban*, ed. C. D. Chavel (Jerusalem, 1964), 283 ff.

[70] Safed, fo. 7a; *SR*, 26b.

[71] Ibid. (It appears also, in other connections, in Safed, fos. 5d–6a; *SR*, 21a–22b; Safed, fo. 6d; *SR*, 24a–25b.)

[72] Safed, fo. 6c; *SR*, 24b. Safed, fo. 7b; *SR*, 26b. Safed, fo. 12b; *SR*, 50a. Safed, fo. 12d; *SR*, 52b. Safed, fo. 13c; *SR*, 55b. Safed, fo. 13d; *SR*, 56a. Safed, fo. 15d; *SR*, 65a. Safed, fo. 16a; *SR*, 65a–b. Safed, fo. 16b; *SR*, 66a–67a. Safed, fo. 18d; *SR*, 76b. Safed, fo. 21b–d; *SR*, 86b–89a. Safed, fo. 22a; *SR*, 89b–90a. Safed, fo. 24b; *SR*, 99b. Safed, fo. 25b; *SR*, 103b. Safed, fos. 26d–27d; *SR*, 108b–113b. Safed, fo. 28b–c; *SR*, 109a–117b. {On *demut* see now Dan, *Torat ha-Sod shel Ḥasidut Ashkenaz* (above, n. 52), 224–9; id., *Toledot Torat ha-Sod ha-'Ivrit* (above, n. 31), vi. 613–19.}

[73] Safed, fo. 27c; *SR*, 112b.

stand in endless array before the Kavod,[74] drawing their sustenance from the absorption of the heavenly light that streams forth from the Kavod,[75] and in turn transferring this vitality to their earthly counterparts.[76] Although one passage would suggest that they are made of some emanation of that Divine light,[77] the substance of the *demuyot* nevertheless remains shadowy. For this reason, and owing also to the congenital inability of Ḥasidei Ashkenaz to adhere to any fixed scheme or terminology, the term *demut* alternates with those of *mazzal* and *malakh*, but with differing connotations. At times, the *mazzal* or *demut* is distinguished from the *malakh*, the former referring to the soul-images mentioned above, whilst the latter term indicates the active guardian angels of the Bible and Midrash, who may assume, when on terrestrial missions, the shape of their ward.[78] On other occasions the two terms are identified, albeit in different ways. Thanks to the quest for a traditional name for a somewhat *nouveau arrivé* celestial entity,[79] and in view of the long association of a person's 'angel' with his fate, the *demut* is often simply labeled *malakh*,[80] but, in other instances, the *demuyot* (or *mazzalot*) are viewed as being substantively angels. Human faces have simply been imposed upon the well-known categories of *malakhei ḥabbalah ve-raḥamim* as if there were a resistance to the idea that good and bad could have undifferentiated representation before God.[81]

[74] Safed, fo. 12b; *SR*, 50a. Safed, fo. 27c; *SR*, 112b.

[75] Safed, fo. 13c; *SR*, 55b.

[76] Safed, fo. 13c; *SR*, 55b. Safed, fo. 28c; *SR*, 116b.

[77] See the image of the flame, Safed, fo. 13c; *SR*, 55b (cf. Safed, fo. 3d; *SR*, 12a).

[78] Safed, fo. 15d; *SR*, 64b–65a (see *Ha-Targum ha-Arami ha-Mekhuneh Targum Yonatan ben 'Uzi'el 'al Ḥamishah Ḥumshei Torah*, ed. D. Rider [Jerusalem, 1974], 52, Gen. 33: 10). Safed, fos. 15d–16a; *SR*, 65a.

[79] The entries s.v. *mazzal* in J. Levy, *Wörterbuch über die Talmudim und Midraschim* (Berlin, 1924), M. Jastrow, *A Dictionary of the Targumim, the Talmud Babli and Yerushalmi and the Midrashic Literature* (London, 1903), and E. Ben-Yehudah, *Milon ha-Lashon ha-'Ivrit ha-Yeshanah ve-ha-Ḥadashah* (Jerusalem, 1908–59), and in the *'Arukh ha-Shalem* (above, n. 68), to which may be added *Bava Batra* 12a and *Ḥagigah* 5a, yield no such concept. A. Kohut's attempt (*Jüdische Angelologie* [Leipzig, 1866], 92–3) to prove such a concept on the basis of *Shabbat* 146a is unconvincing. Rashi, in three places, interprets this astral body as *malakh* (*Shabbat* 53b, 61b, *Megillah* 3a), but makes no claims as to the prototype. The Targum on Eccles. 7: 15 (cited in the *'Arukh*) has, perhaps, such a concept, but this passage is without influence.

[80] Safed, fo. 13c; *SR*, 55b. Safed, fo. 16b; *SR*, 66b. Safed, fo. 21b; *SR*, 86b–87a.

[81] (*a*) Safed, fo. 7b; *SR*, 26b. Safed, fo. 28c; *SR*, 116b. I have declined to interpret Safed, fo. 7b; *SR*, 26b as a state of pre-existence and thus to find a hint to pre-determination, for the only other passage which contains this image (Safed, fo. 28c; *SR*, 116b) is clearly one of coexistence, the fate of the spiritual entity being subject to immediate alteration by human conduct.

(*b*) Two further meanings of *demut* should also be noted—see p. 173 above. *Mazzal* may also refer either to the guardian angel of a nation (Safed, fo. 26b; *SR*, 107a) or to the more pedestrian (at times almost pedantic) *genius loci* (Safed, fo. 18b; *SR*, 75b).

Though of celestial nature, and perhaps coeval with the soul,[82] the *demut* is not one's other, higher soul,[83] the reunion with which is the goal of spiritual ascent. The *demut* is a counter-shape and plays no role in the religious experience of Ḥasidei Ashkenaz. Its functions are numerous. There is an antecedent image corresponding to every change in man, and it is by inspection of these images that angels obtain their foreknowledge of human events;[84] and their perception by man is, perhaps, the source of visions, prophetic or magical.[85] Every deed on earth is reproduced by the *demut* before the heavenly throne,[86] and conversely, every act to which the *demut* is subjected in heaven takes place subsequently on earth,[87] thus providing for the Ḥasidim—who, for all their opposition to anthropomorphism, were incurably pictorial-minded—a vivid portrait of both the immediacy of Divine omniscience and of the medium of Divine providence. Finally, the ingestion of light by the *demut*, mentioned above,[88] gave expression to the conviction (perhaps the experience?) that the source of life is a repose in the Divine light and a perpetual infusion of it.[89]

Because of the profound relationship between the mirror-image of man and his actual well-being and fate, the doctrine of *demut* bulks large in the teachings of Ḥasidei Ashkenaz. But as was their wont, they entertained alongside it, and not always discerningly,[90] other, substantially different types of celestial shapes: mirror-images that are not of men, and images of men which mirror nothing.

The objects of prophetic vision must clearly encompass such configurations as the human form seated on the throne, which, needless to say, stands in no relationship to any earthly counterpart.[91] Conversely, counter-images, usually called *mar'ot* or *dugma'ot*,[92] to set them off from the more clearly

[82] Safed, fo. 27c; *SR*, 112b. Safed, fo. 19b; *SR*, 79a; cf. above, p. 168.

[83] The problem of what corresponds to the *demut* before and after death, and how it differs from the soul, engenders occasionally a sliding of terms (of *nefesh* and *mazzal*), e.g. in the sources listed above, n. 82, in Safed, fo. 25b; *SR*, 103a–b, and in the obscure phrase in Safed, fo. 2c, ולמה נקרא גוף שגוף האדם מצויר אחר גוף של מטה היא הנשמה (all manuscripts are identical with the printed text, except MS London, Beth Din 70, which reads אחר גוף שהוולד של מטה). But this should not obscure the essential distinction. {*SR* at p. 7b reads: אחרי הגוף של מעלה היא הנשמה.}

[84] Safed, fo. 26d; *SR*, 109a–b.

[85] Safed, fo. 6c; *SR*, 24b. Safed, fo. 14d; *SR*, 60b. Safed, fo. 18c–d; *SR*, 76a–b. Safed, fos. 26d–27b; *SR*, 109a–114a.

[86] Safed, fo. 14d; *SR*, 60a.

[87] Safed, fo. 26d; *SR*, 109a–b. Safed, fo. 21d; *SR*, 87a.

[88] See above, p. 174.

[89] I suspect that the shade referred to in Safed, fo. 22a; *SR*, 90a–b is the one cast by the falling of the heavenly light on the *demut*, and hence its absence is an indication that the *demut* is no longer within the rays of the Kavod. Cf. I. Tishby, *Mishnat ha-Zohar* (Jerusalem, 1961), ii. 92. The text, however, is not clear, and the numerous manuscript variants yield no better reading.

[90] Safed, fo. 21b; *SR*, 86b–87b. Safed, fo. 18a; *SR*, 74a–b.

[91] Safed, fo. 21b; *SR*, 86b–87a.

[92] Safed, fo. 14b–c; *SR*, 69a. Safed, fo. 18a–d; *SR*, 73b–76b.

Divine *demuyot*, are claimed for every terrestrial object, animate or inanimate. It is these forms, rather than the semi-divine archetypes, which (more appropriately) may be subject to the command of sorcery. This ethereal world makes the justice of Divine judgment more manifest by freeing its evidence from the ravages of time and nature.[93] Finally, it serves the purpose of providing for the somewhat fastidious hasidic mentality a buffer-state between the transcendental and the mundane, a medium via which the pure could act upon the impure without any contaminating encounter.[94]

The origins of the concept of *demut* may lie ultimately in the Platonic theory of ideas, in astral correspondence, or in astrological stars;[95] but in the *Ḥokhmat ha-Nefesh* it has been reduced to passivity,[96] as an instrument of Divine action and an object of supernatural perception. But if the German Pietists unwittingly borrowed from Plato, they had their revenge on the pagan: for their *demuyot* did not establish unity in the teeth of diversity, but rather multiplied the multiplicity by two.[97]

[93] Safed, fo. 18a; *SR*, 74a. The passage from *Ḥagigah* 16a preoccupied the minds of Ḥasidei Ashkenaz; see Safed, fo. 2d; *SR*, 8a, and Safed, fo. 5d; *SR*, 21b for alternative explanations, i.e. that of ריח הגוף.

[94] Safed, fo. 14b–c; *SR*, 59a.

[95] G. Scholem, *Major Trends in Jewish Mysticism* (New York, 1941), 117. Joseph Dan has drawn my attention to A. Wertheimer, ed., *Battei Midrashot: 'Esrim ve-Ḥamishah Midreshei Ḥazal* (Jerusalem, 1950), i. 44.

[96] See especially Safed, fo. 13c; *SR*, 55b, the reduction of the *mazzal ha-rakia' ha-taḥton* to mere receptivity.

[97] This article, which has been delayed for technical reasons since 1967, has been overtaken in the press by J. Dan's *Torat ha-Sod shel Ḥasidut Ashkenaz* (Jerusalem, 1968). {The 1967 issue of the *Journal of Jewish Studies*, in which this essay first appeared, saw the light of day in 1969.}

METHODOLOGICAL ISSUES

WHILE I have dealt with *Sefer Ḥasidim* from time to time, the leading scholar of German Pietism of this generation has unquestionably been Ivan Marcus. His work *Piety and Society: The Jewish Pietists of Medieval Germany* made a considerable impression when it appeared in 1981. It was and still is widely cited; indeed, one might say without exaggeration that it has, over the years, achieved semi-canonical status.* Nonetheless, I have deep reservations regarding the methodology of his study as well as his manner of reading and interpreting *Sefer Ḥasidim*.

I would like, in the two following essays, to set forth my difficulties and proffer some ground rules that I believe should be employed in drawing inferences from *Sefer Ḥasidim*. These principles, if used flexibly, should be helpful in analyzing any aggregated and associative work and can be put to good use, in my opinion, in finding the contemporary agenda in ethical works and in drawing historical inferences from writings that employ standard terminology and seek to advance what to all appearances are traditional moral goals.

I realize that I am a minority of one; nevertheless, I hope that my distinguished colleague will engage me in a methodological discussion to our mutual benefit and that of other students of German Pietism.

* See e.g. E. Shoham-Steiner, 'The Humble Sage and the Wandering Madman: Madness and Madmen in an Exemplum from Sefer Hasidim', *Jewish Quarterly Review*, 96 (2006), 38.

CHAPTER EIGHT

On Reading *Sefer Ḥasidim*

IN HIS INFLUENTIAL BOOK *Piety and Society: The Jewish Pietists of Medieval Germany*, Ivan G. Marcus writes:

The question is, What is the character of the group portrayed in *Sefer Ḥasidim* as non-Pietists? Haym Soloveitchik has recently observed that *Sefer Ḥasidim* applies the term "wicked" to cases of learned rabbis who wrote liturgical poems [*piyyutim*] but who are simply non-Pietists, that this usage indicates that "wicked" denotes those who do not follow the Pietists' Way, and that most references to sinners, corrupt communal leaders and criminals should be discounted or at least not taken at face value:

> No doubt [terms such as "wicked"] refer at times to violent and immoral individuals but the widespread presence of *resha'im* [wicked] according to the hasidic account leads us to one of two conclusions: either the political and spiritual leadership in thirteenth-century Germany was frequently in the hands of evil men or the Pietists used this term after their own fashion.

Soloveitchik concludes that *Sefer Ḥasidim* does not contain a reformist program for the amelioration of society from social and economic wrongs. To him, the terms "wicked" and so on refer mainly not to social but to religious deviance. Those to whom the author of *Sefer Ḥasidim* assigns such epithets are in the main simply non-Pietists, and the character of Jewish society in medieval Germany cannot be inferred from the way *Sefer Ḥasidim* describes non-Pietists.

There is merit in being cautious about how *Sefer Ḥasidim* should be used to write the social history of medieval German Jewry. The book, we too are arguing, is a program of a particular radical religious point of view, not a documentary record of everyday events written for its own sake. Caution is warranted, but evenhanded caution is in order. The difficulty with Soloveitchik's analysis is that while it insists on giving full weight to some data (those who wrote *piyyutim* are called "wicked") it advocates discounting other data (corrupt communal leaders are also called "wicked"). But there is no more reason for discounting the one than the other. The fact that scholars and synagogue poets are described as being "wicked" (which we agree clearly means "non-Pietists") does not prove that all or even most cases of the wicked are to be leveled to mean simply "non-Pietists", regardless of the specific accusations made about their behavior. Allegations of murder, apostasy, obstruction of justice and other types of wrongdoing are no less (and no more) credible than references to talmudic scholars who wrote poems but who were not Pietists. Moreover, there is no way of classifying the majority of general references to the "wicked", which lack any detailed accusations, as being of the scholar-poet or criminal variety of non-Pietists.

To concede that "wicked" may refer at times "to violent and immoral individuals" but then to argue that "the Pietists' indictment [of scholars and lax communal leaders] was more a product of their outlook than a reflection of reality" is a bit arbitrary. Less arbitrary would be the realization that Judah views society in *Sefer Ḥasidim* as being fundamentally divisible into two camps, Pietists and non-Pietists, and that the latter consists of a spectrum of deviance away from pietism. At one end are the scholars and observant Jews who would be called "righteous" and "pious" if they were being judged by one another, i.e. by other non-Pietists. According to the pietistic standards of *Sefer Ḥasidim*, however, they are the "wicked" simply because they are non-Pietists. The existence of such non-Pietists, however, does not mean that credence should not be given to descriptions of other non-Pietists who are alleged to be at the other end of the spectrum: corrupt communal leaders or the criminal element. The author of *Sefer Ḥasidim* condemns all non-Pietists: talmudic scholars who are filled with erudition but deficient in pietism, and authors of liturgical poems as well as would-be rapists, murderers and informers, those who violate the communal ban and do not give their fair share of taxes and who deserve "to be in Hell with Christians"—and everyone in between. Non-Pietists' books, for example, are called "impure" [*sifre pissul*] and, like Christians' books, are to be burned. In the social order posited by Judah in *Sefer Ḥasidim*, Pietists are the "good Jews"; non-Pietists—of all varieties—are the "bad Jews."[1]

Passing the issue that I never questioned that there were sinners and wicked men in Ashkenaz—I only doubted whether the religious, intellectual, and lay establishment in Ashkenaz was so *frequently* populated by sinners as *Sefer Ḥasidim* would give us to understand[2]—far more important is the methodological question of how one reads *Sefer Ḥasidim*. Marcus insists on the need of often taking such terms in *Sefer Ḥasidim* as *resha'im* (wicked people),

[1] I. G. Marcus, *Piety and Society: The Jewish Pietists of Medieval Germany* (Leiden, 1981), 61–2. The central chapter of Marcus's book had appeared a year earlier as an essay entitled 'The Politics and Ethics of Pietism in Judaism: The *Hasidim* of Medieval Germany', *The Journal of Religious Ethics*, 8 (1980), 227–58. The essay was translated into Hebrew and appeared in I. (Y.) Marcus, ed., *Dat ve-Ḥevrah be-Mishnatam shel Ḥasidei Ashkenaz* (Jerusalem, 1987), 253–78.

[2] See above, p. 33: 'No doubt they refer at times to violent and immoral individuals, but the widespread presence of *resha'im* according to the hasidic account leads us to one of two conclusions: either the political and spiritual leadership in thirteenth-century Germany was *frequently* in the hands of evil men or the Pietists used this term after their own fashion' (emphasis added).

peritsim (immoral people, ones who do not stick to the straight and narrow), *einam mehugganim* (dishonest people or people who act improperly/immorally), and the like quite literally, and to see in them a reflection of a wayward, indeed criminal, segment of the Ashkenazic community. I couldn't agree with him more. He also draws attention to the fact that these same terms are used to describe people who were fully religious but opposed the distinctive tenets of the Pietists, i.e. non-Pietists. This again is unquestionable, and I devoted many pages to proving this point in my 1976 essay, 'Three Themes in *Sefer Ḥasidim*'.[3] He then proceeds to say that the common terminology is not fortuitous, but rather reflects an identity of perception. The Pietists saw the world the way sects, as defined by Michael Hill,[4] do, as being divided into two groups—we and all others. They viewed all non-Pietists as being one and alike, whether they were religious or not, and in a limited sense not differing from the Gentiles. This allows all texts in which *resha'im*, *peritsim*, and the like are mentioned, whether they refer to actual murderers and wastrels or to scholars and religious poets who opposed the Pietists, to be cited interchangeably as evidence of the exclusivity of the Pietists. It is with this equation and its consequences that one may take issue.

Words, let us remember, may be ambiguous or undifferentiated. The Bible has one word for both tree and wood—*'ets*. This does not mean that biblical man did not distinguish between a piece of wood and a tree, but rather he used the same word ambiguously. The Eskimos are proverbially said to have seven different words for snow, we have but one. Not that we distinguish among seven types of snow and use one word ambiguously; rather, all snow is the same to us, and we use that word in an undifferentiated manner. The same holds true in daily life. If a child falls down an improperly maintained elevator shaft, the grieving parents may cry out at the landlord 'Murderer!', and at that moment the word is being used without differentiation. As time passes, the grieving parents themselves realize that criminal negligence is one thing and murder another.

So, too, with the German Pietists. No doubt in their bitter moments, and there were many, their opponents appeared to them as the vilest of men, no better than thieves or murderers, perhaps even worse, for not only were they sinning themselves, but in frustrating the Divine will they were causing others to stumble. But in his quieter moments, the Ḥasid knew that he and his pious, religious, though non-Pietist, neighbor prayed in one synagogue, observed

[3] Above, pp. 23–9.

[4] *The Religious Order: A Study of Virtuoso Religion and Its Legitimation in the Nineteenth-Century Church of England* (London, 1973). See below, p. 243.

the same Sabbath, worshipped the same God, shared daily the same treatment by their Gentile neighbors and a common fate in times of social unrest or religious turmoil.

Sefer Ḥasidim, like life, has varied moods; and, as in life, the same words mean wholly different things at different moments. Only context can tell us what those words mean, not social theory. The latter can suggest fruitful possibilities, but it can never determine the meaning or significance of a specific case.

As context alone tells us the meaning of certain words, meaning is then a conclusion that we draw from the text, and drawing conclusions from the text of so aggregated and heterogeneous a work as *Sefer Ḥasidim* is no simple matter. In a previous essay, when discussing the alleged negative attitude of *Sefer Ḥasidim* to lending money at interest to non-Jews, I suggested and employed three guidelines in drawing inferences from that work.[5] It is useful, perhaps, to reproduce that passage.

There is equally no ground for claiming that the German Pietists opposed usury. In a large, multifaceted, and formless work such as the *Sefer Ḥasidim* (Book of the Pious) one can find any and every idea. The controlling question is what degree of importance this idea has in the movement's ideology, and if it is not important, whether it at least has a distinct, clear place in their thought. *Sefer Ḥasidim* is, furthermore, amorphous and associative: central assertions and parenthetic asides are found alongside one another and their disentanglement poses major methodological problems. For our present discussion, three criteria may serve to winnow the trivial from the essential: purpose, reiteration, and intensity. That is to say: What is the purpose of the passage? Does the idea expressed recur with any degree of frequency in the literature of the movement? Finally, does one sense in its formulations an emotional involvement, whether identification or disgust?

In light of these considerations let us investigate the remarks of *Sefer Ḥasidim* cited as proof of the Pietists' opposition to usury. They are found in the section entitled 'On Torah Study':

'מרבה הונו בנשך ובתרבית לחונן דלים יקבצנו, מסיר אזנו משמוע תורה גם תפילתו תועבה' (משלי כח, ח ט) סמכם להודיע שלא יאמר אדם 'אני לוקח ריבית וחפץ אני לתת הריבית לגבאי צדקה למי שיחונן דל', מוטב שלא יקח ריבית. לפי שכתוב (ויקרא כה, לז) 'ובמרבית לא תתן אכלך', וכתיב 'תרבית' (הרי כתיב) לגבי ריבית לכך בתחיית המתים יהיה

[5] 'The Jewish Attitude to Usury in the High and Late Middle Ages (1000–1500)', in D. Quaglioni, G. Todeschini, and G. M. Varanini, eds., *Credito e usura fra teologia, diritto e amministrazione: Linguaggi a confronto (Sec. XII–XVI)*, proceedings of an international conference held at the Istituto Trentino di Cultura, Trento, Sept. 4–5, 2001 (collection of the École Française de Rome 346) (Rome, 2005), 119; repr. in *Collected Essays*, i (Oxford, 2013), 48.

מת 'ולא יחיה' שכתוב ביחזקאל (יח, יג) ובנשך נתן ותרבית לקח וחי לא יחיה את כל התועבות האלה עשה מות יומת דמיו בו. לכך 'מרבית' 'תרבית' ראשי תיבות מת. ואל יאמר אקח ריבית ואתן ללומדי תורה. 'ובתרבית' ב' יתר: שני ריביות מישראל ואף מגוי, מי שיכול להתפרנס משדותיו. ועוד ב' ריבי[ו]ת מוקדמת ומאוחרת.

'He that augmenteth his substance by interest and increase, gathereth it for him that is gracious to the poor. He that turneth away his ear from hearing the law, even his prayer is an abomination' [Prov. 28: 8–9]. The two verses were joined together so that one should not say, 'I want to give money earned in usury to charity'.

'You should not lend thy food at interest [*marbit*]' [Lev. 25: 37]; and elsewhere [Lev. 25: 36] usury is called not *marbit* but *tarbit*—the first letters of the two words spell *met* ['dead' in Hebrew]—to teach you that the usurer will not be resurrected, as is clear from Ezekiel [18: 13]: 'He [that] hath given at interest and hath taken interest, shall he live? He shall not live!' That is why the beginning letters spell 'dead'. One should never say, 'I will take interest and give it all to charity'. And in that verse it further says *u-ve-tarbit*; the *bet* in that word is superfluous. *Bet* numerologically is 2; this is a numerological reference to a twofold ban: on usury from a Jew and that from a Gentile. . . . It also refers to the twofold ban on both 'advance' and 'delayed' usury.

Having previously emphasized in #807 the importance of supporting scholars, he [the Ḥasid] hastens to add in #808 that this support should not come from usury. Then he proceeds to decode, in good hasidic, numerological fashion, the various hints and references embedded in these verses. One is the non-resurrection of those guilty of the sin of usury, the second is the ban on both Jewish and Gentile usury, and, in addition, the ban both on 'early usury', i.e. interest paid prior to the repayment of the capital, and on 'late [delayed] usury', i.e. interest paid well after the repayment of the capital. The purpose of the passage is not to condemn Gentile usury; this injunction is mentioned in passing as one of several numerological hints found in the biblical verses about usury. There is nothing unique in this use of the numerological reference of *ke-neged*: it was a favorite hermeneutical device of the Pietists. Literally hundreds of similar numerological allusions are expounded in the pages of *Sefer Ḥasidim*. Nor is there any further criticism of usury from a Gentile in the vast literature of that movement. Quite the contrary: in the only other place where usury is mentioned, in #1958, it is described as a 'fence' (*seyyag*) against charging interest to another Jew. In other words, usury from a Gentile was forbidden by rabbinic law not because it was intrinsically wrong, but for fear that the Jew would get accustomed to practicing usury and would eventually, from habit, charge Jews too.[6]

[6] See *Sefer Ḥasidim*, ed. J. Wistinetzki (Berlin, 1891). This edition was photo-offset in Frankfurt am Main in 1924 and provided with indices and a large and important introduction by J. Freimann. It was printed from MS Parma 1133, hence the common abbreviation *SHP*, to distinguish it from the briefer edition first published in Bologna in 1538, *SHB*.

I would like to suggest three more controls that may be profitably employed in assessing the meaning of words and passages in *Sefer Ḥasidim*: context, linguistic resources, and contemporary understanding of the proof text. Both here and in the passage above, I am not laying down rules but suggesting guidelines to be used with discrimination.

1. Context: first, as I have said above, in clarifying the meaning of ambiguous terms; second, in noting the specific framework in which the narrative is set and which determines the meaning of the passage, something which, as we shall soon see, is not always done.

2. Literary skill and resources: What were the linguistic resources available to the author attempting to write, for the first time in Ashkenazic history, moral and expository prose? Did there exist in the Hebrew language that they knew an alternative phrase to the one they used, so that the choice of one term over the other is revelatory? Take, for example, such a simple word as *tsaddik*. It can be translated as 'righteous'; it can also mean the 'non-wicked', the innocent, as in Abraham's plea for the men of Sodom: 'Will you sweep away the innocent with the guilty?'[7] (*ha-af tispeh tsaddik im rasha'*; Gen. 18: 23), and equally it may mean the one who is in the right in a dispute, whose claim has been vindicated, as in Deuteronomy 25: 1 (*ve-hitsdiku et ha-tsaddik*). There is no word in biblical, mishnaic (*leshon ḥakhamim*), or rabbinic Hebrew for an 'ordinary' man, someone neither particularly good nor particularly bad. There is no *ma'aseh be-veinoni eḥad* ('Once upon a time, an average man . . .'). Yiddish later develops the phrase *a poshiter yid*, 'a simple Jew', which then enters Hebrew as *yehudi pashut*. Every now and then, the Ḥasid struggles to find some circumlocution for the ordinary man,[8] but finds it cumbersome and immediately reverts to the ambiguous antonyms *tsaddik/rasha'* (one who is righteous/wicked), *tov/ra'* (one who is good/bad), *hagun/eino hagun* (one who acts properly or morally and one who doesn't).

[7] I have here used the translation of the Jewish Publication Society (JPS) as it brings out more clearly the meaning of the Hebrew than does the King James Version; *The Tanakh: A New Translation of the Holy Scriptures according to the Traditional Hebrew Text* (Philadelphia, 1995).

[8] See #1695 end: **אע"פ שאינו יודע כל כך ואינו צדיק כל כך** ('even though he isn't that much of a scholar or that much of a *tsaddik*'). See also #881: **מעשה שאדם אחד שקיבל צדיקים עמו ולא היה צדיק המקבל צדיקים** ('Once a man hosted *tsaddikim* in his home, and he was not a *tsaddik* who hosted the *tsaddikim* [i.e. the man who hosted the *tsaddikim* was not himself a *tsaddik*].') One finds occasionally *hedyot* (commoner) contrasted to *tsaddik* or to *tov*, as in ##898, 1300, 1628, 1629, and possibly #1945. However, this contrast could not replace the natural antonymic pairs of *tsaddik/rasha'*, *tovim/ra'im*, and *mehugganim/einam mehugganim*, and these dyads populate *Sefer Ḥasidim*.

3. Contemporary understanding of the proof texts: *Sefer Ḥasidim* cites and comments on the widest variety of talmudic and midrashic sources, but unless there is some indication that they are reading it in a distinctive fashion, one must read these texts in the same way as their contemporaries did. The closer to home these contemporaries are, and especially if they are of the same culture, the stronger the evidence must be that the Pietists read that text differently from their confrères. If they quote a passage from the *Torat Kohanim*, for example, and we have a commentary on that work by a pupil of a contemporary Kalonymide, we should presume that they understand that text as did the commentator, unless it can be shown otherwise.

Consistent use of these principles may alter the conclusions sometimes drawn from *Sefer Ḥasidim* by even so fine a historian as Marcus. Let us examine, in this light, his analysis of philanthropy as an example of the 'exclusivist scale of values' of the Pietists. I choose this area because we are here in general agreement as to the conclusion. The entire second section of 'Three Themes in *Sefer Ḥasidim*' pointed out the self-righteous elitism of the Ḥasidim. As for charity, I wrote: 'Need I mention the sensitive, yet at the same time elitist, doctrine of charity set forth in *SH*, ##857–929, 1675–1719, which, if implemented, would have slashed severely the alms available to the non-hasidic poor?'[9] Admittedly I spoke of 'elitism' and Marcus speaks of 'exclusivity', and there is a considerable difference between the two as we shall see. However, both of us point to the fissure between the Pietists and the larger community, to the former's clear awareness of their alterity and their abiding sense of superiority to the common herd. Wherein we differ is how one arrives at such a conclusion. Put differently, how does one read a work like *Sefer Ḥasidim*; indeed, how should a historian read traditional ethical works altogether?

Marcus opens with the statement that 'the ideal recipient [of charity] in *Sefer Ḥasidim* is not one's family per se, but a needy Pietist [*tsaddik ve-tsarikh*]' (*Sefer Ḥasidim* Parma [*SHP*], ##857, 917).[10] I do not believe that the texts cited support this statement,[11] but the statement is scarcely evidence of exclusivity. 'Ideal recipient' states a preference, not a preclusion. For much the same reason, I do not see how any of the statements made in this paragraph and the

[9] Above, p. 39 n. 88.

[10] *Piety and Society* (above, n. 1), 101. The bracketed numbers are the sections in *Sefer Ḥasidim* that Marcus cites to document his statement.

[11] See below, pp. 193, 195, for my reservations.

following one are evidence of exclusivity.[12] Seven major claims are, however, made in the subsequent three paragraphs with characteristic force and verve. I will present them in the order in which they appear in my colleague's book,[13] and then regroup them for the purposes of analysis.

[1] One is obligated to support one's own Pietist relatives even if funds from other sources become available. When relatives are not involved, one is to give charity to Pietists in need. [2] One recipient may give a contribution to someone else, but only to another Pietist in need; [3] money can be given to a needy Pietist either directly or indirectly but only by means of another Pietist or Sage. [4] Moreover, giving money to a non-Pietist is a sin; [5] not giving charity to a non-Pietist is itself an act of pietism. [6] One should go to great lengths, even leaving town, 'to avoid supporting non-Pietists including one's own father'. [7] Unless a non-Pietist threatened to murder someone if a Pietist does not give him charity, a Pietist must not yield to threats to commit a sin. Even if he should threaten to apostatize, the Pietist is to resist helping a non-Pietist: 'Let the non-Pietist go to Hell.'

I regroup these statements for analysis:

1. Marcus pointedly writes: 'Moreover, giving money to a non-Pietist is a sin;

[12] Marcus continues:

> If one's relatives are Pietists and in need, there is no conflict between giving to one's relatives and to fellow Pietists. Pietist relatives have priority over Pietists who are not related to the donor. But when one must choose between poor relatives who are non-Pietists and those who study Torah for pietistic reasons, the Pietist is to ignore the relative. Even if they say that they will study properly in the future, they are not to be considered, because their motives for saying so are suspect: perhaps they are making the pledge to study in order to get the charity. Similarly, a father cannot favor one of several children in his will just because he loved that child more than the others, but only if that child was more pietistic.

In matters of charity, family has halakhic priority over strangers, just as local need trumps that of an adjacent community (*Bava Metsi'a* 71a). Favoring Pietist non-relatives over non-Pietist relatives is a statement of preference, not of exclusivity. It asserts who stands first in line; it says nothing about who is precluded from standing in the line. See below, pp. 193, 195. Only the last statement would appear to be exclusivist. However, it is based on #1703, and that passage is ambiguous, as it concludes: 'and he [the son who fulfills the Will of the Borè] will give more charity, therefore he [the father] should give him more'. It is not clear whether the controlling factor is the pietistic one or the consideration of the greater benefit for the poor. This type of ambiguous contrast—A rather than B and C, leaving the reader at a loss whether B and C are to be understood jointly or alternatively, or even that C is a passing thought and the intended contrast is only between A and B—is characteristic of speech and occurs frequently in *Sefer Ḥasidim* as its diction is that of the spoken rather than the written word (see above, p. 85, and below, n. 48). See #888, for example, which is a case of choosing A and B over C and D. However, it is clear that the Ḥasid is not contrasting two groups with different sets of traits, as the simple language would have it, but rather privileging one group over the other. One doesn't know whether the choice is between *tsaddikim* and non-*tsaddikim* or between family and strangers.

[13] *Piety and Society* (above, n. 1), 101–2.

not giving charity to a non-Pietist is itself an act of pietism' (*SHP*, ##840, 917, 1705).[14] These two claims are indeed exclusivist, and the evidence cited for them merits study. Admittedly, in #840 the terms *peritsim* and *einam mehugganim* appear, but these are hardly religious, law-abiding 'non-Pietists'; they are explicitly described as being wastrels and whoremongers, who will use the money for immoral purposes. The passage reads:

> טוב מלא כף נחת שאדם נותן ליראי שמים עניים שירדו מנכסיהם ממלא חפנים עמל שנותן לעניים שאינם מהוגנים ולא עוד אלא שנחשב לו עון כי מה שיתנו לפריצים יתנו לזונות או בבליעות ומקים מורדים להקב"ה בעולם.

'Better is a handful with quietness'—that a man gives to God-fearing [*yir'ei shamayim*] poor who have lost their money—'than both the hands full with travail' [Eccl. 4: 6] —who gives to the poor who are *einam mehugganim*. Yea, it is viewed as a sin, for what he gives to the *peritsim* they will spend on whores or gluttony, and he raises up [i.e. sustains] those who rebel in this world against God.

Section 1705 opens with a citation from *Torat Kohanim*, as the modern editor of *Sefer Ḥasidim* (*SHP*), J. Wistinetzki, noted. It reads:

> ומניין אם החזקת בו אפילו [ע"ב] ארבע וחמש פעמים חזור והחזק בו ת"ל [ויקרא, כה: לה] 'והחזקת בו'; יכול אפילו אתה מפסידו לתרבות רעה ת"ל [שם, שם] 'עמך'. ואפילו אם הוא אביו אם נותן לו מסייע לעוברי עבירה הוא לפי שהוא גורם ואפילו נותן לו לאכול ומצד אחר באים לו מעות שהוא נותן לתרבות רעה.

And whence do you learn that he is duty-bound to sustain [the poor man] even four or five times [i.e. even if this is the fourth or fifth time that he has fallen on the dole]? Learn it from [Lev. 25: 35] 'help him'[15] [i.e. an unqualified imperative that applies in all cases]. One might think that this is so even if he is *mafsido le-tarbut ra'ah*—learn from 'with thee' [i.e. lives as you do, that is to say, conducts himself properly]. Even if he [the poor man] is his father, if he gives him [charity], he aids sinners in achieving their ends. Even if the father spends the charity money on food, that [simply enables him] to spend the money coming from other sources on bad ways.

The passage states that one need not or ought not to give charity to one who is *mafsido le-tarbut ra'ah*, but how the author understood this unusual phrase cannot be determined from the text. The mid-thirteenth-century Ashkenazic commentary on *Torat Kohanim*, written by no less a figure than a pupil of the Kalonymides,[16] explains it as either referring to someone who regularly

[14] Ibid. 102.

[15] A biblical citation must be translated as the Pietists understood the verse, so in a number of instances in this essay, as here, I have substituted my own translation for that of both the King James Version and the JPS *Tanakh* (see above, n. 7, and below, n. 29).

[16] E. E. Urbach, *Ba'alei ha-Tosafot: Toledoteihem, Ḥibbureihem, Shitatam* (rev. edn., Jerusalem, 1986), 312–15.

transgresses the Law and thus falls outside the imperative of charity, or one who will use the money for whoring or gambling.[17] The first interpretation seems forced, as the technical term for a transgressor is either *rasha'*, *'avaryan*, *mumar le-te'avon*, or *mumar le-hakh'is*.[18] If one wishes to attribute literary flourish to the *Torat Kohanim*, one might yet extend this meaning to the idiomatic phrase of *yatsa le-tarbut ra'ah* (he has fallen on bad ways), but scarcely to the very unidiomatic *mafsido le-tarbut ra'ah*. The second interpretation (which is also that of Ravad of Posquières[19]) is of a wastrel, who spends his money on whores and gambling, and who will misuse the funds to his own detriment. It fits well the language ('wastes it [the charity] on [his] bad ways'), matches the Pietist's addendum ('spend the money . . . on bad ways'), and corresponds to the contemporary description in #840 just cited.[20] I see no reason not to assume that the author of *Sefer Ḥasidim* understood this passage as did his contemporary Kalonymide disciple. Neither of his two interpretations precludes charity from a Jew of good standing who is not a Pietist.

Section 917 documents the second major claim: 'not giving charity to a non-Pietist is itself an act of Pietism'. It reads:

> כתיב [משלי כז יד] 'מברך את רעהו בקול גדול בבקר השכם קללה תחשב לו', מי שאמר לשליח צבור לברכו שכך וכך יתן לו או שכך וכך יתן לו או לצדקה בבקר השכם ללכת, או יש לו לשלם באותו יום והעניים מצויים ואמרו שעובר בבל תאחר, או שיודע עניים צדיקים וצריכים והוא אומר מוטב שאתן לכיס של צדקה של צבור שהרי שליח צבור יברכהו בקול רם ויענו בקול רם אמן, והצדיקים העניים בלילה ילינו מבלי בגדים לכסות והגבאי לא יתן להם מה שצריכים, או בלילה לא היה להם מה לאכול, או שהשכים בבקר ואמר תן לי הכלים שעושים בהם מלאכה ביום, אף על פי שיברכו בלילה על שהשאילו כסות לילה, קללה תחשב לו, ולכך סמכו (שם, כז יג) קח בגדו כי ערב זר: אלא יתן לטובים בסתר והם יברכוהו וכתיב (שם כא יד) מתן בסתר יכפה אף וכתיב (דברים כד יג) ושכב בשלמתו וברכך ולך תהיה צדקה. והבורא (יודע רואה לנותנים אם טובים ואינו חפץ כשמברכים אותו

[17] *Sifra de-Vei Rav hu Sefer Torat Kohanim 'im Perushei Rabbotenu ha-Rishonim, Ravad ve-ha-Rash mi-Shants* (Jerusalem, 1959), fo. 117d, *parshta* 5: יכול את מפסיד לתרבות רע: כלומר יכול אפילו עובר עבירה שהוא נפסד מדרך החיים. פי' אחר: יכול אפילו מטה ידו בשביל עבירות זנות וקוביא, תהא מצוה להחזיק בו? ת"ל עמך, בדומה לך.

[18] See below, p. 206.

[19] *Sifra de-Vei Rav hu Sefer Torat Kohanim 'im Perush Rabbenu Avraham ben David*, ed. I. H. Weiss (Vienna, 1862), fo. 117d, *parashah* 5.

[20] It is possible that the Ḥasid is ignoring the present tense (*mafsido*) and taking it to refer to the past, i.e. he has fallen into poverty because he had squandered his money on bad living and gambling. See #853, where one is told not to help such a person. See also the truncated passage at the closing of #898: אם אדם נעשה עני על ידי מעשיו הרעים או ששיחק בקוביא והפסיד ('If a man became impoverished thanks to his wicked ways or he gambled away his money'); the missing conclusion is the one stated in #853, as the editor Wistinetzki already suggested, i.e. he is not to be given charity. (See analogously #1687, where the Ḥasid advises collecting loans from a gambler as swiftly as possible, for the sooner a gambler is penniless, the better it is for him.)

ונותנים לשאינו מהוגנים) [יודע מי שנותן לטובים ואינו חפץ שיברכוהו בקול רם וגם רואה לנותני' לשאינם מהוגנים כדי להתכבד].[21]

It is written, 'He that blesseth his friend with a loud voice, rising early in the morning, it shall be counted as a curse to him' [Prov. 27: 14]. Someone who says to the cantor [or sexton] to bless him for he will give a certain sum to him or to charity, and gets up in the morning and departs [without paying the pledge]; or he has the money to pay the same day, and there are poor [that need the money immediately], transgresses the injunction against delayed payment of vows. Or if he knows that here are righteous poor [*'aniyyim tsaddikim*] who are in need and he says [to himself], better that I give to the communal charity chest for then I will be blessed publicly, and the congregation will answer [after my blessing] 'Amen'. And the righteous poor will pass the night without clothes and the sexton will not give what they need or they will not have anything to eat in the night. Or [after being blessed for giving the poor clothes in which to pass the night], he rises up in the morning and says to the poor [to whom he has also lent money], give me as security the tools of your day labor, even though he was blessed for giving them night clothes, it [the blessing] shall be counted as a curse and that is why the next verse in Proverbs speaks [of loans]: 'take his garment that is surety for a stranger'. But rather [than public blessing for giving to the communal chest], he should give to the poor and they will bless him, and it is written: 'A gift in secret pacifieth anger' [Prov. 21: 14], and it is written: 'and it shall be righteousness unto thee' [Deut. 24: 13]. And the Creator knows who gives to the good ones [*tovim*] and does not wish to be publicly blessed, and He sees those who give to the *einam mehugganim* so as to attain public honor.

The Pietist is bothered by the verse in Proverbs: why should one be cursed for loudly blessing a friend early in the morning? He accounts for it by any number of explanatory examples, all of which boil down to vowing charity in the evening and annulling its value by one's conduct the following morning. After vowing in the evening, the donor departs without paying his vows at all; or he departs and delays his payment to a later date; or after doing an act of charity in the evening by returning to debtors their night clothes to sleep in (see Exod. 22: 25–6; Deut. 23: 12–13), he arises in the morning and departs, taking with him the tools the poor need for day labor; or (here the Pietist emphasizes the word 'loudly' in the verse in Proverbs) he gives in the evening to a less worthy cause because of public approval, and the poor, whose aid should have been the object of his charity, pass the night without clothes or food. This last point is reiterated at the end.

The terms *tsaddikim*, *tovim*, and *einam mehugganim* are used, but the

[21] The emendation is according to the parallel text in *SHB*, #1048. It is clear from the double verb *yodea' ro'eh* in the text of *SHP* that an elision has occurred.

context leaves their specific meaning open. Nor need it be provided, for these terms are used for contrast. The 'act of Pietism', the pietistic imperative outlined in #917, does not lie in 'not giving charity to non-Pietists', but in foregoing public acclaim for the sake of giving to the better cause.[22] The example given is of the good and bad or better or worse individuals, and the Pietist clearly thinks that worthy beneficiaries (*tsaddikim*, *tovim*) are more deserving of support than unworthy ones (*einam mehugganim*), but the moral message is that of always giving alms to the better though less popular cause. How one defines better and worse recipients is not indicated, as it is irrelevant to the point being made by the author. Marcus's interpretation, to my thinking, transfers the moral of the passage to one of the examples and then proceeds to interpret that example in terms of Pietist and non-Pietist.

2. 'One recipient', Marcus writes, 'may give a contribution to someone else, but only to another Pietist in need; money can be given to a needy Pietist either directly or indirectly but only by means of another Pietist or Sage' (##1700, 1683, 1684). One should go to great lengths, even leave town, 'to avoid supporting non-Pietists, including one's own father' (##1679, 1705). 'One is obligated to support one's own Pietist relatives even if funds from other sources become available' (#1683). Three Pietistic imperatives, strongly exclusivist, are stated. Let us take each claim separately and assess the documentation.

(*i*) 'One recipient may give a contribution to someone else, but only to another Pietist in need' (##1700, 1693, 1683, 1684). The entry '1693' is a typo and I do not know what passage Marcus has in mind.[23] A study, however, of the sources shows that the other three cases have a common framework—the money under discussion was earmarked by the donor specifically for Pietists or for a cause which would be a 'great *mitsvah*'.

(*a*) Section 1700 reads:

אם נותנים לראובן *שהוא צדיק ולכך נתנו לו*, הוא יכול לתת לצדיק אחר מזה שנתנו לו ולא לרעים, והנותן נותן על מנת שיתן לבני ביתו.

If they give to Reuven *because he is a tsaddik and for that reason they gave to him*, he is permitted to give [the money] to a *tsaddik* other than the one they gave it to

[22] *SHB*, #1048.

[23] #1693 reads:

כתיב הרחוקים מצדקה [ישעיה מו: יב]. אם בא אדם לתת צדקה לעניים אז יזהר האדם שלא ימצא שם אדם כדי שלא יתביישו העניים

The Bible says, 'who are far from charity' [Isa. 46: 12]: if one seeks to give charity to the poor, he should take care that no one be present [when he gives it], so as not to embarrass the poor [recipients].

> [i.e. he may transfer it to another *tsaddik*] but not to the bad ones [*ra'im*]. And he who gives money [to a *tsaddik*] gives it with the intention that the money may be given to members of his [the *tsaddik*'s] household. [italics mine]

(*b*) Section 1683 reads:

> אחד אמר לחכם פלוני הלך לעולמו *ואמר לי לתת כך וכך* על פיך *לעניים טובים* למי אתן, אתן לפלוני ופלוני שהם טובים אם טוב בעיניך, אמר לו החכם אם אתה הייתה רגיל לתת לקרוביך ואתה רוצה להקל מעליך בממון של פלוני שנתן לצדקה כשהלך לעולמו ואתה עשיר דע כי עון הוא לתת שנמצא שאתה גוזל לעניים ואם אתה לא תמעט מלתת לקרוביך מה שהיית רגיל הרי נחלוק להם ואם לאו לא נחלוק להם.

> Someone said to the Sage, 'X died, and [before his death] he told me to *give a certain sum of money to the good poor*; to whom shall I give it? I will give it to Y and Z, who are good people [and who also are the speaker's relatives].' The Sage said, 'If you are accustomed to giving to your relatives, and if you wish to lighten your load by using the money of X, who gave it to charity before his death, and you are wealthy, know that it is a sin to give to them and that you are stealing thereby from the poor. If, however, you will not diminish your customary charity to your relatives, then you may allot to them [X's money]; if not [i.e. if you intend to diminish your charity to them], you may not allot [them the money].' [italics mine]

(*c*) Section 1684 reads:

> אחד היה לו כסף ואמר לחכם *תחשוב למי אתן שיהא מצוה רבה*, אמר לו החכם לפלוני ופלוני שהם עניים וטובים וגמר בלבו ואמר כן יהיה למחר בא לפני החכם אמר לו יש עני אחד אם היית ממעט לאותם שאתמול אמרת כדי שניתן גם לאחר אמר לו כיון שאינו יותר טוב מאותם שאמרתי לך וכבר גמרתה אל תמעט לאלה אלא אם יש לך מעות אחרים תן לו ואל תמעט לאלה.

> Someone had money and he said to the Sage, 'Think of [a cause] to which I should give so that it would be considered a "great *mitsvah*" [*mitsvah rabbah*].'[24] The Sage said, 'Give it to X and Y, who are good poor.' And the questioner firmly resolved and said, 'So be it.' The next day he came to the Sage and said, 'There is a poor man [to whom I would like to give charity]; if you were [to allow me] to diminish the amount of charity to those that you spoke of yesterday, I could also give to him.' He [the Sage] said, 'Since he is no better than those that I told you about and you have already firmly resolved [to give to them], you may not diminish [their allotment]. However, if you have other money, give it to him, but do not diminish [anything destined for] the others.' [italics mine]

Money earmarked for Pietists must end up in the hands of Pietists, and

[24] The classic case in the Talmud of *mitsvah rabbah* is that of ransoming captives who were otherwise destined for slavery or death; see *Bava Batra* 8a–b and *Mishneh Torah*, 'Matenot 'Aniyyim', 8: 10: ואין לך מצוה רבה כפדיון שבוים.

money earmarked for an especially worthy cause must be given to those who especially merit it.[25] These three passages do not equally document Marcus's second claim, that 'money can be given to a needy Pietist either directly or indirectly but only by means of another Pietist or Sage'.[26] Perhaps it is documented by the reference that was erroneously registered as #1693, though I do not know of any passage in *Sefer Ḥasidim* which restricts the 'middleman' to a Pietist or Sage, only to trustworthy individuals (*ne'emanim*),[27] a limitation dictated by common sense.

(*ii*) Marcus writes: 'One should go to great lengths, even leave town, to avoid supporting non-Pietists, including one's own father' (##1679, 1705).

(*a*) Section 1679 reads:

אחד בא אצל חכם אמר לו נדרתי עשרים ליטרין לתת למי *שיהיה נראה בעיני צדיק* ושואל אני אם אוכל להרויח במעות עד שיבא שום אדם טוב ואתן לו אמר לו כן. בא אחר *ואמר כדברי זה* אמר לו אסור אתה להרויח אלא יהא מונחים בידך אל תרויח בהם. בא שלישי ושאל לו *כדברי אילו*, אמר לו הביאם מיד למקום שתמצא עניים טובים או תתנם מידך לצדיקים שבעירך שישמרו אותם עד שיבאו לידם עניים טובים.

אמרו לו תלמידיו דבריך הולכים בשלשה דרכים, למה חלקת דבריך? אמר להם כי למי שהוא צדיק ואני יודע כשיבאו לידו עניים טובים אני יודע שבשביל ריוח שלו לא יעכב המעות בידו ויתנם מיד להם לכך אמרתי לו תרויח בהם והוא נאמן שכל מה שירויח לא יקח אלא שלו. לאותו שאמר אסור אתה להרויח ידעתי כי נאמן הוא ואם יבאו עניים שיתנם להם אם לא ירויח בהם ואם ירויח בהם אם יבא לו עניים יאמר אמתין עד שיבאו יותר טובים ועוד שאינו כל כך עשיר שמא לא יהיו לו מזומנים המעות כשיבאו עניים טובים. ולאותו שאמרתי תסירם מידך מיד שאינו נאמן לעכבם בידו ועוד קרוב לעירו מזומנים עניים טובים, ועוד אם יוכל אדם לשלוח ליד טובים אפילו הם למקום[!] רחוק אין לעכבם בידו כדכתיב (משלי כא כא) רודף צדקה וחסד אם אין עניים טובים בעירו שיתן לעיר אחרת.

Someone came to the Sage and said, 'I vowed to give twenty pounds *to one who seems to me to be a tsaddik*, and I ask whether I may invest the money until a good [poor] man appears', and he [the Sage] replied, 'Yes.' Subsequently a second person came and *said the same thing* [i.e. raised the same question], and he [the Sage] said, 'You are not allowed to invest it; the money must remain in your possession—don't invest it.' A third person came along *with the same question* and he [the Sage]

[25] As for the view that *tovim* are an especially worthy cause, see above, p. 190 and below, p. 197.

[26] *Piety and Politics* (above, n. 1), 102.

[27] As in #1680, end. I suspect that Marcus had this section in mind, for there is there a statement that 'had the inquirer given it [the money] to a trustworthy *tsaddik* to distribute to the poor', the Sage would have ruled differently. However, I fail to see how one can take *tsaddik* here as meaning 'Pietist', for if so, the adjective 'trustworthy' is not only superfluous but insulting. The concluding, summary sentence, 'he should give it to the good poor or give it to trustworthy individuals to give to the good ones [*tovim*]', renders accurately the meaning of *tsaddik* in the exemplum.

replied, 'Bring the money immediately to a location where good poor people are found or give it to *tsaddikim* in your city, who will keep the money safe until good poor people appear.'

His [the Sage's] pupils said to him, 'Your rulings go in three [different] directions; why did you so differentiate in your rulings'? He replied, 'The one who is a *tsaddik*, I know that when good poor people present themselves he will not retain the money to increase his own profit, but will give them the money immediately. To him I said, "You may invest it." He [also] may be relied on to retain only that which is his [i.e. the profit of the investment, but not the principal]. The one to whom I said it was forbidden to invest is one that I know to be reliable [to the extent that] if he does not invest the money, should the [good] poor present themselves, he will give them the money. However, should he invest the money, he will say [to himself], "I will wait until even more worthy poor people present themselves." Moreover, he is not so wealthy, and if he has invested the money and good poor people appear, he may not have the liquidity to give [them all] the money [that he originally received, twenty pounds]. As to the one that I told to dispose of the money immediately, he cannot be trusted to retain the money. Moreover, good poor people are to be found close to his city [i.e. close by].'

Moreover [it is not clear whether the Sage is still speaking, or, what appears more probable, the author/editor of *Sefer Ḥasidim*], if one can send to good people even if they be found in a distant place, he should not retain the money [that he has vowed to charity], as is written, 'He that pursueth righteousness and mercy' [Prov. 21: 21][28]—if there be no good poor people in one's city, he should give it to [the righteous poor] in another city. [italics mine]

All three cases in this exemplum are equally instances where the donor stated at the outset that he wished the money to be given to a *tsaddik*, i.e. they all treat restricted funds. Moreover, no extreme demand would appear to be made by *Sefer Ḥasidim* of 'leaving town', as claimed by Marcus, 'to avoid supporting non-Pietists'. *Sefer Ḥasidim* simply states that when there are no hometown Pietists, money allocated to Pietists must be sent to a different town where Pietists are to be found. Stated in halakhic terms: fulfilling the donor's intent trumps the well-known rule of charity allocation that local needs have priority (*'aniyyei 'irkha kodmim*—'the poor of your city come first'[29]).

(*b*) Section 1705 is cited as proof of the 'father rule' ('One should go to great lengths, even leave town, to avoid supporting non-Pietists, including one's

[28] Whenever possible, I have cited the King James translation, but here I have changed the verb from 'followeth' to the more literal 'pursueth'. The Pietist emphasizes the need to traverse distance so as to realize the act of mercy righteously.

[29] *Bava Metsi'a* 71a.

own father'). I have already cited that passage above and need only repeat the controlling sentence.

> One might think that this is so even if he is *mafsido le-tarbut ra'ah*—learn from 'with thee' [i.e. lives as you do, that is to say, conducts himself properly]. Even if he is his father, if he gives him [charity], he aids sinners. Even if the father spends the charity money on food, that [simply enables him] to spend the money coming from other sources on bad ways.

The father is either a criminal and thus beyond the pale of charity, or, more probably, he will use the money for immoral purposes, such as whoring and gambling.

(*iii*) Marcus writes: 'One is obligated to support one's own Pietist relatives even if funds from other sources become available' (#1683). I have already cited #1683 above and simply point out that the opening sentence reads: 'Someone said to the Sage, "X died, and [before his death] he told me to *give a certain sum of money to the good poor.*"'

Barring one instance, where the money will be spent on gross dissipation, all the passages cited in this section treat, as noted, money that has been given specifically to Pietists. The moral of these exempla is that care must be taken in the transfer of restricted funds to see that the intention of the donor is maintained.

The first sentence in this section ('one recipient may give a contribution to someone else, but only to another Pietist in need') should, to my mind, read: 'A needy Pietist who has received money restricted to needy Pietists may transfer it only to another needy Pietist.' The second sentence ('One should go to great lengths, even leave town, to avoid supporting non-Pietists, including one's own father') should, I believe, read: 'If one earmarks money for Pietists one should go to great lengths, even send it to another town, to ensure that it is given to Pietists, as stipulated by the donor.' The third sentence ('One is obligated to support one's own Pietist relatives even if funds from other sources become available') should, to my thinking, read: 'If one receives money earmarked for Pietists, and one has been supporting Pietist relatives of one's own, one may not use that money as a substitute support for those relatives, but must give it to other Pietists.' To use money, the *Sefer Ḥasidim* teaches, in a way that diminishes one's own obligations is an abuse of the fiduciary role of the distributor. The goal of charitable distribution is always to increase the sum of money available for philanthropy, not to enable the distributor to reduce his own burden, even if technically speaking he may still be complying with the donor's instructions.

3. 'When relatives are not involved', writes Marcus, 'one is to give charity to Pietists in need' (##1680, 1689).

This statement, like those in the first two paragraphs of the section on philanthropy, advances a preference not an exclusion. Pietists have priority; others are not barred.[30]

4. A passage in *Sefer Ḥasidim* deals with the choice one must make between giving to a *rasha'* or a *tsaddik* when under threat, and Marcus forcefully concludes his section on philanthropy with its analysis.[31] 'Unless a non-Pietist threatened to murder someone if a Pietist does not give him charity, a Pietist must not yield to threats to commit a sin. Even if he should threaten to apostatize, the Pietist is to resist helping a non-Pietist: "Let the non-Pietist go to Hell"' (#857). The passage reads:

> אדם צדיק וצריך לצדקה שתתן לו ואם רשע זולל וסובא עומד ואינך יכול לתת אלא לאחד מהם והנה הרשע אומר אם לא תתן לו ישתמד או יעשה עבירה אחרת ולא רציחה תן לצדיק והרשע ילך לגיהינם, אבל אם בא לעשות רציחה כדי לפדות הנקי שלא יהא נרצח, תן לו.

A *tsaddik* is in need of charity and a wicked man [*rasha'*], 'a wastrel and a drunkard' [Deut. 21: 20], stands [before you to receive charity], and you can only give to one of them, and the *rasha'* says that if you do not give him [the money], he will convert to Christianity or commit another offence, but not that of murder, give to the *tsaddik* and let the *rasha'* go to Hell. However, if he is about to commit murder, give him [the money] as ransom for the innocent man, so that he will not be killed.

As the *rasha'* under discussion is a wastrel, a blackmailer, a potential convert, and quite capable of murder, I would suggest that the phrase *ve-ha-rasha' yelekh la-Gehinom* is best translated as 'Let the wicked man go to Hell'.[32] The context, to my mind, clearly indicates that *rasha'* here means 'wicked', in the ordinary sense of the word, and the contrasting term *tsaddik* means simply an honest man, an upright individual. No clearer example could be given of the

[30] See above, p. 185 and n. 11. Section 1689 is a typo; I do not know what passage Marcus has in mind. As for #1680, see also my remarks above, n. 27.

[31] *Piety and Society* (above, n. 1), 102.

[32] If the reader is put off by the blunt expression ילך לגיהינום ('he should go to Hell'), MSS Jewish Theological Seminary 2499 and Vatican 285, #110 have a slightly more literary formulation: תן לצדיק והרשע [ילך] בחמת רוחו לגיהנם ('and the *rasha'* should go in the bitterness of his spirit to Hell', based on the verse in Ezek. 3: 14: ואלך מר בחמת רוחי, 'and I went in anger and in the bitterness of my spirit'). Vatican 285 has been published twice: once by Mosheh Hershler in *Genuzot: Kovets 'Et li-Genuzot Rishonim*, 1 (1984), 125–62 and again in *Sefer Ḥasidim: Kitvei Yad le-Rabbi Yehudah he-Ḥasid, Parma ve-Roma*, Otsar ha-Posekim edn. (Jerusalem, 2015). In the latter edition, the passage is numbered #125.

straightforward use of these terms, and consequently of their inherent ambiguity in *Sefer Ḥasidim*.

Terminology was never a hasidic strong point,[33] and, not surprisingly, they never coined terms which firmly distinguished between 'pious' and 'Pietist'. Their bent of mind did not tend to fixed terms, and they never gave themselves a fixed name, as did, for example, the Polish hasidim or the Sabbatians. *Tsaddikim*, *tovim*, *mehugganim*, *yir'ei ha-Shem* were all used interchangeably. They added new content to these old words, but did not and could not remove their old contents. The result: they called themselves by a host of shifting names, and they called all other ordinary, law-abiding Jews by the same names. The terminological ambiguity is ours to resolve.

How does one resolve that ambiguity? How does one go about reading *Sefer Ḥasidim* or any ethical text in a traditional society, using as it does stock terms and repeating common themes? Context, in the several senses outlined, is one tool; comparison of the interpretation of the same 'canonical' citations in one work with that of other works is a second; identifying terms charged with special meaning is a third.

Most ethical works, if they had any practical purpose, had a 'front', addressed some common human failings which they felt especially needed correction at that time, or some communal breaches which needed urgent mending, and advanced a program which would achieve these ends. Identifying this 'front' is the first task of a historian, for it is these needs and breaches which are the contemporary moment in these seemingly timeless moral exhortations.

Often this can be accomplished only by identifying loaded terms. Given the very restricted vocabulary of rabbinic Hebrew, any bearer of a new vision of Jewish religious life had to reach into the pre-existing vocabulary and press old words into new service. Standard words must take on new meanings in the writings of any group that seeks religious reform, with denotations and connotations known both to writer and reader at that time, but devoid of them in prior or subsequent times. To give a contemporary example from the ideological struggle of the modern Orthodox and the *ḥaredim* (ultra-Orthodox): the term *ben Torah* has now a very specific connotation, down to the hat worn—ordinary or black and distinctively broad-rimmed—the type of *kippah* worn—black or stitched woolen—and the wearing of the shirt collar—on top of or under the jacket—all of which identifies where one stands on the contem-

[33] See above, p. 26 n. 5 (end) and below, p. 202.

porary religious spectrum. A hundred years ago, that term was an uncommon expression for a scholar or a 'knowledgeable and scrupulously observant Jew', and some fifty years hence it may well revert to its traditional, non-denominational meaning.[34] These charged words are usually linked to the 'front' of the movement—to the critique of, and the point of struggle with, the established mores, to the specific ethical/religious agenda which the writer or movement is seeking to advance.

Let us take the above topic of charity and attempt to resolve the ambiguity of the term *tsaddik* in the writings of the German Pietists. Let us try to identify in those passages a specific, charged denotation, i.e. instances when it clearly refers to the Pietists and, consequently, evidences their values. Very early in their discussion of charity, they cite *en passant* a section of the Talmud Yerushalmi which attracted the attention of other medieval Talmudists.[35] Like so many other passages in the Yerushalmi, it is in an unedited state, and while the question is clear, the resolution is anything but that. The passage reads:

> ירושלמי: ר' חייא בר אבא אזל לחמא יהבון ליה פריטין למיפלגיה ליתמי ולארמלתא ונפק (ופלגיטן) ופלגינון לרבנן. מהו שיהא צריך תחותיהון? ר' יעקב בר חמא ר' דוסא בשם ר' אליעזר כל המעות ישנו אם לא נתנו לגזברים ואם נתנו לא ישנו. הרי למדנו שאין צדקה אלא במי שנותן לתלמידים חכמים צדיקים שעוסקים לשמה

R. Ḥiyya b. Abba went to Ḥama; [there] they gave him money to distribute to orphans and widows. He proceeded to distribute it to scholars. Must he replace the money [with an equivalent sum to be distributed to widows and orphans as originally intended]? R. Dosa said in the name of R. Eli'ezer: 'One may shift charity money to a different purpose so long as it has not yet been received by the *gizbar* [treasurer or director of the charity]; once received by the *gizbar*, it may not be shifted [to another purpose].' From this we learn [the Pietist concludes] that there is no charity other than giving it to scholars who are *tsaddikim* and who study Torah *li-shmah* [lit. 'for its own sake'].[36]

[34] See Y. Hazani, 'Mi-Mitos le-Etos: Ben Torah, Ben Navi ve-Talmud Torah (He'arot Mispar 'al ha-Av, ha-Em ve-ha-Ben)', *Derekh Aggadah*, 10 (2007), 95–137, which, among other things, lists and comments on all the occurrences of *ben Torah* in the classical literature.

[35] The unit on charity begins with #857. Our passage is #860. In reality, the unit begins at #851 or #852; however, the scribe only gives it a title five or six sections later. This is a frequent occurrence in *SHP*; the scribe or editor wakes up to the fact that a new unit is beginning a few sections after it has begun.

[36] Yerushalmi, *Megillah* 3: 1, Academy of Hebrew Language edn. (Jerusalem, 2001), col. 764; Romm edn. (Vilna, 1922–8), fo. 24a. I cite the passage as quoted by *Sefer Ḥasidim* in MS Parma 1133. For the variant readings of the Yerushalmi passage, see *Ahavat Tsiyyon vi-Yerushalayim, Megillah*, ed. B. Ratner (Vilna, 1912), 66–7.

Ravad of Posquières commented on this passage and interpreted it as ruling that the money must be replaced, and his words bear citation:

> נראה כי ר׳ יעקב בר אחא בא לסייע דברי מי שאומר צריך להפריש אחרים תחתיהם, כלומר, שלא יפסידו היתומים והאלמנות שהופרשו להם המעות. ו[י]שלמו להם מן הנדבה [מה] שהיו הרבנים נוטלים ממנה, לפי שלא כדין עשה ר׳ חייא כשחילק אותם הואיל וליתומים ואלמנות נתנו מתחילתן. כך נראה לי.
>
> אלא שיש לבעל הדין לחלוק ולומר מפני שרבי חייא בר אבא מדעת עצמו עשה ,שלא מדעת בני העיר. אבל אם עשה (כדעת) [מדעת] בני העיר לא היה צריך להשלים אחרים תחתיהם. אלא שאין הדעת מקבלת ואין השכל מורה כן שיהיו הצבור יכולים לגזול נדבתן של אלו וליתן לאלו כדי שיחסרו אלא שנתייחדו להם הנדבה לכתחילה.

It appears that R. Ya'akov bar Aḥa was cited as support for the opinion that money had to be restored so that the orphans and widows should not lose [the money], as it was specifically designated for them. And they should reimburse them from the community chest the sum that was given to the scholars. For R. Ḥiyya acted improperly when he gave it [to the scholars], since it was given from the very outset to the orphans and widows.

Though one could argue that the duty of restitution arises from the fact that R. Ḥiyya b. Abba acted [i.e. took earmarked money from the communal chest] without consulting the community, and had he consulted the community, he would not have had to make a restitution, however, the mind cannot accept, nor can reason ever rule, that the community may steal the charity donation of these [donors] and give to others, in such a manner that the [intended] recipients should lose that which has been given specifically for them.[37]

Some halakhists arrived at conclusions similar to that of Ravad;[38] others at ones at variance with him. Rabbenu Tam, for example, contended that once the money has entered the communal chest, the administrators of the fund may use it for any communal purpose they deem fit.[39] His position was endorsed by a number of halakhists with varying degrees of modification.[40] The German Pietists saw things differently from all medieval halakhists: the money clearly need *not* be replaced for R. Ḥiyya never breached his fiduciary role. On the contrary, he acted quite correctly, indeed, could not have acted otherwise. The very point of the Yerushalmi is that one *should* give scholars money that had been earmarked for widows and orphans.[41] The Ḥasid's

37 *Temim De'im* (Venice, 1622), #116.

38 See e.g. *Ḥiddushei R. Yosef Megas 'al Massekhet Bava Batra*, ed. Y. Politansky and Y. Dehan (n.p., 2015), 8b, s.v. *u-mistabra lan*.

39 Tosafot, *Bava Batra* 8b, *u-le-shanotam*; *Shitah Mekubbetset*, *'Arakhin* 6a, s.v. *le-shanotah*.

40 See *Ḥiddushei ha-Rashba 'al Massekhet Bava Batra*, ed. M. L. Katsenelenbogen (Jerusalem, 1997), 8b, s.v. *u-le-shanotan* and notes ad loc.

41 It will not do to argue that the Pietist here was the captive of his simplicity and piety and could

attitude to widows and orphans is not as harsh as it appears at first blush —when he says 'there is no charity other than giving it to scholars who are *tsaddikim* and who study Torah *li-shmah*', he is prioritizing rather than precluding. He is not denying widows and orphans access to charity—that would be absurd—but stating that scholars unquestionably come first, and where there are insufficient funds to go around, the widows and children should be left out in the cold. Widows and orphans are the classic cases throughout the Bible and in Jewish tradition of vulnerability, of needing special protection and help, and therefore are the preferred recipients of charity. The Pietist thought otherwise. Where they stand vis-à-vis scholars in his scale of values is crystal clear.

Previously, I faulted Marcus for citing instances of priority as evidence for exclusivity.[42] Am I not doing here the same thing? First, as will be clear as we proceed, I am claiming that the Pietists were elitist rather than exclusivist. Second, not all preferences are equal. To prefer poor scholars over the ordinary poor is of no matter—personal choices were never disallowed in charity. To prefer poor scholars over widows and orphans is altering the traditional hierarchy of priorities. To prefer scholars to the extent of overriding the stipulation of the donor is pre-emptive entitlement and goes far beyond simple preference.[43]

It is not, however, scholars per se, 'scholars' as the term is commonly understood, who hold this pre-emptive position, but scholars who are also *tsaddikim she-'osekim ba-Torah li-shmah* (who engage in Torah study for its own sake). It is this group alone that is so remarkably privileged in hasidic thought. In view of their unique entitlement, their precise identification merits our attention.

The *tsaddikim* are characterized as studying Torah *li-shmah* (for its own sake). *Li-shmah*, however, has many meanings, the most common of which is 'without any ulterior motive'.[44] Does it have distinctive denotations in hasidic thought? If yes, what are they, and when is the term being used distinctively?

not conceive of an *amora* of the Talmud acting incorrectly. Such a qualm could have been allayed by claiming, as did R. Menaḥem ha-Me'iri, that R. Ḥiyya acted as he did because there were no poor people around at the time to receive the restricted money, so R. Ḥiyya supported scholars with these funds, intending to make an equivalent sum available to the poor whenever they appear. See *Bet ha-Beḥirah 'al Massekhet Bava Batra*, ed. A. Sofer (Jerusalem, 1956), 8b, s.v. *u-miktsat ḥakhmei.*

[42] Above, p. 195.

[43] The case here at bar is not exclusivist, because if no scholars are around, the ordinary poor receive the charity. Giving to non-Pietists is not a 'sin'. See above, p. 186.

[44] See N. Lamm, *Torah li-Shemah: Torah for Torah's Sake in the Works of Rabbi Hayyim of Volozhin and His Contemporaries* (New York, 1989), 190–229.

Context, parallelism, and clustering may here be useful as both tools and controls.

Two sections later, *Sefer Ḥasidim* cites another passage from the Yerushalmi that speaks of the importance of giving money to scholars rather than spending it on buildings, and the idea of studying *li-shmah* occurs again:

> ולא יבנה אדם בתי כנסיות אלא אותם פשיטי[ם] יתן ליראי יי' העוסקין בתורה לשמה וכן אמ' ר' חמא ב"ר [חנינא לר' אושעיא] כמה בתי כנסיות בנו אבותי, [אמר] לו ר' אושעיא כמה נפשות אבדו אבותיך, שלא נתנו אותן מעות לתלמידי חכמים שיעסקו בתורה.

One should not build synagogues but rather give the money to God-fearers who study Torah *li-shmah*. And this [we have learned from the Yerushalmi, where] R. Ḥama b. R. [Ḥanina] said [to R. Oshaya], 'How many synagogues my ancestors built!', R. Oshaya replied, 'How many souls did your ancestors destroy in not giving the money to scholars so that they could study Torah?'[45]

There is a second unit on charity in *Sefer Ḥasidim*, in sections 1675–1718, and the same passage from the Yerushalmi (this time in the original Galilean Aramaic[46]), and the same moral lesson to be derived from it, are repeated (#1707). It reads:

> רבי חמא ב"ר חנינא ור' הושעיא רבא הוו מיטיילין באילן כנישתא דלוד אמ' ליה ר' חמא ב"ר חנינא לר' הושעיא רבא כמה ממון שקעו אבותיי כאן. [אמר] ליה כמה נפשות שקעו אבותיך כאן; מי לא הוון בני אינשא דילעון באוריתא. ר' אבין עבדון ליה תרעא לסידרא רבא, נחית ר' מני לגביה, אמ[ר] ליה חמית מה דעבדית, אמ[ר] ליה וישכח ישראל עושהו ויבן היכלות, מי לא הוון בני אינשא דילעון באוריתא.

Rabbi Ḥama b. R. Ḥanina and R. Hoshea' Rabba were strolling among the synagogues of Lod. R. Ḥama b. R. Ḥanina said to R. Hoshea' Rabba, '[See] how much money my ancestors sunk in [i.e. invested] here?' He replied, 'How many souls did they sink in [i.e. buried]? Were there no people who labored in study of the Torah [i.e. giving the money to them would have been far better]?' R. Avin had them make gates for the Sidra Rabba. R. Mani met him. He [R. Avin] said, 'See what I have done!' He [R. Mani] replied, 'For Israel hath forgotten his Maker and buildeth temples [Hos. 8:14].'

The Pietist then restates the principle in his own words, with a concluding admonition:

[45] #862.

[46] Yerushalmi, *Shekalim*, 5: 6, Academy of Hebrew Language edn. (Jerusalem, 2001), col. 622; Romm edn. (Vilna, 1922–8), fos. 23b–24a. For the Roman system of patronage and *euergetism* reflected in R. Ḥama's remarks, see Y. Wilfand, *Poverty, Charity and the Image of the Poor in Rabbinic Texts from the Land of Israel*, The Social World of Biblical Antiquity, 2nd ser., 9 (Sheffield, 2014), 264–6.

הרי מי שיש לו ממון לא יאמר אעשה בבית הכנסת ובית המדרש אלא יתן לצדיקים שיעסקו בתורה. ולא לאותן שגורסין קושיות כדי שיהו העולם סבורין שיודע כל התלמוד ולא עסקו אלא ראו קושיות וגירסות להראות חריפותו, אלא יתן ליראי יי׳ הלומדים לקיים המצות.

From this one sees that someone who has money should not say, 'I will build a synagogue or a study hall', but rather should give to *tsaddikim* so that they may study Torah. And not to those who recite questions [i.e. contradictions between different passages in the Talmud] so that people will believe that they know the entire Talmud and [in reality] they did not study Talmud but saw [in other books] these questions and [different] versions [of the talmudic *sugya*]; rather, he should give it [his money] to God-fearers [*yir'ei ha-Shem*], who study for the purpose of fulfilling the commandments [*ha-lomedim le-kayyem ha-mitsvot*].

In the first passage (#862), the Pietist advocates that they should rather give the money to *yir'ei ha-Shem*, who study Torah *li-shmah*. *Yir'ei ha-Shem* (God-fearers) is often a technical term for the Pietists.[47] In the parallel passage (#1707), the formulation is 'he should give [the money] to *tsaddikim* to enable them to study Torah'. Not to those, it adds, who ask questions which they plagiarized to impress people. Rather, he should give to *yir'ei ha-Shem*, who study for the purpose of fulfilling the commandments (*ha-lomedim le-kayyem ha-mitsvot*). *Tsaddikim* seems here (#1707) to be synonymous with *yir'ei ha-Shem*, and this matches the use of *yir'ei ha-Shem* made by the Pietist in his parallel restatement of the Yerushalmi in #862.

The identical talmudic text is commented on in both sections on charity in *Sefer Ḥasidim*, the identical moral is drawn, and the identical substitution is made of 'God-fearers' for the simple term 'scholar' found in the citation. If one leaves aside the very real digression about plagiarists (and a digression it is[48]), the two passages (##862, 1707) seem to be alternative formulations of the same principle. *Li-shmah* seems interchangeable with *le-kayyem*, just as *tsaddik* is with *yir'ei ha-Shem*. If this be so, then these two passages on charity and the preceding one of #860, where the *tsaddikim* who study Torah *li-shmah* are privileged over widows and orphans in matters of philanthropy, seem to be referring to one and the same group—and a highly privileged one at that.

[47] See above, p. 26 n. 52 (end).

[48] Not to give preference in charity to charlatans or four-flushers is common sense and needed no proof from the Yerushalmi. As I noted in 'Piety, Pietism, and German Pietism' (above, p. 85), the diction of *Sefer Ḥasidim* is that of the spoken word, in which grammatically incorrect and unclear contrasts, together with shifts of grammatical construction in mid-sentence (anacoluthons), abound without causing confusion. One understands the intent of the speaker from his intonation. Here the negation (*lo she-yiten*) begins in a dismissive tone—it goes without saying that one shouldn't give priority to charlatans or four-flushers who pretend to be scholars; the next sentence is said in earnest: *ela she-yiten* . . . The point being made here is that priority is restricted to scholars who study to fulfill the commandments, as is clear from #862. See also above, n. 12.

The theme of 'studying for the purpose of fulfilling' (*lilmod 'al menat le-kayyem*) repeats itself frequently in *Sefer Ḥasidim*, and in the opening sections of the Bologna edition of *Sefer Ḥasidim* (*SHB*), which comes close to being a programmatic presentation of the principles of Pietism, one finds an entire section devoted to it.[49] One also finds them inveighing against scholars who do not study Torah so as to fulfill its demands. There are rotten apples in every barrel, but when they state that there are '*hosts* of scholars who study *all* day and do not fulfill the Law',[50] they clearly have some common phenomenon in mind. Yet *Sefer Ḥasidim* levels no charges of hypocrisy against scholars, or even against some scholars. The concentration of the charge in this term alone, and its absence elsewhere, makes one suspect that this indeed is a charged word—one that had clear and specific meaning to its user, and one that denoted a 'front' that the Ḥasidei Ashkenaz sought to alter or a specific value or norm of conduct that was specifically theirs.

In an earlier essay, I wrote:

With their congenital inability to adhere strictly to any terminology, the Pietists used the term *she-lo li-shmah* at times as synonymous with *lilmod she-lo 'al menat le-kayyem* (study without the intention of fulfilling the Law),[51] which in their hands meant not simply study by the religiously lax, but the reduction of *talmud Torah* (Torah study) to a purely intellectual experience. Any expansion of the Divine norm was certainly in consonance with the goals of Ḥasidut, and the Pietists had no quarrel with the new *pilpul* (tosafist dialectic) as such. But the purpose of dialectic to them was not simply the solution of logical difficulties, but the detection by man of new demands made upon him by God. One thought in order to discover to what to submit. Unlike early Polish hasidim, the German Pietists did not seek to empty *talmud Torah* of its intellectual content, for that would have been self-defeating. They rather demanded *in* study the ongoing experience of law as an imperative. Only then was study integrated with and productive of religious growth, and anything less than that bordered on the criminal. A scholar who attained a deeper understanding of the halakhah—that is to say, a fuller comprehension of the Divine demands—but whose religious observance did not intensify concomitantly could only be viewed, in the final analysis, as being in a state of rebellion.[52] *Talmud Torah* could not coexist with a static religious commitment.[53]

[49] *SHB*, #17. As for the fact that the first 152 sections of *SHB* were authored by conventional rather than German Pietists, see above, pp. 81–9.

[50] *SHB*, #17.

[51] *SHP*, ##754, 756 (note contrast); *SHB*, #17. Compare *SHP*, #862 with #1707: אלא . . . יתן [הצדקה] ליראי ה' העוסקין בתורה לשמה / אלא יתן ליראי ה' הלומדים לקיים המצוות. (MS Oxford, Bodley 875, which contains the first 152 sections of *SHB*, reads at fo. 134v: אלא לומד על מנת לקיים לשמור ולעשות זו היא תורה לשמה.)

[52] *SHB*, #17; *SHP*, ##1474 (end), 1475.

[53] Above, pp. 47–8. The essay was first published over forty years ago.

This still seems to me to be the thrust of the concept in hasidic thought, and this view seems to have been shared by the more conventional pietists in the Franco-German community, whose thought is reflected in the first 152 sections of *SHB*, what I have called *Sefer Ḥasidim I*.[54] The agenda of the German Pietists, however, went a step further, as we can see from the one example of not studying *li-shmah* that they provide us with. A few sections into the unit that treats *talmud Torah*, we find:

> אם חשב אדם ללמוד לשמה כיצד יחשוב בלבו כל מה שאלמוד אקיים. . . אם יקיים הרי היא לשמה, אבל למד 'המרצה מעות מידו לידה כדי להסתכל בה לא ינצל מדינה של גהינם'[55] והוא צופה, הרי יענש גם על מה שלמד.

Should someone intend to *study li-shmah*, how does he go about it? He should seriously intend that 'everything that I study, I will fulfill' . . . and should he fulfill, that is *li-shmah*. However, if he has learnt [the talmudic dictum] 'one who passes money [more slowly] from his hand to her hand in order to gaze at her will not be saved from the judgment of Gehinom' and, [nevertheless,] does gaze, he will be punished also for what he had learnt [i.e. he is ever more culpable, for now he has done something in full awareness of its illicit nature].[56]

The eye automatically lingers on a pleasing sight, but combating the most elementary impulses and reflexes of man was central to the hasidic agenda. Indeed, control of automatic reflexes was the very ark of the hasidic covenant, and minimizing the occasions that might trigger such reflexes was central to the hasidic way of life. This melded well with another hasidic goal, that of cultivating responsibility for one's thoughts. Fleeting feelings and thoughts leave no fingerprints in most people; they are subject to what Freud once called *Ungeschehenmachen* (making something 'unhappen'). Mentally undoing what one has actually done is the mark of neurosis; what one has criminally done, the mark of a pathology; mentally undoing what one has thought is simply human nature. When I finally arrive at my destination, after driving close to an hour in the heavy traffic of the East River Drive, I have mentally sent some drivers to an insane asylum, others to Hell, and occasionally even strangled one of them. Yet when I step out of the car in the parking lot, I have no sense of guilt at all. Automatically, I've wiped out any trace of these thoughts from my mind and feel no sense of sin for having entertained them. Many saints are not blessed with this erasure mechanism; thoughts to them

54 Ch. 3 above.

55 *Berakhot* 61a, *'Eruvin* 18a. For the variant readings of *yinakeh/yinatsel*, see *Dikdukei Soferim*, ed. R. N. N. Rabbinovicz, *Berakhot* (Munich, 1867), 61a (p. 352), n. 8.

56 *SHP*, #754. For the attitude of the conventional pietists, see above, Ch. 1, Afterword, sect. A, #3.

are morally as real and as culpable as deeds. Religious virtuosi often share this mentality.

Instilling, first, a sense of responsibility for one's thoughts, a sense of guilt at harboring these normal passing ideas and sensations, and then training oneself to avoid and, if necessary, conquer these natural reflexes was one of the major goals of Ḥasidei Ashkenaz. They adopted a policy of 'custody of the eyes', of walking with their eyes cast down, lest their eyes alight upon a pleasing forbidden object, such as, indeed first and foremost, the face or form of a woman. This made them into objects of mockery in the Jewish community, and the Ḥasidim spoke repeatedly of the humiliation which must be endured to persist in this practice.[57] It entailed constant vigilance and exertion, and the effort expended, coupled with the ridicule it elicited, made its practice one of the great divides between the Pietists and the rest of the community.[58] *Le-kayyem* and *li-shmah* often denote this endeavor and function as charged words, words that denote the marrow of the movement's aspirations, the most salient facet of its religious agenda. When they do so function, as here, statements that *tsaddikim ha-lomedim li-shmah* or *tsaddikim ha-lomedim le-kayyem* have priority over widows, orphans, and the abject poor are chilling.

One might conjecture that this extreme privileging of *tovim* and *mehugganim* arose from discrimination experienced by the German Pietists in the distribution of charity of the time. However, not a whisper of such an injustice or even a hint of such a bias is to be found in *Sefer Ḥasidim*. That work exudes a strong sense of religious and political disinheritance[59] but not disenfranchisement at the communal dole. Neither hurt nor loss nor even *ressentiment* and its insidious after-effects are at work here, but simply outlook, the values and priorities of the hasidic movement, which makes it even more disturbing.

Indeed, from the numerous exempla given where money is earmarked for the *tovim*, *mehugganim*, and *tsaddikim*,[60] one gets the impression that there was considerable support for the German Pietists in the general community. A Ḥasid who spent hours in protracted prayer and contemplation and avoided all small talk and social intercourse found himself inevitably in strait-

[57] See above, pp. 29–30. [58] See above, pp. 29–30. [59] See above, pp. 51–5.

[60] ##905, 918–21, 1679, 1683, 1695, 1700. One might contend that the sections on charity in *Sefer Ḥasidim* are in-house directives, guidance for Pietists only. I find this difficult to reconcile with the numerous dicta about reckoning with sensitivities of the poor and of the newly poor from all walks of life, and with practical advice given on a wide range of problems which parents, teachers, and householders encounter in daily living. The opening sections of *SHP* and *SHB* are indeed directed to those aspiring to Ḥasidut, as are many specific directives. However, there are hundreds of pages of dicta and exempla that to all appearances seem addressed to those in the wider community who are seeking ethical and religious guidance.

ened circumstances, if not outright poverty. His needs and those of his family had largely to be met by the dole. To be sure, the Pietist who hindered communal prayer, lectured his wayward co-religionist, and generally acted as if he were God's older brother was usually put in his place brusquely. Nor was there any lack of public amusement or occasions of mockery by the communal jokers at the expense of the Ḥasid's strange four-fringed garment (*tallit*)[61] and his constant, ever-failing attempt to avoid looking at women. However, this did not mean that many in the community, while scarcely sharing the Ḥasid's values, did not respect his Sisyphean aspirations and admire the meek acceptance of the humiliations that he endured for his convictions. Yet this real—if mute—support in no way altered the Ḥasid's mindset, nor did it affect his chiaroscuro perception of entitlement.

What the Pietists are, at most times, is elitist, and philanthropy graphically illustrates this. *Sefer Ḥasidim* introduces into charity the notion of merit, indeed makes it central. And merit, even conventionally defined as a criterion for charity, is a new and radical concept. There are two passages in the talmudic literature that do introduce the notion of merit. However, they are so outweighed by innumerable other passages that they are not even mentioned in Yael Wilfand's comprehensive survey, *Poverty, Charity and the Image of the Poor in Rabbinic Texts from the Land of Israel*, not even in her chapter on 'Rabbinic Approaches to Examining the Eligibility of Applicants for Alms'.[62] And correctly so. If one scours rabbinic literature long enough, one chances upon traces of almost any idea. These wisps are written off as stray and idiosyncratic notions that managed somehow to register themselves in that vast corpus. Indeed, the thrust of tannaitic and amoraic literature tends to discourage even serious inquiry into whether those who seek charity are actually in need.[63] Wilfand writes in summary: 'Regarding the Jewish poor . . . the rabbinic texts do not raise religious stipulations that would disqualify an indigent petitioner from receiving support. The sole criterion seems to be economic

[61] *SHP*, #1344; *Teshuvot R. Me'ir mi-Rothenburg* (Budapest, 1895), #287. (The largest collection of the medieval Ashkenazic responsa commonly attributed to R. Me'ir of Rothenburg was first printed in Prague, 1608. The defective text was critically edited by M. A. Bloch and published in Budapest in 1895.)

[62] Above, n. 46; the cited chapter is found at 185–97. I have not reckoned with the passage in *Sukkah* as that hinges upon the interpretation given to it by Rashi. It may be that Wilfand does not cite these two passages as the *derashah* of Rava is Babylonian, and she focuses on Palestine. Similarly, the report of Rabbi, who regretted giving bread to the unlettered poor, is found only in the Bavli, and she uses only Palestinian amoraic traditions of *tanna'im*. However, she does cite on occasion reports of the Bavli for contrast, and this would have constituted a striking divergence of the two streams. More plausibly, she ignored these passages because of their rare occurrence and outlandish character even within the Babylonian tradition.

[63] Ibid. 197.

vulnerability. In other words, the rabbis in no way restrict support for the impoverished in any particular group within the Jewish community.'[64]

If one moves into the medieval period and inspects, for example, Maimonides' *Mishneh Torah*, the only criterion is need.[65] Not surprisingly, as indigence is the controlling principle of the last chapter of tractate *Pe'ah*, which underlies Maimonides' presentation.[66] To broaden the medieval field, we may take the two comprehensive compendia of talmudic and midrashic ethical dicta, the *Menorat ha-Ma'or* of Ibn 'Al-Nakawa and Abohab's work of the same title,[67] and we will not find in the 114 pages on charity in these works a single dictum that would indicate that merit, personal virtue of any sort, plays a role in its allotment. All attention is focused on the importance of charity, the manner of giving it, and the various definitions of need. But it is need and need alone that is the criterion for receiving charity.

To be sure, there is some outer limit of conduct that, if crossed, puts the transgressor beyond the pale of society and stamps him as an outlaw who is to be denied communal aid and excluded from its largesse, of which charity is but one form. This outer limit, however, is a criminal one. Opinions may differ as to where the boundary line is drawn (*mumar le-te'avon* or *le-hakh'is*, for example);[68] however, as the classification is a legal one, it is always formally

[64] Wilfand, *Poverty, Charity and the Image of the Poor* (above, n. 46), 273.

[65] 'Hilkhot Matenot 'Aniyyim', ch. 9.

[66] Ch. 8.

[67] Yisra'el Ibn 'Al-Nakawa, *Menorat ha-Ma'or*, i, ed. H. G. Enelow (New York, 1929); Yitsḥak Abohab, *Menorat ha-Ma'or*, ed. Y. P. Horev (Jerusalem, 1961). On the problematic relationship between the identically titled two works and which one preceded the other, see most recently Y. M. Ta-Shma, 'Ḥidat Sefer *Menorat ha-Ma'or* u-Fitronah', *Tarbiz*, 64 (1995), 395–400; repr. in id., *Keneset Meḥkarim: 'Iyyunim ba-Sifrut ha-Rabbanit bi-Yemei ha-Beinayim*, ii: *Sefarad* (Jerusalem, 2005), 202–8.

[68] The exact definition of 'outlaw' and 'beyond the pale' is subject to controversy. Maimonides does mention *mumar le-hakh'is* (one who violates the law on principle) as being beyond the pale of charity ('Hilkhot Matenot 'Aniyyim', 8: 14). Opinion differs whether this extends equally to a *mumar le-te'avon* (a non-ideological sinner, one who violates the law simply out of greed or for the sake of pleasure). See both *Tur* and *Shulkhan 'Arukh*, 'Yoreh De'ah', 251: 1 and the classic commentators ad loc. Including the *mumar le-te'avon* in the outlaw category, contrary to the simplest reading of the *locus classicus* of *Gittin* 46b, was first advocated by R. Eli'ezer of Metz in his *Sefer Yere'im*, ed. A. A. Schiff (Paris, 1891), #156. He coins a more derisive term for this class of sinners, *'avaryan be-mezid*. His view is cited by R. Mosheh of Coucy in his *Sefer Mitsvot Gadol* (*Semag*), ed. E. Schlesinger (Jerusalem, 1995), *'aseh* #162 (p. 148), and by R. Yitsḥak of Corbeil in his *Sefer 'Amudei Golah* (*Semak*) (Jerusalem, 2005), at the very outset of the unit dealing with charity, #246 (#248). This view of *mumar le-te'avon* is controverted by Ri (*Tosefot R. Elḥanan*, *'Avodah Zarah*, ed. A. Y. Kreiser [Benei Berak, 2003], 26a, s.v. *ani*), and is reflected in the standard *Tosafot* ad loc. Alyssa Gray has recently discussed the doctrine of R. Eli'ezer of Metz in 'R. Eliezer of Metz's Twelfth-Century Exclusion from Charity of the Jewish *Avaryan B'mezid* (Deliberate Transgressor)', in S. A. Farmer, ed., *Approaches to Poverty*

determined and never left to personal opinion. Such exclusions are found in the criminal code defining societal outlaws. These extreme cases of banishment from the intra-Jewish support system are taken for granted, and they make no appearance in discussions of charity in ethical works, and in legal codes on philanthropy these exclusions are noted only in passing.

The centrality of merit expresses itself in *Sefer Ḥasidim* in many and startling ways. Confronted with a dying man who has collected charity but will not live to distribute it, the Ḥasid advises him to mandate its use for providing for an orphan's dowry, and then concludes, 'provided they are *tsaddikim*'.[69] Far more significant than this overt qualification are the unwitting ones. Famous and oft-quoted talmudic dicta, such as גדול המעשה יותר מן העושה—'Greater is the reward that awaits the one who pressures others to give to charity than that which awaits the contributor himself'—is taken as matter of course as referring to forcing contributions for *tsaddikim*. Wishing to get across the message that the objects of such forced exactions must be the wealthy and not the poor, the Ḥasid writes: דוקא אם מעשים העשירים לתת לצדיק עני . . . אבל אם מעשה את מי שאינו יכול להתפרנס, הרי הוא כאילו גזלן. ('This holds true only if he forces rich people to contribute to a poor *tsaddik* . . . but if he forces someone who cannot support himself [i.e. has difficulty supporting himself], it is as if he were a strong-armed robber.'[70]) The well-known dictum: אמר רב אליעזר אין הצדקה משתלמת אלא לפי החסד שבה שנא[מר] זרעו לכם צדקה קצרו לפי חסד—'R. Eli'ezer stated: The reward of charity depends entirely upon the extent of the kindness with which it is extended, for it is said, "Sow to yourselves according to charity, but reap according to kindness [Hos. 10: 12]"'—is taken as self-evidently referring to kindness benefiting a *tsaddik*: שכל מי שמהנה צדיק כפי הנאה שנהנה ('Anyone who benefits a *tsaddik* [will be rewarded] in proportion to the benefit that accrued [to the *tsaddik*]').[71]

Emphasizing, as do many medieval writers, that preventing a person from falling upon dole by helping him to support himself is an act of the highest charity,[72] the Ḥasid automatically thinks in terms of helping a *tsaddik*. He writes: יש צדקה שאינה נראית כצדקה והיא לפני הקב"ה צדקה מעולה, כגון עני צדיק שיש לו חפץ למכור. . . שאין חפיצים לקנות, והוא קונהו מידו. ('There is charity which does not appear as charity but in God's eyes it is the highest charity. For example, there is a

in Medieval Europe: Complexities, Contradictions, Transformations, c. 1100–1500 (Turnhout, 2016), 67–92. I wish to thank Yehudah Galinsky for drawing my attention to this article.

[69] #925. I believe the ellipsis had *tsedakah min ha-muvḥar*, as evidenced by the ending. As this remains a conjecture, I have not included it in the text.

[70] #912.

[71] #879. Why they construe 'kindness' as 'benefit' is beyond my comprehension, but this in no way affects my argument.

[72] For talmudic precedents, see e.g. *Shabbat* 63b; *Sanhedrin* 76b.

poor *tsaddik* who has some object to sell . . . but no one is interested in buying it, and he buys it from him.'[73])

Similarly, when the Ḥasid thinks of need, he thinks of the need of the *tsaddik*. When, for example, he decries giving to lesser causes for the sake of acclaim and neglecting worthy causes, he does not think of widows and orphans, so frequently mentioned in the Bible, but of needy *tsaddikim*.[74] When the Ḥasid is given money for *mitsvah rabbah* (a great *mitsvah*), neither the redemption of captives, the classic case of *mitsvah rabbah* of the Talmud, nor the indispensable bridal dowry for the impoverished, nor even the leprous poor of his time come to mind, only the needy *tsaddik*.[75] When in an elaborate exemplum he seeks to bring home the importance of paying one's charitable vows immediately, he concludes, 'he should [swiftly] give them to good poor people or to a reliable man, who will give it to good people'.[76]

So significant is this idea in the hasidic *Weltanschauung* that it raises issues of theodicy. Perplexed how it could be that a greater *hagun* (worthy person) received less charity than a lesser *hagun*, the Ḥasid attributed it to God's seeking to deny the greater reward to the community, so He deprived them of the opportunity of contributing to the greater *hagun* by sending them a lesser one. A similar explanation is provided by another hasidic mentor, the Ḥakham,[77] when confronted with a donor who waxed rich when he gave to non-*mehugganim* and became poorer when he gave to *mehugganim*. In the era of the Jewish badge of shame, the rise of ritual murder accusations and those of Host desecration, the differences in communal charity allocation would seem to be the least of God's ways that needed justification. Indeed, even in contemporary America, where the Jewish community is unburdened by such existential concerns, I have difficulty imagining that the head of the famed *ḥaredi* yeshivah in Lakewood would have theological problems because the Westchester Torah Academy raised more funds than did his institution.[78]

[73] #884. [74] #917, discussed above, pp. 192–3. [75] #1684, discussed above, p. 191.

[76] #1680: ויתנם לתת לעניים טובים או יתן לנאמנים שיחלקו לטובים.

[77] I have used the term 'the Ḥasid' for the authorial voice in the dicta of *Sefer Ḥasidim*, the one who stands behind the numerous hasidic instructions and rulings. When a guide is mentioned in that work, he is often called 'the Ḥakham', one who is learned in the Will of the Creator. See Marcus's enlightening discussion in *Piety and Society* (above, n. 1), 71–4.

[78] ##913, 1706. The one possible exception to merit would seem to be #1695. However, since the *tsaddik* has support from another source, he is strictly speaking not in need. The distinction here is not between the greater need of an ordinary man and the lesser need of a *tsaddik*; that would eventuate in the hasidic ruling that the *tsaddik* trumps the ordinary man. Here the *tsaddik* has another source of charity; forgoing that source and drawing upon the new source would condemn the ordinary man to hunger, which is a wholly different matter. When the Ḥasid is not contemplating the proper allocation of charity but administering penance, distributing the penitent's ill-gotten gains,

The questions occupying every allotment committee, namely those of competing priorities, are strikingly absent in *Sefer Ḥasidim*. In a work that seeks to give practical guidance, one finds no discussion of the competing claims of the orphan as against the widow, the obligatory bridal dowry as against the child support. No indication is given how to assess the significance of the same need to different people. In brief, all that we would most expect to find in *Sefer Ḥasidim* with its psychological sensitivity is missing there. Two leitmotifs run through its discussion of charity—minimizing the embarrassment of the recipient, especially of one who has fallen from high estate, and the significance of merit. The former is a long-standing concern in classical Jewish literature on charity,[79] the latter a radical innovation. At times, this latter mindset makes one recoil. In reply to the question whether it is preferable to give money to a scribe to copy books or to *tovim* who have no clothes, *Sefer Ḥasidim*, wishing to emphasize that the physical needs take precedence on occasion over religious ones, cites Isaiah, who said, 'When thou seest a naked man, thou shouldst clothe him.'[80] The Ḥasid did not notice that Isaiah spoke of naked men, not of naked *tovim*. It is he who, upon seeing a poor man in tatters, instinctively takes his religious and moral temperature and structures his exemplum accordingly.

Take merit conventionally, and translate *tsaddik* simply as 'pious' or 'upright', and the step taken by Ḥasidei Ashkenaz is still a radical, indeed a portentous, one. One can take a measure of its chilling influence on a pupil of R. Yehudah he-Ḥasid. R. Yitsḥak of Vienna opened his great multi-volume halakhic compendium, *Or Zarua'*, with the laws of charity, and prefaced it with a collection of aggadic dicta on *tsedakah*. Twenty-one citations are listed, and, under the influence of the movement, three talmudic passages are cited one after another. (The first passage is cited with Rashi's explanatory remarks, which I have placed in italics):

1. וא[מר] ר[בי] אלעזר כל העושה צדקה ומשפט, כאלו מלא כל הארץ חסד, שנא[מר] 'אוהב צדקה ומשפט, חסד ה' מלאה הארץ'. שמא תאמר כל הבא לעשות צדקה ומשפט וחסד מספיקין בידו' *וממציאין לו אנשים מהוגנים* ? ת"ל 'מה יקר חסדך ה', *צריך לתת לבו ולרדוף אחרי[הם] לפי שאינ[ם] מצוי[ים] תמיד לזכות בה למהוגנין*.[81]

R. El'azar stated: He who does charity and justice, it is as though he had filled all the

he speaks of giving to 'orphans and poor children', with no proviso of merit (#630). The 'deserving poor', however, are not far from his mind, and he soon reverts to stating, 'buy books from which God-fearing people or poor orphans can study'.

[79] On the shifting attitudes to the newly poor, see A. M. Gray, 'The Formerly Wealthy Poor: From Empathy to Ambivalence in Rabbinic literature of Late Antiquity', *AJS Review*, 33 (2009), 101–33.

[80] #1696; Isa. 58: 7.

[81] *Sukkah* 49b.

world with kindness, for it is said, 'He loveth charity and justice, the earth is full of the loving kindness of the Lord' [Ps. 32: 5]. Lest you say whoever wishes to do good succeeds without difficulty *and finds worthy recipients* [*mehugganim*], Scripture teaches us, 'How precious [i.e. how rare] is Thy loving kindness O God': *he must make an effort and pursue* [i.e. search for] *them because one is not always fortunate to give to worthy recipients.*

R. Yitsḥak Or Zarua', as is his wont, has interwoven Rashi's comments with the text of the Talmud. Rashi introduced the notion of *mehugganim* for exegetical reasons. What is so difficult, he asked himself, about finding poor people that one needs Divine assistance? Obviously, something over and above simple need is being discussed here. Seeking, as any good commentator does, to interpret from within and not from without, to explain a text with another passage in the same corpus, Rashi scanned the Talmud for other possible qualifications, and his mind's eye alighted on the words of Rava in *Bava Batra*. I don't believe that Rashi's explanation reflects any personal view of his, as he is simply operating here in his usual commentarial mode. Moreover, *mehugganim* may well mean to his thinking simply those who are honestly in need, as opposed to those who are freeloading.[82] The invocation of the passage written by R. Yitsḥak Or Zarua' is another matter, as it must be judged by the company it keeps; placed alongside the next two quotations, one sees that it forms part of a triad of exclusion.

2. **ובפ[ר]ק ק[מא] ד[בבא] בתרא, אמר ר' יצחק מאי דכתיב 'רודף צדקה וחסד ימצא חיים צדקה' וכו', משום דרודף צדקה ימצא צדק[ה], אלא הקב"ה ממציא לו מעות כדי לעשות מהם צדקה. רב נחמן בר יצחק אומר הקב"ה ממציא לו בני אדם מהוגנים לעשות בהן צדקה לקבל מהם שכר. לאפוקי מדרבא, דדריש רבא מ[אי] ד[כתיב] 'יהיו מוכשלים לפניך בעץ אפך עשה בהם'? אמר ירמי' לפני הקב"ה, רבש"ע אפילו בשעה שכופין את יצרם לעשות צדקה, הכשילם ב[בני] א[דם] שאינם מהוגנים כדי שלא לקבל עליהם שכר.**[83]

R. Isaac said: What is the meaning of the verse 'He that followeth after [i.e. pursueth] righteousness findeth righteousness, life, and honor'? Because a man has pursued

[82] See *Bava Metsi'a* 24a, where the Talmud advises that one should not speak about one's largesse in receiving guests, and Rashi (s.v. *be-ushpiza*) explains that this is to forestall people who are not *mehugganim* from constantly frequenting his table and consuming his financial resources (**כדי שלא יקפצו בו בני אדם לא מהוגנים לבוא תמיד אצלו ויקחו את ממונו**). This interpretation is suggested by *'Arakhin* 16a, as pointed out somewhat elliptically by *Tosafot*, *Bava Metsi'a* 23b, s.v. *be-ushpiza*, and more clearly by *Tosafot ha-Rosh 'al Bava Metsi'a*, eds. M. Hershler and Y. D. Grodzitski (Jerusalem, 1959), 23b, s.v. *be-ushpiza*. On the shifting attitudes to possible freeloaders, see the fine article by Elliot Horowitz, '"Ve-Yihyu 'Aniyyim (Hagunim) Benei Betekha": Tsedakah u-Fikuaḥ Ḥevrati bi-Kehillot Yehudei Eiropah bein Yemei ha-Beinayim le-Reshit ha-'Et ha-Ḥadashah', in M. Ben-Sasson, ed., *Dat ve-Khalkalah—Yaḥasei Gomlin: Shay le-Ya'akov Kats bi-Mel'ot lo Tish'im Shanah* (Jerusalem, 1995), 209–31.

[83] *Bava Batra* 9b.

righteousness [*tsedakah*, i.e. charity], shall he find righteousness? The verse comes to teach us that if a man pursues [i.e. is anxious to give] charity, God furnishes him with money to give. R. Naḥman said: God sends him men who are fitting recipients of charity [*mehugganim*], so that he may be rewarded for assisting them. This is to exclude who? This is to exclude [those people mentioned by Rava]. For Rava taught: What is the meaning of the verse 'Let them be made to stumble before Thee: in the time of thy anger, deal with them' [Jer. 18: 23]? Jeremiah said, 'Holy One Blessed be He, Sovereign of the universe, even at a time when they conquer their evil inclination and seek to do acts of charity before Thee, cause them to stumble through men who are not fitting recipients [*she-einam mehugganim*], so that they should receive no reward for assisting them.'

3. ורבי נמי קאמר התם 'אוי לי שנתתי פתי לעם הארץ'[84]

Rabbi [i.e. R. Yehudah the Prince] said, 'Woe is me that I have given my bread to a man without learning.'

Just how alien these notions are to other medieval scholars can be seen from the fate of these three maxims in other works of the period. Maimonides omits them entirely in the last chapter of 'Hilkhot Matenot 'Aniyyim'. This, however, says little, as he is highly selective. Hundreds of other aggadic dicta on charity are also omitted. The same holds true to a lesser extent for the much-reprinted *Ma'alot ha-Middot*.[85] The *Menorat ha-Ma'or* of R. Yisra'el Ibn 'Al-Nakawa and R. Yitsḥak Abohab's work of the same title, however, are sweepingly comprehensive compendia of aggadic stories and dicta, and the fate of those maxims in these two works is indicative. Charity takes up sixty-seven pages in Ibn 'Al-Nakawa's work, and thirty-seven small-print pages in that of Abohab. Ibn 'Al-Nakawa omits entirely both the dictum of R. Yehudah the Prince and that of R. El'azar in *Sukkah*. The passage in *Bava Batra* is handled surgically. The opening positive statement of R. Isaac is cited not from *Bava Batra* but from the *Pesikta*.[86] This allows him to omit—without charges of censorship by partial quotation—the subsequent dicta of R. Naḥman and Rava, clearly implying that charity should be given only to the meritorious, found in *Bava Batra* but not in the *Pesikta*. Abohab cites the story

[84] Ibid. 8a.

[85] Yeḥiel b. Yekuti'el ha-Rofè, *Ma'alot ha-Middot* (Jerusalem, 1955), 34–41. The work is entitled *Sefer Bet ha-Middot* in the first two of its many printings, Constantinople 1512 and Cremona 1557. There are few differences, if any, between the early editions and the modern ones.

[86] Ibn 'Al-Nakawa, *Menorat Ha-Ma'or* (above, n. 67), 84. One cannot claim that the omission of the *Bava Batra* passage was an oversight, as the passage which immediately follows Rava's remark in *Bava Batra*, that of R. Yehoshua b. Levi, is cited on p. 89.

and dictum of R. Yehudah the Prince; however, he explains it as being true in an instance of triage only.[87] If the available funds suffice to support only a limited number of applicants, scholars take priority over ignoramuses, as they would in the redemption of captives.[88] The passage in *Sukkah* is presented as referring to charity given gracefully and compassionately, and thus is unrelated to any issue of merit.[89] The passage in *Bava Batra* is explained away (by emphasizing the word 'pursue') thus:

> הרודף *בכל כחו* לחלק צדקה *יותר ממה שיש לו*, הקדוש ברוך הוא מרבה שכרו וממציא לו מעות לתת לאנשים מהוגנים שיקבלוהו כדגרסינן בפרק קמא דבתרא אמר ר' יצחק מאי דכתיב וכו'

Someone who pursues *with all his might* the distribution of charity, *over and above what he possesses* [i.e. more than what he can reasonably afford], God increases his reward by giving him yet more money that he can give to people who are *mehugganim*, as we find written in the first chapter of *Bava Batra*: 'R. Yitsḥak said . . .'. [emphasis mine]

The satisfaction that one has from knowing that one's money is supporting a virtuous man is the special reward given by God for supererogatory philanthropy.[90] Neither R. Yisra'el Ibn 'Al-Nakawa nor R. Yitsḥak Abohab, bent though they were on comprehensiveness and fidelity, could entertain the thoughts which came so naturally and so often to the German Pietists.[91]

[87] Abohab, *Menorat ha-Ma'or* (above, n. 67), 412. He is here following the lead of R. Yom Tov b. Avraham al-Sevilli, commonly known as Ritva. See below, n. 92.

[88] *Horayot* 13a.

[89] *Menorat ha-Ma'or* (above, n. 67), 403–4.

[90] Both authors do mention *hagun* once in their works. Abohab states that one who gives to a *hagun* is rewarded by not suffering the forced exactions of Gentile rulers (p. 401). Giving to those of merit is an added virtue which does not go unrewarded. I do not know what generated this remark. Ibn 'Al-Nakawa (p. 83) adds the qualification of *hagun* as a trait demanded of an agent (*shaliaḥ*) who is employed to transmit money to the communal chest—which goes without saying.

[91] I have doubts about the correct interpretation of the words of the only other medieval ethicist who cites this passage, the famed Catalan pietist, Rabbenu Yonah mi-Gerundi, in his *Commentary on Avot*, 1: 2. He writes:

> ומענין גמילות חסדים הוא להשגיח לעניים ולבחור בין טוב ורע ולהקדים הצנוע והירא שמים על (ה)אחרים שאינם כמותו. ואם בכולם *נעשה צדקה*, וכמו שאמר ירמיהו ע"ה ויהיו מוכשלים לפניך בעת אפיך עשה בהם, אפילו בשעה שיעשו צדקה הכשילם (שיתנום במקום שאינו הגון) [בבני אדם שאינם הגונים].

> One of the characteristics of *gemilut ḥasadim* is to observe carefully the poor and choose between the good ones and the bad and to give preference to the modest and God-fearing over others unlike them. *And if to all he has done charity* [*sic*], as Jeremiah said, 'Let them be made to stumble before Thee: in the time of thy anger, deal with them', even at a time when they conquer their evil inclination and seek to do acts of charity before Thee, cause them to stumble through men who are not fitting recipients [*she-einam mehugganim*]. [italics mine]

The problematic phrase 'and if to all he has done charity' is found in the best manuscripts and in most recent editions. *Perushei Rabbenu Yonah mi-Gerundi 'al Massekhet Avot*, ed. M. S. Kasher and Y. Y.

Needless to say, no halakhist cited R. Yehudah the Prince's regrets at having given an ignorant pauper food to eat. Maimonides, of course, omits it, as does R. Ya'akov b. Asher in his *Tur*. Ritva comments on the passage in *Bava Batra* and confines it to an instance of triage.[92] R. Yosef Karo, in his famous commentary on the *Tur*, the *Bet Yosef*, realizing that the statement from a person as authoritative as R. Yehudah the Prince might be taken as a halakhic mandate, cited it in order to restrict it by invoking Ritva's qualification.[93] This maneuver is repeated in his *Shulḥan 'Arukh*.[94]

Belkhrovits (Jerusalem, 1966), 4–5 (based on MSS Madrid G-IV-5, fo. 3a and Vatican 277, fo. 62a); *Massekhet Avot 'im Perushei Rishonim*, ed. M. L. Katsenelenbogen (Jerusalem, 2005), i. 126 (based on MS Parma, De Rossi 1203). I was unable to obtain B. D. Kohen's edition, published in Jerusalem in 2006; however, it is based on MSS Florence, Biblioteca Medicea Laurenziana 155 and London, British Library 235, and both (the former at fo. 3a, the latter at fo. 139a) have the same readings as the preceding manuscripts, as does Jerusalem, National Library of Israel 1998=8 (formerly Livorno, Talmud Tora 14), fo. 52b. (Most manuscripts read *'oseh tsedakah* rather than *na'aseh tsedakah*, and that of Florence has *ve-'al kulam 'oseh tsedakah*.) Katsenelenbogen takes it to mean 'and if [he gives] to all [indiscriminately], he has done charity [but not *gemilut ḥasadim*]'. This interpretation goes against the immediately following citation of Rava, which speaks specifically of charity. Moreover, it inverts the relationship between *tsedakah* (charity) and *gemilut ḥasadim* ('deeds of loving kindness', as translated by G. E. Moore, *Judaism in the First Centuries of the Christian Era: The Age of the Tannaim* [Cambridge, Mass., 1946], ii. 171–4). The latter is viewed as a more comprehensive mode of aiding one's fellow man than charity. For example, charity can be extended only to the living; *gemilut ḥasadim* encompasses both comforting the living mourners and honoring the dead by attending their funeral.

The *Commentary of Rabbenu Yonah* found in the standard Romm Talmud was taken from the defective Altona 1848 or Lemberg 1864 editions and lacks that gnomic phrase. By all rules of editing, the more difficult reading found in the best manuscripts is to be preferred over the smoother one of the older prints, as one can readily see why an editor would elide this problematic phrase, but scarcely why he would add it to a perfectly comprehensible sentence. If the older prints do have the correct reading, Rabbenu Yonah endorsed the principle of merit advanced by the German Pietists. This would go against everything that we know of his attitude toward the teachings of that group (see above, pp. 98–9). However, as the matter now stands, one might think that one ethicist in the Middle Ages did, in fact, share the views of Ḥasidei Ashkenaz on this issue. Note should be taken, however, that R. Yonah endorsed only the principle of merit; he did not share their views as to how 'merit' is defined. There is no evidence from his other writings that he understood *tov*, *yere shamayim*, and *tsanua'* (good person, God-fearing, and modest) in the same sense as they did. (My personal feeling is that the manuscript versions already contained a prior elision which rendered the meaning of the text obscure, and some copyist or the editors of the early printed versions eliminated the problematic phrase to render the passage comprehensible.)

92 *Ḥiddushei ha-Ritva 'al Massekhet Bava Batra*, ed. Y. D. Ilan (Jerusalem, 2005), 8b, s.v. *ve-'ammei ha-arets*. The only other work which cites Rava's midrashic dictum (but not the passage in *Sukkah* or Rabbi's regretful remark) is in the aggadic peroration of *hilkhot tsedakah* in the *Orḥot Ḥayyim*, *Ḥelek Sheni*, i. 446. However, its author, R. Aharon ha-Kohen of Lunel, draws no conclusions from it. He does not state that one should therefore restrict one's charity to the virtuous poor, or how he defines 'virtuous'. He leaves the passage in its pristine, aggadic form.

93 *Bet Yosef*, 'Yoreh De'ah', #251, s.v. *katav ha-Ritva*.

94 'Yoreh De'ah', 251: 11. It seems wise to preclude here a possible misunderstanding. R. Mosheh of

Taken on its own, the criterion of merit is new and chilling. In the hands of the Pietists it is fraught with danger. And the danger lies in that very ambiguity which I have striven to emphasize. An open-ended criterion has been created by a movement with separatist and elitist tendencies—a movement which experienced its moments of humiliation and bitterness, and fluctuated between harshness and tenderness. And there is nothing whatsoever to prevent this criterion from being used in an arbitrary and partisan fashion.

The attitude of Ḥasidei Ashkenaz towards philanthropy, like its posture in many other matters, is uncharitably elitist and potentially exclusivist to a frightening degree.

I have said 'like its posture in many other matters'. On what basis have I said it? Attempting to answer this question allows us to continue to pursue one of our previous lines of inquiry: how one reads *Sefer Ḥasidim* or other ethical works to find their distinct message. Only now I wish to focus not on the meaning of a passage of *Sefer Ḥasidim*, but on its weight, the importance that we should assign to what is expressed there. Again, the aggregated and heterogeneous nature of *Sefer Ḥasidim* presents us with problems.

At the outset of the essay, I mentioned that in a previous study I had suggested several guidelines for interpreting and drawing inferences from that work. Two are relevant here:

1. Reiteration: Does the idea expressed recur with any degree of frequency in the literature of the movement?

Coucy, in his *Sefer Mitsvot Gadol* (above, n. 68), in *'aseh* #162 and again in #332, cites the opinion of Rabbenu Tam that if one vows to give money to charity, the discretionary right of distribution does not become that of treasurers of the community chest, but is retained by the donor. He may choose to give the money to someone who, in his eyes, is an upright or righteous individual (*hagun*), and he is entitled to withhold the funds until such a person appears on the scene.

ואומר רבינו יעקב שנדרי צדקה שאנו עכשיו נודרין לדעת עצמינו ואנו כגזברין עליה, ואם אנו ממתינים עד שיבואו עניים הגונים אין כאן בל תאחר (עשה ס׳ קסב). וכבר ביארנו בהלכות צדקה בשם ר״ת כי הנדרים שאנו נודרין עכשיו, אנו נודרין לדעת עצמנו ואנו כגזברים עליהם. ואם אנו ממתינין עד שנמצא הגון לקבל צדקה אין כאן בל תאחר (לאו של״ב).

First, even assuming that *hagun* here means 'righteous', this is not a ruling about allocation, but about retention of rights. It is not a dictate regarding to whom the charity *should* be given; it is a statement that the discretionary power of allocation remains in the hands of the donor. Personal preferences on the part of the donor, as opposed to the communal administrators, is perfectly permissible. Second, *hagun* may simply mean one who, in the donor's opinion, is genuinely poor (one who is 'upright' in his request for charity) as opposed to someone whom he views as a freeloader; see above, n. 82. (The same report of Rabbenu Tam's ruling is found, unsurprisingly, in the *'Amudei Golah*, more commonly known as the *Sefer Mitsvot Katan* [*Semak*], by R. Yitsḥak b. Yosef of Corbeil [Jerusalem, 2005], #246 [#248].)

2. Intensity: Does one sense in its formulations an emotional involvement, whether identification or disgust?

I would like to add here three more indicia:

3. Going against the grain of a canonical text: If the author is aware that there is a talmudic or midrashic dictum contrary to the manner of conduct that he is advocating and seeks to interpret it away, he believes deeply in what he is espousing.
4. Spread (if possible): Given that *Sefer Ḥasidim*, be it in the version of Parma or Bologna (and the other manuscripts of any heft are no different), is an agglomeration of various 'booklets' (*maḥbarot*, *kuntresim*) of the Pious, a medley of overlapping and randomly stitched together hasidic sources, one strongly prefers that the idea to which we attach importance be spread across the collection, to appear in a number of those booklets and not be concentrated in just one of them. One must, however, acknowledge that, given the unpredictable and amorphous nature of *Sefer Ḥasidim*, this indicator is a high bar, at times too high to be met.
5. Proportionality: there must be a clear correlation between the magnitude of a claim made by the historian and the strength of the evidence adduced.[95]

Let us turn again to the opening passage of the section on charity and see how one can further interrogate *Sefer Ḥasidim*. Section 857 reads:

> A *tsaddik* is in need of charity and a wicked man [*rasha'*], 'a wastrel and a drunkard' [Deut. 21: 20], stands [before you to receive charity], and you can only give to one of them, and the *rasha'* says that if you do not give him [the money], he will convert to Christianity or commit another offence, but not that of murder, give to the *tsaddik* and let the *rasha'* go to Hell. However, if he is about to commit murder, give him [the money] as ransom for the innocent man, so that he will not be killed.[96]

The first question to be asked when encountering such a passage in a traditional literature is: Is such a question and answer (irrespective of the tone) in any way distinctive, something that would be of aid in characterizing the work? The answer is clearly no. The question of triage is a permanent one in human affairs, be it school, family, or government. How far should one go to accommodate the disruptive, even the wicked? Nor is there anything distinctive in their drawing the line where they do.

[95] This essay does not invoke this principle, but the following essay does. See below, p. 225.

[96] The original Hebrew text is cited above, p. 195.

This, however, was not the only position of the Pietist movement. In #1704 we find:

לאחד היו לו שני בנים צדיק ורשע והיה נותן מזונות לרשע לא לצדיק כי הרשע היה אומר כל זמן שאתה מספיקני לא (יצא) [אצא] לתרבות רעה ואחרים אמרו לו לא תחמול על הרשע אלא על בנך הצדיק. ועל זה חלוקים דוד ושלמה: דוד מינה שבואל על האוצרות כדי שלא יהא כהן פסל מיכה, ושלמה הסירו וחזר לקדמותו.

Someone had two sons, a *tsaddik* and a *rasha'*, and he would give food to the *rasha'* and not to the *tsaddik*, for he said, 'As long as I support him, he will not fall on bad ways.' Others said to him, 'Do not have mercy on the *rasha'*; rather [have mercy] on your son, the *tsaddik*.' In this matter, David and Solomon disagreed. David appointed Shebuel [as the head] of his treasures so that he should not revert to being a priest in service of the idol of Micah [Judg. 18: 30], and Solomon removed him, and he returned to his previous state [of being a priest in the service of Micah].

This is an obscure reference both to a passage in *Bava Batra* (110a) in the Bavli and a passage in *Berakhot* (9: 3) in the Yerushalmi.[97] In Judges 18: 30, we read: 'And Jonathan, the son of Manasseh, he and his sons were priests to the tribe of Dan until the day of the captivity of the land.' In 1 Chronicles 26: 24 we read, 'and Shebuel the son of Gershom, the son of Moses, was ruler of the treasures.' For reasons that are irrelevant to our discussion, the Talmud takes Shebuel and Jonathan to be one and the same person. Jonathan became a priest in the service of the idol of Micah for personal gain. King David, the Bavli explains, seeking to pry him away from the idolatrous service and knowing that he liked money, made him head of his treasures. If this be so, how could Jonathan or Shebuel be priest until the Exile, as the verse in Judges attests? To this the Yerushalmi replies that when Solomon became king, a changing of the guard took place and Shebuel/Jonathan lost his post and returned to his bad ways of serving the idol of Micah.

Again, the mode of interpreting these canonical passages in *Sefer Ḥasidim* is in no way unique to the German Pietists. It is the product of the tendency in traditional Jewish thinking to see the actions of great figures in the Bible as governed not by personal inclination but by a moral or religious perspective. If Solomon dismissed Shebuel, it had to have been that he disagreed with David as to the treatment of wayward individuals. One should not tempt them to better their ways, but one should let them go their own way, even to perdition. It also reflects the tendency in a religious society to find in the sacred literature

[97] The complementary statements of the Bavli and the Yerushalmi may well have come to the attention of the Pietist because Rashbam, in his commentary on *Bava Batra* ad loc., s.v. *she-shav*, cites this passage in the Yerushalmi as rounding out the narrative in the Bavli.

the answer to the questions of their time, or, at the very least, to find their problems reflected in the timeless, all-answering canon.

Clearly, divergent views in the movement existed as to how one handles errant children and #857 adopts the harsher view. To infer the position of a movement from a single passage and from a book as amorphous as *Sefer Ḥasidim* is hazardous. Sections 182–5 tell us clearly where the Pietists stood on the matter. They read:

182. אם יש לאדם בנים ואחד מהם זולל וסובא אל יעקור את עצמו ואת בניו בשביל האחד ולבסוף יצא לתרבות רעה, לכך מוטב לו שקודם יעשה כאילו לא היה בנו מעולם ולא יעשה לו רעה ולבניו בשביל האחד.

183. לאחד נשתמד בנו והלך בין הגוים ועשה כמעשה הגוים. היו אביו ואמו עסוקים להוציאו ולהביאו בביתם ולנדור לו ממון שישוב אמ[ר] להם החכם חדלו לכם פן תתחרטו ויעשה יותר ברע כי שמעתי שרוצה לתת עיצה רעה ולהסית ולהדיח את אחיו ואת אחיותיו ללכת בין הגוים. ועוד הוא אומר כשהיה יהודי היה משליך בקדירה בשר נבילה מוטב שתעזבוהו בין הגוים ולא יחטיא אחרים ולא יאכיל את כל בני הברית דברים האסורים אפרים חבור עצבים הנח לו (הושע ד: יז) מוטב מלקרבו ויחבר אחרים אל עצבים.

184. ואם לחכם תלמידים ואחד עוסק לקנטר את הרב ואת חביריו מוטב לגרש האחד לתקנת הטובים שנאמ׳ גרש לץ ויצא מדון (משלי כב: י) וכן לעניין עבדים ושפחות אע״פ שאינו גונב לו ואינו מקנטר אותו אלא אותם שבבית ומבקשים נקמה על אותם שיש בידו למחות ואינו מוחה או בידו לגרש. אבל במינקת לא יוכל לגרש כשהתינוק מכיר את מניקתו (כתובות ס׳ ע״א).

185. ואם יש לו לאדם בנים ואחד מהם בעל מחלוקת או שירא פן יחטיא אחיו מוטב שידחה את הרשע בשתי ידים ואל תאמר והרי אמרו תהא שמאל דוחה וימין מקרב (סוטה מז ע״ב) במקום שחב לאחרים יותר יבא לרעה אם לא ירחקוהו שהרי דוד לפי שקירב את אבשלום הרי כמה נפשות נהרגו בשבילו לכך אל יניח אדם אף לבנו שלא יבא לידי מכשול.

182. If a man has two sons and one of them is a wastrel, he should not bleed himself and his children white in supporting the wastrel, who will [eventually] fall on bad ways [anyway]. Therefore, it is best that he should act early as if he [the wastrel] is not his son, and he should not do himself and his children damage because of that one [son].

183. Someone's son converted and went to live with Gentiles and adopted their ways. His father and mother were occupied with trying to get him to leave the Gentiles and come home, vowing to give him money. The Ḥakham said to them, 'Desist, lest (they) [you] will regret it. He will [only] do more harm. For I heard that he intends to give them [his brothers and sisters] wicked advice and entice them to live among the Gentiles.' He [the Ḥakham] also said, 'When he was Jewish, he used to throw non-kosher food into the pots. Better that he should

remain with the Gentiles and not lead others astray and cause Jews to eat forbidden foods, as is written [Hos. 4: 17], "Ephraim is joined to idols: let him alone." This is preferable to [attempting to] attract him for he will [only] join others to idols.'

184. If a *ḥakham* [here any teacher, not necessarily a hasidic one] has pupils and one of them hassles the teacher and his friends, it is best to expel him for the benefit of the good ones, as it is written [Prov. 22: 10], 'cast out the scorner and contention shall go out'. However, in the case of a wet-nurse, one cannot expel her once the baby identifies her as his wet-nurse [and will refuse to suckle from other wet-nurses—*Ketubbot* 60a].

185. If a man has sons and one is very quarrelsome or he fears he will cause others to sin, better that he rejects that son 'with two hands' [i.e. swiftly and entirely]. Do not counter [that the Talmud says], 'The left hand should reject, while the [stronger] right hand should pull the person closer.'[98] In an instance where he damages other people, not rejecting him will lead to no good, for David did not reject Absalom and how many people lost their life because of this [indulgence]? Therefore, he should not go easy even on his son, lest it become [a major] stumbling block.

In reading a work like *Sefer Ḥasidim*, one must often ask four questions to sort out the different levels at which ideas can be entertained: Is this a passing thought (of which there are any number in this work)? Is it a thought seriously entertained but only abstractly, or is this a thought that the author seeks to impress upon his readers to stir them to action? Finally, is this an idea that lies at the heart of the thinker's agenda, a message which his movement flies on its mast, as is, for example, avoiding looking at women for German Pietism?

Clearly, sacrificing the wicked or the wayward for the good of others does not play the same role in the Ḥasid's thought as does 'custody of the eyes'. It is not a hallmark idea of his movement. It is equally clear from its reiterations in *Sefer Ḥasidim* that it is not a passing thought of the Pietists.[99] Nor is it simply a theoretical position of Ḥasidei Ashkenaz. In sections 182–5, the Ḥasid strives to get this point across to his readers, to have them internalize the message, by giving, in good exemplum fashion, a series of concrete examples as to how this rule should be enforced in the family, in school, and in the running of

[98] *Sotah* 47b.

[99] It should be emphasized that all the above cases are ones of triage—a forced choice between two undesirable options. Keeping the wicked has negative consequences; others suffer because of his continued presence. If there is no loss to others, the Ḥasid is in favor of keeping the sinner if feasible, as in #892. (The fifth word in the printed text, *'oseh*, is a misprint for *'osher*, as found in the manuscript from which it was published [Parma, De Rossi 1133] and corroborated by JTS Boesky 45.)

the household. We also have 'spread'—the theme is expressed in several of the different booklets that make up *Sefer Ḥasidim* (##182–5, 857, 1705). We have, in addition, 'intensity'. The Ḥasid's fourfold reiteration and different exempla evidence his desire to have a varied audience absorb this message, to see that this principle is followed in diverse situations of real life. Finally, there is 'going against the grain'. The Pietist is aware that there is a well-known rabbinic dictum against outright rejection of the wayward and in favor of the carrot-and-stick approach—'rejecting with the left hand while attracting with the [stronger] right'. Indeed, the Talmud goes so far as to rebuke Elisha for dismissing Geḥazi 'with two hands [i.e. swiftly and entirely]' (2 Kgs 5: 26).[100] No one goes lightly against a talmudic pronouncement. Only if the author is deeply convinced of his position, and of the need to maintain it despite what the sacred sources seem to opine, will he engage the maxim and seek to limit its applicability.[101]

Note also that there is not a word of sympathy for the parent who is told to cut his child dead. A brief, matter-of-fact statement, 'He should act early, as if he was not his son', without any accompanying remark there or in sections 183 and 185 that would indicate that he understands the sacrifice he is demanding of a father and mother. There is no difference in word or in tone between the demand to dismiss a student or a servant and that to 'dismiss' one's own child. It is moments like this that make the reader feel that there is some ice in the Pietist's veins.

Are there other such moments?

In ransoming captives when the money is limited, the Mishnah establishes certain priorities, one of which is that scholars take precedence over ignoramuses (*'ammei ha-arets*), to the extent that a bastard scholar takes precedence over an ignorant high priest. A woman takes precedence over a man in matters of ransom generally, and if both are in need of clothes (*kesut*) to cover their nakedness, the woman again takes precedence; if both lives are at stake (*le-haḥayot*), a man takes precedence over a woman.[102] There is an astonishing passage in the Yerushalmi which rules that if one must choose between clothes for the wife of a scholar (*ḥaver*) and the life (*ḥayyei*) of an ignoramus, the clothes for the wife come first.[103] R. Mosheh Margoliot, the author of the standard commentary on the Yerushalmi, felt that it was impossible to take this passage literally; clearly the term *ḥayyei* here must mean sustenance over

100 Above, n. 99. 101 See above, p. 215. 102 *Horayot* 12a.

103 *Horayot* 3: 5; Academy of Hebrew Language edn. (Jerusalem, 2001), col. 1428; Romm edn. (Vilna, 1922–8), fo. 18a. In light of my remarks (below, p. 201), we should add that *ḥaver* can also mean 'scholar'.

and above what is needed for survival, for it is a universal principle in Jewish law that all rules yield to the imperative of saving a life (*pikuaḥ nefesh*).[104] R. Shabbetai Kohen, the great commentator on the *Shulḥan 'Arukh*, neutralized the ruling by another route. He invoked and applied here a well-known ruling that one of the fines mentioned in the Talmud for disrespecting a scholar no longer applies, as no one in post-talmudic times is worthy of the appellation 'scholar'.[105]

Sefer Ḥasidim reproduces in full this Yerushalmi passage with no qualms whatsoever. One might argue that this is simply one of many citations of classical texts found in *Sefer Ḥasidim* for no visible purpose and without any sign that the writer identifies with its message. They appear to be simply carried in the skiff as ballast[106] or cited because of some associative thinking known to the hasidic author/compiler but not to us. However, *Sefer Ḥasidim* does take this passage seriously for it adds further conditions for its application:

> **דוקא כשאשת חבר כחבר וטובה למקום וטובה לבעלה וטובה לטובים, אז כסות אשת חבר קודמת לחיי עם הארץ. ודוקא מה שצריכה לכסות שאי אפשר בלא כסות, אבל להתקשט, חיי עם הארץ קודם.**

[The preference given to the wife of a scholar applies] only if she conducts herself as would a scholar and acts well to God [i.e. fulfills fully her religious obligations] and well to her husband and to other good people; then her garments take precedence over the life of an illiterate. And the term 'garments' is restricted to essential clothes [without which she would be dressed immodestly]; but if the garments in question are ornamental, the illiterate's life has precedence.

Wise qualifications indeed, but which leave the operative principle fully in place.

I have cited ##182–5. It pays to cite the section that opened this small subunit, #181:

> **כתיב (משלי כח, יז) 'אדם עשוק בדם נפש עד בור ינוס ולא יתמכו בו'. אם בורח רוצח אליך אל תקבלהו בין יהודי בין גוי כמעשה דר' טרפין בנידה (ס"א ע"א). אם *יברחו* רשעים וחטאים אצלך *לחסות בצל כנפיך* אל תהי עליהם מגן שאם תקבלם יהפך הדבר שיהו לך לסטן או לזרעך. כי כאשר יבא רשע בעיר אם תוכל למחות בידו אל תתנהו לבא בעיר וכל שכן בביתך שאם תקבלהו הוא או זרעו יהיה לך או לזרעך לשיכים בעיניכם לצנינים בצדיכם שגרמת רעות לעיר שדר בה.**

The Bible says: 'A man oppressed by bloodguilt will flee to a pit; let none give him support [Prov. 28: 17]'.[107] If a murderer flees to you, do not accept him, be he Jewish or

104 *Mar'eh Panim* on *Horayot* 3: 5.
105 *Shakh*, 'Yoreh De'ah', 251: 16.
106 G. Scholem, *Major Trends in Jewish Mysticism* (New York, 1941), 89.
107 For clarity's sake, I have used here the JPS translation (above, n. 7).

Gentile, following the precedent of R. Tarfon [*Niddah* 61a]. If *resha'im* and sinners should *flee* to you *seeking refuge* under your wing, do not protect them [i.e. take them in], for if you receive them [i.e. allow them residence], in the end they will become an implacable adversary of yours or of your seed. When a *rasha'* comes to your city, if you can prevent him from settling, do not allow him to settle. For if you accept him, he or his seed will become "barbs in your eyes and thorns in your side", for you caused bad things in the city in which he [will] dwell. [Italics mine]

It is always wise to compare the precedent—talmudic, midrashic, or biblical—invoked by an ethicist with the case at hand to measure just how close to or wide of the mark are the proof texts cited. It is often a good indicator of how traditional or how novel the ideas being advanced are. Some men suspected of murder sought refuge in the house of R. Tarfon, and he refused to allow them in. The Talmud explains that even though one can in no way presume their guilt, nevertheless one may and should act with caution. The application is to Jews *fleeing persecution* and asking to be allowed to settle in the safe Jewish community. (*Ḥerem ha-yishuv* dictated that no Jew could settle in another community without its consent.[108]) Are we dealing here with people suspected of murder? It scarcely seems so. The Ḥasid doesn't speak of any physical danger, but of their becoming a 'thorn in one's side'; the new settlers will constitute a stumbling block for the Ḥasidim in the town. It seems very much to be the conflict between the Sons of Light and those of Darkness that I sketched in 'Three Themes in *Sefer Ḥasidim*'.[109]

One could argue that the Ḥasid is referring not to upright non-Pietists but to undesirables, to morally or religiously deficient individuals who will have a bad influence on the town. Yet note the formulation 'an implacable adversary of yours *or of your seed*'. The struggle that he anticipates may well be decades away—a generation or two after the acceptance of the fugitives. Nevertheless, he advocates denying them shelter now. Let them be massacred rather than risk spiritual or ethical problems in the distant future—a ruling without parallel in Jewish ethical literature, ancient, medieval, or modern.

The Ḥasid here, I would add in conclusion, is only following in the path of his master, the movement's founder, as I wrote in the aforementioned essay:[110]

Few lines harsher than those of R. Yehudah he-Ḥasid have been penned in Jewish ethical writings. Unable to comprehend how Abraham could have sought mercy for the sinners of Sodom, he wrote:

108 See *Encyclopaedia Judaica* (Jerusalem, 1972), xiii. 356, s.v. *ḥerem ha-yishuv*.

109 Above, pp. 31–8.

110 Above, p. 40.

'Wilt Thou destroy [the *place* and not spare it for the fifty righteous]?' [Gen. 18:24] Explanation: He [Abraham] is not concerned about the wicked [*resha'im*] if You kill them, but do not overturn the city; leave it for the righteous and their seed. And this is what [he says], 'Shalt Thou destroy the entire city? Leave the land alone and kill the inhabitants.'[111]

I doubt whether we will ever fully understand that compound of texts known as *Sefer Ḥasidim*. At every turn, we confront its inexplicable use of biblical citations, its long chains of biblical verses, and catenations of various talmudic or midrashic texts that to our thinking are wholly unrelated. And we can only ask ourselves, 'What in the world were their authors' thought processes?' If we cannot yet address the underlying question of how they thought, I believe that we can begin to address the question of what was the upshot of this mode of thinking. What did the German Pietists think? I have attempted to set forth some initial guidelines for drawing inferences from this puzzling collection, and essayed to formulate some criteria for assessing the weight that we should attach to the different strands of moral dicta; how one goes about winnowing the significant from the casual and distinguishing between the essential and the significant in that baffling agglomeration of booklets known as *Sefer Ḥasidim*.

[111] *Moshav Zekenim 'al ha-Torah*, ed. D. Sassoon (London, 1959), 24; MS Cambridge, Add. 669.2, fo. 9v {= *Perushei ha-Torah le-Rabbi Yehudah he-Ḥasid*, ed. Y. S. Lange (Jerusalem, 1975), 22}:
האף תספה רשע עם צדיק. פי[רוש] על הרשעים איני חושש אם תמיתם, רק את העיר אל תהפוך ותניח לצדיקים ולזרעם. וזהו "התשחית בה[ן] [=בחמישים] כל העיר"? הקרקע תניח ובני העיר תמית.
For more textual detail, see above, p. 40 n. 91.

CHAPTER NINE

Sefer Ḥasidim and the Social Sciences

This essay links naturally with the preceding one as it treats the evidence advanced for some of the currently reigning ideas in the study of German Pietism. The texts of the movement are available to all. The question is, how does one read them? And how does one use notions and models drawn from the neighboring disciplines of sociology and anthropology?

A century ago, Ya'akov Naftali Simhoni (Simchovitz) drew attention to the great influence that German Pietism had on Ashkenazic Jewry.[1] Important articles were subsequently written, yet no full-length study appeared on that movement. Ivan G. Marcus's book *Piety and Society* filled a large gap.[2] Drawing upon past studies, he melded them critically with his own extensive researches, and the result was a rich portrait of Ḥasidei Ashkenaz. Penance, so central a theme of the Pietists' teachings and certainly their most lasting legacy to the Ashkenazic community, received here its first full analysis. The relationship between sin, atonement, and Pietism was analyzed, and the theme of reward and punishment, which so preoccupied the thoughts of the Pietists, as it did the minds of all medieval men, finally received the attention it merited in Jewish historiography. Indeed, I would venture to say that Part I of Marcus's study is required reading for all those who wish to know the hasidic aspiration.

Marcus also has many important things to say about the exclusivist tendencies of the Pietists and their tense relationship to the surrounding society. I agree with some of his arguments, indeed, advocated some of them myself in an article long ago.[3] Further on in the book, he discusses 'atonement as sectarian initiation' at length. Here I must demur. Marcus proceeds to portray the Pietists as a sect, as defined by sociologists of religion; indeed, his use of

[1] 'Ha-Ḥasidut ha-Ashkenazit bi-Yemei ha-Beinayim', *Ha-Tsefirah* (1917), 12–32. It was reprinted in I. G. Marcus, ed., *Dat ve-Ḥevrah be-Mishnatam shel Ḥasidei Ashkenaz* (Jerusalem, 1985), 47–79.

[2] *Piety and Society: The Jewish Pietists of Medieval Germany* (Leiden, 1981).

[3] 'Three Themes in *Sefer Ḥasidim*', reprinted with revisions as Chapter 1 above.

atonement as initiation is part of this attempt to depict the Pietists as sectarians.[4] Here, I'm afraid, my demurral becomes dissent. In his introductory remarks, he is duly cautious about the use of these categories, but these caveats seem to be lost in the vigor and force of the actual presentation. Marcus, I feel, has sacrificed his numerous insights for the sake of sociological and anthropological models, and the complexities and ambiguities of the movement, of which he is aware, have lost much of their vibrancy in the attempt to align them with constructs drawn from neighboring disciplines. I have long advocated several of these ideas; my argument is not with some of my colleague's basic notions but with his constructs, more precisely, with what I believe to be the sway of the model over the evidence. I would like to examine the proofs adduced for three major theses of the book: the three-stage evolution of German Pietism, penance as a rite of passage into the pietistic fraternity, and finally, the sectarian nature of *Sefer Ḥasidim*.

I. The Three-Stage Evolution

Marcus vigorously presents an original, striking portrayal of a three-stage development of German Pietism. Impelled by an inner, almost dialectical force, Pietism moved from personal eschatology to social radicalism and religious exclusivism, and then, defeated in achieving its wider goals, it reverted to a conservative soteriology. The riveting developments outlined, the sharp contrasts made between the positions of R. Shemu'el he-Ḥasid, R. Yehudah he-Ḥasid, and R. El'azar of Worms—tradition, radicalism, and reaction—are based naturally upon an analysis of their writings. Authorship is a thorny problem in the study of German Pietism. Unless one can identify what each of these figures wrote, any development depicted remains in the realm of pure conjecture. Realizing the centrality of literary attribution, Marcus devotes a full-length appendix to this question.[5] As much of the argument of the book hinges on these identifications, it merits the closest of studies.

Let us begin, as does the author, with the Kalonymide tradition of personal eschatology. This rests upon the attribution of the first thirteen sections of

[4] *Piety and Society* (above, n. 2), 55–108. A large part of this section (pp. 58–65, 87–108) appeared the year before as 'The Politics and Ethics of Pietism in Judaism: The *Hasidim* of Medieval Germany', *Journal of Religious Ethics*, 8 (1980), 227–58.

[5] *Piety and Society* (above, n. 2), 136–43. A dozen years later, Marcus modified his position in his 'The Historical Meaning of *Hasidut Ashkenaz*: Fact, Fiction or Cultural Self-Image?', in P. Schäfer and J. Dan, eds., *Gershom Scholem's Major Trends in Jewish Mysticism 50 Years After* (Tübingen, 1993), 103–16. This, however, did little to neutralize his argument in *Piety and Society* and in the *Journal of Religious Ethics*, which had achieved semi-canonical standing.

Sefer Ḥasidim printed from the Parma manuscript (*SHP*), the *Sefer ha-Yir'ah*, to R. Shemu'el he-Ḥasid. At the very beginning of the manuscript, the name Shemu'el appears, and underneath it a phrase from Psalms (25: 14), *sod ha-Shem li-yere'av* ('the secret of the Lord is with them that fear him'). A scholar by the name of Y. L. Margeshes suggested to Wistinetzki, the editor of the work, after it had gone to press, that 'Shemu'el' numerologically equals the phrase *sod ha-Shem li-yere'av*. Wistinetzki cited Margeshes's remark in an addendum on the last page of the book.[6] Avraham Epstein, the leading scholar of German Pietism at the turn of the twentieth century, linked this *gematriyah* to a report that R. Shemu'el he-Ḥasid, Yehudah's father, had authored a short pietistic work, and concluded that the first section of *SHP*, which refers to itself as *Sefer ha-Yir'ah*, constituted a part of this work.[7] R. Shemu'el—in good Kalonymide fashion—marked his authorship numerologically by the verse in Psalms. This is all presented by Marcus, who writes candidly, 'Although the evidence is extremely skimpy, it is enough to suggest the likelihood, at least, that Samuel was the author of *Sefer ha-Yirah*.' The question of proportion between the strength of the evidence and the importance of the claim arises.[8] If the determination is purely bibliographical, as it was in Epstein's classic study, nothing is risked by thin evidence; for, if incorrect, one simply subtracts some thirteen pages from R. Shemu'el's oeuvre. In Marcus's case, the authorial identification is of major significance, seeing that it serves as the first tier of a three-stage development, and one wishes for more than 'extremely skimpy evidence' for its existence. Marcus proceeds to say that this is Kalonymide tradition, which makes R. Yehudah's position not only radical but also revolutionary. I know of no evidence supporting *Sefer ha-Yir'ah* being a Kalonymide tradition, nor have I found in Marcus's study any argument for this.

One can, however, eliminate the Kalonymide tradition and retain a two-phased evolution of German Pietism of great significance. This evolution hinges on the thorny problem of single or collective authorship of *Sefer Ḥasidim*, which has puzzled scholars for well over a century. Marcus addresses the question directly and advances two arguments in favor of a single author. He states that *Sefer Ḥasidim* was composed by R. Yehudah he-Ḥasid, for the

[6] *Sefer Ḥasidim*, ed. J. Wistinetzki, 2nd edn., with an introduction and appendices by J. Freimann (Berlin, 1924), 490. The first printing of the text was in Berlin in 1891. A smaller edition—some 60 percent in size of the Berlin one—had appeared in Bologna in 1538 (*SHB*).

[7] *Kitvei R. Avraham Epstein*, ed. A. M. Habermann (Jerusalem, 1950), 259–60; repr. in Marcus, ed., *Dat ve-Ḥevrah be-Mishnatam shel Ḥasidei Ashkenaz* (above, n. 1), 25–46. The article first appeared in *Ha-Goren*, 4 (1903), 81–101.

[8] See Ch. 8 above.

'ascription to Judah is so firmly grounded in so many early sources that it must be taken seriously'.[9] What the early sources, however, attest to is that R. Yehudah he-Ḥasid wrote *a Sefer Ḥasidim*. Indeed, our printed *Sefer Ḥasidim* refers to such a *Sefer Ḥasidim*, writing 'this is already written [i.e. found] in *Sefer Ḥasidim*'.[10] The question at issue is whether that agglomeration of hasidic 'booklets' (*maḥbarot, kuntresim*) which has come down to us—be it in the form of the Bologna edition of *Sefer Ḥasidim* of 1538 (*SHB*) or that of the far larger Parma manuscript published by Wistinetzki in 1891 (*SHP*)—was authored by R. Yehudah he-Ḥasid. And the early sources have nothing—could have nothing—to say on this issue, as they could not know which of the numerous hasidic collections that were in circulation in the Middle Ages (found today in two different print editions and in numerous manuscripts, many of which have their own medley of hasidic sources[11]) were destined to survive and remain at our disposal.

Let us focus, as does Marcus, on *SHP*, the largest and richest collection. My colleague argues that passages in our *Sefer Ḥasidim* are found in R. Yehudah's *Commentary on the Pentateuch*. This is correct. There are three, possibly five, such parallel passages. Do three to five passages justify attributing the remaining 1,856 other passages to R. Yehudah he-Ḥasid? Do they do so any more than the five or so parallel passages from the works of R. El'azar of Worms found in *Sefer Ḥasidim* justify attributing the work to him?[12] On the basis of parallel passages, our *Sefer Ḥasidim* could be a joint work of both men, and equally a collection compiled by an unknown editor which included citations from the works of the two. Let us quintuple, for argument's sake, the number of parallel passages and assign them to either figure; this would still not justify assigning the remaining 1,830 or so passages —an agglomerated medley on the widest variety of topics—to the assignee. To my eye, at least, *SHP* is much too rambling and variegated a work to be assigned without far more evidence to any single individual.

Marcus then argues that R. El'azar usually 'signed' his name on all his works by use of name acrostics, and the absence of such a signature in *Sefer Ḥasidim* is evidence that he is not its author. This is true, but R. El'azar would scarcely sign his name on a joint work when his 'co-author' didn't and

[9] *Piety and Society* (above, n. 2), 137. I cite Marcus's text as published. As he uses the English form of Hebrew names and I the Hebrew one, this results in occasional dissonance between the text and the citation. I ask the reader's forbearance. [10] *SHP*, #1589. [11] See above, pp. 124–5.

[12] See Freimann's discussions (introduction to *SHP*, 13–14) and that of Epstein (above, n. 7, 260–1, nn. 27, 28). Neither scholar concludes that *SHP* is the product of R. Yehudah he-Ḥasid; both believe that it is a compound work involving numerous hands and cannot be assigned to any one person.

wouldn't (R. Yehudah he-Ḥasid was opposed to such authorial markings[13]), nor would these name acrostics appear in a compilation by an editor which incorporated, among many other things, selections from R. El'azar's works.

The first to point out that R. El'azar differed ideologically with his revered teacher, R. Yehudah he-Ḥasid, was H. H. Ben-Sasson.[14] He pointed out the absence of any social critique, let alone any goal of egalitarian distribution of wealth—so noticeable in R. Yehudah's writings—in the works of R. El'azar, such as the *Sefer Roke'aḥ*[15] and the *Ḥokhmat ha-Nefesh*.[16] Marcus is in full agreement with Ben-Sasson on this matter. He criticizes Ben-Sasson for claiming that R. El'azar (often called, in good rabbinic fashion, by the name of his famous work, *Roke'aḥ*) shared R. Yehudah's sharp critique of the communal and religious establishment. He first claims that the passages of the *Roke'aḥ* cited by Ben-Sasson do not deal with communal leadership, but rather with 'the divinely arranged trial which lies in store in each generation for *the Righteous person*'.[17] He further argues that by comparing the passages from the writings of these two authors, one sees that Roke'aḥ borrowed from R. Yehudah and not the reverse.[18] This issue, to my mind, is beside the point. The question is not who took from whom, but whether or not there is a sharp critique of the religious and communal authorities in the works of Roke'aḥ. If there is, Roke'aḥ then does not fit into the reactionary mode of Pietism that Marcus has attributed to him.

I think Marcus is correct that R. El'azar has borrowed themes of R. Yehudah; however, as I noted in 'On Reading *Sefer Ḥasidim*', one of the criteria for identifying positions in as amorphous and associative a work as *Sefer Ḥasidim* (and in places, Roke'aḥ's writings in the *Ḥokhmat ha-Nefesh* do not differ much from *Sefer Ḥasidim*) is that of intensity: is this simply one of many notions that has made its appearance in that baffling, multifaceted work, or is there an emotional involvement of the author with the idea being expressed? Are these abstract notions or do they yield the feeling that they are products of actual experiences?

13 See M. Beit-Arié, 'Ideals versus Reality: Scribal Prescriptions in *Sefer Hasidim* and Contemporary Scribal Practices in Franco-German Manuscripts', in G. Sed-Rajna et al., eds., *Rashi, 1040–1104. Hommage à Ephraïm E. Urbach: Congrès européen des études juives* (Paris, 1993), 559–66.

14 'Ḥasidei Ashkenaz 'al Ḥalukkat Kinyanim Ḥomriyyim u-Nekhasim Ruḥaniyyim bein Benei Adam', *Zion*, 25 (1970), 62–79.

15 *Sefer ha-Roke'aḥ*, ed. B. S. Shne'orson (repr. Jerusalem, 1960); *Ha-Roke'aḥ ha-Gadol* (Jerusalem, 2014). (As to the first edition [Fano, 1505], see above, Ch. 1, n. 9.)

16 Safed edn. (1913); Sodei Razaya edn. (Jerusalem, 2006). The latter is a somewhat superior text of the *Ḥokhmat ha-Nefesh* that was published by the Makhon Sodei Razaya in the second volume of *Sifrei ha-Ra mi-Germaiza, Ba'al ha-Roke'aḥ* (Jerusalem, 2006), sect. 2, 1–132.

17 *Piety and Society* (above, n. 2), 139. Caps and italics are those of Marcus.

18 Ibid. 139–41.

To demonstrate that R. El'azar took from R. Yehudah's works, Marcus takes four passages from the writings of R. Yehudah and aligns them with a lengthy citation from *Ḥokhmat ha-Nefesh*. One passage deals with the idea that 'Two [righteous people] in each generation sustain the world'; the other three passages treat the righteous versus the wicked. Let us focus on the latter group, as this group should reveal if the establishment, both communal and religious, bulks large in the description of the wicked, and resolve the question whether R. El'azar was indeed critical of the contemporary powers that be.

Marcus cites:

1. At the Creation, God decreed [*gazar*] people's livelihood [*parnasatan*] for all generations and who would tend to their economic needs. He also decreed that some people should be reduced from a position of greatness and who would ruin them, who would be their 'thorns' [*kotsim*], as it is written, 'thorns and thistles shall the earth bring forth' [Gen. 3: 18], (meaning that there is a thorn) for a Righteous person in each generation [*be-khol dor la-tsaddik*].[19]
2. The following is found in a book of R. Judah the Pietist: 'Thorns and thistles are numerically equivalent to (the word) generations [*dorot*], which means that there is not a generation [*dor*] which lacks Wicked people who attack the Righteous: Abraham had Nimrod, Isaac had the Philistines, Jacob had Esau, Moses had Datan and Aviram.'[20]
3. He also decreed, 'Thorns and thistles [*kots ve-dardar*] shall the earth bring forth' [Gen. 3: 18], (meaning) that in each generation [*she-be-khol dor va-dor*], in each town where there is a Righteous person, there also will be a Wicked person to make him suffer.[21]

[19] *SHP*, #1171. (In the citations, I have changed the system of transliteration employed by my colleague to align it with the one employed in the rest of this volume.)

[20] *Hadar Zekenim* (Livorno, 1843), 3a [Rosh]. Thus Marcus sources the passage. It is not entirely clear that this passage in the *Hadar Zekenim* was authored by R. Yehudah he-Ḥasid rather than by R. Eli'ezer b. Yo'el, the famed Talmudist, Ravyah. The passage in Hebrew reads:

'בזיעת אפיך': נמצא בספרו של ר' יהודה החסיד: שזו קללה אינה מתקיימת אלא בעובדי אדמה ולא בשרים ובמלכים. אבל בעצב תלדי בנים מתקיימת בכל הנשים, לפי שהאשה חטאה והחטיאה, גדולה קללתה.'וקוץ ודרדר': [ב]גימ[טריא] דורות: שאין דור שאין בו רשעים וקמים כנגד[!] צדיקים—אברהם נמרוד, יצחק פלישתים, יעקב עשו, משה דתן ואבירם. עד כאן לשון אבי העזרי.

I assume that Marcus takes Ravyah as citing both commentarial remarks in the name of R. Yehudah. This is open to question, however, as the point being made here is methodological rather than empirical; the actual authorship is immaterial. There is a one-line version of this theme in the so-called *Perush ha-Roke'aḥ 'al ha-Torah* (Benei Berak, 1979), i. 86, which was not authored by Roke'aḥ but by a member of the hasidic movement (J. Dan, 'He'arah', *Kiryat Sefer*, 59 [1981], 644). See also *Tosafot ha-Shalem: Otsar Perushei Ba'alei ha-Tosafot*, ed. Y. Gliss (Jerusalem, 1982), i. 140–1. The so-called *Perush ha-Roke'aḥ* was published from MS Oxford, Bodley 268, and thus corresponds to Gliss's entry #8 on p. 141. See Gliss, pp. 18, 21.

[21] *SHP*, #1049.

Marcus then compares them with a lengthy passage from the *Ḥokhmat ha-Nefesh*, which treats these themes.[22] He opens with the passage in *Sefer Ḥasidim* which parallels the first theme in the *Ḥokhmat ha-Nefesh*, namely, that the existence of two righteous people is what sustains any generation. This is followed by a partial citation of the subsequent passage from the *Ḥokhmat ha-Nefesh*, which deals with the righteous and the wicked. Let us omit the opening passage, as it has no bearing on the issue here at bar, and cite in full the subsequent passage on the eternal strife between the good and the bad:

Thorns and thistles shall (the earth) bring forth [Gen. 3: 18]. It was decreed that for each generation [*kol dor ve-dor*] there should be a thorn [*kots*] accompanying it, (as implied in the expression 'but the ungodly, they are as thorns' [2 Sam. 23: 6]). And God planted (the thorns) in each generation. There was Abraham, and Amrafel was his thorn; there was Isaac and the shepherds of Gerar were his thorn; there was Jacob, and Esau was his thorn; there was Moses and Aaron and there were Datan and Aviram; there was David and there were Do'eg and Aḥitofel; (there was) Solomon and there was Solomon's adversary [i.e. Hadad the Edomite, see I Kings 11: 14; etc.] There was Hezekiah and there were Shevna and the king of Assyria; there was Mordecai (and there was) Haman.

It is always the case that *when a town has a Righteous man who is a good influence, he has a wicked thorn*. There were the prophets of the Lord (and) their thorn was the prophets of Baal. When the community is good, they do what the prophets (of the Lord) say (and) ignore the prophets of Baal; but if the community is not worthy, the prophets (of the Lord) will not be respected and their words will not be heeded.[23] [italics are those of Marcus]

Here ends Marcus's citation. The passage continues thus:

Similarly the Righteous man in the city will seek to benefit [i.e. improve] it in all ways he deems fit [*mezakkeh le-khol ḥeftso*]—benefiting both himself and others. And he will have a thorn in the city who shall overturn his words and aggravate him in every way that the wicked can aggravate the good. *If that were not bad enough, the good man will speak justly and rule truthfully and justly, while the evil man will pervert justice and*

22 Safed edn., fo. 23a; Sodei Razaya edn., 94a–b. On the two editions, see above, n. 15. Marcus does not document this citation. Two notes before, after citing the *Hadar Zekenim*, he writes, 'Cf. HN 25a (23a)', which means *Ḥokhmat ha-Nefesh* (Lemberg, 1876), fo. 25a (Safed edn., fo. 23a). This reference, apparently, was intended to document our passage and somehow ended up in a preceding note. (The Lemberg and Safed editions are identical in pagination, even in font[!]; they differ only in the numbering of the pages. The Lemberg edition is two numbers higher than that of Safed; thus fo. 25a in the Lemberg edition will be fo. 23a in the Safed edition.)

23 Safed edn., fo. 23a; Sodei Razaya edn., 94a–b. The Hebrew original of this passage and its continuation (cited immediately after) is found above, Ch. 1, n. 70.

his words will be wrong, and the words of the good man will go unheeded while those of the evil man [*will be accepted*]. And he will lead the public astray. And all this was predetermined then [after Adam's fall, by the curse] 'Thorns and thistles it shall bring forth to you'. And this takes place because the people of the city are deemed [by God] unworthy of heeding the good man and so He inclines their hearts after the wicked so that they should stumble. And He makes the words of the wicked man successful [i.e. attractive], so that they should be drawn to him and stumble. If that were not bad enough, *the wicked man will yet write books which will last for generations and write piyyutim* [*liturgical poems*] *which will be recited by* [*succeeding*] *generations, but not so the good man* [i.e. he will neither write books nor compose liturgies, or, if written, they will remain unread and unrecited]. And all this happens because future generations are also unworthy, and so God allows all this to come to pass in order that they too shall stumble. . . . And because He knows posterity to be unworthy, he allows the dishonest *to write books and piyyutim, for had the* [*future*] *generations been worthy He would have allowed the good men to write the good books and the piyyutim.* 'Thorns and thistles', in *gematriyah*, is the numerical equivalent of 'posterity'. And thus a wicked man is enabled [by God] to *earn* [*richly*] *in this world in an iniquitous way and to establish a synagogue or a cemetery or some other important thing*, for posterity is unworthy [to benefit from] the deeds of the good, and God does not want the deeds of the good to [benefit] the dishonest. [italics mine]

The difference in the way the notion of 'thorns and thistles' was entertained by the two leading figures of German Pietism couldn't be starker. R. Yehudah expounds briefly a biblical interpretation (whose examples go no further than Moses) which has a one-line contemporary moment to it. R. El'azar of Worms runs the biblical examples all the way down to the book of Esther, and then explodes in anger with a long list of the tribulations of the just and pious at the hands of religious leaders, judges, poets, and scholars, and equally at the hands of communal leaders and benefactors. The emotional involvement of R. El'azar in this passage is evident, as is the contemporary import of his descriptions. For evidence just how aptly these descriptions reflect the communal and religious claims of the Pietists and their rejection by the authorities, I refer the reader to my essay 'Three Themes in *Sefer Ḥasidim*'.[24] R. El'azar invokes 'thorns and thistles' once again in the same work when speaking of the wicked frustrating the good people's endeavor to institute the Will of the Creator.[25] It seems difficult not to conclude that he shared R. Yehudah's critique of the communal and religious establishment.

[24] Ch. 1, pp. 30–3 above.

[25] *Ḥokhmat ha-Nefesh*, Safed edn., fo. 19a; Sodei Razaya edn., 78a–b.

Marcus then argues against R. El'azar's involvement with *Sefer Ḥasidim* because the penitential sections of that work (with confession to a hasidic sage) are so different from the private penitentials (without confession or sage) of R. El'azar, and to the extent that there is some likeness, R. El'azar clearly borrowed from what is found in *Sefer Ḥasidim*. He advocated penance manuals rather than sage penance. This is a very important point that Marcus has proven beyond question and we are all indebted to him for this insight. Ben-Sasson has also shown that R. El'azar differed with his teacher regarding egalitarian distribution of wealth and social protest. I widened the gap between these two religious mentors by pointing to the disinterest that Roke'aḥ had in the quality of human relationships, even on a one-to-one basis: 'The *Hilkhot Ḥasidut* of R. El'azar is a propaedeutic to spiritual ascent and self-perfection, in which man's dealings with his brethren hardly figure.'[26] Differing, however, on penance, economic equality, and even on social relations does not mean that Roke'aḥ differed with his teacher about the central tenet of German Pietism, the Will of the Creator (*retson ha-Borè*), or about the religious radicalism evinced by R. Yehudah and his followers in enforcing its mandate, so vividly portrayed by Marcus.[27] One can accept Marcus's argument, as I do, that R. El'azar reworked R. Yehudah's sage penance, but this does not disassociate him from the rest of *Sefer Ḥasidim* and its outlook. Similarly, three small blocks of *Sefer Ḥasidim* on penance, interspersed with alien material, seem to reflect the notions of penance of R. Yehudah he-Ḥasid rather than those of R. El'azar.[28] This, however, in no way proves that the remaining 1,869 sections of that maddening agglomeration of texts on every topic under the sun that we call *Sefer Ḥasidim* are equally the work of R. Yehudah he-Ḥasid.

What can be said is that the works unquestionably authored by R. El'azar center entirely on the moral and religious development of the individual. This exclusive emphasis of Roke'aḥ admits of a simpler interpretation. If one decides to go public and prefaces a legal code (*Sefer Roke'aḥ*) with a set of ethical teachings—*Hilkhot Ḥasidut*—as does R. El'azar, and in so doing

[26] Above, Ch. 1, n. 29. Moshe Idel has recently advanced the idea that these two leaders differed also on theurgy and, to some extent, on anthropomorphism. See his ''Al Zehut Meḥabreihem shel Shenei Perushim Ashkenaziyim la-Piyyut ha-Aderet ve-ha-Emunah ve-'al Tefisot ha-Te'urgiyot ve-ha-Kavod etsel R. El'azar mi-Worms', *Kabbalah: Ketav 'Et le-Ḥeker ha-Mistikah ha-Yehudit*, 29 (2013), 67–208, and my remarks above, pp. 148–51. Susan Weissman has shown that R. Yehudah he-Ḥasid and R. El'azar of Worms differed on the matter of man's relationship with ghosts, the dead, and the nature of Divine Judgment; see below, p. 234.

[27] *Piety and Society* (above, n. 2), 92–102, and cf. above, pp. 30–3.

[28] *SHP*, ##17–26, 37–8, 41–3.

implicitly claims for them a normative status on a par with that of laws of the Sabbath, the author can formulate these moral imperatives in a pietistic manner. There is universal agreement with the general principles—fear and love of God, humbleness, restraint of one's desires, and the like—so the author can distribute the emphases in the presentation to give these axioms a pietistic bent. However, he cannot incorporate the novel and sometimes startling dictates of the Will of the Borè as there is no consensus, to put it mildly, as to their very existence.

That R. El'azar believed in the Will of the Borè, I doubt not for a moment, otherwise how could he have been counted among the German Pietists? Yet there is not a reference to that Will, or to any of its numerous prescriptions, in his writings. He shared, to all appearances, the Pietists' aspiration for religious reform on the communal level, for he was angry and resentful about the defeat and humiliation of these well-intentioned souls by the religious and communal establishment.[29] Indeed, his anger at the 'wicked' opponents of the righteous attained astonishing dimensions.

In his *Ḥokhmat ha-Nefesh*, R. El'azar discusses the eternal bliss of the souls of the righteous, which in hasidic thought meant an eternity of gazing from close quarters upon the supernal Kavod and basking in its glory.[30] The proximity to the Kavod was strictly allocated on the basis of merit and merit alone.[31] He writes:

> ויש קרוב לכבוד ויש רחוק: וכל מי שאין בו קנאה, ומזכה אחרים, ורדף צדק, והצנע לכת ואינו מתלוצץ, ושונא רעים, ואוהב צדיקים ואינו גונב, ועוצם עיניו מראת ברע הוא יהיה קרוב.

'There are those that are placed close to the [supernal] Kavod and there are those who are placed far away [from the Kavod]. Anyone without jealousy, who acts for the good of others and pursues justice, who walks humbly and is not given to levity, who hates the wicked and loves the righteous, who does not steal and closes his eyes so as not to look upon the bad [i.e. at women other than his wife], he will be [placed] close [to the supernal Kavod]'.[32]

[29] In my 1976 essay 'Three Themes in *Sefer Ḥasidim*' (Ch. 1 , pp. 51–5), I suggested a reason for the underlying strata of bitterness in Roke'aḥ's remarks. As I noted there parenthetically, this in no way conflicts with his understandable anger at the way some of his and R. Yehudah's well-meaning followers were treated by the establishment.

[30] See above, pp. 161–2, for the various editions of that work and the ones selected for citation.

[31] On Kavod, see G. Scholem, *Major Trends in Jewish Mysticism* (New York, 1941), 111–14; J. Dan, *Torat ha-Sod shel Ḥasidut Ashkenaz* (Jerusalem, 1978), 104–68; id., *Toledot Torat ha-Sod ha-'Ivrit* (Jerusalem, 2011), v. 209–58.

[32] Safed edn., fo. 14a; Sodei Razaya edn., 57b–58a. On the contemporary meanings of the terms *mezakkeh aḥerim*, *resha'im*, and *tsaddikim*, see above, pp. 32–6.

No other work—to the best of my knowledge—in the entire ethical or kabbalistic literature of the Jews prescribes hatred of the wicked as a necessary requirement for beatitude, or even as a trait that commends one for such bliss.[33]

Nevertheless, there is not a word of these feelings in R. El'azar's *Hilkhot Ḥasidut*, the opening section of his *Sefer ha-Roke'aḥ*. Reaching out to a wider audience, he equally avoided in that work any mention of the *retson ha-Borè*, let alone of the new norms which this Will had imposed. His restraint was wisdom. The dictates of the Borè, so reverently decoded by the Pietists, were swiftly consigned to oblivion. The *Hilkhot Ḥasidut* of R. El'azar achieved the widest diffusion and ultimately shaped the moral posture of European Jewry.[34]

Marcus concludes his argument:

A third consideration also indicates the usefulness of this working hypothesis as well. When we operate on this assumption, we find a consistent set of differences between *Sefer Ḥasidim*, on the one hand, and El'azar's known works, on the other. In light of these differences it is possible to reconstruct a dynamic movement from radical to reactionary phases of the religious revival which occurred in medieval European Judaism. The hypothesis 'works' and provides us with a new understanding of the texts and the historical development of German-Jewish pietism.

Precisely why wariness is in place. Only too often have the minds of historians proven to be far clearer and more orderly than the historical process that they describe.

Marcus has analyzed and highlighted important elements in hasidic thought, such as atonement, personal eschatology, and what he terms 'sectarianism', but in so far as I can read the evidence, one cannot speak of a neat, three-stage development. There are numerous strains of thought in the movement, some contradictory, some complementary, perhaps coeval with one another, perhaps sequential, and, excepting penance and social justice, one cannot assign with a reasonable degree of probability the other strains of thought to any of the three known leaders of Ḥasidei Ashkenaz, R. Shemu'el, R. Yehudah, and R. El'azar. The most that can be said of R. El'azar is that when he decided to go public, his works were conservative and centered on personal spiritual ascent.

33 My claim of absence of such a notion in the kabbalistic literature is based on the replies to my query by Moshe Idel and Daniel Abrams.

34 J. Dan, 'Goralah ha-Histori shel Torat ha-Sod shel Ḥasidei Ashkenaz', in E. E. Urbach, R. J. Z. Werblowsky, and Ḥ. Wirszubski, eds., *Meḥkarim be-Kabbalah u-ve-Toledot ha-Datot Muggashim le-Gershom Shalom* (Jerusalem, 1968), 87–99.

I would suggest that, in wrestling with questions of authorship in *Sefer Ḥasidim*, we move away from attributions of this paragraph or that small packet of paragraphs to R. Yehudah or R. El'azar to that of thematic analysis. I have attempted to do this in my study of what I called *Sefer Ḥasidim I*. I analyzed the first 152 sections of the Bologna edition of *Sefer Ḥasidim* (*SHB*) and arrived at the conclusion that the positions in those passages were incompatible with the rest of that volume, and even more so with the much larger *Sefer Ḥasidim* printed from the Parma manuscript (*SHP*). It was the work of conventional pietists who shared several of the aspirations of the Ḥasidei Ashkenaz, but who had no truck with their radical social perspective, their notion of the Will of the Borè, their extreme penance, or their esoteric traditions of prayer.[35] And indeed, a number of manuscripts of *Sefer Ḥasidim*, including the oldest dated one, contain only those 152 sections.[36] A student of mine, Susan Weissman, took the large subject of ghosts, the relationship between the living and the (very active) dead, and the notions of Final Judgment in *Sefer Ḥasidim* and found them to be consonant with what we have of R. Yehudah's thoughts on these subjects, but strongly at odds with the writings of both his pupils, R. El'azar of Worms and R. 'Azri'el of Bohemia, the author of the *'Arugat ha-Bosem*, not to speak of the thought of the Tosafists, both German and French.[37] Thus, we may legitimately attribute, certainly as a working hypothesis, other statements found in *Sefer Ḥasidim* on these subjects to R. Yehudah he-Ḥasid, even though they have no corroboration in his other writings. However, this tells us nothing about whose views are reflected in the pronouncements of *Sefer Ḥasidim* about such subjects as books, marriage, raising of children, or whatever.

Put differently, there is an atmospheric unity to the various Books of the Pious that we have in print and manuscript (barring *Sefer Ḥasidim I*), just as there is a linguistic commonality—they all share the same bad Hebrew, poor syntax, and clumsy expression. Is there, however, a common *Weltanschauung*? This can only be answered, I suggest, by analyzing major topics of that work—for example prayer, one of the largest subjects of discussion in the book and about which there is a great amount of theoretical writings in

35 Above, pp. 80–90.

36 Oxford, Bodley Opp. 340 (Neubauer 875) (the oldest extant manuscript, copied in 1299); MSS Moscow, RSL Günzburg 103; Milan, Biblioteca Ambrosiana X 111 Sup; Nîmes, Bibliothèque Municipale 26 (contains *SHB*, #1–62). (I should add that MS Oxford, Bodley 453 does not contain any copy of *Sefer Ḥasidim*.) See above, pp. 123–4.

37 'Ghost Tales in *Sefer Ḥasidim*: An Examination of the Role of the Dead and Notions of the Afterlife among the German Pietists and Jews of Medieval Ashkenaz' (Ph.D. diss., Yeshiva University, 2013), published as *Final Judgement and the Dead in Medieval Jewish Life* (Oxford, 2019).

the esoteric literature of the movement.[38] If we seek to attribute an entire collection, be it that of Parma or Bologna, we shall seek and never find. If we essay to find whose voice or voices speak in the wide array of subjects in those collections, we may succeed, in part, in our quest.

II. Penance

My distinguished colleague has some very important things to say about penance; indeed, his is the first thorough study of this central but much-neglected field of hasidic thought. Rather than making it the focal point of his study, he chose to link it to anthropology and 'sectarianism', and devotes a full chapter to its exposition.

It may well be that the two of us have differing notions of the social sciences and their use. My colleague has written a study fusing anthropology and history, *Rituals of Childhood: Jewish Acculturation in Medieval Europe*.[39] To my mind, the power of the social sciences lies in their ability to explain—at the very least, to order—large bodies of data, for example the anthropological distinction between guilt and shame cultures. If, however, one takes a single ritual and assigns to its various parts symbolic significance, how does this differ from what a preacher does? Anthropology is one thing, anthropological homiletics another. The book, however, was well received, and I may well be as wrong in the matter of the penitential 'rites of passage' of the German Pietists—to which I now turn—as I apparently am in the initiatory rite of Jewish schoolchildren.

Marcus interprets penance in light of van Gennep's famous concept of 'rites of passage'.[40] The argument rests on two explicit assumptions: first, that penance was the initiation rite into the sectarian Pietist movement; second, that penance in the *Sefer Ḥasidim* is restricted exclusively to Pietists or to those 'who would like to be initiated into pietism'.[41] The two assumptions are intertwined, and the first hinges upon the second. If penance was practiced equally by non-Pietists, its practice could not serve as a sectarian initiation, for non-sectarians were practicing it too. Both assertions are, to my mind, problematic. Moreover, the stages of passage—separation, transition, and incorporation—are supported by questionable evidence.

[38] See the remarks of I. Gruenwald, 'Social and Mystical Aspects of *Sefer Ḥasidim*', in K. E. Grözinger and J. Dan, eds., *Mysticism, Magic and Kabbalah in Ashkenazi Judaism: International Symposium held in Frankfurt a.M.*, Studia Judaica 13 (Berlin, 1995), 110–15.

[39] New Haven, 1996.

[40] *Piety and Society* (above, n. 2), 77.

[41] Ibid. 75.

So as not to tax the reader's patience, I will spell out my reservations about the first two stages, then examine each piece of evidence adduced for the third and most documented stage: incorporation.

Marcus writes, 'The act of separation is clearly indicated in *Sefer Ḥasidim* by the description of how a Sage meets a penitent. Invariably, a confession to a Sage begins with the formula, "If so-and-so comes to inquire [of a Sage] how to atone".'[42] To my mind, this simply states that someone has requested penance for a sin, and I fail to see how the other five passages cited in the supporting footnote evidence an act of separation.[43] Approaching a Sage for penance does not mean separating oneself from the community, nor does it mean accepting the myriad novel dictates of the Borè. It simply demonstrates that the person seeks to expiate his sin and is willing to be guided by the Sage in this matter. Of all the innovations of the Pietists, penance, as we shall soon see, aroused the least question or opposition.

'Transition' founders upon the same issue. None of the passages cited gives any indication that these requirements are rites unique to Pietists and not simply the demands made on a person who seeks to expiate a specific sin and whose religious ambitions go no further.[44] Humiliation is, indeed, the hallmark of the Pietist, but the humiliation flows from his observing the strange, new prescripts of the Borè: wearing a distinctive *tallit*, reducing all social relations to a bare minimum, even to the extent of not playing with one's own children,[45] to focus his thoughts more intently on God, and, above all, observ-

[42] *Piety and Society* (above, n. 2), 78.

[43] *SHP*, ##19 (pp. 23–4), 21, 52, 112=629, 630.

[44] Ibid., ## 976, 39, 43 (p. 41), 19 (end), 32, 21, 113, 112. To further argue that humiliation is equated by the Pietists with death, and this meets 'Mircea Eliade's conception of religious initiations as requiring ordeals of symbolic death', seems to my untutored eye as pushing the envelope a bit far. First, *Sefer Ḥasidim* never states that to become a Pietist one need suffer humiliation; it simply states as a sad fact that this will inevitably be the Pietist's lot. Second, as emphasized in the text, the humiliation experienced by the Ḥasid is not occasioned by penance but by his antisocial behavior and, above all, by his refraining from looking at women. Finally, as Wistinetzki already noted, the passage in *Sefer Ḥasidim* cited by my colleague (#976) draws upon the famous tannaitic dictum in *Bava Metsi'a* (58b) that '[If] one humiliates his fellow man publicly, it is as if he shed his blood'. This dictum is a general one—true in all times and places—and is cited hundreds (if not thousands) of times in the rabbinical and ethical literature of the past millennium, all unrelated either to pietism or to initiatory ceremonies of any sort.

[45] See *SHP*, ##278, 339, 770, 986. *Le-tayyel* in Mishnaic Hebrew and Aramaic means primarily to relax, amuse oneself, play, as in **אוכל ושותה ומטייל בסוכה** (*Sukkah* 28b). This meaning still obtained in rabbinic Hebrew in the high Middle Ages in Ashkenaz; see e.g. *Tosafot*, *Betsah* 12b, s.v. *dilma*, end, where playing ball is described as *tiyyula be-'alma*; and it is in this sense that it is generally employed in *Sefer Ḥasidim*. When joined to the verb *la-lekhet*, as in #20 (p. 24 bottom), it means walking, or better yet, going for a stroll. See above, Ch. 1, n. 113.

ing 'custody of the eyes', avoiding looking at women at all costs. Each of these, but especially the last, earned the penitent the mockery of much of the community, even, one may assume, of many of the learned and the scrupulously observant.[46] These were the hallmarks of a Ḥasid, for which he paid a high personal and social price. I know of no evidence that penance per se ever provoked public or even private reprobation, nor does Marcus offer any. Indeed, if subsequent history is any guide, of all the hasidic practices, penance was the one that the Ashkenazic community was most attuned to and which it adopted with alacrity.[47] Marcus's underlying assumption that every person who went to the Sage for penance was interested in becoming a Pietist is dubious.

Expiation of sin is a common reaction to guilt, and in a society in which public expiations were part of the fabric of religious life for centuries, nothing would be more natural than this.[48] Few, if any, of the very numerous passages dealing with penance in *Sefer Ḥasidim*, or in the literature of the movement generally, indicate that the penitent is a would-be German Pietist. No doubt someone who wished to be such a Pietist would have to do penance for all his unwitting transgressions of the Will of the Borè, not to speak of his all-too-human failings,[49] but this scarcely means that all or even a significant number of those who did penance were seeking to be such Pietists.

Indeed, if one surveys the now readily available transcriptions of all penance manuals of Ḥasidei Ashkenaz in print and manuscript,[50] one will immediately see that there is no penance prescribed in any for transgressing the wishes of the Borè as outlined in *Sefer Ḥasidim*. Expiation is demanded for clear halakhic breaches, for common breaches in social and religious decorum which all would agree were transgressive—for example talking and acting improperly in the synagogue or making a hurtful remark to another—but

[46] See above, Ch. 1, nn. 55–60, and see Scholem, *Major Trends in Jewish Mysticism* (above, n. 31), 92–3.

[47] See Y. Elbaum, *Teshuvat ha-Lev ve-Kabbalat Yissurim: 'Iyyunim be-Shitot ha-Teshuvah shel Ḥakhmei Ashkenaz ve-Polin 1348–1648* (Jerusalem, 1992), 11–43.

[48] The twelfth century witnessed no sharp change from the outer to the inner forum, from penance to repentance. Public penance continued to be practiced in the thirteenth century. See M. C. Mansfield, *The Humiliation of Sinners: Public Penance in Thirteenth-Century France* (Ithaca, 1995); S. Hamilton, *The Practice of Penance, 900–1050* (Woodbridge, 2001); R. Meens, *Penance in Medieval Europe, 600–1200* (Cambridge, 2014).

[49] See above, Ch. 1, n. 47 and p. 120, item 2.

[50] E. Kozma, 'The Practice of *Teshuvah* (Penance) in the Medieval Ashkenazi Jewish Communities (A *tesuva* [vezeklés] gyakorlata a középkori askenázi zsidó közösségekben)' (Ph.D diss., Eötvös Loránd University, Budapest, 2012). The Hebrew section at the end of the thesis contains an annotated edition of all penitentials in print and manuscript.

which in the Pietists' eyes were grave sins,[51] and for wicked thoughts, such as of murder,[52] or impure imaginings of a sexual nature.[53]

The passages cited as evidence for 'transition'—'a process by which the non-Pietist enters the Pietist fellowship'—give, to my mind, no such indication.[54] The same holds true for the proof texts cited for 'incorporation'.[55] Let us analyze one by one the passages advanced for the latter.

1. Marcus writes:

The initial phase of being accepted is at the point when the penitent agrees or refuses to accept preliminary penance by which to demonstrate contrition:

> Someone apostatized reverted back to Judaism and agreed to do penance as the Sages would instruct him. From the moment he agrees (to do so) [*misha'ah she-kibbel*], one may drink wine and pray with him if he completes a quorum (for prayer),[56] so long as he acts like other Jews. (#209)

All the passage says is that one's legal status as an apostate is nullified by his internal regret and reacceptance of Judaism, and that penance, for all its importance for the health of the soul and in avoiding the fires of Hell, has no bearing on his formal standing as an upright and fully privileged Jew.

2. Marcus continues:

To refuse to undergo the test of demonstrating contrition leads to the sinner's not 'being accepted' by the Sage into the company of Pietists:

> For if he does not do this, we do not accept him [*ein mekabbelim oto*]. This was also said formerly 'Whoever accepts (upon himself) the requisites of membership in rabbinic fellowship [*ḥaverut*] except for one thing, is not accepted (as a Fellow).' (#43)

By way of introduction one should observe that the penance of the German Pietists consists of several components, two of which were: physical expiation (the amount of suffering should be proportionate to the pleasure derived from the sin) and taking measures to ensure that one is not involved in situa-

[51] ##1484, 224, 1589. See the 'Takkanot Shum' of 1221–3, to which R. El'azar is one of the signatories, in L. Finkelstein, *Jewish Self-Government in the Middle Ages* (repr. New York, 1964), 231, 249. See now R. J. Barzen, *Taqqanot Qehillot Šum. Die Rechtssatzungen der jüdischen Gemeinden von Mainz, Worms und Speyer im hohen und späten Mittelalter*. Monumenta Germaniae Historica. Hebräische Texte aus dem mittelalterlichen Deutschland 2 (forthcoming). See also R. Yitsḥak of Corbeil, *'Amudei Golah (Semak)* (Constantinople, 1509–16); ed. D. Harpenis (Satmar, 1935), #11 end.

[52] Kozma, 'The Practice of *Teshuvah*' (above, n. 50), 61–2.

[53] Ibid. 77–9.

[54] See above, pp. 236–7.

[55] *Piety and Society* (above, n. 2), 80–1.

[56] That is to say, he may be counted as one of the ten Jews necessary for a quorum of prayer, which would not be the case were he still viewed as an apostate.

tions which could lead again to this temptation to sin (this is called 'fence penance').[57]

Let us read now the entire passage, which deals initially with 'fence penance':

המורה ישאל לו תחילה אם מתחרט: אם יאמר כן, אם בעון אשה הוא, יאמר לו תחילה אם מתחרט אתה, יש לך להרחיק מאותה אשה מלראותה ומלדבר עמה שנה אחת. אם תעשה זה ותעמוד בזה, אז אתן לך דברים להסיר עונך, שאין עון סר בלא נזק שנאמ[ר] (ישיעיהו ו: ז) הנה נגע זה על שפתיך וסר עונך וחטאתך תכופר. ואם יאמר תן לי כפרות אחרות וזה לא אוכל לעשות, אין נזקקין לו, שאין תשובה אלא בשב ממעשיו ועושה סייג. שכבר אמרו השב מן הריבית אפילו מן הגוי לא יקח ריבית.[58] ומנזיר נוכל לדעת שהרי כל הרואה סוטה בקילקולה יזיר עצמו מן היין[59] שנאמ[ר] (הושע ד: יא) זנות יין ותירוש יקח לב, ואין נזיר לחצאין[60] שאם נזיר באחד נזיר בכולן, ולמה אסר בחרצנים עד כל משרת ענבים (במדבר ו: ג ד)? מכאן שיש לו לאדם לעשות סייגים. ואם לא יעשה כן, אין מקבלין אותו. וכן אמרו מי שקיבל עליו דברי חבירות חוץ מדבר אחד אין מקבלין אותו[61] וכן גר.[62]

ואין לומר שאנו נועלים דלת בפני השבים[63] כשבא לפני המורה להורות ולא אמרו תקנת מריש[64] אלא בבאין לדין אבל לצאת ידי שמים[65] אין אומרים לו אלא אמת[66] שישיב מן הגזילה. ואם אין הנגזל רוצה לקבל, יתן גזילה לצדקה שלא יהנה ממה שגזל שנאמ' ויתנו שכרי שלשים כסף ואשליך אל בית האוצר, מן הדין לא היו שלו וניתן לאוצר. ואחר שנראה (שישב) [ששב] ממעשיו הראשונים. והרבה סייגים ואחר כך יתן הרב דין מה שכתבתי למעלה.

The Teacher should begin by asking him if he repents, and if the answer is 'Yes', and it was sinning with a woman, he should say to him at the outset, 'If you indeed regret your actions, you must keep a distance from that woman and refrain from seeing her or speaking with her for a year. If you will successfully do this despite its difficulties, then I will give you a penance [i.e. a regimen of physical expiation] which will remove your sin, for sin cannot be removed without damage [i.e. physical pain], as the Bible says . . . And if he [the sinner] says, 'Give me some other form of penance because I cannot keep this' [i.e. refrain a full year from seeing the woman or speaking with her], then one has no further dealings with him. For there is no repentance without making a 'fence' [around the sin, i.e. avoiding situations that in themselves are permissible, but which may lead to repeating the sin]. For the [Talmud says,] one who repents lending at usury must refrain from taking interest even from loans to Gentiles [which is permitted]. And we can also see this [the need for fences and its indispensability] from the laws of the Nazirite. The Talmud says that one who sees a woman committing adultery should abstain from wine like a Nazirite, as the Bible says . . . And there is no partial acceptance of Nazirism. The Nazirite must abstain from everything [forbidden

[57] Marcus has superbly expounded the various forms of penance; see *Piety and Society* (above, n. 2), 39–43.
[58] *Sanhedrin* 25a.
[59] *Sotah* 2a.
[60] *Nedarim* 83a.
[61] *Bekhorot* 30b.
[62] Ibid. MS Jewish Theological Seminary, Boesky 45 erroneously reads 'נר'.
[63] *Bava Kamma* 67a.
[64] *Sukkah* 31b.
[65] See above, Ch. 1, n. 28.
[66] Thus in MS Parma, De Rossi 1133, fo. 15b.

to a Nazirite]—not only wine [which intoxicates] but also from any contact with the dead. And why is he [the *nazir*] forbidden to drink everything connected with wine from 'the kernels [of the grape] to the liquor of grapes [i.e. water in which grapes have been soaked]' [Num. 6: 3–4]? [Water in which grapes have been soaked is a fence around wine-drinking;] from here we see that a man must make 'fences' [around objects of forbidden desire]. And if he refuses to act in this way, we don't accept him [*ein mekabbelim oto*]. In a similar manner [to no half-Nazirism], they [the Sages of the Talmud] also said, 'One who accepts [upon himself] the requisites of membership in the rabbinic fellowship [*ḥaverut*] except for one thing is not accepted. Similarly with a convert [i.e. a would-be convert who accepts all the laws of the Torah barring one is not accepted as a convert].

And do not argue [that by insisting that a penitent accept the entire set of penances] we are breaching the talmudic warning against 'locking the door on those who would repent' [i.e. making it so difficult that few if any will become penitents]. Nor can you argue from the halakhic ruling that if one stole a board and used it in the construction of a building, the repentant thief is not bound to tear down that section of the building to return the stolen board to its owner [so as not to make repentance for stealing so onerous that people will refrain from repenting]. For this law of the non-return of the board is only in human courts, as it were, but [by the higher moral law, which we call] 'law of Heaven', we tell him that in truth he must restore what he has stolen. And if the person from whom he has stolen refuses to accept the board, he [the penitent thief] must distribute its value to charity, as the Bible says . . . And after we see that he has repented his former ways and [created] many 'fences', the rabbi should impose on him the [physical penances] that I have stated above.

The Pietists are introducing the radical notion of penance, and a multiple form of penance at that, something that has no precedent in the canonized literature. They are well aware of the objections that will be raised. One may, perhaps, understand the need for various forms of penance, but must one insist on all the different forms as a *sine qua non*? Doesn't this result in making repentance far too hard for most, and thus 'locking the door on those who would repent'—something the Talmud warned against, indeed, it waived certain halakhic requirements to forestall such a consequence?

Their reply to this objection is that there is a higher norm known to Pietists, 'the law of Heaven', which overrules the talmudic ruling about the non-return of the stolen board. They also argue that the manifold penances of their authoritative, esoteric tradition form a whole, constitute a package deal, as it were—it is all or nothing—and they proceed to give three precedents for such package deals—Nazirism, the *ḥaverut* (fellowship) of Talmud, and conversion.

Factually I fail to see how the acceptance into the talmudic community or fellowship of *ḥaverut* conforms in any way to van Gennep's rite of passage, seeing that all that is required is a simple statement by the candidate before three of the group members (*ḥaverim*) that he will abide by their standards of tithing and ritual purity.[67] The main issue, however, is methodological. If one accepts, as the Pietists do, that each component of their penance is essential, the multiple requirements are then a necessity. The refusal to give instruction about penance to someone who announces in advance that he will execute only part of it is a reasonable policy and, without further evidence, it does not in itself indicate the existence of a 'fraternal association', let alone rites of incorporation into a sect. To be sure, *ḥaverut* is cited as an example, but this is only one of three different talmudic examples to illustrate or prove that partial acceptance of a set of requirements is inadmissible. Multiple talmudic or biblical citations are characteristic of *Sefer Ḥasidim*. What criterion is being used to determine which of these citations should serve as the basis of analogy? In the absence of such a yardstick, one could equally argue that the Ḥasidim thought of themselves as Nazirites. Admittedly, the *retson ha-Borè* has nothing in common with the demands of Nazirism of ritual purity and abstention from wine, but then neither does it partake in any way of the requirements of ritual purity and tithing that constitute *ḥaverut*. One is no more distant than the other from the norms of the Will of the Creator.

3. Marcus proceeds:

But once the process of atonement is complete, in principle, even when the penances themselves are not all done, the former non-Pietist is to be treated like a Pietist. Thus, Pietists are not to recite blessings over a Wicked person [*rasha'*] unless he repents.

> A man should not bless a wicked person (*rasha'*): 'May God lengthen your life', unless he repents of his ways. For (otherwise), he is deserving of a curse, not a blessing. (#388)

Marcus cites no further proof texts for this point. This passage in and of itself is evidence of the harsh posture of the Ḥasidim towards *resha'im* which I have discussed,[68] but what does this have to do with 'incorporation'?

4. 'After the repentance occurs', writes Marcus, 'the non-Pietist becomes one with the Pietist community':

[67] *Bekhorot* 31b; *Mishneh Torah*, 'Hilkhot Ma'aser', 10: 1; 'Hilkhot Mishkav u-Moshav', 10: 5. I should add that the question is not the nature of *ḥaverut* as seen by historians (though I am unaware of anyone construing it in the terms of van Gennep), but what Ḥasidei Ashkenaz or other medieval Jews would have taken it to be, namely the image of the institution that emerges from talmudic texts—Mishnah, Tosefta, and the Gemara as read by contemporary Talmudists. See above, p. 185.

[68] Above, pp. 197–214.

If there are normally ten Righteous men available (for a quorum in the synagogue) but one should be out of town, and there is need for a quorum [*minyan*], he should not invite an Evil person [*ra'*] (to join) because his prayers would be sinful unless he repents of his evil conduct. (#1573)

This passage, too, stands alone, unaccompanied by any other sources. As such, it is a clear manifestation of the Pietists' elitism and was one of the main causes of their clash with non-Pietists;[69] however, I fail to see how this documents 'incorporation' as understood by van Gennep or other anthropologists.

5. 'The same principle', Marcus continues, 'underlies the thought that the Pietist should pray that Sinners [*ḥot'im*] should return [i.e. repent] to the Will of the Creator [i.e. become Pietists].' Section 1922 is cited as evidence. It reads:

שני משומדים אחין היו, חקר החכם אחד [את] אבותם, מה גרם? כשהיתה הגזירה, אמרו הקהל 'מה נעשה?' אמר הרב: 'ממני תראו וכן תעשו'. לקח שתי וערב ונשא כדי שלא יהרגוהו גוים. אנסוהו עם בני עירו. לכך נשתמדו בניו. לכך יתפלל אדם שלא תבא תקלה על ידו, וכל היוצא ממנו שלא יהו מחטיאים, וכל החוטאים שישובו (כן)[70] לרצון הבורא.

Two brothers were both apostates, and the Sage probed the past of their parents [to find out] what [might have] caused this [double apostasy. He discovered that] there had been a religious persecution, and the community turned to the rabbi [the father of the future apostates] and asked, 'What should we do?' The rabbi replied, 'See what I do and do likewise.' He took a cross and carried it so that they [the Christians] should not kill him. And they baptized all the Jews by force. [The father subsequently returned to Judaism. Nevertheless,] because of this, his own children subsequently apostatized. Therefore, one should always pray that he [himself] should not prove a stumbling block to others, that his descendants should never cause others to sin, and that all sinners should return to the Will of the Creator.

The sinners in this passage are two apostates, so to pray that they repent of their wickedness would scarcely be unique to Pietists, nor are such hopes indicative of 'incorporation'. Furthermore, the Ḥasid never had hopes so high that he prayed that these apostates should yet become Pietists, but simply that they return to the faith of their fathers. The Will of the Borè here means simply the will of God, i.e. the Torah, in other words, a return to Judaism. *Retson ha-Borè* here has the same conventional meaning as it has, for example, in sections 114, 244, and 305.[71] As the one who first drew attention to the

[69] See above, pp. 34–40.

[70] Thus in the parallel passage in MS Cambridge University Library 379,2, fo. 46d, #542.

[71] See above, Ch. 1, n. 10. The reverse at times equally holds true. See above, Ch. 1, n. 52, where the conventional *retson ha-Kadosh Barukh Hu* in #1344 is clearly being used for the covert Divine Will of the Pietists, the *retson ha-Borè*: ורוב ראשי הקהל טובים וברצונם לתקן רצון הקב"ה ואין יכולים מפני הגאים.

significance of the phrases Will of the Borè and *yir'ei ha-Shem*,[72] I must emphasize what I wrote in the preceding essay, 'On Reading *Sefer Ḥasidim*', namely, that the Pietists took old phrases and endowed them with new meaning; however, they neither could nor did seek to empty those terms of their old meanings. *Yir'ei ha-Shem*, *resha'im*, *tsaddikim*, *retson ha-Borè* are used throughout *Sefer Ḥasidim* both in their conventional sense and as expressions freighted with unique contemporary meaning. Distinguishing between the radically differing denotations of these key phrases lies at the heart of interpreting *Sefer Ḥasidim*.[73]

6. Marcus concludes:

> Once the new Pietist has been incorporated into the Pietist fellowship, it is as difficult for him to leave it as it was for him to join. New social pressures will help him remain a Pietist:
>
> > Just as a person is initiated into [*le-hikkanes*] pietism with difficulty, so it is increasingly difficult for him to stop (being a Pietist) because of shame. (#982)

Undoubtedly. However, penance is never described as one of the initiatory practices that invite ridicule—it is for custody of the eyes and the like[74] that he suffered ridicule, and a return to looking at women would ordinarily awaken the barbed mirth of his co-religionists.

III. Sectarianism

Marcus, following a contemporary sociologist, sees the sect (as distinct from the religious order) as possessing two salient traits: a sharp division of the world into a we–they dichotomy and the possession of an independent source of authority. He then proceeds to characterize the German Pietists as a sect.[75] In law one can postulate that there are three requirements for the charge of first-degree murder; in theology one can postulate that there are a certain number of tenets of the faith. These are normative systems, and the supreme authority in each can decree the requisite conditions for any formal status. However, in an empirical discipline like sociology, every third sociologist of religion has his own definition of 'sect'. What is gained by saying that Ḥasidei Ashkenaz meet the definition of sect as defined by Michael Hill in his *The Religious Order: A Study of Virtuoso Religion and Its Legitimation in the Nineteenth-Century Church of England*?[76] They don't meet the widely

[72] See above, Ch. 1, pp. 8–16, 26 n. 52.
[73] Above, p. 196.
[74] See above, Ch. 1, pp. 29–30.
[75] *Piety and Society* (above, n. 2), 58–9.
[76] London, 1973. Surprisingly, this book does not appear in the bibliography of *Piety and Society*.

differing requirements of 'sect' as defined by Max Weber, Ernst Troeltsch, Rodney Stark, Brian Wilson, and other sociologists, as there is no agreement as to the meaning of the term.

Let us even accept that there could be, at least lexically, a common definition of 'sect'—and lexical consensus is often enough for a historian—its use as an analytical term would depend, first, on the intensity with which the required traits are embodied in the out-group; second, on the extent to which its waywardness is minimized or even outweighed by other characteristics of its adherents, and, finally, on the historical context that determines the differing importance attached at the time to each of these traits. For example, David Berger has argued powerfully that the current beliefs of a major sector of Lubavitch render their adherents a dissident sect lying beyond the pale of Judaism. There is much merit to his argument theoretically.[77] Were we living in a theological age as did Jews in Europe for centuries, incessantly struggling with a strong Christian drive to convert them, Berger's argument about dead messiahs and human beings being part of the living Deity might well have found a receptive audience, and Lubavitch followers may have been declared sectarians and written out of the fold. A hedonistic age, however, is the one in which we live, with little interest in theological niceties, and assimilation into an accepting, pluralistic society rather than conversion to Christianity currently constitutes the major danger to Jewish survival. Religious observance, now ever more rigorously practiced by the Orthodox, has for many become more difficult as Orthodox Jews have entered professions that demand frequent travelling to places such as China, Japan, India, and numerous cities scattered over America and Europe which have no indigenous Jewish settlements that can provide them with the necessities of the Jewish life. The hyper-religious compliance of the Lubavitcher hasidim, their unremitting outreach and warm embrace of Jews of every imaginable stripe, and the Habad houses they have established the world over which service the religious needs of locals and transients currently outweigh their questionable theology.[78]

Let us begin with the first characteristic that Marcus employs. The sect sees itself as set apart from the rest of the world, who constitute an indiscriminate mass of Others. The Puritans saw the adherents of the Protestant Church of England as no different from those who adhered to the Roman Church. To be sure, Marcus warns about pushing the analogy too far, but proceeds, to my mind, to do just that. For example, in the chapter on the 'politics of piety', he insists that every use of the terms *resha'im* or *ra'im* means

77 *The Rebbe, the Messiah and the Scandal of Orthodox Indifference* (Oxford, 2002).

78 In effect, these countervailing forces were noted by Berger himself, 137–9.

non-Pietists, for Ḥasidei Ashkenaz grouped together fully observant Jews and religious deviants. Indeed, all non-Pietists were, in his words, 'comparable in some respects to Christians'.[79]

I would simply point out that sectarianism or radical exclusivity bordering on sectarianism requires demographic mass, which the Ḥasidim, unlike the Puritans or Baptists, lacked, for they were few and scattered in the tiny Jewish communities of Germany. Secondly, it is true that facing inward, when their thoughts were directed towards the Jewish settlement, especially the manner of conducting communal affairs, the Pietists were separatists; however, this absolute division could not be maintained, for never for a moment could the Ḥasid forget the omnipresent, ever-threatening Other—the Gentile. Fear is a great leveler. The stronger the antagonism between one group and another, the less significant are the undeniable social hierarchies within the weaker one. The more isolated and endangered a group feels, the less important do the internal religious tensions appear to its members. The sheer need for mutual support, for defense and succor, for simple body warmth to survive against an unremittingly and increasingly hostile world drew the Ḥasid and non-Ḥasid together. The age of blood libel and ritual murder was scarcely an opportune time for the development of separatist tendencies in Ashkenaz. The significance of ideological differences dwindled among German Jews of the thirteenth century as they faced the growingly aggressive, even lethal antisemitism of their infinitely more numerous Christian neighbors.

I think, however, that most sociologists of religion would agree that the term 'sect' demands a claim to possessing 'a different source of religious authority', as Marcus puts it. He cites Hill as contrasting the religious order with the sect thus:

> [The order] exists only as part of a Church and has to be sanctioned by that Church. Thus, it is based ultimately on an external source of Authority. The sect, on the other hand, contains its own authority.

Marcus continues:

> From Hill's point of view, the Franciscans are an order for two reasons: they think of themselves as Christians, as well as Franciscans; their source of authority, the Pope, is the same as the ultimate authority of the Church, of which they are a part. In contrast, the Cathari or a host of other 'heretical' dissenters can be thought of as sectarian because they claimed to be the true Christians in contrast to all others; and they claimed to possess a higher source of religious authority, independent of the existing ecclesiastical hierarchy.[80]

[79] *Piety and Society* (above, n. 2), 59–65. The quotation is at p. 64.

[80] Ibid. 58.

The Cathars, the Waldensians, and their like were persecuted and exterminated by the Church, but who ever persecuted the German Pietists? The most that happened to some of them was that they were thrown out of the synagogue. And for good reason, as they tried to draw out the daily service for many hours and sought to deny non-Pietists any religious role in the Divine service.[81] However, if they went off and formed their own *minyan* (a quorum of ten men necessary for communal prayer) and spent most of the day in prayer and numerological calculations,[82] who bothered them? Many made pests—occasionally intolerable pests—of themselves by constantly rebuking others for their religious laxity and exhorting their neighbors to greater levels of observance.[83] There were undoubtedly angry exchanges of words and here and there some fisticuffs; but no more.

Clearly the Establishment didn't view the German Pietists as sectarian. How could they? The leaders of the movement had the bluest blood in Ashkenaz. They were the keepers of the esoteric lore of Ashkenaz, the arcane secrets which opened the Heavenly Gates of Prayer. The Kalonymides were among the greatest religious poets of the Ashkenazic community, and the family's migration from Lucca to Mainz marked in many ways the beginnings of Ashkenazic culture. If this were not enough, the Kalonymides also contributed some of the most famous Talmudists of the German high Middle Ages. They had a superabundance of both social and cultural capital. They had natural access to the corridors of political power, and, as the wealthy usually wish to marry upwards socially, there is every reason to imagine that many sought and some succeeded in linking themselves by marriage to this family, which in turn both provided the family with financial capital and afforded its members the wherewithal to devote themselves to scholarship, prayer, and meditation. It would be hard to find less probable sectarians. The impeccable credentials of the movement's leaders threw a protective mantle around those who walked in their footsteps.

Wherein lay their sectarianism? Marcus would have it, in their esoteric lore, and he cites the several passages in which they trace the antiquity of their traditions and their sacred nature.[84] I don't see how their claim of possessing esoteric truth of Divine origin differs in any way from the parallel claims of the Provençal, Catalan, or Spanish kabbalists.[85] If anything, the doctrines of Provençal mystics were far more radical and 'heretical' than anything enter-

81 See above, Ch. 1, pp. 31–8.

82 See above, p. 34.

83 Ch. 1, n. 76.

84 *Piety and Society* (above, n. 2), 65–71.

85 See now O. Yisraeli, 'Jewish Medieval Traditions concerning the Origins of the Kabbalah', *Jewish Quarterly Review*, 106 (2016), 26–41.

tained by the German Pietists. R. Yitsḥak Sagi Nahor in the early thirteenth century admonished his followers against disseminating their secrets of the Godhead lest they be misunderstood and taken for some form of polytheism.[86] No one ever objected to R. Yehudah he-Ḥasid's or R. El'azar of Worms's dissemination of the esoteric lore of the Kalonymides. R. Mosheh b. Ḥisdai of Taku (Tachau) thought that the radical anti-anthropomorphism of the Pietists was both wrong and wrongheaded, and that their source of authority and inspiration, R. Sa'adyah Gaon, had created out of thin air some new-fangled entity, a semi-divine/quasi-divine, visible Kavod (Glory) that was the object of the numerous prophetic visions of an anthropomorphic God found in the Bible. To him this was pure invention, indeed, the product of 'alien wisdom'. However, there were never charges of heresy on his part,[87] and if he did level such an accusation (the one extant manuscript of his polemical work is incomplete), no one, to the best of my knowledge, paid any attention to it. One cannot advance a claim of sectarianism on the basis of the *Ketav Tamim* of R. Mosheh, nor does Marcus attempt to.

As to the covert Will of the Creator (*retson ha-Borè*), this was not part of their esoteric tradition but of the unique insight of the Ḥasid to discern the Divine wishes embedded in the canonical literature and in the daily affairs of men. They speak of truths embedded in Scripture that are destined to be discovered only generations later. Not only in Scripture but also in the Talmud and Midrash.[88] Marcus seems to agree with this view,[89] though in one passage he includes the *retson ha-Borè* in the traditions of Kalonymide arcana.[90] Let us,

[86] G. Scholem, *Meḥkerei Kabbalah*, ed. M. Idel and Y. Ben-Shelomoh (Tel Aviv, 2001), 7–39; id., *Origins of the Kabbalah*, ed. R. J. Z. Werblowsky (Philadelphia, 1987), 393–414.

[87] The expression *dat ḥadashah* on p. 83 of his *Ketav Tamim*, published in *Otsar Neḥmad*, 3 (1860), 58–92, seems to me to be more a derogatory remark than a charge of heresy. I doubt that he seriously put R. Sa'adyah Gaon's Kavod on the same plane as Christianity. (A facsimile edition of the solitary manuscript was published by Merkaz Dinur entitled *R. Mosheh Taku, Ketav Tamim, MS Paris H711*, introd. J. Dan [Jerusalem, 1984]. The cited passage is found on fo. 31a.) See E. Kanarfogel, 'Varieties of Belief in Medieval Ashkenaz: The Case of Anthropomorphism', in D. Frank and M. Goldish, eds., *Rabbinic Culture and Its Critics: Jewish Authority, Dissent and Heresy in Medieval and Modern Times* (Detroit, 2008), 117–59; J. Davis, 'Drawing the Line: Views of Jewish Heresy and Belief among Medieval and Early Modern Ashkenazic Jews', ibid. 161–5. See, however, J. Dan, *Toledot Torat ha-Sod ha-'Ivrit* (Jerusalem, 2011), v. 455–79.

[88] *SHP*, #1514, 1826, 1829, 1831, and see above, Ch. 1, nn. 1, 7, 9. Contrast the authority claimed for their esoteric traditions cited by Marcus and the absence of such claims in the two introductory passages in *SHP*, #1 and #28. (Section 28 is the introduction to another set of *maḥbarot* [notebooks] of *Sefer Ḥasidim* [see the heading— זה ספר חסידים] that the author/compiler of *SH I* subsequently lifted and used as an introduction to his work. See above, Ch. 3, p. 91.)

[89] *Piety and Society* (above, n. 2), 63–8.

[90] Ibid. 70.

for argument's sake, assume this to be so; what is heretical in the *retson ha-Borè*? These are supererogatory requirements, demands for behavior above and beyond the traditional call of religious duty. Novel, to be sure, and occasionally strange, but containing nothing antinomian, to put it mildly.[91] The German Pietists could be adversely viewed as eccentrics, but scarcely as religious reprobates. Their unique doctrines of the *retson ha-Borè* were without influence, but not their inclination towards stringency (*haḥmarah*). The Pietists, in fact, were norm-intoxicated, and in their quest to insure perfect compliance with the traditional halakhic norms, they developed a policy of systematic stringency in all matters of halakhah and of erecting fences (*seyyagim*) about the law, to which the larger community for centuries responded favorably. So much so that by the sixteenth century this hasidic policy had transformed the Ashkenazic norms of religious observance.[92]

If, in characterizing the German Pietists, I had to choose between the two groups contrasted by Michael Hill (in the above citation[93]), my choice would be the opposite of that of my distinguished colleague. I would opt for 'religious order' rather than for 'sect'—for German Pietism was a group or movement with religious demands far greater than those made of ordinary adherents to the faith, but one that fully recognized the binding power of the halakhah, indeed, ringed its norms with hedge after hedge to insure its perfect observance.[94] This band of elite souls only felt, as do religious virtuosi the world over, that far more had been expected of man than that which had been explicitly mandated by Revelation—in the Pietists' case by the Written and Oral Law. Their undoing lay in that they were situated in a religion, if you wish, in a 'church', in the sociological sense of the word, which did not admit any soteriological distinction between elites and masses, one that did not recognize a lower and higher path to eternal bliss.

They were further hampered by the fact that the Ashkenazic community was animated by a proud sense of *kehillah kedoshah*, of being a 'sacred community' that scrupulously fulfilled its religious duties. Unlike most medieval Jewish communities, Ashkenaz did not entertain the notion of elite religious observance as opposed to that of the common folk. There was one religious standard for all.[95] Thus, the Pietists were members of a religious culture

[91] As for the so-called antinomian dimension of *din shamayim*, see above, Ch. 1, n. 28, and pp. 59–60. [92] See above, pp. 15–16. [93] p. 245. [94] See above, pp. 12–16, 58–60.

[95] J. Katz, 'Alterations in the Time of the Evening Service (*Ma'ariv*): An Example of the Interrelationship between Religious Customs and their Social Background', in id., *Divine Law in Human Hands: Case Studies in Halakhic Flexibility* (Jerusalem, 1998), 107–11. (Katz's article originally appeared in Hebrew: 'Ma'ariv bi-Zemano ve-Shelo bi-Zemano: Dugmah le-Zikah bein Minhag, Halakhah ve-Ḥevrah', *Zion*, 35 [1970], 35–60; our passage is at pp. 47–52; republished in id., *Halakhah*

that did not so much seek to reduce the religious virtuosi to the level of the common folk as it invested the deeds of the common folk with an aura of correctness and a normative value that elevated them to the same rank as that of the elite. This self-image had been intensified by the unparalleled devotion to God that it had displayed in the First Crusade—murder of their own children lest they be raised as Christians, followed by the mass suicides of the parents. So deep did this feeling run that the intellectual leaders of Ashkenaz, the Tosafists, had difficulty in entertaining the notion that large swaths of the community had failed in their religious observance. Indeed, they went so far as to reinterpret the law to justify many communal practices, treating a contradiction between popular practice and a talmudic dictum much as they would treat a contradiction between two talmudic dicta—conflicts to be resolved through dialectical distinctions.[96] Announcing to a *kehillah kedoshah* that it was in fact deeply sunk in sin as it daily transgressed a covert Will of the Borè, unknown to its members or to its revered forefathers, was one of the most bizarre and futile undertakings of the Jewish Middle Ages.

ve-Kabbalah: Meḥkarim be-Toledot Dat Yisrael 'al Madureiha ve-Zikatah ha-Ḥevratit [Jerusalem, 1984], 175–201. The cited passage is at pp. 187–91.) H. Soloveitchik, *Yeinam: Saḥar be-Yeinam shel Goyim—'al Gilgulah shel Halakhah ba-'Olam ha-Ma'aseh*, rev. edn. (Jerusalem, 2017), 87–148; id., *Ha-Yayin bi-Yemei ha-Beinayim—Yein Nesekh: Perek be-Toledot ha-Halakhah be-Ashkenaz* (Jerusalem, 2008), 360–2.

96 H. Soloveitchik, 'Religious Law and Change: The Medieval Ashkenazi Example', *AJS Review*, 3 (1978), 153–96 (repr. in id., *Collected Essays*, i [Oxford, 2013], 239–57, and see the next essay in that volume, '"Religious Law and Change" Revisited', 258–77).

PART II

RAVAD AND PROVENÇAL STUDIES

CHAPTER TEN

Ravad of Posquières: A Programmatic Essay

WHO WAS R. AVRAHAM BEN DAVID OF POSQUIÈRES? 'The greatest of Maimonidean critics.' That he was great is unquestioned; that he wrote strictures (*Hassagot*) on the *Yad ha-Ḥazakah* is common knowledge, but it is not to these *Hassagot*, I suggest, that he owes his pre-eminent place in medieval halakhic thought. Ravad of Posquières the Maimonidean critic is a creation of the sixteenth century. What led me to this conclusion, and, if it is correct, who then is Ravad, are the successive subjects of this essay.

In the course of study it became apparent that the doctrines cited so often in Ravad's name in the novellae of Ramban (Nahmanides) or those of Rashba (R. Shelomoh Ibn Aderet) can seldom be traced back to the *Hassagot*. A systematic check of sixty consecutive references in the *Ḥiddushei ha-Ramban* yielded only eight corresponding doctrines in the glosses. Of fifty citations in Rashba's work, seven were found in the *Hassagot*. Moreover, of these seven, only two are explicitly taken from Ravad's glosses.[1] The other five, though appearing in R. Avraham's *Hassagot*, may well have originated in his other

Professors Shraga Abramson, Jacob Katz, Yaakov Sussman, Israel Ta-Shma, Isadore Twersky, Ephraim E. Urbach, Rabbi Dr Aharon Lichtenstein, and the much-lamented Professor Haim-Hillel Ben-Sasson were kind enough to comment on the manuscript. For the perversities still remaining, I bear sole responsibility. {The respective publishers of both this article and Ch. 12 transliterated R. Avraham b. David's name as Rabad, employed q rather than k for *kof*, used double rather than single quotation marks, etc. I have taken the liberty in this volume of my *Collected Essays* to align throughout (other than in a bibliographical reference to the articles) the rules of transliteration, punctuation, and the like with those followed in the preceding volumes. Here and there in the notes, I have added a word or phrase. These inserts are bracketed. I have also omitted n. 44, as I found it redundant.}

[1] *Ḥiddushei ha-Rashba*, *Berakhot*, ed. Y. Bruner (Jerusalem, 2007), 42b, s.v. *u-le-'inyan* 45a, s.v. *sham*.

works. Be that as it may, forty-three of the fifty references of Rashba are not traceable to the *Hassagot*. The *Torat ha-Bayit*, the *Ḥiddushei ha-Ritva*, and the *Sefer ha-Terumot* were subjected to the same test and the results found to be similar.

Nor did Provençal literature upon inspection present a different picture. The *Sefer ha-Hashlamah* never once mentions Ravad's glosses. So startling is his absence at times that some ninety years ago one editor was led to suggest that the author was unacquainted with the *Hassagot*.[2] Ravad's Maimonidean strictures were known to R. Me'ir ha-Me'ili, but 85 percent of his numerous references to Ravad are to doctrines never articulated in these strictures. Only twenty-five (at most) of some 225 references to Ravad in the *Sefer ha-Mikhtam* are culled from the *Hassagot*. And while citations of Ravad are common enough in R. Manoaḥ's *Sefer ha-Menuḥah*, references to the *Hassagot* are strikingly infrequent.[3] Clearly, medieval Talmudists (*rishonim*) did not draw their knowledge from anything Maimonidean.

Conversely, if I encountered a gnomic gloss of Ravad and turned to *rishonim* for enlightenment, I inevitably came away empty-handed. True, these scholars will often expound Ravad's doctrine at length and from their presentation one can understand the terse notes in the *Yad*; but it is clear that these men drew their information from elsewhere, and their comments were not designed to clarify these glosses. Hundreds, possibly thousands of Ravad's doctrines are commented upon in the works of the *rishonim*, but rarely does one find explicated a passage from the *Hassagot*. The *Hassagot* are his least cited work. Indeed, they are one of the least studied works of the Middle Ages. And, as we shall see, justly so.

Were Ravad's glosses at least well known? As acquaintance presumes dissemination, manuscripts might provide a rough answer. Neubauer's catalogue of the Bodleian Library lists no fewer than forty-seven manuscripts of the *Mishneh Torah*, but not one single copy of the *Hassagot*, even though that great collection possesses a representative sampling of Ravad's other works, both

[2] *Sefer ha Hashlamah le-Seder Nezikin*, ed. Y. Lubetzki (Paris, 1895), introduction, pp. 9–10. (See Y. Lubetzki, *Bidkei Batim* [Paris, 1896], 41); correct, however, *Kesef Mishneh*, 'Ḥamets u-Matsah', 4: 4 according to *Sefer ha-Menuḥah* ad loc. (Constantinople, 1718). That commentary is now conveniently found in the Shabsi Frankel edition of the *Mishneh Torah*.

[3] Of the fifty-three references to Ravad in the *Sefer ha-Menuḥah*, ed. E. Hurvitz (Jerusalem, 1970), two are practical rulings and fifty-one doctrinal positions. Three of the latter refer explicitly to Ravad's strictures; two more may also have reference to them; the remaining forty-six recount positions not articulated in the *Hassagot*. In R. Manoaḥ's commentary on *Sefer Mo'ed* (above, n. 2) {and see Shabsi Frankel's edition of the *Mishneh Torah*}, the references to the *Hassagot* are more frequent. They are cited on a dozen occasions, but references to Ravad's other writings total more than twice that number.

real and pseudepigraphic. It may be noted that six manuscripts of the *Haggahot Maimuniyot* are found in Bodley. In the catalogue of the British Library thirteen manuscripts of the *Mishneh Torah* are to be found, but none of the *Hassagot*. There are two, possibly three, manuscripts of the *Haggahot Maimuniyot*. Zotenburg's catalogue of the Bibliothèque Nationale describes fifteen manuscripts of the *Yad ha-Ḥazakah*, one of the *Hassagot*, and one of the *Haggahot Maimuniyot*. That one manuscript of the *Hassagot* is not found in a copy of the *Mishneh Torah*, but is rather lodged between Ibn 'Ezra's commentary on the Pentateuch and the correspondence of R. Yonatan of Lunel with Maimonides. The catalogue of the Institute of Microfilmed Hebrew Manuscripts of the National Library of Israel in Jerusalem gives us a rough comprehensive figure of all surviving manuscripts of the *Yad* and the *Hassagot*, whether of volumes, individual books, or even fragments. Listed there are 438 different manuscripts of the *Mishneh Torah*, thirty-two of the *Haggahot Maimuniyot*, and twelve of the *Hassagot*. Of these twelve, six (at most)[4] are

It may be argued that citation is not a reliable guide. A man need not cite an author when reacting to his stimulus. And, thus, while R. Manoaḥ may indeed have drawn heavily on Ravad's other writings, this does not preclude his work from being, among other things, a quiet reckoning with the glosses from Posquières. In fact, it would be surprising if this were not the case. To more accurately gauge the extent to which the Maimonidean commentator, R. Manoaḥ, reckoned with the Maimonidean critic Ravad, a study was made of Hurvitz's edition of the *Sefer ha-Menuḥah* on the preliminary assumption that every remark of R. Manoaḥ that forfends, explains, or even encompasses a remark made by Ravad in his *Hassagot* was indeed occasioned by these notes (though it may equally have been generated by R. Manoaḥ's own perception, Ravad's other writings, or the positions or remarks of other Provençal scholars). The following results were obtained: of the fifty-seven *Hassagot* contained in the sections of the *Yad* commented upon by R. Manoaḥ, only twenty-two could possibly be viewed as having been taken into consideration by him. The contents of the other thirty-five glosses were wholly ignored in the *Sefer ha-Menuḥah*. (A cursory glance at the sizeable sections of R. David ha-Kokhavi's *Sefer ha-Batim*, ed. M. Y. Blau [New York, 1978], which appeared just as this article was going to press, taken together with smaller sections previously available, yielded a far better average. Yet even here the ratio of non-Maimonidean citations to Maimonidean ones runs roughly two and a half to one.) {Further study has validated the impression that R. David ha-Kokhavi used the *Hassagot* of Ravad more than other medieval scholars. His work seems to be the exception which confirms the rule. Another edition of the *Sefer ha-Battim*, edited by M. Hershler and Y. Hershler, was published in Jerusalem in 1983.}

[4] Actually only MS Leipzig, Karl Marx University Library, 1104, has the *Hassagot* as we would envision them. The other five are in the following state: in MS Rome, Biblioteca Angelica, Or. 63 the *Hassagot* are not glossed to the text, but were copied out at the end of the manuscript (fos. 417–39). If one imagines that location plays no role in use and reference, may I remind him of the differing degrees of acquaintance that talmudic scholars to this day possess of the *Haggahot Maimuniyot* and the *Teshuvot Maimuniyot*. MS Vatican, Apostolica, 171, a potpourri of philosophical and belletristic miscellanea, contains in its ninth section the text of the *Hassagot* on part of *Sefer Madda'*. The interest here appears philosophical rather than halakhic. The same holds true, one suspects, for the glosses in

actually glossed to the *Yad*; the other six are separate works. Twenty-seven of the thirty-two copies of *Haggahot Maimuniyot* are marginalia of the *Yad*.[5] The one significant collection not on film in Jerusalem is that of the Jewish Theological Seminary of America. Its librarian, Dr Menahem Schmelzer, informs me that their holdings contain 128 manuscripts of the *Mishneh Torah*, one separate manuscript of the *Hassagot*, and on the margin of one copy of the *Yad* a set of the *Haggahot Maimuniyot*.

In other words, 558 of 564 scribes or owners of the *Mishneh Torah* did not view the *Hassagot* as a desirable (let alone necessary) complement to that work. Yet what little effort was required for a scribe of the *Yad* to have added the *Hassagot*—eight to ten lines a chapter—to his voluminous transcriptions? All the above figures are subject to endless qualification, but their general import seems inescapable, especially as it corroborates our previous impression: the *Hassagot* were a sparsely disseminated work. Throughout the medieval period, when Ravad's influence was both massive and decisive, his glosses on the *Mishneh Torah* were little known and of less influence.

the great Ashkenazic copy of the *Mishneh Torah* made by Berakhiah ha-Nakdan in Paris in the year 1242 (MS Cambridge, University Library, Add. 1564). This huge manuscript of the entire *Yad ha-Ḥazakah* contains the glosses on *Madda'* and the beginning of *Sefer Ahavah*. It stops abruptly in the middle of 'Hilkhot Keri'at Shema'. Did the scribe (or owner) lose interest in these notes once out of the philosophical waters of *Madda'*? At any rate, over 80 percent of this text of the *Mishneh Torah* is without *Hassagot*. MS Parma, De Rossi, 1383 contains *Sefer Zemanim* with some thirty-five scattered glosses of Ravad, clustered heavily in 'Hilkhot Ḥamets u-Matsah'. The printed text contains 219 glosses of Ravad for the same text. Lastly, MS Modena, Biblioteca Estense, S.8.18 (Bernheimer 18): this is a manuscript of the *Yad* (*Nashim, Kedushah, Hafla'ah*) in which the *Haggahot Maimuniyot* are integrated within the text. Another hand added, on the margin, Ravad's glosses together with other sundry notes.

(It cannot be argued that the paucity of manuscripts of the *Hassagot* is due to the fact that these glosses were incorporated into the *Migdal 'Oz* and *Maggid Mishneh*, for yet fewer manuscripts of those works are found. Not one manuscript of the *Migdal 'Oz* exists [not surprisingly], and only five manuscripts of sections of the *Maggid Mishneh*.)

5 Manuscripts of the *Haggahot Maimuniyot*: (*a*) The Bodley collection actually has seven manuscripts, as MS Oxford, Bodley, 610, registered in the catalogue as *Teshuvot Maimuniyot*, contains also *Haggahot Maimuniyot*. MSS London, British Library, 494 and 495 are *Haggahot Maimuniyot*; MS 501 is problematic. The Bibliothèque Nationale contains, in reality, two manuscripts of the *Haggahot*, 344 and 354. (*b*) I have discounted three manuscripts in the catalogue of the Institute of Microfilmed Hebrew Manuscripts for the following reasons: I have not included in the count two very similar manuscripts: Florence, Biblioteca Medicea Laurentiana, Plut. II. 21 and Parma, De Rossi, 214. As they contain exclusively *Teshuvot Maimuniyot* and not *Haggahot*, it seemed improper for our purposes to juxtapose them to Ravad's notes. Neither have I counted MS Budapest, Hungarian Academy of Sciences, 2° 1, as I have found there nothing worthy of the name *Haggahot Maimuniyot*. On the other hand, I have added to the toll MS Livorno, Talmud Tora (Bernheimer 11), currently found in the National Library of Israel and entered as 1987 = 8.

If not a Maimonidean critic, who then was Ravad? And if not a Maimonidean critic, how did he come to be identified as one? The answers to both questions are, I believe, simple.

It is difficult to label individual *rishonim*, but two figures certainly lend themselves to swift portrayal. The greatest codifier of the Middle Ages, in a sense its greatest author, is Maimonides, and Rashi is its greatest commentator. R. Menaḥem le-Vet ha-Me'iri (Mei'ri) does indeed entitle Maimonides 'the greatest of authors' (גדולי המחברים), yet the designation 'the greatest of commentators' (גדולי המפרשים) he bestows not upon Rashi but upon Ravad.[6] As a son of Provence he was correct in his evaluation. It was Ravad's commentaries that first broke free from the geonic moorings, and it was these exegetical works that heralded the intellectual independence of Europe.[7]

In evaluating the early literature of Provence, far too much emphasis has been placed upon agreement or disagreement with the Geonim. Disagreement is a pallid form of independence, for, in a sense, one only demonstrates one's subservience to a thinker when one spends one's time seeking to refute him. It is the universe of discourse rather than the positions adopted therein that is determinative. The central question to be asked in assessing the intellectual dependence of southern Europe is whether its frame of reference is geonic. Do the writings of R. Sherira, R. Natronai, and R. Ḥai serve as the point of departure of the discussion; are the categories employed those of the Geonim; and do areas outside the geonic purview bulk large in the author's concerns? Seen from that perspective, Provence, for all its independence in many areas of religious practice, still revolved in a geonic orbit. Ravad changed all that. The effects are noticeable simply on a technical level. Remove the Geonim from the *Eshkol* and the work collapses; subtract the Geonim from the *'Ittur* and it limps badly; take away the Geonim from Ravad and the loss is

6 When referring on occasion to Ravad's strictures, Me'iri calls their author 'the greatest of the glossators' (*gedolei ha-magihim*). My point is not that Me'iri was oblivious to Ravad's talents as a critic, but that he viewed him as *the* talmudic commentator. (When chronicling the history of halakhah in his introduction to *Avot*, R. Menaḥem took a less Provençal and more European perspective and placed Ravad alongside Rashi, Ibn Megas, and R. Me'ir Abulafia as one of the leading talmudic commentators.) Whichever evaluation of Ravad we choose as the most reflective of Me'iri's views, the one he adopted throughout his multi-volume oeuvre or that in his brief survey in *Avot*, the commentarial activities of Ravad remain the man's claim to fame in R. Menaḥem's eyes. See *Bet ha-Beḥirah 'al Avot* (Jerusalem, 1964), 54. {MS St Petersburg-Firkowitz, II a 9/1 corroborates the editor's emendation of *harkavat perush u-fesak*. See below, p. 293 n. 5.}

7 Sometimes, as in several chapters of *Niddah*, *Mikva'ot*, and *Yadayim* and a half-chapter in *Sukkah*, Ravad's exegesis took the form of commentary-codes. I include these, naturally, in his commentarial oeuvre, though for brevity's sake I will sometimes simply say 'commentaries' rather than 'commentaries and commentary-codes'.

barely noticeable. The student of Geonica has no reason to rejoice in Ravad's advent. Before Ravad, Provençal writings are a storehouse of geonic literature. After him the geonic material in Provençal works dwindles radically.[8] When geonic dicta then appear, they are generally summed up rather than cited, conceived as doctrines to be juxtaposed, not as precious decisions to be preserved and discussed. Ravad disrupted the geonic transmission.

The revolution that he wrought, however, would not have been effective had it been simply negative. R. Yitsḥak of Fez had discarded the Geonim before him. He had attempted to decide talmudic controversies independently of their writings, but there is little indication that he essentially understood those controversies differently. There is no evidence that he read the sources afresh, or that he sought to expand the traditional perimeter of halakhic concerns. Unable to pose a positive alternative, Alfasi could not succeed in his dislodgement of the past. Weighty and influential as his work was, his contemporaries and successors—R. Yitsḥak Ibn Gi'at, R. Yehudah Albargeloni (of Barcelona),[9] and R. Avraham Av Bet Din of Narbonne—swiftly restored the Geonim to their pre-eminent place. It was Ravad who broke the geonic domination.[10] Anyone who compares several pages of the *Eshkol* with those of Ravad's commentaries or commentary-codes will perceive immediately the difference between a perception of the Talmud mediated by the Geonim and a direct encounter between the intellect and the sources. Ravad takes a tractate or a field in its entirety as his subject, interprets it *in toto* in his own categories, and dwells at length on those topics which *he* finds stimulating. In Ravad's

[8] And any study of the thirteenth-century literature will evidence that it is not the tosafist movement which effected this displacement in Provence.

[9] Professor Shraga Abramson once remarked to me that a good deal of Alfasi's importance is his removal of the Geonim, and a great deal of the point of the *Sefer ha-'Ittim* is their restoration. For all other remarks in the paragraph I bear full responsibility.

[10] (*a*) The absence of Geonica in Ravad's commentaries is nigh total. No code (unless it is apodictic, as is Maimonides', rather than discursive) can, however, dispense with precedent. Despite this fact the absence of prior doctrines in Ravad's commentary-codes is striking. Hundreds of rulings are laid down in the *Ba'alei ha-Nefesh*, yet the Geonim (including here R. Ḥanan'el and R. Yitsḥak of Fez) are cited on fewer than a score of occasions. Most of these citations, furthermore, occur where Ravad has something to say on the matter, e.g. rejecting a doctrine outright, conjecturing as to its source, illuminating an obscurity, rejecting a popular misapprehension, or simply juxtaposing differing views so as to set the stage for a decision based on his own argumentation. Rare indeed is that geonic ruling which is cited simply as a halakhic datum.

(*b*) What *Katuv Sham* (ed. M. Z. Ḥasida [repr. Jerusalem, 1969], 138; ed. Ḥ. Freiman [Benei Berak, 1990], 305) and Rosh on *Sanhedrin* 4: 6 actually say {and this has often been misunderstood} is that discarding geonic doctrine as convincingly as he, Ravad, did was simply a *davar shelo nimtsa* {an impossibility; more politely, the rarest of things}. He who tried it, did so at great peril {for he would be held liable for any error on his part by the losing party.}

writings one witnesses a mind working unaided and untrammelled in (what to his view is) virgin territory. And subsequent generations found in *his* interpretation, in *his* categories—in brief, in *his* conception of the field—greater stimuli, more fruitful points of departure, than in the works of the Geonim, which now began to appear distant. And Ravad's impact upon talmudic studies was correspondingly massive, not only in Provence, but south of the Pyrenees as well. Hundreds upon hundreds of his original insights were assimilated, adapted, and extrapolated by the scholars of Spain, whose school dominated halakhic thought for centuries.

His accomplishments are thus greater and lesser than those of Rashi. Greater in that his work was innovative rather than consummatory. Ravad did not possess a comprehensive exegetical tradition upon which to build, or perhaps chose basically not to employ it. He began anew and his achievements on the whole were his and his alone. Yet his attainment was at the same time lesser than Rashi's, for despite multiple shafts of genius he could not hope to match singlehandedly the scope of Rashi's oeuvre or the totality of coherence which that scholar achieved when he distilled and transformed the centuries-old traditions of the Rhineland. Nor could Ravad dream of matching the luminous clarity of Rashi's presentation or the limpidity of his prose. His work was thus less definitive than Rashi's and far less comprehensive, but more original.

It was this almost unparalleled capacity to confront talmudic texts unaided, to wrest their meaning single-handedly, that allowed Ravad to penetrate into those areas where no commentarial tradition was available—halakhic *midrashim*, tractates *Kinnim* and *'Eduyot*—and to range far and wide over the Yerushalmi and the Tosefta. His activities in these fields were not accidental. Since, ultimately, he studied *Bava Metsi'a* aided only by his own intellect, there was no basic difference between that tractate and the *Sifra*. Ravad's proclamation at the head of *'Eduyot*, 'I have received no guidance in these [matters] from either rabbi or teacher' (כי אין עמי בכל אלה לא מפי רב ולא מפי מורה), described in the broadest sense his entire life's work. In some areas he literally possessed no guides, while in others he basically dispensed with them. If the Tosefta, Yerushalmi, and *Sifra* could yield their secrets to a man from Posquières, could anyone now imagine that the Bavli was decipherable only with the help of the geonic code?

Sometime late in the second quarter of the twelfth century, Europe declared her independence of Babylonian tutelage, and within the wondrous span of sixty years achieved it. North of the Loire it was the dialectical revolution of Rabbenu Tam which heralded the advent of European halakhic thought; south of the Loire it was the commentarial labors of Ravad. Both were bringing a newly forged vision of Truth and each was well aware of the fact. Not by accident does the same imperious sense of self stamp everything that these two titans wrote. Both personalities exuded power and boldness, and in one as in the other this was often translated into impatience with others, and, at times, into plain irascibility.[11] Having broken the Talmud to their harness, they did not suffer kindly opposition from mere mortals. Not that they overthrew the past—Heaven forbid; they simply rendered much of it irrelevant. And it is not for the meek to discard 500 years of tutelage.

Though Ravad's greatness may lie largely in the innovative nature of his work, his ongoing importance rests upon his substantive achievement. Hundreds upon hundreds of his insights were adopted and elaborated upon by the Spanish school and thus shaped the contours of the halakhah. Indeed any penetrating study of the halakhic literature of the thirteenth and fourteenth centuries—piercing the anonymity of the myriad 'there are those that say' (*ve-yesh omerim*) and 'there are those that explain' (*ve-yesh mefarshim*)—might disclose that, in many areas, the basic perception of the Talmud Bavli for the past 600 years has been that of Rashi, R. Ḥanan'el, and Ravad, as amended by the schools of Ramerupt-Troyes (Rabbenu Tam and Ri ha-Zaken) and Gerona (the school of Ramban). It is to these seminal writings of Ravad that subsequent writers make constant reference, and it is upon them that his position in the history of halakhah rests.

Without for a moment equating the scope or (as we shall see later) the density of Ravad's oeuvre with that of Rashi, we are still led to ask: if Rashi had written extensive glosses on the *Halakhot Gedolot* and the *She'iltot*, would anyone characterize him as a geonic critic? Yet this is precisely what happened to Ravad. To judge Ravad by his Maimonidean strictures is, to switch the analogy, like judging Mommsen or, better yet, Wilamowitz by his book reviews. Medieval commentators ignored the *Hassagot*, for they had twenty-fold material at their disposal. Why struggle to infer Ravad's conception of a talmudic discussion (*sugya*) from a gnomic gloss when a shelf row of his commentaries lay at hand? Indeed, since (as we shall see) his glosses were a random lot and do not reflect a quarter of his talmudic positions, any information gathered from them would be haphazard and incomplete. And so, they were simply ignored.

Great as were Ravad's accomplishments in the field of exegesis, his works,

[11] Some of these parallelisms, together with others, were noted by Isadore Twersky in *Rabad of Posquières: A Twelfth-Century Talmudist* (Cambridge, Mass., 1962), 235–6, a definitive portrait of the regnant perception of the man.

as I have noted, did not attain that scope or total cohesion which was Rashi's when he consummated the work of centuries, nor did they ever approach that wondrous felicity of presentation which again was Rashi's alone. Indeed, Ravad's commentaries are singularly lacking in literary grace. He belonged to that small band of writers whose style is improved by adrenalin. He is never clearer, weightier, or more epigrammatic than when in a combative position. One can, at times, get as clear a picture of Ravad's views from a terse note tossed off in exasperation as from a full paragraph in his non-polemic works. In his talent for pregnant statement he probably has no equal, but he was excelled by many in the art of straightforward presentation.

Crucial aperçu rather than comprehensive exposition was Ravad's commentarial forte, though this may have been as much a question of temperament as of talent. It was the difficult nub of a talmudic discussion that held his interest more than the task of detailed and often routine explication of an entire *sugya*; and his policy in *'Eduyot* and *Sifra* of commenting exclusively upon passages not sufficiently discussed in the Talmud reflects in a heightened fashion this exegetical inclination.[12] He was, moreover, wholly alien to the impulse that so animated Rashi—of guiding the ordinary student through a *sugya* by forfending imperceptibly a host of minor errors. Concern for the average may be attention to the mediocre or solicitude for the all too human, and Ravad and Rashi were not the first thinkers who divided along this line. Ravad was a problem solver (and polemicist) not a pedagogue. As the ongoing accompaniment to the Talmud, his works were inevitably displaced by those of the Tsarfati, but his numerous distinctive interpretations could not be displaced; that in itself should have ensured him a visible place in halakhic history.

It was Ravad's ill fate, however, to be followed by Ramban and Rashba.

The great creative period of the Tosafists in France was the twelfth century. The thirteenth century simply edited, abridged, or rearranged the intellectual accomplishments of its predecessors. Though the magnitude of the accomplishments of Rabbenu Tam and R. Yitsḥak ha-Zaken (Ri) was partially obscured by the tendency of later editors to present many of their views simply as

[12] This same proclivity, however, rendered Ravad so effective in commentary-codes, where line-by-line *explication de texte* was out of place. The central topics (or problems) in a field had to be isolated, the controlling passages in the *sugya* explained, and the merits of the conflicting views weighed. In such works Ravad was, as it were, the master of ceremonies, and his style is at all times, if not quite felicitous, clear, sinewy, and decisive. {To forefend charges of contradiction, I would add that what I argue below (Ch. 11) is that Ravad frequently changed his views, not that he did not express trenchantly whatever view he held at the time.}

'reply may be made' (*ve-yesh lomar*), no one has imagined that R. Perets of Corbeil or R. Eli'ezer of Tuchheim were major creative Tosafists. Men of modest stature, they could not obscure the great figures who had preceded them. The only two names that one carries away from a study of the standard *Tosafot* remain those of Rabbenu Tam and Ri. In Spain, the creative period stretched from the days of Ramban to those of Ritva or possibly R. Nissim of Barcelona.[13] Their successors, R. Yitsḥak Perfet, R. Shim'on Duran, R. Ḥasdai Crescas, R. Yitsḥak Abohab, were (in matters of talmudic commentary) men of lesser mold and could not displace the writings of Ramban and his school. It was Ravad's misfortune, however, to be followed by two giants—Ramban and Rashba. These two thinkers fused Ravad's insights with their own extrapolation of the tosafist dialectic and transformed both. The end result was greater than that which Ravad had created, and, in the course of time, his works fell into desuetude.

Provençal pride in its most illustrious son could yet have ensured the preservation of his oeuvre, but here fate dealt the final blow. France and Germany had their Poland, Spain its Mediterranean; but Provence was childless. When the time came for Ashkenaz to go into exile, it transported its culture to the empty spaces of central and eastern Europe. When Sepharad's days were up, the Spaniards took their classics with them to the far ends of the Mediterranean. Provence fell on evil times just as halakhic thought was flourishing south of the Pyrenees. The affinity between the two cultures was great, and Provence was absorbed by Spain with startling rapidity. In exile, Sepharad and Ashkenaz preserved, if not their cultural identity, at least their heritage. Provence did not; and 95 percent of its halakhic literature was swept away, unknown until the present century. The only Provençal writings preserved and destined to achieve currency were those appended to Sephardic works—Razah on Alfasi, Ravad on Maimonides. Provençal Talmudists survived as critics, not as creators.

And even that was not a foregone conclusion! The *Yad ha-Ḥazakah* underwent six editions before Ibn Naḥmias, seeking to produce a 'compleat Maimonides', commentaries and all, printed the *Hassagot* partially as marginalia, partially imbedded in the *Maggid Mishneh* and *Migdal 'Oz*. Another sixty-five years were to pass before the *Hassagot* assumed the format that we now know—that of separate marginalia in all fourteen volumes of Maimon-

[13] To a lesser extent, Ran did in certain tractates—*Shevu'ot* and *Ḥullin*, for example—obscure Nahmanides' accomplishments. But these are fine points and do not affect the basic state of affairs. (I do not here wish to enter into the problem of the exact nature of R. Nissim's contribution to halakhah in these two tractates, if a creative contribution he did indeed make.)

ides' work.[14] From that moment on, however, the image of the *Yad* became fixed. Since Talmudists tend, when studying a *sugya*, to forget the names of the various proponents of alternative explanations mentioned in novellae, Ravad was visible as a distinct entity only in the *Hassagot*. And as the *Hassagot* overflow with personality (it is probably the most personal work of the Middle Ages, certainly the most personal work in the average Talmudist's library), Ravad became stamped in rabbinic consciousness as the Ba'al ha-Hassagot and has remained so to this day.[15]

The scholars of *Ḥokhmat Yisra'el* did not spend time studying the *ḥiddushim* of Ramban and Rashba. They had more interesting things to attend to. They saw Provence primarily as the port of disembarkation of Maimonidean

14 See Shlomo Zalman Havlin's introduction to the Makor photostat of the Constantinople edition of the *Mishneh Torah* (Jerusalem, 1972); E. E. Urbach, 'Hassagot ha-Ravad le-Mishneh Torah la-Rambam bi-Defusim u-ve-Khitvei-Yad', *Kiryat Sefer*, 33 (1958), 360–3, and the literature there cited.

15 Moving, as my remarks do, from 1375 to 1509, from the surmised year of Ran's death to that of the publication of Soncino's *Yad ha-Ḥazakah*, they entail perforce a degree of compression. Some of the process outlined above began, not surprisingly, already in the fifteenth century. As the writings of Ramban's school gained currency around the Mediterranean littoral and supplanted Provençal works, Ravad's role as a talmudic commentator became progressively obscured and his image as Maimonidean critic loomed progressively larger, especially among jurists and responders, to whom the Maimonidean code was central to their labors. This is discernible if one simply takes the responsa of R. Asher or those of Aderet and notes the number of Ravad citations taken from his Maimonidean strictures as opposed to those from his other writings, and then compares those results with the percentages obtained from a similar study of the responsa of the Duran dynasty. Had printing not intervened, two images would have emerged from a study of medieval literature. The responsa literature of the fifteenth century would have shown Ravad primarily as critic, and the earlier literature would have yielded Ravad the commentator. It was the latter perception, the perception of their immediate predecessors, that naturally guided the men of the sixteenth century, printers not historians, and they proceeded to stamp Ravad's image for posterity: The *Mafte'aḥ ha-She'elot ve-ha-Teshuvot: She'elot u-Teshuvot ha-Rosh* (Jerusalem, 1965) lists eleven citations of Ravad, and five of them are noted as being culled from the *Hassagot*. The first entry contains no actual quotation of his words and, as Ravad expressed this opinion on a number of occasions, R. Asher may indeed have drawn his knowledge of Ravad's views from the Maimonidean *Hassagot* or equally from his *Hassagot* on Alfasi (*Ketubbot* 87a), or from the *Katuv Sham* (above, n. 10) ad loc. The second entry refers to a doctrine enunciated by Ravad in five separate works (see below, n. 38), and the citation of R. Asher (כמו שכתוב שטר על שמו) shows him to be referring to *Temim De'im* in Tam Ibn Yaḥya, *Tummat Yesharim* (Venice, 1622), #65 end. Thus only three of the eleven are certain references to the *Hassagot*. And the third reference, for the purpose of this essay, bears citation. After leveling an extensive critique of a Maimonidean doctrine, R. Asher writes ואחר שנשאתי ונתתי בדברים הללו בדקתי בהשגות שהשיג הראב"ד ז"ל על הרב ומצאתי כתוב שם וכו' ('After I weighed carefully these matters, I checked in the *Hassagot* that Ravad critiqued the master [i.e. Maimonides] and I found written there'). (I would like to thank the Makhon le-Ḥeker ha-Mishpat ha-'Ivri at the Law School of the Hebrew University for making available to me their card indices of medieval responsa, which allowed me to check my own impressions.)

thought in Europe, where the sons of light and darkness then waged battle over philosophy and rationalism. Of Provence qua Provence, in halakhah, they knew little and, possibly, cared less. So, to them, too, Ravad was primarily the author of the *Hassagot*, and his strictures a prelude to the Maimonidean controversy. Though violently at odds in all else, rabbis and *maskilim* were in agreement that, for better or worse, Ravad of Posquières was a Maimonidean critic. And this perspective has dominated historical studies to our day.

The Ba'al ha-Hassagot, who has merited such great attention, is no medieval figure but a sixteenth-century creation, and this 'modern' Ravad, while quite well known, was in fact singularly uninfluential. A doctrine of Ravad which was not incorporated into the writings of the school of Ramban or those of R. Asher (Rosh), but became known through the exclusive agency of the *Yad*, was without influence. I have not found a single such view that won acceptance.[16] Nor is the reason difficult to find. Ravad lacked a constituency. In a controversy where both arguments were of equal merit, Ashkenaz would follow the Tosafists and R. Asher, the Sephardim Maimonides or the school of Ramban. Ravad commanded no similar allegiance, for Provence had long ceased to exist. In halakhic impact, Ravad either made it early (as the *gedol ha-mefarshim*) or not at all.

It has sometimes been contended that by challenging Maimonidean finality these abrasive strictures prevented a petrification of the halakhah, and that this in itself would guarantee the *Hassagot* a prominent place in the history of halakhah. This assumes that Maimonides failed in his goal because he was criticized. I would suggest that he failed because his work was outmoded even before completion. While Maimonides was hewing in granite the upshot of talmudic discussions, a new Talmud was being written in northern France. Dialectic, dormant for some three-quarters of a millennium, was rediscovered by Rabbenu Tam and R. Yitsḥak ha-Zaken, and the two proceeded to do to the work of Abbaye and Rava what those *amora'im* had done to the Mishnah. Anyone who comes to the *Mishneh Torah* from studying a *sugya* with the writings of the Tosafists, with their vast collation of data, their discovery of hidden problems, and proffer of multiple solutions, will find Maimonides' presentation thin and simplistic. Valid, at best, but far from the final word. On a practical level, moreover, the *Yad* had ceased to sum up the state of halakhic affairs. By dint of the tosafist method thousands of inferences were being drawn from

[16] Needless to say, when Ravad simply expressed a mainstream opinion against a maverick Maimonidean doctrine (e.g. *kol ha-poshe'a mazik*, 'Hilkhot Sekhirut', 2: 3), his view prevailed. But it prevailed not because of the agency of his note, but because the weight of medieval halakhic thinking was against the other position.

the Talmud of which Maimonides (and the Geonim) had never dreamt. How skeletal and inadequate a code the *Yad* had become by the first quarter of the thirteenth century can be seen by comparing the several laws regulating the purging of vessels (*hag'alat kelim*) given by Maimonides in 'Hilkhot Ḥamets u-Matsah' (5: 21–6) with the extensive section 464 in *Sefer Ravyah*. Or compare what is probably the most comprehensive set of rules in *Mishneh Torah*, 'Hilkhot Malveh ve-Loveh', with the massive *Sefer ha-Terumot* of R. Shemu'el ha-Sardi (of Cerdagne), the joint product of French, Provençal, and Spanish thought around the year 1225. The future lay with European dialectics. Nahmanides defended the codifiers of the old world, but he thought and wrote like a denizen of the new. A century later, after the dialectical labors had been completed, the task of scholars became to do for the new Talmud what the great men of Muslim Spain had done for the old. So, R. Asher wrote the *Alfasi* of the tosafist Talmud and R. Ya'akov Ba'al ha-Turim penned its *Mishneh Torah*. Maimonides' *Mishneh Torah* was a magnificent monument to a lost world, outmoded even as it was unveiled. Ravad's *Hassagot*, unknown to most in the Middle Ages, had nothing to do with muffling the Maimonidean impact. When has criticism ever stopped an idea whose time has come?

The Maimonidean orientation has hung around the neck of Provençal studies like an albatross. Not only has it obscured the central role of Ravad in Jewish intellectual history, but it has disoriented the very legitimate study of Ravad as Maimonidean critic.

No halakhist penned a more savage polemic than did Rashba in his *Mishmeret ha-Bayit*, but his strident tone has aroused little comment among historians. Yet the sharpness of Ravad's notes has stirred endless discussion, both critical and apologetic. Indeed, evaluation of his polemical manner has been viewed as one of the central problems of Ravad studies. The differing reactions may partially be due to the fact that the *Mishmeret* was written as a defense, while the *Hassagot* opened a controversy. But basically the indifference to Aderet's tone stemmed from the fact that no one thought that an assessment of Rashba—one of the great talmudic commentators and possibly the greatest jurist and responder of the Middle Ages—would be seriously affected by the consideration that he could wield a nasty pen when irritated. If Ravad's place in history depends on his glosses, the spirit in which they were written is indeed crucial. Is this a work of jealousy, correction, or creation? If, however, these strictures are the medieval equivalent of review essays of a revolutionary scholar whose pathbreaking commentaries fill some dozen volumes, their significance, no less than that of Rashba's polemics, dwindles radically. Objectivity then comes easier. Many scholars have felt attracted by Ravad—his forceful personality still communicates itself over a distance of 800 years. But, thinking that his place in history stemmed from these strictures and fearing that their acerbic tone would deny him his due meed, effort upon effort was made to downplay their stridency. One can now admit to the full measure of tartness and spleen present in the *Hassagot* without this detracting a whit from Ravad's immortality.

Acerbic the notes certainly are, and it will do us no good to minimize this fact, but are they destructive? Is Ravad a captious critic out to spike Maimonides at every turn? His place in history is, as I have said, unaffected by this question, but any evaluation of his character hinges on the answer.

In seeking to demonstrate that Ravad was not motivated by jealousy or obscurantism, many arguments have been advanced, and scholarship is, no doubt, much the richer for this. The question itself, however, could have been resolved quite simply—by placing the *Hassagot* within the framework of his other writings. Among the arguments advanced for the objectivity of the *Hassagot* is the claim that several of those glosses reflect views that Ravad espoused elsewhere. This is correct. The number of correspondences runs well into the hundreds.[17] Indeed, if one investigates those areas in which we possess (from other sources) comprehensive information about Ravad's views, the correspondence between those writings and the glosses runs to about 70–80 percent.[18] Even the most vociferous Maimonidean advocate will admit that at least 10–15 percent of Maimonides' statements that are commented upon by Ravad are difficult or surprising by all accounts, and that a critical note is only natural. More significantly, investigation of Ravad's other writings reveals that in his *Hassagot* he registers roughly only one-quarter of his divergent views. Even a cursory study of his work on *Bava Kamma* or *'Avodah Zarah*, his *Ba'alei ha-Nefesh* and *Ḥibbur Lulav*, or the *Ḥiddushei ha-Rashba* on *'Eruvin* will show that his views differed from those of Maimonides on hundreds of other occasions. Had Ravad been out to ax Maimonides he could have covered the margins of *Mishneh Torah* with animadversions, rather than pen the two or three notes per chapter that he did. This in itself indicates how random are his strictures and why *rishonim* used them so little.

Indeed, it would seem that Ravad didn't read the full text of the code that he glossed. How else can we explain the fact that often the most startling doctrines of Maimonides escaped his strictures? After studying the *Ba'alei ha-*

[17] See the appendix below.

[18] *Lulav*, shofar, and *ḥamets u-matsah*, for example.

Nefesh, can anyone imagine that Ravad agreed with Maimonides' peculiar calculation of *yemei niddah* and *yemei zivah* (one of the most basic problems in *issurei bi'ah*)? Does anyone believe that Ravad concurs with Maimonides' ruling of *leḥi ha-'elyon*, or with his incomprehensible doctrine of *ḥosheshin le-zera' ha-av* in the matter of *oto ve-et beno*, or with his stamping prayer as being a pentateuchal rather than rabbinic imperative?[19] Yet on all these (and many other) classically difficult or tendentious rulings of Maimonides no remark whatsoever of Ravad is to be found, not even a neutral 'there are those who disagree' (*ve-yesh ḥolkin*). The *Hassagot* betoken a penetrating reading of many sections of the *Mishneh Torah*, not a thorough reading of the whole. Far from being Ravad's crowning achievement, as we have been led to believe, the *Hassagot* actually are the somewhat random, if copious, notes made by a supreme scholar on a work which came his way towards the close of his life. Certain sections interested him deeply—Maimonides' treatment of *tum'ah ve-taharah*, for example, a field where Ravad had no one in Provence with whom to spar. Sheer curiosity as to just how successfully the Egyptian rabbi had mapped that jungle impelled him to review, in effect, the whole of *Seder Toharot*. Other sections—'Hilkhot Shabbat', for example—interested him less. And he recorded his reactions in a highly personal and rather unsystematic fashion. Anyone who has labored a lifetime in a field and has developed strong views both about his metier and himself, and then comes across a brilliant work which states different conclusions in an annoyingly apodictic fashion, will, if he is a

[19] (*a*) 'Hilkhot Issurei Bi'ah', 6: 2–7; 'Hilkhot Sheḥitah', 8: 23, 12: 9; 'Hilkhot Tefillah', 1: 1. This observation, that Ravad often does not gloss the most difficult Maimonidean doctrines, I heard many years ago from my father.

(*b*) Reply could be made to my rhetorical query that the *ba'alei ha-kelalim* clearly believed so. They, however, were jurists rather than historians, and of the sort that look for rules of thumb. And silence as consent is as good a rule as any. Let us further remember just how few of Ravad's other writings were actively circulating. The *Ba'alei ha-Nefesh* was published just once (and then as an addendum to another work) prior to 1762, and his *Ḥibbur Lulav* and notes on Alfasi and R. Zeraḥyah were to be found only in Tam Ibn Yaḥya's *Tummat Yesharim*, published in Venice in 1622, and not too much could be inferred from *Kinnim* and *'Eduyot*. Ravad as a distinct entity was visible only in the *Hassagot*, and their conclusion, given the bent of mind of one in search of judicial rules, a natural one. Sometimes *rishonim* do infer Ravad's position from his Maimonidean silence (e.g. R. Yehudah b. R. Asher, *Zikhron Yehudah* [Berlin, 1846], #55; *Teshuvot ha-Rivash* [Vilna, 1878], ##14, 445; *Teshuvot ha-Rivash ha-Ḥadashot* [Munkács, 1901], #6; this responsa collection is now viewed as having been written by Rivash's son-in-law and his contemporaries. The responsa have been given a new edition by D. Metzger and published as an addendum to the *Teshuvot ha-Rivash* [Jerusalem, 1993] as *Teshuvot Meyuḥasot le-Rivash*); the temptation to do so, especially when amassing precedent, is great. Considering, however, the hundreds, possibly thousands, of instances where no such argument is advanced, it is clear that this is an occasional reflex rather than a habitual, let alone permanent, posture.

born note writer, fill the margins with all kinds of remarks . . . And if his personality is strong and his pen biting, those notes will not be too different from what we find in the *Hassagot*. Wrenched from their context, these brilliant marginalia raise all sorts of problems; placed in their proper framework (Ravad's massive writings known to medieval scholars), their nature appears evident and their significance minimal. By studying the Maimonidean critic while neglecting the Provençal Talmudist, historians may have saddled themselves with a problem of their own making, attempting to understand the tip while oblivious to the rest of the iceberg. It was, after all, the Provençal Talmudist who became the Maimonidean critic.

Though in no sense an oeuvre, the *Hassagot* nevertheless repay deep study. Small etchings they may be in comparison with Ravad's other rich canvasses, but the hand of the master is still everywhere discernible. Nor do I wish to downplay the role of Ravad as polemicist. He was a man who walked alone and if someone collided with him on the way he could get very irate. Misinterpretation appeared to him as an indignity done to truth; and error could assume, at times, the form of a personal affront. Nothing, then, was more natural for him than to give error and its propagators a sound thrashing. The study of Ravad as critic must, however, be carried out within the context of Provençal polemics, and here again the preoccupation with Fustat has worked distortion. It has been said in defense of the *Hassagot* that Maimonides treated his own opponents in no better a fashion. This would seem somewhat beside the point. If an English rabbi should write a biting criticism of a Kurdish *ḥakham*, should he be judged by British or Persian standards? The polemical style of twelfth-century Provence, both among Jews and Gentiles, is the backdrop we must seek. The violent language of Placentius, Ravad's great contemporary in Roman law in neighboring Montpellier, comes immediately to mind,[20] and the centrality of R. Zeraḥyah of Lunel (Ba'al ha-Ma'or) in any such study becomes apparent. The latter, too, wrote a major work of criticism —on Alfasi—and, more significantly, waged an ongoing battle with Ravad over the course of a lifetime, in his parallel commentary on *Kinnim*, in his strictures on the *Ba'alei ha-Nefesh*, and, of course, in the violent and fascinating *Sefer Divrei ha-Rivot*—the most personal and revealing document to

[20] P. Tisset, 'Placentin et l'enseignement du droit à Montpellier: Droit romain et coutume dans l'ancien pays de Septimanie', *Recueil de mémoires et travaux de la Société d'histoire du droit et des institutions des anciens pays de droit écrit*, 2 (1951), 77–8.

survive the Middle Ages. If one must have a foil in Ravad studies, the proper figure is the Ba'al ha-Ma'or, not Maimonides. Ravad's contact with the latter was a chance literary encounter in the closing years of his life; with the former a lifelong, personal quarrel that shaped a good part of both his and R. Zeraḥyah's oeuvres. And a study of this polemic may prove axial in evaluating Ravad, both the critic and the man.[21]

Besides serving as precious indicia of personality, Provençal polemics merit study as a literary genre. Ravad's *Hassagot* on Alfasi are as much in the nature of collected essays on *Seder Nashim* as anything else, and the same holds true, though this is less generally realized, for large sections of the *Sefer ha-Ma'or*. The setting down of major insights, self-contained analyses, in what is ostensibly a gloss and critique of another work is a distinctly Provençal idea, and it resulted in a series of works in which creativity and captiousness—personal antagonism, reasoned objection, and independent achievement—are peculiarly interwoven. Ravad was one of the creators of this genre of literature, his ready pen probing in turn R. Meshullam of Lunel, R. Yitsḥak of Fez, R. Zeraḥyah ha-Levi of Lunel (Razah), and finally Maimonides, and the *Hassagot* is one of his more brilliant creations. He was possibly the greatest—certainly the wittiest[22]—halakhic polemicist of the Middle Ages, and a study of the evolution of his technique is needed if we are to form any precise opinion of his posture towards specific contemporaries. It is thus within the broader context of the Provençal literature of controversy that the problem of the *Hassagot* must be treated.

If the literary form of the *Hassagot* can be properly understood only within the framework of Ravad's other writings, how much more so is this true for their halakhic content! Marginalia cannot be studied in isolation. The *Hassagot* possess a twofold importance in an evaluation of Ravad. First, in the

[21] (*a*) This essay (excepting some minor revisions) was written in Spring 1974. Since then I. M. Ta-Shma has published an important article on this topic in his 'Sifrei ha-Rivot bein ha-Ravad le-vein Rabbi Zeraḥyah ha-Levi (ha-Razah) mi-Lunel: Hebbetim Bibliografiyim ve-Sifrutiyim', *Kiryat Sefer*, 52 (1977), 557–77 {repr. with revisions in *Rabbenu Zeraḥyah ha-Levi Ba'al ha-Ma'or u-Venei Ḥugo: le-Toledot ha-Sifrut ha-Rabbanit be-Provence* (Jerusalem, 1992). I have discussed the relationship between Razah and Ravad at length; see Ch. 11 below.}

(*b*) I exempt R. Efrayim of Kala' Ḥamad from the comparison, because of the dissimilar nature of his work. Can anyone imagine Ravad's or R. Zeraḥyah's notes being incorporated by a scribe into the text of Alfasi? Or that future generations should have to labor to disentangle the two?

[22] Brevity is the soul of wit, but Ravad is so brief that the wit often went unnoticed. See, for example, his *double entendre* in the *hassagah* in 'Ḥovel u-Mazik', 8: 15 (אין כאן לא מלח ולא תבלין) already noted by B. M. Lewin, *Otsar ha-Ge'onim*, x: *'al Bava Kamma* (Jerusalem, 1943), introduction, p. 8; and again in his critique of Maimonides' directions for the knotting of the *tsitsit* ('Hilkhot Tsitsit', 1: 8), where he writes: זה הסדר אין לו לא שורש ולא ענף, a standard phrase, but one referring at the same time to Maimonides' opening formulation of ענף שעושין על כנף הבגד . . . הוא הנקרא ציצית.

invaluable information they provide of his wondrous achievements in tractates *Zera'im*, *Kodashim*, and *Toharot*, which are only partially visible in his works on *'Eduyot* and the *Sifra*. Second, in the multiple glimpses that they afford of Ravad's views in his closing years, glimpses which allow us to trace at times the evolution of his thinking over the course of a lifetime, and to marvel at the mental vigor and flexibility of that titan in his old age. The *Hassagot* are a random but still invaluable set of X-rays of the mind of the greatest Provençal Talmudist as his end drew near, and the results obtained from them take on significance only when plotted on the curve of Ravad's intellectual growth. It is to the manner of reconstructing this graph, to the way in which one goes about composing an intellectual portrait of Ravad, that we must now turn.

Writings must be assembled before they can be studied. And more works of Ravad exist than is commonly imagined. Unlike a bibliographical essay, however, a programmatic one such as this can only touch upon some of the more salient facts. The commentaries on tractates *Bava Kamma* and *'Avodah Zarah* are considered the two works to have been preserved intact. Technically speaking this is correct, but a comparison of the work on *Bava Kamma* with citations thereof in the *Shitah Mekubbetset* shows that R. Betsal'el Ashkenazi copied out the overwhelming majority of the commentary. If so, we possess, in effect, Ravad's commentary on *Ketubbot*, *Bava Batra*, and *Bava Metsi'a*, and the latter work proves itself one of his ripest compositions. As the *Hassagot* on Alfasi are basically collected essays on some tractates of *Seder Nashim* and contain some of Ravad's profoundest writings, we have, then, Ravad's own words on *Ketubbot*, *Gittin*, *Bava Kamma*, *Bava Metsi'a*, and *Bava Batra*, and, to a lesser extent, on *Yevamot*, *Shevu'ot*, and *Makkot*. Certainly, enough material exists for us to form a clear picture of his achievements in these fields, if his Maimonidean glosses and those on the *Sefer ha-Ma'or* (not to speak of the numerous citations by other medieval scholars) are integrated, as they should be, with the above material.

Other than the *Ḥibbur Lulav*, the *Derashah 'al Rosh ha-Shanah*, and several important fragments in the *Temim De'im*, we have for *Seder Mo'ed* only other people's reports of Ravad's doctrines. This, however, does not preclude a serious appreciation of his accomplishments. His commentaries on *Berakhot* and *'Eruvin* influenced all subsequent literature, and Rashba, Me'iri, and R. Me'ir of Narbonne (Ba'al ha-Me'orot) cite them extensively. Ravad's work on *Mo'ed Katan* can be reconstructed in startling detail from the *Sefer ha-Mikhtam*, Ramban's *Torat ha-Adam*, and the *Hilkhot Semaḥot* of R. Me'ir of Rothenburg. And a similar process in many other tractates would yield equivalent results.

Not that this reclamation poses no problems. Reports sometimes vary, and there is a tendency in law to give point and clarity to doctrines that did not originally possess them. But these difficulties are—with proper methodological care—superable, especially if one is attuned to the differences between the climate of halakhic opinion of twelfth-century Provence and that of later ages. By a careful study of the literature of the thirteenth and fourteenth centuries of Provençal, Spanish, and even German origin, the bulk of Ravad's commentarial oeuvre can be reconstructed.

How is this material to be evaluated; how is Ravad to be assessed? Very simply. Achievement is the difference between what a man finds and what he leaves. Ravad's works must, then, be placed over and against those of his Provençal predecessors—R. Avraham of Narbonne and R. Yehudah of Barcelona—and the results compared.[23] R. Yehudah is generally classified as a Spanish scholar and is distinguished by his absence in most Provençal studies. No doubt there is a great deal of Spain in his work, but till the thirteenth century Barcelona faced north. Both culturally and politically it was more linked to France than to Spain. Much of Provençal history in the twelfth century is the struggle between the counts of Toulouse and Barcelona for hegemony of Languedoc. Barcelona dated its documents by the reigns of the kings of France and acknowledged them fealty. The language of Catalonia was then closer to Provençal than to Spanish. Its poetry is troubadour, like that of Provence, rather than epic as in Spain. Nothing was more natural than for R. Avraham of Narbonne to have studied in Barcelona, or for Ravad to have included that city in his Provençal itinerary. The Pyrenees, like the English Channel, was a geographical obstacle not a national boundary, and it should come as no surprise if Barcelona halakhically was then part of Provence.[24]

[23] Ideally one would like to compare Ravad with R. Mosheh b. Yosef (Rambi), but unfortunately too little of his work has survived to make the comparison meaningful. Professor Ya'akov Sussman has queried whether there is not a still-undetected Provençal commentarial tradition which underlies much of the more prominent writings of the twelfth century. I would be the first to endorse the quest for such a substratum. But if its uncovering is, as I suspect, as difficult as that of eleventh-century Ashkenaz (see my 'Can Halakhic Texts Talk History?', *AJS Review*, 3 [1978], 185 {repr. in *Collected Essays*, i (Oxford, 2013), p. 210}), it would be best to leave it for a later phase of investigation and begin with the clearly defined *Sefer ha-'Ittim* and the *Eshkol*. This Provençal tradition (if it existed) was common to both Ravad and his predecessors and consequently the contrast between these writers remains illuminating. (The phrase 'undetected Provençal tradition' does not intend to imply those places where someone wrote *ve-anu mefarshim* [and we interpret] and the like—such a narrow conception would not carry us very far. It comprehends primarily an exegetical substratum implicit in Provençal practices and forming the underpinning of the edifices of Ravad and his contemporaries.)

[24] This was already noted by B. Z. Benedikt, 'Entsiklopedyah le-Toledot Gedolei Yisra'el', *Kiryat*

The measure of Ravad's accomplishments can be taken only by a penetrating comparison of his work on *'Eruvin* with the parallel sections in the *Sefer ha-'Ittim* and the *Sefer ha-Eshkol.* In the same spirit the *Ḥibbur Lulav*, the *Ba'alei ha-Nefesh*, and the last two chapters of his commentary on *'Avodah Zarah*, to give just a few examples, should be contrasted with the treatment of these problems by his father-in-law, R. Avraham of Narbonne. A bibliographical essay that determines, on the basis of testimonia and manuscripts, those doctrines belonging to Ravad and those authored by R. Avraham of Narbonne is, then, a major desideratum.[25] These two writers tended to be interchanged in rabbinic literature because of the similarity of their acronyms (ר"א אבד and ראב"ד). As the essence of Ravad's accomplishment lies precisely in the increment that accrued to the halakhah between ר"א אבד and ראב"ד, this confusion of names greatly hinders any historical assessment of the rabbi from Posquières. Great rigor must characterize our analysis of the understanding of the *sugya* and of the tractate that Ravad *found* and of the understanding that he *bequeathed* to his successors, for what is at stake in this 'before and after' study of the state of halakhic thinking in Provence may be no less than the intellectual birth of Europe, or of southern Europe at the least.

In order to separate Ravad's distinctive accomplishment from the general advance made by halakhic thought in the latter half of the twelfth century, the appropriate sections of his writings should be placed alongside those of his contemporary—R. Yitsḥak ben Abba Mari of Marseille. Only against the background of the *'Ittim* and the *Eshkol*, on the one hand, and the *'Ittur*, on the other, can the particular attainments of Ravad be discerned. And comparison with R. Zeraḥyah ha-Levi of Lunel (Razah or Ba'al ha-Ma'or) and his commentarial achievements becomes ever more insistent. So preoccupied have halakhists been (from the very outset) with Razah the critic that Razah the exegete went unnoticed. While his work is indeed a strident critique of Fez, he also poured into those glosses (in true Provençal style) the work of a lifetime in Talmudics.[26] And the bulk of *Sefer ha-Ma'or* consists of discussions

Sefer, 24/1 (1947), 8, and again in id., 'Al Sefer ha-Tashlum le-Hilkhot ha-Rif al Rabbenu Efrayim', *Kiryat Sefer*, 26 (1950), 325 n. 18 {repr. in id., *Merkaz ha-Torah be-Provence*: *Asufat Ma'amarim* (Jerusalem, 1985), 222–42}. See A. Castro, *The Structure of Spanish History* (Princeton, 1954), 103, 324.

[25] Y. Ḥ Kafiḥ's editions, *Teshuvot u-Fesakim shel R. Avraham b. R. David, Ravad* (Jerusalem, 1964) and *Teshuvot u-Fesakim shel R. Avraham b. R. Yitsḥak, Ravi* (Jerusalem, 1962), while useful, are inadequate and do not meet our need.

[26] The Venetian printers who, in 1552, appended Razah's notes to Alfasi occasioned no misconceptions. Razah is indeed a critic of Alfasi, and most citations of his doctrines in medieval literature are drawn from the *Sefer ha-Ma'or*.

of *sugyot* unrelated to anything contained in Alfasi.[27] Razah, no less than Ravad, worked independently of the Geonim. Only, unlike Ravad, in cutting the Babylonian anchor he relied heavily on northern French tools. What is the measure of their respective accomplishments and what is the role of each in the emerging European exegesis?[28] Is one root of their bitter animosity the common purpose that these two men shared?

Ravad's impact should be measured in three ways. The first is his influence upon Provençal thought; and here the literature of the thirteenth century, the *Sefer ha-Me'orot*, the *Sefer ha-Mikhtam*, and the works of Me'iri, for example, provide the framework for study. Yet another source exists—the so-called *Ḥiddushei ha-Ritva 'al Bava Metsi'a*; a Narbonnese pupil of R. Shelomoh of Montpellier is the real author of that work.[29] We thus possess for *Bava Metsi'a* both a rich commentary of Ravad and a subsequent Provençal work relatively free of Spanish influence, and the relationship between the two works should prove revelatory. On the other hand, Ravad's startling absence from the writings of R. Yonatan of Lunel[30] and R. Avraham of Montpellier, and his absence, at times, in R. Meshullam of Lunel (Ba'al Sefer ha-Hashlamah) in places where we would most expect him, may be simply a matter of delayed diffusion or may betoken a more basic cleavage in Provençal thought. And again the relative roles of Ravad and Razah in the exegetical perception of thirteenth-century Provence must be evaluated.

The second area of impact was the most important. It was through his influence on the school of Ramban (*Bet Midrasho shel ha-Ramban*) that Ravad shaped the halakhah for close to a millennium. A study should be made of Ramban, Rashba, and their disciples to determine to what extent their grasp of a tractate was influenced by Ravad's writings. It is, I suspect, the workings of the tosafist dialectic upon the commentarial base of Rashi, Ravad, and

27 Israel Ta-Shma has brought home forcefully the full extent of R. Zeraḥyah's non-Alfasi-oriented notes in his 'Rabbenu Zeraḥyah ha-Levi Ba'al ha-Ma'or u-Venei Ḥugo: le-Toledot ha-Sifrut ha-Rabbanit be-Provence' (Ph.D. diss., Bar-Ilan University, 1974), {published as *Rabbenu Zeraḥyah ha-Levi, Ba'al ha-Ma'or u-Venei Ḥugo: le-Toledot ha-Sifrut ha-Rabbanit be-Provence* (Jerusalem, 1992).}

28 Assessment of R. Zeraḥyah's attainments is complicated by the fact that he assimilated the works of others. His writings contain, in unidentified form, for example doctrines of R. Mosheh b. Yosef (Rambi) and R. Efrayim, as Ravad and Nahmanides already noted. This is a serious but not insuperable obstacle in the path of evaluation.

29 *Bet ha-Beḥirah—Bava Metsi'a*, ed. K. Schlesinger (Jerusalem, 1969), introduction, pp. viii–xi; *Ḥiddushei ha-Ritva ha-Ḥadashim 'al Bava Metsi'a*, ed. S. A. Halpern (London, 1962), introduction, p. 9.

30 See e.g. R. Yonatan's *Commentary on Bava Kamma*, ed. S. Friedman (Jerusalem, 1969), and introduction, pp. 41–3.

R. Ḥanan'el that is in many places the tale told by Spain. If true, all this requires far more detailed and rigorous formulation. It may prove crucial to contrast, for example, the writings of Rashba on *Shabbat* with his work on *'Eruvin*. Any reconstruction of Ravad's writings will quickly show that there were areas of greater and lesser accomplishments. Though he was almost unexcelled in talent and moved easily in areas where others had feared to tread, Ravad's final output was uneven. He started *ab novo*, for he lacked or declined to employ an exegetical tradition, and he never approached the commentarial enterprise with anything resembling Rashi's quiet, but at the same time awesome, singlemindedness. He may well have written commentaries on most of the Talmud, but they were of unequal density. The one on *Bava Kamma*, for example, is thin on substance (and this is probably what led historians to downplay his exegetical activity). *Berakhot*, *'Eruvin*, and *Mo'ed Katan* were areas where he labored mightily; *Shabbat*, *Pesaḥim*, and *Megillah* —areas where he produced relatively little work. Is the absence of a Ravad stratum in *Shabbat* noticeable in the works of the school of Ramban? If yes, how so, and what is its significance? And if this absence proves unimportant, does this not call into question our entire contention of the centrality of Ravad's commentarial enterprise for Ramban and his disciples?

Finally, there is Ravad's impact on codification. This really breaks down to the three or four areas where he composed commentary-codes. In these fields—*Lulav*, *Niddah*, *Mikva'ot*, for example—his influence was enormous, indeed possibly controlling, but his role in halakhah is not determined by it. His impact here is neither (if one be permitted the terms) *Shas*-wide nor *seder*-wide, often not even tractate-wide; it is topical and local, even if massive and all-pervasive.

Only by charting where halakhic thought stood when Ravad began, where it stood upon his death, and what his successors did with his legacy will any clear picture of his role in the history of the halakhah emerge. It should be evident from the above that I have, as Frost once put it, 'a lover's quarrel' with much of halakhic historiography, believing as I do that the most fruitful approach at present is the thematic study rather than the biographical one. Legal literature is couched in the idiom of the inevitable. No jurist, certainly no religious jurist, dreams of interpreting the law according to his personal inclination; he seeks simply to discover what the sources say on the matter. And if he is of any stature, his words will read as a series of objective and ineluctable conclusions. Only by comparing his solution with those of others does its subjectivity become apparent. Law leans towards continuity and has an antipathy to radical change; thus, the revolutionary jurist must disguise his innovations—at times even from himself. Only by aligning a man's interpretation with those of his predecessors can its innovative character be discerned, and only by studying its impact upon his successors can its significance be evaluated. The subjective, the revolutionary, the historic in law reveals itself only to a thematic treatment. An approach which surveys the works of a thinker without placing the opinions there articulated in a historical continuum finds itself inevitably at a loss when called upon to assess the man and his contribution. Only after a number of thematic studies are completed, and we then possess both a rough chart of legal developments and some intimations of the roles played by pivotal figures, will biography, to my thinking, become a fully productive genre of halakhic historiography. But, as I have indicated, mine is a minority opinion.

Charting Ravad's accomplishments in terms of predecessors and successors is to see the man from the perspective of the immanent evolution of the discipline, to study what forces in halakhic thought came to the fore in his personality and how he transformed his heritage. But R. Avraham of Posquières was not just a significant point on the curve of halakhic development; he was an inhabitant of twelfth-century Provence. The contemporary moment in Ravad's works must equally be apprehended for any full appreciation of the man, and this moment is to be found less in his commentaries, which we have hitherto concentrated on, than in his other writings—above all his responsa.

And what a wealth of material and perspectives awaits us there! As this aspect has been generally neglected, I would like to breach the format of this programmatic essay and conclude it with three brief examples of how Ravad's writings are anchored in Provençal life and thought. In a previous essay I noted in passing that placing R. Avraham's writings in the context of general (i.e. Gentile) Provençal law, specifically within the period of the penetration of Roman law, allows us to give some rough date to several of his works. The *Commentary on the Sifra* was written during the second third of the twelfth century, when Roman legal terminology had begun to penetrate the *Septimanie*. The *Commentary on Bava Metsi'a* shows itself to be a later work, written sometime in the last third of the century, when Roman law began to affect day-to-day practice in Posquières. Similarly, inspection of Ravad's writings on the topic of surety (*'arev*) shows him to be employing terminology of Roman law when seeking to articulate anew the concept of accessorial security, after certain halakhic developments had rendered the standard Aramaic expressions meaningless.[31]

More significant than these sundry borrowings, these occasional aids in solution, are the thoughts which living in an alien world engendered. Much of medieval writing is a response to just such stimuli. Section 50 of the *Temim De'im* provides a good example. The inquiry put to R. Avraham as to whether a debtor can be compelled to redeem a gage did not arise in a vacuum. In Germanic law a pawn is a quit-payment, with no further obligation incumbent upon the debtor. In gaging, the debtor sold the pawn to the creditor in exchange for the money received, reserving to himself only the right of repurchase, a right that he might or might not excercise. It is difficult, however, to run separate businesses—one for Jews and one for Gentiles. Business is business, and habits are habits. The daily practice of treating one set of gages as a sale with the right of repurchase inevitably led to someone questioning whether the other set was so radically different. And the question, once asked, as asked it was all over Europe—Spain, Provence, Germany[32]—admitted no simple answer. True, Jewish law, at first glance, is incurably obligational. Pawns are never *Sachhaftung*, but simply accessorial to the ongoing personal obligation. But by holding the pawn, the creditor holds in his hands the means of payment. Why should he not be told to look there for satisfaction? Does he have the right to reject the pawn and insist on another form of payment, that is, cash? Put concisely in halakhic terms, a pledge is certainly an *apotiké*; is it an *apotiké meforash*? And if it is an *apotiké meforash* (as the *'Ittur* tells us the sages of Narbonne thought),[33] just how does a formula of *lo yehe lekha pera'on ela mi-zeh* ('you may only collect from this [piece of property]') give rise to a personal obligation? To use for a moment northern French terminology, is there a *shi'abud ha-guf* (personal obligation) in an *apotiké meforash*, and if there be only a *shi'abud nekhasim* (a lien on property which subjects it to collection without any obligation on the part of the debtor to repay the loan), isn't that *Sachhaftung*?[34] Is the Jewish gage, after a closer look, really so different from the Germanic one?

[31] H. Soloveitchik, ''Arev be-Ribbit', *Zion*, 37 (1972), 13–14 nn. 46, 47; and id., 'A Note on the Penetration of Roman Law in Provence', *Tijdschrift voor Rechtsgeschiedenis*, 40 (1972), 227–9.

[32] 'Potiké', in *'Ittur*, ed. R. M. Yonah (repr. New York, 1955), fo. 64, col. 2; *Sifran Shel Rishonim*, ed. S. Assaf (Jerusalem, 1935), #5; *Temim De'im* (above, n. 15), #50; *Sefer Ravan*, ed. S. Albeck (Warsaw, 1905), #111.

[33] 'Potiké', in *'Ittur* (above, n. 32), fo. 64, col. 2. {*Apotiké* is a mortgage, liened real estate. Under certain circumstances, this restricts the creditor from collecting from any other liened real estate. *Apotiké meforash* is a mortgage explicitly restricted to a specific piece of property.}

[34] See Aryeh Leib ha-Kohen, *Ketsot ha-Ḥoshen* (New York, 2014), 386: 5.

Ravad threw up his hands at the problem and decided to let the Gentiles solve de facto the riddle of their own making. He replied: ובמשכונא של קרקע, במקום שאין מנהג לישראל הולכין אחר מנהג של גויים, והם נהגו וכו. ('And as regards mortgages: in those places where there is no distinct Jewish custom, one follows the customaries [*coutumiers*] of the Gentiles, and their practice is etc.') The reply is revealing, especially his concluding remark: וכן אני אומר בכל דבר שאין דינו מפורש אצלנו ואין לנו בו מנהג ידוע, שהולכים בו אחר המנהגות שלהם, וקרוב דבר זה לדינא דמלכותא והם דנים על פי מנהגות ('and I [further] say that in all [monetary] matters in which we have neither a clear halakhic ruling nor a customary practice, we should follow their [i.e. the Gentiles'] customaries, and this is analogous to [the talmudic ruling that] "The law of the kingdom is the law [i.e. it binds Jews]", and they [i.e. the Gentiles] rule according to what is found in their customaries')—all of which would be inconceivable north of the Loire, and which accurately reflects the relative merits of the Provençal and Champagne systems of justice at the time. Ravad's remarks here should be correlated with his views on solidarity of sureties in the *Hassagot 'Hilkhot Malveh ve-Loveh'*, 25: 10. Both opinions reflect the rather favorable assessment of the Provençal exile that he gave expression to when he commented on the words of the *Sifra*:

> וישבתם לבטח בארצכם [ויקרא כו ה]: בארצכם אתם ישובים לבטח ולא בחוץ לארץ.
> פי[רוש:] הגרים החוצה לארץ אינם בכלל ברכה

'and ye shall dwell in your land safely' [Lev. 26: 5]: in your land you shall dwell safely but not in other lands [*ḥuts la-arets*]. Explanation: those who live in *ḥutsah la-arets* are not included in the Divine blessing [of safety; i.e. those who live outside Israel have no Divine promise of security, though they may well in fact enjoy it].[35]

The initial query (regarding redemption of gages) should furthermore be placed alongside the suit between Aimery de Clermont and the Abbot of Aniane in the year 1203, which Eduard Meynial has noted:

> However, at the beginning of the thirteenth century the cartulary of Aniane provides us with a very interesting example of this 'romanization' [i.e. penetration of Roman law]. Aimery, creditor of the abbot, claims the right to demand of the abbot to repurchase the pawn that he has gaged to him. The abbot declines to repurchase. If one treats a pledge as a sale with right of repurchase [as in Germanic law] . . . the abbot is correct, for the repurchase is a right which the vendor need not exercise. If, however, the pawn is subjected to Roman rules, the abbot is wrong, for repurchasing the pledge is simply repaying the debt; the existence of the pledge, since it did not extinguish the

35 Ravad's commentary on the *Sifra*, published as *Sifra de-Vei Rav: Hu Torat Kohanim 'im Perush R. Avraham ben David* (Vienna, 1862), 'Behar', 4: 4.

debt, does not deprive the creditor of the right to insist on payment when the contracted time is up.[36]

Moving from the opposite directions, halakhah and Provençal law met here in a point of common perplexity. In Ravad's case it is the encounter of an obligational system of gage with the notions of *Sachhaftung*; in the suit of Aniane it is the movement of a system (the Germanic one) rooted in *Sachhaftung* towards the concept of *obligatio*.

Material problems no less than contemporary concepts elicited response from Ravad, and I would like to end with a brief study of the practical import of one of his better-known Maimonidean notes. In his *hassagah* on 'Hilkhot Mekhirah', 6: 12, Ravad explains Shemu'el's famous ruling **המוכר שטר חוב לחבירו וחזר ומחלו, מחול** ('If someone sells to another a note of indebtedness and subsequently waives it, the debt is waived') after this fashion: **מפני שהלוה אומר ללוקח אני לא שיעבדתי לך את עצמי לפיכך אם כתב לו שטר חובו הריני משועבד לך ולכל הבאים מכוחך אינו יכול למחול במשכר שטר חובו.** ('Because the debtor can say to the purchaser [of the debt], "I never indebted myself to you". For this reason if the debtor wrote in the note of indebtedness ["I am indebted] to you and to all who are empowered by you", the creditor cannot annul the debt after he has sold the debt.')

These are some of the most seminal words ever penned on the nature of obligation and, together with those of Rabbenu Tam,[37] they have given birth to an entire literature. But the *lefikhakh* ('therefore') suggests a practical purpose to his remarks, and this finds corroboration in the fact that Ravad saw fit to reiterate this proviso on no fewer than four other occasions.[38] Clearly Ravad's doctrine must be studied not only from the perspective of the development of halakhic thought, but also in the context of twelfth-century Provence. It should be linked with another ruling of his, reported in *Sefer ha-Terumot*:

> **נשאל הראב"ד ז"ל: המוכר שטר לחבירו, ויש משכון ביד המלוה ומסרו ביד הלוקח אם יכול המוכר שהוא המלוה למוחלו (ללוקח) [ללוה] אם לאו? והשיב שאינו יכול למחול מאחר שהמשכון מוחזק ביד הלוקח. והביא ראיה ממה שכתב הרי"ף בכתובות משום דמתנת שכיב מרע עשאוה כמתנה דאורייתא דכמאן דמטיא ליד המקבל דמי, ולפיכך אין היורש מוחלה. מדקאמר [הרי"ף] 'דמטיא לידיה דמקבל דמי', שמע מיניה אם יש משכון ביד המלוה ומסרו ללוקח, שאינו יכול למוחלו. ע"כ**

[36] E. Meynial, 'De l'application du droit romain dans la région de Montpellier au XIIe et XIIIe siècles', *Atti del Congresso Internazionale di Scienze Storiche (Roma, 1–9 Aprile 1903)*, ix: *Storia del dritto* (Rome, 1904), 147–69.

[37] *Piskei ha-Rosh*, *Ketubbot* 9: 10.

[38] References in *Bet ha-Beḥirah*, *Bava Metsi'a*, ed. K. Schlesinger (Jerusalem, 1959), 67 nn. 475, 477, and the *Ḥiddushei ha-Rashba le-Rabbenu Shelomoh Aderet*, *Gittin*, ed. Y. Sklar (Jerusalem, 1986), s.v. *ve-katav ha-Ravad*.

Ravad was asked, if someone sold a debt to another person and the creditor passed on the debtor's pawn to the purchaser, can the original creditor waive the debt? And he [i.e. Ravad] replied: 'He cannot waive the debt since the purchaser has now the pawn.' And he [i.e. Ravad] cited a proof from what R. Alfas said about gifts made in contemplation of death, that such oral gifts were as valid as one made in consonance with the laws of the Torah, for such a gift is seen as 'having come into the hands of the receiver [of the gift]'. One may infer from this [Ravad contends] that if the original creditor passed on the pawn to the purchaser, he cannot waive the debt.[39]

I, for one, am at a loss to understand how the case discussed by Alfasi has any bearing upon the question at hand. If Ravad, however, says that it is relevant, I defer to his judgment, but I remain no less perplexed. Assuming that one can indeed make deductions about the problem under discussion from R. Yitsḥak of Fez's language about gifts made in contemplation of death, what weight should this inference carry with someone who penned massive criticisms of Alfasi? If Ravad had intuitively felt that renunciation could take place with gaged debts, nothing that Alfasi might have said, even explicitly, would have swayed him. Clearly Ravad was not deducing anything from R. Yitsḥak's remarks, as he contended. But, having arrived intuitively at a doctrine of non-renunciation, and lacking any proof for his position, he seized upon a formulation of Alfasi as precedent and *asmakhta* (support).

Behind these two rulings stands the problem of credit circulation. In a society where trade has achieved some vigor, one standard form of payment is the transfer of notes of indebtedness. We do it daily when we endorse checks, which are simply notes of indebtedness. When the payee endorses it, he transfers it to another in exchange for something received. Notes of indebtedness were hardly as common in twelfth-century Provence as in our day, but then neither was money. There was a dearth of currency at the time in Provence,[40] and a double burden was thus thrust upon notes of indebtedness (*shitrei ḥov*). They became a basic vehicle of exchange. Shemu'el's ruling that the debt may be renounced by the original creditor even after he has sold it to another mortally impedes the free movement of credit. If a debt, once sold, can yet be

[39] *Sefer ha-Terumot*, Giddulei Terumah edn. (Venice, 1643), 51: 6: 3.

[40] J. de Malafosse, 'Contribution à l'étude du crédit dans le Midi au Xe et XIe siècles: les sûretés réelles', *Annales du Midi*, 63 (1951), 105–48. It is this state of affairs that R. Mosheh b. Todros refers to when he writes (*Sifran Shel Rishonim* [above, n. 32], #33, p. 36; {*Sefer ha-Terumot* (above, n. 39), fo. 237a}): שהעולם דחוק וחסר, וכל העם נמנעין מלהלוות אלו את אלו. שאין הפרוטה מצויה להלוות איש את אחיו ולא להטיל מלאי להתעסק בו ('For the world [i.e. general society] is hard-pressed and lacking in means, and most people refrain from lending to each other for there is a dearth of coinage [which prevents] both extending credit to one another and investing in a silent partnership.') {See below, pp. 342–5.}

renounced by the original creditor, no one will accept a transferred note of indebtedness, or if they do, it will be only at great discount. The fact that Shemu'el's ruling awakened no surprise in talmudic times[41] and no efforts were made to neutralize it in practice shows that credit circulation played a small role in the talmudic economy.[42] This was hardly the case in the high Middle Ages. The very first formularies of notes of indebtedness that we possess contain clauses to order or to bearer (נכ"ז);[43] that is to say, they anticipate the need for the sale of such notes and attempt to allow for it. Ravad's remarks in the *Hassagot* are an attempt to validate these clauses; his responsum in *Sefer ha-Terumot* seeks to preclude renunciation even in notes lacking such clauses. Both rulings seek to open the arteries of credit blocked by Shemu'el's ruling. The two dicta כמאן דמטיא ליד המקבל דמי ('as if it came into the hands of the [receiver of the gift]') and לא לך שיעבדתי את עצמי ('I have not indebted myself to you'), though poles apart conceptually, are a two-pronged attempt to wrestle with the problems that presented themselves as Jews moved from an agricultural to a credit economy.

Ravad's neutralization of Shemu'el's ruling went yet further: it transformed the note of indebtedness from a personal document into a monetary instrument. If such a note can be used to collect from the original parties only, it is of personal but not economic significance. A possessed money before, B did not. After the loan, B possesses money, A has a piece of paper. Money has changed hands but no more of it is in circulation. If, however, A can transfer this note and proceed to purchase things with it—in other words, if A retains his buying power at the same time that B has acquired it—every loan with a note of indebtedness then doubles in effect the volume of currency in circulation. Ravad's famous doctrine of לא לך שיעבדתי את עצמי ('I have not indebted myself to you'), with all its conceptual significance, was at the same time an attempt to validate the coin minted by a society suffering from a dearth of currency.

If we obey Ranke's instruction of viewing each culture on its own terms and each as worthy of its own history, the works of Ravad will reveal to us the declaration of European independence from geonic thought, the discovery of

[41] As did, for example, the injunction against usufruct from possessory mortgages; *Bava Metsi'a* 67b: *ela be-mai neikhol?*!

[42] Rabbah b. Rav Huna's suggestion (*Ketubbot* 86a) is for novation (to another specific party, naturally) and not for the creation of a negotiable instrument.

[43] A. Gulack, *Otsar ha-Shetarot* (Jerusalem, 1926), 206–7; J. Brissaud, *History of French Private Law* (Boston, 1912), 536–7.

self and of the power to reason so characteristic of the twelfth century, the emergence of distinctive European categories of talmudic discourse, the penetration of Roman law, the encounter between halakhic and Germanic conceptions, and the adjustments in the halakhah as the economy was moving from agriculture to credit. This and much more awaits us in Ravad's writings if we will only free ourselves from our Maimonidean orientation and begin to see Ravad of Posquières as he was—a twelfth-century Talmudist of Provençe.

APPENDIX TO NOTE 17

The following is a random list of some hundred correlations (whole or partial) which come readily to mind. The number could easily be tripled.

הלכות תשובה	פ"ד הל"ג	דרשת הראב"ד לראש השנה (לונדון, תשט"ו) עמ' כ"ח.
הלכות תלמוד תורה	פ"ז ל"ז	ספר המכתם, מועד קטן (ניו יורק, תשי"ט) ט"ז ע"א.
הלכות תפילה	פ"א הל' י'	כתוב שם, ברכות, כ"א ע"א.
	פ"י הל' י"ג	(בפירוש אנשי משמר) כתוב שם, ברכות, ריש פרק קמא.
הלכות ברכות	פ"א הל' י"ס	ספר המאורות, ברכות (ניו יורק, תשכ"ד) מ"ז ע"ב.
	פ"ה הל' ט"ו	כתוב שם, ברכות כ"א ע"א.
	פ"ו הל' ב'	תמים דעים ס' ס"ו, ס"ז.
	פ"ו הל' י"ג	תמים דעים, ס' ס"ו.
	פ"ו הל' ט"ז	תמים דעים, ס' ס"ו.
	פ"ח הל' י"א	כתוב שם, סוף פ"ק דברכות.
הלכות ציצית	פ"א הל' ז'	תמים דעים, ס' ל"ט.
הלכות יום טוב	פ"א הל' י"ז	כתוב שם, ריש פ"ק דביצה.
	פ"ג הל' ח'	כתוב שם, ביצה, ט' ע"א.
	פ"ח הל' ד'	מכתם, ביצה, ו' ע"א; מועד קטן ח' ע"ב.
	פ"ח הל' ח'	מכתם, ביצה, ו' ע"א; מועד קטן ח' ע"א.

הלכות חמץ ומצה	פ״א הל׳ ו׳	כתוב שם, פסחים, מג ע״א.
	פ״א הל׳ ח׳	כתוב שם, פסחים, ז ע״א, כ״ח ע״א.
	פ״ג הל׳ ג׳	כתוב שם, פסחים, י״ג ע״א.
	פ״ה הל׳ כ׳	כתוב שם, פסחים, לו ע״א.
	פ״ו הל׳ ה׳	תמים דעים, ס׳ ז.
	פ״ח הל׳ י״ד	כתוב שם, פסחים קי״ז ע״ב.
הלכות שופר	פ״א הל׳ א׳	דרשת הראב״ד לראש השנה, עמ׳ לג לד.
	פ״א הל׳ ה׳	דרשת הראב״ד, עמ׳ ל״ז מ׳.
	פ״ג הל׳ ד׳	דרשת הראב״ד, עמ׳ מ״ו מ״ח.
	פ״ג הל׳ י״ג	דרשת הראב״ד, עמ׳ מ מ״א.
הלכות לולב	פ״ז הל׳ ב׳	תמים דעים (בתמת ישרים, ונציה, שפ״ב) ס׳ רכ״ח.
	פ״ת הל׳ א׳	תמים דעים (שם) ס׳ רל״ג.
	פ״ה הל׳ ג׳	תמים דעים (שם) ס׳ רכ״ט: פירוש הר אב״ד על בבא קמא (לונדון, ת״ש) צ״ו ע״א.
	פ״ח הל׳ ה׳	תמים דעים (שם) ס׳ רכ״ח. כתוב שם, סוכה, ל״ג ע״א; פירוש על ספרא (ווין, תרכ״ב) אמור, פרק ט״ו ה״ז.
	פ״ח הל׳ ו׳	תמים דעים (שם) ס׳ רכ״ח.
	פ״ח הל׳ ז׳	תמים דעים (שם) ס׳ ר״ל.
	פ״ח הלף ט׳	תמים דעים (שם) ס׳ רכ״ז, רל״ג (רל״ב): כתוב שם, ריש פרק לולב הגזול.
הלכות תענית	פ״א הל׳ ט״ו	ספר ההשלמה, תענית, (גנזי ראש ונים, ירושלים, תשכ״ג), עמ׳ קנט; ספר המאורות (ניז יורק, תשכ״ז) תענית, י׳ ע״ב.
הלכות אישות	פ״ה הל׳ ט״ו	תמים דעים, ס׳ ג׳.
	פט״ז הל׳ כ׳	השגות על הרי״ף, כתובות פ״ז ע״א; כתוב שם, שם.
הלכות איסורי ביאה	פ״ה הל׳ י״ב	בעלי הנפש, שער הפרישה (דפוס ירושלים, תשט״ו, עמ׳ י״ט).

	פ"ה הל' י"ג	שער הפרישה (שם, עמ' ט"ו י"ח).
	פ"ט הל' ו'	שער הכתמים (שם, עמ' ע"ד).
	פי"א הל' י"ב	שער הפרישה (שם, עמ' ט"ו י"ח).
הלכות מאכלות אסורות	פ"ט הל' י'	תמים דעים, ס' כ"א (ועיין ס' ז').
	פי"א הל' כ"א	פירוש הראב"ד על עבודה זרה (ניו יורק, תשכ"א) ע"ד ע"ב, ד"ה ושל חרס, וד"ה אמר רבא.
	פי"ב הל' י'	פירוש על ע"ז, ס' ע"א, ד"ה מצדה טהור.
	פט"ו הל' י"ד	כתוב שם, סוף ע"ז: פירוש על ע"ז, ע"ב ע"ב.
	פ' ט"ז הל' זי	כתוב שם, פסחים, כ"ו ע"ב.
הלכות שחיטה	פ"ג הל' ד'	ספר המאורות, חולין (ניו יורק, תשכ"ד) ל"ב ע"ב.
	פ"י הל' ט"ז	חמים דעים, ס' י"א.
	פ' י"א הל' י"ג	תמים דעים, ס' י"ב.
הלכות כלאים	פ"י הל' ב'	פירוש על ספרא, קדושים, פרק ד' ה' י"ח.
הלכות חרומות	פ"ז הל' ח'	כתוב שם, פסחים, מ"ח ע"ב.
הלכוח בכורים	פ"ו הל' י'	תמים דעים, ס' ז'.
הלכות מקוואות	פ"ב הל' י"ז	(דק"ל כלישנא בתרא) בעלי הנפש שער הטבילה (שם,עמ' צ"ז).
	פ"ג הל' י"ב	בעלי הנפש, שער המים (שם, עמ' קכ"ו).
	פ"ט הל' י"א	בעלי הנפש, שער המים (שם עמ' ק"ב, קי"ד, קכ"ה).
	פ' י"א הל' ג'	תמים דעים, ס' ס"ז.
	פ' י"א הל' ז'	(שההלכה כר"י . . . אבל צריך שיהא שם רביעית) תמים דעים, ס' ס"ז (ע"ש היטב).
	פ' י"א הל' ח'	(השגה שנייה) תמים דעים, ס' ס"ז.
הלכות נזקי ממון	פ"ב הל' ט'	כתוב שם, בבא קמא, י"ז ע"ב.
	פ"ב הל' י"ד	פירוש לב"ק, י"ח ע"א: כתוב שם, סוף כיצד הרגל.
	פ"ב הל' י"ח	פירוש לב"ק כ"ג ע"א.
	פ"ב הל' י"ט	פירוש לב"ק, כ"ג ע"ב.

	פ״ג הל׳ ד	פירוש לב״ק, כ׳ ע״א.
	פ״ד הל׳ ב	פירוש לב״ק, נ״ה ע״ב.
	פ״ד הל׳ ו	פירוש לב״ק, ט׳ ע״ב.
	פ״ה הל׳ א	פירוש לב״ק, כ״ג ע״ב.
	פ״ט הל׳ י׳	(רישא) פירוש לב״ק ל״ה ע״ב (בית הבחירה על ב״ק [ירושלים, תשכ״ז] ל״ה ע״א).
	פ״ט הל׳ י׳	(בא״ד ״ואי תימא״) פירוש לב״ק, ס״ב ע״א.
	פ׳ י״ב הל׳ ח׳	פירוש לב״ק, ט׳ ע״ב.
	פ׳ י״ב הל׳ י״ז	פירוש לב״ק, נ״א ע״ב.
הלכות גניבה	פ״א הל׳ ג׳	פירוש לב״ק, ע״ט ע״א.
	פ״ב הל׳ ו׳	פירוש לב״ק, ע״ט ע״א.
	פ״ד הל׳ ב׳	פירוש לב״ק, ק״ז ע״ב.
הלכות גזילה ואבידה	פ״ד הל׳ י״ג	(בס״ד ״מ״מ מכל זה״) השגות על הרי״ף, שבועות, ריש פרק כל הנשבעים.
	פ׳ י״ג הל׳ כ׳	השגות על הרי״ף, גיטין, נ״ב ע״ב.
	פ״ד הל׳ כ״ב	(שתי ההשגות) פירוש לב״ק, כ״ז ע״א.
	פ״ז הל׳ ז׳	פירוש לב״ק, כ״ו ע״א.
	פ״ז הל׳ י״ט	פירוש לב״ק, ס״ב ע״א.
	פ״ח הל׳ ד׳	השגות על הריף, בבא קמא, קי״ז ע״א: פירוש לב״ק, קונטרס כענין ישראל שאנסוהו (עמ׳ שנ״ג ואילך).
הלכות מכירה	פ״ג הל׳ י״ב	כתוב שם, ב״ק, י״ב ע״א.
	פ״ו הל׳ י״ב	(בא״ד ״לפיכך״) תמים דעים, ס׳ ס״ה.
	פ״ט הל׳ א	(״ואם רצה ממשכך״) שיטה מקובצת, בבא מציעא, נ״ז ע״ב בשם הראב״ד.
הלכות זכייה ומתנה	פ״ו הל׳ י״ז	השגות על הרי״ף, כתובות, ק״ב ע״ב.
	פ״ט הל׳ ז׳	השגות על הרי״ף, ב״ב, קמט ע״ב.
	פ׳ י״ב הל׳ ו׳	שיטה מקובצה, ב״ב, קכט ע״ב בשם הראב״ד.
הלכות שלוחין ושותפין	פ״ג הל׳ ה׳	תמים דעים, ס׳ ס״ב (בס״ד).

	פ״ג הל׳ ז׳	(בין לפירוש הב״י והגר״א, בין לפירוש הדרישה והש״ך) תמים דעים, ס׳ ס״א.
	פ״ג הל׳ י״א	תמים דעים, ס׳ ס״ב.
הלכות עבדים	פ״א הל׳ ח׳	שיטה מקובצת, בבא מציעא, ע״ג ע״ב.
	פ״ז הל׳ ח׳	השגות על הרי״ף, גיטין, מ׳ ע״א.
	פ״ח הל׳ ט״ו	(בין לכ״מ בין ללח״מ) השגות על הרי״ף, גיטין, ל״ז ע״נ.
הלכות שכירות	פ״ב הל׳ ז׳	(״ורבותי הורו״) פירוש לב״ק, קו ע״ב. (״ועוד ודאי שלר״) שיטה מקובצת, ב״מ, צ״ז ע״ב.
	פ״נ הל׳ י״ב	כתוב שם, שבועות, מ״ו ע״ב.
	פ״י הל׳ א׳	השגות על הרי״ף, שבועות, סוף פרק שבועת הדיינים; כתוב שם, שבועות שם; פירוש לב״ק, מ״ט ע״א.
הלכות שאלה ופקדון	פ״ה הל׳ ו׳	פירוש לב״ק, ס״ב ע״א.
	פ״ה הל׳ ז׳	(רישא) פירוש לב״ק, ס״ב ע״א.
הלכות מלוה ולוה	פ׳ י״ג הל׳ ד׳	פירוש לב״ק, ס״ב ע״א.
	פ׳ י״ד הל׳ ג׳	א״א אורבך, מתשובותיהם של תכמי פרובנס, מזכרת לזכר מרן הרב יצחק אייזיק הלוי הרצוג. (ירושלים, תשכ״ב), עמ׳ 405.
	פ׳ ט״ו הל׳ א׳	השגות על הרי״ף, שבועות, ריש פרק שבועות הדיינים.
	פ׳ ט״ו הל׳ ז׳	השגות על הרי״ף, כתובות, פ״ז ע״א; כתוב שם, שם.
	פ׳ י״ח הל׳ ד׳	השגות על הרי״ף, גיטין, מ״א ע״א.
	פ׳ כ״א הל׳ ג׳	כתוב שם, בבא מציעא, ט״ו ע״א ד״ה עוד כתב.
	פ׳ כ״א הל׳ ד׳	שיטה מקובצת, בבא מציעא, ק״י ע״ב.
הלכות טוען ונטען	פ״א הל׳ ז׳	השגות על הרי״ף, גיטין, נ״ב ע״ב. השגות על הרי״ף, שבועות, מ״ב ע״ב.
	פ״א הל׳ ח׳	(בא״ד ״ולאו דחייה״) פירוש לב״ק, ל״ה ע״ב.
	פ״ב הל׳ ה׳	השגות על הרי״ף, כתובות, פ״ו ע״א; כתוב שם, שבועות, סוף כל הנשבעין.

	פ"ה הל' ב'	שיטה מקובצת, ב"מ, ה' ע"א.
	פ"ט הל' ה'	השגות על ה ריף, שבועות, מ"ו ע"ב.
הלכוח נחלות	פ' י"א הל' ז'	(בא"ד "ואם חב") השגות על הרי"ף, גיטין, נ"ב ע"א.
	פ' י"א הל' ח'	השגות על הרי"ף, גיטין, מ' ע"ב.
הלכות סנהדרין	פ' כ"ו הל' ג'	השגות על הרי"ף, שבועות, סוף פרק שבועת הערות.
הלכות עדות	פ' י"ב הל' ב'	השגות על הרי"ף, מכות, סוף פרק קמא.
הלכות אבל	פ"ו הל' י"ז	מכתם, מו"ק, כ"ב ע"א.

AFTERWORD

I can best give sense of the purpose and nature of this essay by describing its genesis. In mid-December 1973 I developed an infection of the inner ear, which lasted for some three and a half months. This can be a nasty business, with dizziness and nausea for weeks. I was lucky; if I lay perfectly flat on my back, I suffered nothing. As there is just so much time that one can gaze at the ceiling, I began to mull over and piece together my impressions of Ravad of Posquières that had accumulated over some two decades of Talmud study and which, I knew, differed greatly from the reigning view both of talmudic scholars and of academicians. The impression of Ravad that I had received from the writings of the school of Nahmanides was not that of a great critic of Maimonides; indeed, his critiques of Maimonides scarcely figured in their works.

I lay on my back and passed before my mind's eye the *Ḥiddushei ha-Ramban* or those of the Rashba or Ritva on a particular tractate, trying to recall where Ravad was cited in these works and whether that doctrine was found in Ravad's *Hassagot* on *Mishneh Torah*. Then, reversing the procedure, I tried to recall and test whether the *Hassagot* of Ravad that originated in this tractate were to be found in these novellae. So I proceeded from tractate to tractate. There were tractates with which I was fully conversant and tractates in which my acquaintance was restricted to specific chapters. My choice of which novellae or set of novellae to use in any specific tractate depended on the degree of my familiarity with them—it could be those of the Rashba on one tractate, those of the Ritva on another. The editions of these works that were then available were I. Z. Meltzer's edition of the *Ḥiddushei ha-Ramban*, the Tet-Vav Shitot edition of the *Ḥiddushei ha-Rashba*, and the Kur le-Zahav edition of the *Ḥiddushei ha-Ritva*. To claim that the editorial work in the volumes of the Talmudists of Ramban's school was, shall we say, 'sparse' would be an understatement. The *Ḥiddushei ha-Rashba* on *Bava Kamma* did not even provide the pages (*dappim*) of passages in the Talmud cited by Rashba. If Rashba wrote 'as is said in the chapter *Ha-'Or ve-ha-Rotev*', you had to sit and turn the pages of the chapter in tractate *Ḥullin* until you chanced upon the passage to which he was referring.

When I felt well enough to get around the house, I sat down at my desk and wrote up the product of my protracted ruminations, and then added, almost as an afterthought, the footnotes. I don't believe I spent more than two to three weeks documenting the essay. This study was impressionistic in the simplest sense of the word. It reflected the image of Ravad that had emerged, not from any research, but from fusing a number of half-conscious assessments made over the course of some twenty years of study. If my readers found a persuasive correspondence between my portrayal and the picture of Ravad that had evolved from their study of the Ramban's school, the footnotes were superfluous; if they found differently, lengthy footnotes would not have helped, for I would be documenting what they knew to be false. For they, no less than I, had for decades studied the same sources and had formed their own impression of Ravad, which would be contradicting mine.

Understandable as this manner of going about things may be, it can be an invitation to serious error, and made all the more open to revision by the outpouring, over the past thirty-five years, of new editions of the writings of the school of Nahmanides. These works are the staple of talmudic study in yeshivot the world over. Sales are guaranteed as year in, year out, every entering cohort purchases these necessary tools. And the editions are of high quality. The introductions list the names and places of the authorities cited in the work. The notes on the citation in the body of the text are full and usually provide a reliable guide to the history of this doctrine in the medieval halakhic literature of western Europe. The information provided about the antecedent views of the Geonim is generally less comprehensive; nevertheless, the material cited usually supplies sufficient points of departure for arriving at the full range of the available sources. The doctrines of Ravad, found so richly in the writings of Ramban and his disciples, have been fully contextualized and open to historical evaluation. To my thinking, it is from these works that the major criticism of the essay should be launched.

There are thirty-six references to Ravad in the *Ḥiddushei ha-Rashba* on *Shabbat*. You can be sure that I did not remember all of them. I doubt that I remembered half of them. The crucial question is: is my overall impression of Ravad's role and impact confirmed by the new editions or not? Unfortunately almost no historical work has been done on Ravad since I published the essay in 1980, until very recently.

A few years ago, Dr S. Yahalom published a major work, *Bein Gironah le-Narbonnah: Avnei Binyan li-Yetsirat ha-Ramban* (Jerusalem, 2013), on the influence of Provençal scholars upon the thought of Ramban.[44] It was deeply researched and has proven to be a major resource for scholars. Beside probing and tracking Provençal influences, Dr Yahalom also sought to sort out the old but painful problem of distinguishing between ר"א אבד and ראב"ד, the first the acronym of Ravad of Posquières's father-in-law, R. Avraham, Av Bet Din of Narbonne, the latter that of Ravad himself. All available manuscripts were tracked down and used with precision, and for the first time we have a solid basis for assessing the work of these two scholars.[45] The book is a major accomplishment.

I would simply like to correct three misstatements or misconceptions that appear in that work, errors that affect the correctness of my writings but in no way weaken the book's central argument or diminish its many merits. Yahalom states that I wrote that Ravad's *Commentary on Bava Metsi'a* is a thin work, and then proceeds to disprove this. I wrote that Ravad's *Commentary on Bava Kamma* was thin of substance, and that his *Commentary on Bava Metsi'a* is one of his richest works. Second, Yahalom, in rejection of my central claim that Ravad's *Hassagot* had little influence in the Middle Ages, attempts to show that some thirteenth- and fourteenth-century Provençal scholars do cite that work. To my thinking this is beside the point. I addressed the historical importance of Ravad. The cited scholars were without influence. Indeed, most were unknown until the last century. To speak of historical importance means to speak of Nahmanides and his school. Yahalom further states that I argued that it was the abrupt, haphazard nature of the *Hassagot* on *Mishneh Torah* that led Nahmanides and his school (*Bet Midrasho shel ha-Ramban*) to

[44] It may be that Ravad only gave strong expression to a prior Provençal attempt to neutralize Shemu'el's crippling ruling. See Meiri's formulation in *Bet ha-Beḥirah, Bava Metsi'a* (above, n. 38), 20b, s.v. *din zeh* (pp. 67–70) and the similar position of the *'Ittur* noted there. {I don't see such a reference in the editor's notes, nor am I aware of such a doctrine accepted by the author of the *'Ittur.*} Attention may also be drawn to the earlier neutralization of Shemu'el's dictum in loans involving possessory mortgages. See *Bet ha-Beḥirah*, ibid., p. 70 and notes ad loc., to which may be added *Sifran shel Rishonim* (above, n. 32), 7–8, and, as E. E. Urbach has pointed out to me, *Shenaton Mishpat 'Ivri*, 2 (1975), 45.

[45] Yahalom, *Bein Gironah le-Narbonnah*, 11–36.

ignore them. This is only partially correct. I gave two reasons for the indifference to the *Hassagot* in the late Middle Ages. First, why struggle to infer Ravad's doctrine from the terse language and fragmentary nature of his Maimonidean glosses when his full commentaries on most of the Talmud were readily available? Second, Nahmanides' school had extrapolated Ravad's insight into doctrines that surpassed the latter's formulations and expressed those aperçus with far greater felicity than their author ever did. I further added:

> Provençal pride in its most illustrious son could yet have preserved Ravad's oeuvre, but here fate dealt the final blow. France and Germany had their Poland, Spain its Mediterranean; but Provence was childless. When the time came for Ashkenaz to go into exile, it transported its culture to the empty spaces of central and eastern Europe. When Sepharad's days were up, the Spaniards took their classics with them to the far ends of the Mediterranean. Provence fell on evil times just as halakhah was flourishing south of the Pyrenees. The affinity between the two cultures was great, and Provence was absorbed by Spain with startling rapidity. In exile, Sepharad and Ashkenaz preserved, if not their cultural identity, at least their heritage. Provence did not; and 95 percent of its halakhic literature was swept away, unknown until the present century. The only Provençal writings preserved and destined to achieve currency were those appended to Sephardic works—Razah on Alfasi, Ravad on Maimonides. Provençal Talmudists survived as critics, not as creators.[46]

Yahalom then proceeds to draw a conclusion about the scope of the commentarial work of both R. Avraham Av Bet Din and Ravad. Drawing on the films at the Institute of Hebrew Microfilmed Manuscripts and the new editions of the Gerona school (*Bet Midrasho shel ha-Ramban*), put out by the Makhon ha-Talmud ha-Shalem and Mossad Harav Kook, Yahalom arrives at a shrunken list of tractates that Ravad commented upon and an expanded one of those of R. Avraham Av Bet Din.

I wrote an essay claiming that the school of Nahmanides did not draw on the *Hassagot* of Ravad when they discussed and developed his ideas. I have, over the past four to five decades, asked at least a dozen or so Torah scholars of stature whether they shared my perception of the insignificance of the *Hassagot* in the thought of *Bet Midrasho shel ha-Ramban* in Gerona and Barcelona, and they ratified my views. This may well be anecdotal evidence; however, the simple fact is that I set forth this claim in print some forty-five years ago, and it has gone unchallenged. If Dr Yahalom wishes to challenge this conclusion, he must show from the writings of that school that they,

[46] Above, p. 262.

indeed, drew upon the *Hassagot* in their discussions. Instead he claims that whenever there is a clear source (such as a *hassagah*) and no text of an extant commentary, methodologically one should assume that the source is the known *hassagah*. I fail to see the basis for such an assumption. A reason was given for the disappearance of Ravad's commentaries—the intellectual restatement of Ramban's school. Restatements replacing originals is a common occurrence in the Middle Ages. For example, with the exception of five to six tractates, all the *Tosafot* written at the feet of the great Ri ha-Zaken of Dampierre (d.1189) have disappeared, supplanted by the restatements of lesser scholars, such as R. Perets of Corbeil and R. Eli'ezer of Tuchheim of the third quarter of the thirteenth century.

Moreover, this assumption entails a drastic shrinkage of Ravad's oeuvre and historic accomplishments. It further challenges all medieval accounts, reports which we have no basis for not crediting. The great series of Talmudists who constituted the *Bet Midrasho shel ha-Ramban*, Ramban himself, his pupils and pupils' pupils Rashba, Rah, and Ritva all cite Ravad's commentaries on most of the tractates of the Talmud and speak of Ravad as the greatest of Provençal commentators (*gedol ha-mefarshim*).[47] R. Me'ir ha-Me'ili of Narbonne, in the third quarter of the thirteenth century, corroborates this account, writing in the introduction to the *Sefer ha-Battim* that Ravad commented on 'most of the Talmud'.[48] The same assertion is made by R. David of Estella and reiterated by R. Ḥasdai Crescas.[49] I can't see why any scholar would wish to construct the intellectual world of Narbonne and Gerona in the thirteenth century, the world of Nahmanides and his school, going against this consensus.

Finally, talent will out; if someone has something to say, he says it. Ravad had many, many things to say and said them with unparalleled bite and force. By Dr Yahalom's account, Ravad did not comment on most of *Seder Mo'ed*, precious little on *Seder Nashim*, and, other than *Kinnim*, wrote nothing on *Seder Kodashim*. This simply doesn't square with the picture that emerges from the writings of the *Bet Midrasho shel ha-Ramban*, let alone from his glosses on the *Mishneh Torah*. These great glosses were not simply a response to Maimonides' formulations in his code; they are far, far too rich for that. They are the product of a lifetime of study of the Bavli, Yerushalmi, Tosefta, and *midreshei halakhah*. Yahalom seems to be taking one of the half-dozen or so

47 On the term *gedol ha-mefarshim*, see above, n. 6.

48 *Sefer ha-Battim* (above, n. 3), 26; in Hershler's edition, the passage is found at i. 72.

49 *The Medieval Hebrew Chronicles*, ed. A. Neubauer (Oxford, 1893), ii. 131; *Sefer Or Adonai* (Vienna, 1860), fo. 2.

greatest Talmudists of the past millennium and cutting him down to a figure half the size of R. Zeraḥyah, Ba'al ha-Ma'or. To my untutored eye, this seems the ultimate insult.[50]

Conversely, this entails augmenting R. Avraham Av Bet Din's contribution to halakhah. By Dr Yahalom's account, R. Avraham did write commentaries on as much or more of the Talmud than did Ravad. A close study on my part of the Av Bet Din's *Sefer ha-Eshkol* has yielded almost nothing of intellectual significance. Dr Yahalom tries to explain away this absence of content by claiming that it is an early work. I say to him now what I said to Rabbi Buckwold, 'Spare me the roundabout. The truth will do. The author of the *Eshkol* simply had little to say.'[51] If one seeks brilliant insights into almost every tractate of the Talmud, one finds them in abundance in Ravad's writings. R. Avraham's predecessor, R. Yosef Ibn Megas of Lucena, had some brilliant things to say and he said them; R. Avraham's successor, Ravad, had many brilliant things to say and he said them. Between R. Avraham Av Bet Din and Ravad of Posquières something of great significance was said about the Talmud in twelfth-century Provence, and Nahmanides and his school built on it and their joint effort transformed the halakhah.[52] If Ravad didn't say these brilliant things, then R. Avraham must have done so. Dr Yahalom now has the task of turning R. Avraham into a major halakhic thinker. I wish him success in his endeavors.

[50] See Ch. 11 below for a study of these two figures.

[51] Below, p. 378.

[52] We are, more or less, in possession of the same small corpus of writings of Ri Megas as Maimonides had, and they are indeed brilliant. However, his corpus is small and that of R. Yitsḥak b. Abba Mari of Marseille, the *'Ittur*, was uninfluential; so, all the other brilliant things said in Provence in the twelfth century had to be said either by the Av Bet Din or Ravad.

CHAPTER ELEVEN

The Literary Remains of the *Gedol ha-Mefarshim*

A Study in Personal Rivalry and the Repulsion of Opposites

THE PRECEDING ESSAY was subjected to an extensive critique by Rabbi E. A. Buckwold. His criticism focused on the section of the essay that treated Ravad the decisor (*posek*) and the social and economic realities of Provence, rather than Ravad the man, the critic, and the talmudic commentator. This essay is an extension of my characterization of Ravad in the 'Programmatic Essay'; I have therefore adjoined it to that study and placed my reply to Buckwold's criticism afterwards.

THE PRECEDING ESSAY, 'Ravad of Posquières: A Programmatic Essay', was, as I wrote in its preface, written in spring 1974 (it was published only in 1980).[1] I followed it up with a close study of Ravad's *Commentary on Kinnim* together with the counter-commentary of his contemporary, R. Zeraḥyah ha-Levi of Lunel. This work was upended by the appearance in 1977 of Israel M. Ta-Shma's superb essay on Ravad's controversies with R. Zeraḥyah ha-Levi.[2] In the early 1980s I worked on Ravad's bitter critique of R. Zeraḥyah entitled *Katuv Sham*, and was struck by the differences between both the various manuscripts and the early and late printed editions. Then I labored on the numerous and conflicting printed texts of the *Ba'alei ha-Nefesh* and the equally conflicting versions in the manuscripts. This project was set at naught by the appearance in 1992 of Ephraim A. Buckwold's outstanding edition of

[1] 'Ravad of Posquières: A Programmatic Essay', reprinted with revisions as Ch. 10 above.

[2] I. M. Ta-Shma, 'Sifrei ha-Rivot bein ha-Ravad le-vein Zeraḥyah ha-Levi mi-Lunel', *Kiryat Sefer*, 52 (1977), 557–77; reprinted with revisions in *Rabbenu Zeraḥyah ha-Levi, Ba'al ha-Ma'or u-Venei Ḥugo* (Jerusalem, 1992). The essay would have been yet better had full use been made of Alexander Marx's 'R. Abraham b. David et R. Zaraḥyah ha-Levi', *Revue des Études Juives*, 59 (1910), 200–24.

the *Ba'alei ha-Nefesh*.[3] Though the long immersion in the self-standing works of Ravad (as opposed to purely commentarial ones on the Talmud, on which I had worked for the original essay on Ravad[4]) didn't eventuate in any critical edition, it proved of use in assessing his personality, intellectual profile, and the manner in which he went about recording his thoughts.

Ravad was called by all the famous Talmudists of the great Catalan school (*Bet Midrasho shel ha-Ramban*) 'the greatest of the Provençal commentators' (*gedol ha-mefarshim*), and all admitted their profound debt to his writings.[5] Why we possess next to nothing of those commentaries is understandable, and I attempted to address it in my programmatic essay, writing:

The great creative period of the Tosafists in France was the twelfth century. The thirteenth century simply edited, abridged, or rearranged the intellectual accomplishments of its predecessors. But though the magnitude of the accomplishments of Rabbenu Tam and of R. Yitsḥak of Dampierre was partially obscured by the tendency of later editors to present many of their views simply as 'reply may be made' (*ve-yesh lomar*), no one has imagined that R. Perets of Corbeil or R. Eli'ezer of Tuchheim were major creative Tosafists. Men of small stature, they could not obscure the great figures who had preceded them. The only two names that one carries away from a study of the standard *Tosafot* remain those of Rabbenu Tam and Ri. In Spain, the creative period stretches from the days of Nahmanides to those of Ritva or possibly R. Nissim of Barcelona (Ran). Their successors, R. Yitsḥak Perfet, R. Shim'on Duran, R. Ḥasdai Crescas, and R. Yitsḥak Abohab, were (in matters of talmudic commentary) men of lesser mold and could not displace the writings of Ramban and his school. It was Ravad's misfortune, however, to be followed by two giants—Ramban and Rashba. These two thinkers fused Ravad's insights with their own extrapolation of the tosafist dialectic, and transformed both. The end result was greater than that which Ravad had created, and, in the course of time, his works fell into desuetude.

Provençal pride in its most illustrious son could yet have preserved Ravad's oeuvre, but here fate dealt the final blow. France and Germany had their Poland, Spain its

[3] *Ba'alei ha-Nefesh le-Rabbenu ha-Ravad 'al Hilkhot Niddah, Mikva'ot u-Kedushah* (Benei Berak, 1992; repr. with addenda and corrigenda in 2013.)

[4] Above, pp. 253–86.

[5] The phrases *gedolei ha-mefarshim*, *mi-gedolei ha-mefarshim*, and *gedol ha-mefarshim* alternate freely in the writings of R. Menaḥem le-Vet ha-Me'iri (Mei'ri) and the members of the School of Ramban (*Bet Midrasho shel ha-Ramban*), R. Shelomoh Ibn Aderet (Rashba), R. Aharon of Barcelona (Rah), R. Yom Tov al-Sevilli (Ritva), and R. Nissim of Barcelona (Ran). No one questioned that Rashi was the commentator par excellence of the Talmud; the above phrases implicitly mean the greatest Provençal commentator. Or, to be more precise, as was Me'iri (*Bet ha-Beḥirah 'al Avot* [Jerusalem, 1964], 54): the greatest commentator whose commentaries dealt exclusively with the text and who avoided giving any rulings as to the final outcome of the talmudic discussion (*sugya*) was Rashi. The greatest commentator who interwove commentary and the final halakhic upshot of the *sugya* was Ravad of Posquières (*harkavat perush u-fesak*).

Mediterranean; but Provence was childless. When the time came for Ashkenaz to go into exile, it transported its culture to the empty spaces of central and eastern Europe. When Sepharad's days were up, the Spaniards took their classics with them to the far ends of the Mediterranean. Provence fell on evil times just as halakhah was flourishing south of the Pyrenees. The affinity between the two cultures was great, and Provence was absorbed by Spain with startling rapidity. In exile, Sepharad and Ashkenaz preserved, if not their cultural identity, at least their heritage. Provence did not; and 95 percent of its halakhic literature was swept away, unknown until the present century. The only Provençal writings preserved and destined to achieve currency were those appended to Sephardic works—Razah on Alfasi, Ravad on Maimonides. Provençal Talmudists survived as critics, not as creators.[6]

This leaves, however, unaccounted Ravad's hundreds, indeed thousands, of brilliant insights that we find in his *Hassagot* on *Mishneh Torah*, especially in the areas of *Zera'im*, *Kodashim*, and *Toharot*, with their sovereign command of the Yerushalmi, Tosefta, and all *midreshei halakhah*. These brilliant, biting Maimonidean critiques (*Hassagot*) were equally known to all the great Talmudists of Ramban's school, Rashba, Ritva, Rah, and Ran. Their content did not come in one blinding flash to Ravad as he scrutinized Maimonides' masterpiece very late in his life (the *Mishneh Torah* arrived in Provence no earlier than 1193, five years before Ravad's death). It had been built up over a lifetime of creative endeavors which either were not inscribed by Ravad (something difficult to imagine for so vast and varied an oeuvre, even for a thinker with as much difficulty in writing as Ravad) or were simply not preserved in the least by his successors (something equally difficult to conceive). Barring the commentaries on *Bava Kamma* and *'Avodah Zarah* (which are thin and somewhat abridged) and fragments on several other tractates, what we have is his commentaries on tractate *Kinnim* and on the *Torat Kohanim*—two classic works which lay well off the beaten track, scarcely enough to sustain a reputation as the greatest of commentators—and his commentary-code on menstrual abstinence, the famous *Ba'alei ha-Nefesh*.

Yet if we survey the literary remains of Ravad and take stock of his extant writings, we confront debris, and the riddle of the vast phantom oeuvre remains. How could it come to pass that what should have been the oeuvre of one of the greatest and most far-ranging Talmudists of the past millennium never got inscribed or, if inscribed, was lost to posterity?

I have no solution to this problem.

This essay attempts first to study the literary remains of the *gedol ha-mefarshim*. Passing over the talmudic commentaries, which I discussed in the

6 Above, p. 261–2.

above-cited programmatic essay, it examines the few works of Ravad that have come down to us and probes whether they have a coherent, unified text or whether every text of Ravad's oeuvre is 'open' and in flux to this day. Is there nothing stable in his literary legacy? I then seek to study the bitter rivalry that developed between Ravad and R. Zeraḥyah ha-Levi of Lunel, the author of the *Sefer ha-Ma'or*, a rivalry that consumed and embittered much of Ravad's life.

The following is an expanded form of a lecture that I gave at the Inauguration of the Merkin Family Research Professorship in 1990, and then at City University of New York Graduate Center in New York at the behest of Mark Mirsky in 1992.

Ravad, Ba'al ha-Hassagot—'author of the *Critiques*'—is the cognomen given to Ravad of Posquières (d.1198) for the past 500 years. It was coined soon after the publication of Ibn Naḥmias's edition of the *Mishneh Torah* in 1509, which published Ravad's white-hot and often stinging glosses on Maimonides for the first time (the Rome printing of *c.*1480 didn't have the *Hassagot*), and the reputation was 'sealed', as it were, by the Constantinople 1574 printing, which had a much fuller text of Ravad's *Hassagot*, supplied by no less a Talmudist than R. Yosef Karo. Nevertheless the characterization *ba'al ha-hassagot* well suits Ravad, and is confirmed by his works uncovered three centuries later: his sharp attack on R. Zeraḥyah ha-Levi, author of the *Sefer ha-Ma'or* (Ba'al ha-Ma'or, d. before 1186), in their controversy over a well-known passage in *Bava Metsi'a*, entitled *Sefer Divrei ha-Rivot*,[7] and most certainly by his savage critique of the *Sefer ha-Ma'or*, the *Katuv Sham*.[8]

I use the word 'savage' advisedly. Medieval polemics could be sharp. Witness the *Mishmeret ha-Bayit*—Rashba's reply to the critique of R. Aharon of Barcelona (Rah) of the *Torat ha-Bayit*. It pales, however, before the *Katuv Sham*, a work whose animosity is almost painful, but, as we shall see, understandable, indeed, I would venture to say, perhaps even justifiable.

The *Katuv Sham* gets its name from the opening words of almost every critique of the *Sefer ha-Ma'or*, the life work of R. Zeraḥyah b. Yitsḥak ha-Levi of Lunel (Razah). Ravad refuses throughout to even mention R. Zeraḥyah's

[7] *Sefer Divrei ha-Rivot*, ed. B. Drachmann (Philadelphia, 1908); repr. as *Sefer Divrei ha-Rivot* in Avraham b. R. David, *Teshuvot u-Fesakim*, ed. Y. Ḥ Kafiḥ, 2nd edn. (Jerusalem, 1992), 101–25.

[8] The existence of a much fuller version was signaled by A. Marx in his famous essay 'R. Abraham b. David et R. Zaraḥyah ha-Levi' (above, n. 2). The manuscript is currently registered as JTS Rabbinica 750 (MS 6591).

name, and when some personal reference is necessary, he takes refuge in the chilling neutral 'this man' (*zeh ha-ish*). In one passage, he also makes a wholesale attack on R. Zeraḥyah's distinguished father, R. Yitsḥak b. R. Zeraḥyah of Gerona, a relation of Nahmanides and scion of one of the most prestigious families of that city.

Ravad's critique reads:

> יש כאן הפוך בני מעין לההיא [סוגיא]. אי זה דרך עבר רוח האמת מאת כל הגאונים ז"ל עמודי עולם ומאת כמה גדולים וחכמים וישישים אשר נהגו כמנהג הזה, לדבר אתו(?). והנה שם השם רוח שקר בפיו, וזאת העדות על(!) כל שקריו ופחזותיו אשר אסף רוח בחפניו להנבא שקרים ולהתעות הפתיים והסכלים בעדיי אחרים אשר נתעטר בהם ספר המירוס אשר חיבר.
>
> וברוך יי' אשר החייני והעיר את רוחי ועזרני לגלות שקריו ולהחזיר עטרה ליושנה ולהושיבה במקומה, ולא עזב תורת אמת אשר נתן לנו ביד כסילים להתעות בהם כהתעות שיכור בקיאו.
>
> ועתה אשוב לדבר על השקר אשר כתב בכאן(!)[9] ואע"פ שהוא דבר מפורסם *לכל איש* אשר בו רוח חיים . . .
>
> והראיה שמביא מילדותו [שז' ברכות בלבד אמרו] (ל)[ה]ציבור [במוסף של ר"ה] וכו' ובזקנתו נשתנה המנהג. [יש להשיב] השנוי ההוא מאביו יצא ששנה המנהג בעירו על דרך הרב אבן גיאת ז"ל אע"פ שלא היה הוא מודה בדבר. אבל רצה אביו להתגדר בדברים זרים, ומצא נערים ושאינן בני תורה והנהיגן כרצון רוחו, ואח"כ באו שם אנשי תורה משאר מקומות ולא שמעו למנהגיו הזרים והחזירו המעשה לאמיתו ולמנהגו. וגם הוא קם תחת אביו לשנות דתות ולהחליף מנהגות, ויאבד הוא ואלף כיוצא בו, ואות מן ההלכות לא תבטל ומנהג אחד לא ישתנה.

He has turned the *sugya* upside down [lit. 'inverted stomach', which would render an animal *trefah*; see *Ḥullin* 56b]. What [ill] wind swept the truth away from all the Geonim, the Pillars of the Earth, and from great men, wise men, and sages who [are alleged to] have acted in this way, to speak to him[?] Behold, God filled his [i.e. Zeraḥyah ha-Levi's] mouth with falseness, and this attests to all his lies and irresponsible statements, who gathered wind [i.e. lies] in the cup of his hands, to prophesy falsely and to mislead fools and stupid people with ornaments of others with which he decks himself [i.e. even his misstatements are not original but taken from others] in the book of Hamiram [Homeros] [which is fit to be burnt; see *Yadayim* 4: 6; *Ḥullin* 60b][10] . . .

[9] i.e. *kan*. This use of *be-khan* (for *kan*) is common in writings of northern France, Languedoc, and Catalonia, as is *le-sham*, e.g. in *Perush Talmidei Rabbenu Yonah mi-Gerundi* (of Gerona) and Alfasi on *Berakhot* 2b (Romm edn.): כמו שיוצא לשם בדיעבד.

[10] It is difficult to translate these paragraphs with any degree of certainty as to the exact meaning of every sentence. The passage is a mosaic of derogatory phrases from, and allusions to, the classical sources. How they fuse into sentences with clear and distinct meaning is not always clear. Bergmann reads *sefer ha-mesuras* instead of *sefer ha-mirus*, 'the castrated [or upside-down] book'. I cited the passage as found in the readily available Freiman edition.

And now I shall return to the lies that he has written here, even though their falseness is widely known to every living creature . . . The proof that he cited from [what he witnessed] in his youth, that the congregation [in its silent prayer recited only seven blessings in the *musaf* 'Amidah of Rosh Hashanah (but not *Malkhuyot*, *Zikhronot*, and *Shofarot*)] etc. [Reply can be made:] this change was originated by his [R. Zeraḥyah's] father, who changed the practice of the city [of Lunel] on the basis of what [R. Yitsḥak] Ibn Gi'at said, even though he [R. Yitsḥak] would never have agreed [to such a change, i.e. his opinion was purely theoretical and was never intended to be applied, as it would run counter to universal practice]. His [i.e. R. Zeraḥyah's] father, however, wished to stand out from the crowd with strange [i.e. new and unfounded] religious practices. And he found youths and ignoramuses and he led them [in every which direction] that he chose. [Fortunately,] scholars from other cities settled [in Lunel] and they paid no attention to his [i.e. R. Zeraḥyah's father's] strange practices, and they restored the rite to its true and long-practiced form [i.e. reciting these three added *berakhot* also in the silent prayer]. And now he [R. Zeraḥyah] has succeeded his father in attempting to change religious rites and to alter long-established practices. Better that he be blotted out and a thousand others like him rather than one letter of the Law be abrogated or [long-hallowed] practices be altered.[11]

Admittedly this is extreme even for the *Katuv Sham*, and as true as may be the angry and grossly intemperate image it yields of Ravad in the stormiest moments of his life, nevertheless, as Ta-Shma pointed out in the above-mentioned essay, in this case it was R. Zeraḥyah who opened the quarrel not Ravad. Indeed, Ba'al ha-Ma'or attacked Ravad's writings for much of his life, criticizing him and his works incessantly.

Ravad wrote a commentary on *Kinnim*, one of the most baffling sets of *mishnayot* in the entire Talmud,[12] a commentary that had won the admiration of his father-in-law, R. Avraham Av Bet Din of Narbonne. R. Zeraḥyah wrote a critique of it. Ravad altered a passage in light of the critique and Razah offered a counter-interpretation of that passage.[13] Ravad advanced an interpretation of a well-known passage in *Bava Metsi'a*[14] and R. Zeraḥyah wrote down or spelled out to others orally his strictures. Ravad then wrote his famed *Ba'alei ha-Nefesh*, and Ba'al ha-Ma'or sat down and critiqued it.

[11] *Katuv Sham*, ed. B. Bergmann (Jerusalem, 1957), 72–3; *Katuv Sham*, ed. Ḥ. Freiman, 2nd edn. (Benei Berak, 2003), 112a–b. The only flaw in Freiman's edition is that he chose from the several manuscripts the smoothest version, and provided no apparatus of variant readings, not even noting them in his otherwise informative notes. However, the clearest text is not necessarily the most authentic. Though there are no differences in meaning—*Katuv Sham* is a remarkably clear work—there are authentic readings that remain unrecorded in this fine edition. See n. 10 above.

[12] See the remarks of the author of the *Tif'eret Yisra'el* cited below, n. 27.

[13] See below.

[14] 96b–98b.

Actually R. Zeraḥyah wrote a double-barreled critique of both the *Kinnim* commentary and a simultaneous 'early publication' of the *Ba'alei ha-Nefesh*, as if to say that whatever R. Avraham wrote was in need of correction. He entitled his joint correction *Sela' ha-Maḥloket*[15] and further subtitled it, as it were, 'Purging the Dross', writing in the opening lines of the introductory poem: מצרף לכסף וכור לזהב / להסיר בדיליהם וכל סיג בהם התערב ('Refining silver and [purging] furnace for the gold | to remove all the dross and all the base metal in which it is enmeshed').[16]

Ravad retracted some of his positions in the *Ba'alei ha-Nefesh* in light of the criticism, and Razah immediately noted with satisfaction, some might say patronizingly, the corrections that Ravad had made as a consequence of his criticism,[17] and further critiqued some of the new interpretations that the other had offered.[18]

Ba'al ha-Ma'or finally finished his life's work, the *Sefer ha-Ma'or*. Ravad's response was, in effect, 'You have been criticizing me for my entire lifetime, now it's my turn to write a critique of your *chef-d'œuvre*.' His extraordinary outburst at R. Zeraḥyah's father was generated, Ta-Shma points out, by a nasty put-down by Ba'al ha-Ma'or in their controversy over a well-known *sugya* in *Bava Metsi'a*.[19] He demeaned Ravad's father as a plebeian, perhaps even an ignoramus:[20] R. Zeraḥyah came from a distinguished Catalan family whose lineage went back at least four generations, and, in all probability, he was among the founding fathers of the Gerona community. He was also at home in philosophy and *belles-lettres* and was himself a religious poet of no mean stature. He demeaned Ravad's common lineage and his ignorance of Andalusian Jewish culture, the culture of *adāb*, the medieval Arabic counterpart of the nineteenth-century German *Bildung*—the forging of a moral and

15 Ta-Shma, 'Sifrei ha-Rivot' (above, n. 2), 559 n. 9.

16 *Ba'alei ha-Nefesh*, ed. Buckwold (above, n. 3), introduction, p. 4; text, p. 189.

17 ומצאנו הכל מתוקן ומוגה כדברינו . . . ובזה שמחנו. *Ba'alei ha-Nefesh*, ed. Buckwold (above, n. 3), introduction, p. 13.

18 Ibid., n. 35; text, p. 4 (very bottom of page), 190. Printed also in *Ba'alei ha-Nefesh*, ed. Y. Ḥ. Kafiḥ (Jerusalem, 1964), 162–4.

19 96b–98b.

20 *Sefer Divrei ha-Rivot* (above, n. 7), 48; *Sefer Divrei ha-Rivot*, in *Teshuvot u-Fesakim* (above, n. 7), 121: אני בן תלמיד חכם ובן בנו. In Provençal sources of the twelfth century, Ravad's father is not called 'R. David', nor is his grandfather ever mentioned. R. Zeraḥyah ha-Levi signs his name 'R. Zeraḥyah b. R. Yitsḥak b. R. Zeraḥyah'. It may well be that Ravad's outburst here was an overreaction, seeing that Razah's father had attempted to alter the 'Amidah of Rosh Hashanah. However, one must remember that Razah's put-down had been festering for years, and that Ravad's sense of being disdained by the illustrious families of Lunel had equally been present for much of his life. Decades of sensed rejection and humiliation by the patriciate of Lunel can only too readily cloud one's judgment.

intellectual self at home with the finest values of the civilization in which the individual is imbedded.[21]

Ba'al Ha-Ma'or finished his life's work. Ravad had difficulty finishing anything. He was perhaps hypersensitive to criticism; he was also hyper-responsive. No sooner did he hear a critique than he began to contemplate its merit. If he saw merit in the counter-argument advanced, he began thinking about reinterpretation, and revision soon followed in its wake. Far more important, he himself was rarely satisfied with what he wrote and was constantly revising his work, so much so that in important places the original version is scarcely discernible.

But we are running ahead of ourselves. Let us leave aside his commentaries on individual tractates of the Talmud, as I discussed them elsewhere in this volume.[22] Let us address the three above-mentioned works, beginning with the *Katuv Sham*.

The Literary Remains of the *Gedol ha-Mefarshim*

Katuv Sham

The *Katuv Sham* is not to be found in the first printing of the *Sefer ha-Ma'or* (1509). In 1910 Alexander Marx, in a famous article in the *Revue des Études Juives*,[23] drew scholars' attention to a manuscript in the collection of the Jewish Theological Seminary and described in detail its text, which was far more extensive than anything then available. He also analyzed trenchantly the rich personal details contained in that version and demonstrated its indispensability for any assessment of both the *Katuv Sham* and Ravad's relationship to Razah.

In the 1930s and early forties, M. Z. Ḥasida copied out a fuller manuscript of the *Katuv Sham*, found in the library of the Hebrew University (now the National Library of Israel). He typed up his transcriptions, mimeographed them, and traveled about Mandatory Palestine, pre-Holocaust Europe, and America selling his wares in an attempt to put bread on his family's table.[24] In 1957 the *Katuv Sham* on tractates *Rosh Hashanah* and *Sukkah* was published

21 On *adāb*, see B. Safran, 'Baḥya ibn Pakuda's Attitude toward the Courtier Class, in I. Twersky, ed., *Studies in Medieval Jewish History and Literature* (Cambridge, Mass., 1979), i. 154–96, and A. Tanenbaum, 'Arrogance, Bad Form, and Curricular Narrowness: Belletristic Critiques of Rabbinic Culture from Medieval Spain and Provence', in D. Frank and M. Goldish, eds., *Rabbinic Culture and its Critics: Dissent and Heresy in Medieval and Early Modern Culture* (Detroit, 2008), 57–82. Most recently, N. Alshaar, ed., *The Quran and the Adab: Literary Tradition in Classical Islam* (Oxford, 2017).

22 Above, pp. 251–68.

23 'R. Abraham b. David' (above, n. 2).

24 Ḥasida used MS 120 = 4 of the National Library of Israel. He entitled his mimeographed sheets

by Bernard Bergmann from the manuscript described by Marx, and, needless to say, it contains large sections of the text of tractates in which Ḥasida's text was deficient.[25] In *Sukkah*, for example, Ḥasida's text skips from folio 9b to 32a, while the *Hassagot* published by Bergmann on this section are extensive and revelatory. Scholars noticed that neither the manuscripts of the Jewish Theological Seminary nor that of the National Library of Israel contained the full text of the *Katuv Sham* on tractates *Yevamot*, *Ketubbot*, *Gittin*, *Kiddushin*, *Bava Kamma*, *Bava Metsi'a*, *Bava Batra*, *Sanhedrin*, *Shevu'ot*, and *Makkot*.

Another thirty-five years were to pass before the full text of the *Katuv Sham* appeared in 1990. For fear, apparently, of a backlash because of the harsh light it casts on Ravad thanks to his intemperate attacks on the author of the *Sefer ha-Ma'or*, R. Zeraḥyah ha-Levi, no editor of the work was registered either on the title page or on its flipside; it simply reads, '[published by] the Makhon le-Ḥeker Kitvei Yad 'al Shem Maran ha-Ḥatam Sofer'. There was no reaction, and some fifteen years later the editor, Ḥayyim Freiman, signed the introduction, finally taking responsibility and receiving deserved praise for the fine notes that he had appended to the text and for the scouring of recent publications of medieval sources for citations from the *Katuv Sham*.[26] One had to wait until 1990, close to a millennium after its composition, to get the full text of the *Katuv Sham*.

Commentary on Kinnim

This commentary on what is arguably the most obscure and gnomic mishnaic tractate[27] was one of Ravad's earliest and most original works. It won the awed approval of his father-in-law, the famed scholar-kabbalist, R. Avraham of Narbonne. This commentary is not found in the early editions of the Talmud. It first appeared in Constantinople in 1751, when it was bound with the

Ha-Segullah. The first seven volumes, containing the material 'published' between 1934 and 1942, were, for several decades, held in the Rara division of libraries. In the late 1950s, with the advent of photostatic printing, they were readily available until replaced in the early 1980s by the far fuller version of Freiman (see below).

[25] *Katuv Sham*, ed. B. Bergmann (Jerusalem, 1957), 47–109; ed. Ḥ. Freiman, 2nd edn. (Benei Berak, 2003), 116–27. See above, n. 11.

[26] A new edition of *Katuv Sham* has appeared as part of the *Sefer Ba'al ha-Ma'or 'al Massekhtot ha-Shas*, 3. vols, ed. D. Bitton [Jerusalem, 2005]. However, no information is provided as to what its text is based on—what manuscripts were used—so I have addressed only the edition of Freiman.

[27] See, for example, the opening statement of R. Yisraél Lipschütz, the mid-nineteenth-century author of the famed Mishnah commentary, the *Tif'eret Yisra'el*, that he has yet to see a commentary on the tractate which successfully disposes of the difficulties generated by the gnomic text. He writes:
והנה באתי עד הלום, לפרש בעזרת אבינו שבשמים, מסכת קינין החמורה שבחמורות שבכל הש"ס, בפירוש מספיק מזוקק שבעתיים, אשר עד הנה לא זכיתי לראות עוד על מסכת זו פירוש שלם אשר יפלש כל סתרי תעלומותיו.

enigmatic work currently known as *Shitah Lo Noda' le-Mi 'al Kiddushin*. The editors of the Romm Talmud reprinted this text. Some twenty years later, the editors of the Romm Mishnah drew upon a Jerusalem manuscript. The text of Ravad's commentary there differs widely from the text printed in the Talmud, so much so that often the initial version can barely be discerned.

The Romm editors noticed this and, with their usual thoroughness, printed the two texts alongside one another and prefaced the work thus:

אמרו המדפיסים: פי' הראב"ד והרז"ה הדפסנום ע"פ כתב יד שהיה ביד בעל מלאכת שלמה ז"ל. וההוספות והשנוים שמצאנו בו נגד הנדפסים מכבר הצגנום בחצי מרובעים. והנוסחאות שנדפסו כבר הצגנום בחצאי עגולים, והמעיין יבחר לו את הנוסחא הישרה.

Printers' note: We have published the commentaries of Ravad and Razah from a manuscript that was in the possession of the author of the *Melekhet Shelomoh*.[28] The passages [in our text] which differ from the previously published edition, or those which are not to be found [in the previous edition] at all, we placed in square brackets, and [in juxtaposition] we placed the text of the previous edition in round brackets. The reader may [thus] choose [for himself] the proper text.[29]

Though two texts have come down to us, there was yet an earlier version. Ravad, in his commentary on the *Torat Kohanim* (*Sifra de-Vei Rav*), presents one interpretation of a certain phrase (*atsmah shel ḥattat*) and then another, and writes of the second view: 'There is much in this interpretation that needs scrutiny, and I have already written [on it] in another notebook [version] of the *Kinnim* commentary.' He is referring to the very first *mishnah* of *Kinnim*; the second opinion is, not surprisingly, that of his critic R. Zeraḥyah ha-Levi of Lunel (Razah), in his counter-commentary on this passage. However, neither of the two printed versions has any treatment of R. Zeraḥyah's views. Obviously, Ravad referred to a fuller version than what has come down to us, one that, at least in part, took R. Zeraḥyah's strictures into consideration.

Ba'alei ha-Nefesh

There are multiple versions of the *Commentary on Kinnim*; nevertheless, each version is a full work. Not so in the case of Ravad's most influential and arguably greatest work, the *Ba'alei ha-Nefesh*.

Though begun apparently early, alongside the *Commentary on Kinnim*,[30] it

[28] R. Shelomoh 'Adani, a pupil of R. Yosef Ashkenazi. See G. Scholem, 'Yedi'ot Ḥadashot 'al R. Yosef Ashkenazi, "ha-Tana mi-Tsefat"', *Tarbiz*, 28 (1959), 59–89.

[29] *Kinnim, Shishah Sidrei Mishnah*, Romm edn. (Vilna, 1885).

[30] See the laudatory poem on the *Kinnim* commentary of Ravad's father-in-law, R. Avraham, Av Bet Din of Narbonne: לדלות מקינים ופתחי אסורות, a clear allusion to קינין ופתחי נדה הן הן גופי תורה (*Avot* 3: 18).

was unfinished at the time of Ravad's death in 1198. He worked intermittently on it throughout his life.[31] The first edition of the *Ba'alei ha-Nefesh* appeared in Venice in 1602, in a work entitled *'Avodat ha-Kodesh* by Rashba which contained the *Hilkhot Niddah* and *Mikva'ot* of the *Torat ha-Bayit* and the *Ba'alei ha-Nefesh*. In 1741 R. Yeshayah Bassano published in Venice for the first time Razah's *Hassagot* on the *Ba'alei ha-Nefesh*. He further compared the Venice edition with a manuscript in his possession, noticing that his manuscript contained numerous passages not found in the first edition, to put it mildly. Quantitatively, the additions are so massive in certain places as to constitute a different text. For example, the third chapter of the famous penultimate section, the *Sha'ar ha-Mayim*, is two and a half times as long in the later edition as in the first.[32] It also contains new interpretations that at times complement, at times conflict with, the text of the first edition.

R. Yeshayah also noted that some citations of the *Ba'alei ha-Nefesh* in the *Bet Yosef* differed considerably from the printed text. He transcribed the variant passages and published them in 1741 as corrigenda and addenda to the *Ba'alei ha-Nefesh*, together with Razah's *Hassagot* on that work. In 1762 R. Avraham Mencke decided to publish (in Berlin) a single volume of both the *Ba'alei ha-Nefesh* and Razah's *Hassagot*, which had been printed by Bassano some twenty years earlier. He printed the text of the *Ba'alei ha-Nefesh* according to Bassano's corrigenda and addenda. The Berlin edition states explicitly that, in addition to its innumerable errors, the 1602 edition also suffered from lacunae, or, as the editor put it, 'it was missing a number of pieces [*ḥatikhot*]' and that he had set matters right by incorporating into the text the *haggahot* (corrections, glosses) to the *Ba'alei ha-Nefesh* that were published in Venice in 1741.

R. Mencke inserted most of the additional passages of Bassano into the text of the *Ba'alei ha-Nefesh*, occasionally preceding them with a parenthetical abbreviation (נ"א = o.v., i.e. other versions) or following them with a brief note, 'until here the gloss'. The Berlin text became, in effect, the basis of all subsequent editions. However, since the notations 'o.v.' and 'gloss' were not uniformly entered, passages both supplementary and dissonant entered the Berlin text unmarked and unbracketed.

Scholars noticed that R. Yosef Karo's famed commentary on the *Tur*, the *Bet Yosef*, has quotations from the *Ba'alei ha-Nefesh* that match neither the text of Venice 1602 nor that of 1741. In 1964 Rabbi Yosef Ḥayyim Kafiḥ published

[31] *Ba'alei ha-Nefesh*, ed. Buckwold (above, n. 3), introduction, pp. 13–14.

[32] Compare Venice, 1602, with Venice, 1741.

from his private manuscript collection a text identical with MS National Library of Israel, 120 = 4, which contained the passages cited in the *Bet Yosef*.[33] He published the new passages in bold and the standard text in petite, and one glance at the pages will show the massive differences between the texts.

Clearly, our printed text is a conflation of different recensions. 'Recension' is perhaps a misnomer: 'text in flux' or 'text in transit' would be more appropriate. Ravad continued to revise the text of the *Ba'alei ha-Nefesh* even after he had 'published' it, that is to say, permitted others to copy it. He had not the time, quite possibly not the patience, after he had made a change, to edit the entire manuscript in order to fully align it with the most recent alteration. What we possess is not so much recensions as different snapshots of the text in various stages of its evolution. Rashba and Ramban had one such still shot, R. Yosef Karo possessed another, R. Yeshayah Bassano yet a third, the printers of the first edition a fourth, and, by the nature of things, one can assume that yet others await us in the manuscripts.

Just how unstable that famous work is can be seen from R. Ephraim A. Buckwold's superb 1992 edition of the *Ba'alei ha-Nefesh*. On the basis of all the then available manuscripts and scouring of the rishonic literature for all statements about Ravad's halakhic stand on the issues of menstrual purity, Rabbi Buckwold has shown us just how many drafts Ravad wrote and how he was loathe to accept anyone's position on these matters without thinking it through again and again.[34] There is nothing stable in the greatest of Ravad's works, the *Ba'alei ha-Nefesh*. In a sense, what we have in the *Sha'ar ha-Mayim* section of that work are numerous notebooks and not a unit of a book—rapid, at times abrupt, inscriptions of new interpretations that flowed from a ceaselessly creative mind.

The source of this fluidity was Ravad's preternatural speed in rethinking his position. No man was quicker to disavow, even mock, a position he had vigorously advocated and to admit the error of a position he had once embraced. He treated his former self no better than others.

In the bitter exchange between Ravad and the author of the *Sefer ha-Ma'or*, R. Zeraḥyah ha-Levi, Ravad's rejoinder to R. Zeraḥyah's telling characterization of him as 'the wise man [scholar] whose wisdom boils him [keeps him in steady boil] and whose insight gives him no rest'[35] was, 'Say what you

[33] Above, n. 18.

[34] *Ba'alei ha-Nefesh*, ed. Buckwold (above, n. 3), text, pp. 16, 26–8, 35–6, 54–5, 60–1, 101–6, 119–30, 133–52, 154–68.

[35] *Sefer Divrei ha-Rivot*, ed. Drachmann (above, n. 7), 20; *Sefer Divrei ha-Rivot*, ed. Kafiḥ (above, n. 7), 110: החכם אשר חכמתו מרתיחתו / ותבונתו לא מניחתו.

wish about me; I at least admit to error and my work shows my openness to criticism.'[36]

There is, in fact, nothing stable in any of the works of Ravad that have come down to us. No text is uniform, all have alternative versions. No surviving manuscript of any commentary or code that Ravad wrote is complete; there are gaps in all the surviving editions and in the manuscripts that lay behind them. All are, in effect, drafts. Though we well understand that Ravad's strength in rethinking was the source of his weakness in inscription, nevertheless one feels that the *gedol ha-mefarshim* of Provence deserved better at the hand of Fate.

Ravad–Razah: A Study in Personal Rivalry and the Repulsion of Opposites

Personal Rivalry

A starker contrast between two towering contemporaries can scarcely be found in the history of the halakhah. On the one hand, the humbly born R. Avraham b. David of Posquières, irascible, teeming (boiling) with creativity, and proud disowner of any secular education, philosophical or literary; on the other, R. Zeraḥyah ha-Levi of Lunel, author of the *Sefer ha-Ma'or*, scion of a distinguished Narbonnese family, and accomplished Talmudist and liturgist. Not a major poet, but one who had proven his skills in all forms of medieval *piyyut*—*seliḥah*, *pizmon*, *zulat*, *me'orah*, *nishmat*, and *azharah*.[37] The wide reception given to his *piyyut* and the numerous liturgical rites that have incorporated them show the answering echoes of assent that his words evoked in a varied range of congregants. R. Zeraḥyah was an exemplary product of Andalusian culture and a proud advocate of its *adāb*, the medieval Islamic version of the nineteenth-century German *Bildung*.[38]

Nothing could be more elegantly telling than Razah's salutation to Ravad in their famous exchange over a well-known passage in *Bava Metsi'a*[39]:

[36] The quotation marks here do not represent a direct translation of Ravad's words but the crux of his reply. See *Sefer Divrei ha-Rivot*, ed. Drachmann, 7, ed. Kafiḥ, 105: ידעתי כי יד המידה השביעית נוגעת בו. Indeed, as Ta-Shma remarked to me, few medieval halakhic works have the high degree of internal consistency as the *Sefer ha-Ma'or*. The instances that Ta-Shema adduces ('Sifrei ha-Rivot' [above, n. 2], 565) and which reflect changes in Ba'al ha-Ma'or's position are simply the exceptions which prove the rule. They form a minute percentage of the halakhic positions set forth in the *Sefer ha-Ma'or*.

[37] Y. Meisils, *Shirat ha-Ma'or: Piyyutei R. Zeraḥyah ha-Levi mi-Lunel* (Jerusalem, 1984).

[38] See above, n. 21.

[39] 96b–98b.

שלום לך ולתורתך / והשקט והנחה מחמתך ועברתך /
החכם אשר חכמתו מרתיחתו / ותבונתו לא מניחתו

Peace unto you and unto your Torah [i.e. your teachings]
And quiet and rest [for you] from your anger and wrath
The wise man [i.e. scholar] whose wisdom keeps him at a boil
[i.e. keeps him in a constant state of inner turmoil]
and whose wisdom gives him no rest

Nothing could be more elegant and derisive than the poem R. Zeraḥyah placed at the end of his critique of Ravad's *Ba'alei ha-Nefesh* (I quote selections):

Lines 1–3:

לבי המתק את מענך / כי קדוש מחניך / ותנה תחת ללשונך / צוף דבש עם מנך
השמר מהתרגזך, / הס מהעלות שאננך / לפני שרים, שרי קדש / ירז נגדם משמניך
שוכני מגדל ירחונך.

My dear, sweeten your response and keep your dwelling pure
[i.e. don't use foul language][40]
And put honey under your tongue / honey from the comb [S. of S. 4: 10]
Keep your rage and your turmoil under control [see 2 Kgs 19: 28; Isa. 37: 29]
Your sturdiness will waste away [see Isa. 20: 16] [when standing]
Before nobles, the holy [i.e. learned] nobles / who dwell in your [city,] Lunel

Lines 5–6:

בהם תמשול על ילדי יום / גם תסתולל בזמנך / מתירושך ודגניך / לא ירעיבך ויענך
לבני עירך ושכניך / תשרוק תחרק את שינך / הם דלי תורה / עבה ממתניהם קטנך

Over mortals [i.e. simple people] you can rule
And act rudely whenever you wish.
Your wine and wheat [i.e. your sustenance] you will have
He [God] will not make you hungry / And cause you to suffer.
Raise a hue and grind your teeth at your fellow citizens and neighbors
They are poor in knowledge of the Torah
and your pinky is larger than *their* thigh [but not the thigh of the nobles of Lunel] . . .

The concluding two lines:

האומרים חדש יינך / בראות חדש קנקניך / כן צעיר לימים צעיר לחכמות הנה הינך.
אם תגביה כנשר / ובין כוכבים שים קנך.

They say your wine is new when [all] they see is your new earthen containers.

[40] This may appear as an overly sharp translation. However, I do not see how one can avoid translating the clear imputation of the verse in Deut. 22: 14–15, ויד תהיה לך מחוץ למחנה ויצאת שמה חוץ. ויתד תהיה לך על אזנך, והיה בשבתך חוץ וחפרת בה וכסית את צאתך . . . והיה מחניך קדוש.

> Yes, [indeed,] young in years, young in wisdom, that's what you are,
> If you shall lift up your perch and place your nest among the stars
> [With the unspoken but clear association of the next verse in Obad. 1: 4,
> משם אורידך —'From there I will take you down'].[41]

Ravad moved from Lunel to the neighboring forest village of Posquières—*kiryat ye'arim, gevul Lunel*.[42] He may have done so to breathe the fresh forest air; he may have sought to build a larger structure to house the numerous students who were flocking to his yeshivah. Jewish students often lived in their teacher's home,[43] and Ravad, independently wealthy, supported his students and believed he could get a better price for a building in the local village than in the small, cramped Jewish quarters of Lunel. He may also have sought to escape the patrician society of Lunel, which looked down upon his plebeian origins and was convinced that he never could or ever would be original, and that the students who were flocking to his study were buying into an illusion.

Their anger was only heightened by the fact that R. Avraham, Av Bet Din of Narbonne, had chosen him, Ravad, as a son-in-law over the scions of the patriciate of his own city—arguably the most prestigious Jewish community of southern France and Catalonia—and, of course, over the aristocracy of Lunel. R. Avraham had further reached deep into the common herd and selected the 'uncultured' Ravad and chosen to reveal to him the esoteric lore (*sod*, what we call today kabbalah[44]) of which he, the Av Bet Din, was the

The real question is not how I or some of my readers understand the biblical references, but how Ravad understood them, and here I believe the answer is obvious. Ravad, perhaps, was thin-skinned; however, if he was, R. Zeraḥyah ha-Levi was more than aware of this fact.

41 *Ba'alei ha-Nefesh*, ed. Buckwold (above, n. 3), 189; ed. Kafiḥ (above, n. 18), 134–5.

42 R. Menaḥem b. R. Shelomoh ha-Me'iri, *Magen Avot*, ed. Y. H. Last (London, 1908), 103: מה שכתב הרב ז"ל בצאתו מעיר קרית יערים היא פושקיירישׂ. I. Twersky, *Rabad of Posquières: A Twelfth-Century Talmudist* (Cambridge, Mass., 1962), 32.

43 See M. Breuer, 'Le-Ḥeker ha-Tipologyah shel Yeshivot ha-Ma'arav bi-Yemei ha-Beinayim', in I. Etkes and Y. Salmon, eds., *Studies in the History of Jewish Society in the Middle Ages and Modern Period Presented to Jacob Katz on his 75th Birthday* (Jerusalem, 1980), 48–54.

44 I use the term 'kabbalah' on the authority of Gershom Scholem, whose lectures on the mystical teachings in Provence were entitled 'Ha-Kabbalah be-Provence', both in the series that he gave at the Hebrew University in the academic years of 1964–1966 and in the dactylographed transcription of the lectures by Rivkah Shatz (a practice then common in European universities) and sold in the bookstore of the Student Union of the Hebrew University (the Akademon). Almost all references to *ruaḥ ha-kodesh* and the like in the halakhic writings of Ravad, for instance his gloss on *Mishneh Torah*, 'Hilkhot Lulav', 8: 5, or *Temim De'im* in Tam Ibn Yaḥya, *Tummat Yesharim* (Venice, 1643), #50, are simply the medieval equivalent of our modern expression 'with God's help'. See Twersky, *Rabad of Posquières* (above, n. 42), 291–300. The one place where Ravad allows his esoteric traditions to intrude upon his halakhic thinking, and with characteristic boldness, is in his *hassagah* on ''Avodah, Bet ha-

guardian, and to make him, rather than some distinguished member of the Jewish intellectual and spiritual aristocracy, the link of that generation in the tiny circle of initiates of the mystical tradition.[45]

And the Av Bet Din chose wisely. It was Ravad who was to write commentaries on most of the Talmud,[46] and he would bear the cognomen, given to him by both R. Menaḥem le-Vet ha-Me'iri and the great school of Gerona (*Bet Midrasho shel ha-Ramban*), 'the greatest of the talmudic commentators'. That wide and weighty recognition, however, was in the future. During his lifetime, Ravad felt systematically belittled, demeaned, and abused by the aristocratic establishment of Lunel.[47]

המשלתני כיורה רותחת, מעלה עשן בחמתי ועברתי, וריח שמני הפכת לחלבונה, וכאלה רבות . . . ותכת[ו]ב עלי כי (נחמסו) [נחפשו] עקביה ונגלו שוליה . . . ועוד קראתני בתוכה ממשל משלים, ועשיתני כמשחק קוביא ואוחזי העניים וסדן הריחיים יסוב על צירו כל היום ואינו הולך לא לפנים ולא לאחור . . . ביזיתני, ביישתני וקללתני ועשיתני אפיקורס ומגלה פנים בתורה [שלא כהלכה] ומבזה את רבותי.

You have compared me to a boiling pot that raises smoke in anger and rage, and the smell of my perfume [see S. of S. 1: 3] you have turned into the foul-smelling [plant],

Beḥirah', 6: 14. For one exposition of the meaning of Ravad's *hassagah*, see H. Pedayah, *Ha-Shem ve-ha-Mikdash be-Mishnat R. Yitsḥak Sagi Nahor: 'Iyyun Mashveh be-Khitvei Rishonei ha-Mekubbalim* (Jerusalem, 2001), 42–55.

45 See G. Scholem, 'Te'udah Ḥadashah le-Toledot Reshit ha-Kabbalah', *Sefer Bi'alik* (Tel Aviv, 1934), 141–62.

46 R. David ha-Kokhavi (of Estella), scion of the Rav Av Bet Din, writes in his *Kiryat Sefer* (A. Neubauer, ed., *Medieval Jewish Chronicles* [Oxford, 1997], ii. 231):

ובעיר נרבונא וגבוליה ולונל וגבולו קמו חכמים חדשים ונבוני לחש [וז"א כנראה, מקובלים] שמשו בצרפת וספרד וח[י]דשו דברים רבים לברר בד[ב]רי התלמוד ודיניו ולי[י]שב המאמרים הנראים כסותרים אזה את זה. ומהם אשר ב[י]ארו באור רחב קצת מסכתות מן התלמוד כגון ר' אברהם אב בית דין והוא חיבר ספר האשכול. ובימים ההם הופיע בגבול לונל אור בהיר (הוא) הרב הגדול רבינו אברהם בר דוד מפושייקיירש היה חכם גדול בקי בשני התלמודים ותוספתא וספרא וספרי *ופ[י]רש ר[ו]ב התלמוד*, וחיבר גם כן פירוש תורת כהנים.

And at that time in Narbonne and her borders and in Lunel and her borders there arose new scholars and kabbalists who served in France and Spain and originated many [new] things in the words of the Talmud and its laws to resolve apparent problems—things [i.e. statements] that appear to contradict one another. And some wrote commentaries on some talmudic tractates, as R. Avraham Av Bet Din, and he wrote commentaries on some tractates. And in those days, there appeared *on the border of Lunel* a great light, R. Avraham b. David of Posquières, who was a great scholar and had full command of both Talmuds [i.e. Bavli and Yerushalmi], Tosefta, *Sifra*, and *Sifrei*, and wrote commentaries on most of the Talmud. He also wrote a commentary on the *Torat Kohanim*.

And the most important piece of evidence is the cognomen given to him by the great school of Ramban, *gedol ha-mefarshim*, together with Me'iri, who places Ravad alongside Rashi as the two *gedolei ha-mefarshim* (ibid. 228). See I. Twersky, *Rabad of Posquières* (above, n. 42), 32, and see above, p. 290.

47 *Sefer Divrei ha-Rivot* (above, n. 7), ed. Drachmann, 30–1, ed. Kafiḥ, 114–15.

the galbanum [*ḥelbonah*], and many [insults] like these ... You have written about me, for her traces have been searched out [i.e. your malicious correspondence about me has been revealed] and her private parts exposed ... In addition, you have [in those letters] turned me into a spinner of tales, a card-shark and illusionist, and [compared me to] a wooden pole that serves to rotate all day the fixed, heavy round stones of a flour mill but does not move forward or backward ... You have humiliated me, shamed me, cursed me, turned me into a heretic, [portrayed me as] a person who misinterprets the Law and is contemptuous of his teachers.

From a distance of over 800 years these seem like words of a paranoid; paranoids, however, also have enemies. More importantly, we must never forget that what has survived the depredations of time and the carelessness of man are the elegant and sophisticated put-downs of R. Zeraḥyah ha-Levi. No record remains of the coarser remarks and epithets hurled at Ravad over the course of his lifetime by the cruder scions of the aristocracies of Narbonne and Lunel, who were enraged at the Av Bet Din's choice of Ravad as his son-in-law and as his heir in the mystical tradition of Provence.

Ravad, one of the greatest Talmudists of the past millennium, was one of the Nefillim, sons of the giants (*benei ha-'anakim*). Such men cannot be measured by the yardstick of the 'merely' superbly talented, such as R. Zeraḥyah ha-Levi of Lunel. Ravad had the greatness, the tragedy, and the loneliness which, at times, is the fate of Nefillim. I don't know whom Rashi and Rambam had to talk to. However, the absence of serious interlocutors does not necessarily lead to a punishing sense of solitariness, the demeaning sense of inarticulateness—the inability to express the full depths of one's insights—and the unsettling awareness that all one's ideas were tentative and subject to swift revision. Temperament bulks large in such a reaction. The one figure who most resembles Ravad in his pugnacious, explosive personality, in his difficulty focusing on a single task, and in his inability to inscribe the stream of ideas that flowed from his ceaseless creativity, R. Ya'akov Tam of Ramerupt, better known as Rabbenu Tam, was fortunate in having been able to discuss his ideas with the immortal R. Yitsḥak of Dampierre, the famed Ri. Whether this made him a milder person than Ravad, I have no idea.

Repulsion of Opposites

The one sad, central fact of Ravad's intellectual life, however, is clear. He never found, as had R. Zeraḥyah in the *Sefer ha-Ma'or*, a vessel into which to pour the insights of a lifetime.

One of the sources fueling Ravad's agitation and distemper was the profound frustration which came from an inability to weave the thoughts of his teeming mind into a single garment. If a man has good in him and it doesn't come out, that good can prove corrosive. Had it not been for the appearance of *Mishneh Torah* very late in Ravad's life (some five years, at most, before his death[48]), who would ever have known of his wondrous achievements in *Zera'im*, *Kodashim*, *Toharot*, Yerushalmi, Tosefta, and the full range of *midreshei halakhah*? As stimulated as he was by Maimonides' work, the thousands of new doctrines that he propounded in his critiques were not the product of an inspired reading, in his old age, of *Mishneh Torah*. They were the fruit of a lifetime of creativity, thoughts which, for whatever reason, he had never inscribed.

While Maimonides, Rashi, and Ba'al ha-Ma'or all occasionally changed their minds in the course of their lives (how could they not), Ravad's fertile, teeming mind found no rest—'The scholar whose wisdom keeps him at a boil and whose insight gives him no rest', as his literate opponent aptly characterized him.[49] He was always dissatisfied with his own answers, not to speak of those of others. He seems not to have operated on a single topic or work; multi-focused, Ravad seems to have worked simultaneously on any number of problems.

This combination of restless creativity and difficulties of writing, especially of sustained composition, often leads to a dangerous disproportion between personal accomplishment and literary legacy, an imbalance that is strikingly noticeable, as I have already noted,[50] in the works of Ravad's greatest contemporary, Rabbenu Tam (d.1171), whom he resembled in so many ways. Anyone who has repeatedly experienced the voltage of Ravad's brief notes and then surveys his literary legacy will feel that the creativity of the man was far greater than his literary output. Unlike Maimonides and Rashi (and one is forced to add, *pace* Ravad, Ba'al ha-Ma'or), Ravad never found an appropriate format in which to systematically cast his life's work. His genius was of the type that needs a better receptacle for his insights than he was able to provide. And one wonders what the final image and impact of Rabbenu Tam would have been had he not been followed by the more orderly genius of Dampierre.[51] Ravad had no such luck. Unlike Rabbenu Tam, Ravad of Posquières had no disciples capable of inscribing his thoughts.[52]

48 H. Gross, 'R. Abraham ben David aus Posquières: Ein literarische Vertrag', *Monatsschrift für Geschichte und Wissenschaft der Judenthums*, 22 (1874), 20; *Iggerot ha-Rambam*, ed. Y. Shilat (Jerusalem, 1995), ii. 510, 501; 474–5 and n. 3 ad loc.

49 Above, p. 304.

50 Above, p. 308.

51 Above, p. 261.

52 On the inscriptions of Ri's disciples, see my 'The Printed Page of the Talmud', in S. Mintz, ed., *Printing the Talmud: From Bomberg to Schottenstein* (New York, 2005), 40; repr. in my *Collected Essays*, i (Oxford, 2013), 7–9.

The reader may ask: if Ravad had such great difficulty ordering and recording his thoughts, whence the sobriquet 'the greatest of Provençal scholars'? The answer is simple. It was, as I have already noted,[53] Ramban and his school that perceived the depths of thought in Ravad's brief, at times gnomic, statements, built upon them, and transformed the halakhah. There was also the element of his style and temperament. As I wrote in the programmatic essay on Ravad:

Indeed, Ravad's commentaries are singularly lacking in literary grace. He belonged to that small band of writers whose style is improved by adrenalin. He is never clearer, weightier, or more epigrammatic than when in a combative position. One can, at times, get as clear a picture of Ravad's views from a terse note tossed off in exasperation as from a full paragraph in his non-polemic works. In his talent for pregnant statement he probably has no equal, but he was excelled by many in the art of straightforward presentation.

Crucial aperçu rather than comprehensive exposition was Ravad's commentarial forte, though this may have been as much a question of temperament as of talent. It was the difficult nub of a talmudic discussion that held his interest more than the task of detailed and often routine explication of an entire *sugya*; and his policy in *'Eduyot* and *Sifra* of commenting exclusively upon passages not sufficiently discussed in the Talmud reflects in a heightened fashion this exegetical inclination. He was, moreover, wholly alien to the impulse that so animated Rashi—of guiding the ordinary student through a *sugya* by forfending imperceptibly a host of minor errors. Concern for the average may be attention to the mediocre or solicitude for the all-too-human, and Ravad and Rashi were not the first thinkers who divided along this line. Ravad was a problem solver (and polemicist) not a pedagogue.[54]

Opposite Types

One of the most frequent charges that Ravad leveled against Ba'al ha-Ma'or was that of plagiarism, first and foremost of Ravad himself,[55] but also of 'the Frenchman',[56] of Rabbenu Ya'akov (Rabbenu Tam),[57] of R. Yitsḥak Ibn

[53] Above, pp. 260–1.

[54] Above, pp. 261–2.

[55] *Katuv Sham*, ed. Bergmann (above, n. 11), XXX; ed. Ḥ Freiman (above, n. 25), 127a: **בחושך שמו יכוסה, ולמה כיסה מי הוא המפרש וכבר נודע כמה שנים כי אני הוא המפרש.**

כולה מילתא דידי ועוד הוספתי ראיות בהלכה מה שלא כתב זה (ibid. 136a).

גנוב הוא מאיתי שכבר כתבתי אותו בהלכות איסור והיתר לפני האב ר' משולם (ibid. 87a).

זה ארבעים שנה כתבתיה כן בהלכות הרב במסכת כתובות (ibid. 323b).

אני מעיד עלי עדות שמים והארץ כי מכמה שנים ס[י]פר לי התירוץ הראשון שהיה משתבח בו, ואמר כי אדוני הרב ש[י]בחו. ואני זכור שקראתי עליו [משלי י: כו] 'כחומץ לשיניים וכעשן לעיניים', והקשיתי עליו כל מה שהוא מקשה עתה על עצמו (ibid. 276a).

[56] Ibid., *ad libitum*.

[57] *Ha-tsarfati* or *ha-rav ha-tsarfati* in Ravad's writings can refer to Rashi, Rashbam, or Rabbenu

Gi'at, of R. Efrayim of Kala' Ḥamad, of Rabbenu Ḥanan'el—of who not. He accuses him of 'adorning himself with other people's ornaments' and similar metaphors.

While Ta-Shma has correctly shown that there is no actual proof that the two studied together in Narbonne at the feet of R. Avraham Av Bet Din,[58] I share the view of Isadore Twersky and Alexander Marx that they were, indeed, confrères.[59] I find it difficult to imagine so intense, lifelong an animosity without a deep personal aversion. Be that as it may, I also believe that the clash was not simply of two radically different temperaments, but also of intellectual types that were polar opposites.

With the exception of Handel, Beethoven read (remember, he was deaf) little of the music of others. Quite apart from personal taste, he didn't care to do so as there was little he could do with such music, for it failed to stir any creative spirit within him. Indeed, he saw the compositions of others as a negative, as they cramped his creativity. Mozart, on the other hand, read and listened to other composers' works, and his genius could transform them into something distinctly Mozartian. He did not even disdain to borrow a theme from a children's jingle, 'Ah! Vous dirai-je maman' (the French version of 'Twinkle, Twinkle, Little Star'). The end result is scarcely a masterpiece, but its widespread popularity for over two centuries shows that it has its touch of magic, and after a few bars anyone will recognize the hand of Mozart. Rashi too, be it as a talmudic or Torah commentator, could appropriate anybody's interpretation, transform it, and make it his own.

Ravad was a loner's loner. Whether he had some commentarial tradition we shall never know, because he basically declined to use it. He had to wrest the meaning from the sources first-hand and not receive it from others as inert information. He couldn't be simply a link in a chain, a stage in a development. He had to stand alone and do it by himself, for all the pain and frustration it caused him. To such a temperament, R. Zeraḥyah was bereft of creativity, indeed, was its antithesis. He couldn't work on his own, he needed the constant draw of other people's writings. When he wasn't stealing he was lean-

Tam. Its referent can be determined only by the context. One of Ravad's monikers for the Ba'al ha-Ma'or is זנב הצרפתי, e.g. in his statement זה אין לו [ז"א אינו שלו] אלא מה (שמנו) [ששנו] אחרים *ונעשה זנב הרב הצרפתי* (*Katuv Sham*, 29a); the emendation ששנו is that of Marx ('R. Abraham b. David' [above, n. 2], 209 n. 4), and in והצרפתי נשתבש בפירושה *וזה הזנב* הולך אחריו ולא ידע בין טוב לרע. (ו)הוא סבור לתפוש על הרב [ז"א האלפסי] והנה הוא נתפש (*Katuv Sham*, 43a).

58 Ta-Shma, 'Sifrei ha-Rivot' (above, n. 2), 563.

59 Twersky, *Rabad of Posquières* (above, n. 42), 13–14: Marx, 'R. Abraham b. David' (above, n. 2), 200.

ing—on the works of others. He was also a scavenger. Let others do the pioneer work of the first commentary, as did he, Ravad, on *Kinnim*, and then R. Zeraḥyah would come in and write a counter-commentary.

R. Zeraḥyah ha-Levi scarcely lacked creativity. Much of the *Sefer ha-Ma'or* is unrelated to the Rif, but is a storehouse of independent essays that range broadly over a wide gamut of talmudic issues, including those of *Kodashim* and *Toharot*. He employs a wide range of literature, both past and contemporary, without always mentioning the source, as did many medieval thinkers. He did not, as did Mozart and Rashi, transform all that he touched. Far from it. However, R. Zeraḥyah did enough for him to be counted among the mighty.

When strong personal dislike is joined to a deep sense of being belittled, set upon, and used,[60] perspective can be lost. Moving boldly into areas where others had feared to tread—*Kodashim*, *Toharot*, Yerushalmi, Tosefta, *midreshei halakhah*—Ravad explored new continents and illuminated dark places. Like most explorers of wild lands, he was a man who was wont to stride alone, and if someone collided with him on the way, he could get very irate. And the cultured, elegant, richly talented Rabbenu Zeraḥyah ha-Levi of Lunel ensured for him a lifetime of such collisions.

60 See above, p. 307.

CHAPTER TWELVE

A Response to R. Buckwold's Critique of 'Rabad of Posquières: A Programmatic Essay', Part I

I WOULD LIKE FIRST TO APOLOGIZE to R. Buckwold for my delay in replying to his extensive critique of my article on Ravad of Posquières in the Jacob Katz *Festschrift*.[1] A chapter in a book that I was finishing had grown out of all proportion, and I decided to publish it as a separate work.[2] At the time, I thought that with a little rearranging and a touch of replastering the structure of the original work could be retained, and the book finished within several months. In fact, the book had to be entirely reorganized and new chapters written. This has taken some two and a half years, and it is only now that I am free to address his scholarly critique.

It is a pleasure to have an essay in the history of halakhah scrutinized and evaluated by a genuine *talmid ḥakham*; to have an article on Ravad evaluated by the editor of an outstanding edition of the *Ba'alei ha-Nefesh* is a double blessing.[3] Rarely have I had so learned a reader or a disputant of such distinction.

R. Buckwold's article contains many substantive criticisms and, if I read it correctly, it is also undergirded by a twofold anger. First, my contention that Ravad was a revolutionary and that he dispensed with 'geonic tutelage' strikes him as a gross, even disrespectful, misinterpretation of Ravad. How could

[1] My essay is reprinted as Chapter 10 above. For R. Buckwold's response, see E. A. Buckwold, 'Rabad—Disrupter of Tradition? A Response to Haym Soloveitchik's "Rabad of Posquieres: A Programmatic Essay"', *Torah u-Madda Journal*, 12 (2004), 24–73.

[2] *Yeinam: Saḥar be-Yeinam shel Goyim—'al Gilgulah shel Halakhah be-'Olam ha-Ma'aseh* (Tel Aviv, 2003).

[3] *Ba'alei ha-Nefesh le-Rabbenu ha-Ravad 'al Hilkhot Niddah, Mikva'ot u-Kedushah* (Benei Berak, 1992).

anyone 'dispense' with the Geonim? How could anyone 'render the Geonim irrelevant'? He is equally upset at my claim that Ravad 'transformed his heritage' or that the revolutionary jurist 'disguises his revolution—at times even from himself'.

The second aspect of my article that has awakened his wrath is my contention—in his view—that some of Ravad's doctrines were forged in part in response to contemporary problems, to historical conditions of his time. Though he is courteous enough not to say so explicitly, this smacks to him of attributing to Ravad tendencies best associated with Reform or Conservative Judaism. He vigorously denies any such agenda on the part of Ravad and proceeds to expose what he believes are the subtle ways in which I have insinuated these heretical notions into my presentation of Ravad and his work.

I would like to begin by addressing the latter half of his article—his underlying anger at my 'Reformist' portrait of Ravad—and then turn to his specific critiques of my essay.

Passing for the moment the issue whether or not I actually contended what he attributes to me (we will deal with that later on), his outrage is nevertheless misplaced. In the matter of response to contemporary problems, one has to clearly distinguish between the realms of ritual and civil law, between the areas of 'Oraḥ Ḥayyim' and 'Yoreh De'ah' and that of 'Ḥoshen Mishpat'. The Reform movements of the past two centuries have centered on ritual law; adjustments of 'Ḥoshen Mishpat' are an ongoing enterprise of halakhah. Suppose religious Jews were to insist on having all their business litigation adjudicated by rabbinic courts, or that the State of Israel were to hand civil litigation over to rabbinic courts: does R. Buckwold not think that efforts would be made in the halakhah to justify the existence of corporations, of stock markets, of credit cards? What would he say of a decisor or respondent (*dayyan* or *meshiv*) who, upon being asked to adjudicate the inheritance of Walter Annenberg, were to rule that Mr Annenberg had all the while been a pauper, and that there were precious few assets to be divided among his heirs? Most of Annenberg's famous business acquisitions were exercises of the purest *asmakhta*; the bulk of his assets were in stocks and securities—intangible goods (*davar she-ein bo mamash* or *davar she-lo ba la-'olam*) which are not subject to acquisition; and as for his famous art collection, almost all of it had been acquired from Gentiles, and the proper modes of acquisition (*kinyan*) had never been employed.

The world of affairs is not under Jewish control; corporations exist, as does the stock market, and they will not disappear because the halakhah refuses to recognize them. The Sages of the Talmud (*Ḥazal*) realized this and grappled with these problems, as did the Geonim and medieval Talmudists (*rishonim*), as R. Buckwold himself states further on in his essay.[4] If halakhah is to regulate the office no less than the home, it must come to grips with an alien reality and give it recognition in its thinking. Both modern Orthodox and most *ḥaredi* communities have no need for any work on 'Ḥoshen Mishpat' similar to the *Mishnah Berurah* on 'Oraḥ Ḥayyim', for halakhah stops at the office door. In their personal life they live lives of scrupulous religiosity; in their business affairs they live like pagans, by the law of the Gentiles. That they do so is understandable; less understandable are those who take their paganism as a mark of purity. *Seder Nezikin* exists for them as a beautiful world of theory, not as a regulative system. One does not sully this pure world with the dross of daily affairs. Living in an open society in a modern democratic state, such a bifurcation between the public and private spheres is possible, and the binding force of 'Ḥoshen Mishpat' is entirely optional. This was not the case in the closed corporate states of the Middle Ages. Each group was charged with regulating the affairs of its members, and if it ceased to do so, its self-government and survival were seriously endangered. Self-government was a prerequisite for Jewish continuance, which meant grappling with intractable economic realities and finding halakhic categories on the basis of which to adjudicate the issues that arose from their existence. To say that Ravad wrestled with the dearth of currency in his time or with the urgent need for greater credit mobility is not to discredit him. It simply means that he lived in an era where it was axiomatic that the full spectrum of one's activities fell within the orbit of halakhah, and that God's word was not to be consigned as now to the inner sanctums of the home and synagogue.

R. Buckwold further feels that the response to contemporary problems yields a false or specious halakhah. To my thinking the problem of sale of notes of indebtedness (*mekhirat ḥov*), like that of credit cards today, is simply a challenge to halakhic thinking, as is a problem or objection (*kushya*) posed in the study hall (*bet midrash*). Both stimuli can generate a correct response or a specious one, and instances of good and bad replies can be found in abundance for each of the two catalysts. The fact that a theorem is a response to a contemporary *kushya* scarcely invalidates it; similarly a response to a contemporary challenge is not disqualified by its origins. A reflexive, undiscriminating reaction to the phrase 'a halakhic response to a contemporary problem', while readily understandable, advances the comprehension of neither halakhah nor its history.

The difference between the response to a theoretical question and a practi-

[4] p. 46 and cited below at p. 340.

cal one is primarily the time frame. The theoretical question can be answered at one's leisure, and, as happens only too frequently, the proper reply can occur to the thinker only after a long while. A responsum, however, must be written in a brief space of time. The world cannot come to a standstill while judges ponder problems for years. There is, moreover, no guarantee that the correct proof will occur to the respondent in the short time allotted to him. It is this pungent awareness of the constraints of practical decision-making that, arguably, led the greatest Ashkenazic respondent of modern times, Ḥatam Sofer, to assert that the intuition of a *posek* is far more important than his argument. The argument may well be faulty, but if the intuition is correct, the *pesak* will be justified in the course of time.[5] This is hardly a prescription for a *rosh yeshivah*, and any *dayyan* of a lesser mold would be well advised to see that his arguments are sound. However, Ḥatam Sofer's remarks do highlight the frequent limitations in judicial rationales, limitations that one must occasionally reckon with.

Let me now turn to the specific critiques. First, however, a note on procedure.

I will first reproduce both my original statement and the entire text of R. Buckwold's criticism and then respond to the latter. As R. Buckwold's critique often incorporates large sections of my original article, this results in overlap. I doubt whether readers will view themselves as twice blessed by these repetitions.[6] I beg their forbearance. Most of my readers have no access to the Katz *Festschrift*, where my essay originally appeared, nor could I assume that they have retained a copy of my learned colleague's critique. The only way that I could ensure that the reader held in his or her hand all the data necessary for an informed judgment is to present the texts in full.

As these quotations lengthen the reply considerably and as there is a limit to any reader's patience, I have decided to divide my reply and will treat, in this chapter, only the matter of Ravad's response to economic realities. The second installment of my discussion, in the following chapter, will, among other things, address the nature of 'revolutions' in halakhah, what it means to dispense with a literature of half a millennium, the issue of precedent and innovation, and how in law the new wears necessarily the guise of the old. The reader will then be able to judge whether my sins in these areas are as scarlet as R. Buckwold takes them to be.

[5] Shelomoh Sofer, *Ha-Ḥut ha-Meshullash* (Tel Aviv, 1963), 97–9.

[6] In the interest of keeping the citations within manageable size, I have not reproduced R. Buckwold's footnotes, except on two occasions when I address them.

EXAMPLE 1[7]

May a creditor insist on payment of a debt in legal tender, even when he holds a pawn as security?

I Wrote[8]

More significant than these sundry borrowings, these occasional aids in solution, are the thoughts which living in an alien world engendered. Much of medieval writing is a response to just such stimuli. Section 50 of the *Temim De'im* provides a good example. The inquiry put to R. Avraham as to whether a debtor can be compelled to redeem a gage did not arise in a vacuum. In Germanic law a pawn is a quit-payment, with no further obligation incumbent upon the debtor. In gaging, the debtor sold the pawn to the creditor in exchange for the money received, reserving to himself only the right of repurchase, a right that he might or might not exercise. It is difficult, however, to run separate businesses—one for Jews and one for Gentiles. Business is business, and habits are habits. The daily practice of treating one set of gages as a sale with the right of repurchase inevitably led to someone questioning whether the other set was so radically different. And the question, once asked, as asked it was all over Europe—Spain, Provence, Germany[9]—admitted no simple answer. True, Jewish law, at first glance, is incurably obligational. Pawns are never *Sachhaftung*, but simply accessorial to the ongoing personal obligation. But by holding the pawn, the creditor holds in his hands the means of payment. Why should he not be told to look there for satisfaction? Does he have the right to reject the pawn and insist on another form of payment, that is, cash? Put concisely in halakhic terms, a pledge is certainly an *apotiké*; is it an *apotiké meforash*? And if it is an *apotiké meforash* (as the *'Ittur* tells us the sages of Narbonne thought),[10] just how does a formula of **לא יהיה לך פרעון אלא מזה** ('you may only collect from this [piece of property]') give rise

[7] In my original essay, I used three examples to demonstrate Ravad's strong ties to intellectual currents and commercial problems in Provence at the time (see pp. 278–80 above). Keeping my wording, R. Buckwold structured his critique around those three points. In my response I have preserved his structure, and reply separately to each of his critiques of my three examples.

[8] Above, pp. 276–8.

[9] |**orig. n. 32**| (reference is to original note numbers in 'Ravad of Posquières: A Programmatic Essay', printed as Ch. 10 above). *'Ittur*, Potiké, ed. R. M. Yonah (repr. New York, 1955), fo. 64, col. 2; *Sifran Shel Rishonim*, ed. S. Assaf (Jerusalem, 1935), #5. *Temim De'im* (above, p. 263 n. 15), #50; *Sefer Ravan*, ed. S. Albeck (Warsaw, 1905), #111.

[10] |**orig. n. 33**| *'Ittur*, Potiké, fo. 64, col. 2. {*Apotiké* is a mortgage, liened real estate. Under certain circumstances, this restricts the creditor from collecting from any other liened real estate. *Apotiké meforash* is a mortgage explicitly restricted to a specific piece of property.}

to a personal obligation? To use for a moment northern French terminology, is there *shi'abud ha-guf* (personal obligation) in an *apotiké meforash*, and if there be only a *shi'abud nekhasim* (a lien on property which subjects it to collection without any obligation on the part of the debtor to repay the loan), isn't that *Sachhaftung*?[11] Is the Jewish gage, after a closer look, really so different from the Germanic one?

Ravad threw up his hands at the problem and decided to let the Gentiles solve de facto the riddle of their own making. He replied: **ובמשכונא של קרקע, במקום שאין מנהג לישראל הולכין אחר מנהג של גויים, והם נהגו וכו'**. ('And as regards mortgages: in those places where there is no distinct Jewish custom, one follows the customaries [*coutumiers*] of the Gentiles, and their practice is etc.') The reply is revealing, especially his concluding remark: **וכן אני אומר בכל דבר שאין דינו מפורש אצלנו ואין לנו בו מנהג ידוע, שהולכים בו אחר המנהגות שלהם, וקרוב דבר זה לדינא דמלכותא והם דנים על פי מנהגות** ('and I [further] say that in all [monetary] matters in which we have neither a clear halakhic ruling nor a customary practice, we should follow their [i.e. the Gentiles'] customaries, and this is analogous to [the talmudic ruling that] "The law of the kingdom is the law [i.e. binds Jews]", and they [i.e. the Gentiles] rule according to what is found in their customaries')—all of which would be inconceivable north of the Loire, and which accurately reflects the relative merits of the Provençal and Champagne systems of justice at the time. Ravad's remarks here should be correlated with his views on solidarity of sureties in the *Hassagot 'Hilkhot Malveh ve-Loveh'*, 25: 10. Both opinions reflect the rather favorable assessment of the Provençal exile that he gave expression to when he commented on the words of the *Sifra*:

> **וישבתם לבטח בארצכם [ויקרא כו ה]: בארצכם אתם ישובים לבטח ולא בחוץ לארץ. פי[רוש:] הגרים החוצה לארץ אינם בכלל ברכה**
>
> 'and ye shall dwell in your land safely' [Lev. 26: 5]: in your land you shall dwell safely but not in other lands [*ḥuts la-arets*]. Explanation: those who live in *ḥutsah la-arets* are not included in the Divine blessing [of safety; i.e. those who live outside Israel have no Divine promise of security, though they may well in fact enjoy it].[12]

The initial query (regarding redemption of gages) should furthermore be placed alongside the suit between Aimery de Clermont and the Abbot of Aniane in the year 1203, which Eduard Meynial has noted:

> However, at the beginning of the thirteenth century the cartulary of Aniane provides us with a very interesting example of this 'romanization' [i.e. penetration of Roman

[11] |**orig. n. 34**| See R. Aryeh Leib ha-Kohen's *Ketsot ha-Ḥoshen* (New York, 2014), 386: 5.

[12] |**orig. n. 35**| Ravad's commentary on the *Sifra* published as *Sifra de-Vei Rav: hu Torat Kohanim 'im Perush R. Avraham ben David* (Vienna, 1862), 'Behar', 4: 4.

law]. Aimery, creditor of the abbot, claims the right to demand of the abbot to repurchase the pawn that he has gaged to him. The abbot declines to repurchase. If one treats a pledge as a sale with right of repurchase [as in Germanic law] . . . the abbot is correct, for the repurchase is a right which the vendor need not exercise. If, however, the pawn is subjected to Roman rules, the abbot is wrong, for repurchasing the pledge is simply repaying the debt; the existence of the pledge, since it did not extinguish the debt, does not deprive the creditor of the right to insist on payment when the contracted time is up.[13]

Moving from the opposite directions, halakhah and Provençal law met here in a point of common perplexity. In Ravad's case it is the encounter of an obligational system of gage with the notions of *Sachhaftung*; in the suit of Aniane it is the movement of a system (the Germanic one) rooted in *Sachhaftung* towards the concept of *obligatio*.

R. Buckwold Wrote[14]

The last major theme of the 'Programmatic Essay' is Ravad's supposed contribution to the development/evolution of Halakhah. According to Professor Soloveitchik, Ravad covertly 'transformed his heritage following the pattern of the revolutionary jurist [who] must disguise his innovations'.

In arguing his case, Professor Soloveitchik offers us 'three brief examples of how Ravad's writings are anchored in Provençal life and thought'. These examples are intended to reveal non-Halakhic considerations that actually lay behind what appears to be strictly Halakhic argumentation and reasoning.

Examination of these sources, however, reveals that they offer no basis for such claims.

Example 1—'Section 50 of the *Temim De'im* . . . The inquiry put to R. Abraham as to whether a debtor can be compelled to redeem a gage.' Prof. Soloveitchik offers an interesting approach to the source of the question:

In Germanic law a pawn is a quit-payment, with no further obligation incumbent upon the debtor. In gaging, the debtor sold the pawn to the creditor in exchange for the money received, reserving to himself only the right of repurchase. . . . It is difficult, however, to run separate businesses—one for Jews and one for Gentiles. . . . The daily practice . . . inevitably led to someone questioning whether the other set was so radically different. . . . True, Jewish law, at first glance, is incurably obligational. Pawns are never *Sachhaftung*, but simply accessorial to the ongoing personal obligation. . . . Does he have the right to reject the pawn and insist on another form of payment, i.e. cash?

[13] |**orig. n. 36**| E. Meynial, 'De l'application du droit romain dans la région de Montpellier au XIIe et XIIIe siècles', *Atti del Congresso Internazionale di Scienze Storiche (Roma, 1–9 Aprile 1903)*, ix: *Storia del dritto* (Rome, 1904), 147–69.

[14] 'Rabad—Disrupter of Tradition?' (above, n. 1), 40–5.

> Put concisely in halakhic terms, a pledge is certainly an *apotiké* [mortgage]; is it an *apotiké meforash* [a specified mortgage]? . . . Is the Jewish gage. . . really so different from the Germanic one?

Soloveitchik further explains:

> The initial query (regarding redemption of gages) should furthermore be placed alongside the suit between Aimery de Clermont and the Abbot of Aniane in the year 1203. . . . Moving from the opposite directions, halakhah and Provençal law met here in a point of common perplexity. In Ravad's case it is the *encounter of an obligational system of gage with the notions of Sachhaftung*. . . . [Emphases mine—EB]

How did Ravad respond? According to Soloveitchik:

> Ravad threw up his hands at the problem and decided to let the Gentiles solve de facto the riddle of their own making. He replied: ובמשכונא של קרקע, במקום שאין מנהג לישראל הולכין אחר מנהג של גויים, והם נהגו וכו'. ['With regard to a land security, where there is no established Jewish practice, we follow Gentile practice . . .']

Soloveitchik comments:

> The reply is revealing, especially his concluding remark: וכן אני אומר בכל דבר שאין דינו מפורש אצלנו ואין לנו בו מנהג ידוע, שהולכים בו אחר המנהגות שלהם, וקרוב דבר זה לדינא דמלכותא והם דנים על פי מנהגות ['and so I say in any issue where the rule is not stipulated by us (in talmudic law) and we have no known common practice, we follow their (the Gentile) common practice, and this is close to the law of the land since they rule according to their practices']—*all of which would be inconceivable north of the Loire, and accurately reflects the relative merits of the Provençal and Champagne systems of justice at the time.* ('Programmatic Essay', pp. 32–33) [Translations and emphases mine—EB]

R. Buckwold's Reservations

Before zeroing in on this source, it behooves us to comment on Soloveitchik's suggestion that Ravad was drawn to apply the talmudic principle of 'the law of the land is the law' (*dina de-malkhuta dina*) because of the superior system of justice in southern France. Had he lived in northern France—where we are to assume the Gentile justice system was less satisfactory—he would have ruled otherwise. In other words, Ravad widened the authority of Gentile law because he was favorably impressed by the merits of the Gentile justice system in which he found himself.

This suggestion is highly untenable, for two reasons: (1) Rashbam, one of the great scholars *north of the Loire*, preceded Ravad in stating that the law of the land extends to dealings between individuals, and includes common practice. (2) This very ruling of Ravad greatly limits the authority of local civil law, in that it cannot overrule explicit talmudic law or even Jewish custom! Based on Ravad's explicit opinion here, later halakhic authorities ruled to limit the authority of the law of the land, contrary to the broader ruling of a Tosafist opinion of R. Yitsḥak b. Perez, specifically referring to the Gentile practice of pawns. R. Yitsḥak b. Perez definitely did not live in Provence or Champagne.

Now, let us examine the sources. Here is the responsum from which Soloveitchik quotes—in its entirety:

שאלה: ראובן שמשכן לשמעון ביתו סתם ולא קבע לו זמן, אם יכול שמעון לכוף את ראובן לפדותו ולמשכנו עוד כל הלואתו עוד כל הלואתו במלאת שנתו. וכן אם הלוהו על המשכון סתם, [אם] יתבענו אחר ל' יום ויכוף אותו לפרעו או לא.

תשובה: כי מקומות יש בברצלונה ובספרד [ש]כופין על המשכונא סתם לפדותה אחר שנה או אחר [ה]זמן שיפסקו זה עם זה, אבל בנרבונה אין כופין לא בבית ולא בשדה ולא בכרם.

ובמשכון אחר לא שמעתי מנהג, ולפי המשנה [ההלכה] משלושים יום ואילך מוכרו בבי"ד, שלא נחלקו חכמים על דברי רשב"ג פרק המקבל (בבא מציעא דף קיג.) אלא בענין שצריך להחזיר לו משכנו, אבל באחר לא נחלקו.

ובמשכונה של קרקע במקום שאין מנהג לישראל, הולכים אחר מנהג הגויים, והם נהגו שאם לא התנה בשעת הלואה אינו יכול לכופו לפרוע [לפדותו]. וכן אני אומר בכל דבר שאין דינו מפורש אצלנו ואין לנו בו מנהג ידוע, שהולכים בו אחר מנהגות שלהם, [ש]קרוב דבר זה לדינא דמלכותא דינא, והם דנין על פי המנהגות.

QUERY: Reuven 'pawned' his house to Shimon inexplicitly without specifying a (repayment) date. Can Shimon force Reuven to redeem it at the end of the first year and not just continue holding on to it as a *mashkonah* (a land 'pawn')?

Also, if he (Shimon) lent him (money) on the basis of a pawn inexplicitly (without specifying a repayment date), can he make a demand after thirty days and force him (Reuven) to pay, or not?

RESPONSE: There are places, in Barcelona and in Spain, where (borrowers) are forced to redeem a *mashkonah* (land 'pawn') after a year (for a loan in which no repayment date was specified) or alter the time set between the two sides. However, in Narbonne they do not force (the redemption) neither by a house nor by a field nor by a vineyard.

And regarding other pawns, I have not heard of any common practice, and according to the Mishnah from thirty days on (the lender) sells it in court. For the Rabbis did not disagree with R. Shimon b. Gamliel, in chapter *Ha-Mekabbel* (*Bava Metsi'a* 113a), except on the issue of having to return the pawn, but other than that they did not disagree.

And regarding a *mashkonah* (a land 'pawn') in a place where there is no common practice of Jews, we follow the common practice of the Gentiles, and their practice is that if (the lender) did not specify (a repayment date) at the time of the loan, he cannot force (the borrower) to pay [or to redeem it]. And so I say on any issue where the rule is not stipulated by us (in talmudic law) and we have no known common practice, we follow their (the Gentile) common practice, and this is similar to the law of the land since they rule according to their common practices.

On examination of this responsum, we discover that neither the questions addressed to Ravad nor his responses bear any resemblance to the issue presented in the 'Programmatic Essay'.

1. Note that there are actually two discrete questions, and two discrete answers. Only the second question involves a pawn (*mashkon*). On this question, Ravad replies that since there is a clear halakhah, based on the Talmud, *Gentile rules and practices have no bearing on the decision.*

2. Contrary to Soloveitchik's reading, the ruling of Ravad to follow Gentile practice has nothing to do with a regular pawn at all, but rather with a '*mashkonah* of land'—an arrangement in which the lender uses the borrower's land, 'eating its fruits', while deducting minimal rental payments from the debt. This is both a form of strong pressure on the borrower to come up with the cash, and also gradual payment, if only partial. This is not a normal pawn (*mashkon*). It is rather referred to as a *mashkonah* or *mashkanta*.

A *mashkonah* (land 'pawn') is different from a normal pawn for several reasons:

(i) Land generates income. (The pressure on the borrower is thus very strong, for until he redeems his land, he loses its profits.)

(ii) Land cannot be physically moved to the control of the lender, but rather the lender must take control of the land by utilizing its productivity, thereby profiting from the income.

(iii) Since usury is halakhically prohibited, a minimal rental payment is continuously deducted from the debt.

3. Both questions raised were only in a specific context: any לא קבע לו זמן [where no repayment date was set]. This crucial detail is missing in Prof. Soloveitchik's presentation.

The logic behind the query is clear: Does the omission of a repayment date mean that the lender relinquishes his right to demand payment? The concept of a lender's relinquishment of his right to demand payment is found in the Talmud Yerushalmi, even in a case where the lender is not in possession of a pawn or *mashkonah*. It is also clear from this source that even though the lender loses his right to demand payment, *the obligation of the borrower remains*. This concept of relinquishment is also found, as Soloveitchik correctly notes, in the form of the talmudic concept *apotiki mefurash* [a specified mortgage where the lender has no right to demand any other form of payment]. Ravad himself clearly explains the legal understanding of such an agreement as the lender's relinquishing of his right to demand payment:

והוא מחל לשעבודיה שאר ארעתיה ואפילו זוזי לא בעי למיתבעיה

He (the lender) relinquishes his right to subject the other lands (of the borrower besides the specified mortgage) for payment of the debt, and even money he doesn't want to demand.

(Indeed, this rationale is especially clear in light of Ravad's perspective of a borrower's obligation, which will be discussed below in Example 2. Ravad states that even though a lender may sell his power to demand a debt, the actual obligation of the borrower to his lender cannot be sold. The obligation of a borrower, in Ravad's opinion, is his own personal obligation, not the possession of the lender. Clearly then, the lender may relinquish his saleable right of demanding payment, while leaving intact the personal obligation of the borrower. 'True, Jewish law . . . is incurably obligational'?)

The basic question—whether or not the omission of a date for payment demonstrates the lender's relinquishing his right to demand payment—has three possible variations, as can be seen in the questions and answers in Ravad's responsum:

a. *When the lender holds no pawn or mashkonah*, no question is asked since it would be unreasonable for a lender to relinquish his only form of pressure on the borrower.

b. *When the lender holds a pawn*, the question does arise. Since the pawn constitutes pressure for payment, it is possible that the lender relinquished his right to demand payment. Ravad answers, however, that there is a clear talmudic ruling that the lender does not relinquish his right to demand payment (unless there is local Jewish practice to the contrary).

c. *When the lender holds a mashkonah (a land pawn)*, Ravad differentiates between this case and the above case of a pawn. Here he finds no halakhic ruling (unless there is local Jewish practice that defines the lender's intention) since the pressure on the borrower is great: the more the payment is delayed, the more income the borrower loses, and the more the lender profits from the produce of the land. Indeed, the lender's right to demand payment is not crucial, and perhaps the absence of a date shows that he relinquished it.

In summary: The questions addressed to Ravad relate to a situation in which a date is absent from the agreement of a *mashkonah* (a land pawn) and of a pawn: May the lender force a payment in cash (or sell the pawn)—and when—or must he continue holding on to the *mashkonah* (a land pawn) or to the pawn? Ravad answers that if there is a local Jewish practice, the practice defines the inexplicit agreement.

Where there is no local Jewish practice: in the case of a pawn, we find a talmudic ruling that he can force a payment after 30 days. Gentile law and practice cannot change this ruling.

As to a *mashkonah* (a land pawn), there is no talmudic ruling. Therefore, the practice of the Gentiles defines the inexplicit agreement, based on the talmudic principle of 'the law of the land is the law'.

Soloveitchik's account of the suit between Aimery de Clermont and the Abbot of Aniane in the year 1203 is most interesting. However, we are not shown even a remote parallel in the writings of Ravad.

My Reply

R. Buckwold prefaces his critique of the gaged loan with one directed against my remarks about *dina de-malkhuta dina*. He cites the ruling of Rashbam, who lived north of the Loire, as disproving my thesis, and follows up both in the text and in a lengthy footnote (n. 86), disputing the radical nature of Ravad's ruling, not to speak of his alleged esteem for the judicial practice in the surrounding society.

In the preface to this section of the essay, I wrote, 'I would like . . . to conclude it [i.e. the essay] with three brief examples of how Ravad's writings are anchored in Provençal life and thought'. I clearly was far too brief. Let me begin by noting that Ravad does not say that the case at bar of following Gentile practice in some instances of *mashkona* (we will discuss the meaning of the term later) is one of *dina de-malkhuta dina*, rather that 'this matter is *akin* to *dina de-malkhuta dina*' (*קרוב* דבר זה לדינא דמלכותא דינא). And in a gloss on *Mishneh Torah*, 'Hilkhot Malveh ve-Loveh', 25: 10, which I also cited (and which R. Buckwold ignored), and in which he states that one follows Gentile custom in the matter of solidarity of sureties, Ravad does not mention *dina demalkhuta dina* at all (זה אינו מחוור אלא לפי המנהג ולמידין מן הגוים לישראל). Why the 'akin' in the case at bar and his silence in the case of sureties?

Very simple. All cases of *dina de-malkhuta dina* involve commands of a sovereign ruler. His authority to issue these commands may stem from the traditional prerogatives of a ruler—presumed, in medieval political theory, to have consent of the entire realm as Rashbam would have it, or as a consequence of rabbinic ordinance (הפקר בית דין הפקר) as Rabbenu Tam advocated—from the implicit powers of a ruler parallel to those of a Jewish king (*mishpetei ha-melukhah*), as is reported in the name of Ri; from the ownership of all the lands of the realm as a king had in a feudal structure, and obedience to his commands was a precondition to the right of settlement as R. Eli'ezer of Metz, and more famously R. Nissim of Barcelona (Ran), held, or some variation of the above.[15] This may be, and indeed swiftly was, extended to rulers of all sorts—dukes, barons, local potentates, and also to town councils (*raat*) when cities achieved local autonomy and self-government. And it is this sovereign authority, the traditional prerogative of the king to confiscate and award property, that Rashbam refers to when he writes the passage that R. Buckwold cited:

כל מסים וארנוניות[!] ומנהגות של משפטי המלכים שרגילים להנהיג במלכותם דינא הוא שכל בני המלכות מקבלים עליהם מרצונם חוקי המלך ומשפטיו

All taxes, *arnonas*, and customary practices of the Crown, that is to say, that which kings are accustomed to instituting in their kingdoms, are the law—for all the subjects of the Crown accept of their own free will the laws of the king and his judgments.

The *coutumiers* (*minhagot*) that Ravad is referring to, however, were not the product of any legislation, nor were they the consequence of the will of any sovereign body; they were simply the local customs as known by all and, if questioned, as attested to by the elders. The *coutumiers* were not something ordained from above; quite the contrary: legislation was an innovation and an anathema, and was out of the question. *Coutumiers* were the time-honored practices of some locale that throughout much of western Europe were held to have prescriptive force, for people must act in the present as they have acted in the past. Three different *coutumiers* could obtain under the same ruler if three places under his sway had differing traditions, as they often did; conversely, the lands of three different rulers could and did have the same *coutumier*. It is this fundamental difference that led Ravad on one occasion to analogize local *minhagot* to *dina de-malkhuta dina* (as both they and the *minhagot* of a royal power, as Rashbam puts it, flow from being time-honored) but not identify it

15 Rashbam, *Bava Batra* 54b, s.v. *ve-ha-amar*; *Teshuvot Ba'alei ha-Tosafot*, ed. Agus, #12; *Ḥiddushei ha-Ritva*, *Bava Batra*, 5th edn., ed. M. Y. H. Blau (New York, 1995), 55a, s.v. *hanei telat*; and see Ramban's statement in the name of his teachers, **שקבלו מדעת הצרפתים**, in *Sefer ha-Terumot*, Giddulei Terumah edn. (Venice, 1643), #46: 8: 5; *Or Zarua'*, *Bava Kamma*, #447; *Perush ha-Ran 'al Nedarim*, 28a, s.v. *be-mokhes*.

with that principle (for a *coutumier* does not eventuate in any sovereign power to tax, issue coin, execute, confiscate, and the like). And on a second occasion, in the matter of sureties, he refrained from analogizing them to *dina de-malkhuta dina* altogether. In the matter of local *coutumiers*, we are here in a grey area, and the direction in which one turns in grey areas indicates how one is inclined.

Furthermore, the halakhah, like common law, tends to be casuistic, that is to say, it tends to decide things on a case-by-case basis. A decisor can, if he so chooses, expand his ruling into a general formulation, or he can leave it to others to enshrine the ruling not simply as precedent but as archetype. Ravad was asked about a secured loan both of mobilia and real estate in which no date of repayment was specified. He replied fully to the question at hand and to variants thereof. He could have stopped there; but he didn't. He proceeded to enunciate a general principle applicable to *all lacunae* in Jewish law, something he was not asked about and something he obviously felt quite at ease promulgating.

> וכן אני אומר בכל דבר שאין דינו מפורש אצלנו ואין לנו בו מנהג בדבר שהולכים בו אחר המנהגות שלהם.

Similarly, I am of the opinion that in all matters where there is neither a clear halakhic prescription nor an established Jewish practice, we should follow the customary practices [*coutumiers*] of the Gentiles.

Gentile law, he announced, should fill the interstices, the blank spaces of halakhah. This is no minor assertion; small wonder that Ramban, when he referred to this responsum in his reply to an inquiry of R. Shemu'el ha-Sardi (of Cerdagne), the author of the *Sefer ha-Terumot*, wrote: דבר זה אתה יודע שכבר נשאל הראב"ד ומה שנסתפק בו והורה עליו *בעמעום* ('As you know, Ravad was already asked about this case and his doubts and final ruling were *murky*').[16] Ramban's pupil, Rashba, spoke pointedly against analogizing regnant Gentile law to royal law and enactments, and even claimed that rulings of the royal courts which constitute expansions or interpretations of the royal wish were not halakhically binding:

> ועוד אני אומר שעל דיני הגויים [לא] אמרו דינא דמלכותא דינא, שאין מקפיד על דינין ידועין, שזה בא ומחדש ומפרש דינין לפי דעתו ושכלו, ואחר כך בא אחר ומהפך דבריו. אין למלך קפידא כלל, אלא אם כן הם נימוסין ידועין עשויין מצד המלכות שלא ידונו אלא כך . . . ודינא דמלכותא דינא אבל דיני אומתו לאו דינא.

[16] *Teshuvot ha-Ramban*, ed. C. H. Chavel (Jerusalem, 1975), #40, p. 66. R. Shemu'el, who subsequently cited Ravad's ruling, graciously omitted the word *be-eimmum*. See *Sefer ha-Terumot* (above, n. 15), #49: 53: 3.

Moreover, I believe that *dina de-malkhuta* does not apply to [all] laws of the Gentiles. He [i.e. the king] doesn't pay any attention to well-known laws [emanating from a different source] that this one [i.e. the judge] creates (and) [or] interprets simply in accordance with what he thinks, and later another judge reverses his decision. The king couldn't care less about these laws, only about those rulings well known as enactments of royal making and bearing the instruction [of the Crown] to rule thus . . . [The maxim] *dina de-malkhuta dina* was said about laws of the Crown, not the laws of the nation [i.e. emanating from the subjects of the Crown.][17]

Rashba reiterated even more forcefully his critique in another responsum against the mandatory force of the now transcribed local *coutumiers* and parts of Roman law that had filtered into law books:

> ולענין[18] דינא דמלכותא דינא שאמרת, בודאי לא אמרו אלא במאי דאיכא הורמנא דמלכא ובדברים שהם מדיני המלכות . . . אבל דינין שדנין בערכאות אין אלו משפטי המלוכה אלא הערכאות דנין לעצמן כמו שימצאו בספרי דיינין, שאם אין אתה אומר כן, בטלת חס ושלום דיני ישראל.

Regarding what you wrote about *dina de-malkhuta*, certainly this law refers to those laws where there are royal edicts . . . however, those laws [or rulings] that emerge from popular [or merchant] courts, these are not royal laws but [simply] what those courts find in the judges' books [or handbooks]. For [if one does not discount these rulings] one has put an end [to the effective rule] of Jewish law.[19]

Me'iri, though a proud defender of Provençal traditions in general and of Ravad's writings against the critiques of Ramban in particular, nevertheless wrote: אבל מה שהם עושים מתורת נימוס הידוע להם בספריהם, אין זה נקרא דינא דמלכותא ('However, what they [the Gentiles] do because of a law which they find in their books [of law], this is not included in *dina de-malkhuta*').[20]

A characteristically bold doctrine of Ravad, voluntarily enunciated far beyond the immediate, local need of the case at bar; a parallel ruling of his in the matter of solidarity of sureties and a positive assessment on Ravad's part of the security of the Provençal exile of his time (as reflected in his *Sifra* commentary); taken together with an effective court system of civil law, which Provence in the mid-twelfth century possessed but scarcely Champagne—all this led me to write what I did in the essay.

17 *Teshuvot ha-Rashba*, ed. A. Zelaznik (Jerusalem, 1997), vol. iii, #109. The emendation *lo* is that of the editor.

18 Ibid., #149.

19 R. Menaḥem le-Vet ha-Me'iri (Me'iri), *Magen Avot* (London, 1908), and #21 in particular, which is a lengthy, detailed reply to Ramban's extensive critique of Ravad's *Ḥibbur Lulav*, printed in Chavel's edition of the *Teshuvot ha-Ramban* (above, n. 16), 223–64.

20 *Bet ha-Beḥirah, 'Avodah Zarah*, ed. A. Sofer (New York, 1961), 16b, s.v. *ha-Mishnah ha-shevi'it*, p. 41.

R. Buckwold's approach is not to ask: What concretely did Ravad have in mind when he wrote of *minhagot*; what concretely was Rashbam thinking of when he wrote of מנהגות של משפטי המלכים (customary practices of the Crown)? The first would have led him to books on French private law in the Middle Ages and the nature of *coutumiers*; the second, to medieval political theory and rationales of royal power.[21] (Without the notion of *consensus fidelium*, the universal agreement that is postulated in medieval political theory and which need not actually exist, one is perplexed by Rashbam's continuation: שכל בני המלכות מקבלים עליהם מרצונם חוקי המלך ומשפטיו—'for all the subjects of the Crown accept of their own free will the laws of the king and his judgments'. Did they run a referendum in medieval times on royal edicts?) In either case R. Buckwold would swiftly have realized how different the two rulings of Ravad and Rashbam were. He, furthermore, declined (barring a passing reference to Rabbenu Yonah in a footnote) to place the remarks of Ravad in their medieval context, in the writings of his Provençal and Catalonian successors. This would have led him to such books as Shemu'el Shilo's comprehensive study of the topic, entitled, not surprisingly, *Dina de-Malkhuta Dina*,[22] which would provide him with a fuller and clearer halakhic and historical understanding of that concept. It would have made him equally cognizant of the boldness of Ravad's ruling. He relied, rather, upon the sixteenth- and seventeenth-century commentators on Alfasi and the *Shulḥan 'Arukh*,[23] who could not know of the nature of *coutumiers*, and thus elided the dramatic expansion contained in Ravad's ruling, treating it as dealing directly with the classic instance of sovereign edicts.

This problem runs like Ariadne's thread through much of R. Buckwold's presentation. To give another example from the topic under discussion: R. Buckwold points out that Ravad's doctrine, far from being an expansion of *dina de-malkhuta dina*, is actually a restrictive one. He writes:

> This very ruling of Ravad greatly limits the authority of local civil law, in that it cannot overrule explicit talmudic law or even Jewish custom! Based on Ravad's explicit opinion here, later halakhic authorities ruled to limit the authority of the law of the land, contrary to the broader ruling of a Tosafist opinion of R. Yitsḥak b. Perez, specifically referring to the Gentile practice of pawns.

[21] The best introduction is J. Gilissen, *La Coutume*, Typologie des Sources du Moyen Âge Occidentale 41 (Turnhout, 1982). On political theory, see F. Kern, *Kingship and Law in the Middle Ages* (repr. New York, 1970), 70–5, 149–66.

[22] Jerusalem, 1975. The immediately related pages are 60–2, 185–6. See also his index under the entries *nimusei ha-goyyim*, *dinei ha-goyyim*, and *minhagei ha-goyyim*.

[23] Both in the above-cited text and in his lengthy n. 86.

R. Buckwold then proceeds to treat R. Yitsḥak's ruling as one of many halakhic positions advanced by *rishonim*, on a par with the other positions of the Tosafists or of Ramban and his school. Let us look more closely at that doctrine and the use that R. Buckwold makes of it, for it illustrates the difference between writing history and doing law and also the dangers that attend a would-be historian of halakhah (or would-be critic of a historian of halakhah) in viewing the medieval *rishonim* from the vantage point of the *Shulḥan 'Arukh*.

The doctrine of R. Yitsḥak b. Perets, a late thirteenth-century English scholar, is a radical one. It states that *dina de-malkhuta dina* overrides not just Jewish customary practice but even explicit talmudic dictates! Taken at face value this would mean that someone seeking a *yadin yadin* degree (rabbinic ordination for adjudicating cases in civil law) would do better to study in an American law school than in a yeshivah. Not surprisingly, many decried this doctrine.[24] It merits further inspection.

The doctrine is found in the printed *Mordekhai* on *Bava Kamma* and in the *Mordekhai* only.[25] No other medieval collection cites him. Inspection of Avraham Halperin's critical edition of the *Mordekhai* on *Bava Kamma* reveals the following. Fourteen of the eighteen manuscripts of the work on *Bava Kamma* do not have this passage at all, including that at the Academy of Sciences, Budapest, 2° 1, the oldest and far away the best manuscript. Of the four remaining, three have the manuscript as a gloss and one (Jewish Theological Seminary [JTS] Rabbinica 674) has the passage in the text, though marked **תוס'** ('add.'), that is to say **תוספת** ('addition').[26] Thus, as Halperin and Urbach already noted, one can trace the progress of the gloss into the text.[27] As luck would have it, a manuscript similar to the one in the JTS library had found its way to the printers in Constantinople of the first edition of the *Mordekhai* in 1509.[28] They published what they possessed and accurately marked it with the note **תוס'**, i.e. **תוספת** (a marking that is still found in the standard Romm edition). However, many famous doctrines of the Ba'alei ha-Tosafot are

[24] e.g. R. Shabbetai ha-Kohen in *Siftei Kohen* (*Shakh*), 'Ḥoshen Mishpat', 66: 39: **אלא אפי' לשאר פוסקים דאמרי' ד"ד בכל דבר היינו מה שאינו נגד תורתינו אלא שאינו מפורש אצלינו, אבל לדון בדיני עכו"ם נגד תורתינו חלילה.** ('Even according to the other opinions, who claim that *dina de-malkhuta dina* applies in all spheres, this is true only for what does not contradict our holy Torah, but simply fills a lacuna; however, to rule according to Gentile law contrary to our Torah, God forbid!') See also Rama, 'Ḥoshen Mishpat', 369: 11 end, and authorities there cited.

[25] *Mordekhai* on *Bava Kamma*, ed. A. Halperin (Jerusalem, 1992), ii. 188, #154.

[26] Ibid., 'Textual Variants', n. 45.

[27] Ibid., introductory volume, i. 29–30; E. E. Urbach, *Ba'alei ha-Tosafot*, rev. edn. (Jerusalem, 1980), 512 nn. 4, 5.

[28] 52d, end of #153 and closed by *ad kan leshono*, end of #154.

equally found in the printed *Mordekhai* with the marking *tosefet*, for the author was killed in the Rintfleisch pogrom of 1298, and his students added to the unfinished oeuvre the notes R. Mordekhai had assembled but had not yet integrated into his work.[29] Subsequent halakhists, therefore, had no way of knowing that this note was not an integral part of the *Mordekhai*. Thus, through the agency of the printed *Mordekhai*, and only via this sixteenth-century print, did the doctrine enter the halakhic mainstream, especially in the writings of such Polish Talmudists as R. Mosheh Isserles and the commentators on the *Shulḥan 'Arukh*.

If viewed from the vantage point of modern times, the post-*Shulḥan 'Arukh* period, had Ravad's doctrine dealt with the rule of a sovereign power (as it did not), it would indeed have been a restriction of R. Yitsḥak's position, as R. Buckwold describes it. In the Middle Ages, R. Yitsḥak's doctrine simply didn't exist. It achieved no recognition in the literature of the *rishonim*, was registered in no halakhic work of the period. It is a report of a scribe on a ruling of a none-too-famous Talmudist (to put it mildly) that, at a much later date and by sheer accident, made its way into the first edition of an influential text. Once a doctrine enters the legal mainstream, it is given full faith and credence; historically, however, it cannot be equated to, or used as a yardstick to measure, major doctrines of medieval halakhists or be called a 'tosafist' opinion.

In fact, one doesn't even know if R. Yitsḥak b. Perets ever intended the wider rule that later authorities attributed to him. He never enunciated a general principle as did Ravad. True, he cited the Talmud in *Gittin* 9b as proof. Yet he adjudicated a specific case only, and one charged with meaning, even with danger, in the England of his time. He ruled on the right to sell a pawn after a year and a day had elapsed since the time of the loan, a right that the king of England had specifically given Jews and expected them to exercise, to put it mildly.[30] In England, Jews and all that they possessed were, by R. Yitsḥak's time, the property of the king, not only theoretically—as may equally have been the case in some other parts of western Europe—but practically. Lest the reader suspect that I am exaggerating, the words of the greatest English jurist of the Middle Ages, Henry de Bracton, a contemporary of R. Yitsḥak, should be cited: 'The Jew can have nothing that is his own, for whatever he acquires he acquires not for himself but for the King; for Jews live not for themselves but for others, so they acquire not for themselves but for

[29] S. Cohn, 'R. Mordekhai b. Hillel', *Sinai*, 12 (1943), 143–4.

[30] H. G. Richardson, *English Jewry under the Angevin Kings* (London, 1969), 108–9.

others.'[31] The mandate of Henry III in 1253 to his justices, who had 'custody of the Jews', put it very simply: 'The King has provided and ordained that no Jew remain in England unless he do the King service, and that from the hour of his birth every Jew, male or female, serve us in some way.'[32]

Jewish moneylending was under extraordinarily close and brutal supervision in England, without parallel in western Europe.[33] A failure to maximize one's income in an intra-Jewish transaction resulted in less money being available for lending at interest to Gentiles. This, in turn, meant less income for a grasping, ruthless Crown. All Jewish financial transactions, whether between one Jew and another or between Jews and Gentiles, were effectively under royal scrutiny. If all that a Jew owned was, both legally and in fact, the property of the Crown, the writ of *dina de-malkhuta* ran in every financial transaction of a Jew. Would R. Yitsḥak have ruled the same way in instances where the Crown was not breathing down the neck of a community that had been literally shattered by brutal royal exactions,[34] as, say, in a case of abutment of two Jewish properties (*bar metsra*)? The halakhist looks at how the case has been subsequently interpreted and has his answer; the historian is barred from doing so and, despite the argument from *Gittin*, he must leave the question unanswered.

Let us now address R. Buckwold's substantive critique of my analysis of the gaged loan.

1. He challenges my analogy between Ravad's ruling and the case of Aimery of Clermont and the Abbot of Aniane. He points out that the latter case dealt with pawns (*mashkon*), that is to say mobilia (*metaltelin*), whereas Ravad's ruling dealt with a '*mashkona* of land', as he calls it, more properly, a possessory mortgage, where the creditor takes possession of the real estate—home or field—of the borrower. ('Contrary to Soloveitchik's reading, the ruling of Ravad to follow Gentile practice has nothing to do with a regular pawn at all, but rather with a "*mashkona* of land"' [p. 322]. And again: 'Soloveitchik's

[31] Henrici de Bracton, *De legibus et consuetudinibus Angliae*, ed. and trans. T. Twill, Rolls Series 70 (London, 1883), vi. 50–1. Scholars debate whether or not such a formulation implied a legal status of serfdom similar to the 'serfdom of the chamber' in the German Empire. What this formulation meant practically is clear to all. On the issue of serfdom, see R. R. Mundhill, *England's Jewish Solution: Experiment and Expulsion 1262–1290* (Cambridge, 1998), 54–5 and the literature there cited.

[32] *Select Pleas, Starrs, and other Records from the Rolls of the Exchequer of the Jews, A. D. 1220–1284*, edited for the Selden Society by J. M. Rigg (London, 1902), 47–8.

[33] C. Roth, *History of the Jews in England*, 3rd edn. (Oxford, 1964), 38–67, and, more recently, Mundhill, *England's Jewish Solution* (above, n. 31), 45–71.

[34] See R. Stacey, '1240–1260: A Watershed in Anglo-Jewish Relations?', *Historical Research*, 61/145 (1988), 135–50.

account of the suit between Aimery de Clermont and the Abbot of Aniane in the year 1203 is most interesting. However, we are not shown even a remote parallel in the writings of Ravad' [p. 324].) Once again, I wrote too briefly. Having spent a number of years studying securities in loan arrangements both in Jewish and Germanic law for a study that I published,[35] I assumed knowledge of its fundamentals on the part of my readers. I should have stated that in Germanic law there is no difference between a pawn of land and one of mobilia. In both cases the borrower had willingly parted with possession of his property, and as there was no clear distinction in Germanic law between ownership and possession, he who yielded up possession of either land or mobilia surrendered his ownership of it, and was left with only a right to redeem his former property, which he had willingly alienated.[36] For this reason I treated the two cases as identical, and I pointed out that, as habits are habits, the inability to demand payment from a Gentile debtor in an instance of secured debts gave rise to questions both in Ashkenaz and in Provence whether a demand for repayment existed in Jewish law as regards both *mashkona* and *mashkon*. (Truth to tell, I am a bit surprised by R. Buckwold's objection, for he has read, as we shall see,[37] Malafosse's article on possessory mortgages, where the Germanic concept of pawn is clearly spelled out and applied to the 'land pawn'.)

2. R. Buckwold then writes, 'Contrary to Soloveitchik's presentation the query was not: May a pawn be considered "quit-payment"? For if it were, Ravad's answer—ולפי ההלכה משלושים יום ואילך מוכרו בבית דין—would not prove anything.'[38] I request the reader to read my remarks in the text (above, p. 317). I never contended that the question posed to Ravad was one of quit-payment. I said that in Germanic law pawns were quit-payment, while halakhah views

[35] *Halakhah, Kalkalah ve-Dimmuy 'Atsmi: ha-Mashkona'ut* (Jerusalem, 1980).

[36] For the English reader, see R. Hubner, *A History of Germanic Private Law* (repr. New York, 1968), 374–84; J. Brissaud, *A History of French Private Law* (repr. New York, 1968), 427–33. A vigorous synthesis (still valuable in its general outlines of the Germanic law of pledges) was made over a century ago by the polymath J. H. Wigmore (the author of the famous work on evidence): 'The Pledge-Idea: A Study in Comparative Legal Ideas', *Harvard Law Review*, 10/6–7 (1897), 321–50, 389–417. {To what extent *Schuld* and *Haftung* are still relevant categories in current German legal scholarship is an open question. See F. H. Stewart, 'The Contract with Surety in Customary Bedouin Law', *UCLA Journal of Islamic and Near Eastern Law*, 3 (2002–3), 223–8. These controversies, however, do not affect my argument. As I pointed out in 'Pawnbroking: A Study in *Ribbit* and of the Halakhah in Exile' in *Collected Essays*, i (Oxford, 2013), 82 n. 56, §A, §B, 'Even those who disagree with the categories of *Schuld* and *Haftung* agree on the basic rules of pawnbroking that obtained in Germanic law. How one conceptualized them is a modern question asked by legal historians.' See in the pawnbroking article the appendix to n. 56, at pp. 152–3.}

[37] See above, pp. 317–8.

[38] n. 91 in Buckwold's essay.

all loans as obligational. However, once the question arose whether or not a debtor can be forced to redeem his pawn by paying his debt in legal tender, there are *indigenous* categories in the halakhah, such as *apotiké meforash*, that would yield the same result as quit-payment.

3. I cannot grasp R. Buckwold's presentation of *apotiké meforash*. He links this institution with the ruling of the Yerushalmi in *Shevi'it* (**המלוה את חבירו על מנת שלא לתובעו, השביעית משמטו**—'one who loans to another on the condition that it would not be annulled in the sabbatical year, [nevertheless] the sabbatical year annuls the debt') as understood by Ri Corcos (cited by my critic in note 93 of his article), who states that, according to the Yerushalmi, the debtor is 'morally bound' (*mi-din shamayim*) in such a case to repay the loan and, conversely, the creditor has the right of self-help (*iy tafas lo mapkinan mineih*). By virtue of this linkage, the same right of self-help and 'moral duty' of payment should exist in the instance of a destroyed *apotiké* (**נסתחפה שדהו**). However, I have not found any such rulings in the classic sources. Needless to say, I fail equally to understand his next paragraph (in parentheses), further relating Ravad's position about the personal nature of debt (**לא לך שיעבדתי את עצמי**) to his remarks in *Bava Metsi'a* about *apotiké meforash*. All Ravad says in that passage is that in an *apotiké meforash*, the creditor has restricted his property lien to a single piece of real estate. Finally, the linkage is problematic methodologically (see below, p. 359 and n. 48 there).

R. Buckwold then points out in considerable detail (pp. 312–24) that the responsum makes reply to three different situations: where there is a talmudic ruling on the case (as in a *mashkon*), where there is a Jewish practice (as in possessory mortgages with a stipulated time), and, finally, where there is neither Jewish custom nor any talmudic ruling (as in an open-ended possessory mortgage). He goes to great lengths to explain each and every one of the three cases discussed by Ravad in this responsum and why the last case is truly problematic. His implicit criticism is that I had claimed that Ravad made the entire question of demanding payment in the instance of securities dependent on Gentile practice, which he clearly did not.

I have little quarrel with the substantive portion of these remarks, but again I fear that my brevity was, perhaps, detrimental. I wrote:

> Ravad threw up his hands at the problem and decided to let the Gentiles solve de facto the riddle of their own making. He replied: **במשכונא של קרקע, במקום שאין מנהג לישראל הולכין אחרי מנהג הגויים** ('And as regards mortgages: in those places where there is no distinct Jewish custom, one follows the customaries [*coutumiers*] of the Gentiles, and their practice is etc.') The reply is revealing, especially his concluding remark:

וכן אני אומר בכל דבר שאין דינו מפורש אצלנו ואין לנו בו מנהג ידוע, שהולכים בו אחר ('and I [further] say that in all [monetary] matters in which we have neither a clear halakhic ruling nor a customary practice, we should follow their [i.e. the Gentiles'] customaries, and this is analogous to [the talmudic ruling that] "The law of the kingdom is the law [i.e. it binds Jews]", and they [i.e. the Gentiles] rule according to what is found in their customaries'.).

Having quoted the two passages where Ravad states explicitly that whenever there is a Jewish practice, not to speak of a talmudic ruling, one ignores the Gentile practice, and also states that his practical ruling affects only the instance of the possessory mortgage, I didn't think that it was necessary to summarize in English what had just been said in clear and simple Hebrew. Rereading my formulation in light of R. Buckwold's agitated remarks, I realize two things. First, that it would have been wiser to restate in English what had just been cited in Hebrew and, more significantly, that the Hebrew citation that I gave of Ravad gives the impression that he invoked the Gentile *coutumier* in all cases of possessory mortgages, when in fact he did so only in the case of one without a term limit. I would now add the following sentence: 'Ravad ruled that when there was a halakhic ruling (as in the case of a mobilia pawn), we naturally follow the halakhah; where there was Jewish custom (as in a possessory mortgage with a term limit), we follow Jewish custom; where there was neither (as in a possessory mortgage without a term limit), Ravad had no answer and decided to let the Gentiles solve de facto the problem of their own making', and continue on as in the text.

R. Buckwold is particularly offended by my suggestion that the question whether there is a right to collection in a gaged loan was generated by Gentile practice. To him this impugns the integrity of halakhic discourse. I don't see why it does. Suppose contemporary Jewry were to return to having their business affairs regulated by the halakhah. Would not the question immediately arise whether an endorsed check that has been given to a third party has met the requirements of *ketivah u-mesirah* (endorsing the note and handing it over to the purchaser) needed in the sale of loan documents?[39] Endorsement is common practice in the surrounding society, so the question naturally arises: What is its standing in the halakhah? The overwhelming bulk of Jewish credit was extended to Gentiles, and in these numerous transactions gaged loans were not collectible. Nothing was, then, more natural than to ask: What is the standing of gaged loans in Jewish law? R. Buckwold goes on at length to show that there are good halakhic grounds for serious doubt about collection in

39 *Bava Batra* 77a–b, see *Tosafot* s.v. *amar Amemar*, 'Ḥoshen Mishpat', 66: 1.

an open-ended possessory mortgage. Of course there are; otherwise Ravad would not have been stumped. Why does grappling with contemporary realities, which by definition are of Gentile manufacture, impugn the integrity of the halakhah? Only if one assumes that any contact of civil law with the nitty-gritty of actual business undermines its purity. I don't share my learned critic's assumption.

My argument in the matter of the gaged pawn (both of mobilia and of real estate) was that the question of the right to demand cash payment arose in Jewish communities of both Ashkenaz and Provence because (1) no such right existed for the creditor in the innumerable loans that Jews extended to Gentiles, for such transactions were governed by Germanic law; (2) there were concepts indigenous to the halakhah which might preclude such a right; (3) Ravad fell back on Gentile law for resolution of the instance where he could find no guidance in either normative halakhah or common Jewish practice, and (4) as a result, the halakhic system of obligation intersected here with the Germanic one of *Sachhaftung*, parallel to the intersection of *Sachhaftung* and the Roman system of *obligatio*, reflected in the suit between Aimery and the abbot. I fail to see how R. Buckwold's lengthy excursus affects in the slightest any of these four points.

No less important is that R. Buckwold missed entirely the final, fifth, point of my brief presentation. Ravad did not simply rule on a case of a possessory mortgage in an open-ended loan. He proceeded to issue a sweeping, unqualified ruling that Gentile law should fill in *all* the lacunae in halakhic civil law and practice.[40] This is the same as a contemporary decisor ruling that all gaps in 'Ḥoshen Mishpat' should be filled by the Uniform Commercial Code (UCC). (Admittedly, the *coutumiers* were far, far less comprehensive than is the UCC, but so too was twelfth-century halakhah, especially Provençal halakhah, as compared to the halakhah of today.) No wonder that Ramban called Ravad's response *'im'um* ('obscurity'; the colloquial 'murky' might be a better translation), and Rashba wrote about this radical notion: שאם אין אתה

[40] Later scholars (e.g. R. Shabbetai ha-Kohen [Shakh] in his *Siftei Kohen*, 'Ḥoshen Mishpat', 66: 39), seeking to neutralize the radical nature of Ravad's ruling, interpreted it as being similar to the talmudic passage in *Bava Metsi'a* 83a, which rules that the conditions of work customary in a locale are viewed as being implicit in any contract of labor. Ravad, however, did not analogize the 'land pawn' to the labor agreements in *Bava Metsi'a* but to *dina de-malkhuta dina*. The ruling in *Bava Metsi'a* states a judicial construction of the intentions of the parties at the time of contract, that is to say, it construes a mutually agreed-upon condition. *Dina de-malkhuta*, on the other hand, states the power of an outside authority to obligate the parties, irrespective of their intentions, real or constructed. (The Talmud refers to presumed intent in terms of *minhag ha-makom*, i.e. local custom or practice, not *dina de-malkhuta*, law of the kingdom.)

אומר כן, בטלת חס ושלום דיני ישראל ('For [if one does not discount these rulings] one has put an end to [the effective rule of] Jewish law'). This danger, however, gave Ravad's bold soul no pause. This doctrine is, as R. Buckwold emphasizes, restrictive of the one commonly attributed to R. Yitsḥak b. Perets, which would have the UCC overrule literally a *setam mishnah*, the most authoritative source in rabbinic law. However, to be less extreme than a ruling that many halakhists considered to be off the wall is not yet a sign of moderation. Needless to say, Ravad had to have had a positive assessment of contemporary Gentile law to have allowed its astonishing, massive infusion into Jewish judicial praxis.

If there is any defect in my presentation of this responsum in my essay, it lies in my failure to spell out the wholly unsolicited and radical nature of Ravad's ruling. The final section was an add-on, as it were, to an article whose purpose was to challenge the regnant image of the past half-millennium of 'Ravad the Maimonidean critic' and replace it with that of 'Ravad the talmudic commentator', upon which role his central influence on halakhah was based. Preoccupied as I was to portray Ravad's boldness in commentary, I failed to do that same boldness justice in the realm of adjudication.

EXAMPLE 2

Why may a creditor waive the debt after he has sold it (together with the note of indebtedness) to a third party?

I Wrote[41]

Material problems no less than contemporary concepts elicited a response from Ravad, and I would like to end with a brief study of the practical import of one of his better-known Maimonidean notes. In his *hassagah* on 'Hilkhot Mekhirah', 6: 12, Ravad explains Shemu'el's famous ruling המוכר שטר חוב לחבירו וחזר ומחלו, מחול ('If someone sells to another a note of indebtedness and subsequently waives it, the debt is waived') after this fashion: מפני שהלוה אומר ללוקח אני לא שיעבדתי לך את עצמי לפיכך אם כתב לו שטר חובו הריני משועבד לך ולכל הבאים מכוחך אינו יכול למחול במשכר שטר חובו. ('Because the debtor can say to the purchaser [of the debt], "I never indebted myself to you". For this reason if the debtor wrote in the note of indebtedness ["I am indebted] to you and to all who are empowered by you", the creditor cannot annul the debt after he has sold the debt.')

[41] 'Ravad of Posquières', pp. 278–80 above.

These are some of the most seminal words ever penned on the nature of obligation and, together with those of Rabbenu Tam,[42] they have given birth to an entire literature. But the *lefikhakh* ('therefore') suggests a practical purpose to his remarks, and this finds corroboration in the fact that Ravad saw fit to reiterate this proviso on no fewer than four other occasions.[43] Clearly Ravad's doctrine must be studied not only from the perspective of the development of halakhic thought, but also in the context of twelfth-century Provence. It should be linked with another ruling of his, reported in *Sefer ha-Terumot*:

> נשאל הראב״ד ז״ל: המוכר שטר לחבירו, ויש משכון ביד המלוה ומסרו ביד הלוקח אם יכול המוכר שהוא המלוה למוחלו (ללוקח) [ללוה] אם לאו? והשיב שאינו יכול למחול מאחר שהמשכון מוחזק ביד הלוקח. והביא ראיה ממה שכתב הרי״ף בכתובות משום דמתנת שכיב מרע עשאוה כמתנה דאורייתא דכמאן דמטיא ליד המקבל דמי, ולפיכך אין היורש מוחלה. מדקאמר [הרי״ף] 'דמטיא לידיה דמקבל דמי', שמע מיניה אם יש משכון ביד המלוה ומסרו ללוקח, שאינו יכול למוחלו. ע״כ

Ravad was asked, if someone sold a debt to another person and the creditor passed on the debtor's pawn to the purchaser, can the original creditor waive the debt? And he [i.e. Ravad] replied: 'He cannot waive the debt since the purchaser has now the pawn.' And he [i.e. Ravad] brought a proof from what R. Alfas said about gifts made in contemplation of death, that such oral gifts were as valid as one made in consonance with the laws of the Torah, for such a gift is seen as 'having come into the hands of the receiver [of the gift]'. One may infer from this [Ravad contends] that if the original creditor passed on the pawn to the purchaser, he cannot waive the debt.[44]

I, for one, am at a loss to understand how the case discussed by Alfasi has any bearing upon the question at hand. If Ravad, however, says that it is relevant, I defer to his judgment, but I remain no less perplexed. Assuming that one can indeed make deductions about the problem under discussion from R. Yitsḥak of Fez's language about gifts made in contemplation of death, what weight should this inference carry with someone who penned massive criticisms of Alfasi? If Ravad had intuitively felt that renunciation could take place with gaged debts, nothing that Alfasi might have said, even explicitly, would have swayed him. Clearly Ravad was not deducing anything from R. Yitsḥak's remarks, as he contended. But, having arrived intuitively at a doctrine of non-renunciation, and lacking any proof for his position, he seized upon a formulation of Alfasi as precedent and *asmakhta* (support).

42 |**orig. n. 37**| *Piskei ha-Rosh, Ketubbot*, 9: 10.

43 |**orig. n. 38**| References in *Bet ha-Beḥirah, Bava Metsi'a*, ed. K. Schlesinger (Jerusalem, 1959), 67 nn. 475, 477, and the *Ḥiddushei Rashba le-Rabbenu Shelomoh Aderet, Gittin*, ed. Y. Sklar (Jerusalem, 1986), s.v. *ve-katav ha-Ravad*.

44 |**orig. n. 39**| *Sefer ha-Terumot* (above, n. 15), (Venice, 1643), 51: 6: 3.

Behind these two rulings stands the problem of credit circulation. In a society where trade has achieved some vigor, one standard form of payment is the transfer of notes of indebtedness. We do it daily when we endorse checks, which are simply notes of indebtedness. When the payee endorses it, he transfers it to another in exchange for something received. Notes of indebtedness were hardly as common in twelfth-century Provence as in our day, but then neither was money. There was a dearth of currency at the time in Provence,[45] and a double burden was thus thrust upon notes of indebtedness (*shitrei ḥov*). They became a basic vehicle of exchange. Shemu'el's ruling that the debt may be renounced by the original creditor even after he has sold it to another mortally impedes the free movement of credit. If a debt, once sold, can yet be renounced by the original creditor, no one will accept a transferred note of indebtedness, or if they do, it will be only at great discount. The fact that Shemu'el's ruling awakened no surprise in talmudic times[46] and no efforts were made to neutralize it in practice shows that credit circulation played a small role in the talmudic economy.[47] This was hardly the case in the high Middle Ages. The very first formularies of notes of indebtedness that we possess contain clauses to order or to bearer (נכ"ז);[48] that is to say, they anticipate the need for the sale of such notes and attempt to allow for it. Ravad's remarks in the *Hassagot* are an attempt to validate these clauses; his responsum in the *Sefer ha-Terumot* seeks to preclude renunciation even in notes lacking such clauses. Both rulings seek to open the arteries of credit blocked by Shemu'el's ruling. The two dicta כמאן דמטיא ליד המקבל דמי ('as if it came into the hands of the [receiver of the gift]') and לא לך שיעבדתי את עצמי ('I have not indebted myself to you'), though poles apart conceptually, are a two-pronged attempt to wrestle with the problems that presented themselves as Jews moved from an agricultural to a credit economy.

45 |**orig. n. 40**| J. de Malafosse, 'Contribution à l'étude du crédit dans le Midi au Xe et XIe siècles: les sûretés réelles', *Annales du Midi*, 63 (1951), 105–48. It is this state of affairs that R. Mosheh b. Todros refers to when he writes (*Sifran Shel Rishonim* [above, n. 9], #33, p. 36 {*Sefer ha-Terumot* (above, n. 15), fo. 237a}): שהעולם דחוק וחסר, וכל העם נמנעין מלהלוות אלו את אלו. שאין הפרוטה מצויה להלוות איש את אחיו ולא להטיל מלאי להתעסק בו. ('For the world [i.e. general society] is hard-pressed and lacking in means, and most people refrain from lending to each other for there is a dearth of coinage [which prevents] both extending credit to one another and investing in a silent partnership.')

46 |**orig. n. 41**| As did, for example, the injunction against usufruct from possessory mortgages; *Bava Metsi'a* 67b.

47 |**orig. n. 42**| Rabbah b. Rav Huna's suggestion (*Ketubbot* 86a) is for novation (to another specific party, naturally) and not for the creation of a negotiable instrument.

48 |**orig. n. 43**| A. Gulack, *Otsar ha-Shetarot* (Jerusalem, 1926), 206–7; J. Brissaud, *History of French Private Law* (above, n. 36), 536–7.

Ravad's neutralization of Shemu'el's ruling went yet further: it transformed the note of indebtedness from a personal document into a monetary instrument. If such a note can be used to collect from the original parties only, it is of personal but not economic significance. A possessed money before, B did not. After the loan, B possesses money, A has a piece of paper. Money has changed hands but no more of it is in circulation. If, however, A can transfer this note and proceed to purchase things with it—in other words, if A retains his buying power at the same time that B has acquired it—every loan with a note of indebtedness then doubles in effect the volume of currency in circulation. Ravad's famous doctrine of **לא לך שיעבדתי את עצמי** ('I have not indebted myself to you'), with all its conceptual significance, was at the same time an attempt to validate the coin minted by a society suffering from a dearth of currency.

R. Buckwold Wrote

Example 2:

In his *hassagah* to 'Hilkhot Mekhirah', 6: 12, Ravad explains Shemu'el's famous ruling —**המוכר שטר חוב לחבירו וחזר ומחלו, מחול** ['One (a lender) who sells a note of indebtedness to another individual and subsequently forgives the debt, it stands forgiven']—after this fashion:

> **מפני שהלוה אומר ללוקח אני לא שיעבדתי לך את עצמי לפיכך אם כתב לו שטר חובו הריני משועבד לך ולכל הבאים מכוחך אינו יכול למחול במשכר שטר חובו.**
>
> [Because the borrower says to the buyer (of the note), I did not subject myself to you. Therefore, if he (the borrower) wrote in the note of indebtedness: 'I am hereby obligated to you (the lender) and to all (subsequent buyers of the note) who take your place', he (the lender) is not able to forgive the debt after selling the note of indebtedness.]

These are some of the most seminal words ever penned on the nature of obligation and, together with those of Rabbenu Tam, they have given birth to an entire literature. But the *lefikhakh* ('therefore') suggests a practical purpose to his remarks, and this finds corroboration in the fact that Ravad saw fit to reiterate this proviso on no fewer than four other occasions. Clearly Ravad's doctrine must be studied not only from the perspective of the development of halakhic thought, but also in the context of twelfth-century Provence.

Soloveitchik goes on with his third example, which will be discussed later. He concludes:

Behind these two rulings stands the problem of credit circulation . . . There was a dearth of currency at the time in Provence, and a double burden was thus thrust upon notes of indebtedness (*shitrei ḥov*) . . . Shemu'el's ruling המוכר שטר חוב לחבירו וחזר ומחלו, מחול [One (a lender) who sells a note of indebtedness to another individual and subsequently forgives the debt, it stands forgiven] mortally impedes the free movement of credit. . . . Both rulings seek to open the arteries of credit blocked by Shemu'el's ruling. The two dicta . . . are a two-pronged attempt to wrestle with the problems that presented themselves as Jews moved from an agricultural to a credit economy. Ravad's famous doctrine of לא לך שיעבדתי את עצמי ['I did not obligate myself to you'], with all its conceptual significance, was at the same time an attempt to validate the coin minted by a society suffering from a dearth of currency. ('Programmatic Essay', pp. 34–5). [Translations mine—E.B.]

R. Buckwold's Reservations

1. Let us assume that the economic background presented here is accurate. Of course, healthy commerce is of great importance in Halakhah. Rabbinic enactments made to insure healthy commerce (משום תקנת השוק) are common in the Mishnah and Talmud. Rabbinic authorities continued to make such enactments throughout Jewish history long after the completion of the Talmud. And no attempt was made to disguise them in any way. Why then would Ravad have had to disguise his ruling as if its source was actually the Talmud and talmudic logic? Interestingly, Rosh explains the enactment of *ma'amad sheloshtan* (selling credit orally in the presence of the borrower, the original lender, and the buyer of the credit) as coming to solve problems of commerce very similar to those mentioned in the 'Programmatic Essay'. A note of admission, *odita*, from the lender-seller stating that the credit was transferred to the buyer via *ma'amad sheloshtan* (even though this actually wasn't done) would have sufficed as a simple solution for a secure transfer of credit.

2. Ravad's ruling can be understood quite simply and compellingly without reference to economic conditions in Provence. Here is the gist of the ruling: if the borrower obligates himself to repay all who buy the loan, then the original lender loses his right to cancel the debt. This ruling has a very strong basis: (1) Simple logic dictates that since the borrower specifically obligated himself to the buyers of the credit, his obligation to them is absolute—leaving the original lender powerless to cancel this obligation. (2) Ravad cites talmudic sources for this ruling—sources which are strangely absent from the 'Programmatic Essay'.

Indeed, Rashba (Responsa vol. 3 section 20) exclaims in a rare form of praise for this ruling of Ravad: דברי הראב"ד נכונים וברורים, חזקים כראי מוצק ('Ravad's words are correct and clear, strong as a "cast metal mirror" [an expression taken from Job 37: 18, expressing solidity and clarity]').

3. Despite the clear and simple logic in this ruling, as mentioned above, Ravad's own rationale is actually more complicated. It is based, Ravad explains, on his reasoning, which differs from Rambam's, for this ruling of Samuel—why, indeed, does the original lender have the power to cancel the debt that he had sold? Ravad explains: מפני שהלוה אומר ללוקח אני לא שעבדתי לך את עצמי—'Because the borrower says to the buyer [of the note], I did not obligate myself to you'.

Soloveitchik appears to regard Ravad's reasoning as strikingly innovative: 'these are some of the most seminal words ever penned on the nature of obligation'. He proceeds to explain what, in his view, was the real reason behind this reasoning: 'an attempt to validate these clauses . . . to open arteries of credit blocked by Shemu'el's ruling'.

In truth, Ravad's logic is based on the fundamental principle that a monetary obligation is not the possession of the lender, but rather a personal obligation of the borrower. Rabbenu Tam independently articulated the same principle.

Indeed, this concept of personal obligation was not an invention of Ravad and Rabbenu Tam. It can be found in the Talmud itself: פריעת בעל חוב מצוה—'payment of debt is a *mitzvah*' (*'Arakhin* 22a, *Ketubbot* 86a). This means that payment of a debt can be enforced only as a *mitzvah* is enforced. Ravad and Rabbenu Tam logically concluded that this *mitzvah* of the borrower is not the property of the lender, and therefore cannot be sold by him. Subsequently, the original lender retains the power to cancel the obligation. This is Samuel's ruling.

4. If one is searching for novelty in Ravad's ruling, it is his reliance on his own rationalization of Samuel's ruling. After expressing his disagreement with Rambam, Ravad continues: לפיכך ['therefore'] the stipulation הריני משועבד לך ולכל הבאים מכחך ['I am hereby obligated to you (the lender) and to all (subsequent buyers of the note) who take your place'] prevents the original lender from having the power to cancel the debt.' The לפיכך ('therefore') implies that, according to Rambam's rationalization of Samuel's ruling, this stipulation will not prevent the original lender from having the power to cancel the debt. Ravad thus forces into the mouth of Rambam a dissenting opinion that Rambam himself never uttered!

Indeed, Rav Yosef Karo (in both his *Kesef Mishneh* and *Bet Yosef*) disagrees with Ravad on this point. He claims that the rationale of Ravad's ruling is so clear that Rambam and Alfasi would also accept the implications of the proviso הריני משועבד ('I am hereby subjected . . .').

If Soloveitchik's hypothesis were correct—that Ravad's ruling sought 'to open the arteries of credit blocked by Shemu'el's ruling'—we run into a major paradox: by forcing a dissenting opinion into Rambam's mouth, Ravad was essentially hindering the application of his own ruling!

And indeed, this is what happened. Even though Rav Yosef Karo ruled clearly that in such a case the borrower must pay according to all opinions, this ruling was contested by the *Keneset ha-Gedolah* and the *Giddulei Terumah*, basing themselves on Ravad's implication that Rambam disagrees.

With the outlook of Prof. Soloveitchik, Ravad was playing the game for the wrong side. The words he wrote in his *Hassagot* had the potential to cripple the economy of Provence! This clearly disproves the contention that Ravad was motivated by an ulterior motive: to help solve the problem of credit circulation.

5. Actually, Soloveitchik's basic claim that 'Shemu'el's ruling ['a lender who sells a note of indebtedness to another individual and subsequently forgives the debt, it stands forgiven'] mortally impedes the free movement of credit' is highly questionable for a very practical reason: Halakhah requires the lender-seller to reimburse the buyer for the loss he caused by forgiving the debt. This serves both as a powerful deterrent not to forgive the debt, and as security for the buyer of credit in case the debt is forgiven. Our system of commerce today in the usage of checks and their transfer is similar. A personal check may be cancelled, but the writer of the check is required to reimburse the holder of the check. The fact is that our check system most definitely does not impede the free movement of credit.

My Reply

I turn first to a footnote because it contains a telling criticism of my article. R. Buckwold writes: 'Let us assume that the economic background presented is accurate', and in a footnote (n. 96) he points out that the article of Malafosse in the *Annales du Midi* that I cited in documentation 'speaks of a dearth of currency . . . during the 10th and 11th centuries', whereas Ravad lived in the twelfth.

R. Buckwold is absolutely correct. The article makes no mention of any shortage of coin in the twelfth century. Indeed, the error goes deeper. Even if the article had made such a claim, it would have been wholly inadequate for my purposes. Malafosse was a historian of law, and his article is devoted to demonstrating that even though the Germanic notions of pawn prevailed at the time in Provence, there existed a late Roman substratum in the legal culture of the time that still viewed pawns as accessorial to a debt. Passing remarks by a legal historian about economic conditions cannot be used to demonstrate economic facts, unless they are fully documented—as they are not in the cited article. I can only apologize to my readers for this error.

Where does the issue of coin stand in light of recent research, the most recent of which is Marc Bompaire, 'La circulation monétaire en Languedoc (Xe–XIIIe siècles)' *thèse dactylographée*, 3 vols. (University of Paris IV, 2002)? (It will soon be published in the series Cahiers Ernest Babelon.) Briefly put, despite the absence of any mints west of the Rhône and the small amount of coin emanating from the mints of Narbonne (where R. Mosheh b. Todros sat as judge), it would seem that the currency of Montpellier (the Melgeuilean *denier*, minted at Melgeuil, the seat of the Count of Montpellier) made up for any local dearth of currency. This seems to be certainly so in the neighboring zone where Ravad was active—Posquières, Lunel, and Montpellier—but far less certain in the Narbonnais, where R. Mosheh b. Todros (cited in my footnote) sat as judge, and he may well be referring to a lack of coinage.[49]

[49] Unfortunately the rest of R. Buckwold's critical note 96 is of lesser quality.

(*a*) He proceeds to remark that the statement of R. Mosheh b. Todros that I cited, שהעולם דחוק וחסר וכל העם נמנעים מלהלות אלו את אלו שאין הפרוטה מצויה להלוות איש את אחיו ולא להטיל למלאי להתעסק בו, can be understood as referring simply to general poverty. The phrase שהעולם דחוק וחסר can, indeed, mean that when standing alone; less so if followed by a statement that Jews are refraining from lending to one another. This would indicate, not that there is no money, but rather that loan money is not readily available; in colloquial English 'things are tight'. Be that as it may, R. Mosheh goes on to explain his words, and note that he doesn't say that there is no money for personal consumption (which would be a mark of poverty), but that there is no money with which to extend credit or to use for investment purposes. Moreover, the Provençal Jewish community is not known to have been poor. These two facts, taken with the assumption (and probably the fact in the Narbonnais) of the lack of coin, is what led me to read R. Mosheh's words in this light.

(*b*) R. Buckwold then goes on to add parenthetically: 'Even taken literally, the פרוטה is the smallest copper coin and has the most minimal value, which is of no commercial value.' First, I did not take *perutah* literally. Second, I fear he is confusing Roman coinage current in talmudic times (the *dupondius* or *perutah* of local minting which was of copper or bronze) with Provençal coinage of the Middle Ages. The Talmud and Midrash cannot be used as sources for medieval numismatics. The Roman Empire fell a while ago, and with it went its currency. Ravad lived half a millennium after its fall, and in his day and that of R. Mosheh b. Todros, the *perutah*, which was called denarius (or *denier* in France) and was made of silver (not copper), was the *only* coin in circulation in twelfth-century Provence, indeed, in all of western Europe. See e.g. P. Spufford, *Handbook of Medieval Exchange* (Suffolk, 1986), introduction, p. xix.

(*c*) R. Buckwold further states that the *perutah* was 'of the most minimal value'. Does he know the purchasing power of the denarius in mid- to late twelfth-century Provence? Is he aware of 'cut coinage', denarii regularly sliced in half or in quarters to make smaller coins? (The English 'farthing' was a sliced quarter of the denarius.) Or is his statement made on the basis of 'logic' סברא alone? {There is considerable information on medieval prices readily available at <http://www.florilegium.org/files/COMMERCE/p-prices-msg.html>.}

(*d*) As to the date of the arrival of the *Mishneh Torah* in Provence, see below, p. 353.

Would I retract my analysis? In principle, no, as I see no shame in halakhists being aware of contemporary needs. In practice, equally no. Admittedly, I must change my concluding sentence and add a penultimate one, but in no way need I alter the thrust of my remarks, for Ravad's ruling was of great economic significance and, as we shall see, he was acutely aware of this.[50] In my essay, I spoke not only of 'dearth of currency' but also of the 'circulation of credit' and the need for 'unclogging the arteries of credit blocked by Shemu'el's ruling'. The question is not only how much money is in circulation but also how much credit is available. If someone can loan out money and can then use the note of indebtedness at full or almost full value to do further business, the transferability of such notes doubles, in effect, the capital available to the businessman. The creditor can further replenish the store of money that he has lent by selling the note of indebtedness, extend credit a second time, and then repeat the entire process. Salability of debts both eases the natural shortage in cash flow from which all businesses suffer frequently, and at the same time increases noticeably the volume of credit and commerce. Either way or both ways, Ravad's rulings were fraught with practical significance, which does him and his ruling no disservice. As a result of R. Buckwold's timely correction, my concluding three sentences now read:

> If, however, A can transfer this note and proceed to purchase things with it—in other words, if A retains his buying power at the same time that B has acquired it—every loan with a note of indebtedness then doubles in effect the volume of currency in circulation. It equally doubles the financial resources available to the individual businessman, for after extending money in credit, A can replenish his capital by transferring the note of indebtedness and lend it once again. Ravad's famous doctrine of **לא לך שיעבדתי את עצמי** ('I have not indebted myself to you'), with all its conceptual significance, was equally an attempt to increase dramatically the sum total of credit available for Jewish economic activity and enabled his co-religionists to participate in the massive expansion of European commerce in the twelfth and thirteenth centuries, what Robert Lopez has called 'the Commercial Revolution of the Middle Ages'.[51]

To return to the text.

1. R. Buckwold then writes:

> Of course, healthy commerce is of great importance in Halakhah. Rabbinic enactments made to insure healthy commerce (**משום תקנת השוק**) are common in the Mishnah and Talmud. Rabbinic authorities continued to make such enactments throughout Jewish history long after the completion of the Talmud. And no attempt

[50] See below, pp. 349–50.

[51] R. S. Lopez, *The Commercial Revolution of the Middle Ages: 950–1350* (New York, 1971).

was made to disguise them in any way. Why then would Ravad have had to disguise his ruling as if its source was actually the Talmud and talmudic logic?

(*a*) I never said that Ravad 'disguised' his rulings in the matter of sale of debt (*mekhirat ḥov*). Underlying R. Buckwold's remarks are two assumptions. The first is the meaning of my statement in the previous section of the essay, 'Law leans towards continuity and has an antipathy to radical change; thus the revolutionary jurist must disguise his innovations—even from himself', which R. Buckwold misunderstood and which I will deal with in the second part of my reply.

Even if I had intended what R. Buckwold thinks I did, why would Ravad here, of all places, have 'disguised' his new doctrine? It is a major contribution to the theory of obligations; why would he not proclaim it from the rooftops? What need had he to insinuate it into the halakhic process?

(*b*) The second tacit assumption of R. Buckwold's critique is that an idea generated by a contemporary problem is somehow specious and illegitimate and must be camouflaged if it is to enter the legal mainstream. I addressed this in my preface. Does R. Buckwold believe that the entire legal corpus of the American court system is specious or disguised? Never was there a decision more tailored to a specific situation than John Marshall's decision in *Marbury v. Madison*.[52] Does anyone doubt that that decision, which established the principle of judicial supremacy, is a lasting contribution to American legal thought? Does R. Buckwold imagine that the responsa literature of the past thousand years is bereft of merit, and that it is composed of meretricious, clandestine arguments? A contemporary problem, as I said before, is simply a challenge to a system, as is a good *kushya* in the *bet midrash* or a good article in a law review. The quality of the response depends on the caliber of the responder, not on where the challenge comes from.

(*c*) Truth to tell, I never claimed that Ravad's solution stemmed simply from a pressing contemporary problem. I wrote: 'Ravad's famous doctrine of לא לך שיעבדתי את עצמי ('I have not indebted myself to you'), with all its conceptual significance, was *at the same time* an attempt to validate the coin minted by a society suffering from a dearth of currency' (italics now added). If an idea is a major contribution to halakhic thought, is it the worse for being, *at the same time*, a solution to a pressing contemporary problem? Must important halakhic ideas, to R. Buckwold's way of thinking, be inutile or of utility by

[52] See e.g. L. D. Kramer, *The People Themselves: Popular Constitutionalism and Judicial Review* (Oxford, 2004), 114–27. *Marbury v. Madison* is given only as an example; I pass the issue whether or not the significance commonly attributed to the case is correct historically.

coincidence only? And had this major contribution arisen *solely* in consequence of grappling with contemporary problems, why would it be the worse for this fact?

(*d*) R. Buckwold then asks: Why would Ravad need to validate sale of debts by written instrument when he could always have used an *udita* (a document stating that the debtor has admitted his indebtedness in the presence of witnesses)?

In the view of Alfasi and Maimonides, for example, sale of debts is a rabbinic ordinance (*mi-de-rabbanan*).[53] Do we recite a blessing on endorsing checks as we do over the lighting of Hanukkah candles? There is no religious merit in transferring a debt; why then the ordinance? Because of commercial necessity, as it became increasingly difficult for business to be shackled by the law of the Torah, which precluded the sale of debts. So the Sages (*Ḥazal*) legitimated the sale of debts. (In financial matters, they had the full right to institute what they deemed best.) Why, however, did they trouble themselves to introduce that practice when they could have used an *udita*? Any businessman could provide the answer. Business is complicated, and if an important need exists, there is generally a need for alternative methods to deal with that exigency. What holds true for *Ḥazal* holds equally true for Ravad.

2. My learned critic then points out that there is talmudic proof from *Gittin* 13b that Ravad himself adduced in his other writings for the inability of the original creditor to waive the lien if the note of indebtedness contains a clause to bearer. R. Buckwold then wonders why I did not refer to this passage of Ravad and subtly hints that I was out to demonstrate how Ravad made up halakhic doctrines out of whole cloth and cunningly infiltrated them into the halakhic system. In fact I did refer to it, as we shall soon see. The reason I did not reproduce and discuss this passage is simply that Ravad employed in *Gittin* a line of reasoning *different* from that which he had enunciated in his famous Maimonidean gloss—לא לך שיעבדתי את עצמי—which was the subject of my discussion, as I wrote at the outset: 'I would like to end with a brief study of the practical import of one of his better-known Maimonidean notes. In his *hassagah* to "Hilkhot Mekhirah", 6: 12 etc.' The relationship between the two arguments will be discussed in the next section.

My critic further states that 'simple logic' dictates Ravad's position. I refer the reader to Ramban's dissent from Ravad's position (*Ḥiddushei Ramban, Gittin* 13b) and that of Rosh (*Ketubbot* 9: 10), and to Rashba's lengthy argument defending that position (*Ḥiddushei Rashba, Gittin*, ad loc.). None of

[53] See e.g. Alfasi on *Ketubbot* 85b (44a in Romm edn.); Maimonides, 'Hilkhot Mekhirah', 6: 12.

them perceived the issue as being one of 'simple logic'. Rashba firmly believed Ravad's view to be correct; he scarcely viewed its correctness as being self-evident.

R. Buckwold further points out that Ravad's position here won the fulsome praise of Rashba. Let me first point out that Rashba is praising Ravad's argument from *Gittin* not that of the *Hassagot*; indeed, Rashba, in that responsum, refers to his defense of the doctrine in his *ḥiddushim* on *Gittin*. More importantly, even had Rashba referred to the argument in the *hassagah*, this would in no way conflict with anything that I said—unless one assumes that a creative halakhic response to a contemporary problem must be halakhically baseless, and therefore 'disguised' and slipped surreptitiously into the system.

3. (*a*) R. Buckwold then writes that Rabbenu Tam arrived at the same doctrine as Ravad. I concur, and so stated in my essay: 'These are some of the most seminal words ever penned on the nature of obligation and, together with those of Rabbenu Tam, have given birth to an entire literature'. R. Buckwold further objects to my high regard for the distinction between **שיעבוד הגוף** (*in personam*, personal indebtedness) and **שיעבוד נכסים** (*in rem*, a lien on property of the debtor), and claims they are obvious inferences from the Talmud. I would simply suggest that many important ideas, once formulated, seem obvious. Indeed, it is their subsequent self-evidence which makes these ideas great. I suppose that, after hearing a brilliant resolution of a contradiction in the *Mishneh Torah*, one could say it's obvious that the two rulings deal with different cases or involve different principles.

But why suppose and conjecture? Rabbenu Tam's famous distinction was made very late in his life. To solve the problem of **המוכר שטר חוב לחבירו וחזר ומחלו, מחול**, he at first answered that the sale of debts was only a rabbinic enactment (*mi-de-rabbanan*). He then retracted that opinion as a result of a question from his pupil, R. Eli'ezer of Metz, the author of the *Sefer Yere'im*. Only later, and unbeknownst to Ri, did Rabbenu Tam develop his theory of two separate and distinct liens **שיעבודים**. For this reason the famous distinction is not found in the standard, printed *Tosafot*, which are based on the *Tosafot* of the academy (*bet ha-midrash*) of Ri. Not knowing Rabbenu Tam's theory of two liens, which R. Buckwold considers elementary, R. Shimshon of Sens (Rash mi-Shants) reports in his *Tosafot* on *Ketubbot*, written at the feet of Ri:

> הרבה היה תמי' ר', היאך יכול למכור את החוב? דבשלמ' כשיש לו קרקעות ללוה, מכר (ללוה) [לו] שעבוד על אותם קרקעות, אבל כשאין לו כלום, מה מוכר לו. ואם המכר קיים מדאורייתא, [ו]חזר ומחלו, אמאי מחול?

And my teacher was greatly puzzled. How can the [original creditor] waive the debt? I well understand that if the debtor has real estate, the creditor has sold [the purchaser] the lien on the real estate; however, if the debtor has nothing, what has [the creditor] sold [the purchaser]? If the sale [of debts] is valid pentateuchally, and the creditor then waives it, why is the debt waived?[54]

Anyone familiar with the language of the *Tosafot* knows how very rare, indeed, almost unique, is the phrase והרבה היה תמי' ר' ('And my teacher [i.e. Ri] was greatly puzzled'), and how much perplexity had to exist to generate so unusual a phrase. What is obvious to R. Buckwold was clearly not obvious to Ri. He found Shemu'el's ruling to be self-contradictory. Baffled, he asked: What has been sold and what remains unsold? Clearly the debt hasn't been sold, for otherwise the original creditor could not waive the debt. Yet no less clear is the fact that the debt has been sold, for if no waiver takes place, the buyer can collect the debt and demand of the court that it execute judgment on the property of the debtor. Answering that sale of debt is a rabbinic enactment solves only part of the problem—why the debt can be waived; it doesn't explain why a defective sale will be enforced if no such waiver has taken place. By advancing the existence of two separate and distinct liens, one which is alienable and another which is not, the puzzle of Shemu'el's ruling resolves itself.

The distinction between *in personam* and *in rem* (as שיעבוד הגוף and שיעבוד נכסים are known in other systems of law) is fundamental to any understanding of obligations. To take a simple example from the tiny compass of our discussion: One would not be able to explain *apotiké meforash*. One would know, of course, the law of לא יהיה לך פרעון אלא מזה but one would be unable to explain it conceptually or integrate it in any theory of obligations.

Let us now turn to Ravad's Maimonidean gloss. Both Ravad and Rabbenu Tam shared the same insight—the personal nature of debt, something separate and distinct from the lien on property which can be readily sold.[55] Rabbenu Tam arrived at that doctrine from grappling with Shemu'el's paradoxical ruling; is there any reason to assume that Ravad arrived at his conclusion differently? All halakhists grappled with this perplexing, self-contradictory halakhah. Alfasi and Maimonides gave their solutions; Ravad and Rabbenu Tam adduced theirs. The theory of obligation *in personam* is an immanent halakhic development. It was also of great practical significance, and Ravad hastened to announce it in his Maimonidean gloss. There are two parts to the famous *hassagah*: first, the theoretical solution to the problem raised by Shemu'el's ruling—a product of Ravad's commentarial genius, to which the bulk

[54] *Tosefot ha-Rashba mi-Shants le-Massekhet Ketubbot* (Jerusalem, 1973), 85b, s.v. *ha-mokher*.

[55] Whether the shared legal aperçu resulted in identical legal doctrines is not here our concern. On this, see *Ketsot ha-Ḥoshen* (above, n. 11), 'Ḥoshen Mishpat', 66: 26.

of my essay was devoted; second, the practical implications of that doctrine, which Ravad took care to spell out even in the compass of a brief gloss (לפיכך אני אומר וכו'), indicating his vibrant awareness of contemporary need—this was the subject of the essay's brief concluding section.

Indeed, Ravad addressed on more than one occasion the ubiquitous clause to bearer that had been appended to loan documents since geonic times,[56] but whose halakhic validity had yet to be proven. The first time was in his commentary on *Gittin*; the second time in his Maimonidean gloss. The two formulations of Ravad can be viewed as alternative or complementary. Alternative, if we have here two independent aperçus, each yielding the same practical conclusion which he was at pains to point out, seeing its great practical import. Or, as I would take it, complementary, if the gloss on Maimonides contains a rationale that solves not only the paradox of Shemu'el's ruling but also a problem with, or a limitation of, the rationale that Ravad previously advanced in *Gittin*.

Over the course of years, Ravad realized that his application of Amemar's statement in *Gittin* in the matter of *ma'amad sheloshtan* to the sale of a note of indebtedness would not work according to the doctrine that the sale of debt is a rabbinic enactment (*mi-de-rabbanan*). If debts cannot be sold in principle, as, for example, דבר שלא בא לעולם (futures) cannot, no statement of the debtor can effectuate the sale. If the object is not subject to alienation (אין קניין נתפס עליו in Rosh's phrase, as we shall see), concessions by any party are irrelevant. One must assume that in principle debts are salable, i.e. מכירת חוב מן התורה, but that some waivable right of the debtor impedes the alienation. This means that there must be another rationale for Shemu'el's problematic ruling and one that is linked to debtor rights. In time, he realized that this right rested on the personal nature of indebtedness, in the language of the famous *hassagah*—לא לך שיעבדתי את עצמי. It was this that allowed waiver of the debt (by the original creditor) to take place even after the sale, and it was this that the debtor could renounce by accepting the clause הריני משועבד לך ולכל הבאים מכחך ('I am indebted to you and all who represent you').

In fact, Ravad validated the widely used clause to bearer no fewer than four to five times, as he took care in his *Ḥibbur Harsha'ah* to add a concluding note stating that the addition of the clause foreclosed the option of waiver (*Temim De'im*, #65). Furthermore, in section 64 he provided yet another means to invalidate such a waiver, namely, by tacking on to the bill of sale the formula of *harsha'ah*, תלך ותדון עמו ותזכה לעצמך וכו'. Even though the point had already

[56] A. Gulack, *Otsar ha-Shetarot* (above, n. 48), 206–7.

been made in the body of his essay, Ravad took the trouble to reiterate at the end of that work the effectiveness of this technique. He subsequently reproduced both points in his *Hassagot* on Alfasi.[57] We have thus no fewer than five different occasions when Ravad deals with the problem of waivers. He offered two different techniques of circumvention and over the course of years proposed two complementary rationales for that of לא לך שיעבדתי את עצמי, one of which constituted a major breakthrough in the theory of obligations.

My erudite critic faults me with not citing the Ravad passage in *Gittin*: 'Ravad cites talmudic sources for this ruling—sources which are strangely absent from the "Programmatic Essay"', and adds in a footnote that Ravad's proof is cited by Rashba in his *ḥiddushim* on *Gittin*. I request the reader to read my remarks at p. 337, where I wrote, 'But the לפיכך suggests a practical moment to his remarks, and this finds corroboration in the fact that Ravad saw fit to reiterate this proviso on no fewer than four other occasions'; and note 38 cites the *Ḥiddushei ha-Rashba* on *Gittin*. Seeking to keep my references to a minimum, I refrained from citing separately the *Temim De'im* and the *Hassagot* on Alfasi, but made reference to Schlesinger's note in the *Bet ha-Beḥirah*, where both sources are cited. Perhaps I should, indeed, have set forth all this material in detail, as the three or four attempts of Ravad to validate the widely added clause indicate his concern for the resolution of the pressing problem of waiver. However, this was the concluding point of my essay (the entire section on contemporary import, exclusive of quotations, is less than 1,600 words); introducing the other rationales advanced by Ravad would have complicated the presentation. I would have had to raise the issue of alternative or cumulative explanations, and then spell out the nature of Amemar's ruling in *Gittin*, the potential problem in Ravad's rationale, its resolution by the personal nature of debt, and the difference between the procedural claim of לאו בעל דברים דידי את (in the matter of *harsha'ah*) and the substantive one of לא לך שיעבדתי את עצמי. Seeing that the point of the conclusion was, as I explicitly stated, to illustrate the practical dimension of a famous *hassagah*, I decided to confine my remarks strictly to the *hassagah* and leave any larger discussion of the evolution of this doctrine for another time. As the full spectrum of Ravad's writings vividly evidences his deep disquiet with the option of waiver and his ongoing concern for its circumvention, I never dreamt that by counting and referring to these passages but not actually citing them I would be suspected of suppressing evidence.

(*b*) My learned colleague then goes on to claim that no creativity was needed

57 Alfasi on *Ketubbot* 85b (45a in Romm edn.).

to infer the distinction between *in rem* and *in personam*, for the personal nature of the debt, its non-salability, is rooted in the elementary principle of פריעת בעל חוב מצוה, and Rabbenu Tam and Ravad logically concluded from the existence of such a *mitsvah* that the debt cannot be sold. Before addressing the substance of this strange claim, let us address its documentation, found in note 100. R. Buckwold writes: 'This reasoning is explicit in the novellae of Rashba (*Bava Batra* 147b) in the name of Rabbenu Tam. (This is one of the earliest sources we have on this ruling of Rabbenu Tam.)' When seeking to document a doctrine of Rabbenu Tam, one goes first to Franco-German sources, the ones closest to Rabbenu Tam and his traditions. As this was a late doctrine of Rabbenu Tam and unknown to Ri and his *bet midrash*, our standard *Tosafot* do not report it. However, it is found in the *Tosefot Rosh*, both in *Kiddushin* (47b, s.v. *tsarikh*) and in *Ketubbot* (85b, s.v. *ha-mokher*), as well as in his universally known *Pesakim* (*Ketubbot* 9: 10), by whose agency it entered the halakhic mainstream. No mention is made in any of the three sources of פריעת בעל חוב מצוה being part of Rabbenu Tam's reasoning. (I cite, as an example, the text in *Ketubbot*: והא דאמרי' אם חזרו ומחלו מחול היינו טעמא, דשני שיעבודים יש לו למלוה על הלוה, אחד שיעבוד נכסיו ועוד שגופו משועבד לפרוע לו, ושיעבוד נכסיו יכול המלוה למכור אבל שעבוד של הלוה אין קנין נתפס עליו וכו'.) The argument of פריעת בעל חוב is an addition or sophistication of Rashba; he added something to clarify Rabbenu Tam's theory. What was it?

R. Buckwold believes that it proves not only the personal nature of the debt but also its non-salability, and writes: 'This means that the payment of a debt can be enforced only as a *mitsvah* is enforced. Ravad and Rabbenu Tam logically concluded that this *mitsvah* of the borrower is not the property of the lender and therefore cannot be sold to him. Subsequently, the original lender retains the power to cancel the obligation.' I must admit that I simply don't understand what he says. The dictum פריעת בעל חוב מצוה simply states that paying one's creditor is a *mitsvah*; it says nothing about who that creditor is. If B becomes the creditor, rather than A, the *mitsvah* is to pay B. The original creditor hasn't sold anyone's *mitsvah*; the debtor must, as before, pay his creditor, only the identity of the creditor has changed. Is פריעת בעל חוב (debt payment) some *mitsvah* that must be performed 'on the body of the creditor' (בגופו של מלוה)?! It is not even a *mitsvah* that the debtor himself must bodily perform (בגופו של לוה). The debtor may ask a friend to pay the debt at the friend's own expense. The friend can then proceed to pay the creditor's creditor, and by virtue of the principle of שיעבודא דרב נתן, the debt is paid and the *mitsvah* fully performed. Reply will be made that to pay off a person's debt is to pay the person himself. Indeed it is, but this equivalence makes sense in terms of extinction of debt in monetary terms, that is to say, from the point of view of civil law. There is, however, no such equivalence of one body to another body in the realm of מצוה שבגופו. There is no way that one person's taking of a *lulav* is the equivalent of another's doing so. Clearly, 'debtor' and 'creditor' and the modes of debt payment are first defined by the categories of the civil law ('Ḥoshen Mishpat'); the religious imperative (*mitsvah*) and its manner of realization follow then in their wake.

Rashba addresses a different issue entirely. (I cite, for the reader's convenience, his words):

> וטעמא שיכול לחזור ולמחול אע"פ שמכירתן מן התורה, לפי שאין אדם יכול למכור אלא זכות השעבוד שיש לו בנכסי אביו, אבל חיוב הגוף שחבירו מחוייב לפרוע לו חובו, כדאמרי' פריעת בעל חוב מצוה, אינו יכול למכור וכו'.

The reason why [the original creditor] can waive the debt even though the sale of the debt is pentateuchally valid is that one can only sell the indebtedness that he possesses in his father's property [the subject there under discussion], but the personal obligation borne by the debtor—as in the dictum 'payment of a debt is a religious obligation'—cannot be sold, etc.

Rashba detected a gap in Rabbenu Tam's argument. While the fact of שיעבוד נכסים is well documented in the Talmud, not so שיעבוד הגוף. The phrase is not found in the Talmud, and even if it were, how does this personal lien express itself legally? In collection—never, for one collects the 'cloak' (*gelima*), not the shoulders (*katfa*) (an allusion to a standard phrase in a note of indebtedness, 'you may collect even from the cloak on my shoulders').[58] One doesn't collect the body of the debtor, as there is no enslavement for debt; collection is always made from the debtor's property. Perhaps, then, no שיעבוד הגוף exists; rather, there are two שיעבודי נכסים: one lien *in rem* of real estate, which is not extinguished by sale or inheritance; a second lien *in rem* of *mobilia*, which is extinguished by sale or inheritance. To close this gap in Rabbenu Tam's position, Rashba introduced the halakhah of פריעת בעל חוב מצוה. The personal lien is attested to by this religious imperative.[59] Put differently: שיעבוד נכסים is a precise legal term; שיעבוד הגוף is a metaphor coined for contrast to שיעבוד נכסים. It refers not to any lien on a body but rather to a personal obligation stemming from the commandment of פריעת בעל חוב. The phrase of Rashba, כדאמרי' פריעת בעל חוב מצוה, is cited as evidence for the preceding clause, אבל חיוב הגוף שחבירו מחוייב לפרוע לו, not for the subsequent one, אינו יכול למכור. The non-salability of debts is not inferred from the *mitsvah* of פריעת בעל חוב for it can't be; it is inferred from Shemu'el's ruling that המוכר שטר חוב לחבירו וחזר ומחלו, מחול.

58 *Bava Batra* 157a: מיניה אפילו מגלימא דעל כתפיה.

59 Cf. *Tosafot*, *Ketubbot* 86a, s.v. *peri'at*.

4. R. Buckwold then goes on at great length to argue against any contemporary importance to Ravad's theory. His argument is ahistorical. It assumes that Maimonides' code had the commanding position in Provence in the 1190s that it had a half-century or so later, not to speak of its importance in the time of the author of the *Kesef Mishneh*, in the sixteenth century. If an analogy must be had to a contemporary critique by a denizen of one halakhic culture of a newly arrived code authored by a scholar of another culture, more apt is the instance of R. Mosheh Isserles' *Mapah* on R. Yosef Karo's *Shulḥan 'Arukh*. Rama did not think that by his glossing he was implicitly strengthening in the Ashkenazic world the position of R. Yosef Karo's decisions, or that he would best refrain from glossing an ambiguous ruling, for any time he glossed a passage, the legal inference would be that the *meḥabber* disagreed with that position.

Truth to tell, even that analogy is too strong for the case at hand. R. Yosef Karo achieved towering status in the entire Jewish world upon the publication of his *Bet Yosef*. Indeed, it was the status achieved by the *Bet Yosef* that guaranteed the universal acceptance of the *Shulḥan 'Arukh* as *the* code of Jewish law or as *the basis* of any code of Jewish law. The *Mishneh Torah* rode on no such wave when it reached Provence. It was the massive work of an unknown Egyptian rabbi. Maimonides responded to the twenty-four questions of the scholars of Lunel in 1199 and apologized for the delay of several years (*kamah shanim*). It is difficult to push back the inquiry of Lunel before 1195/6, for in that year (4956 by the Jewish calendar) Maimonides replied to the scholars of Montpellier and wrote that it was clear from their inquiries (about astrology) that they had not yet seen his *Mishneh Torah*. Even those who argue that Maimonides may have been incorrect in his inference (about the scholars of Montpellier not having seen the *Mishneh Torah*) do not advance the arrival of *Mishneh Torah* in Provence before 1193.[60] Ravad died at most five years after its arrival, in 1198, and, as I wrote in the essay, one can only 'marvel at the mental vigor and flexibility of that titan in his old age'. When Ravad was writing, Maimonides was an unknown quantity. His code achieved *qualified* dominance in Provence only a generation or two later. And we must be on guard not to retroject the subsequent onto the precedent. The *Mishneh Torah* arrived both in Provence and soon after in Ashkenaz. In Ashkenaz, it had a muffled impact only; in Provence, its influence was far greater. However, all

[60] H. Gross, 'R. Abraham ben David aus Posquières: Ein literarische Vertrag', *Monatsschrift für Geschichte und Wissenschaft der Judenthums*, 22 (1874), 20; Y. Shilat, ed., *Iggerot ha-Rambam* (Jerusalem, 1995), ii. 510, 501, 474–5 and n. 3 there. From R. Buckwold's remarks in n. 96 end, it is clear that he is unaware of the late arrival of the *Mishneh Torah* in Provence.

this was in the future. When Ravad wrote his *Hassagot*, he could not have known whether the work would prove fascinating but jurisprudentially peripheral, or whether it was destined to be deeply influential.

Frankly, I don't think Ravad thought about posterity or impact when he penned his massive and sometimes acerbic notes on the *Yad*. Towards the end of his life, he encountered a work of unimaginable scope which both fascinated and antagonized him. Fascinated because here was a man who had taken, as he had, the totality of halakhah for his subject, and had succeeded, as he, Ravad, had not, in getting it all together, in inscribing all his insights in one comprehensive and coherent work. Antagonized, for the *Mishneh Torah* was unreferenced and had an annoyingly apodictic tone, as if to say, there was nothing more to be said. Ravad thought that a great deal remained to be said, about the Talmud, about the Yerushalmi, and about *midreshei halakhah* generally, and about the specific rulings in the *Mishneh Torah* in particular. And he proceeded to say it in that rapid-fire, trenchant style of which he was the master. Like a match that combusts from surface friction, Ravad's intellect ignited quickest and burnt most brightly when it moved against the grain of another work. And one could not dream of a more stimulating or frictional work than the *Yad*. Brilliant and naturally combative, Ravad had finally found an opponent of equal stature, and I seriously doubt whether he thought about strengthening anyone's hand when he penned, hastily and in creative excitement, his white hot, immortal glosses.

I would add that, in my experience, people who write angry critiques of other people's writings don't usually think that they are empowering thereby the objects of their censure.

5. R. Buckwold then proceeds to his final point, namely that checks, no less than bills of indebtedness, can be cancelled, but that has not impaired their widespread use in business.

His mode of argument reflects the academic, more accurately, the ivory-towered way of viewing the real world. The first assumption is: to have a good legal claim to something is the same as actually possessing it. To be sure, the buyer can sue, but who buys something that he may easily lose and will have to sue for reimbursement? More concretely: a businessman buys a five-year bill of indebtedness. When the due date arrives, he discovers that the debt no longer exists, and the money that he needs and has counted on now receiving will not be forthcoming. He must now find swiftly new money elsewhere, and as for the debt, his only recourse is to track down the seller after a five-year hiatus. If he succeeds in finding him, he must then litigate to recover his money, and most probably the case will be heard in the seller's jurisdiction. With such a prospect, someone may yet buy a bill of indebtedness, but only at great discount. Between a right to a thing and its possession falls a long shadow.

The second ivory-towered assumption is: anything that is identical legally is identical in reality. The practical difference between a check and a bill of indebtedness is that a personal check is generally cashed within a few days; most business checks are cashed within twenty-four hours, many on the very day of receipt. Bills of indebtedness, on the other hand, don't come due for months, years, or even decades. Checks, bills of business loans, and mortgages are legally identical; in reality they are polar opposites. Checks are not bills of indebtedness, but their opposite—instruments of payment, 'private legal tender' if you wish, which the recipient hastens to cash, that is to say, turn into genuine legal tender. Loan contracts and mortgages are indeed bills of indebtedness. They document the giving of moneys and provide legal assurance that, at some time in the future when the debt falls due, there is proof of its existence. That future date may be and usually is a number of years away. The further away the date of collection, the greater the danger of waiver. If the innumerable mortgage companies that advertise in the real estate section of the Sunday *New York Times* were able to cancel at will the debt in the mortgages that they have issued, the secondary market for mortgages, let alone Fannie Mae, would be considerably smaller, if they would exist at all.

EXAMPLE 3

May a creditor who has received a pawn as security for a debt, and then sold that debt, still waive the repayment, even though he has transferred the pawn to the purchaser?

The text of what I wrote in the essay is given in the citation of Example 2, as the two parts formed a single argument. R. Buckwold chose, quite legitimately, to focus on each part separately.

R. Buckwold Wrote

Example 3:

Another ruling of Ravad, reported in *Sefer ha-Terumot* [51: 6: 3]:

נשאל הראב״ד ז״ל: המוכר שטר לחבירו, ויש משכון ביד המלוה ומסרו ביד הלוקח אם יכול המוכר שהוא המלוה למוחלו (ללוקח) [ללוה] אם לאו? והשיב שאינו יכול למחול מאחר שהמשכון מוחזק ביד הלוקח. והביא ראיה ממה שכתב הרי״ף בכתובות משום דמתנת שכיב מרע עשאוה כמתנה דאורייתא דכמאן דמטיא ליד המקבל דמי, ולפיכך אין היורש מוחלה. מדקאמר [הרי״ף] ׳דמטיא לידיה דמקבל דמי׳, שמע מיניה אם יש משכון ביד המלוה ומסרו ללוקח, שאינו יכול למוחלו. ע״כ

[Ravad was asked: One sold a note of indebtedness to another individual, and also transferred to the buyer (of the note) a pawn he was holding; can the seller (of the note), who is the (original) lender, forgive the debt, or not? He (Ravad) responded that he (the lender who sold the note) cannot forgive the debt, since the pawn is being held by the buyer. He (Ravad) brought proof (to this ruling) from what the Rif (Alfasi) wrote in *Ketuvot* (f. 44b edn. Wilno, in explanation of the talmudic passage *Bava Batra* 147b, see fn. 104): 'Because a gift (a note of debt) given by a *shekhiv mera*—a deathly ill person—was made to be considered as biblical law, as if it (the note of debt) came into the hands of the recipient, and therefore the heir cannot forgive the debt.' From what he (Alfasi) says: 'as if it came into the hands of the recipient', we conclude that if there is a pawn in the hands of the lender and he transfers it to the buyer (of the note) then he cannot forgive the debt of the borrower.]

Prof. Soloveitchik comments:

I, for one, am at a loss to understand how the case discussed by Alfasi has any bearing upon the question at hand. If Ravad, however, says that it is relevant, I defer to his judgment, but I remain no less perplexed. Assuming that one can indeed make deductions about the problem under discussion from R. Yitsḥak of Fez's language about gifts made in contemplation of death, what weight should this inference carry with someone who penned massive criticisms of Alfasi? If Ravad had intuitively felt that renunciation could take place with gaged debts, nothing that Alfasi might have said, even explicitly, would have swayed him. Clearly Ravad was not deducing anything from R. Yitsḥak's remarks, as he contended. But, having arrived intuitively at a doctrine of non-renunciation, and lacking any proof for his position, he seized upon a formulation of Alfasi as precedent and *asmakhta* (support).

Prof. Soloveitchik continues to explain the secret lying behind Ravad's intuition: 'There was a dearth of currency at the time in Provence . . . Both rulings seek to open the arteries of credit blocked by Shemu'el's ruling. The two dicta . . . are a two-pronged attempt to wrestle with the problems that presented themselves as Jews moved from an agricultural to a credit economy.'

R. Buckwold's Reservations

1. As to Soloveitchik's claim that Ravad had no sources—and simply used Alfasi as a fig leaf—we would refer readers to a talmudic source identified by

Ramban. By comparing the talmudic passages *Kiddushin* 47b–48a with *Kiddushin* 8b, Ramban reaches the conclusion that a pawn transfer removes from the original lender the power to cancel the debt. Why Ravad did not accept this talmudic source remains an open question. But one thing is certain: his unwillingness to accept it contradicts Soloveitchik's theory that an ulterior motive drove him to point to a far-flung pseudo-source. Had Ravad merely been looking for additional leverage to neutralize Samuel, this talmudic source would have served him well (much better than Alfasi), since there is no obvious reason why it is not good evidence.

2. A strong rationale for this exception to the rule is also explained by Ramban. The Talmud rules clearly that the lender has a certain ownership of the pawn, as the potential payment is already in his hands. Ramban's opinion is that this includes a pawn given at the time of the loan. It follows that since the lender has ownership of the pawn, he can transfer it by sale together with the loan. Once the pawn is sold (with the loan) and is now owned by the buyer, it clearly follows that the original lender loses his right to cancel the loan. When the original lender exercised his ownership of the pawn by selling it, it is as if he received payment of the debt in the pawn he sold.

Indeed, Ravad could easily have offered this clear rationale since he shared the view that lender ownership also extends to a pawn given at the time of the loan (*Katuv Sham*, p. 130).

The major question to be asked on Ravad is not: How did he rely on a seemingly weak source in Alfasi? But, rather: Why did he not rely on the above reasoning? Apparently this rationale did not suffice for Ravad. Even though the lender enjoys a certain ownership of the pawn and thereby we may consider the loan as if it were already repaid, in actuality it is not really repaid. Can a loan be considered as if it were repaid in the context of the original owner losing his power to cancel the loan?

Ravad found an answer to this question in Alfasi. The case under discussion involves a *shekhiv mera'* who bequeaths a note of indebtedness to another individual. In this instance, the Talmud tells us, even Samuel will agree that the heirs of the lender will have no power to cancel the debt (*Bava Batra* 147b). Alfasi explains why: לידיה דמקבל דמי ('It is as if [the loan money] came into the hands of the recipient [beneficiary]'). We see in Alfasi's reasoning that even though the debt was not actually paid, the halakhic recognition that 'it is as if [the loan money] came into the hands of the recipient' is enough to cancel the power of the original lender. If so, concludes Ravad, a pawn transfer (as the lender enjoys a certain ownership of the pawn and the power to sell this ownership) will certainly cancel the power of the original lender.

3. 'What weight should this inference carry with someone who penned massive criticisms of Alfasi?'

A great deal. See Ravad's introduction to his *Hassagot* on the *Hilkhot Alfasi* cited above (see p. 38 and n. 75). In the eyes of Ravad, Alfasi is a towering and revered authority whom he refers to as ha-Rav (or 'Adoni ha-Rav'). (See n. 68 for discussion in the literature.) His opinions are not merely cited, but studied in depth by Ravad. Indeed, Ravad is actually one of the great commentators on Alfasi, even in his so-called *Hassagot* on Alfasi. Ravad wrote the *Katuv Sham*, a work on the entire Talmud, whose main purpose was to defend Alfasi and to explain his rulings.

4. The economic background presented—the dearth of currency—lacks proper substantiation (see n. 96), and the basic premise that Samuel's ruling 'mortally impedes the free movement of credit' is questionable (see p. 48, point 5).

My Reply

1. I never spoke of Ravad's invocation of Alfasi as a 'fig leaf', nor did I speak of any 'secret' lying behind Ravad's ruling. Similarly, I never used the phrase 'ulterior motive', as I don't share R. Buckwold's assessment of the responses of halakhah in the realm of civil law to challenges from the real world. To his thinking, the product of such a response is inevitably false, so fig leaves are needed to hide the dark secret of its origins.

I pointed out that Ravad confronted the problem of credit circulation and a dearth of currency, and that this challenge—*coupled with the classically difficult ruling of Shemu'el*—led, in the instance of sale of notes of indebtedness, to a major breakthrough in the theory of obligations; in the instance of a loan with a pawn, to a problematic argument.

2. R. Buckwold then writes that Ravad's position was validated by Ramban from a passage in *Kiddushin*, and Ravad could easily have cited it. This argument needs to be addressed from the point of view of both method and substance.

(*a*) Method: R. Buckwold claims that Ravad knew of the passage subsequently advanced by Ramban, that he further perceived a flaw in Ramban's explication of the proof text, and then tried to resolve that problem with a citation from Alfasi. The assumption of R. Buckwold is that any convincing proof of a Talmudist's position adduced by another Talmudist, be it a decade or a half-century or centuries later, was known to the first Talmudist but rejected by him. This indeed is how one 'does law', 'does Talmud', and 'does philosophy'. One postulates total knowledge on the part of great thinkers, and then one proceeds to analyze their positions. Every new argument is judged first on its own merit, and if it passes muster, it is then retrojected onto the original proponent of the position.[61] If a modern philosopher advances a better argument for a Platonic position than the one Plato himself gave, one assumes that Plato knew it and rejected it, and the question is: Why? In such an approach, all jurists, Talmudists, or philosophers of all ages engage in one ongoing debate of the perennial problems in their field. That is why the discussants over the ages have used the present tense in their analyses: 'Ramban thinks', 'Kant says', and the like.

This is good law, good Talmud, and good philosophy; it is bad history. A historian looks at a thing as it is at the time of its occurrence or formulation, and the first thing that he takes care not to do is to project the subsequent onto the precedent—the present onto the past. History means seeing things as they evolve; it entails a realization that institutions and ideas often achieve clarity only slowly. A correct position may be intuited, but only later will the convincing argument for that position be discovered—something that Ḥatam Sofer also realized from experience. He was not a historian, nor would he have wished to be one, to put it mildly. However, he knew precisely what he was doing and, more significantly, what he was not doing; he distinguished sharply between what he saw clearly and what he only intuited. As he answered the endless questions that were addressed to him, Ḥatam Sofer felt the presence of Divine guidance. Yet he realized that this guidance directed him only to the correct ruling, not to the correct *ratio*.[62] In decision-making (*pesak*), with its inevitable constraints of time and attention, the reach at times outstrips the grasp, and the greatness of a judge is measured by how royal his reach is.

How sovereign the reach of Ravad was, we cannot say. Too few of his responsa have survived. We can say that in our case, his legal vision was true. For a historian, however, if Ravad did not advance the passage in *Kiddushin* in

[61] This mode of reasoning repeats itself in R. Buckwold's presentation of Ravad's understanding of *apotiké meforash* (above, p. 353). He injects a Yerushalmi, together with the interpretative remarks of R. Yosef (Ri) Corcos (n. 93), into Ravad's reasoning with no evidence that Ravad, at the time of his writing on *Bava Metsi'a*, knew of this passage in the Yerushalmi or, more importantly, employed it in his argument. If R. Buckwold's reasoning is correct, and I have my doubts on the matter (see above, p. 353), this is good law, but bad history.

[62] Above, n. 5. What is remarkable in the passage is that Ḥatam Sofer employed this insight into the secondary role of the *ratio decidendi* (the grounds of the decision) and his intense sense of Divine guidance to shape his manner of replying *ab initio*, *lekhatḥilah*. The passage reads:

his reply, it had not occurred to him at the moment. If he did not invoke his doctrine about pawn ownership, it was not part of his argument. The question for a historian is not: 'What is the best argument that can be made for Ravad's position?', but 'What did Ravad actually think?' Ravad wrote short responsa, longer responsa, and very long responsa, all as occasion demanded.[63] He also did not write in runes. He could express himself with remarkable bite and clarity. Indeed, no one in the history of halakhah could say more in fewer words than he. In his glosses on the *Mishneh Torah*, he often formulated memorable doctrines in ten to fifteen words. If the writer could express himself well and the surviving text isn't fragmentary, then what isn't there can't be entered on his ledger. I have my doubts, as we shall soon see, about R. Buckwold's legal conjectures on this topic, but at the moment this is of no matter.

וכחצים ביד גבור עד מהרה ירוץ דברו עפ"י רוב עוד באותו יום שבאה השאלה השיב תשובתו הרמה. ופעם שאלו אבא מאוה"ג זצ"ל "אבי, היאך אתה מרהיב בנפשך עוז להורות חצים למרחוק ולהשיב לשואלים דבר ה' מיד בבוא השאלה לידך אפילו בחמורות, ולא תתיירא שבחיפזון תחטיא המטרה?" והשיב לו ידעתי בני ידעתי, כי לא דבר קטן הוא ושמעתתא בעי צלותא. אבל דע בני, בכל דור ודור העמיד ה' איש על העדה אשר יצא לפניהם להאיר להם הדרך, להשיב על שאלותם ולהתיר ספיקות שלהם. ויען כי רובם ככולם שואלים דבר ה' מפי, נראה בעליל כי מן השמים מסכימים על זה. ובו"ה למדתי כל הצורך וכוונתי היא בלתי לה' לבדו ולא זולת, ע"כ אינני חושד להקב"ה שיכשילני ח"ו, ובוודאי יסכים להוראתי. ואם הראיי' לפעמים אינו אמת, מ"מ הדין אמת הוא. וסיפר אבא זצ"ל שפעם באה שאלה חמורה מהגאון בעל אמרי אש זצ"ל בעת ישבו לסעודת צהריים, ומיד אחר הסעודה השיב לו כדרבו והראה תשובתו לאבא זצ"ל. ואחרי ימים, בא מכתב מהגאון הנ"ל ופקפק על איזה דברים, והשיב לו גם על זה מיד. וגם זאת התשובה הראה לאבי זצ"ל. ושאל לאביו הקדוש "אבי, הלא ידעתי איך חשוב רבי מאיר א"ש [אייזנשטאט] בעיניך לת"ח גדול . . . ואתה כותב במהירות כ"כ, ועתה הרע בעיניך על שפקפק בדבריך." וענה לו "בני, הדין דין אמת ומה לי אם איזה ראי' להדין אינה מדוקדקת כ"כ, ות"ח כמוהו צריך להבין זאת." ואחר זמן באה תשובת הגאון הנ"ל והתנצל הרבה שח"ו לא על עיקר הדין פקפק, כי הדין דין אמת . . . רק איזה ראי' מפוקפק הי' אצלו.

And my father told me that once he [Ḥatam Sofer] received a serious question from the author of the *Imrei Esh*. It arrived at dinnertime. Immediately after [dinner], he [Ḥatam Sofer] replied to [the inquirer] and showed his response to father. Some time later, a letter came from [the author of the *Imrei Esh*], who questioned some things [that Ḥatam Sofer had written]. He [my father] asked his sainted father, 'My father, I know how much you esteem R. Me'ir Eisenstadt [the author of the *Imrei Esh*] and consider him a great scholar . . . and [yet] you answered him so quickly; and now, are you disquieted by the fact that he doubted some of what you wrote'? And he [Ḥatam Sofer] answered, 'The ruling is correct. And of what matter is it that some of my proofs aren't that convincing? A scholar of [R. Me'ir Eisenstadt's stature] should have understood this.'

As I said at the outset of my essay (p. 316), this manner of conduct is no prescription for lesser mortals, but the essential aperçu as the litmus test of adjudication (*hora'ah*) remains. Finally, one cannot help reflecting that, unlike R. Me'ir Eisenstadt, most people did not question the reasoning of R. Mosheh Sofer. If most of the great responsa of Ḥatam Sofer reflect only his initial thoughts, one can only gasp in astonishment at how much halakhah has lost by not being privy to his fully considered arguments.

[63] See *Ravad: Teshuvot u-Fesakim*, ed. Y. Kafiḥ (Jerusalem, 1964).

What does matter is that he is here 'doing' law and Talmud, but not history. I was writing history.

(*b*) Substance. In the opening paragraph of point 2, R. Buckwold restates Ramban's 'strong rationale' for the inability to waive a sold debt if the sale included a transfer of the pawn to the purchaser, the crux being, in his words, 'When the original lender exercised his ownership of the pawn by selling it, it is as if he received payment of the debt in the pawn he sold' and, therefore, he cannot waive the debt at some later date. R. Buckwold locates a problem with this argument and contends that Ravad similarly perceived this problem and resolved it with the citation from Alfasi.

I have found no such rationale, strong or weak, in Ramban (nor, I may add, in the writings of his school, Rashba, Ritva, and Ran.) For the reader's convenience, I transcribe the words of Ramban.

At *Kiddushin* 8b Ramban writes:

> ומיהו מדאשכחן לקמן בפ' שני (מו ע"ב–מח ע"ב) שמקדש בשטר חוב דמן הדין מקודשת היא בין במלוה בשטר בין במלוה על פה אלא משום דלא סמכא דעתה ממחילה כדשמואל, ש"מ דכל שקונה שעבוד על הלוה מקודשת, דהא התם לית ליה למלוה עליה דלוה אלא שיעבודא גרידא ולא מצי לזבוני בנכסים דידיה כלום, ואפילו הכי מקודשת מן הדין, והלכך מלוה שיש עליה משכן כיון שקנה מקצת קנין ואינו יכול למחול לאחר מכירה, אשה מתקדשת בו.

However, we find further on [in this tractate, i.e. *Kiddushin* 46a–48b] that a debt can serve as the *kesef kiddushin* [the money or object of value, e.g. a ring, given to the woman by the man to effectuate the marriage], irrespective of whether it is a debt that places a lien on the property of the debtor, as does a debt attested to by a document, or a debt that only imposes a duty of repayment [*in personam*], as does one unattested to by such a document. The reason that an *in personam* debt is ineffective in *kiddushin* is that a woman would not rely on such debt as she would fear that the creditor would waive it. We may conclude that an *in personam* debt is a valid *kinyan kesef*, even though there is no lien whatsoever on any property. Therefore, one who gives as *kesef kiddushin* an unattested loan for which the debtor has deposited a pledge, since . . . the creditor cannot waive it after sale of the debt, the *kiddushin* is valid.

At 48a, Ramban writes (and R. Buckwold cites it in n. 107):

> למדנו שהמוכר שטר חוב לחבירו וחזר ומחלו, לעולם החוב מחול. ואם הניח לו משכון עליו ומכרו ומסר ללוקח משכונו וחזר ומחלו אינו מחול, שאם [לא] כן, היאך מתקדשת בו לדברי חכמים, אלא שמע מינה מחלו אינו מחל.

(The correction of [לא] is that of R. Buckwold, ibid., and is necessitated by the context.)

And we have learnt that one who has sold a debt and then waives it, the waiver is fully valid. If [however] he had received a pawn and [the creditor] transferred it to a buyer, the waiver is not valid. For if you do not rule thus, how can the woman be married? Infer from this that the waiver is invalid.

The Talmud, in *Kiddushin* 8b, states that if a creditor used as *kesef kiddushin* a pawn obtained as a result of a loan to a third party, the *kiddushin* is valid. Yet the Talmud rules in *Kiddushin* 48a that if a creditor used as *kesef kiddushin* an outstanding loan to a third party, i.e. transferred that loan to the woman, the *kiddushin* is not valid, as we assume that the woman would not consent to its acceptance, seeing that the creditor could yet waive the debt and she would end up having received nothing. The question naturally presents itself: Why is it that when a pawn is employed, the *kiddushin is* valid? If the debt is waived, the woman must equally surrender the pawn to the former debtor.[64] The clear inference is that when the creditor transfers the pawn to the woman, he loses thereby the right to debt-waiver.

Ramban simply states the inference; he gives no rationale for it. The 'strong' rationale, together with its problems and solution, is entirely of my learned critic's making. The passages in *Kiddushin* are thus dispositive of the question; yet Ravad didn't cite them. The reason, R. Buckwold suggests, is that Ravad anticipated not only Ramban's thinking but also that of R. Buckwold. Ravad also noticed the difficulty that my critic perceived in his own rationale and he, R. Avraham b. David of Posquières, invoked Alfasi's formulation to alleviate it. Having solved R. Buckwold's problems, Ravad rested content and didn't bother to cite the passage in *Kiddushin* which would have solved the problem that had actually been put to him.

Well, it's a thought—and one, I suspect, that no one has had before.

Ravad adduced a passage from Alfasi whose relevance is problematic, and I concluded that we are dealing with an intuited position rather than a well-argued one. R. Buckwold believes that to so state is to claim that Ravad adduced a 'far-flung pseudo-source' or used Alfasi as a 'fig leaf'. This assumption that any awareness of, or concern for, practical need automatically yields false and cunning interpretations leads my erudite critic to read my words rather oddly. He cites a sentence of mine: 'But, having arrived intuitively at a doctrine of non-renunciation, and lacking any proof for his position, he seized upon a formulation of Alfasi as precedent and *asmakhta* [support]', and proceeds to write: 'Prof. Soloveitchik continues to explain the secret lying behind Ravad's intuition: "There was a dearth of currency at the time in Provence".'

64 This is true whether the *kesef kiddushin* is the debt itself, but the woman received the pawn together with the debt, as Ramban holds, or the *kesef kiddushin* is the pawn which the woman received together with the loan, as Rashba ad loc. would have it.

How can there be a 'secret' behind an 'intuition'? Intuition is instinctive. The word means 'the act or process of coming to direct knowledge without reasoning or inference'.[65] When talking about a halakhist's intuition, we are referring to his halakhic intuition. Ravad's instinctive conclusion (later validated by Ramban) was that a gaged debt, once transferred, cannot subsequently be waived. In support of his halakhic intuition, he adduced a dubious proof.

R. Buckwold is of the opinion that anything that does not correspond to some preconceived notion of perfection is ipso facto specious and deceitful. To my thinking, to point to a flawed proof is simply to say that Ravad, or any other mortal, did not have at all times plenary inspiration, and in the short space that is allotted to a *posek*, he invoked the best source that he could think of. I'm sorry if this shocks R. Buckwold. It would not have shocked Ḥatam Sofer. Ravad was here, as it were, on the side of the angels, both as far as the correctness of his halakhic intuition is concerned and in his attempt to alleviate the financial pressures that his community faced.

Perhaps once again I was too brief in my concluding section and should have added a sentence or two to explain that Ravad's halakhic instinct was justified in time by Ramban, that his inner gyroscope had guided him to the right destination. After all, the argument from *Kiddushin* is scarcely news to me; I alluded to this ruling of Ravad and to the proof from *Kiddushin* subsequently adduced by Ramban in a publication that appeared some thirty-five years ago.[66] Should I republish the essay, I probably will add a passage about intuition and argument, reach and grasp, in halakhic thought and decision-making.

3. The force of this argument hinges on the merits of R. Buckwold's argument in the opening section of his article about Ravad's relationship to his predecessors, to which I shall reply at length in the second half of my response. In it, I shall specifically address his criticism here.

4. (*a*) There was, indeed, no dearth of currency. This, however, does not reduce the great practical significance of Ravad's ruling. It validated the ubiquitous clause to bearer and thereby doubled the capital available to most

[65] The definition is from Webster's *Third International Dictionary*.

[66] 'Pawnbroking: A Study in *Ribbit* and of the Halakhah in Exile', *Proceedings of the American Academy of Jewish Research*, 38–9 (1972), 221 n. 35 end. I noted that Rashi, in a responsum, does not seem to be aware of a possible proof from the passage in *Kiddushin* 8b. I added that Ravad's reply (which we have been discussing here) is a parallel instance of a great Talmudist not citing in a responsum a dispositive proof that was later adduced by Ramban and his school. {In the first volume of this series (Oxford, 2013), it appears in the appendix to n. 81, §1, p. 159.}

merchants, expanded dramatically the scale of the loan market, and 'unclogged the arteries of credit blocked by Shemu'el's ruling'.

(*b*) I have already addressed (p. 355) the matter of cancelled checks and noted my distinguished colleague's grasp of the realities of the mortgage and money market.

R. Buckwold then concludes his critique with this vigorous peroration:

> Having now reviewed all three examples in the 'Programmatic Essay' purportedly showing that 'Ravad's writings are anchored in Provencal life and thought', we may say without hesitation: 'There are no bears here, not even a forest!'

Indeed, my article has no bears; I leave it to my readers to decide whether or not it has substance.

(*To be continued*)

CHAPTER THIRTEEN

A Response to R. Buckwold's Critique of 'Rabad of Posquières: A Programmatic Essay', Part II

IN THE PRECEDING ESSAY I addressed what it means for a major halakhist to respond creatively to contemporary problems, a matter that agitated R. Buckwold. I now turn, as promised,[1] to other issues which incensed my distinguished critic. I claimed that Ravad and Rabbenu Tam were revolutionaries, that they dispensed with 500 years of geonic tutelage, and that the innovative, the new in law often wears the guise of the old, all of which incurred R. Buckwold's wrath.[2] It seems wise to preface my reply to him with some introductory remarks.

The current Lithuanian school of Talmudics draws many of its assumptions from the work of the Gra, R. Eliyahu, Gaon of Vilna (d.1797). Nevertheless, some of the premises of the Gra's work need articulation, and the wider world of Lithuanian Torah students might benefit from familiarity with them, as they will help us understand the mind-frame of Ravad and the other great medieval halakhists.

The *Be'urei ha-Gra* is an anti-legal work. It is a work of *Quellenforschung*, not of jurisprudence. The Gaon cites the *Massekhet Soferim*, for example, as the source of a halakhah in the *Shulḥan 'Arukh*. That, indeed, is the earliest source in classical rabbinic literature that mandates or mentions this practice. However, I do not follow this practice because it is found in the *Massekhet Soferim*; many things are found there which no one follows. I adhere to its dictate because it is reproduced in the *Minhagei Maharil* and is cited by Ramah. The latest normative source is what is binding in law, not the earliest one.

The Gaon denied that there was any legal system in the ordinary sense of

[1] Above, pp. 314–15, 345.

[2] E. A. Buckwold, 'Rabad—Disrupter of Tradition? A Response to Haym Soloveitchik's "Rabad of Posquieres: A Programmatic Essay"', *Torah u-Madda Journal*, 12 (2004), 24–73.

the term. Precedent counted for nothing—the decisions of hundreds of decisors (*posekim*) in the past 300 to 400 years were to be ignored. Custom, regardless of how venerable and cherished, was irrelevant: *piyyut* (liturgical poetry), recited for well over a millennium, and to many central to the holiday experience of prayer, was to be jettisoned; 'Ve-Yir'u 'Einenu', recited since the time of the early Geonim, if not earlier, should be elided from the prayer book. The only criterion for adjudication (*pesak halakhah*) was intellectual truth shorn of the dross of habit and sentiment. The sole gauge was the correct upshot of the talmudic sources as interpreted by the binding sources and, on rare occasions, by the decisor using his own interpretative skills.

And what was to the Gra a binding source? The classic medieval commentators on the Talmud—the *rishonim*—that were available to him, all of whom had passed on by 1375 or so,[3] and a dozen or so authorities after that date: R. Shelomoh Luria's *Yam shel Shelomoh*, and several of the great commentaries on the *Tur* and *Shulḥan Arukh*, such as the *Bet Yosef*, *Shakh*, *Bet Shemu'el*, and *Magen Avraham*. Notably absent was the vast responsa literature of Lithuania, Poland, Russia, Galicia, not to speak of that of the Sephardic world, which R. Shabbetai Kohen, author of the *Shakh*, deployed so effectively in his commentary on the 'Ḥoshen Mishpat'. The vast system of 'modern' case law plays no role in the Gaon's system, nor has it played a role in the subsequent two centuries in Lithuanian jurisprudence, in the rulings and responsa of R. Yeḥi'el Mikhel Epstein, the author of the *'Arukh ha-Shulḥan*, in the Russian Empire, of R. Avraham Yeshayahu Karelitz, the Ḥazon Ish, in Israel, and of R. Moshe Feinstein, whose *Iggerot Mosheh* was normative in America. Barring an occasional reference, noticeable by their absence are 500 years of halakhic writings—novellae (*ḥiddushim*) and commentaries (*be'urim*) of the early modern and modern era, that is to say, the literature of the *aḥaronim*. Missing also is half a millennium of responsa (*she'elot u-teshuvot*), including the great responsa of R. Yeḥezk'el Landau, R. Yosef Sha'ul Natanson, R. Ya'akov Ettlinger, those of R. Mosheh Sofer, R. Yehudah Asad, the *Tsemaḥ Tsedek* of R. Menaḥem Mendel of Lubavitch, not to speak of the vast responsa literature of the Sephardic world.

R. Buckwold is shocked at my statement that the great *rishonim*, such as Ravad, Rabbenu Tam, and Ri ha-Zaken, ignored 500 years of post-talmudic and geonic tutelage. If one wishes to see a large and burgeoning Torah community that has equally discarded 500 years of tutelage, one just needs to look around oneself; in some instances, to look in the mirror.

Do the writings of the Ḥazon Ish and R. Moshe Feinstein reflect any dis-

[3] The last date that we have of any deed or ruling by Rabbenu Nissim of Barcelona is 1371.

dain for the respondents (*meshivim*) of the past? Not that I or anyone else has noticed. There is no disrespect; there is no intentional disowning of the titans of the past. Rather, the problems which bothered the generations of scholars in Lithuania before 1880 are not the problems which bothered the post-1880s Talmudist. No doubt, we—that is to say, the Lithuanian Torah world—are the losers in not studying the writings of R. Shemu'el ha-Levi Edels (Maharsha, d.1631) and R. Me'ir of Lublin (Maharam Lublin, d.1616), whose detailed analyses of Rashi and the *Tosafot*—the staples of all talmudic studies—have been printed in the back of the standard Talmud for centuries. However, these writings do not excite the imagination of modern Talmud students, and all exhortations to engage their thought are useless. Students and scholars are and must be egoists; they must pursue the types of problem which stimulate their mind, otherwise the field comes to a standstill.

Do the *ḥiddushei Torah* of Reb Ḥayyim of Brisk, R. Shimon Shkop, and R. Eli'ezer Gordon cite various *aḥaronim*? They certainly do, indeed, far more than is generally realized. For example, the one surviving *Tagbuch*, or diary as it were, of R. Ḥayyim (the notebook in which he jotted down some of his thoughts), cites no fewer than seventeen *aḥaronim*.[4] However, when R. Ḥayyim resolves a contradiction in the *Shulḥan 'Arukh* between R. Yosef Karo's ruling that women do not generally recite *birkot ha-mitsvot* and his decision that women do recite the *birkot ha-Torah* in the morning service (*shaḥarit*) by contending that *birkot ha-Torah* are not made on the *mitsvah* of *talmud Torah*, but on the *ḥeftsa* of Torah—that is to say that to the Gentile the Torah is but a scroll of parchment, whereas to a Jew it is a scroll of Divine, binding revelation, i.e. the *berakhah* in the *shaḥarit* service is a blessing on Israel's election—you may be sure that he was not involved in any enterprise of resolving contradictions of the *Shulḥan 'Arukh*—there are far more pressing contradictions in that work than this one[5]—but employing these two conflicting determinations as a hook on which to hang his own analysis, the product of his new approach. When he cites Maharam Schiff's commentary in his discussion of *ketav 'al gabei ketav*, he is not returning to the days of *pilpul*, but is using that work to clarify a point necessary for his analysis.

R. Buckwold is wroth with me for writing that 'R. Yitsḥak of Fez [Alfasi]

4 *Kitvei Rabbenu Ḥayyim ha-Levi*, ed. Y. Lichtenstein (Jerusalem, 2018), index, s.v. *Aḥaronim*.

5 On the contradiction between the views in 'Ḥoshen Mishpat' and in 'Yoreh De'ah' regarding the status of pawns in Jewish–Gentile commercial relations involving usury, see H. Soloveitchik, 'Pawnbroking: A Study in *Ribbit* and of the Halakhah in Exile', *Proceedings of the American Academy of Jewish Research*, 38–39 (1972), 203–68; reprinted in an expanded form in *Collected Essays*, i (Oxford, 2013), 57–166.

had discarded the Geonim before him [i.e. Ravad]. He had attempted to decide talmudic controversies independently of their writings.'[6] First of all, this is not my insight (as I noted in a footnote), but that of the late Shraga Abramson. What Professor Abramson had in mind was that R. Alfas made up his own mind on halakhic issues, whereas R. Yehudah of Barcelona, the author of the *Sefer ha-'Ittim*, the figure to whom Abramson contrasts Alfasi, restored the Geonim to their authoritative position. To be sure, there were instances when R. Alfas had no specific view on the matter, and he followed a view of a Gaon that he considered weighty. Much as R. Moshe Feinstein in America or the Ḥazon Ish in Israel would rule like the Rama or Shakh in instances where they had no specific view on the issue at stake. However, on most issues their rulings and those of R. Yeḥi'el Mikhel Epstein, the author of the *'Arukh ha-Shulḥan*, reflected their own view as to the correct halakhic position in the issue at bar.

Let me expand on the matter of Alfasi. Maimonides, who was scarcely given to compliments, writes of R. Alfas that his mistakes do not amount to ten, or, in another instance, to thirty.[7] I once heard from my father that he and my grandfather once very quickly ran up a count of well over thirty places where Maimonides disagreed with R. Alfas. My father commented that when R. Alfas ruled like Rav Huna, whereas Maimonides ruled in accordance with Rav Sheshet, Maimonides did not view this as an error. This is an adjudicative call, and opinions will differ among decisors, great and small. What was in Maimonides' view an error was of the same type as Alfasi's holding that one should blow the shofar on the Sabbath in the congregation where the greatest scholar of the generation prayed.[8] And such deviances are rare indeed in the writings of Alfasi, be it his *Halakhot* or his responsa. Maimonides viewed R. Alfas as the *posek* par excellence, an adjudicator with perfect judicial pitch.

This comes out very clearly if one contrasts his assessment of Alfasi with that of the only other predecessor whom Maimonides admired greatly, R. Yosef ha-Levi Ibn Megas. The latter is praised for his exceptional insight and penetration and for a method that made him unique in the preceding half-millennium of Talmud studies.[9] Rambam does not say that R. Yosef ha-Levi had perfect judicial pitch, nor does he say that Alfasi had a unique

[6] 'Rabad—Disrupter of Tradition?' (above, n. 2), 36–7.

[7] *Mishnah 'im Perush Rabbenu Mosheh ben Maimon*, ed. Y. Ḥ Kafiḥ (Jerusalem, 1963), i. 25. *Teshuvot ha-Rambam*, ed. Y. Blau (Jerusalem, 1957), vol. ii, #251 (p. 459).

[8] *Perush ha-Ran on Alfasi* (Romm edn.), *Rosh Hashanah* 5a, s.v. *ve-nir'eh*; *Milḥamot ha-Shem* ad loc. and see *Ha-Ma'or ha-Katan* ibid.

[9] Mishnah, ed. Kafiḥ (above, n. 7), i. 25: וחי ה' כי הבנת אותו האיש בתלמוד מפליאה כל מי שמתבונן מדבריו ועומק עיונו, עד שאפשר לי לומר עליו 'לפניו לא היה מלך כמוהו' בשיטתו.

method of talmudic analysis. The *posek* par excellence of the preceding four or five centuries was, in his eyes, Alfasi. (Let us remember that there is no mention of the Geonim in the 'history of the halakhah' that Maimonides presented in his introduction to the *Mishneh Torah*.)

A towering adjudicator, Alfasi made up his own mind, as do Lithuanian *posekim* today. If anyone in the past millennium refused to follow other people's views and decried innumerable views that he himself had formerly advocated, it was Ravad of Posquières,[10] and no one has demonstrated this better than R. Buckwold in his superb edition of Ravad's *Ba'alei ha-Nefesh*.[11]

Let me turn now to R. Buckwold's further critiques. He cites as proof of my error the remarks of Ravad's father-in-law, R. Avraham Av Bet Din of Narbonne, who wrote: 'We rely on all rulings of the Gaon R. Isaac [Alfasi], for he knew all the teachings of the Geonim who preceded him and would select the principal [opinion].'[12]

Robert Brody has estimated that some 5,000 responsa or fragments of responsa of the Geonim have come down to us, principally through the cartons of *shemot* (discarded papers that have the name of God inscribed on them) found in the Cairo Genizah, which have been aptly called 'sacred trash'.[13] Would it be rash to assume that R. Alfas, seated in Fez and heir to centuries of geonic communication with and tutelage of the Maghreb, had many of these responsa? Such a corpus will have every opinion on the spectrum. (Just open a page in the *Otsar ha-Ge'onim* and see how many differing opinions are registered there.) To say that Alfasi, as R. Avraham, Av Bet Din of Narbonne, puts it, 'would select the principal [opinion]'[14] can mean no more than that he systematically chose the opinion at which he had independently arrived. He didn't proffer a legal holding because it was a geonic opinion; he arrived at what he believed to be the correct ruling and used the geonic decision as a peg on which to hang his opinion.[15]

[10] I have discussed at length this aspect of Ravad in the essay 'The Literary Ruins of the *Gedol ha-Mefarshim*', Ch. 11 above.

[11] *Ba'alei ha-Nefesh le-Rabbenu ha-Ravad 'al Hilkhot Niddah, Mikva'ot u-Kedushah* (Benei Berak, 1992; repr. with addenda and corrigenda in 2013).

[12] R. Avraham b. R. Yitsḥak, *She'elot u-Teshuvot*, ed. Y. Ḥ Kafiḥ (Jerusalem, 1962), #16. The editorial addition is that of R. Buckwold and is fully warranted.

[13] A. Hoffman and P. Cole, *Sacred Trash: The Lost and Found World of the Cairo Genizah* (New York, 2011).

[14] As translated in Buckwold, 'Rabad—Disrupter of Tradition?' (above, n. 1), 37. The bracketed 'opinion' is the addition of R. Buckwold and is justified by the context.

[15] To prevent misunderstanding, it is advisable to distinguish between two separate meanings of the term 'independence of the Geonim'. It is one thing to say that Kairouan (in what is now Tunisia) or Lucena (in Muslim Spain) were, from the latter half of the ninth century, when they first emerge

In the same fashion, *mutatis mutandis*, when a Lithuanian *posek* invokes a responsum mentioned in the *Pitḥei Teshuvah* and rules accordingly, or when a Lithuanian *rosh yeshivah* rules in 'Yoreh De'ah' according to the view of the *Semak* (mentioned but rejected by Shakh[16]), he is providing what he believes to be the correct solution to the question being posed to him; he is not endorsing or even invoking in any real sense the *Semak* as authority. Again, I urge R. Buckwold to simply look around him and see the sincere, deferential choreography of 'revolutionary' Lithuanian *posekim*, proud members of a traditional society or one that still takes its reverences seriously.

I would, once again, urge R. Buckwold to stop taking his (and my) community for granted, as part of the natural order of things, but to see them as others view them, most notably Polish, Hungarian, and Sephardic scholars. They look askance at the religious *suffisance* of these leaders, who are operating independent of the mandate of centuries of Jewish practice and thought. They act as if they were the only inhabitants of a 'post-rishonic' world.

And why do the Lithuanians operate in such a fashion?

In part because of the heritage of the Gra; in part despite the heritage. What you see in the *New York Times* is what you get. What you see in a work of art is not what you get or not just what you get. *The Brothers Karamazov* is about a murder; it is also about more than that. This is true *a fortiori* of the Talmud. There is an obvious surface meaning; the question is what is beneath the surface. One can assume that the Gemara is like the face of a watch—underneath the surface there is a vast, complicated set of gears, an indescribably delicate and refined mechanism that dictates the movement of the two

from the mist, independent of the Geonim; it is another to say that Alfasi was independent of the Geonim. The first means that neither Tunisia nor al-Andalus reflexively sent all its queries to Baghdad. They attempted from the outset to resolve their financial, and perhaps religious, problems on their own—have their cases adjudicated by local scholars. However, both settlements acknowledged that the Geonim were the final arbiters of all religious questions, and should a query be sent to the Geonim and a ruling issued contrary to those of the local Jewish communities, that ruling would prevail. When one speaks of Alfasi (and a fortiori of the *rishonim*, who include, of course, Ravad) as being independent of the Geonim, one means that they, ever so politely, ignore their predecessors and adjudicate questions on their own. Study a page of the Talmud with the *Otsar ha-Ge'onim* and with the *Ḥiddushei ha-Ritva*, and you realize that each lives in a separate world of discourse—the concerns of one are scarcely those of the other. (It is not our task here to define the difference between the approach of the Geonim and that of the *rishonim*.) As for Ravad, anyone who has studied some ten pages of the *Ba'alei ha-Nefesh* knows that if there was anyone in the past millennium who made up his own mind, it was Ravad of Posquières. He followed no one's views, not even those he himself had advocated only a brief while before. I have expanded on this trait of his in 'The Literary Remains of the *Gedol ha-Mefarshim*', above, pp. 303–4, 309.

[16] The *Semak* was a very influential code until the *Shulḥan 'Arukh* and the *Mappah* appeared, not afterwards.

hands of the watch. Hundreds of tiny pieces control the movement of those two paltry hands. This is a thumbnail description of the assumption of *pilpul* of the early modern period.[17] The position of Rav Papa in a talmudic discussion (*sugya*) is dictated by a technical assumption implicit in another position of Rav Papa in a different *sugya*, and the anonymous objector in the first *sugya* is the same anonymous objector in the third *sugya* and who entertains a different assumption about the basic nature of the mechanics of a *sugya*. Similarly, the second objection raised in the *sugya* is related to a fourth *sugya* . . . and so it goes. Thus the back and forth of a specific *sugya* is actually the product of the integrated mechanics of five other *sugyot*.

It is easier to illustrate this with an example of someone who partially broke out of the system than with an analysis of Maharam Schiff's use of what the school of *pilpul* called a 'Regensburger'.[18] One of the towering figures of the past several centuries is R. 'Akiva Eger. His notes on the Talmud, especially his great annotations of the *Shulḥan 'Arukh* and the *Mishnayot*, are constantly being issued, reissued, amplified as more and more volumes of his library surface and their pages—covered with his notes—are discovered. Yet his formal essays or lectures (*ma'arakhot*), his *derush ve-ḥiddush*,[19] his model of analysis of a broad-ranging *sugya* with its rich interweaving with other *sugyot*, are scarcely studied. Indeed, I would doubt if most contemporary talmudic scholars could fully master a *ma'arakhah* of his.

When R. 'Akiva Eger's mind moves across a text, like a match across a fricative surface, it ignites with ideas and insights that speak to us directly. His piercing mind perceives all types of qualifications and questions that the text poses. However, when he sets out to give a formal lecture or class, as it were, the *derekh ha-pilpul* (the 'way of *pilpul*', i.e. the pilpulistic mode of thought) in which he was raised and trained takes over.[20] Every *sugya* is related to any number of *sugyot* by all types of assumptions of talmudic mechanics; and after a column or two of—what appear to us to be—arid concatenations, we tire of the argument or lose track of it entirely. From a biased Lithuanian perspective, one might say, R. 'Akiva Eger was a great mind who had received a bad education.

A similar experience can be had when using the writings of R. Aryeh Leib of Volozhin (d.1785), better known as Sha'agat Aryeh. He holds a place of

[17] See e.g. S. Z. Dimitrovski, ''Al Derekh ha-Pilpul', in S. Lieberman et al., eds., *Salo Baron Jubilee Volume*, 3 vols. (Jerusalem, 1975), iii. 111–81 (Hebrew volume).

[18] Ibid. 143–4.

[19] *Derush ve-Ḥiddush R. 'Akiva Eger*, 2 vols. (Jerusalem, 1997).

[20] A rough translation of *derekh ha-pilpul* might be 'the mode of post-medieval scholastic dialectics'.

honor in the Lithuanian pantheon, indeed, is viewed as one of the founding fathers of the school. Many a bar mitzvah boy has discussed Sha'agat Aryeh's analysis of the laws of *tefillin*. Yet I wonder how many scholars have worked through many of his analyses. Turn to the similar *teshuvot* of his grand-nephew, R. Ya'akov of Karlin (d.1836), who inherited his predecessor's intellectual fearlessness, his sovereign control of the field, and his imperial disposition, and the material reads easily. The *Mishkenot Ya'akov*[21] is the *Sha'agat Aryeh*[22] passed through the simplifying filter of the Gra, who insisted that there is no subtext in the Talmud, there is only the text, and that must be totally mastered in all its simplicity. The Talmud is not a watch and there are no hidden mechanisms. And should one have asked and still ask: 'What is left to be said about the simple meaning of a talmudic *sugya*?'—the work of R. Ya'akov's humble, soft-spoken brother, R. Yitsḥak of Karlin (d.1841), the *Keren Orah*,[23] demonstrated and continues to demonstrate just how much remains to be discovered in the simple understanding of the Talmud.

Together with the attention to variant readings and to underprivileged texts of the classical literature, this lack of hidden mechanics in a *sugya* was a central part of the legacy of the Gra. This was supplanted by a wholly different agenda in the closing decades of the nineteenth century. The Lithuanian scholars of the 1880s, be it R. Yomtov Heller of Białystok, R. Ḥayyim of Brisk (Brest-Litovsk), R. Yosef Rosen (otherwise known as 'the Rogatchover') of Dvinsk (Daugavpils), R. Shimon Shkop, or R. El'azar Yehudah of Telz (Telšiai), all believed that the Talmud, indeed, resembled a clock, as the school of *pilpul* had assumed. There was a complex world hidden from view that governed the discussions of the Talmud. However, they differed radically with the school of *pilpul* as to what that hidden world was. It was not a mechanical world, but one of ideas and judicial principles. The specific dicta of the Talmud on any topic were but concretions of a central concept, and the task of the scholar was to decode what principles were being instantiated in the different rulings spelled out in the *sugya*. Once decoded, rulings seemingly contradictory proved to be unrelated for they were concretions of different principles. Conversely, rulings seemingly unconnected could be vitally germane to one another as they were instantiations of different aspects of one and the same underlying principle. These fundamental principles could be legal ones, very much akin, if not identical, to those of positive or formalist jurisprudence—as they were with R. Ḥayyim, and in a different sense with

21 Ya'akov of Karlin, *Mishkenot Ya'akov*, 2 vols. (Jerusalem, 1979).

22 *Sha'agat Aryeh*, ed. H. H. Eichhorn (Lakewood, 2015).

23 New York, 1983.

R. Shimon—or they could be philosophical ones, as they were with R. Yosef Rosen.[24]

A half-dozen or so works of the past, such as the *Ketsot ha-Ḥoshen*[25] and the *Netivot ha-Mishpat*,[26] shared de facto this assumption; but the vast majority of works written in the preceding half-millennium had nothing to offer in decoding the underlying principles of the *sugya*, and so were and are simply ignored. Not disrespected, just unused.

Having addressed the two major sources of R. Buckwold's disquiet, I would like to turn to a number of his lesser criticisms, both his assumptions and his mode of argument. He cites Menaḥem ha-Me'iri's introduction to *Avot*[27] in explanation of the absence of written talmudic commentary in the time of the Geonim, and states that, as the language of the Talmud was understood by all, there was no need for commentary.

First, Me'iri's introduction to *Avot*, valuable as it is in some of the information it contains, is not a work of history and is of limited historical use. He lived some 250 years after R. Sherira and Rav Ḥai Gaon and some 2,500 miles west of Baghdad, and his knowledge was worn and hand-me-down, traditions that had been passed on, embellished, or diminished as transmissions tend to be over centuries. As a historical source, it has to be placed along other reports, and its accuracy evaluated. There is, here, the issue of misplaced authority. Me'iri was in one sense a great Talmudist;[28] that does not make him a great historian or even a reliable historical reporter. There is no intrinsic reason to credit his traditions over those of his contemporary Provençal confrère, Menaḥem b. Zeraḥ, with his tale of sixty scholars in the *bet ha-midrash*

[24] R. Yosef Rosen assumed that underlying many discussions of the Talmud were such philosophical issues as, for example, whether time is a series of discreet points or a continuum. The question whether a noticeable taste in food (*noten ta'am*) is a factor which hinders its legal absorption into the large mass into which it has fallen (*bittul*) is a question that makes sense only in the universe of discourse of *kashrut*. The question about the nature of time is understandable to someone who has never even heard of halakhah—in other words, the question did not arise from the data, but is a question external to the data, which is being used to explain them. If the nature of time is, indeed, at bar in the *sugyot* that R. Rosen cites, the talmudic discussion (*masa u-matan*) then should revolve around this question. However, I was unable to find one discussion in the copious talmudic sources cited by R. Rosen in his *Tsofnat Pa'ane'aḥ: Ḥiddushim u-Ve'urim 'al Massekhet Makkot*, ed. M. M. Kasher (New York, 1959) that I could construe as being a discussion of philosophical principles that he adduces. The discussions of that tractate have, to my limited understanding, little to do with the principles said to be at bar in these *sugyot*.

[25] Aryeh Leib ha-Kohen, *Ketsot ha-Ḥoshen*, vol. i (Lemberg, 1788), vol. ii (Lemberg, 1899).

[26] Ya'akov mi-Lissa, *Netivot ha-Mishpat* (Sudlikov, 1809).

[27] Buckwold, 'Rabad—Disrupter of Tradition?' (above, n. 2), 25–9. The correct bibliographical entry for the work cited in n. 54 is: *Bet ha-Beḥirah le-Rabbenu Menaḥem ha-Me'iri 'al Massekhet Avot*, ed. S. Z. Havlin and A. Shoshanah (Jerusalem, 1995).

[28] See below, pp. 399–401.

of Ri ha-Zaken, each responsible for one tractate, and as the Ri pored over the Talmud line by line, each line would be read out before the assembled sixty and checked against all other passages in the Talmud.[29] It was a little unfair for one scholar to have to handle all of the voluminous tractate of *Shabbat*, while his colleague got away with only having to command the thirteen and a half folios of *Horayot*. This is simply a pictorial way, common to exemplum literature and folklore, of stating that in Ri's *bet ha-midrash* every line of the Talmud was examined comparatively.

R. Buckwold further takes me to task for counting only explicit references to the Geonim in the writing of Ravad and not the anonymous 'there are those that say' (*ve-ika man de-mefarshei*). There are, he points out, twenty references to the Geonim in the *Ba'alei ha-Nefesh* and no fewer than eighty references to anonymous commentators.[30] Around a century and a half to close to two centuries separate Ravad (d.1198) from Rav Sherira (d.1004) and Rav Ḥai (d.1038), and if the writings of both Me'iri and R. Shemu'el of Cerdagne teach us one thing, it is that there was far more adjudicatory activity and exegetical creativity in Provence and Catalonia than the writings of Nahmanides and his school would lead us to believe.

Nothing illustrates this better than the writings of Menaḥem ha-Me'iri, the *Shitah lo Noda' le-Mi 'al Massekhet Kiddushin*, first published in Constantinople in 1751, and the so-called *Perush ha-Ritva 'al Bava Metsi'a*, published in Venice in 1622 and repeatedly reprinted in the collected writings of Ritva until a half-century ago.[31] From the innumerable doctrines cited—alas, anonymously, or hidden behind meaningless monikers—there seems to have been a steady stream of interpretative Talmudics. The quality was uneven, as might be expected in any large-scale enterprise of many hands over the course of two centuries. However, that it contained works of brilliance is beyond question. Are we to assume that there was creativity in Provence and Catalonia in the twelfth and thirteenth centuries in the tractate of *Kiddushin* but not in that of *Gittin*; in *Bava Metsi'a* but not in *Bava Kamma*? The dearth of works of significance in twelfth- and thirteenth-century Provence and Catalonia, as compared with Ashkenaz, is due to a simple fact. Far more medieval works of Ashkenaz have come down to us from these centuries than of Provence and Catalonia, as I explained in a previous essay:

29 *Medieval Jewish Chronicles and Chronological Notes*, ed. A. Neubauer (Oxford, 1893), ii. 241.

30 Buckwold, 'Rabad—Disrupter of Tradion?' (above, n. 2), 30–1 and n. 34.

31 The genuine *Ḥiddushei ha-Ritva* on that tractate was first published in London as *Ḥiddushei ha-Ritva ha-Ḥadashim 'al Bava Metsi'a* by A. S. Y. Halperin in 1962.

France and Germany had their Poland, Spain its Mediterranean; but Provence was childless. When the time came for Ashkenaz to go into exile, it transported its culture to the empty spaces of central and eastern Europe. When Sepharad's days were up, the Spaniards took their classics with them to the far ends of the Mediterranean. Provence fell on evil times just as halakhah was flourishing south of the Pyrenees. The affinity between the two cultures was great, and Provence was absorbed by Spain with startling rapidity. In exile, Sepharad and Ashkenaz preserved, if not their cultural identity, at least their heritage. Provence did not; and 95 percent of its halakhic literature was swept away, unknown until the present century. The only Provençal writings preserved and destined to achieve currency were those appended to Sephardic works—Razah on Alfasi, Ravad on Maimonides. Provençal Talmudists survived as critics, not as creators.[32]

In light of this, why must I assume that the eighty or so interpretations that Ravad cites and rejects are all geonic or mostly so? To be sure, such a massive repudiation would speak much for his independence of the Geonim, but there is no need to push things that far.

R. Buckwold further argues that to cite a view anonymously is to give it greater weight and authority, much like a *setam mishnah*. He further compares it to the actions of R. Yosef Karo and R. Mosheh Isserles. They often simply issue a ruling without sourcing it, which of course endows the opinion with unchallenged authority.[33] The answer to this objection is, in my view, obvious. According to the traditional view, there was no written record of controversies until the time of R. Yehudah ha-Nasi. He believed that the need of the hour demanded the writing down of some summary of the Oral Law,[34] and he issued a straightforward dictate (a *setam mishnah*), which, understandably, became the most binding source in halakhah. Similarly, when we know the conflicting views of Geonim and *rishonim* on a matter, and R. Yosef Karo and Rama forgo all mentioning of various authorities and simply issue a ruling that accords with one of these views, the halakhah then speaks in one voice—which increases the sense of the ruling's binding power. (Think of the importance of unanimity in *Brown vs. the Board of Education*, the historic Supreme Court decision which banned segregation in public schools.)

32 Above, p. 262.

33 Buckwold, 'Rabad—Disrupter of Tradition?' (above, n. 2), 60–1 n. 37, 63 n. 49.

34 For a comprehensive study of the subject of the inscription of the Oral Law, see Y. Sussman, 'Torah she-be-'al Peh—Peshutah ke-Mashma'ah: Koḥo shel Kutso shel Yod', in D. Rosenthal and Y. Sussman, eds., *Meḥkerei Talmud*, iii (Jerusalem, 2005), 209–384. See also N. Danzig, 'Mi-Talmud be-'al Peh le-Talmud bi-Khetav: 'al Derekh Mesirat ha-Talmud ha-Bavli ve-Limudo bi-Yemei ha-Beinayim', *Bar Ilan: Sefer ha-Shanah*, 30–31 (Ramat Gan, 2006), 49–112.

However, if neither of these circumstances exists and someone just writes, 'There are some who say', how does this lend any authority to what follows?

R. Buckwold is equally wroth with me for writing that 'the revolutionary Talmudist often conceals his revolution even from himself'. This to him smacks of deceit and of an evil intent to subvert the system from within. In his formulation, 'He [Soloveitchik] claims to have discovered great halakhic authorities—Ravad being a case in point—who "*disguise innovations—at times even from* [themselves]", implying the disguising innovation was done consciously [i.e. was intellectually dishonest].'[35] I respectfully disagree.

One of the mysteries of human society is why people listen to the policeman. Certainly, it is not because of his physical power, even when joined by his fellow officers, as they constitute an infinitesimal percentage of the population. Anyone old enough to have witnessed the disintegration of the Soviet Union, as soldiers and police refused to obey orders to fire on the crowd, has dramatic evidence of the mystery of 'legitimacy'. A state, as Max Weber once defined it, is an institution that has a monopoly on the legitimate use of force. But what is legitimacy and how does one acquire it? One of the most ubiquitous sources of legitimacy is usage—the present receives its empowerment from the past, and so it seems only right and natural to do things in the way they always have been done.

This is one reason why law draws consistently on precedent. The task of a legal system is making and enforcing norms, and thus it is preternaturally sensitive to the issue of legitimacy, as it is only too well aware that it lacks the power for brute force. Without legitimacy, the enforcement arm of the state will be exposed as an emperor without clothes, or more accurately without arms. For this reason, law tends to be quite conservative in creating new forms. It tends to adopt forms of the past even though the reasons for the law's enactment would dictate new forms. This was noted by Ri ha-Zaken close to a millennium ago.[36] It also avoids creating new terms and tends to pack new notions into old words creating linguistic ambiguity, which allows it to issue a new ruling under the guise of simply reproducing an old one. Thus, it preserves its flexibility without sacrificing its legitimacy. This terminological ambiguity is one of the key points in the Lithuanian school, as it sees its task in unpacking the different notions present in a single term, and by so doing resolving seeming contradictions.

35 Buckwold, 'Rabad—Disrupter of Tradition?' (above, n. 2), 52. See also R. Buckwold's concluding paragraph—his peroration, as it were—on p. 73.

36 *Yeinam: Sahar be-Yeinam shel Goyim—'al Gilgulah shel Halakhah be-'Olam ha-Ma'aseh* (Jerusalem, 2016), 159.

It is customary to mischaracterize the approach of R. Ḥayyim of Brisk as that of *shenei dinim*, 'two [different] principles [in the same term]'.[37] The truth of the matter is that there could be five *dinim* in a single term, though if one is rigorous in defining a halakhic principle, as some proponents of the Lithuanian method were often not,[38] finding two genuine halakhic principles in the same term is an accomplishment.

R. Buckwold then takes me to task for not studying the *Sefer ha-Eshkol* on *'Avodah Zarah* and asks me to join him in its study. I decline his kind offer, as I have been there before. I had hoped, when I began my researches in the history of halakhah, to open up not only eleventh-century Ashkenaz, but equally eleventh-century Provence, convinced as I was that the great work of the 'long twelfth century' in Ashkenaz (roughly 1050–1200) could not be understood without knowing what had transpired in the preceding 125 years (*c.*925–1050). Similarly, the great writings of Ravad and R. Zeraḥyah ha-Levi could not be understood without knowing what had preceded them—from the days of R. Yehudah Albargeloni (i.e. from Barcelona) and R. Yosef Ibn Megas, *c.*1050–1150. I began with Albeck's edition of the *Sefer ha-Eshkol* and addressed the tractate of *'Avodah Zarah*. I found nothing. He scarcely says anything, other than making a banal observation here and an obvious remark there. Lengthy quotations from geonic responsa constitute the only substantive material in that work, and, not wishing to omit a precious word of such revered texts, he can copy an extensive responsum for the sole purpose of a half a line that is relevant.

37 I first encountered this characterization in S. Y. Zevin's *Ishim ve-Shitot: Shurat Ma'amarin 'al Ishei Halakhah ve-Shitoteihem be-Torah* (Tel Aviv, 1952), 48 ff. I can only say from personal experience that I never heard in my home Reb Ḥayyim's approach to 'learning' as being so characterized, nor did I hear it so characterized from distinguished *rashei yeshivah* and outstanding alumni of Mir, Brisk, and Telz, such as R. Noaḥ Bornstein, R. Henokh Fishman, R. Yeruḥam Gorelik, R. Yehudah Leib Arnest, and R. Shemu'el Volk. I heard the phrase quite often, as one might expect; however, I never heard R. Ḥayyim's method characterized with this phrase.

38 No two cases are identical; the contexts of any two cases are by definition different. The controlling question is: What are the dominant traits of the case that determine to what precedent it should be analogized? There are endless differences between the vast proffer of precedents. A difference of color is irrelevant to laws of debt collection, but quite relevant to contracts and the laws of contamination (*tum'at tsara'at*). A difference in size may be insignificant to the obligations of filial piety, but not to those of the *lulav* and *etrog*. The test of whether a difference is, indeed, a halakhic one—and not simply a logical or factual one—is: does it make a halakhic difference? (A more difficult thing to prove than one might imagine.) The universe of the *Ḥiddushei Rabbenu Ḥayyim ha-Levi* seems to be a small and restricted one, and in many ways it is. However, it is a purely halakhic one. No difference is admitted except those which can be proven to make a halakhic difference, something that some of R. Ḥayyim's contemporaries occasionally ignored. R. Ḥayyim's contribution lay not in

R. Buckwold strives at length to explain the reasons for the barrenness of the writings of R. Avraham Av Bet Din of Narbonne. Spare me the roundabout. The truth will do—he had little to say. All he can do is quote endlessly. Serious thinkers don't quote. They summarize briefly and then move on to express their own thoughts. A thinker who has something to say says it, as did, brilliantly, R. Avraham's older contemporary from Lucena, R. Yosef ha-Levi Ibn Megas, and R. Avraham's successor, Ravad of Posquières.

Unsurprisingly, Ravad rarely quoted, either in his commentaries or in his self-standing works, such as his *Commentary on the Sifra de-Vei Rav (Torat Kohanim)*,[39] or in his famed composition on the laws of sexual abstention during the period of menstrual 'impurity', the *Ba'alei ha-Nefesh*. However, there is no doubt as to the frequency or brilliance of his interpretative insights. No one has demonstrated it better or brought it more vigorously to contemporary attention than R. Buckwold in his superb edition of the *Ba'alei ha-Nefesh*.[40]

making distinctions—that was part of the new wave in Lithuania in the closing decades of the nineteenth century—but in the rigor with which the halakhic validity of the difference is tested.

[39] *Sifra de-Vei Rav: Hu Torat Kohanim 'im Perush R. Avraham ben David* (Vienna, 1862).

[40] See above, n. 11.

CHAPTER FOURTEEN

Jewish and Roman Law: A Study in Interaction

THIS ESSAY was not written for students of the halakhah, but for students of medieval Provençal law. In studying the role of the surety (*'arev*) in usury loans, I corresponded with André Gouron, the well-known authority on Roman law in Provence. He apparently informed the editors of the Roger Aubenas Festschrift of my work; otherwise I am at a loss how they knew of me as I had never had any dealings with them or with that distinguished authority on medieval Provençal law. Given the target audience of the *Collected Essays*, I should have translated my Hebrew essay on surety and *ribbit* that I published in *Zion*, as that study is geared to halakhists and historians of halakhah, and there is an interesting story to be told. However, once I no longer simply reproduced a study but translated it, I felt that I would have to update it. I taught courses on pawnbroking regularly, and this compelled me to keep a finger in that pie—watching, for example, the shifting attitudes toward *Schuld* and *Haftung* in the historiography of Germanic law. However, I never taught surety and have no idea of the developments in this field in Germany or France in the past forty-five years. I have decided to reprint this essay, written initially in English, which presents the implications which the Hebrew sources have for the history of Provençal law in the twelfth century.

Six terms appear in this essay with which the reader who is not a student of Roman or medieval law may not be familiar. *Caution d'influence*, 'surety of pressure', means that the surety did not assume any debt, but gave his assurance to the creditor that he would use his considerable leverage to ensure that the debtor repaid the loan. If the collection was delayed or frustrated, the surety could be penalized. *Caution d'obligation* is a surety who assumes the obligation to pay the debt. 'Surety of substitution' is roughly an *'arev kablan*, that is to say, the surety was not a co-debtor but replaced the debtor, thus becoming the one and only person from whom the creditor could collect. 'Benefit of discussion' is the right of the surety in Roman law to be

In view of the forum, I have kept the Hebrew references to a minimum. Anyone wishing to check my manner of reading the medieval rabbinic sources can do so in my larger, detailed study ''Arev be-Ribbit', *Zion*, 37 (1972), 1–21. On a few occasions of special interest, I have referred the reader to notes in that article.

'second in line', as it were. The halakhic term is *tove'im le-loveh teḥilah*, that is to say, the surety, who was a co-debtor, could insist, nonetheless, that an attempt had to be made first to collect from the debtor. Only if that failed could the creditor turn to the surety for satisfaction. *Nova constitutio* (new law) was the term used for rulings from Roman law that had begun to penetrate Provençal law in the course of the twelfth century. *Renunciatio* was renunciation by the debtor of rights given him by the 'new' Roman law. In the subject here under discussion, he waives his right to 'benefit of discussion'.

I AM NOT A HISTORIAN of Provençal law but a student of the halakhah (Jewish law). In the course of studying the laws regulating usury (*ribbit*), more specifically, the problem of personal surety in usury contracts, certain peculiar developments in Provençal halakhic thought came to my attention which were not explainable by indigenous forces. The geographical distribution of the discussion seemed oddly disproportionate, the fictions too blatant, the types of problem that were raised seemed inappropriate for the period, and the terminology was occasionally alien. I was compelled to look outside Jewish law for possible stimuli. Placing the Jewish developments within the context of twelfth-century Provençal law shed light on a number of seemingly inexplicable points. The Jewish literature, on the other hand, provided new information about the Gentile law of the time and yielded fresh corroboration for theories of the penetration of Roman law in Provence. However, at the same time this material seemed to point to an earlier date for certain legal developments than is generally accepted. It is these findings that I would like to bring to the attention of the scholars of Provençal law.

Interest (*ribbit*) between one Jew and another was strictly forbidden by the Talmud. In its view, just as the Bible banned usury loans between one Jew and another, so did it forbid Jews from serving as sureties in such transactions.[1] Once a Divine injunction was imposed, there could be no room for development in this matter in the halakhah, other than in the realm of legal fiction to evade the norm. This is not to say that such forbidden loans were never made or that people did not guarantee them; those cases, however, would rarely come before the courts, for no court would enforce such contracts. Indeed, it would most probably punish the parties. If a case of this sort did reach the courts, it would not be legally significant, for it would be an open and shut case, and no record of it would be preserved.[2]

[1] *Bava Metsi'a* 75b.

[2] No Jewish court records of the Middle Ages have come down to us. What we possess are

Loans between Jew and Gentile were a different matter. According to the halakhah, Gentiles could both lend to Jews and borrow from them at interest. What of a Jew serving as a surety in such a transaction? The Talmud devotes several lines to this problem,[3] and the scholars of twelfth-century Provence (this term in Jewish intellectual history refers both to Provence and the Bas-Languedoc, the communities of which formed one culture[4]) treated the matter at length. North of the Loire, in the great academies of Champagne and Île-de-France, hardly a word is to be found on the subject.[5] This silence of the north, this bifurcation of interests, is striking and highly atypical. In many, if not most, issues it was the schools of Champagne and Paris that paved the way in halakhic discourse. Even if one cannot demand creativity on any specific matter ('the spirit bloweth where it listeth'), one could expect at least discussion. Surety was as essential a part of the northern credit system as of the southern, perhaps even more so.[6]

The answer lies in the unequal spread of the 'surety of obligation' in general law, taken together with certain basic facts of the development of Jewish legal thought. Surety in medieval Jewish law was obligational and had been for over a millennium. Among Gentiles the surety of obligation first appeared in Provence in any significant fashion in the latter half of the twelfth century,[7] while in the north the older form of surety, *caution d'influence*, began its retreat only around the second quarter of the thirteenth century.[8] The twelfth

responsa and notes made by rabbis' pupils and contemporaries of important or problematic decisions. A self-evident decision would have left no imprint on these sources. {What the sources do register, at times, is rabbis decrying a widespread breach of the usury injunction or the appearance of a new legal fiction, which the courts have to assess.}

3 *Bava Metsi'a* 71b.

4 See H. Gross, *Gallia Judaica: Dictionnaire géographique de la France d'après les sources rabbiniques*, 3rd edn., with a bibliographic supplement by S. Schwarzfuchs (Paris, 2011), 489. Culturally Barcelona was equally part of Jewish Provence. The ambiance of the term 'Provence' in medieval Hebrew is well illustrated by the case at hand. The scholars who participated in the deliberations about surety were from Barcelona, Narbonne, Montpellier, Lunel, Posquières, and Marseilles. There was constant contact between these talmudic centers.

5 There are exactly two *en passant* remarks about the matter in the literature before the exile of 1306. The first is a reference of a line and a half in an early twelfth-century gloss from Champagne. The second is a remark by a late thirteenth-century editor of the tosafist glosses, who lived, apparently, in Normandy. See below, n. 9, and my article in *Zion* (above, introductory note), nn. 4, 8a.

6 See M. Castaing-Sicard, *Les Contrats dans le très ancien droit toulousain, Xe–XIIIe siècle* (Toulouse, 1959), 379; R. J. Aubenas, *Cours d'histoire du droit privé, anciens pays de droit écrit* (doctorat) (Aix-en-Provence, 1952–61), vii. 22.

7 Castaing-Sicard, *Les Contrats dans le très ancien droit toulousain*, 380–3; M.-L. Carlin, *La Pénétration du droit romain dans les actes de la pratique provençale, XIe–XIIIe siècle* (Paris, 1967), 199–203.

8 In addition to the material now conveniently gathered in the *Recueil de la Société de Jean Bodin*

century was the great creative period of Jewish legal thought in both southern and northern France. The thirteenth century occupied itself with digesting and transmitting the works of its predecessors. The latter half of the thirteenth century in the north was the age of editors and abridgers. Now in a Jewish–Gentile transaction the procedure to be followed, unless otherwise stipulated, would be the Gentile one. In other words, throughout the period of halakhic creativity and a good deal afterwards, to serve in northern France as a surety in a Jewish–Gentile loan meant to serve as a *caution d'influence*. As surety in Jewish law is pure obligation, serving as a *caution d'influence* meant not serving as a surety at all. No halakhic problems of usury could arise. There is nothing in Jewish law preventing a Jew from pressuring his co-religionist to pay his debt to a Gentile. Only when the surety assumed the debt could the issue of *ribbit* arise.[9] This happened in Provence during the course of the twelfth century, the century of its greatest halakhic creativity. A discussion of the problems that the recent assumption of obligation engendered was not only natural but pressing.

The Talmud had ruled that it was forbidden for a Jew to serve as a surety in a usury loan for a co-religionist to a Gentile creditor, for in Gentile law (i.e. Persian law of the third and fourth centuries) the surety did not possess the benefit of discussion,[10] as he did in Jewish law. If the creditor could move directly against the surety, this loan halakhically constituted not one loan, but two: the first between the Gentile creditor and the Jewish 'surety', the second between the Jewish 'surety' and the Jewish debtor. This second loan between two Jews, being one of usury, was forbidden. Only if the Gentile creditor, in the Talmud's words, 'agreed to abide by Jewish law in the matter of surety', that is, consented to benefit of discussion, would the assumption of surety be permissible. For then and only then would there be no loan relationship between the surety and the debtor.[11] But Provençal law, like the Persian law of

pour l'histoire comparative des institutions, 29 (Brussels, 1971), see F. Oliver-Martin, *Histoire de la coutume de la prévôté et vicomté de Paris* (Paris, 1930), ii. 520–3; F. de Fonette, *Recherches sur la pratique de la vente immobilière dans la région parisienne au moyen âge, fin Xe début XIVe siècle* (Paris, 1957), 103.

[9] The remark of the Norman scholar in the latter half of the thirteenth century (above, n. 5) was probably engendered by this shift; see n. 8a in my article in *Zion* (above, introductory note).

[10] I have here oversimplified for clarity's sake. The Persian surety of talmudic times was a surety of substitution (*'arev kablan*). However, as halakhic thought until the mid-thirteenth century treated both a co-debtor and a surety of substitution as equally falling within the ban of usury, I have chosen to discuss the talmudic ruling in terms of a surety without the 'benefit of discussion', as this corresponds to the Provençal practice.

[11] *Bava Metsi'a* 71b. (Strictly speaking, if the surety was one of substitution, the two-stage nature of the loan was an immediate fact. If he was a co-debtor, then the two-stage nature of the loan was

old, made no allowance for any benefit of discussion, certainly not before the influence of Roman law began to be felt. This being so, the rise of the Roman surety of obligation in Provençal law posed serious problems for the Jewish community.

In many places, the surety no less than the pawn was the standard security for a loan,[12] and loans without security were not easy to come by. The Jews in Provence in the twelfth century were hardly a creditor class.[13] Indeed, one scholar of the time, R. Mosheh ben Todros, appealing to his colleagues of the Narbonne court not to rule illegal certain procedures which the Jews had adopted to procure loans from the Gentiles, wrote:

> All the elders and scholars who preceded us [did not seek to forbid this practice]. Perhaps they allowed it because of the need of sustenance. For [it is a matter of sustenance] in many ways: the people are hard pressed and in want, and everyone refrains from lending to one another, for money is not available either to loan from one another or to invest in an enterprise. And on a number of occasions someone will ask his friend to arrange for him somehow a loan from a Gentile,[14] to do business with it [the money] and earn some sustenance.[15]

So long as the surety in Gentile law was a *caution d'influence*, one Jew could readily help his neighbor and guarantee his loan to his Christian creditor. But with the emergence of the *caution d'obligation* in a system which knew not the benefit of discussion, such aid was henceforth precluded. Jews could no longer turn to their relatives and friends for aid. Only Gentiles could now guarantee a Jew's loan. This new development sharply constricted access to credit, increased the dependence on Christians, and severely restricted mutual

only potential—if the creditor chose to collect from the surety first. This distinction, however, was not made by twelfth-century scholars. Possibly they did not perceive the difference. More plausibly they viewed the usury injunction [*lo tesumun*, Exod. 22: 24] as forbidding Jews from entering into such contracts even if collection ultimately was made from the debtor.)

[12] Above, n. 6.

[13] Castaing-Sicard, *Les Contrats* (above, n. 6), 229–332; P. Wolff, *Commerces et marchands de Toulouse (vers 1350–vers 1450)* (Paris, 1954), 19–20, 356; J. de Malafosse, 'Contribution à l'étude du crédit dans le Midi aux Xe et XIe siècles: Les Sûretés réelles', *Annales du Midi*, 63 (1951), 141 n. 6.

[14] *Le-tsaded lo halva'ah*; the English slang 'to angle a loan for him' might be a good literal translation.

[15] S. Asaf, ed., *Sifran shel Rishonim* (Jerusalem, 1935), #33 (p. 36); *Sefer ha-Terumot*, Giddulei Terumah edn. (Venice 1643), 237a. {See now M. Bompaire, 'La Circulation monétaire en Languedoc (Xe–XIIIe siècles)', thèse dactylographée, 3 vols. (University of Paris IV, 2002).}

מאחר דדשו בם רבים ונהגו בה היתרא כל הזקנים והחכמים שהיו לפנינו וכן בכל סביבותינו.
[ו]איפשר שהם התירו משום חיי דברייתא מכמה פנים. שהעולם דחוק וחסר, וכל העם נמנעין
מלהלוות אלו את אלו. שאין הפרוטה מצויה להלוות איש את אחיו ולא להטיל מלאי להתעסק בו.
וכמה פעמים יבקש אדם מרעהו ומאת קרובו לצדד לו ההלואות מן הגוים כדי להטפל בהם וחי בהם.

assistance among Jews, a standard defense mechanism of every minority. The only solution was to ask the Christian creditor to agree to a benefit of discussion. But the lack of ready funds made it a creditor's market. Why should he agree to restrict the number of parties against whom he could initiate action?

Interestingly a doctrine arose at this time in Narbonne that contended that serving as a surety of obligation for a Jewish debtor to a Gentile was forbidden only by rabbinic ordinance and not by a biblical one.[16] The injunction was man-made and not of Divine origin. Caution must be used, however, before we engage in any simplistic sociology of law. The theory upon which this view based itself is a plausible one indeed, and there may even be echoes of it north of the Loire,[17] which at the time was free of the same economic pressures. However, as the severity of a rabbinic ordinance is far less than that of a biblical one, there can be no doubt that this view allowed scholars far greater room to maneuver. Unfortunately, the sources are silent as to whether it won adherents.

Other solutions were found. The Narbonne court reports a peculiar practice.[18] A debtor in a *ribbit* loan would appoint his surety, who often had arranged the loan for him, to also serve as his agent. That is to say, the surety would go to pick up the money from the Gentile creditor. The creditor would give the loan to him, viewing him as his own agent to transfer the money to the debtor, while actually he was the agent of the debtor; that is to say, he was legally not only the surety but also the debtor. Practically, this made no difference to the Christian creditor, as he could still collect from either of the two. From the Jewish legal point of view this is sheer nonsense. Few things in the halakhah are so distinct as the difference between debtor and surety. No one person can function simultaneously as both. R. Mosheh ben Todros, who had entered pleas for other practices, admitted that this one was difficult to defend.[19]

But if the arrangement lacked a basis, it had a clear purpose—to avoid problems of usury created by the rise of the *caution d'obligation*. The difficulties had stemmed from the fact that where there was no benefit of discussion, the relationship between surety and debtor was (from a halakhic perspective) that of creditor and debtor. If, however, the surety was also the agent of the debtor, and therefore legally identical with the debtor, there could be no loan relationship between the two. A person cannot loan money to himself. This arrangement is, of course, nonsense and no scholar, however incompetent,

16 *Sifran shel Rishonim*, 35–6; *Sefer ha-Terumot*, 237a.

17 Rashbam, *Bava Batra* 173b, s.v. *gemar u-mesha'abed*.

18 *Sifran shel Rishonim*, 35–6; *Sefer ha-Terumot*, 237a.

19 Ibid.

could have thought it up. It seems, rather, to have been a popular invention, perhaps of a clever if not too educated businessman. As the distinction between debtor and creditor in Jewish law is so sharp, it is difficult not to imagine that the stimulus came from without. It may have been suggested by the Provençal practice of having the debtor assume also the obligations of the surety,[20] which apparently in olden times were severe. Or it may have been suggested by a new term then gaining currency, *fidejussor et debitor*.[21] This phrase, to be sure, meant something totally different, but frequent contact may have suggested to some hard-pressed Jewish businessman the way out of his usury dilemma. The court of Narbonne denied the practice, but it is hard to imagine that Jews ceased to apply to Christians for credit, and one suspects that this court ruling was simply disregarded. It comes as no surprise if in the thirteenth century a scholar from Narbonne describes this arrangement as being universal practice.[22]

Just as the Narbonne court had tried to forbid Jews from serving as guarantors to Gentile creditors, so voices were soon heard somewhere in Provence against the reverse situation. Objection was raised against Jews serving as sureties for Christians borrowing at interest from Jews. Where precisely these views arose we do not know; the objection is cited anonymously by a thirteenth-century scholar who studied in Lunel and Narbonne and later resided in Montpellier and Posquières.[23] The relationship between surety and debtor here is not problematic. The two parties are Jew and Gentile and if a usurious loan relationship exists between them, it is entirely licit. Obviously what is being assessed here is the relationship between surety and creditor. If the surety does not possess the benefit of discussion, and the creditor can initiate suit against him directly, then he is unquestionably viewed as the debtor. Indeed, exposure to direct action of the creditor is a standard way of defining a debtor. But the new doctrine contended that even if the surety possessed the benefit of discussion, nevertheless a forbidden usury relationship

[20] Carlin, *La Pénétration du droit romain* (above, n. 7), 203. I have, however, found no report of this in the Narbonne area.

[21] Castaing-Sicard, *Les Contrats* (above, n. 6), 388–9; Carlin, *La Pénétration du droit romain* (above, n. 7), 203–5. Professor A. Gouron has drawn my attention to the statute given by the viscount of Béziers to the citizens of Carcassonne on July 12, 1165 found in *Histoire générale de Languedoc, avec des notes et les pièces justificatives*, ed. C. de Vic and J. Vaisette, edn. privat, vol. v, no. 666 (1298).

[22] *Ḥiddushei ha-Ritva 'al Bava Metsi'a* (Amsterdam, 1722), 71b, s.v. *aval*. For the Provençal origin of this work, see *Ḥiddushei ha-Ritva ha-Ḥadashim* (London, 1962), ed. A. Halperin, introduction, pp. viii–ix. That the author is from Narbonne was determined by K. Schlesinger in his introduction to *Me'iri 'al Bava Metsi'a* (Jerusalem, 1969), 9.

[23] R Avraham b. David, Ravad of Posquières; on him see below, n. 31.

existed between surety and creditor, for, as its advocates trenchantly put it, 'the surety has not [by virtue of the benefit of discussion] stepped out of the category of a debtor'.[24] Here is a doctrine that runs against plain Hebrew and against a crystal-clear distinction in halakhah between debtor and surety. Not until the eighteenth century, when the analytical school of jurisprudence in halakhah began to question external forms and seek underlying conceptual identities, was a similar doctrine of the essential identity of debtor and surety ever propounded again.[25] Two questions pose themselves. What induced people in twelfth-century Provence to suddenly doubt the validity of traditional legal terminology, and what was it in the halakhic climate of opinion that gave meaning to this newly found doubt?

Truth to tell, accessorial surety is highly problematic, and not by accident is it a fairly late development in most legal systems. How does the giving of money by the creditor to the debtor create an obligation on the part of the surety? The surety in Jewish law need do nothing except be physically present at the time of the loan. How does sheer physical presence create obligation? Two explanations were current in twelfth-century Provence as to the mechanics of surety. One view (the dominant one in halakhah to this day) proposed that the obligations of the surety flowed from what is termed in common law 'valuable consideration'. The surety obliged himself in exchange for a benefit received from the creditor. He received vivid recognition of his good standing in the community for, on the basis of this trust in him, the creditor gave a loan to the debtor.[26] Another opinion asserted that surety rested on a judicial construction which viewed the money given to the debtor as having been given equally to the surety.[27]

In most matters there is no difference between these two views, and indeed they are used interchangeably in the halakhic literature of the time.[28] In the matter of usury, however, this theoretical controversy is of crucial import. If the surety's obligations flow from valuable consideration, then the surety is

[24] R. Avraham b. David, *Sifra de-Vei Rav: Hu Torat Kohanim 'im Perush R. Avraham ben David* (Vienna, 1862), fo. 109c.

[25] R. Ephraim Navon, *Maḥaneh Efrayim* (Constantinople, 1738), 'Hilkhot Ribbit', #11.

[26] R. Yitsḥak b. Abba Mari, *Sefer ha-'Ittur*, ed. Me'ir Yonah (repr. New York, 1955), s.v. *'arev*. Similarly in the Provençal commentary on *Kiddushin* printed in the Romm edition of the Talmud under the title *Tosafot Ri ha-Zaken*, 7a.

[27] See Ravad's remarks in the commentary on *Kiddushin* written by a pupil of R. Shelomoh of Montpellier and printed at the end of the *Teshuvot Ri Berav* (Venice, 1663), fo. 92, s.v. *ten*.

[28] Good examples are to be found in the *Ḥiddushei ha-Rashba*, *Kiddushin*, ed. E. Lichtenstein (Jerusalem, 1999), 6b, s.v. *ten*; 8a, s.v. *ha*; *Tosafot Bava Metsi'a* 71b, s.v. *metsa'o* and s.v. *kegon*. As to Ravad, see my article in *Zion* (above, introductory note), 9 n. 31.

not a party at all to the loan. Because of a benefit received, the guarantor has contracted independently to pay the creditor a sum equal to the debt in the event of the debtor's default. Usury, halakhically, means *repayment*, not simply execution of a contract for an equivalent amount of money.[29] If, however, the obligation of the surety flows from a judicial construction which sees in him, no less than in the borrower, a recipient of the money lent, legally he, too, has then received a loan. His payment is indeed a repayment and falls under the ban of usury. And it could quite well be argued that the surety (even one with benefit of discussion) 'had not stepped out of the category of debtor'.

Significantly, the latter opinion, which views the surety as having legally received the money, is one which appears in the halakhic literature of several countries. Yet nowhere did it occur to scholars to draw the necessary inferences about surety loans. The distinction in halakhah between debtor and surety is so clear and commonplace a notion that no one realized that this common judicial construction actually undermined an important allowance in Gentile–Jewish credit relations. One suspects that the breakthrough in Provence was facilitated by the term *fidejussor et debitor*, which occurred in contracts signed daily by the Jews. To be sure, it there meant something totally different. It was there to indicate the new dimension of obligation that was being added to the old *caution d'influence*. But hearing a surety regularly being called a debtor led Jewish scholars analyzing a purely obligational system of surety to question whether the time-old surety was not, indeed, a debtor—in the deepest and most essential sense of the word.[30]

If my interpretation is correct (it is, after all, only a conjecture) then before us is a form of influence to which we should perhaps be more attentive—not the transfer of content but the effect of stimuli. Attention is usually focused on tracing how one group received and adopted an idea from another. This is undoubtedly the most important form of influence, but it does not exhaust the catalogue of effects one world may have on another. When societies live side by side, when two, at times mutually exclusive, systems of law are thrust into daily contact, what may occur is that terms, phrases, even institutions of one will be noted or absorbed by members of the other. These foreign concepts awaken internal associations and lead people to probe anew immanent

29 Those arguing for the permissibility of the arrangement cited the talmudic passage (*Bava Metsi'a* 69b), 'The Bible only forbade interest from the debtor', i.e. an outside party may contract to pay the interest on someone else's loan.

30 When *fidejussor et debitor* or the like began to appear in the northern regions (see e.g. J. Yver, *Les Contrats dans le tres ancien droit normand, XIe–XIIIe siecles* [Domfront, 1926], 146–8; Olivier-Martin, *Histoire de la coutume de la prévôté et vicomté de Paris* [above, n. 8], 522), halakhic thought was in sharp decline and few if any new ideas were being propounded.

problems of their own system which they might otherwise never have re-examined.

The person who wrestled most with the problem of surety in Jewish–Gentile loans was the greatest talmudic scholar of twelfth-century Provence, R. Avraham ben David of Posquières (d.1198), more commonly known by his acronym, Ravad.[31] In his commentary on the *Sifra*, he cites both opinions as to the essential nature of a surety at length and says that he finds it impossible to decide between them. Interestingly, in presenting the view permitting Jews to serve as sureties in such loans and emphasizing the accessorial nature of the Jewish surety, Ravad wrote *ikar shi'abud ha-ḥov* ('the main lien of the debt')[32]—this phrase is not talmudic and strictly speaking makes no sense. It can be understood only as a translation of *debitor principalis*. Ravad could not, for stylistic reasons, translate *debitor principalis* into Hebrew,[33] so he transformed *debitor* into an abstract noun and translated *debitum principale*. He was led to this by the fact that the new doctrine, which saw the surety as essentially a debtor, not only challenged standard halakhic terminology but also denied the traditional yardstick employed in determining the status of 'debtor'. A debtor had hitherto been defined as any party whom the creditor could sue directly, and for that reason a surety without benefit of discussion was viewed by all as a debtor. The standard halakhic phrase was 'going against the debtor first'. But in contending that all sureties, even those with the benefit of discussion, were essentially debtors, the proponents were in effect saying that that sequence of action was a procedural matter only and was not indicative of the essential nature of the obligation. The traditional phrase 'going against the debtor first' was thus rendered substantively meaningless, and Ravad, struggling now to express the accessorial nature of the surety, fell back upon an apt juridical term then making its rounds in the Gentile world—*debitor principalis*.

[31] See I. Twersky, *Rabad of Posquières: A Twelfth-Century Talmudist* (Cambridge, Mass., 1962).

[32] *Sifra de-Vei Rav* (above, n. 24). I have followed here the readings of both MS British Library Or. 10750 (written in 1406), fo. 166, and Jewish Theological Seminary Ac. 02145, fo. 168. The printed edition transcribes accurately MS Bodley 423 (fo. 325) and reads *ha-'ikar le-shi'abud ha-ḥov*. This phrase is syntactically superior but no less alien, and it confronts us with the same difficulties. The *lectio difficilior* of the above two manuscripts is an accurate translation of a basic term in Roman law; the other seems to be a scribal emendation to turn a meaningless term into a partially comprehensible phrase. The term makes neither linguistic nor legal sense. *'Ikar* and *tafel* are categories in *birkot ha-nehenin*, for example, but are unheard of in the world of financial obligations. Granting even their existence, how does R. Avraham know that a non-*'ikar shi'abud* or a *shi'abud tafel* is exempt from the usury injunction?

[33] The Hebrew translation would have read *ki ha-loveh hu 'ikar ha-loveh*, which is nonsense.

In the course of time, Ravad came around to the view that a surety with the benefit of discussion (the classic Jewish surety) was simply a guarantor and not a debtor. This allowed Jews to serve as sureties for their Gentile friends who sought a loan from other Jews. However, as Provençal law did not yet allow the surety the benefit of discussion, the Jew would have to explicitly stipulate this right. That this would be impolitic is an understatement. One serves as a surety quite often simply as a favor to the debtor, who otherwise could not get a loan, and the reward received is gratitude and, at times, the hope that the favor will be returned. When a Jew borrowed from a Christian and asked another Gentile to serve as his guarantor, the Gentile surety exposed himself to direct action by the creditor. Yet when the situation was reversed, and a Gentile turned to his Jewish friend and asked him to serve as his surety, the Jew would have to insist on his receiving the benefit of discussion. Such an unequal state of affairs could only awaken resentment. Voices were soon heard contending that for various reasons the Jewish guarantor was permitted to forgo such a stipulation.[34] For a while Ravad inclined to such a view, but in time came to feel that the reasoning was inadequate and insisted on the unpleasant stipulation.[35] That the ordinary surety abided by this ruling and risked good relationships with his Gentile neighbors seems quite doubtful. General developments in Provence, however, came to the aid of the rabbinical establishment. The penetration of Roman law was granting to guarantors in many places the benefit of discussion. Reviewing the problem in a late work of his, the commentary on *Bava Metsi'a*, Ravad reiterated the permissibility of a Jew serving as a surety in Jewish–Gentile usury loans, spoke of the theoretical need to ask the Gentile debtor to agree to the benefit of discussion, and then added:

> And nowadays, when we see that the Gentiles also rule thus: that if one can collect from the debtor one does not collect from the surety, it is as if he [the Gentile] has agreed [to a benefit of discussion].[36]

The reception of Roman law was, as we know, very uneven. In cities right around Posquières, such as Saint-Gilles and Montpellier, the right of the *nova*

[34] *Sifra de-Vei Rav* (above, n. 24), fo. 109c–d.

[35] *Temim De'im*, in Tam Ibn Yaḥya, *Tummat Yesharim* (Venice, 1622), #47.

[36] *Sefer ha-Terumot* (above, n. 15), fo. 237d. The same text is cited by Rosh (*Pesakim*, *Bava Metsi'a* 5: 53) and Rashba (*Ḥiddushei ha-Rashba 'al Bava Metsi'a*, ed. E. Lichtenstein [Jerusalem, 2006], 71b, s.v. *ela 'arev*); *Shitah Mekubbetset 'al Bava Metsi'a* (Amsterdam, 1722), fo. 157c. (In the latter work the word *dayni* [rule] is missing. However, I would not adopt this reading as opposed to the independent corroborative testimony of Rosh, *Sefer ha-Terumot*, and the *Ḥiddushei ha-Rashba*.)

constitutio was explicitly rejected.[37] In other places this right was admitted in theory but cancelled in practice by the technique of *renunciatio*.[38] In effect, many sureties in Provence were as bereft of the benefit of discussion in the thirteenth century as they had been in the twelfth. Ravad of Posquières's disposal of the problem had been premature. The need for stipulating benefit of discussion in usury contracts was as real as ever. Yet no further discussion of the problem is found in the halakhic literature of Provence. This strange silence of thirteenth-century scholars is linked to certain developments in the history of the halakhah and not to outside forces. There is an inward turn in the halakhic thinking of the period; it becomes less receptive to external influences. But this is a matter for another essay and another forum.

I have, up to now, attempted to portray a chapter in the history of the halakhah which is comprehensible only in light of the general developments in Provence. We may now ask what light, in turn, does the halakhic material shed on Provençal law?

First, we have evidence that the benefit of discussion was actually practiced in Posquières toward the close of the twelfth century.[39] The occurrence of the *nova constitutio* in the statutes always leaves open the question whether this procedure was actually followed.[40] Ravad, in his commentary on *Bava Metsi'a*, had no interest in abstract Gentile law, but was concerned—indeed, had to be concerned if he was to rule on it in matters of usury—with what employing a Gentile surety practically entailed. One may infer without hesitation that in Posquières the benefit of discussion was a fact of life.

Second, the standard term in halakhah for benefit of discussion is, as I have said, 'going after the debtor first' or 'summoning the debtor first'. Ravad used none of these terms but rather his own periphrasis, 'if one can collect from the debtor one does not collect from the surety'. This suggests that the practice in Posquières was similar to that which we find in Toulouse some eighty years later.[41] Action may be brought simultaneously against both the surety and the debtor; however, collection may be had from the surety only if the debtor is incapable of paying.

[37] P. Tisset, 'Placentin et l'enseignement du droit à Montpellier: Droit romain et coutume dans l'ancien pays de Septimanie', *Recueil de mémoires et travaux publié par la Société d'histoire du droit et des institutions des anciens pays de droit écrit*, 2 (1951), 82.

[38] Aubenas, *Cours d'histoire du droit privé* (above, n. 6), vii. 61–2; Carlin, *La Pénétration du droit romain* (above, n. 7), 133, 207.

[39] I have spelled out some of these conclusions in a brief note in the *Tijdschrift voor Rechtsgeschiednis*, 40 (1972), 227–9.

[40] [What was note 39a in the original has been amended in this edition to n. 40 and all subsequent notes have been renumbered.] See the cautious language of Carlin, *La Pénétration du droit romain* (above, n. 7), 206.

[41] Castaing-Sicard, *Les Contrats* (above, n. 6), 393–5.

Third, it will be remembered that Ravad of Posquières assumed, in his commentary on the *Sifra*, that Provençal practice was to hold the surety equally responsible as the debtor. The adoption of the benefit of discussion occurred after he had written his work on the *Sifra* and before he had produced his commentary on *Bava Metsi'a*. Yet note that, though old practice had not changed at the time of the *Sifra* commentary, Roman phraseology had penetrated the area and R. Avraham employed it in his discussion. Ravad's writings seem to reflect (and provide further confirmation of) the two-stage penetration of Roman law set forth by A. Gouron.[42] The commentary on the *Sifra* was written during the period of terminological penetration before change had been wrought; the commentary on *Bava Metsi'a* was written in the last third of the twelfth century, by which time changes in actual practice had made themselves felt.

Fourth, some indications *may* be garnered as to when the *caution d'obligation* arose. I said at the outset that Provence produced a varied literature about surety in *ribbit* loans as a result of the problems created by the recent assumption of obligation by the guarantor. Let me spell out more exactly who the parties to this discussion were. The first person was R. Yehudah ben Barzilai of Barcelona, who was active at the end of the eleventh century and the beginning of the twelfth.[43] The second was R. Mosheh ben Todros, a member of the famous court of Narbonne. We know only that he sat on that court together with R. Avraham ben Yitsḥak, who most probably died in 1158.[44]

42 A. Gouron, 'Les Étapes de la pénétration du droit romain au XIIe siècle dans l'ancienne Septimanie', *Annales du Midi*, 69/38 (1957), 103–21.

43 *Sefer ha-Terumot* (above, n. 15), fos. 237d–238a.

44 There is some needless confusion as to the year of R. Avraham's death. The reliable R. Menaḥem ha-Me'iri of Perpignan (d.1315) gives the date as November 1158 in his history of halakhah, which he prefaced to his *Bet ha-Beḥirah 'al Massekhet Avot*. It was published in a separate volume edited by S. Z. Havlin and A. Shoshanah under the title *Sefer ha-Kabbalah le Rabbenu Menaḥem le-Vet ha-Me'iri*, rev. edn. (Jerusalem, 1995), 136. H. Gross, in an early article (1868) in the *Monatsschrift für Geschichte und Wissenschaft des Judenthums*, contended that this must be an error, since R. Avraham, when referring to R. Ya'akov Tam (d.1171), adds 'of blessed memory', and so he suggested amending the text to 1179. We now know that such remarks as 'of blessed memory' were added in the hundreds by later scribes, and no one would now dream (unless he possessed an actual autograph of the author) of inferring anything on the basis of such benedictions. Gross's authority, however, was justifiably great, the exact date of R. Avraham's death of no great interest to anyone, and so few bothered to review his argument in light of what has become common knowledge. Thus one finds 1179 sometimes given as the date of R. Avraham b. Yitsḥak's demise. Ḥ. Albeck, and more recently I. Ta-Shma in a doctoral dissertation under way at Bar-Ilan University, Israel {printed now as *Ba'al ha-Ma'or u-venei Ḥugo* [Jerusalem, 1992], 6–9}, have argued convincingly against this emendation. For earlier references, see G. D. Cohen, ed., *A Critical Edition with a Translation and Notes of the Book of Tradition (Sefer ha-qabbalah) by Abraham ibn Daud* (Philadelphia, 1967), 89, line 475. Nor

Whether R. Mosheh preceded him to the grave or survived him, and if so, by how many years, is unknown. R. Meshullam ben Ya'akov of Lunel, a third party to the deliberation, is reliably reported to have passed away in 1170.[45] The great Ravad of Posquières (d.1198) dealt with the issue in no fewer than four of his works.[46] In one work that I have made reference to, the commentary on the *Sifra*, he anonymously cites the opinions of the other scholars.[47] None of the doctrines adduced are identical with those of the above scholars—in other words, there were at least two other discussants of the problem. Finally, R. Yitsḥak ben Abba Mari of Marseille treated it in his *Sefer ha-'Ittur*, a work written over the course of a lifetime, but still in composition in the year 1189. On the basis of people mentioned in his work with whom he had intercourse, he has been placed roughly in the years 1120–90.[48] Let us discount the testimony of R. Yehudah of Barcelona for two reasons. First, while Barcelona may be, from the perspective of Jewish culture, part of Provence, this is not the case with general law. Catalonia should not be bunched with Bas-Languedoc. Second, his is an isolated instance. It may be that a chance case arose which he happened to treat in his work. There is no evidence of any frequency at this early date.[49] The other authors, however, converge to form a pattern which cuts across the boundaries of Languedoc and Provence. Significantly, these discussions are independent of one another; Ravad, for example, does not

can any convincing argument be made from R. Binyamin of Tudela's itinerary. First, it is not certain, as Albeck has already pointed out, that R. Binyamin actually saw R. Avraham. Second, even assuming that he did, this does not conflict with R. Menaḥem ha-Me'iri's account. R. Binyamin arrived in Rome during the papacy of Alexander III, which would entail a year's sojourn in Provence. See A. Asher, *The Itinerary of R. Benjamin of Tudela* (New York, 1840), i. 32, 38; ii. 17–18. See *Sefer Sha'ashu'im*, ed. I. Davidson (New York, 1914), appendix A. S. W. Baron argues for 1165 as the date of his visit to Rome (*Social and Religious History of the Jews*, vi [Philadelphia, 1958], 435 n. 88), but again, even if correct, we have no idea when R. Binyamin set out on his trip and when he arrived in Narbonne.

[45] The date is given by R. Shelomoh Ibn Verga in his *Shevet Yehudah* (Jerusalem, 1947), 146, and to the best of my knowledge has not been seriously questioned. R. Meshullam's discussion is to be found in the *Sefer ha-Terumot* (above, n. 15), fo. 236c; *Ḥiddushei ha-Ritva 'al Bava Metsi'a* (Amsterdam, 1729), fo. 40d, s.v. *ki*. {In the widely available Kur le-Zahav edition of *Ḥiddushei ha-Ritva*, the passage is found at fo. 88c, s.v. *ki*.}

[46] Commentary on the *Sifra* (above, n. 24), commentary on *Bava Metsi'a* (above, n. 36), *Ḥiddushei ha-Rashba: Bava Metsi'a*, ed A. Lichtenstein (Jerusalem, 2006), 71b (pp. 576–7); *Temim De'im* (above, n. 35) #47 {referenced in *Teshuvot ha-Rashba ha-Meyuḥasot le-Ramban*, ed. A. Zelaznik (Jerusalem, 2001), #223}.

[47] Above, n. 24.

[48] *Sefer ha-'Ittur*, s.v. *'iska*; as to the date, see Ḥ. Michael, *Or Ḥayyim* (Frankfurt am Main, 1891), #1072.

[49] See Castaing-Sicard, *Les Contrats* (above, n. 6), 383, for an instance of obligational surety in Toulouse toward the close of the eleventh century.

know of the arguments of R. Yehudah ben Barzilai or, surprisingly, of those of his teacher, R. Meshullam of Lunel.[50] Neither does R. Yitsḥak of Marseille relate to any of the above doctrines. Clearly, this was not a question which arose in one locale and triggered off academic discussions in numerous talmudic centers, and was, thus, without historical significance. Rather, Jewish scholars from Marseille to Narbonne began to treat independently the problems created by *caution d'obligation.*

It is logically possible to place the writings of R. Yitsḥak of Marseille in the 1180s; the four works of R. Avraham in the last two decades of the twelfth century, and, since we know nothing of R. Mosheh ben Todros's life, we could include his discussion in that period too. R. Meshullam's treatment could be assigned to the closing years of his life, to the late 1160s. However, if we decline to bunch all these writings into the latter days of these scholars' lives and give these works their natural spread, the impression received is that *caution d'obligation* was operative in the mid-twelfth century, somewhat earlier than generally held.[51] This inference would hold irrespective of our conjecture about the role played by the term *fidejussor et debitor*. All the above sources, regardless of the terminology they employ, treat obligational surety. Whether this impression, gathered from the Hebrew sources, has some truth in it or whether all these writings must indeed be packed into the confines of the 1170s and 1180s is a question to be decided by people more learned than I in Provençal law.

[50] See my article in *Zion* (above, introductory note), 11 n. 38.

[51] It may be suggested that since the halakhah was far closer to Roman than to Germanic law, the Jews were especially receptive to the new concepts. There is a measure of truth in this; however, let us remember that, in the case of surety, the rise of obligation posed severe problems of *ribbit*, which makes it rather difficult to imagine that it was the Jews who pressed for this type of surety in their dealings with Gentiles.

CHAPTER FIFTEEN

The Riddle of Me'iri's Recent Popularity

IT IS COMMONLY THOUGHT that the works of R. Menaḥem ha-Me'iri of Perpignan (d. after 1306) were first published in the twentieth century. This is correct if one is referring to the series of Me'iri publications that Avraham Sofer produced from the huge, six-volume manuscript in the Parma Palatina Library (##3551–6), and which contains the *Bet ha-Beḥirah* on most of the tractates of the Talmud. However, a glance at any bibliography, be it the *Bet 'Eked Sefarim*[1] or the *Sarei ha-Elef*,[2] will immediately reveal that the *Bet ha-Beḥirah* on many tractates was already published in the eighteenth century. The commentary on *Megillah* appeared in 1769; on *Shabbat* and *Yevamot* in 1794; on *Nedarim*, *Nazir*, and *Sotah* in 1795.[3] The next century witnessed the republication of these commentaries, and new publications only of the sections on *Yoma*, *Betsah*, and *Avot*. In 1910–13 the *Bet ha-Beḥirah* on *Sukkah*, *Berakhot*, and *'Eruvin* was printed, and in 1928 the commentaries on *Pesaḥim*, *Shekalim*, and *Ḥagigah*. A year or two later Sofer embarked upon his Me'iri enterprise, and volume after volume tumbled from the presses in the following three decades.[4]

[1] C. B. Friedberg, *Bet 'Eked Sefarim*, 2nd edn., 4 vols. (New York, 1951).

[2] M. M. Kasher and J. B. Mandelbaum, *Sarei ha-Elef*, rev. edn., 2 vols. (Jerusalem, 1980). I should add that I have done no genuine bibliographical research, seeking out and handling the various volumes, but have relied on bibliographical guides, library catalogues, and introductions to the various volumes of the *Bet ha-Beḥirah*.

[3] Sections of the *Bet ha-Beḥirah* on *Yoma* appeared in Leghorn in 1766. Me'iri's *Kiryat Sefer* on the laws of *Sefer Torah*, *tefillin*, and *mezuzah* was published in 1863 and reprinted in 1881.

[4] *Sanhedrin* in 1930, *Ta'anit* in 1934, *Ḥallah*, *Shekalim*, *Tamid*, and *Middot* in 1934, *Rosh Hashanah*, *Horayot*, and *'Eduyot* in 1936, *Mikva'ot* in 1940, *Kiddushin* in 1942, *'Avodah Zarah* and *Middot* in 1944, *Ketubbot* in 1947, *Niddah* in 1949, *Bava Batra* in 1956. For a full portrayal of Sofer's work and the history of the huge Parma manuscript and its use by different scholars, together with Sofer's own thoughts about the reasons for Me'iri's strange fate, see Gregg Stern's rich article, 'The Travels of Menachem ha-Me'iri's *Bet ha-Behirah*', in M. Butler and M. E. Frankston, eds., *Essays for a Jewish Lifetime: The Burton D. Morris Jubilee Volume* (forthcoming).

The languid pace of publication, stretching over 200 years, stands out starkly if one compares its history with that of the printing of the novellae (*ḥiddushim*) of R. Shelomoh Ibn Aderet (Rashba) and R. Yom Tov al-Sevilli (Ritva), which Y. M. Ta-Shma has outlined in a superb essay.[5] Until the eighteenth century, the only *ḥiddushim* of Ritva were those on tractate *Kiddushin*, which appeared in 1553. The burning of the Talmud that year followed on its tracks, and most copies apparently went up in flames. Copies of this volume are a rarity. There was one printing in 1523 of the *ḥiddushim* of Rashba on *Berakhot*, *Gittin*, and *Ḥullin*; nothing further appeared for close to two centuries. In 1717 a German printer in Constantinople began printing the *ḥiddushim* of Rashba. He started with *Kiddushin*; three years later, he moved on to *Rosh Hashanah*, *Megillah*, *Sukkah*, *Yevamot*, *Nedarim*, and *Bava Kamma*. In 1729 the *ḥiddushim* of Ritva on *'Eruvin*, *Ta'anit*, *Mo'ed Katan*, *Ketubbot*, and *Bava Metsi'a* appeared in Amsterdam. These publications were warmly received, and printers sought out new manuscripts to meet the demand. In the course of a century, almost all the *ḥiddushim* of Rashba and Ritva saw the light of day.

A different fate awaited Me'iri's *Bet ha-Beḥirah*. Some parts of it were printed in the eighteenth century, a few more in the nineteenth; but they were swiftly forgotten. In fact, the revival of his work did not begin in the 1930s: initially Sofer's publications had little impact. Only in the latter half of the twentieth century did they become popular, and various scholars moved quickly to put out the *Bet ha-Beḥirah* on other tractates of the Talmud and to publish new editions of the works that Sofer had already published, and these editions have been repeatedly reprinted. Why the centuries-long indifference and why the revival of the past sixty years?

The answer to these questions requires two prefaces.

Rhetorical and Glossatorial Presentations

Traditionally, one is introduced to *Tosafot* at an early age. Jewish educators through the ages protested at this and contended that a longer exposure to the Pentateuch (*Ḥumash*) or to the Mishnah would be a far better use of a 9- or 10-year-old's time. There was, however, a method to the tradition's madness. To understand it, one has to understand the difference between a rhetorical mode of presentation and a glossatorial one. An essay is a good example of a

[5] Y. M. Ta-Shma, 'Seder Hadpasatam shel Rishonim', *Kiryat Sefer*, 50 (1975), 325–36; republished in id., *Keneset Meḥkarim—'Iyyunim ba-Sifrut ha-Rabbanit bi-Yemei ha-Beinayim*, ii: *Sefarad* (Jerusalem, 2004), 219–36.

rhetorical presentation. It opens with an introductory paragraph or two, then presents the writer's argument step by step. It finishes with a paragraph summing up the major points of the argument together with its results, preferably with a memorable sentence or two to imprint the conclusions on the mind of the reader. The presentation is self-contained and, properly done, constitutes both a logical and an aesthetic whole. Judicial decisions are such rhetorical presentations; the decisions of a divided court represent conflicting essays, each presenting in full and in the round the view of its author. This mode of presentation was developed by speakers in classical Greece, and employed by both orators and writers in Rome. It was revived in the Renaissance and has become the accepted mode of presentation to this day.

In the Middle Ages, a glossatorial mode of presentation also obtained both among Jews and Christians, and the *Tosafot* are a classic example of this. There is a central text (the Talmud), which is being explicated by the classic commentator, Rashi, with whom the Tosafists are not in agreement. There are, shall we say, eight steps in the talmudic argument. The *Tosafot* will criticize Rashi's interpretation of steps three and seven. Rarely will the *Tosafot* spell out for the reader what the conclusion is of these disagreements. It is expected that the reader will on his own combine steps one, two, four, five, six, and eight of Rashi's interpretation with steps three and seven of the Tosafists and arrive at their legal position. The *Tosafot* often offer alternative solutions (*ve-'od yesh lomar*). The second proffered solution will accept Rashi's understanding of steps one, two, five, and six, as well as the interpretation of the first solution of steps three and seven, but will have its own interpretation of steps four and eight. It too will not spell out the conclusion. One then turns to Rashba or Ritva, great medieval Spanish commentators and staples of yeshivah study, each of whom has his own mix of interpretations of the various steps of the argument. The reader is expected to run swiftly through the sequence of the talmudic argument on his own and arrive at the holdings of the different writers.

In a rhetorical tradition, you know exactly what the different conclusions are. What students must be trained in is seeing what the points of difference in the reasoning are. Whence the incessant question in first-year law, 'Wherein do the three justices differ?' In a glossatorial tradition, you know exactly what the points of difference are, but you generally don't know the conclusion. Whence the incessant questions in early training in Talmud, 'What is the *shitah* [opinion] of the *Tosafot*?' 'What is the *shitah* of Rashba?' Any serious class in Talmud assumes the mastery of this technique. The teacher (*rosh yeshivah*) can remark *en passant*, 'Not to speak of Ramban, who interprets step four in the talmudic discussion altogether differently, as referring to "such and such"', and he takes for granted that the students understand immediately the implications that this difference has for Ramban's holding. Thinking glossatorially means acquiring the skill of seeing swiftly and precisely how the conclusion of an argument is altered by a change in any link of the chain of argument. It is a skill which must be so deeply ingrained that it becomes a constituent of one's thinking. The more swiftly one comes to know the author's opinion, the sooner one can begin evaluating its merits; the more swiftly one has mastered the technique required to play a sonata, the more time and energy are left to address its interpretation. Like any technique that must become reflexive and be performed automatically, whether of piano, ballet, chess, or Talmud, it must be instilled when the mind and body are most pliable—in early youth. A late beginner, as would be a 19- or 20-year-old, can achieve mastery of the glossatorial mode of thinking only by exceptional efforts.

Acculturation and Assimilation

One should distinguish between two separate and distinct processes, acculturation and assimilation. The terms are not important—these two different modes of social integration have been called by different names—but the processes are. Assimilation is a conscious acceptance of the values and way of life of the surrounding culture. Radical assimilation, complete acceptance of the cultural norms of the host society, once resulted in religious conversion to Christianity, nowadays in a total loss of Jewish identity. Examples of partial assimilation would be the movements of *Torah u-madda'* of modern Orthodoxy in the United States and Israel or, previously, of *Torah 'im derekh erets* of Samson Raphael Hirsch in Germany. These two movements have consciously accepted many of the values of Western humanism or of the German notion of *Bildung*—the forging of a moral and intellectual self at home with the finest values of the civilization in which the individual is embedded. Acculturation, on the other hand, is the slow process in which a minority unwittingly absorbs the mores of its environment. Significant areas of feeling, experiencing, and thinking receive their impress from the mold of the environment. Over the course of time, the palate and taste of the community become those of the host society. The grandchildren of the European immigrants now eat pizza and sandwiches; French, Chinese, and Indian restaurants flourish in Jewish religious neighborhoods, as they do in Gentile residential areas. Herring and borscht, the staff of life of their grandparents, have almost disappeared from the Jewish cuisine. The music played at religious weddings, even at those of the ultra-Orthodox community, has religious lyrics, but the beat, rhythm, and 'full blast' volume make it indistinguishable from that of the surrounding culture. Notions of relaxation and vacation of the two adjacent communities have become almost identical. Holy days (*ḥagim, mikra'ei kodesh*), which previously had been 'earned', achieved by dint of grueling, month-long preparation, and were celebrated in the home and local community, are disappearing. Many people, including the earnestly religious, celebrate Passover in a hotel. There is no month-long cleaning of the house from top to bottom to ensure that not a crumb of bread is to be found anywhere. No one now purges the pots and pans in scalding water to make them fit for Passover use. Nor do housewives spend the endless hours necessary for preparing holiday dishes with the restricted ingredients that may be employed on Passover. A holy day has been turned into a holiday.

These transformations of sensibilities have taken place unconsciously, without most people realizing just how Americanized, 'Britishized', or 'Israelized' they have become. This is wholly unrelated to beliefs and ideology. One can separate, indeed segregate, oneself from the general community in education, speech, and dress, as do the hasidim of Satmar in America, who, in addition, impose upon themselves hitherto undreamt-of religious stringencies; nevertheless, over the course of time the taste, the rhythms to which the body syncopates, the sense of humor, and the notions of honor and shame, relaxation and vacation become those of the surrounding society.

One of the marks of the acculturation of the current religious community is the appearance, indeed efflorescence, of secondary literature in halakhah, works that introduce the reader to the laws, say, of the Sabbath, and then systematically set forth its complex regulations. A generation or two ago no such literature, which embodied the rhetorical mode of exposition, existed. There were no secondary texts in halakhah. There were no books that set out to explain to the average reader, step by step and in popular language, the laws governing any subject in halakhah. All study consisted of carefully scrutinizing a classic source, be it the *Ḥumash*, Mishnah, Talmud, or the *Shulḥan 'Arukh*, and all new writings were commentaries on these works, as befitted a glossatorial tradition. One could not approach these new works without first mastering the text upon which they were commenting. Secondary sources simply didn't exist, and their sudden appearance some fifty years ago and remarkable growth over the past few decades is a sure sign of the infiltration of rhetorical notions of presentation in the Orthodox and ultra-Orthodox communities alike.

This acculturation explains the popularity of Me'iri's works in the last fifty or sixty years. Of all medieval halakhic works, his *Bet ha-Beḥirah* is the closest thing to a secondary work. He provides an introduction to topics discussed in the Talmud and does not involve himself with the argumentation of the Talmud, but only with the upshot of the discussion as seen by various commentators. These conclusions are presented in a remarkably clear Hebrew. One can 'read' the *Bet ha-Beḥirah* without having studied the text of the Talmud. Indeed, were one to abbreviate Me'iri (who expresses an unusually wide range of opinions), his work could serve as a substitute for study of the Talmud for those who are only interested in the legal upshot of the talmudic discussions. Such a presentation seems natural to us, but was scarcely so to our predecessors. What scholar, they asked, writes introductions for the layman? What scholar summarizes what the Talmud says? What scholar does not weigh in on the merits of various arguments advanced in a talmudic discussion? It is thus scarcely surprising that Me'iri's writings were ignored for centuries, and came into their own only with the advent of secondary—i.e. rhetorical—halakhic literature in the latter half of the twentieth century.

Objection could be made: Me'iri cites many doctrines that are found in no other source—why didn't scholars draw upon his writings, as later generations drew upon that great collection of medieval commentaries, the *Shitah Mekubbetset*? The answer is that Me'iri, for reasons still unknown, couldn't call a person by his name. He invented a huge number of monikers for various scholars, and while a few scholars have fixed monikers in his writings, as, for example, 'the greatest of commentators' (Ravad of Posquières), 'the greatest of "authors"' (Maimonides), most do not. Many of the monikers change their referents, shift from one scholar to another, as Me'iri moves from one tractate to another. Indeed, on occasion, the same nickname can have multiple referents even within the same tractate. Since readers had no way of knowing who advanced a specific doctrine, they were at a loss as to what specific weight should be assigned to it.

Me'iri, moreover, never quoted, but formulated anew the scholar's position. There is a plus and a minus to this approach. A plus if his formulation is clearer than that of the author; a minus if the original words were freighted with a larger meaning that is absent from Me'iri's restatements. Me'iri also wrote in a remarkably modern Hebrew. Over 600 years separate his Hebrew from the spoken Hebrew of today; nevertheless, this time gap is scarcely felt by the contemporary reader. His Hebrew differs from that of Maimonides; it is cast in a lower diction and is less stately and more 'direct' than the Hebrew of the *Mishneh Torah*, and thus closer to the Hebrew spoken today. I am not a linguist and cannot explain in what this modernity consists. It is, however, manifest and singular and well merits linguistic analysis.

Me'iri's smooth restatements, however, have a downside that goes far in explaining the fate of his work.

Anyone who has studied in a Lithuanian yeshivah or one in a Lithuanian tradition, knows that one 'enjoys' more the writings of R. Yom Tov al-Sevilli (Ritva), a mid-fourteenth-century Talmudist, or those of R. Nissim of Barcelona (Ran), than those of the Tosafists. The formulations of Ritva are closer to their own way of thinking, and as for Ran (especially in his commentaries on the tractate of *Nedarim* and on Alfasi's abridgments of the tractates of *Shevu'ot* and *Ḥullin*), he seems, at times, to be a fully paid-up member of the Lithuanian school.

The tosafist approach is that of scholastic dialectics. One collates all the relevant texts on a given subject, takes note of the contradictions, and seeks to resolve them by making a distinction. One can almost always distinguish between two cases, and so pointing to a factual distinction is but half a solution. One must then show that this difference of fact is of legal significance. Rabbenu Tam and Ri rarely explain the legal significance of their distinctions. They are content to simply state the factual difference (*ve-yesh lomar de-hakha mayrei*). They leave the task of investing these distinctions with legal significance to their successors. However, the men who came after them, such as R. Yehudah Sirleon, R. Mosheh of Coucy, R. Perets of Corbeil, were unequal to this task; they usually simply transmitted the remarks of their predecessors, while here and there adding some new distinction. The true successors of Rabbenu Tam and Ri were Nahmanides and his school—Rashba, Ritva, and Ran. This school not only advanced systematically new and different distinctions, but also gave a jurisprudential dimension to their own distinctions and those of the Tosafists. This is less noticeable in the writings of Nahmanides, for reasons which are here irrelevant, but is salient in the writings of his school, especially those of Ritva and Ran.

The currently dominant Lithuanian school of talmudic analysis also attempts to draw distinctions between ostensibly similar rulings and to uncover the conceptual content of differing legal positions. This is the main reason for the sense of closeness that exists between the two schools, especially in the Lithuanian attraction to the *ḥiddushim* of Ritva and Ran.

Often Rashba, Ritva, and Ran advanced no new doctrine, but rather explained in a revelatory way the doctrine espoused by the Tosafists, and especially that of Nahmanides. It is in their writings that the reader discovers the ideas with which Nahmanides grappled and which he strove to express. In the commentaries of Ritva and Ran, the two last exponents of the school of Gerona, the dialectical movement of the Tosafists received its fullest and most sophisticated formulation. The same cannot be said of the writings of Me'iri. The technical content of the doctrines is expounded with unparalleled clarity, but their conceptual content, the jurisprudential insights that they embody, are entirely lacking. Very often one encounters in the writings of Nahmanides 'loaded words', as it were, phrases in which Nahmanides is struggling to bring forth a new insight, but which require further development and articulation. In the writings of his school, these ideas are set forth in their fullness. However, I doubt whether one could identify from the formulations of Me'iri which doctrine is that of the great Ravad of Posquières and which is that of some mediocre Provençal Talmudist; which doctrine is that of Nahmanides and which that of an insignificant Catalonian scholar—the simple reason being that the jurisprudential insights that mark the conclusions of Ravad and Nahmanides are not to be found in Me'iri's formulations. A host of halakhic doctrines are set forth in his writings with unparalleled clarity, but without depth or legal resonance. Me'iri never pondered what ideas these technical holdings embody—indeed, at times one feels that he is wholly unaware of their existence. This is the third reason for the fate of his works. To a known ruling, Me'iri added nothing; any new ruling that he reported was a technical novelty with little if any legal suasion. It was also an orphaned position, as Me'iri's strange monikers hid the father of the doctrine.[6]

To sum up, Me'iri was over half a millennium in advance of his time in his preternaturally modern Hebrew and in the literary form in which his writings were cast, one that approximates the rhetorical mode of presentation of today. At the same time, he was unaware of, perhaps even indifferent to, the strides made in the sophistication of halakhic thought, not far from his native Perpignan, in Gerona and Barcelona, in the famed schools of Nahmanides and his pupils Rashba, Ritva, and Ran. For over 600 years scholars were understandably indifferent to the *Bet ha-Beḥirah*. Only with the arrival of the era of ArtScroll and Schottenstein did Me'iri's writings come into their own.

[6] I find unpersuasive the explanation given by Moshe Halbertal that the indifference of the school of Nahmanides to Me'iri and to the halakhic writings of thirteenth-century Languedocian thought was the result of their deep antagonism to the Maimonidean stance of these scholars. The works of the thirteenth-century Languedocian scholars were all published by M. Y. Blau in the course of 1960–1985. Does anyone ever cite them? Does anyone even look at them? Contemporary talmudic scholars have no knowledge of the posture that these scholars assumed in the Maimonidean controversy. They ignore them because there is nothing in their writings to which to pay attention. The creative period of Languedocian halakhic thought was the twelfth century; the writings of the thirteenth century are the writings of epigones, and there was no reason for such towering figures as Rashba, Ritva, and Ran to pay them any heed. Gregg Stern (above, n. 4) equally rejects Halbertal's view, for other reasons (nn. 47–9). The latter's views are found in his path-breaking book, *Bein Torah le-Ḥokhmah: Rabbi Menaḥem ha-Me'iri u-Va'alei Halakhah ha-Maimuniyim be-Provence* (Jerusalem, 2000), 217–22.

CHAPTER SIXTEEN

Printing and the History of Halakhah

THIS ARTICLE fits in with my second response to Rabbi Ephraim A. Buckwold. It was originally a lecture delivered at the Van Leer Institute in 1992 on the occasion of the publication of Zeev Gries's *Sefer, Sofer ve-Sippur be-Reshit ha-Ḥasidut*.

OCCASIONALLY one is influenced by works that one has never seen; but not often. This occurs mostly with works which have shaped the climate of opinion of an age, as did once Freudianism or Marxism. However, in scholarly fields this happens much more rarely. Someone who does not follow the history of the printing of halakhic texts cannot know which halakhic works were influential and which were not. The study of the history of printing is no minor matter, and the best evidence for this is the study of the late and much-lamented I. M. Ta-Shma on the printings of the novellae (*ḥiddushim*) of Ramban and his school.[1]

Nowadays, every bar mitzvah boy gets the *ḥiddushim* of Ramban, Rashba, Ritva, Rah, and Ran, and so nothing is more natural than to assume that these works were in the hands of scholars in the centuries that precede us. Nothing could be further from the truth.

One could well argue that there were very few scholars of the boldness and sovereign command of the classical sources of R. Shabbetai Kohen, author of the *Siftei Kohen* (*Shakh*)—certainly if one restricts the list to Ashkenazic Talmudists of the time. Yet R. Shabbetai hardly ever cites in his commentary on 'Ḥoshen Mishpat' the *ḥiddushim* of Ramban. Equally striking is the absence in his discussions of citations from the *ḥiddushim* of Rashba and Ritva. Ta-Shma has shown that, barring Ramban's *ḥiddushim* on *Bava Batra* and his study of indirect causation (*dinei garmi*), which were printed in 1523,

[1] 'Seder Hadpasatam shel Ḥiddushei ha-Rishonim le-Talmud: Perek be-Toledot ha-Pilpul', *Kiryat Sefer*, 50 (1975), 325–36; repr. in id., *Keneset Meḥkarim*, ii (Jerusalem, 2004), 219–38. {For a more comprehensive statement of the origins of the currently dominant Lithuanian approach in Talmudics, see M. Lichtenstein, '"Ve-Et ha-Aḥaronim Ani Hu"—Tekufat ha-Aḥaronim: Megammot ve-Kivvunim', *Netu'im*, 16 (2010), 131–74.}

and the *ḥiddushim* of Rashba on the tractates *Berakhot*, *Gittin*, and *Bava Batra*, no further writings of these authors or of the other great figures of Ramban's school (*Bet Midrasho shel ha-Ramban*) were printed until 1715. No volume of the *Shitah Mekubbetset* was ever published until 1738. In other words, almost the entire revolutionary thought of *Bet Midrasho shel ha-Ramban* was known only through the agency of the *Commentary on Alfasi* of R. Nissim of Barcelona (Ran).

Can we conceive of the *Ketsot ha-Ḥoshen* without Ramban, Rashba, Rah, and Ritva and the *Shitah Mekubbetset*? Their doctrines are writ large on every page of that work. I don't mean to suggest that these works caused a revolution. In the final analysis, a book is simply a book—an inert object. Without genius to perceive the depths found in it, the book remains simply one among many others on the shelf. Genius, however, requires some supportive framework; without that, it does not come to fruition—or it realizes itself in a few striking personalities and in them only.

Take, for example, the case of R. Aryeh Leib (d.1785), the rabbi and head of the court (*rav ve-av bet din*) of the tiny town of Volozhin, not far from Vilna. He had the intellectual power to reopen halakhic discussions that had seemingly ended with the passing of the great medieval commentators (*rishonim*). He had, equally, the independence of mind to proceed to do this. Indeed, given his imperious personality, he felt impelled to do so, despite the fact that most of the central halakhic issues had been sealed and settled in Ashkenaz with the acceptance of the *Shulḥan 'Arukh* and the *Mappah* of Rama, together with the classic commentators R. David ha-Levi Segal (Taz, d.1662), R. Shabbetai Kohen (Shakh, d.1663), and R. Avraham Avli (Magen Avraham, d.1699). However, most halakhists, even those who were his equals in talent, would hesitate to challenge a long-entrenched halakhic consensus, and certainly not do it systematically.

We tend to attribute the low level of halakhic thought in Poland and Lithuania in 1650–1750 to the massacres that attended the Ukranian revolt led by Chmelnitzki (1648–50) and the devastation wrought by the subsequent Swedish invasion. And with justice. However, one should equally remember that the previous century had witnessed the dramatic emergence of Polish halakhic thought—R. Mosheh Isserles (Rama, d.1572), R. Shelomoh Luria (Rashal, d.1574), R. Me'ir (Maharam) of Lublin (d.1617), R. Shemu'el Edels (Maharsha, d.1631), R. Yo'el Sirkes (Baḥ, d.1640), R. David ha-Levi Segal (Taz), and R. Shabbetai Kohen (Shakh). These scholars had edited and elucidated the works of the great medieval commentators of Ashkenaz; they had parsed their thought and analyzed and adjudicated their controversies. There was little for the creative halakhist to do, unless he were to throw down the gauntlet to all who had preceded him—and, barring R. Ḥezkiyah da Silva (rabbi and chief of the court of the AHU communities—Altona, Hamburg, and Wandsbeck—author of the *Peri Ḥadash* [d.1698]) and R Aryeh Leib of Volozhin, who would ever dream of doing so?

And what did the printing, in the eighteenth century, of the *ḥiddushim* of *Bet Midrasho shel ha-Ramban* produce?

First, it opened anew the halakhic discussion. A halakhah is a fact; a halakhic controversy is a problem. It demands analysis and insists on adjudication. With the infusion of thousands of doctrines of Ramban, Rashba, and Ritva, and the hosts of new positions registered in the *Shitah Mekubbetset*, rabbinical scholars were now required to reopen closed issues and weigh the established rulings against the claims of the new doctrines that were streaming into the system. They had to scour the Talmud to see whether there were passages that supported some of the new doctrines and to assess whether the new views of Ramban's school contained juridical insights that set past rulings at naught.

Second, printing introduced a new level of halakhic thinking into the legal discourse. I scarcely think that it is an exaggeration to say that the solutions advanced by the *Bet Midrasho shel ha-Ramban* are more suasive than those of the Tosafists. They are often deeper and formulated with greater precision and sophistication than those of the French Ba'alei ha-Tosafot. Put somewhat simply, one often enjoys a passage in the *Ḥiddushei ha-Ritva* more than one in the *Tosafot*. Hardly surprising, as the members of the school of Ramban were the intellectual heirs of the Tosafists; they constituted the second stage of the tosafist dialectical movement.

In the early phases of an intellectual revolution, the numerous problems raised are often better than the solutions propounded. The weakness of the old views is obvious, but seldom can new views be fully developed and attain their richest and most sophisticated formulations within a generation or two. For this to occur, a long line of major thinkers has to toil to attain that fullness of vision. In the early stages, there is much improvisation in an attempt to answer many of the questions that now flood the field. Over the course of time, as the intellectual tools become more sophisticated, the situation improves: a new equilibrium is established between the existing problems and instruments of solution.

The Ba'alei ha-Tosafot had only one textual tradition, together with the variant readings found in the commentaries of Rabbenu Ḥanan'el of Kairouan. They were compelled to build a new halakhic world unaided by the learning of other cultures and on the basis of one textual tradition only. In contrast, the *Bet Midrasho shel ha-Ramban*, some two centuries later, had not only the commentaries of Rashi, Rabbenu Ḥanan'el, and the Tosafists, but also those of the Geonim, Alfasi, and R. Yosef Ibn Megas of Lucena (Muslim Spain) and the commentaries of the greatest Provençal thinker and commentator, Ravad of Posquières. They approached the halakhah with a far more varied corpus of sources and with an improved and more sophisticated version of scholastic dialectic than that of their French predecessors. One well understands why the infusion of the writings of this school into the halakhic world of the eighteenth century transformed the halakhah.

This is immediately visible in the writings of R. Yehoshua Falk (Penei Yehoshua, d.1756), R. Yeḥezk'el Landau (Noda' bi-Yehudah, d.1793), and, to a lesser extent, R. Yonatan Eibeshutz (Urim ve-Tummim, d.1764). But individual insights, regardless of how trenchant and revolutionary they are, aren't yet a revolution. The way of thought that yielded these insights has to be internalized for the flow of insights to become systematic and halakhic thinking transformed. This occurred in the next generation in the writings of R. Aryeh Leib of Stryj (Ketsot ha-Ḥoshen, d.1813) and his younger colleague, R. Ya'akov Lorberbaum (Netivot ha-Mishpat, d.1832).[2] A new way of thinking came into being with the publication of the writings of the *Bet Midrash* of Ramban in the eighteenth century; and, in the form that it assumed in Lithuania in the latter half of the nineteenth century, it remains the dominant approach in the yeshivah world to this day.

And one cannot understand how all these major developments took place without knowing the 'trivial' details of the history of printing.

APPENDIX

A final word is in place. The sudden infusion of new legal material can work a swift revolution in legal thought, but not in adjudication. Law is based on precedent, and many days have to pass before a 'new' ruling comes to be viewed as an old one, as a controlling precedent. A responsum of the author of the *Ketsot ha-Ḥoshen* provides an excellent example of this process.[3] He was asked to rule in a case that arose in a nearby town upon a controversy between two partners that involved 'negligent misrepresentation' (*mar'eh dinar le-shulḥani*[4]). He discusses in detail the positions of Shakh and Urim ve-

[2] My remarks here about the *Netivot ha-Mishpat* should be qualified by the observations of M. Lichtenstein in the article cited in the previous note, 162–3 and n. 39.

[3] Yehoshua ha-Kohen, *Even Yehoshua* (Stryj, 1847), #76.

[4] *Bava Kamma* 99b.

Tummim, as one would expect of a scholar who had been raised on the close readings of the works of Maharsha and Maharam Lublin, and his entire discussion is according to the ground rules and modes of argument that obtained in his time—without a whisper of his own revolutionary approach.

CHAPTER SEVENTEEN
Angle of Deflection

I
REPLY TO CRITICS
A

In much of my writing on the history of the halakhah, I have employed implicitly or explicitly the principle of 'angle of deflection' or 'measurable deflection'.[1] For example, in the preface to *Yeinam* I wrote:

> To avoid a simplistic sociology of law, anyone claiming that a jurist's thought has been influenced by outside forces or inner ambiguities must be able to point to some obvious flaw in the thinker's argument, a measurable deflection from the expected line of reasoning that indicates that something impinged upon the mind of the jurist and diverted his thought from its normal course.[2]

This principle has been utilized superbly by Mark Cohen in his path-breaking work on Jewish economic activity in the Islamic world.[3] But the principle of angle of deflection still has its critics. Some have seen in it a reflection of legal formalism—not surprisingly, as I was trained in Lithuanian Talmudics, which has a strong bent to formalism. Whether law develops from within, as a consequence of an internal dynamic, or whether its motor force is

[1] Implicitly in my first publication, 'Pawnbroking: A Study in *Ribbit* and of the Halakhah in Exile', *Proceedings of the American Academy of Jewish Research*, 38–39 (1972), 203–68 (repr. in an expanded form in my *Collected Essays*, i [Oxford, 2013], 57–166); explicitly in my subsequent publications on the subject: 'Can Halakhic Texts Talk History?', *AJS Review*, 3 (1978), 152–96 (repr. in *Collected Essays*, i. 169–223); 'Halakhah, Hermeneutics, and Martyrdom in Ashkenaz (Parts I and II)', *Jewish Quarterly Review*, 94 (2004), 77–108, 278–99 (repr. in *Collected Essays*, ii [Oxford, 2014], 228–87); *Ha-Yayin bi-Yemei ha-Beinayim—Yein Nesekh: Perek be-Toledot ha-Halakhah be-Ashkenaz* (Jerusalem, 2008), 186–8; *Yeinam: Saḥar be-Yeinam shel Goyim—'al Gilgulah shel Halakhah be-'Olam ha-Ma'aseh* (Jerusalem, 2016), preface, x–xi. I have used interchangeably the phrases 'angle of deflection' and 'measurable deflection'.

[2] *Yeinam* (above, n. 1), 10.

[3] M. Cohen, *Maimonides and the Merchants: Jewish Law and Society in the Medieval Islamic World* (Philadelphia, 2017).

social pressures and the personal predilections and ideologies of judges is an ancient jurisprudential question. The formalists contend that the judge only applies the rules of the system to a specific case, while the realists contend that in the final analysis the judge rules, be it only unconsciously, in accordance with his personal and ideological inclinations.

The principle of angle of deflection is, however, not a jurisprudential but an evidentiary one. Both formalists and realists agree that the dominant motor force in a system does not operate to the exclusion of all else. The realist admits that on occasion the judge simply applies the rule found in the law books, while the formalist concedes that on occasion the judge rules according to his personal predilections. The rule of the angle of deflection provides the historian with a criterion by which to assess whether or not a specific jurist in a specific case was influenced by outside considerations. How the judicial system works generally is a juridical question; how the system worked in a certain case at a certain time and place is a historical one.

This is not to claim that a decision in which no angle of deflection is to be discerned was determined entirely by immanent developments. It only says that the historian has no basis for claiming that it was a product of outside forces. However, the rule of the angle of deflection is not the only test to ascertain whether a judicial ruling had a clear social purpose. A series of rulings, for example, in favor of debtors is equally valid a way to prove such intent, provided that one defines clearly what one means by the phrase 'series of rulings'. Obviously, one cannot ignore those decisions that supported the creditors' claims. However, one must equally, though this is not often done, take into consideration those decisions which could have been bent to the interest of the debtors, yet the judges chose to adjudicate on other grounds and not use the case in question as an occasion to advance the interest of those desiring inflation and the easing of bankruptcy. That avoidance is understandable, as it is not an easy task, to put it mildly, to compose a decision that will be as persuasive as the one given, but at the same time advance a social agenda not shared by the judge. Yet, unless such an alternative decision is presented, the contention that the decision was a product of the judge's personal inclinations and outlook is simply poor, reductive sociology.

Others have criticized this criterion on other grounds. In a recent review, Ivan Marcus took another historian, who 'took Jewish legal theory [as the] focus of his investigation', to task for writing: 'The task of the historian is to follow and evaluate the manner in which rabbis navigated their path between competing judicial considerations.' Marcus writes:

In this pursuit, Woolf is following the school of the late Jacob Katz and the influential essay by Haym Soloveitchik, 'Can Halakhic Texts Talk History?', *AJS Review*, 3 (1978), 152–96. Most cultural Jewish historians, however, and some legal scholars, do not share this approach because it imposes theological restrictions on more empirical historical methodologies.[4]

If a researcher chooses to focus on the history of Jewish law, how does such a focus impose 'theological restrictions' on him? Isn't Jewish legal history as empirical a discipline as Jewish cultural history?

In a review essay several years ago, Marcus raised more fundamental objections to the principle of angle of deflection, writing:

Soloveitchik then assumes a constant jurisprudential system *at all times* and goes on to argue that historical information can be drawn from halakhic texts only when they deviate from how the rules of Jewish *jurisprudence are supposed to operate. His method assumes that Jewish law as a historical fact operates only the way it is supposed to.* If there are no uniform sets of rules and practices as an historical fact, there can be no meaning to the term 'deviation'. Soloveitchik's rule of inferring historical realia in 'deviations' from a *universal halakhic norm* ...[5] [emphases in the original]

The principle of angle of deflection deals with the judge's breaking elementary logical and legal rules. Should a judge state 'The defendant does and does not exist', wouldn't the most dyed-in-the-wool positivist historian, no

[4] I. Marcus, 'Jeffrey R. Woolf. *The Fabric of Religious Life in Medieval Ashkenaz (1000–1300): Creating Sacred Communities*', *AJS Review*, 40/2 (2016), 441.

[5] 'Israeli Medieval Jewish Historiography: From Nationalist Positivism to New Cultural and Social Histories', *Jewish Studies Quarterly*, 17 (2010), 277–81. The full sentence and the next read (p. 280): 'Soloveitchik's rule of inferring historical realia in "deviations" from a *universal halakhic norm* is an application of Katz's sociological and religious paradigm that Soloveitchik shares and develops. His view is a continuation of Katz's own debate with Haim Hillel Ben-Sasson about how historians should read sources. Ben Sasson's counter-argument that historians should read all sources as historians is worth rereading, a point Moshe Rosman recently made in a different context.' No one ever questioned that historians should read all sources as historians; at bar in the Katz–Ben-Sasson controversy was what inferences can be drawn from legal hypotheticals. Law deals with general rules; no rule obtains universally, and the task of the jurist is to create hypothetical cases which illustrate the limit of rule, i.e. the mandate of the rule cannot obtain in this case. For example, divorce is considered halakhically as detrimental to a woman's status, personally and socially. A halakhist in Poland gave, as illustration of the limits of this rule, a case where a husband is passionately in love with his wife, who with equal passion loves another man. May one infer that some men in that period passionately loved their wives to the extent of sacrificing their own happiness? Ben-Sasson said 'Yes' and Katz 'No', arguing that the 'facts' of the case were logical constructs created to illustrate the limits of a general principle. They cannot, *in and of themselves*, be evidence of a social reality. I fail to see how Rosman's discussion has any bearing on this issue. As to Marcus's presentation in his essay of Katz's oeuvre, I fear that would require more than a footnote to correct.

less than the student of law, wonder whether something was amiss in the judge's ruling and suspect that something or someone was pushing the judge to say things which he ordinarily would never dream of saying?

As to the claim that I 'argue that historical information can be drawn from halakhic texts only when they deviate from how the rules of Jewish *jurisprudence are supposed to operate*', I would simply state that for some 150 years Jewish historians have been drawing conclusions from rabbinic material. I was of the opinion that a number of their conclusions were not valid and that above all their mode of inference was flawed. I wrote a book, *Shut ke-Makor Histori* (*Responsa as a Historical Source*),[6] and there is no mention whatsoever in it of angle of deflection. That principle is one that assesses adjudication, not determination of fact. It answers the question: When is a historian justified in claiming that forces outside the judicial system impinged upon the judge and led him to rule as he did?[7]

As to the claim that this principle assumes 'a universal halakhic norm', a constant jurisprudential system at all times, and that 'it assumes that Jewish law as a historic fact operates only the way it is supposed to', I simply reply: the halakhah, like any legal system, has numerous and varied approaches, and the juridical activity of one age can differ radically from that of another. However, there are certain red lines about which all are in agreement that they cannot be crossed. The first rule is that the judge's reasoning must conform to the elementary rules of logic. To give a couple of examples: Should a judge argue, (1) all revolutionaries have two feet; (2) Goldberg has two feet; (3) therefore, Goldberg is a revolutionary, that judge has crossed the line that separates law from rhetoric. Similarly, should a judge derive Y from X and rule according to Y but not according to X, one of the two rulings must be invalid and the two must be aligned with one another. The second rule is linguistic. One cannot explain words in the Talmud contrary to the way they have been uniformly interpreted by all commentators, medieval and modern. The third is: ignoring judicial hierarchy. An American judge, for example, cannot rule contrary to the Constitution of the United States. Similarly, a halakhist cannot rule contrary to a *setam mishnah* as it has been understood by all commentators. It is angles of deflection such as these that I had in mind and pointed out frequently in my writings.[8] These rules hold true for all times and places, and the halakhah 'as an empirical fact' has always abided by them. Deflections such as the above attest to the fact that some force is impinging upon the thought of the judge and pulling him off the straight and narrow. This is doubly so if there is a series of such deflections in a specific area of the law.

6 *Shut ke-Makor Histori* (Jerusalem, 1990).

7 Ibid. 441.

8 Above, n. 1.

Marcus concludes by contending that '[Soloveitchik] adopts [Jacob] Katz's apologetic stance, since at bottom, the result [i.e. Soloveitchik's book on Gentile wine in Ashkenaz] is to historicize Jewish law about Christian wine in medieval France and Spain.' I have two minor questions. First, why is 'historicization' apologetic? Second, isn't a historian supposed to historicize?

B

I would like to now address Adiel Schremer's critique of my scholarly work, published recently in *Zion*.[9] His presentation of my specific arguments (which I don't recognize) and his disagreement with my interpretation of the sources (which I can't grasp) I will spell out in a future issue of *Zion*. I would like here to address his use of formalism and realism as framework categories in his critique.

As noted above, 'whether law develops from within, as a consequence of an internal dynamic, or whether its motor force is social pressures and the personal predilections and ideologies of judges is an ancient jurisprudential question. The formalists contend that the judge only applies the rules of the system to a specific case, while the realists contend that in the final analysis the judge rules, be it only unconsciously, in accordance with his personal and ideological inclinations.'[10] The controversy in jurisprudence between realists and formalists emerged from the study of civil, criminal, and matrimonial law as obtains in American law, common law, and Roman law.

However, the halakhah, like canon law, deals not only with relations between man and his fellow man but also with those between man and God. Indeed, the large majority of halakhah consists of ritual law. Let's make a rough estimate using Maimonides' comprehensive code, the *Mishneh Torah*. It is divided into fourteen units. Only five of them deal with relationships between man and man—*Nashim*, *Nezikin*, *Kinyan*, *Mishpatim*, and *Shofetim*—that is to say, 37.5 percent. In other words, over 60 percent of the halakhah has little bearing on social and economic relationships. To be sure, there are some topics in ritual law which are fraught with social and economic significance, but despite their importance they are but a very small percentage of the vast ritual corpus of Judaism.

Realism speaks of *Zweckjurisprudenz*—goal-oriented decisions. Can one speak of social and economic policy in whether one recites *borè peri ha-'ets* or *borè peri ha-adamah* on strawberries? In using two or three matzot at the *Seder*?

[9] 'Historyah, Halakhah u-Zehut Datit be-Siaḥ ha-Hilkhati shel Ḥakhmei Ashkenaz bi-Yemei ha-Beinayim', *Zion*, 81 (2016), 31–66.

[10] Above, pp. 407–8.

Whether the fruit of a potted plant with a hole in the base (*'atsits nakuv*) is subject to tithing? Whether the blood of a sacrificed animal may be sprinkled on the altar after sundown (*dam nifsal bi-sheki'at ha-ḥamah*), to take only four of thousands of instances? Would a jurist coming to the halakhah *tabula rasa*, surveying a system of which over 60 percent is ritual, ever assume that the system is predominantly goal-oriented?

I first learnt of Rudolph von Jhering's notion of *Zweckjurisprudenz* when I was in the Semicha Program of the R. Isaac Elchanan Theological Seminary of Yeshiva University in the early 1960s, and read with excitement the writings of Jhering, Karl Llewellyn, and Jerome Frank. I realized that this would mean that the mode of argument in *Nashim* and *Nezikin*, which are goal-oriented, would differ fundamentally from most arguments in the other four *sedarim* of the Talmud. I didn't find the mode of reasoning in areas of *bein adam le-ḥavero* (between man and man) different from that in instances of *bein adam la-makom* (between man and God). I was unable to discover such a difference in my yeshivah days and have not succeeded in discovering it in all the intervening years, and not for lack of trying. Indeed, I would say that I have turned repeatedly to this problem over the course of my academic career.[11]

C

The issue of formalism and realism is a jurisprudential controversy, not a legal one. The relationship of jurisprudence to law is similar, *mutatis mutandis*, to that of philosophy of history to history. Jurisprudence deals with the nature of the human activity called adjudication and the system that such an activity engenders, in other words, the nature of the judicial process; philosophy of history deals with the nature of historical knowledge. The legists—that's the best word that I could find for a group constituted by lawyers, judges, law professors, and historians of law—care as much for jurisprudence as historians care about the epistemological status of historical knowledge. The common denominator of philosophy of history and jurisprudence is that neither is an empirical discipline. Let's leave aside philosophy of history and concentrate on jurisprudence, more specifically the distinction between realists and formalists. The claim that most adjudication—Dr Schremer insists vociferously

[11] Let me be clear what I have in mind. The issue is not whether there were ideological considerations in the formation of some laws of, say, *tum'ah ve-taharah* during the legislative period of the halakhah, in the era of the Sages (*Ḥazal*)—during the time of the Second Temple and the era of the *tanna'im* and *amora'im*. I refer to their interpretation over the following 1,200 years by the Geonim, *rishonim* (medieval Talmudists), and *aḥaronim* (post-medieval, down to and including contemporary, Talmudists) and their rulings in matters of 'Yoreh De'ah' and 'Oraḥ Ḥayyim'.

that *all adjudication*—is goal-driven or a product of internal dynamic is a philosophical claim. It can never even begin to be verified empirically. Realism and formalism deal not with individual cases but with judicial systems as a whole. The number of cases that have been ruled upon, for example, in the American system in municipal, state, and federal courts for some 225 years totals, I am told, well over a million. How could one master even part of such a corpus? Even supposing the existence of a human computer, such as the Gaon of Vilna and Rav 'Ovadyah Yosef, how could either of them have documented his conclusion? How could one even make a representative sampling? Ten thousand cases? That would require some fifteen to twenty thick volumes of justification, at the very least, and it would still be less than 1 percent. What's more, what does one know of the *Weltanschauung* of the tens of thousands of individuals who have sat in judgment over this period? What is known of a Judge Steven Williams, who sat on the district court of Ohio in the 1870s, and thousands like him? One is hard pressed to find such material even on most occupants of the Supreme Court. Read the articles of the realists. What documentation does the average article contain? Some forty cases at most. Even more to the point, what documentation is there of the socio-economic, religious-moral outlook of the judges of those cases? None whatsoever, so far as I could discover. Were this an empirical enterprise, one would imagine the writings of the realists to be replete with biographical material. There is none. Indeed, the only biographical information that I have come across in the discussions of formalism and realism is, for example, 'BA Yale 1982, LLD NYU 1985', i.e. biographical data on the author of the article, not on the judges whose world view and personal predilections are so knowingly discussed. The closest thing to an empirical study that I know of is *The Cheyenne's Way*. However, what can be done with the contemporary observation of the remnants of an Indian tribe on a pitiful reservation cannot be done with American, common, or Jewish law—continental or diasporic in scope and stretching back centuries, in Jewish law, well over a millennium.

Jurisprudents may well divide into realists and formalists; historians of law divide into no two such camps. Historians can neither postulate nor accept a postulate about the uniform conduct of any group over the course of centuries. They can only characterize the underlying reasons of specific rulings in specific cases, or the judicial outlook of a judge in his most notable cases. The claim that all or most opinions in a legal system uniformly derive from one source—be it the goal-orientation of the judge or the inner dynamic of the system—is, to a historian, ludicrous. First, there is no supportive data; there can be no supportive data for so broad a claim. Second, human nature is far too diverse and idiosyncratic for its actions over continents and centuries to be understood by any monocausal explanation. Outside of the natural sciences, universals exist in philosophy and theology, never in the *sciences humaines*, what we call the humanities and the social sciences. Particles have no individuality or choice; human beings do.

No one asks whether Morton Horowitz or G. Edward White (two eminent historians of American law) is a formalist or a realist. Nor has anyone posed that query about Frederick Mailand, Otto Gierke, Karl von Amira, Paul Viollet, or Adhémar Esmein—some of the great historians of medieval law. The categories of realism and formalism are meaningless in the empirical discipline of history. The sooner we banish these misplaced if sonorous terms, the sooner we will be able to treat the genuine methodological problems that confront the writing of the history of halakhah.

Not that these categories are useless to the historian. The postulate of the realists, for example, is useful as a heuristic device, as is Marxism, which postulates the uniform primacy of economic interests. Such notions sensitize the historian to forces which *may* be operative in specific rulings and whose signals he may not otherwise have detected. This postulate of the realists is simply one more instrument in the large toolkit of the historian.

Where does the jurisprudent get his ideas? From his perforce limited knowledge of the system and from his feeling that there is a uniformity in its functioning. The legal term for a judge's reason is called the *ratio* of the decision; its plural form in American law is, forgive the bad Latin, *ratios*. Realist jurisprudents announce that all *ratios* are but rationales. The legist replies, 'That may be true, but not all rationales are equal, and our business is to evaluate them.' This second misapprehension, I believe, underlies a good part of Dr Schremer's remarks and those of some of his confrères. My distinguished colleague thinks that realism frees the judge from making a cogent argument. Since everything is but a rationalization, why trouble oneself with them, and what's the difference between a good rationalization and a bad one? Rashi's reasons didn't really play a role, and Rambam often dispenses with reason altogether and simply rules as he wishes, plucks his decisions, as it were, out of thin air. This is a comforting thought for those who desire to write the history of halakhah but wish to be spared the heavy lifting of serious legal thinking, or for some scholars in Jewish studies who have little skill in handling rabbinic sources but who must draw on such sources for their work.

Unfortunately, this comfort is illusory. Where a judge gets his ideas is as irrelevant as where a historian gets his ideas. The test of a historian's idea is not in its point of origin, but in the degree of persuasive correspondence between his theory and the data it seeks to explain. The test of a judge's ideas is the cogency and power of his argument. There is probably no decision in American history so shamelessly and ingeniously political as that of *Marbury v. Madison*. Yet there has been no more important and influential decision in American history: it established judicial review—the power of the Supreme Court to declare acts of Congress or of the President unconstitutional. Many of Marshall's greatest decisions had a clear political purpose, were part and parcel of the agenda of the Federalist Party to which he belonged—namely, to enhance the power of the federal government at the expense of that of the states. Yet, because of their power and cogency, they carried the day; and the brilliant if irascible anti-Federalist, John Randolph of Virginia, could only cry out at one of Marshall's decisions, 'Wrong, wrong, totally wrong! But no man can tell why or wherein.' He realized only too well that without such a 'why and wherein' these ideas would rule the judicial roost, as indeed they did. The rulings of Holmes and Brandeis had far more pith and power than those of their colleagues, Van Devanter and McReynolds, who represented the majority. Holmes's famous dissenting opinion that freedom of thought is freedom for thought that you hate and Brandeis's similar opinion that the cure for bad speech is more speech, not enforced silence, captured the hearts and minds of the younger generation, and when they attained to a court majority they translated these dissents into law which obtains to this very day. They form one of the cornerstones of the current civil liberties in America. Arguments in law do matter—regardless of which side one takes in *jurisprudential* controversies.

The same fallacy underlies, I believe, my distinguished critic's argument against my criterion of angle of deflection. Dr Schremer has countered that the entire notion of angle of deflection is a formalist one, because the assumption of any realist is that law does not emerge from the sources but from the wishes and goals of the judge, so deflection from the sources is only to be expected, indeed, is inevitable. That may be the position of a jurisprudential realist; it will not be that of any legal scholar or historian. Judges are deemed great and their decisions read and held binding because of the force of their arguments, arguments which have held, at times, for centuries. When a great jurist does make a crude mistake, usually something is up, and the task of the historian is to find out what that something is.

So things stand legally. Is Dr Schremer's criticism of the angle of deflection even valid jurisprudentially? That depends on what one considers an angle of deflection. If I may be permitted to quote what I have said above:

> the halakhah, like any legal system, has numerous and varied approaches, and the juridical activity of one age can differ radically from that of another. However, there are certain red lines about which all are in agreement that they cannot be crossed. The first rule is that the judge's reasoning must conform to the elementary rules of logic. To give a couple of examples: Should a judge argue, (1) all revolutionaries have two feet; (2) Goldberg has two feet; (3) therefore, Goldberg is a revolutionary, that judge has crossed the line that separates law from rhetoric. Similarly, should a judge derive Y from X and rule according to Y but not according to X, one of the two rulings must be invalid and the two must be aligned with one another. The second rule is linguistic. One cannot explain words in the Talmud contrary to the way they have been uniformly interpreted by all commentators, medieval and modern. The third is: ignoring judicial hierarchy. An American judge, for example, cannot rule contrary to the Constitution of the United States. Similarly, a halakhist cannot rule contrary to a *setam mishnah* as it has been understood by all commentators. It is angles of deflection such as these that I had in mind and pointed out frequently in my writings. These rules hold true for all times and places, and the halakhah 'as an empirical fact' has always abided by them. Deflections such as the above attest to the fact that some force is impinging upon the thought of the judge and pulling him off the straight and narrow. This is doubly so if there is a series of such deflections in a specific area of the law.[12]

I believe that even a dogmatic realist would say that errors of this sort place the argument beyond the pale of both law and jurisprudence.

II

OTHER CAUSES OF DEFLECTION

This, however, does not exhaust the reasons why an angle of deflection arises. At times, it comes about because there are no halakhic categories to respond to the challenge, yet the respondent must invoke such categories in his decision if he seeks to have it normatively binding. This occurred frequently in the modern period in dealing with reform movements and, in our day, in treating the halakhic status of women. For example, many of the changes introduced in the Hamburg Temple at the close of the second decade of the nineteenth century by the Reform movement were ones which were halakhically trivial. Some were even practices of long standing in the traditional synagogue. The first reform was praying in German rather than in Hebrew. The permissibility of praying in any language is explicitly stated in a *mishnah* in Sotah.[13] Indeed, the classic commentator on the *Shulḥan 'Arukh*, 'Oraḥ Ḥayyim', R. Avraham

[12] p. 410. [13] *Sotah* 32b.

Avli, stated that it was preferable to pray in a language that one understood.[14] Tens of thousands of Jews had prayed for centuries in Yiddish. The reformers introduced an organ played by a Gentile. However, hadn't R. Mosheh Isserles, in his authoritative glosses on the *Shulḥan 'Arukh*, permitted a Gentile flutist on the Sabbath to introduce a more joyous note of celebration during the marital feast?[15] Moreover, he had stated that the talmudic ban on playing music on the Sabbath for fear that 'one might fix a musical instrument' no longer applied these days! The rabbis who opposed the reforms perceived that the purpose of these changes in the traditional Jewish rite of prayer was to make the Jewish service resemble the Gentile one; this was simply another step in the process of assimilation and the destruction of Jewish distinctiveness. The central issue was the intent of the reformers, not their actions. Who, however, could prove that the purpose of the reformers was not to elevate by music the hearts of the worshippers to a more profound Divine service? The rabbis were thus obliged to demonstrate to the Senate of Hamburg that the deeds of the reformers were contrary to Jewish law. The result was the famous *Eleh Divrei ha-Berit* (*These are the Words of the Covenant*),[16] a collection of responsa, many signed by justly famed scholars, characterized by forced and unpersuasive arguments. All because there were no halakhic categories to address the real question—the illegitimate purpose of the reformers.[17]

The same 'absence of categories' has arisen in our day regarding women reading the Torah or the Megillah. The question is not the halakhic permissibility of these performances—this is obvious—but where the women's movement is headed: will it lead to attempts to alter the halakhic rulings that the Sages (*Ḥazal*) had instituted or had derived from the Bible?

The absence of appropriate categories took another—and tragic—form in the Middle Ages with regards to the question of the religious fate of children in a time of mass persecution. The laws of martyrdom treat under what circumstances an individual is required to lay down his life rather than betray his religion, but they do not discuss what happens to his children's upbringing after his martyrdom. In mishnaic and talmudic times this question did not arise. The Jewish communities of Palestine and Bavel (Babylonia) were very large, and after the death of a martyred family, the community would appoint guardians for their children's upbringing. However, in Islamic lands, and even more so in Christian Europe, the Jews constituted a tiny percentage of the population; pogroms like those of the Crusades, the Armleder, or the massacres that attended the Black Plague wiped out scores of Jewish

[14] *Magen Avraham*, 101: 5. [15] *Mapah*, 368: 2. [16] Altona, 1819.

[17] This characterization is based upon an unpublished study of these responsa.

communities. The surviving children would be brought up in the Muslim or Christian religion. If the children would be Christians and Muslims, what then was the purpose of Jewish martyrdom? The consequence of communal martyrdom was simply the mass conversion of Jewish children!

There were two paths open to medieval Jews: to convert with their children and wait for an opportune moment to return to the Jewish fold or to kill oneself and one's children to prevent them falling into Gentile hands and being raised in their idolatrous faith. Jews in Islam generally chose the first path, for reasons which lie beyond the province of this essay; Ashkenazic Jewry generally chose the second one.

Maimonides opens his *Iggeret ha-Shemad*, in which he defends Moroccan Jews who had publicly attested (literally, 'witnessed'; *shahada* in Arabic) 'There is no God but Allah and Muhammad is his prophet' but continued their Jewish identity in the privacy of their home (*be-tsin'ah*), with these words: 'A contemporary of ours has inquired . . . about the contemporary religious persecution which compels people to admit that Muhammad is a true emissary [of God], that he is a true prophet. Should he admit this so that he can live and his children will not be absorbed into the Gentile population [*yitam'u bein ha-goyim*], or should he rather die and not attest [to Muhammad's prophecy]?' Yet in his lengthy reply he makes no mention of the fate of the children. Correctly so, because their fate is not a halakhic consideration. Whence the deeply problematic *Iggeret ha-Shemad*. Maimonides could not mention the central consideration of both the Moroccan community and himself—the future of Jewish survival—and so he penned a lengthy and unpersuasive responsum.[18]

The same question arose in medieval Ashkenaz. Many communities chose, as I have said, the second path. They killed their children 'lest they be raised in their ways', that is to say, in the religion of their Christian persecutors, and then committed suicide, lest they yield at the last moment to the threat of the Christians and convert. Suicide because of the fear of conversion is highly questionable; murder, not to speak of the murder of children, is out of the question.

One of the most tragic documents that have come down to us from this period is the responsum of R. Me'ir of Rothenburg, the greatest Ashkenazic jurist (*posek*) of the Middle Ages.

> A Jew asked our teacher R[abbi] M[e'ir], may he live [long]: is penance required of someone who slaughtered his wife and four children during the great massacre at

[18] See my extensive analysis in *Collected Essays*, ii (above, n. 1), 288–364.

Koblenz [April 2, 1265], the blood-soaked city, because they asked him to kill them for they saw that God's wrath had been kindled and the enemies [Christians] began slaughtering the children of the living God [i.e. Jews]? He, too, wished to kill himself [and die] with them, but God [wished otherwise] and saved him by the Gentiles [i.e. they stopped him from killing himself].

And he [Rabbi Me'ir] wrote to him: 'I'm at a loss as to how to rule. Certainly, one who kills himself for the Unity of God is permitted to do so. . . . However, to kill other people requires further scrutiny to find allowance. . .

However, the allowance in this matter is widespread and we regularly find that many great people killed their sons and daughters. And [they were] celebrated by Rabbi Kalonymos in his dirge . . .

Whoever imposes penance upon him [i.e. the father who killed his children in a time of persecution] speaks evil of the pious of preceding generations [who did the same], since his intention was to do good, and he hurt those who were most dear to him only out of an abundance of love for our Creator, may He be blessed, and they begged him to do so . . . And one should not be severe with him [the father] at all.

May the Rock of Israel avenge our plight and the plight of his Torah and the blood of his servants swiftly in our days, and may our eyes see it [God's vengeance] and our hearts rejoice.

MbB [= Me'ir ben Barukh], may he [i.e. Barukh] live [long][19]

R. Me'ir's proofs are questionable, indeed, they will not withstand scrutiny, not for lack of stature of the respondent, but for lack of halakhic categories to address the problem.[20] Legal categories occasionally cannot address the existential question of religion and faith. The fate of the children may be irrelevant to the halakhah, but it is vital to Jewish survival. Saving a human life (*pikuaḥ nefesh*) is a halakhic category; saving Judaism (*pikuaḥ nefesh shel Yahadut*) is not. As I wrote: 'Powerful forces were thus at work in medieval martyrdom which could not find expression in the traditional, normative idiom. Ineluctably, they created new idioms or refashioned (if you wish, distorted) old ones. Thus, discussions of martyrdom are often halakhically problematic, if by halakhah one means the classic, talmudic norms that govern quotidian Jewish conduct. Major—indeed overwhelming—considerations do not register, at times, on the legal radar.'[21]

At times, the deflection from the legal straight and narrow lies not in the nature of the question, but in the nature of law itself. Law is a blunt instrument; it speaks a binary language, operates in an either/or manner.

[19] *Teshuvot, Pesakim u-Minhagim R. Me'ir mi-Rothenburg*, ii, ed. Y. Z. Cahana (Jerusalem, 1960), *Teshuvot*, #59. (The emendation and additions are those of the editor, mostly based on manuscripts.)

[20] See *Collected Essays*, ii (above, n. 1), 251–4, 285.

[21] Ibid. 228–9.

A man is either guilty or not guilty; liable or not liable. Law makes subtle distinctions in its argument because it generally cannot make such distinctions in its rulings. Thus, contradictory feelings which often lie side by side in the breast of a single person or of an entire society—understanding and shock, affection and revulsion, bonds of affection and alienation—often fail to find expression in the legal system. Woe to the scholar who, in a subject as emotionally fraught and contradictory as that of the Marranos (the New Christians of Spain post-1391), projects the conclusions of a court in one field of law upon that of another. One can rule that the Marrano is an apostate in every sense of the word in matters of divorce and levirate marriage and then turn around and rule that they must be rescued if endangered, redeemed if they fall captive, and sustained from the communal chest if they fall into poverty. Consistency can only be expected within the same legal field—marital law, fraternal support (charity and the like); and even there, contradictions abound, because they abound in the human heart.[22]

Important as halakhic texts are as a source of history, the historian must always remember that law is a skeletal system only. It structures and supports but is itself encased by living flesh and blood—the habits of conduct and the modes of feeling and believing, in brief, the way of life, of a society. Rarely is this reflected in the legal system. Take, for example, the support and education of children. Halakhically one is obliged to support children only to the age of 6. From 6 to 'adulthood', that is to say, until 12 for a female and 13 for a male, the obligation arises only as 'charity'. This means that support of one's children must take preference over other claims of philanthropy towards which the individual may be inclined. After those ages, there is no obligation whatsoever to support one's progeny.[23] As for education, one can fulfill all one's obligations by teaching children until the ages of 6 and 7,[24] as millions of poor Jews did for thousands of years.

One can know the entire tractate of *Shabbat* cold, and all that one has is an endless series of 'No', 'No', 'No'. One can have a sovereign command of the complex laws of the Sabbath found in the *Shulḥan 'Arukh* and not know of the strange power of rest and renewal possessed by the Sabbath and the central truth of the saying 'More than the Jews have observed the Sabbath, the Sabbath has preserved the Jews.' One can know the entire Talmud with its vast commentarial literature and still not know the centrality of Torah study

[22] This is based on an unpublished essay on the responsa on the Marrano issue.

[23] Maimonides, *Mishneh Torah*, 'Hilkhot Ishut', 12: 14–15; *Shulḥan 'Arukh*, 'Even ha-'Ezer', 71: 1.

[24] *Kiddushin* 29b.

in Judaism, and he who knows not that knows nothing of Judaism or of Jewish history.

These are some of the dangers which attend those who seek to describe Judaism on the basis of legal sources. It is immensely difficult to capture the intimate experiences of Jews in bygone days—relations between parents and children, husbands and wives, for example, not to speak of the value systems of their society: their notions of honor and shame, of self-worth and abnegation, of rest and toil. If one knows how to listen attentively to halakhic sources, one can catch echoes of these values, but any real reconstruction must draw upon a far wider range of sources. If one declines to do so, one's conclusions will be only a sketch; more often than not, a caricature.

A simple example: A purely halakhic view of history could even argue that since there was an opinion in the Talmud that one was obliged to teach children how to swim and this opinion is the view of no less a figure than R. 'Akiva,[25] it is reasonable to assume that the religiously scrupulous and devout (*ḥasidim ve-anshei ma'aseh*) followed this dictum to the letter. And then conclude that Jewish education of the last two millennia has been an abysmal failure for it produced only one international swimming champion, Mark Spitz.

[25] Yerushalmi, *Kiddushin* 1: 7, Academy of Hebrew Language edn. (Jerusalem, 1981), column 1154; Romm edn. (Vilna, 1924), 19a.

Bibliography of Manuscripts

Most manuscripts have been cited by the catalogue number of the Institute of Microfilmed Hebrew Manuscripts at the National Library of Israel, not by the shelf mark of the library of origin, the reason being that, given the Institute's vast collection of microfilms from all over the world, for decades most scholars worked there rather than moving around to different libraries in a host of countries. They naturally cited the manuscripts as they were registered in the Institute's catalogue, and these numbers have entered the scholarly literature.

Generally there are three numbers in the lists below: the catalogue number registered at the Institute in the left-hand column, taken from the catalogues of the respective libraries of origin; the library of origin's shelf mark in the middle column; and the reel number of the microfilm at the Institute in the right-hand column (where the catalogue number is not that of the Institute this is noted in the relevant left-hand column heading).

Where the library of origin did not have a catalogue, the Institute registered the manuscripts by the library's shelf mark, and the only references given below are that library's shelf mark and the Institute's reel number. Where the library of origin arranged its manuscripts by the order of its catalogue, the catalogue number together with the Institute's reel number are the only references.

The collections of London Beth Din and Beth Hamidrash and Jews' College (Montefiore), London have been sold and the manuscripts dispersed, many to private parties. Such manuscripts are nevertheless entered below as they are registered in the card catalogue of the Institute.

Berlin, Staatsbibliothek

Catalogue no.	Shelf mark	Reel no.
160	Or. Qu. 685	1798

Budapest, Library of the Hungarian Academy of Sciences

Catalogue no.	Shelf mark	Reel no.
2° 1		31445

Cambridge, University Library

Stefan C. Reif's catalogue of Cambridge University Library's manuscripts came out long after the microfilms of Cambridge had been accessed by the Institute. These manuscripts were therefore registered at the Institute by Cambridge's shelf mark. For the manuscripts below, Cambridge's catalogue number is in the left-hand column, the shelf mark in the middle, and the Institute's reel number on the right.

Shelf mark	Catalogue no.	Reel no.
Add. 379,2	SCR 363	16298
Add. 669,2	SCR 97	15890
Add. 1564	SCR 254	16476
Add. 3127	SCR 361	17556

Florence, Biblioteca Medicea Laurenziana

Catalogue no.	Shelf mark	Reel no.
—	Gaddi 155	20370
—	Plut. I. 44	17649
—	Plut. II. 21	20366

Frankfurt am Main, Stadts- und Universitätsbibliothek (now Universitätsbibliothek Johann Christian Senckenberg)

Catalogue no.	Shelf mark	Reel no.
oct. 94	hebr. oct. 94	25916

Freiburg, Universitätsbibliothek

Catalogue no.	Shelf mark	Reel no.
98	483, 29	11392

Hamburg, Staats- und Universitätsbibliothek, Levy Collection

Catalogue no.	Shelf mark	Reel no.
213	hebr. 303	26368

Jerusalem, National Library of Israel

Catalogue no.	Shelf mark	Reel no.
—	120=4	B 3
—	1987=8	B 12
—	1998=8	B 1016

Leipzig, Universitätsbibliothek

Catalogue no.	Shelf mark	Reel no.
—	1104	9992

London, Beth Din and Beth Hamidrash

Catalogue no.	Shelf mark	Reel no.
70	70	4737

London, British Library

Catalogue no.	Shelf mark	Reel no.
235	Harley 269	4833
243	Or. 2853	6398
494	Harley 5702	4880
495	Add. 11438	4920
501	Or. 45	5902
737	Add. 27199	5871
789	Or. 10750	8065

Madrid, Biblioteca de San Lorenzo de El Escorial

Catalogue no.	Shelf mark	Reel no.
—	G-IV-5	10074

Milan, Biblioteca Ambrosiana

Catalogue no.	Shelf mark	Reel no.
119	X 111 Sup.	12336

Modena, Biblioteca Estense

Catalogue no.	Shelf mark	Reel no.
18	S.8.18	14964

Moscow, Russian State Library, Günzburg Collection

Catalogue no.	Shelf mark	Reel no.
73	Mos. RSL 73	6753
82	Mos. RSL 82	6762
103	Mos. RSL 103	6783

Munich, Bayerische Staatsbibliothek

Catalogue no.	Shelf mark	Reel no.
15	hebr. 15	1170
42	hebr. 42	1612
81	hebr. 81	23120
232	hebr. 232	1656

New York, Jewish Theological Seminary

Catalogue no.	Shelf mark	Reel no.
2499		28752
Boesky 45		75736
	Ac. 02145	
6591	Rabbinica 750	

Nîmes, Bibliothèque Seguier Municipale

Catalogue no.	Shelf mark	Reel no.
26	—	4424

Oxford, Bodleian Library

Catalogue no.	Shelf mark	Reel no.
268	Opp. 27	16736
423	Or. 593	18411
453	Or. 608	18597
610	Arch. Seld. A. 4	20200
641	Opp. Add. fol. 34	20557
782	Or. 146	20319
875	Opp. 340	21834
1098	Mich. 569	17293
1566	Opp. 111	16934
1569	Opp. 109	16937
1570	Opp. 110	16938
1571	Opp. 493	16939
1943	Opp. 487	19105
1984	Mich. 155	19146
2275	Opp. 614	20967
2393	Opp. Add 4° 100	21673

Paris, Bibliothèque Nationale

Catalogue no.	Shelf mark	Reel no.
344	Heb. 344	2946
354	Heb. 354	2956
363	Heb. 363	20238
407	Heb. 407	27901
711	Heb. 711	1159
850	Heb. 850	14479
1391	Heb. 1391	34252
1408	Heb. 1408	15770

Parma, Biblioteca Palatina

Giovanni B. De Rossi published a catalogue of his personal Hebraica collection in 1803. That collection was acquired by the Biblioteca Palatina. In 2001 a more precise and detailed catalogue was published by Benjamin Richler, long after the collection had been accessed by the Institute. Its card catalogue registers the De Rossi number.

De Rossi catalogue no.	Shelf mark	New catalogue no.	Reel no.
214	Parma 2608	Richler 868	13309
1133	Parma 3280	Richler 1367	13957
1203	Parma 2454	Richler 720	13459
1383	Parma 3060	Richler 763	13826
1390	Parma 2784	Richler 1198	13633

Rome, Biblioteca Angelica

Catalogue no.	Shelf mark	Reel no.
	Or. 63	11710

St Petersburg–Firkowitz

Catalogue no.	Shelf mark	Reel no.
	11 a 9/1	63935

Vatican, Biblioteca Apostolica

Catalogue no.	Shelf mark	Reel no.
Ebr. 171	171	8630
Ebr. 183	183	8698
Ebr. 277	277	334
Ebr. 285	285	8632

Warsaw, Żydowski Instytut Historyczny

Catalogue no.	Shelf mark	Reel no.
204	—	10112

Zurich Zentralbibliothek

Catalogue no.	Shelf mark	Reel no.
D 74		Ph 5330[1]
Heid. 51		2613

[1] Photograph of two pages

Source Acknowledgments

The following essays were originally published as detailed below.

CHAPTER 1: 'Three Themes in *Sefer Ḥasidim*', *AJS Review*, 1 (1976), 311–58.

CHAPTER 2: 'Le Ta'arikh Ḥibburo shel *Sefer Ḥasidim*', in R. Bonfils, M. Ben-Sasson, and Y. Hacker, eds., *Tarbut ve-Ḥevrah be-Toledot Yisra'el bi-Yemei ha-Beinayim: Kovets Ma'marim le-Zikhro shel Ḥayyim Hillel Ben-Sasson* (Jerusalem, 1989), 149–52.

CHAPTER 3: 'Piety, Pietism, and German Pietism: *Sefer Ḥasidim I* and the Influence of Ḥasidei Ashkenaz', *Jewish Quarterly Review*, 92 (2002), 455–93.

CHAPTER 4: Pietists and Kibbitzers', *Jewish Quarterly Review*, 96 (2006), 60–6.

CHAPTER 5: 'The Midrash, *Sefer Ḥasidim*, and the Changing Face of God', in R. Elior and P. Schäfer, eds., *Creation and Re-Creation in Jewish Thought: Festschrift in Honor of Joseph Dan on the Occasion of his Seventieth Birthday* (Tübingen, 2005), 163–76.

CHAPTER 6: 'Two Notes on the *Commentary on the Torah* of R. Yehudah he-Hasid', in M. Schmidman and J. Bleich, eds., *Bernard Lander Festschrift* (New York, 2008), ii. 101–11.

CHAPTER 7: 'Topics in the *Ḥokhmath Ha-Nefesh*', *Journal of Jewish Studies*, 21 [1967], 65–78.

CHAPTER 10: 'Rabad of Posquières: A Programmatic Essay', in I. Etkes and Y. Salmon, eds., *Studies in the History of Jewish Society in the Middle Ages and in the Modern Period—Presented to Jacob Katz on his Seventy-Fifth Birthday by his Students and Friends* (Jerusalem, 1980), 1–41.

CHAPTER 12: 'A Response to Rabbi Ephraim Buckwold's Critique of "Rabad of Posquières: A Programmatic Essay"', Part I', *Torah u-Madda Journal*, 14 (2007), 193–240.

CHAPTER 14: 'Jewish and Roman Law: A Study in Interaction', in *Mélanges Roger Aubenas* (Montpellier, 1974), 711–24.

CHAPTER 15: '*Bet ha-Beḥirah* le-Menaḥem ha-Me'iri ve-Goralo', in M. Idel, J. Cohen, and Y. Kaplan, eds., *Asufah le-Yosef: Kovets Meḥkarim Shai le-Yosef Hacker* (Jerusalem, 2014), 253–9.

CHAPTER 16: 'Hadpasat Sefarim ve-Toledot ha-Halakhah: Nituaḥ le-Dugma', in Zvi Steinfeld, ed., *Sefer Zikaron le-Me'ir Simḥah Feldblum*, Sefer ha-Shanah le-Universitat Bar-Ilan—Meḥkarim be-Yahadut u-Madda'ei ha-Ruaḥ 30–31 (Ramat Gan, 2006), 319–22.

CHAPTER 17: 'Angle of Deflection'. An expanded version of 'Hassakat Maskanot Historiyot me-Sifrut ha-Halakhah', in I. Etkes, D. Asaf, and Y Kaplan, eds., *Avnei Derekh: Massot u-Meḥkarim be-Historiyah shel 'Am Yisra'el—Shai li-Tsevi (Kuti) Yekutiel* (Jerusalem, 2015), 111–18.

The page numbers of the original essays have been shown thus in the text: |99| to enable readers to swiftly find references to passages in these articles registered in the scholarly literature of the past.

Index of Names

W

Weber, Max 244, 376
Weissman, Susan 234
White, G. Edward 414
Wilfand, Yael 205
Williams, Steven 413
Wilson, Brian 244
Wistinetzki, Judah 79, 80, 89–90, 187, 225
  see also Index of Subjects: *Sefer Ḥasidim*, Parma MS of
Wolfson, Elliot 142 n. 16, 150

Y

R. Ya'akov ben Asher (Ba'al ha-Turim) 213, 265
R. Ya'akov Ḥazan of London 95
R. Ya'akov of Karlin 372
R. Ya'akov ha-Kohen 108–9
R. Ya'akov of Ramerupt (Rabbenu Tam) 43, 260, 400
  on charity 198, 213 n. 94
  on credit 73–5, 347, 348, 351–2; personal obligation in 278, 341
  dialectic rediscovered by 259, 264
  on *dina de-malkhuta dina* 325
  ignores the Geonim 365, 366
  importance of, as Tosafist 261–2, 278
  marks birth of European halakhic thought 41, 52, 259–60
  personality of 46 n. 108, 308, 309
  and *piyyut* 56 n. 133
  ratio of distinction not provided by 400
  students of 52, 93, 108
Yahalom, S. 288–91
R. Yehudah of Barcelona (Albargeloni) 258, 271, 368, 377, 391
R. Yehudah he-Ḥasid 55, 57, 107–9
  aristocratic descent of 53–4
  authorship of *Sefer Ḥasidim* 70–1, 76–7, 118, 226, 231–4
  Commentary on the Torah 152–3; contains parallels with *Sefer Ḥasidim* 226; contains reports of his son 157, 159–60; eccentric interpretations of 156–7; as Midrash 21; on Mosaic authorship of the entire Torah 152, 155–6
  compared to St Francis of Assisi 5, 40
  critical of the new dialectic 43, 47, 54
  criticizes the establishment 227
  and R. El'azar of Worms 227–8, 230–1
  esoteric teachings of 53 n. 126, 93, 247
  harsh ethical stance of 40, 221
  radical pietism of 21, 224, 225, 231
  sense of justice of 5–6, 159–60, 227
  testament of 19–20
  Zekher 'Asah le-Nifle'otav 64
R. Yehudah ha-Nasi 211–13, 375
R. Yehudah Sirleon of Paris 21 n. 32, 52, 157, 400
R. Yisra'el Salanter 3, 97, 100
R. Yitsḥak ben Abba Mari of Marseille 272, 291 n. 52, 392, 393
  see also Index of Subjects: *Sefer ha-'Ittur*
R. Yitsḥak ben Asher (Riva) 41, 53
  critique of Rashi's straw man 73
R. Yitsḥak of Corbeil 38 n. 84, 52, 94–5
  alleged pietism of 100, 102, 104, 112
R. Yitsḥak of Dampierre (Ri) 41, 43, 55, 56 n. 133, 290
  on credit 73–4, 347
  on *dina de-malkhuta dina* 325
  importance of 52, 260, 261, 264
  methodology of 400
R. Yitsḥak of Fez (Alfasi; Rif) 279
  cited by Ravad 356, 358, 361, 362
  code of, used by Ramban's school 405
  contrasted with R. Yehudah of Barcelona 368
  independence from Geonim 258, 367–9, 370 n. 15
  Maimonides on 368–9
  Ran's commentary on 400, 403
  Ravad's *Hassagot* on 263 n. 15, 269, 279, 350, 358
  on sale of debts 341, 346, 348, 356, 357
  R. Zeraḥyah of Lunel's critique of 262, 268, 272–3, 312
R. Yitsḥak of Gerona (R. Zeraḥyah ha-Levi's father) 296–8
R. Yitsḥak of Karlin 372
R. Yitsḥak ben Mordekhai (Rivam) 41, 53
R. Yitsḥak ben Perets 321, 329–31, 336
R. Yitsḥak of Vienna (Or Zarua') 52, 73, 74, 108, 209–10

Index of Places

Index of Subjects

H